Glannon Guide
Bankruptcy

Glannon Guide
Bankruptcy

Sixth Edition

Daniel Keating
Tyrrell Williams Professor of Law
Washington University School of Law

Nathalie Martin
Frederick M. Hart Chair in Consumer and Clinical Law
University of New Mexico School of Law

ASPEN
PUBLISHING

To contact Customer Service, e-mail customer.service@aspenpublishing.com, call 1-800-950-5259, or mail correspondence to:

Aspen Publishing
Attn: Order Department
1 Wall Street
Burlington, MA 01803

1 2 3 4 5 6 7 8 9 0

ISBN 979-8-8941-0940-4

Library of Congress Cataloging-in-Publication Data

Names: Martin, Nathalie, 1961- author | Keating, Daniel L. (Daniel Louis), 1961- author
Title: The Glannon guide to bankruptcy / Daniel L. Keating, Tyrrell Williams Professor of Law, Washington University School of Law; Nathalie Martin, Frederick M. Hart Chair in Consumer and Clinical Law, University of New Mexico School of Law.
Description: Sixth edition. | Burlington, MA : Aspen Publishing, 2025. | Series: Glannon guide | Includes bibliographical references and index. | Summary: "Welcome to the new and improved 2025 Glannon Guide to Bankruptcy. This study guide is designed to help you prepare for the introductory bankruptcy and creditors' rights class, as well as a more advanced Chapter 11 class. It is different from the other study guides you may have seen at the bookstore. The goal of this guide is to help you understand your bankruptcy or creditors' rights class from a different point of view and help you do a better job on your exam in this class. It is also designed to help you become a better and more thorough lawyer, although the emphasis is clearly on test-taking" — Provided by publisher.
Identifiers: LCCN 2025041264 (print) | LCCN 2025041265 (ebook) | ISBN 9798894109404 paperback | ISBN 9798894109428 ebook
Subjects: LCSH: Bankruptcy — United States | Bankruptcy — United States — Problems, exercises, etc.
Classification: LCC KF1524.85 .M368 2025 (print) | LCC KF1524.85 (ebook) | DDC 346.7307/8076—dc23/eng/20250903
LC record available at https://lccn.loc.gov/2025041264
LC ebook record available at https://lccn.loc.gov/2025041265

ABOUT ASPEN PUBLISHING

Aspen Publishing is a leading provider of legal education content and digital learning solutions in the United States and globally. Our innovative products and platforms—designed based on best practices in learning science—engage students and enhance outcomes. From textbooks and audiobooks authored by renowned experts to digital platforms and products like LEAF, Connected eBooks, Connected Quizzing, PracticePerfect, and JD-Next, we empower the next generation of legal professionals with innovative, trusted, and accessible resources.

The Aspen Casebook Series, affectionately known as the "red and black" casebooks among law faculty and students, includes hundreds of highly regarded textbooks across more than 80 disciplines. These range from foundational courses like Torts and Contracts to emerging electives such as Sustainability and the Law of Policing. Our study aids, including the popular *Examples & Explanations* series, help law students master complex topics with clarity and confidence.

Aspen's expertise extends to undergraduate education with our Paralegal, Criminal Justice, and Business Law series, offering the same hallmark quality to a broader audience. JD-Next, our groundbreaking online law school prep course and admissions test, provides a realistic preview of law school, equips students with essential skills for academic success, and evaluates their readiness for legal studies.

Aspen Publishing Is Proud to Be a UWorld Company

Since 2003, UWorld has been a global leader in developing high-quality learning tools for students preparing for high-stakes exams. With a commitment to excellence, UWorld has helped millions of students in undergraduate, graduate, and professional programs in fields such as medicine, nursing, finance, and law achieve their academic and career goals.

Founded by Chandra S. Pemmasani, M.D., during his medical residency, UWorld began focusing on medical education and has since expanded into various academic fields, including law. In 2020, UWorld launched its Legal vertical, starting with its comprehensive Multistate Bar Exam (MBE®) Question Bank, followed by the acquisition of Themis Bar Review, which integrated resources to provide a complete bar exam preparation experience. In 2024, UWorld expanded its offerings by acquiring Aspen Publishing, enhancing its suite of legal education products.

Today, UWorld offers an unparalleled range of study materials that blend active learning methods with expert content, ensuring students and educators can access the most effective resources. From bar preparation to law school success, UWorld is committed to supporting the next generation of legal professionals. Learn more at uworld.com.

This book is dedicated to Stewart, my partner in all of life's adventures.
N.M.

To Jane.
D.K.

Contents

Acknowledgments *xix*

Chapter 1: **A Very Short Introduction** 1

Chapter 2: **The Secured Versus Unsecured Distinction: A Brief Introduction** 5
- A. Types of Secured Claims or Liens 6

Chapter 3: **State Collection Law** 9
- A. State Court Collection Process 9
  - *1. The execution process* 9
- B. State Law Exemptions 12
  - *1. State law exemptions and bankruptcy* 15
- C. Fraudulent Transfers Under the Uniform Fraudulent Transfer Act 16
  - *1. The purpose of fraudulent transfer law* 16
  - *2. The history of the Uniform Fraudulent Transfer Act* 16
  - *3. The elements of a fraudulent transfer* 17
- D. The Closer: Chapters 2 and 3 21

Chapter 4: **Introduction to Bankruptcy** 25
- A. The Bankruptcy System: The Basics 26
  - *1. Chapter 7* 27
  - *2. Chapter 13* 28
  - *3. Chapter 12* 29
  - *4. Chapter 11* 29
  - *5. Chapter 9* 30
- B. Definitions and Learning to Read the Code 31

Chapter 5: **Jurisdiction and the Powers of the Bankruptcy Court** 39
- A. Introduction 39
- B. Bankruptcy Court Jurisdiction over Bankruptcy Cases 39
- C. Appeals from the Bankruptcy Court 43

	D. Preemption and the Relationship Between Federal Bankruptcy Law and State Law	45
	E. The Court's Equity Power Under §105(a)	45
	F. Sovereign Immunity of States and Tribes	46
Chapter 6:	**Case Administration and Structure of the Code**	51
	A. Changes in Case Administration Under the 2005 Amendments	52
	1. More documents	52
	a. Overview	52
	b. The details	52
	2. New attorney obligations	54
	3. The creditors' meeting	55
	B. Basic Chapter 7 Administration	55
	C. Basic Chapter 13 Administration	56
	D. Basic Chapter 11 Administration	56
	E. The Structure of the Code	57
	F. The Closer: Chapters 4, 5, and 6	57
Chapter 7:	**The Automatic Stay**	61
	A. Exceptions to the Automatic Stay	62
	B. Multiple Filing Cases: When the Stay Is Not So "Automatic"	68
	1. One prior dismissed case	69
	2. Two or more dismissed cases	69
	3. Extending the 30-day stay under §362(c)(3)	69
	4. Obtaining a stay under §362(c)(4)	71
	5. Which stay does the repeat filer NOT get?	71
	C. Relief from the Automatic Stay	73
	D. The Closer: Chapter 7	74
Chapter 8:	**Property of the Debtor's Estate**	77
	A. Breadth of the Estate	77
	B. Legal and Equitable Interests in Property	78
	C. Retirement Funds	80
	D. Post-Petition Assets	82
	1. Chapter 7 post-petition assets	82
	2. Post-petition assets in a Chapter 13 or a Chapter 11 case	84
Chapter 9:	**Exemptions in Bankruptcy**	85
	A. State Versus Federal Exemption Schemes	86
	B. New Limitations on the Homestead Exemption	91

C. Exemptions for Individual Retirement Accounts 93
D. The Valuation of Exempt Property 94
E. Voiding Involuntary Liens, and Nonpossessory, Non-Purchase-Money Security Interests That Interfere With an Exemption 99
F. The Closer: Chapters 8 and 9 101

Chapter 10: **Priorities** 105

Chapter 11: **The Treatment of Secured Claims in Bankruptcy** 115
A. Secured Credit in General 115
1. *Secured creditor remedies outside bankruptcy* 116
2. *Secured creditor treatment in bankruptcy* 116
B. The Comfort of Being Secured 117
C. Undersecured and Oversecured Creditors: Learning the Lingo 118
D. Practicing the Calculations 120

Chapter 12: **The Avoiding Powers** 123
A. Preferential Transfers 124
1. *Preferential payments and transfers in consumer bankruptcy cases* 131
2. *Defenses to preference actions* 132
3. *Ordinary course of business defense* 132
4. *The new value exception to the preference statute* 133
5. *The substantially contemporaneous exchange for new value exception* 133
6. *Setoff preferences* 135
B. Avoiding Fraudulent Transfers Under the Bankruptcy Code 138
C. Avoidance of Unperfected Security Interests Under the Trustee's Strong-Arm Powers Contained in §544(a) 140
D. The Closer: Chapter 12 141

Chapter 13: **The General Bankruptcy Discharge** 143
A. The Policy Behind Discharge for Individual Debtors 143
B. The Timing of the Discharge 144
C. The Scope of the Discharge 145
1. *Only pre-petition debts are discharged* 145
2. *Only claims are discharged* 145
3. *Not all debtors get a discharge* 146
4. *Some debts are not entitled to discharge* 146

Chapter 14: **Exceptions to Discharge Under §523** 149
A. Taxes 150
B. Exceptions to Discharge Based on Fraud 151
1. *Objections based on actual fraud* 151
2. *Fraud based on the use of a false financial statement* 152
3. *A presumption of fraud for charging luxury goods or taking cash advances within 60 days of the filing* 153
C. Objections to Discharge Based on Fraud in the Fiduciary Capacity, Embezzlement, or Larceny 156
1. *Fraud in the fiduciary capacity and embezzlement* 156
2. *Larceny* 157
D. Forgetting or Simply Failing to List a Creditor on the Bankruptcy Paperwork 158
E. Domestic Support Obligations Under §523(a)(5) and §523(a)(15) 159
1. *The difference between support obligations and property settlement obligations in bankruptcy* 159
2. *Marital obligations and the automatic stay* 163
3. *Two additional reasons why it matters whether a debt is support or a mere property settlement debt* 164
F. Intentional Torts and Debts Stemming from Driving Under the Influence of Alcohol 164
G. Student Loans 165
H. Conclusion 166

Chapter 15: **Objections to the Debtor's General Discharge** 169
A. A Knowing and Fraudulent False Oath in or in Connection with a Bankruptcy Case 170
B. Inexplicable Loss of Money 172
C. Concealment, Loss, Destruction, Falsification, or Mutilation of Records, or a Failure to Keep Records 173
D. Transfers Made with Intent to Hinder, Delay, or Defraud Creditors 174
E. Prior Chapter Discharge Within Past Eight (or Six) Years 178
F. Failure to Complete the Debt Management Course Under §727(a)(11) 179
G. The Closer: Chapters 13, 14, and 15 (CODE READER) 179

Chapter 16: **Keeping Secured Property in a Chapter 7 Case** 183
A. Redemption 184
B. Reaffirmation: When Is It Necessary or Advisable? 189
1. *General principles of reaffirmation* 189
2. *The formal requirements of reaffirmation* 189
3. *When is reaffirmation necessary? The "keep and pay" option* 190
C. The Closer: Chapter 16 193

Chapter 17: **Dismissal** 197
A. Dismissal for Failure to Cooperate in the Case 197
B. Dismissal Under the Means Test: The New Issue in Consumer Bankruptcy 200
C. Dismissal for Abuse of Chapter 7: The Old Standard and the New Means Test 200
1. *The old test* 201
2. *The new test for abuse under §707(b): The means test* 201
a. Income 202
b. Allowable expenses 203
c. Figuring out what's left 205
d. How can the debtor rebut the presumption? 206

Chapter 18: **Involuntary Bankruptcy** 217
A. The Anatomy of an Involuntary Bankruptcy Case 217
B. The Closer: Chapters 17 and 18 222

Chapter 19: **Overview of Chapter 13** 225

Chapter 20: **Chapter 13 Eligibility** 229

Chapter 21: **Secured Creditor Treatment Under Chapter 13** 233
A. Treatment of Personal Property Loans and Other Secured Loans That Are Not Home Mortgages 234
1. *Bifurcation and "stripdown" or "cramdown"* 234
2. *New limitations on stripdown* 236
3. *Valuation* 238
4. *The present value interest rate* 239
B. Treatment of the Home Mortgage in Chapter 13 241
C. Recognizing When Stripdown Applies 242
D. A New Approach to Stripdown 242

Chapter 22: **The Treatment of Priority Claims in Chapter 13** 249
- A. The Closer: Chapters 19, 20, 21, and 22 252

Chapter 23: **The Disposable Income Test in Chapter 13** 255
- A. The Prior Disposable Income Test 255
- B. The New Disposable Income Test 256
  1. *Below-median-income debtors and the new disposable income test* 257
  2. *The debtor's budget and the status quo: Class issues* 259
  3. *Payments to 401(k) plans for below-median-income debtors* 262
  4. *Above-median-income debtors and the new disposable income test* 263

Chapter 24: **The Good Faith Test in Chapter 13** 265
- A. Overlap with the Disposable Income Test and Other Tests 265
- B. Good Faith Factor-Based Tests 266
- C. Multiple Filings 268
- D. Zero Percent Plans 269

Chapter 25: **The Best Interest of Creditors Test** 271
- A. The Closer: Chapters 23, 24, and 25 276

Chapter 26: **Chapter 13 Plan Feasibility** 279
- A. Do the Proposed Payments Meet the Plan Obligations? 279
- B. Can the Debtor Make the Payments? 280

Chapter 27: **Modification of a Chapter 13 Plan or Dismissal of a Chapter 13 Case** 285

Chapter 28: **Overview of Chapter 11 and Its Alternatives** 291
- A. Comparing the Out-of-Court Workout and Chapter 11 293
- B. Introduction to the Basic Chapter 11 Rules and Major Parties-in-Interest 300
  1. *Major players in a Chapter 11 case* 301
     - a. The debtor-in-possession 301
     - b. The United States Trustee's Office 301
     - c. Creditors' committees 302
     - d. Secured creditors 305
  2. *Venue* 307

Chapter 29: **Cash Collateral, Post-Petition Financing, and Other First-Day Orders** 309
A. The Cash Collateral Motion and Order 310
1. What is cash collateral? 311
2. Special rules for the debtor's use of cash collateral 314
3. Cash collateral stipulations 318
B. Post-Petition Financing Orders 321
C. Critical Vendor Orders and the Doctrine of Necessity 327
D. Payment of Other Unsecured Claims Before Confirmation 331
E. Applications to Be Employed as Counsel, Accountant, or Other Professional 332
F. Cash Management Orders 335
G. Utilities 335
H. The Closer: Chapter 29 337

Chapter 30: **The Automatic Stay and Adequate Protection** 339
A. The Scope of the Automatic Stay 339
B. Exceptions to the Automatic Stay 342
C. Relief from the Automatic Stay 344
D. Adequate Protection 351
E. The Closer: Chapter 30 352

Chapter 31: **Operating the Chapter 11 Debtor: The Rights and Goals of the Debtor-in-Possession, and the Grounds for Appointment of a Chapter 11 Trustee or Examiner** 355
A. Activities that the Debtor-in-Possession Can Engage in Without Court Approval While in Chapter 11 356
B. The Appointment of a Trustee 358
C. The Appointment of an Examiner 361
D. Maintaining the Debtor's Operations and Structuring a Successful Chapter 11 Case: The Basic Goals and Requirements 362
E. Overview of Chapter 11 Treatment Rules 367
F. Overview of Chapter 11 Procedural Rules 367
G. The Closer: Chapter 31 368

Chapter 32: **Claims Against the Estate** 371
A. Definition of a Claim 371
B. Administrative Claims Under Chapter 11 375
C. The §506(c) Surcharge 378
D. The Closer: Chapter 32 381

Chapter 33: **Reshaping the Estate Through the Assumption or Rejection of Executory Contracts and Unexpired Leases Pursuant to §365, and Through Asset Sales Pursuant to §363** 383

A. Assumption or Rejection of Executory Contracts and Unexpired Leases 384
  1. *What are executory contracts and unexpired leases?* 384
  2. *Ipso facto clauses* 386
  3. *Rejection of executory contracts and unexpired leases* 391
  4. *Assumption of executory contracts and unexpired leases* 393
  5. *Assuming and assigning executory contracts and unexpired leases* 395
    a. Adequate protection in shopping center leases 396

B. Sales of Assets Pursuant to §363(b) of the Code 398

C. The §363 Sales Process: Seeking Out Highest and Best Bids 402

D. Successor Liability and §363 Sales 404

E. The Closer: Chapter 33 405

Chapter 34: **Introduction to the Plan and the Minimum Chapter 11 Plan Requirements** 409

A. Introduction to the Chapter 11 Plan Process 410
  1. *Consensual plans versus cramdown plans* 410
  2. *Basic Chapter 11 requirements* 411

B. Priority Treatment Under Chapter 11 412

C. The Best Interest Test in Chapter 11: Treatment of General Unsecured Claims 416

D. Feasibility 419

E. Secured Creditor Treatment Under Chapter 11 423
  1. *The treatment of oversecured and undersecured claims after the filing but before confirmation of a Chapter 11 plan* 424
  2. *Secured creditor treatment under the plan* 424

F. The Closer: Chapter 34 426

Chapter 35: **Voting and Classification: Soliciting Votes for the Plan** 429

A. The Disclosure Statement 430

B. Plan Voting 435

C. Classification 436

D. Impairment 440

E. The Closer: Chapter 35 441

Chapter 36: **Forcing the Plan on Dissenting Creditors: A Different Kind of Cramdown** 443

A. Cramdown of a Secured Class 444

B. The Specific and General Requirements of the Fair and Equitable Test 444

1. *Duration of payments to the secured party* 445
2. *General fairness and §1129(b)(1)* 447
3. *The present-value interest rate* 448
4. *Obtaining positive votes from at least one accepting class: If you are stripping down, this is harder than it looks* 450

C. The Absolute Priority Rule When Forcing the Plan on Classes of Unsecured Creditors 452

D. The Closer: Chapter 36 457

Chapter 37: **Small Business Cases Under Chapter 11** 459

A. A Brief History of Small Business Bankruptcy 459

B. Shorter Deadlines for Small Business Debtors 461

C. Additional Reporting Requirements and Oversight 463

D. Simplification of the Plan Process 464

E. Higher Risk of Conversion or Dismissal 464

F. The Small Business Reorganization Act of 2019 ("SBRA") 466

Chapter 38: **Post-Confirmation Issues: The Effect of Confirmation** 473

A. The Confirmation Order Is Res Judicata as to All Issues Dealt with in the Plan and Also Discharges All Claims Except as Otherwise Provided for in the Plan 474

B. Enforcing the Plan 481

C. The Closer: Chapter 38 484

Chapter 39: **Closing Closers: Some Practice Questions** 487

Index 515

Acknowledgments

First, I want to thank my co-author and friend Daniel Keating for working tirelessly and for being the primary driver of this new and improved edition. I also thank my husband Stewart Paley who worked hard on earlier drafts, as well as my now late and deeply missed colleague Frederick Hart, my tireless assistant, Cheryl Burbank, as well as my talented student research assistant Ben Jacobs (UNM School of Law, JD 2017).

N.M.

I would like to thank my friend Nathalie Martin for allowing me to join her as a co-author for this sixth edition. I would also like to thank David Farrell of Thompson Coburn LLP for his review of and suggestions for the chapter about small business bankruptcies.

D.K.

Finally, we are grateful to all those involved in the editorial process at Aspen Publishers, including Eric Song of The Froebe Group in New York for this sixth edition, who made this a better book.

N.M. & D.K.

August 2025

Glannon Guide
Bankruptcy

1

A Very Short Introduction

Welcome to the new and improved 2025 Glannon Guide to Bankruptcy. This study guide is designed to help you prepare for the introductory bankruptcy and creditors' rights class, as well as a more advanced Chapter 11 class. It is different from the other study guides you may have seen at the bookstore. The goal of this guide is to help you understand your bankruptcy or creditors' rights class from a different point of view and help you do a better job on your exam in this class. It is also designed to help you become a better and more thorough lawyer, although the emphasis is clearly on test-taking.

This book is different from the others in another way as well. It has been edited both by other faculty members and students. Our own students have practiced the questions and weeded out the confusing ones, leaving only those that actually help you! We have had both bankruptcy students and those who have never taken a bankruptcy class read the book, to make sure that it is understandable and useful to you, which is the ultimate test of its success.

You might wonder how this guide can help you perform better in your bankruptcy classes. Traditional commercial outlines contain a great deal of black letter law, but not many hypothetical factual scenarios that help you learn to apply the law. Applying the law is what makes the difference between a "B" or a "C" exam and an "A" exam. This guide focuses more on the examples than on the black letter law and teaches the law through both the incorrect and the correct answers to the questions posed. This format allows you to learn the main rules, the exceptions to the rules, and the nuances or gray areas of the law in context. This can be done more easily with the questions offered here than with the outline format. Learning the law from this guide is an interactive process, one you may even enjoy.

This book can also help you learn some of the ever-important language of debtor-creditor law. Studies of learning theory, particularly in the context of foreign languages, suggest that if a word is repeated in different contexts at a certain frequency or interval, students will quickly learn to understand the meaning of that word based upon the context in which it is used. We have attempted to use words over and over again in different contexts, at the intervals suggested by the studies, so that you can master this new language with real understanding of the concepts, not just a surface recognition of them.

If you get lost, go back and read the section again. Try not to let things slip by, and you'll be amazed at your understanding of this subject. You'll note that some words in the guide are italicized. Most of the italicized words are new vocabulary words and are highlighted to allow you to recognize them as new words and help you pay special attention to their context.

This guide is organized primarily around a series of multiple-choice questions. When you use the guide, be sure to read the text offered, try to answer the question without looking at the answers, and then carefully read the explanation provided right below the question. The explanations of the answers are sometimes more important than the text before the question. They should reinforce your learning of the subject of the question. Some questions require that you read a Bankruptcy Code section before attempting to answer the question. (The Code became more difficult to read since its major overhaul in 2005. Some sections are literally incomprehensible, but it is still important to try.) These questions contain the words "CODE READER" in the question preface.

The Glannon series of study guides is unique in its use of multiple-choice and other similar questions to teach the subject matter. One of the signatures of the Glannon Guide Series is the "Closer" question, which is used at the end of the chapter or a series of chapters in order to reinforce the material and apply it in a more complex context. In many Glannon Guides, a Closer question appears at the end of each chapter. Because bankruptcy is an area that is best learned in very small, bite-sized pieces, the chapters in this Glannon Guide are much shorter than in most other books in the series, particularly in the first half of the book, which covers general bankruptcy principles and Chapter 7 and Chapter 13 cases. As a result of these very short chapters, this Glannon Guide will sometimes present you with a Closer question after a series of chapters, rather than after each chapter. By using this technique, rather than presenting you with a Closer question at the end of each chapter, we can keep the chapters short enough so that you can learn each issue in isolation but can then attempt to integrate the materials in a series of chapters with a Closer question at the end of that series.[1]

The materials in this book are organized in a way that is similar to the organization of many bankruptcy and creditors' rights classes. It starts with a few chapters on state court collection procedures, then introduces the Bankruptcy Code system and its definitions, discusses bankruptcy court jurisdiction and

1. Thus, during the first 27 chapters of this book you will find a Closer question, on average, once every three chapters. Once we enter the more complicated area of Chapter 11, you will then find a Closer question at the end of each chapter. We also use the Closer questions in a way that is somewhat different from other Glannon Guides. Generally, they are used either to present the student with more complexity and integration of the subject matter, or to reinforce the policy behind certain bankruptcy rules, so that you can use that knowledge of the policy to reinforce and help you remember the rule.

administration, and then covers various bankruptcy topics that are applicable in any type of bankruptcy. These topics are covered in Chapters 7 through 13. Thereafter, the guide discusses topics in the context of the three main types of bankruptcy cases, known by their chapter numbers within the Bankruptcy Code. Chapter 7 liquidation cases are covered in the guide's Chapters 14 through 18. Chapter 13 individual payment plan cases are covered in the guide's Chapters 19 through 27. Chapter 11 business reorganization cases are covered in the guide's Chapters 28 through 38.

We suggest that you read the chapter or chapters pertaining to each topic right before or after you cover the same material in class. Because every class is different, this may require some skipping around. Undoubtedly, because every textbook is different, this guide will tie concepts together in a way that will be somewhat different from your own course. This is a positive thing because it will help reinforce the materials from different angles.

Whether your teacher chooses to test through essay, multiple-choice, or short-answer questions, answering the questions in this book and carefully reading through the explanations that follow can improve your understanding of this complex area of the law. Using a multiple-choice study guide is also much more fun than simply using a commercial outline, as the interactive format will allow you to see how you are doing as you proceed through the book.

ONE LAST NOTE: You need a calculator and a copy of the Bankruptcy Code in order to make the best use of this book. Some questions will require you to calculate distributions, interest payments, and other numbers. Additionally, no bankruptcy guide worth spending money on will tell you that you can learn bankruptcy law without learning how to read the Bankruptcy Code. This hefty statute, found in Title 11 of the U.S. Code, simply must be mastered (at least on some level) before you can succeed in any bankruptcy course. While reading the Bankruptcy Code may seem hard at first, it becomes much more manageable with practice.

Think of the Code sections as poetry. See what you can glean from the first reading, then go back and see what further understanding you can gain. To help you develop this skill, Chapter 4 includes practice on Code reading, and we cover definitions there. This is a wonderful place to start learning to read the Code. Interspersed throughout the book, we will help you practice this skill by asking you to read a Code section and then apply it to one of the multiple-choice or other questions posed. Taking advantage of this opportunity will help you in this class as well as other Code-oriented classes in the future. Good luck, and we hope you enjoy this unique form of study aid.

2

The Secured Versus Unsecured Distinction: A Brief Introduction

OVERVIEW
A. Types of Secured Claims or Liens
Martin's and Keating's Picks

We can think of no distinction more critical and central to understanding debtor-creditor law than the distinction between the secured and the unsecured creditor. Later chapters will discuss this difference in detail and focus on different situations in which the two types of creditors are treated differently. Most bankruptcy concepts build on this distinction, so it is important to get some idea what it is about right away. As Gordon Gekko — a character in the movie "Wall Street" — said about insider trading, "If you're not inside, you are outside, okay?" So it is with being a secured creditor. You either are one or you are not.

Secured creditors hold particular property or collateral to secure their debt. Think of a real property mortgage on a home to secure the repayment of the home loan. Secured claims can also be secured or collateralized by personal property, including things that are intangible, like trademarks, accounts receivable, or most anything of value. Because unsecured creditors do not have any collateral supporting or backing up their debts, they must go to court to reach any of the debtor's property in order to satisfy their debts. Moreover, the debtor (the one who owes the debt) may not have any property from which an unsecured creditor can be paid. Secured creditors have collateral backing up their debt. As a result, the secured creditor usually has the right to simply repossess the collateral (as long as it is possible without breach of the peace), sell it, and get paid on the debt from the proceeds. Courts need not get involved, unless the collateral is real estate and you are in one of the roughly half the states that require judicial foreclosures of real estate. This ability to collect without courts is one of the most critical differences between being secured and being unsecured under state law.

A. Types of Secured Claims or Liens

There are three basic kinds of secured creditors,[1] and all hold liens in particular property.[2] First, there are voluntary liens or security interests, which are created by contract. The debtor voluntarily gives an Article 9 security interest[3] or a mortgage[4] to a secured party, usually in order to obtain credit but sometimes to secure prior debt. Next, there are involuntary liens, many of which are created through the state court execution process, which is described below. These liens are not created by contract; the debtor must be forced to pay through the judgment, execution, and sale process, all of which occur against the debtor's will. Other involuntary liens include tax liens attachment, and (in the case of real estate liens) simply the docketing of a judgment. Finally, there are statutory or common-law liens, which are also involuntary, and which, as you might have guessed, are created by state statutes or by courts. They give special property rights to certain creditors, by legislative or judicial creation. Examples include landlords' liens in property left on premises, so the property left can be sold and used to pay past-due rent, and mechanics' liens in favor of contractors who have created a benefit on a property owner's land but who have not been paid.

All three types of liens — voluntary, involuntary, and statutory — are aptly named. Together, they make up a descriptive package of creditors who have special collection rights due to their interests in particular property owned by the debtor.

QUESTION 1. All of the following are general categories of liens except

A. a voluntary lien.
B. an involuntary lien.
C. a mechanic's lien.
D. a statutory lien.

---

1. To me, the three categories are voluntary, involuntary, and statutory. Some teachers may believe that there are just two basic types, involuntary and voluntary, with statutory being a subset of involuntary. If you know how each type arises, you should be fine either way.
2. If you remember that a lien or security interest (used interchangeably here) cannot be in the abstract but must be in something specific, this will start to make some sense.
3. Article 9 is part of the Uniform Commercial Code, and covers the subject of voluntary security interests in personal property, as opposed to real estate mortgages.
4. Other state statutes cover voluntary security interests in real estate. They are not included under the scope of Article 9.

ANALYSIS. A mechanic's lien is not a general category of a lien, but rather a specific type of statutory lien, so **C** is the answer. The only general categories of which we are aware are voluntary liens, involuntary liens, and statutory liens. Note how descriptive each name for a type of lien is. Learn how each lien arises, and you'll understand what they are.

Martin's and Keating's Picks

1. Question 1 **C**

3

State Collection Law

OVERVIEW

A. State Court Collection Process
   1. The execution process
B. State Law Exemptions
   1. State law exemptions and bankruptcy
C. Fraudulent Transfers Under the Uniform Fraudulent Transfer Act
   1. The purpose of fraudulent transfer law
   2. The history of the Uniform Fraudulent Transfer act
   3. The elements of a fraudulent transfer
D. The Closer: Chapters 2 and 3
Martin's and Keating's Picks

A. State Court Collection Process

Most likely, your bankruptcy or creditors' rights class will start with an analysis of state law and state court collection procedures before moving on to focus on federal bankruptcy law. This chapter covers the basics of state collection law.

1. The execution process

Unsecured creditors do not have an interest in any particular property of the debtor. If not paid back voluntarily, unsecured creditors generally must go through a long and tortuous process to be paid. Most state court collection procedures focus on getting unsecured creditors paid, as most secured creditors don't need to go to court to get paid.

A creditor can attempt to exert societal pressure or another form of leverage on the debtor to exact payment. If none of that works, the creditor must go to court, get a judgment against the debtor, and get a sheriff to execute or seize property and sell it in satisfaction of the judgment. In your other classes, you have learned how to file a lawsuit and obtain a judgment, but clients do not pay lawyers for pieces of paper. They want money, which can be obtained only through the state court execution process.

Once an unsecured creditor obtains a judgment, which can take quite a while in and of itself, the creditor cannot simply seize any of the debtor's property that it chooses. Rather, it must determine which of the debtor's property is exempt (discussed below), and then get a sheriff to levy or execute on the judgment by seizing nonexempt property. The executing creditor must deliver a group of documents to the sheriff that tell him exactly what the debtor has that can be executed on, where these things are located, and whatever else he needs to know to get the job done. This is not exactly fun work for the sheriff, and the creditor's attorney must to do everything in his or her power to make it easy on the sheriff. Otherwise, the sheriff may return the judgment to the creditor unsatisfied.

As alluded to previously, individuals who owe money (debtors)[1] are entitled to exemptions in some property, a concept discussed later in this chapter. Businesses, however, do not get exemptions and thus have no exempt property. Thus, the sheriff can execute on anything and everything that a business debtor has.[2]

Once the sheriff has located whatever property is available for execution, the sheriff must, in most states, exercise dominion and control over the property. This is necessary in order to create a lien and thus to turn the creditor into a secured creditor.[3] The easiest way to exercise dominion and control over a debtor's property is to throw the property in the sheriff's vehicle and take it back to the sheriff's office. If the property is too big to actually take, then the sheriff can place big notices all over the property. The notices say something like, "The sheriff of so-and-so county has executed on this and, as a result, will soon sell the items." There may be other ways to exercise dominion and control over property to create a lien, such as changing the locks. Regardless of the method, anyone viewing the property should be able to tell that it has a lien on it. There should be no secret liens.[4]

Once the sheriff has exercised sufficient dominion and control over this property, we say that execution or levy has occurred. This is an important moment in the process because at the moment of execution, a lien is created in the property executed on. Before that time, the judgment is just a piece of

1. The word debtor is not pejorative in any way. We are all both debtors and creditors because we all owe money to someone and someone also owes us, at any given time. In fact, if you work, and assuming you are not paid in advance, your employer owes you money (and is your debtor) right now!

2. This is an overview, as the situation is more complicated than this. An individual who runs a sole proprietorship that is not incorporated may be able to save some business assets, called tools of trade, from execution, but a corporation, partnership, or limited liability company will have no exempt property.

3. In some states, the lien arises as soon as the judgment creditor delivers the writ of execution to the sheriff. In these states, a secret lien arises and the state statute must find a way to protect those who deal with the property before the sheriff makes a levy.

4. Secret liens are frowned on because they give potential unsecured creditors the impression that more of the debtor's property is unencumbered, and thus available to pay general unsecured creditors than is actually the case. Despite this, it is hard to eliminate them completely. *See* Footnote 3.

paper. Selling the property at a sheriff's sale is the next step. Once this has been done and the sheriff's fees have been paid, the executing creditor can satisfy its debt from the rest of the proceeds.[5] Only execution can create a lien. Merely having a judgment will never create a lien.

QUESTION 1. Clyde's Shoe Shop was in financial difficulty, and one of its suppliers, Saucy Shoes, has just obtained a judgment against Clyde's. After the writ and other paperwork were delivered to the sheriff, the sheriff proceeded to Clyde's, walked into the premises, and announced loudly in front of Clyde and a few customers, "I am the sheriff of Bernalillo County, and I hereby execute on all the shoes in this store." The sheriff then walked out, leaving the shoes in the store. Which of these statements best describes Saucy's legal position after this act by the sheriff?

A. Saucy is a general unsecured creditor, because it has a judgment against Clyde's but has not executed on any of Clyde's property.
B. Saucy is an involuntary lien creditor now because it has a valid judgment against Clyde's.
C. Saucy is an involuntary lien creditor and thus has a valid lien on the shoes because it has executed on the shoes.
D. It is unclear whether Saucy has a valid lien and security interest in the shoes because it is unclear whether the sheriff has exercised sufficient dominion and control over the shoes to create a valid lien.

ANALYSIS. Try to first find the obviously incorrect answers and eliminate them. One thing that is simply never true is that a creditor has a lien on something merely because the creditor has obtained a judgment. Thus, **B** is the most obviously incorrect answer. The judgment here is just a piece of paper. All three of the other answers are at least plausible, but **B** is incorrect because it is not clear if the execution was successful.

The Barney Fife move in which the sheriff engaged here is ambiguous at best. He declared that he was executing on the shoes. OK, we'll admit that he said this, but is it true? He left the shoes there. He did not load them in his vehicle and take them away, nor did he put tags on them and provide notice to the world through the tags that the shoes were the subjects of a valid lien on the part of Saucy. What does it mean to exercise dominion and control over the shoes and thus create a valid lien on them? Courts disagree on this. Secret or invisible liens about which no one can find out are poor policy, suggesting that **A** is the correct answer because this was not sufficient to create a lien. If the sheriff's actions were not sufficient to create a lien, then **A** would be

---

5. This is much oversimplified, but you get the idea.

true. Because it is unclear, however, the correct answer is **D**. In Credit Bureau of Broken Bow v. Moninger, 204 Neb. 679, 284 N.W.2d 855 (1979), the court found that a sheriff who took similar actions towards a truck, then left the truck with its owner rather than driving it away, had exercised sufficient dominion and control over the truck to create a valid and enforceable lien on the truck. Many courts would decide the same case differently, based on the aversion to secret liens, making **D**, rather than **B**, the best answer. Unfortunately, there is much uncertainty in this area of law. It will help if you can become comfortable with this uncertainty and learn to work with it.

Now let's review the situation with another question.

QUESTION 2. Saucy Shoes could have saved itself some trouble by asking the sheriff to do which of the following when he got to Clyde's premises?

A. Call the office and tell them he was executing on the shoes.
B. Load the shoes into his vehicle and take them back to his office, or put up DO NOT ENTER signs and change the locks.
C. Announce to the customers in Clyde's that he was taking the shoes.
D. Tag all the shoes.

ANALYSIS. **C** is wrong for the reasons stated above. Announcing that he is executing on the shoes does not clearly create a lien that will allow Saucy to sell the shoes in satisfaction of its judgment, so this is not the best thing to do. **A** is wrong because it makes no sense. Why would the sheriff call his office? This will accomplish nothing. **D** says that the sheriff should tag the shoes, but this is not the safest or the easiest way to create a lien. First, it would take as long as loading the shoes into his vehicle and taking them away. Second, think about the purpose of the tags. The purpose is to let people know that the lien is there even though the debtor is still in possession of the goods. The tags would probably go on the boxes and the shoes could be sold without the boxes.

Taking the shoes is the only way to make sure they will not be dissipated before the sheriff's sale, but changing the locks will also probably work to create a lien. While changing the locks will likely create a lien, it will also create more work because the sheriff will probably need to come back to get the shoes to sell them anyway. In any case, **B** is the best answer.

B. State Law Exemptions

As noted previously, once the creditor has obtained a judgment, most states require the creditor to deliver a bunch of documents called a writ package to the debtor. This writ package includes a document that asks the debtor whether any of his or her property is exempt from execution by judgment creditors. Every state allows people to keep some things exempt from creditors' claims, even if they owe other people money. A typical state exemption statute would allow a debtor to keep some equity in a home, some clothing, some equity in a car, etc.

The theory behind allowing the debtor to keep some things is that it will accomplish very little to force people to become homeless, to take away their transportation to work, and to take away their clothing. Items like clothing are presumably needed to hold down a job, and they are also worth very little to a creditor. People should be able to keep enough property to survive, so the theory goes, and to avoid becoming wards of, and charges upon, the state.

State law exemptions vary incredibly from state to state. For example, in New Mexico, each person can keep $60,000 in equity in a home and $4,000 equity in a car, free from any executing creditor. In Delaware, however, there is no allowance for a home (meaning no homestead exemption), and very little exemption for a car or anything else. In Texas and Florida, a debtor can keep unlimited equity in a home, even if the home is worth many millions of dollars.[6] Thus, an unpaid creditor, or the victim of a tort or even a hit-and-run accident, could not force the sale of a million-dollar home in Texas to pay a judgment that a court held was now due and owing.

Keep in mind that whether a debtor has any exempt property is determined based on the debtor's equity in the property, meaning the amount of value in each item over and above any secured loans or liens on the property. This is easy to forget, so it is important to practice using this concept. To determine the debtor's equity, you must value the property and then subtract the amount of any secured creditor claims.

Also keep in mind that the state exemptions never prevent a consensual secured creditor from enforcing its security interest by either judicial or nonjudicial means. One way to remember this is simply to think of the consensual security interest as being ahead of or higher than the exemptions. Another way to think of it is that it is as if the security interest is a voluntary waiver of the exemption in the item pledged as collateral. Either way, the exemptions don't help when a secured creditor is repossessing.

QUESTION 3. The Smiths live in a state in which each debtor can keep $30,000 in equity in a home and $4,000 in equity in a car, as well as all the proceeds in IRAs and other retirement accounts. Janny, a judgment holder, has a $50,000 judgment and is looking for property upon which to execute. You represent Janny. In your depositions in aid of execution,

6. Interestingly, the Florida exemptions are extremely lean other than the homestead exemption and allow the debtor to keep just $1,000 in all personal property of any kind.

you have discovered that the Smiths own a $200,000 home with a $100,000 first mortgage on it, as well as a $25,000 home equity loan on top of that. The Smiths own three cars, a $20,000 Mercedes with an $18,000 loan left to be paid, a $5,000 Chevy Blazer that is all paid up, as well as an old pickup worth $1,000. The Smiths have a $30,000 savings account and $200,000 in retirement funds located in an IRA.

Janny is champing at the bit over the retirement funds and the Mercedes, convinced that these assets will satisfy his judgment. Is he correct?

A. No, because the judgment will be satisfied from the equity in the home, and this equity must be exhausted first.
B. No, because there is no value in either of these things for a judgment holder, as both are fully exempt.
C. Yes, because the retirement funds are unreasonable in light of the Smiths' financial condition.
D. Yes, because the home is fully encumbered.

ANALYSIS. The answer is **B**. There is no value for Janny in either item, as outrageous as this may seem. The Smiths have $200,000 socked away in retirement funds. However, the fact pattern states that all funds held in IRAs are exempt regardless of amount. This is not unrealistic. Many states have a similar exemption. **C** is incorrect because the statute does not put a dollar limit on this exemption, from what you have been told. The policy behind such an exemption is to encourage people to save for their futures. In practice, this type of state law exemption allows careful planners to protect large sums from creditors. **B** said that both the IRA and the Mercedes were unavailable, and the Mercedes is similarly exempt from execution. The debtors have just $2,000 in equity in the car.

Re-read the problem and make sure you understand the concept of equity and how equity is calculated. An item's equity is calculated by subtracting the amount of any liens from the total value of the property. For example, the Mercedes is worth $20,000 and the total secured claims on the Mercedes are $18,000. Thus, the equity in the car is $2,000. Assuming that the Mercedes is one of the two cars the Smiths will choose to keep, there is no value in the Mercedes for Janny. The statute allows the Smiths to keep one car each with up to $4,000 in equity in each. Thus, this Mercedes is clearly exempt. It will make Janny mad to think that Mr. or Mrs. Smith can drive the nice car and not pay him, but that is the law.

As for the other two answers, they are also flawed. Both contain incorrect statements about the home. **D** claims that the home is fully encumbered but it is not. The liens or encumbrances (as they are sometimes called) total $125,000, leaving $75,000 in equity. Fully encumbered means that the liens are as large as the value of the collateral, which is not true here. **A** contains two incorrect statements: first, that the creditor must go after the home equity first and, second, that the home equity is sufficient to satisfy the judgment. There is no requirement that a judgment holder be paid from home equity first. In fact, the judgment holder is allowed to choose which nonexempt assets from which to be paid, although the debtors can voluntarily sell smaller items and pay the judgment, if this will allow them to save their home. Second, the judgment cannot be satisfied from the equity in the home. The home is worth $200,000 and the liens total $125,000. There is $75,000 in equity in the home. Out of the equity, the debtors get the first $60,000 from the sale, on account of the exemptions of $30,000 per person, after secured claims are taken care of.[7] This would leave just $15,000 (assuming there are no costs of sale) to satisfy the $50,000 judgment.

Before moving on, let's use this problem to reinforce what you just learned. Go back and re-read the problem, this time trying to calculate the total amount of cash you could get for Janny if you chose the right items to execute on. Do it now before reading on! Then read the footnote.[8]

1. *State law exemptions and bankruptcy*

The primary role of the state law exemptions is to protect property from creditor executions in cases in which there is no bankruptcy case. These state law exemptions, however, can sometimes be used in bankruptcy as well. Because most of the bankruptcy class is about bankruptcy, students tend to forget that one can use the state exemptions outside bankruptcy and without the need for a bankruptcy.

Just so you know, the Bankruptcy Code has its own set of exemptions, which can be used only in a bankruptcy case. (*See* 11 U.S.C. §522(d).) In some states, these federal bankruptcy exemptions cannot be used at all, even in a bankruptcy, leaving the debtor with only the state exemptions. This is true because Congress allowed states to opt out of the exemption provisions of the Bankruptcy Code. Thus, the state law exemptions are always available to everyone, both inside and outside bankruptcy, and in some states, debtors can choose between the state and the federal exemptions in a bankruptcy case.

The real point here, though, is that the main purpose of the state law exemptions we just talked about is to protect property from creditor executions in cases in which there is no bankruptcy case — cases where a creditor is

7. These would either be satisfied from the sale proceeds or the property would be sold subject to the liens.

8. The nonexempt assets include $15,000 from the house, among other things. The house is worth $200,000, so we take this amount and deduct the $125,000 in total liens, leaving $75,000 in equity. Of that $75,000 in equity, $60,000 is exempt, leaving $15,000 for Janny from the house. The debtors also have $30,000 in savings, which does not fit within any category of the exemptions. Finally, there is $1,000 in equity in the $5,000 car that is not exempt and there is the $1,000 pickup. The debtor can only keep two cars, not three. Thus, the total amount available for Janny (ignoring any cost of sale) is $47,000. Not bad if you know where to look!

executing on assets in a state court proceeding. This confuses students greatly. By the end of the semester, almost all students forget that state law exemptions can be used outside bankruptcy. By then they have all but forgotten about state collection law. To keep this from happening to you, it might help to remember that in this guide, state law exemptions are presented as an integral part of the state law collection process.

C. Fraudulent Transfers Under the Uniform Fraudulent Transfer Act

1. *The purpose of fraudulent transfer law*

As you have seen, a secured creditor often extends credit and takes an interest in certain collateral, and the debtor is allowed to keep and use the collateral as long as he or she does not go into default. If the debtor does default on the loan, the secured creditor can reach the collateral to satisfy the loan.

Unsecured creditors who have no collateral always run the risk that the debtor who owes them money will have no nonexempt or unencumbered assets from which to satisfy their claims. Sometimes the debtor simply has not accumulated much. At other times, however, the debtor may have concealed or transferred away property with the hope of avoiding the claims of executing creditors. Perhaps the debtor has predicted financial problems and tried to conceal property that a creditor might use to satisfy the debt. Or perhaps the debtor has sold property for less than its fair market value. Perhaps the debtor never intended to pay the debt and has manipulated property to become judgment-proof. The law recognizes that this type of thing happens and has provided some protection to unsecured creditors placed in these situations. Transfers of property, either with actual intent to defraud creditors, or for less than equivalent value that results in the debtor becoming insolvent, are reversible or avoidable as fraudulent transfers. Thus, creditors can execute on these assets even though they have passed to a third party.

2. *The history of the Uniform Fraudulent Transfer Act*

The law of fraudulent conveyances goes back to 1570 when the English Parliament passed the Statute of Elizabeth, perhaps the first statute regarding commercial law. The statute made it a crime to make a transfer if the intent of the transferor-debtor was to "hinder, delay or defraud" any creditor. Most states adopted the statute either by legislation or by court decision and, in 1918, the National Conference of Commissioners on Uniform State Laws promulgated the Uniform Fraudulent Conveyances Act (UFCA), which was revised in 1984 and renamed the Uniform Fraudulent Transfer Act (UFTA). Most states have adopted one or the other of these uniform acts, and the differences need not concern us here, as they involve details not necessary to our discussion.

One reason for the change to the UFTA was that the terminology of the UFCA had become considerably outdated and needed a modern overhaul. Also, the Bankruptcy Reform Act of 1978 changed the federal law on fraudulent transfers in significant ways, making it sensible to reconsider state law, as well. Finally, creditor-debtor relationships had become more complicated, making it necessary to revisit the subject in general.

In 2014, the Uniform Law Commission approved a series of amendments to the UFTA that also included changing the statute's name to the Uniform Voidable Transactions Act (UVTA). As of this writing, 22 states have adopted the UVTA to replace the UFTA. However, the amendments to the UFTA that were incorporated into the UVTA are fairly narrow, and the amended and renamed statute retains all of the key concepts of the UFTA. The main difference is to change references from "fraudulent transfers" to "voidable transactions." This is to clarify the confusion that arose with some courts from the fact that a constructive fraudulent transfer under the UFTA (see below) need not involve the traditional elements of a fraud action, especially the intent to deceive on the part of either the debtor or the transferee.

3. *The elements of a fraudulent transfer*

A fraudulent transfer occurs when a debtor either (1) transfers property with the actual intent to hinder, delay, or defraud a creditor, or (2) transfers property without receiving reasonably equivalent value in return, if the transfer leaves the debtor insolvent. The first type of fraudulent transfer is often called "actual fraud" and requires proof that the debtor was trying to defraud creditors by making the transfer. As in all cases that require proof of intent, this is often difficult to prove. If it is proven, the transfer is avoidable irrespective of whether it made the debtor insolvent.

The second type, often called "constructive fraud," does not require any showing that the debtor was acting fraudulently. Thus, this type of transfer does not involve any fraud but is still called a fraudulent transfer. The statute simply takes the position that transfers for less than fair considerations that leave the debtor-transferor insolvent can be avoidable. Typically, this type of transfer arises when the debtor makes a gift of valuable property, or sells property for an amount far below its fair market value, typically to a relative or a friend.

A full discussion of the law of fraudulent transfers is beyond the scope of this book, but the following observations will be helpful when you read the UFTA.

- With regard to the second type of fraudulent transfer, "insolvency" is the balance sheet definition: A debtor is insolvent if liabilities exceed assets. However, there is a presumption of insolvency if the debtor is generally not paying debts as they become due. (UFTA §2.)

- An actionable fraudulent transfer includes not just a "transfer made" but also an "obligation incurred" by a debtor with actual intent to defraud or for less than a reasonably equivalent value in exchange.
- A distinction is made as to which creditors can avoid the transfer. Future creditors (i.e., those who extended credit after the transfer was made) are protected only if the debtor-transferor intended to incur obligations (or should have believed that he or she would incur obligations) beyond his or her ability to repay them, or was left with assets that were unreasonably small in relation to the transaction that was entered into (UFTA §4). Present creditors, however, are protected not only in those situations but whenever the transfer is made either with the actual intent to defraud creditors, or made for less than a fair consideration (UFTA §§4 and 5).
- The definitions section of the act, UFTA §1, is important. There are extensive definitions of "value" (UFTA §3) and a long explanation of when transfers are deemed made (UFTA §6).
- The act treats transfers to "insiders," defined to include relatives, partners, and so forth, somewhat differently (UFTA §1(7)). As to present creditors, transfers to insiders for an antecedent debt are fraudulent if the insider had reason to believe that the debtor was insolvent (UFTA §5). What is unusual about this rule is that most fraudulent transfers are to non-creditors. Under bankruptcy law, pre-petition transfers by the debtor to certain favored creditors are avoidable as "preferences," but for the most part, preferences are not avoidable under state law. The UFTA section on payments to insider creditors is an exception to the general rule that we don't have avoidable preferences outside of bankruptcy.
- The act specifies certain facts that may evidence an actual intent to defraud, including, for example, the debtor-transferor retaining possession, concealment of the transfer, a substantial transfer of all of the debtor's assets, a transfer to an insider, and so forth (UFTA §4(b)). These are frequently called "badges of fraud," a term originating in the early days of the law of fraudulent transfers.
- When a fraudulent transfer is made, a creditor has several options (UFTA §7 and §8). The creditor may bring an action to avoid the transfer or execute on a judgment by levying directly against the transferred asset in the hands of the transferee. The creditor may also petition the court to enjoin the transfer or to have a receiver appointed. Finally, the creditor may recover judgment for the value of the asset transferred, or the amount necessary to satisfy the creditor's claim, whichever is less.
- The key benefit with all of these remedies for the affected creditor is that the remedies are against a party other than the (presumably insolvent) debtor: namely, against the initial transferee from the debtor or against subsequent transferees of the asset, other than good-faith transferees for value. Even the initial transferee from the debtor, if he or she is in good faith, is entitled, to the extent of any value given to the debtor, to a lien on the asset transferred or to a reduction in the amount of the liability on the judgment.

- A transfer made with the actual intent to defraud cannot be avoided if the transferee acted in good faith and gave fair equivalent value, nor can a transfer be avoided if a subsequent transferee gave value and took in good faith.

QUESTION 4. The debtor has been receiving nightly phone calls from credit card companies wondering when he is going to make his payments. In total, his credit card debt is around $12,000. He owns no home, nor does he have any other property secured by a lien. Eventually, one of the credit card companies sues him and receives a default judgment in the amount of $5,000. The day after receiving the judgment, the company plans to execute on the debtor's extremely rare collection of comic books valued at $7,000, his only asset. The debtor, fearful that his Spider-Man issue #1 will be taken from him forever, goes to a local comic book store and sells his whole collection. He tells the dealer—a childhood friend—of his situation and the comic book dealer makes a deal with him. He will "pay" him $6,000 for the entire collection and in two months the debtor can return and pay $6,500 for the entire collection's return. The transaction is memorialized in a contract on the back page of a worthless Archie comic. The debtor agrees and makes the deal. The credit card company gets wind of this contract, and seeks to void the transfer under the UFTA. What fact creates the easiest route to recovery for the creditor?

A. The debtor did not receive reasonable value. Therefore, under the UFTA, the company can force the return of the collection.
B. The dealer is an insider. Therefore, under the UFTA the company can force the return of the collection.
C. Because the contract here proves there was actual fraud, the creditor can use it to prove actual intent.
D. The debtor is insolvent.

ANALYSIS. **A** is almost correct, but not quite. There would be a question as to whether a collection worth $7,000 but sold for $6,000 was sold for fair value, but this probably is reasonably equivalent value, given that reasonable values always fall within a range. More importantly, there is an easier way for the creditor to use the UFTA, so **A** is not the best answer.

B is also close to correct, but not quite. A transfer to a person related to the debtor would be some indicia of fraud, but it is very unlikely that case law would define a childhood friend as an insider. Again, there is an easier way for the creditor to recover. **C** is the correct answer. The UFTA places a burden on the party seeking to undo or avoid the transfer, based on actual fraud, to prove intent to hinder, delay, or defraud the creditor. Fortunately for the creditor, the contract is a real smoking gun. The explicit intent to defraud could not be clearer.

D is incorrect. Although it appears that the debtor is insolvent under the definition of insolvency in the UFTA, because liabilities exceed assets, the problem does not state this explicitly. A failure to pay bills as they become due does raise a presumption of insolvency, but the debtor may be able to overcome it. Also, insolvency itself does not make a transfer fraudulent. The second element, that the debtor-transferor received less than reasonably equivalent value must be present, and, as discussed in the comments to answer **A**, this may not be the case. Thus, the correct answer is **C.**

QUESTION 5. The debtor, who is insolvent, owns a diamond ring that is a family heirloom. The ring is worth \$50,000. As a favor to his sister, the debtor agrees to sell her the ring for just \$10,000. The sister knows that this is a good deal for her, but she is unaware of the debtor's insolvency, and she buys the ring in good faith. At the time of the sale, the debtor has a creditor, Big Bank, to whom the debtor owes \$70,000 on a debt that is overdue. When Big Bank learns about the ring sale, Big Bank wishes to enforce a judgment against the sister because the debtor has no valuable assets and is essentially judgment-proof. For what amount of money may Big Bank enforce a judgment against the debtor's sister?

A. \$70,000.
B. \$50,000.
C. \$40,000.
D. \$10,000.

ANALYSIS. The correct answer is **C**. As explained earlier in this chapter, the creditor may recover judgment for the value of the asset transferred, or the amount necessary to satisfy the creditor's claim, whichever is less. In addition, even the initial transferee from the debtor, if he or she is in good faith, is entitled, to the extent of any value given to the debtor, to a reduction in the amount of the liability on the judgment. Here the value of the asset transferred is \$50,000 and the creditor is owed \$70,000. So we start with the lesser of those two numbers, \$50,000, and subtract from it the \$10,000 that the sister gave the debtor in good faith. That entitles Big Bank, the creditor, to recover \$40,000 from the initial transferee, the sister.

The easiest answer to eliminate here is **D**. That represents the amount that the initial transferee, the sister, paid the debtor in good faith. That amount can be subtracted from a potential judgment against the sister, but it does not represent the amount of the judgment itself. **A** is wrong because that is the amount that the creditor was owed, which here is greater than even the value of the asset transferred. **B** is wrong because although \$50,000 does represent the value of the asset transferred, which is less than what the creditor is owed, that answer fails to subtract the \$10,000 that the sister paid in good faith for the ring.

QUESTION 6. Debtor lives in a house that is worth $225,000. The maximum homestead exemption amount in the state where Debtor lives is $35,000. In addition to his homestead, Debtor has nonexempt assets whose value equals $75,000. Debtor has no secured creditors at this time, and his unsecured creditors are owed a total of $90,000. Debtor gives his homestead to his daughter as a gift. If we assume that Debtor is in good faith when he gives his homestead to his daughter, would that transfer by Debtor qualify as a constructive fraudulent transfer?

A. Yes, because the transfer caused Debtor to become insolvent.
B. Yes, because the transferee in this case was a family member.
C. No, because Debtor made the transfer in good faith.
D. No, because the transfer of exempt property cannot count as a fraudulent transfer.

ANALYSIS. Before getting to the correct answer here, let's see why the other three choices are incorrect. Choice **B** is incorrect because the donee's status as a family member is not a factor in defining what is or is not a constructive fraudulent transfer. Instead, the focus in a constructive fraudulent transfer analysis is strictly on the debtor-transferor's solvency and whether or not the debtor-transferor received reasonably equivalent value in exchange for the transfer. Choice **C** is incorrect because the debtor's good faith is only relevant for actual fraudulent transfers under UVTA § 4(a), but not for constructive fraudulent transfers under UVTA §5(a). Choice **D** is incorrect because even though the transfer of completely exempt property cannot count as a fraudulent transfer under the UVTA, Debtor's homestead in this case represented $190,000 worth of nonexempt property. That leaves **A**, the correct answer. Choice **A** is correct because a constructive fraudulent transfer under UVTA §5(a) includes transfers that cause the debtor to become insolvent, as was true in this case. And, of course, giving something away as a gift means by definition that the debtor-transferor did not receive reasonably equivalent value in exchange for the transfer.

D. The Closer: Chapters 2 and 3

Your neighbor Josh had become your new best friend, at least until he stiffed you on a big loan that you made to him. He built a new patio and decided that he needed one of those new gas grills made of stainless steel, with the ice bucket built in and all the other bells and whistles. He promised to have lots of great parties if he could only buy the grill and, as a result, you lent him $5,000. You did the deal on a handshake, with no paperwork. He was going to pay you back over ten months at $500 a month. Since you lent him the money, he rarely answers the phone, and you haven't seen any of your money. Which of the following statements accurately describes your legal position at this time?

1. You're perfectly safe to go over and repossess the gas grill while Josh is at work, as Josh owes you money and promised to pay you back.
2. If you grab the gas grill from Josh's house, you could be guilty of conversion and convicted of a crime.
3. If you had taken a security interest in the gas grill, then you could repossess it at any time.
4. If you had taken a security interest in the gas grill, you could repossess it at any time, as long as it did not fall within Josh's state exemption.

A. All of the above.
B. 2, 3, and 4.
C. 2 and 3.
D. Just 3.

ANALYSIS. Choice **1** says that you are free to repossess the gas grill at any time. This is incorrect, however, as you failed to obtain a security interest in the gas grill. Consequently, if you do decide to take the gas grill and you are caught, you could be guilty of conversion. This would be a crime. Although you made a loan to Josh, you did not retain any interest in the gas grill and, as a result, Josh alone owns the gas grill. Consequently, choice **1** is incorrect and you can eliminate **A** as a possible correct answer. Choice **2**, on the other hand, describes the opposite perspective and is true. If you take the gas grill you are essentially stealing it at this point because you failed to retain a security interest in it. As a result, choice **2** is correct. This means that the answer must be either **B** or **C**. Choice **3** says if you had taken a security interest in the gas grill you could repossess it and this is correct, something you learned in Chapter 2. As a result choice **3** should also appear in the correct answer.

What about choice **4**? This is probably the trickiest part of the question, as choice **4** states that if you had taken a security interest in the gas grill, you would be able to repossess, but only if it did not fall within Josh's state law exemptions. Choice **4** is incorrect because secured creditors do not need to worry about the exemptions. Their claims come before the exemptions. To get the gas grill as an unsecured creditor, you would have to fulfill the execution process, and even then could not execute on the gas grill unless the gas grill did not fall within any of Josh's exemptions. The exemptions are always something to worry about if you are an unsecured creditor, but are not if you're a secured creditor. As a result, the answer is **C**.

Martin's and Keating's Picks

1. Question 1	**D**
2. Question 2	**B**
3. Question 3	**B**
4. Question 4	**C**
5. Question 5	**C**
6. Question 6	**A**
The Closer: Chapters 2 and 3	**C**

4

Introduction to Bankruptcy

OVERVIEW

A. The Bankruptcy System: The Basics
   1. Chapter 7
   2. Chapter 13
   3. Chapter 12
   4. Chapter 11
   5. Chapter 9

B. Definitions and Learning to Read the Code

Martin's and Keating's Picks

Federal bankruptcy law is a uniquely American phenomenon. It is an intricate system designed, in part, to fuel and support capitalism. You will notice that the system is lenient on debtors in some ways and allows people to get out from under their debts with few societal repercussions. This was much truer before the 2005 amendments to the Bankruptcy Code, which make bankruptcy more difficult to file procedurally and the system more punitive.

Some people really take to bankruptcy law because it raises some of the most fundamental questions about the human condition. What does a person really need? What should happen to a person who does not pay his or her debts? What is gained by continuing to recognize the debts, when a debtor has no money? Should the rules for discharging or releasing debts be different for businesses, compared to individuals with mostly consumer debts? How does American bankruptcy law fit into our overall economic policy?

Bankruptcy law itself is quite technical, but these policy questions drive the system. Just as we saw in our brief discussion of state law, secured creditors have superior rights in bankruptcy when compared to creditors that do not have any collateral. You'll also see that some holders of unsecured debts (unsecured creditors) receive special treatment in bankruptcy (which we call priority treatment) because society finds them important.

Virtually all bankruptcy rules are designed to reflect what we find important as a society. If you can learn the policy behind a bankruptcy rule, it will help you understand and remember the rule. Most bankruptcy courses organize the course materials around two categories of cases: consumer bankruptcy cases and business bankruptcy cases. Many bankruptcy casebooks discuss Chapter 7 liquidation cases first, mostly in the context of consumer cases,[1] and then move into Chapter 13 cases, which are repayment plans for individual debtors. Having tackled consumer bankruptcy, many of these textbooks then move on to Chapter 11, a complex repayment system that is used mostly by businesses.[2] Other casebooks organize the materials around general bankruptcy subject matters such as the automatic stay, and discuss how the subject matter is treated within those subjects. This book starts the bankruptcy material with two introductory chapters. The first describes the different types of bankruptcy in broad terms and also teaches statutory reading through some Code definitions.[3] The second addresses bankruptcy court jurisdiction and administration. We recommend that you work through the definitions section before moving on, but of course, it is up to you. See if you find it helpful and, as with all parts of this book, use it to the extent that it works for you. The jurisdiction chapter can be skipped and read later, depending on when your teacher covers this in class. It seems incomplete not to cover jurisdiction here in the beginning, but it is quite complex and may seem a bit much with no background in the basics.

A. The Bankruptcy System: The Basics

In the United States, all the different kinds of bankruptcy are designed to balance two things: the rights of debtors to a fresh start or a second chance, and the rights of creditors to be paid. This tension is present in all aspects of the system, and all types of bankruptcy send off the same general vibe: Get in trouble with your creditors and this system will help you find a way out. Don't abuse the system, however, or you will not reap its benefits. If you are a cheater and a liar, you could even end up in jail!

1. Chapter 7, the basic straight, liquidation type of bankruptcy, can be used by both individuals and by businesses of all kinds. A debtor need not be totally broke or insolvent to file for Chapter 7 bankruptcy. However, an individual debtor (meaning a person as opposed to a legal entity such as a corporation) is eligible for Chapter 7 relief only if the debtor satisfies the needs-based test described in §707(b), which is called the "means test."

2. Chapter 11 can be used by individuals as well, but this is rare because it is expensive and harder to succeed in than Chapter 13. Normally, only an individual whose debts are too high to qualify for a Chapter 13 will file a Chapter 11 case.

3. We know how much most students hate to read the Code, but we still think it is critical to learning all areas of statutory law. Statutes, if you can learn to read them, are so much handier than common law (cases). Much of what you need to know is right there in one place in the statute, and there is less need to sift through endless case digests.

Bankruptcy cases in the United States fall into two models or categories. They are either "sell-out" or "pay-out" cases.[4] Sell-out or liquidation-style cases (also sometimes called straight bankruptcy cases) are cases in which the assets available for creditors are sold and distributed to creditors, quickly ending the case. Pay-out cases are cases in which the debtor promises, through a plan of repayment, to pay some or all creditors from future income over time. Both the phrases "sell out" and "pay out" can be misnomers, but these are quick generalizations that should help you learn the basics.

1. *Chapter 7*

Most cases filed in the United States are Chapter 7 liquidation cases, or "sell-out" cases. These cases are resolved quickly. In each Chapter 7 case, a trustee is appointed to gather all assets available to pay creditors and to sell them and distribute the proceeds, according to a structured priority scheme. The trustee is a fiduciary for all creditors and is charged with maximizing value for estate creditors. This is often done by rooting around for free assets to distribute. Chapter 7 is primal bankruptcy, the simplest kind.

Chapter 7 is available to both legal entities like corporations and limited liability companies (LLCs), as well as to individuals. If a corporation or LLC files a Chapter 7 case, this is the easiest case of all. There typically are no issues. The corporation is entitled to no exemptions because it will be dissolved or remain in limbo as an empty shell. It will have no ongoing life. For the same reason, it also does not get a discharge. Thus, the two most litigated issues in a Chapter 7 case, exemptions and dischargeability, are not at issue in a corporate Chapter 7 case.

When a natural person files a Chapter 7 case — and these cases amount to the vast majority of all bankruptcy cases filed in the United States — the debtor turns over all nonexempt assets to a bankruptcy trustee who sells them and distributes them to creditors according to the priority scheme. Although these cases fall into the sell-out category of cases, in most of them the debtor has no nonexempt assets; thus, there is no sell-out. Despite the sell-out classification, in such a situation nothing is sold and the debtor loses no property. These are often called no-asset cases.

What issues commonly arise in a natural person's Chapter 7 case? The trustee could disagree with the debtor over what property is exempt and may challenge the value of the debtor's exempt property as too low, thus arguing that there would be assets available to creditors if the property (or some part of it) were sold. The trustee or an individual creditor might object to the debtor's discharge due to wrongdoing on the part of the debtor right before or during the bankruptcy case (if the debtor hid assets, for example). A creditor could also object to the dischargeability of its particular debt, or perhaps the United

4. *See* Elizabeth Warren & Jay Westbrook, The Law of Debtors and Creditors 115 (7th ed. 2014).

States Trustee Program (an arm of the federal Department of Justice) could file an abuse motion to have the case dismissed because the debtor has income over and above his or her expenses and thus could afford a Chapter 13 plan.

As another potential issue in a Chapter 7 case, the trustee could challenge whether a Chapter 7 debtor should file a Chapter 13 instead because he or she can afford to pay a Chapter 13 plan rather than simply discharging most debts.

The duties of the United States Trustee have been expanded under the 2005 Code amendments. These duties are set out in 28 U.S.C. §586. They now include appointing case trustees under Chapters 7 and 11, performing general monitoring of cases and attorneys' fees, appointing creditors' committees in Chapter 11 cases, monitoring overall abuse in the consumer bankruptcy system, certifying credit-counseling agencies, and approving debtor education programs.

In most cases, a Chapter 7 trustee administers the case within 90 days of the filing, there is no litigation, and after these 90 days are over, the debtor obtains a discharge of most of his or her debts.

2. *Chapter 13*

Chapter 13 cases are "pay-out" rather than sell-out cases. As a general matter, the trustee does not sell the debtor's nonexempt assets. Instead, the debtor is allowed to keep them so long as the debtor is paying at least the value of these nonexempt assets to creditors over the course of the plan. In a sense, the debtor is buying back his or her assets from the creditors.

The idea is that the debtor will propose a repayment plan for paying creditors and will make the proposed payments for three to five years. During that time, the debtor will pay all allowed secured claims in full,[5] all priority claims in full, and will pay a distribution to unsecured creditors as well, assuming the debtor has sufficient disposable income to do so.

The case is administered by the Chapter 13 trustee who (like the Chapter 7 trustee) is a fiduciary for creditors, charged with creating the best possible recovery for the debtor's creditors. The trustee may do this by trying to get the debtor to contribute more of his or her income to the plan, by objecting to the debtor's expenses as profligate, or by encouraging the debtor to sell some nonexempt property if this is the only way the plan will work.

In a Chapter 13 case, commonly litigated issues include the following: (1) the value of the allowed secured claims, or really, the value of the underlying collateral (because in some situations the debtor can just pay the value of the collateral, rather than the whole loan, to many of his secured creditors); (2) the priority treatment of certain claims; (3) whether the debtor has

---

5. As you'll learn very shortly, this does not mean that the secured creditor's entire claim will be paid in full. In some cases, the debtor may pay the lesser of the value of the collateral or the amount of the loan, which amount defines the size of the allowed secured claim under §506 of the Code. Part of the secured creditor's claim could be unsecured, and that part would not necessarily be paid in full.

contributed all of his or her disposable income to the plan, which is required under Chapter 13; and (4) the value of exempt property as that bears on the minimum distributions the debtor must pay under the plan. The Chapter 13 trustee plays a substantial role in the success of Chapter 13 cases and will object to the plan if it does not comply with the Code. If all of the rules contained in Chapter 13 of the Code are satisfied, the court approves the plan and the debtor sets out to complete the payments.

3. *Chapter 12*

Chapter 12 is a bankruptcy scheme for family farmers and family fishermen. It is very similar to Chapter 13, but has slightly easier repayment rules and higher debt limits.

4. *Chapter 11*

Chapter 11 is a pay-out-style case, available to individuals but almost always used by business entities like corporations. You can read about big Chapter 11 cases that are pending right now on the front page of the Wall Street Journal. Recent cases include Borders Bookstores, General Motors, CIT Group, Kmart, Enron, WorldCom, United Airlines, and so on. In the past, Federated Stores (Macy's), Texaco, and many others have emerged successfully from Chapter 11.

Chapter 11 cases involve restructuring the debts and other obligations of companies that need help. The general idea, as with Chapter 13, is that the debtor will repay a portion of its debts over time from its future operations. Its plan must pay its priority claims in full. It also must pay all of the allowed secured claims in full but, as in a Chapter 13 case, this does not mean that the secured creditor gets its entire claim paid in full. The debtor must pay the lesser of the value of the collateral or the amount of the loan, which defines the size of the allowed secured claim. Thus, part of the secured creditor's claim could be unsecured, and that part would not necessarily be paid in full. Finally, while Chapter 11 does not technically require it, in most cases the debtor will pay a distribution to the unsecured creditors.[6]

The plan approval process is different in a Chapter 11 case than in a Chapter 13. In a Chapter 11, the debtor solicits votes from classes of creditors, for what it hopes will turn out to be a consensual Chapter 11 pay-out plan. Creditors are placed in classes for the purpose of plan voting. They vote by

---

6. All creditors get to vote on the plan, and most will not vote in favor of a plan that pays them no distribution. Technically, a debtor can get a plan approved without the positive votes of the unsecured creditor class, as long as it pays unsecured creditors at least as much in the plan as they would get in a Chapter 7 case, and as long as no junior classes (including equity interests or owners of the business) receive or retain anything under the plan. There is an exception to this rule if senior classes of claims consent. It is always easier to get the plan approved through positive votes. All these rules are covered in great detail later in this Guide—we just want you to know that the text is simplified for ease of understanding at this early stage.

class under a modified majority rule system.[7] If all classes of creditors vote to go along with the plan, then the court generally approves the plan. If there are holdouts (people who are not in favor of the plan), the court can sometimes force the creditors to accept the plan, assuming that various tests are met by the plan and the debtor.

There is one huge difference between a case under Chapter 13 and a case under Chapter 11. Both are pay-out-style cases, but in a Chapter 13 case, a trustee actively looks over and manages the plan, the plan payments, and the overall case. In a Chapter 11 case, there normally is no trustee in the case at all. The company in bankruptcy is usually run by the same people who were in management before the filing, or by some newly appointed management — but in any event, by management! Some might say that the fox is in the henhouse. The debtor continues to run the company, although it does get a different name. The debtor (in effect, its management) is now called the debtor-in-possession or the DIP. The DIP has, under the Code, all of the duties and powers of a trustee. The DIP is a fiduciary and is charged with creating the best possible distributions (payouts) for creditors. The DIP, then, has many conflicting duties: to shareholders, to management, to creditors, and to employees. Its primary duty, however, is to creditors.

The U.S.-style Chapter 11 case, in which management can stay in place, is unique in the world. You might wonder why we allow this type of thing, rather than just liquidating failing businesses as most of the world does. Keeping the company afloat and allowing it to try to stay in business is often justified on the basis that assets are usually worth more in an ongoing business and, as a result, creditors can often get more in a reorganization plan being paid over time, than they could get in a liquidation.[8] Others justify Chapter 11 as a way to save jobs, and to keep from disrupting communities that might otherwise be left without local industry. In any case, the subject of Chapter 11's existence is controversial and some scholars have called for its abolition. Despite this, Chapter 11 shows no sign of becoming extinct. This has been a drastic oversimplification of Chapter 11, and you'll learn much more about this in Chapters 28 through 37.

5. *Chapter 9*

Chapter 9 is a reorganization-style bankruptcy scheme, similar to Chapter 11, but for municipalities. It has been used over 70 times, but only a few times by large municipalities. The most famous case involved the bankruptcy of Detroit, Michigan. Other municipality bankruptcies in the past have included

---

7. Some might call the applicable rule a mixed majority-plurality rule. What is required is that the debtor obtains positive votes from more than one-half in number and at least two-thirds in amount of all creditors voting within each class.

8. This is perhaps true for many unsecured creditors, but is often untrue for secured creditors, who could take their collateral and realize on it immediately if it were not for the bankruptcy.

Bridgeport, Connecticut; Orange County, California; and Vallejo, California. Of course, like any other bankruptcy debtor, municipalities file for bankruptcy for a variety of reasons. In fact, one town, Washington Park, Illinois, purportedly filed because one of its main sources of income, high license fees for topless bars, was found to be unconstitutional.

B. Definitions and Learning to Read the Code

In this section of this guide, we hope to help you with one of the most difficult skills learned in the bankruptcy class: reading and interpreting the Bankruptcy Code. Most of these questions are not difficult. They just require careful reading. This section is designed to hone your statutory reading skills by asking you interpretive questions about the Code sections you are reading. We work hard on Code-reading skills with our own students, who claim that this process has helped them in their other statutory classes as well.

In approaching these questions, first read the quoted section of the Code and then try to answer the question. If you do this before reading the analysis that follows, you will get much more out of the questions. Eventually, you will be reading the Code with much more confidence and ease. You may even find that you enjoy this.

QUESTION 1. Every debtor hopes to include as many of his debts under his bankruptcy umbrella as possible, so the debts can be discharged and the debtor can move on to his debt-free life. To be included in the bankruptcy, the debts must qualify as claims under §101(5). Under this section, a claim must:

1. Be matured;
2. Be unliquidated;
3. Result from an action or event that occurred before the debtor's bankruptcy filing;
4. If not liquidated by the time distributions of estate assets are to be made, be estimated for the purposes of allowance.

A. 1 and 2 only.
B. 1, 2, and 3 only.
C. All of the above.
D. 3 and 4.

ANALYSIS. This question is hard because you cannot tell whether all of these statements are true or false just by reading the statute. You can tell fairly quickly, however, that 1 and 2 are wrong. As your first Code reading suggests, a "claim" need not be matured (meaning it is already due), so **1** is incorrect. **2** is also false because a claim can be unliquidated (meaning that its amount is still unset), but it doesn't have to be. This means that **A**, **B**, and **C** must be wrong, leaving only **D** as a possible right answer. As it turns out, **3** is true, and so is **4**, but it may not be clear why. Read on to find out.

A big part of the reason a debtor files for bankruptcy is to discharge pre-petition or pre-bankruptcy claims. Only claims that arise before the bankruptcy petition actually get discharged, however. Those that arise after the bankruptcy filing must generally be paid in full by the debtor, without regard to the bankruptcy. This makes sense. One cannot file bankruptcy in the morning and then go out and charge something in the afternoon, hoping to discharge (or become free from) the post-filing charge in the bankruptcy case. Bankruptcy cases clean up the past, but the debtor is expected to proceed at his or her own risk for debts incurred after the filing. The bankruptcy covers all claims arising before the filing. As the Code provides, the concept of a claim is broad enough to include a judgment against the debtor that would have been obtained years after the bankruptcy is filed, but that resulted from a car accident that the debtor caused before his or her bankruptcy case was filed.

Assume a typical automobile accident that takes place soon before one of the parties to the accident files for bankruptcy. Although the other person — the one that did not file (also called the nondebtor party) — was hurt, we would not know the amount of his or her claim. It would be a contingent claim, meaning that perhaps fault had not even been established. It would also be unliquidated, meaning its amount was certainly unknown. Although such a claim would be contingent and unliquidated, it could still be discharged in the debtor's bankruptcy because the events leading to the claim occurred pre-petition. The Code's broad definition of claim allows the debtor to discharge all debts arising from pre-filing events, and thus get a true fresh start, a concept discussed more later. The claim must result from an action or event that occurred pre-petition and may need to be estimated for the purposes of allowance if it is not liquidated in time to be paid (assuming there is going to be a distribution to creditors). That means the answer is **3** and **4**, or choice **D**. 11 U.S.C. §101(5).

Try not to get too frustrated when first attempting to read the Code. This first question demonstrates one of the reasons it is hard. The sections contain words whose meanings you don't know. Little by little, you'll learn the new language. Sometimes a law dictionary can help, too.

QUESTION 2. Under Chapter 12 of the Code, family farmers and fishermen get special privileges when they file a reorganization-style bankruptcy. Which of the following are unquestionably ineligible for a Chapter 12 bankruptcy, because they do not qualify as a "family farmer" under §101(18)?

1. An individual engaged in farming with $15 million in noncontingent, unliquidated debts.
2. Del Monte Fruit Company, a publicly traded company.
3. A corporation owned by the Jones family, whose assets all relate to their farming operation.
4. A corporation owned 100 percent by the Ramos family. Eighty percent of the corporation's assets are used in the farming operation, with the other 20 percent used for commercial leasing.

A. 1 and 2.
B. All of the above.
C. 1, 2, and 4.
D. 1 and 4.

ANALYSIS. An individual engaged in farming whose noncontingent unliquidated debts total $15 million is ineligible for Chapter 12 bankruptcy because the unliquidated debts cannot exceed $12,562,250.[9] Because the question asks which of these is unquestionably ineligible, then **1** is part of the answer, right? This did not help much, as **1** is included in every answer available.

2 says that Del Monte is a corporation. While subsection (A) of §101(18) states that a family farmer must be an individual, if you read further into subsection (B), you'll see that a family farmer can be a corporation or a partnership, but the corporation or partnership must be owned at least 50 percent by one family, it cannot be a publicly traded company, and 80 percent of its assets must be related to the farming operation. Can you find all of these things in the statute? Del Monte Fruit Company is publicly traded, so under subsection 101(18)(B)(iii), it is clearly ineligible for Chapter 12, and **2** should also be in the correct answer.

Under the statute, there is nothing about the Jones family that would seem to make them clearly ineligible for Chapter 12, so **3** should not appear in the correct answer. As for the Ramos corporation, the question states that the corporation uses 80 percent of its assets in farming, but the statute, §101(18)(B) requires that it use "more than" 80 percent of its assets in farming. Thus, the Ramos corporation is clearly ineligible for Chapter 12, and the correct answer is **C**. Gee whiz! This Code reading is pretty precise! This problem demonstrates the importance of careful — even tediously careful — reading.

9. These numbers are adjusted every three years by the Judicial Conference of the United States. *See* 90 Fed. Reg. 8941 (2025), which is why they are so odd and uneven. These are the numbers as of April 1, 2025.

QUESTION 3. For certain purposes, especially when looking at transfers that the debtor may have made before filing his or her bankruptcy, we classify some transferees (people who received the transfers) differently because they have an especially close relationship with the debtor. We call these people who are close to the debtor insiders. Which of these is not an insider under Bankruptcy Code §101(31)?

A. The wife of the debtor.
B. The debtor's landlord.
C. The chief executive officer of the debtor.
D. A person in control of the debtor.

ANALYSIS. If you just pick through the definition of insider, slowly, you see that under §101(31) a debtor's landlord is not considered an insider under the Bankruptcy Code, but the rest of these people are, so the answer is **B**.

QUESTION 4. Different bankruptcy rules apply to a business that qualifies as a small business debtor. Under Bankruptcy Code §101(51)(D), a small business:

A. need not be engaged in business or commercial activity.
B. must have debts of at least $3,424,000.
C. must have debts of less than $3,424,000.
D. must have debts of $3,424,000.

ANALYSIS. Under §101(51)(D), a small business is a person engaged in commercial or business activities (other than merely owning or operating real property) that has aggregate noncontingent, liquidated, secured, and unsecured debts as of the date of the petition or the date of the order for relief in an amount not more than $3,424,000 (excluding debts owed to one or more affiliates or insiders). It also requires that the United States Trustee has not appointed under §1102(a)(1) a committee of unsecured creditors, or that the court has determined that the committee of unsecured creditors is not sufficiently active and representative to provide effective oversight of the debtor. **A** is incorrect, as the small business debtor must be engaged in business. **B** is incorrect because Code §101(51)(D) states that the debts cannot exceed $3,424,000, whereas **B** states that the debtor must have debts of at least $3,424,000. The debts can obviously be less than that. Again, reading carefully, **C** is incorrect because the debts need not be less than $3,424,000. They can be exactly $3,424,000 or any amount less than that, making **D** the correct answer.

QUESTION 5. You will learn a bit of fraudulent transfer law in this book. There is state fraudulent transfer law, as well as federal bankruptcy law on the subject. The point of all this law is to see if the debtor has transferred away assets (either fraudulently or for less than fair value) that could have been used to pay creditors. For the purposes of fraudulent transfer law contained in §548 of the Bankruptcy Code, a transfer under §101(54):

A. cannot include an indirect transfer.
B. must be a transfer of cash only.
C. can include a transfer of a security interest.
D. must be voluntary.

ANALYSIS. A transfer under §101(54) is defined to include every mode—direct or indirect, absolute or conditional, voluntary or involuntary—of disposing of or parting with property or with an interest in property, including retention of title as a security interest and foreclosure of the debtor's equity of redemption. How broad! Certainly it does include transfers that are indirect (**A**), as well as transfers that are not cash (**B**). Thus, both **A** and **B** are wrong. **C** is true. The transfer can be a transfer of a security interest. In fact, this is often the case, so **C** is the correct answer. What about **D**? **D** is incorrect as well, because the statute clearly states that for fraudulent transfer purposes, a transfer can be involuntary.

QUESTION 6. Which of the following obligations would not fall into the category of a "domestic support obligation" under §101(14A)?

A. A claim for back rent awarded to a spouse in a divorce decree and owed by the debtor.
B. A claim for past due legal fees associated with a lawsuit regarding the amount of child support owed.
C. A state government owed money under a family assistance plan.
D. A claim for half the house, awarded in the marital settlement agreement as part of the overall property settlement.

ANALYSIS. Section 101(14A) contains a very broad definition of what constitutes a "domestic support obligation" ("DSO"). The definition covers any support claim that accrues before or after the bankruptcy case, owed to a spouse, a former spouse, a child of the debtor, a parent of a child of the debtor (meaning it covers unmarried ex-partners), a legal guardian of the child, or even a responsible relative, a term not defined in the Bankruptcy Code. A DSO can even include claims held by a government entity as long as the claim is for "support." What is support? Any claim in the nature of alimony, maintenance, or support (including assistance provided by a government), for a spouse, former spouse, or child of the debtor or such child's parent, without regard to how the claim is characterized (*see* 11 U.S.C. §101(14A)).

One thing the definition does not cover is claims for property settlement debts. The distinction between DSOs (like child support and alimony) and property settlement debts is relevant in various parts of bankruptcy law (priorities and dischargeability, to name two), so **D** is the correct answer. The other three choices could all be DSOs, depending on the specific facts involved, so all three are incorrect. The legal fees associated with pursuing child support are almost certainly a DSO, eliminating **B**. The debt described in **C** could be a DSO if it is deemed to be in the nature of support. **A** is tricky in the sense that it sounds like just rent due to a spouse, which could be a property settlement claim, but it is not clear that it is not support. Because we can't really tell what the claim is for, **D** is the better answer as it states outright that it is a property settlement claim.

We hope that this brief foray into statutory reading has convinced you that you can read this and other statutes. If you scan through all of §101, you will notice that there are over 50 definitions. When these words or phrases are used in the substantive sections of the Bankruptcy Code, the definitions found in §101 control. We have looked at only a few of them because our purpose was not to get you to learn all of the definitions, but to get you reading the Code. Hopefully, you are a little more comfortable with reading it as a result of this exercise. We will meet many of the definitions that we did not cover later in these materials, and, for the most part, they will be explained in the context in which they are used. Don't hesitate, however, to go back to §101 whenever you see a word you don't know.

In most cases, you will find that the text in these materials is sufficient to give you an understanding of each topic that is covered. In some instances, however, we will specifically ask that you read a Code section in connection with a particular question. These questions will contain the words (CODE READER) in the preface. With those questions, you will need to read the cited Code section before trying to answer the question.[10]

QUESTION 7. (CODE READER) Alice sells her favorite painting to her friend, Betty, for $1,000 in cash. Betty gives the painting as a birthday gift to her son, Charles. Charles sells the painting to a stranger, Donald, on Craigslist for $800. Donald knowingly gives Charles a bad personal check for $800 that ends up being dishonored. Donald then has the painting stolen from his garage by a thief, Earl. Which of the above individuals qualifies as a "purchaser" for purposes of §101(43)?

10. We strongly recommend that you quickly peruse each Code section after it is cited in this book. This will improve your Code reading and your understanding of bankruptcy law more than anything else we can think of.

A. Only Betty
B. Only Betty and Charles
C. Only Betty, Charles and Donald
D. Betty, Charles, Donald and Earl

ANALYSIS. The term "purchaser," as defined in §101(43), means "transferee of a voluntary transfer." The "purchaser" does not need to pay consideration as our everyday definition of that term would probably require. Nor does a "purchaser" even need to be in good faith, as long as the transfer to that person was voluntary. Therefore, the only person among the four listed that would not qualify as a purchaser would be Earl, the thief. That's because Earl is not the transferee of a voluntary transfer of the painting since he stole the painting from Donald's garage. Even Donald qualifies as a purchaser, despite the fact that he knowingly bought the painting with a fraudulent check, because Charles still voluntarily transferred the painting to Donald in exchange for that bad check. Therefore, the correct answer here is **C.**

Martin's and Keating's Picks

1. Question 1 **D**
2. Question 2 **C**
3. Question 3 **B**
4. Question 4 **D**
5. Question 5 **C**
6. Question 6 **D**
7. Question 7 **C**

5

Jurisdiction and the Powers of the Bankruptcy Court

OVERVIEW
A. Introduction
B. Bankruptcy Court Jurisdiction over Bankruptcy Cases
C. Appeals from the Bankruptcy court
D. Preemption and the Relationship Between Federal Bankruptcy Law and State Law
E. The Court's Equity Power Under §105(a)
F. Sovereign Immunity of States and Tribes
Martin's and Keating's Picks

A. Introduction

Bankruptcy law in the United States is primarily federal law rather than state law. Article I, Section 8, of the U.S. Constitution gave Congress the power to establish uniform laws on the subject of bankruptcy throughout the United States. This has been done over the years through the enactment of a federal statute, originally called the Bankruptcy Act and now called the Federal Bankruptcy Code, or simply the Code. The Code is found in Title 11 of the U.S. Code. When you hear a reference to Title 11, the speaker is talking about the Bankruptcy Code.

B. Bankruptcy Court Jurisdiction over Bankruptcy Cases

The Bankruptcy Act, which was governing federal law until the Bankruptcy Code was enacted in 1978, granted jurisdiction over bankruptcy matters to federal district courts, which then referred bankruptcy cases to specialized courts that had limited power. The judges of these courts, who were called "referees" until 1973, could only decide issues that related very directly to the administration of the bankruptcy estate's assets and not to other types of disputes arising in a more ancillary way, unless the parties (either voluntarily or involuntarily), consented to a broader jurisdiction.

When the current Code was enacted, Congress (in Title 11) granted bankruptcy courts much greater latitude to decide cases and issues that came before them and far broader jurisdiction. Essentially, bankruptcy judges were given jurisdiction to decide all matters that a district judge could decide within the context of bankruptcy cases. However, because bankruptcy judges appointed under the Code are appointed pursuant to the powers contained in Article I of the Constitution rather than Article III, there was some question about how much of that broad grant of jurisdiction was constitutionally valid.

The Supreme Court invalidated this broad grant of jurisdiction in 1982 in Northern Pipeline Construction Co. v. Marathon Pipe Line Co., 458 U.S. 50 (1982). The bankruptcy court in the case had adjudicated a garden-variety state law contract claim involving no real bankruptcy issues. In fact, the only bankruptcy connection in the case was that one of the parties was in a Chapter 11 proceeding in front of the adjudicating court, and was seeking a judgment that presumably would benefit the bankruptcy estate. The nondebtor party to the contract dispute objected to the court's jurisdiction, arguing that the case had nothing to do with bankruptcy and that as a result the court had no jurisdiction to adjudicate it.

The decision was appealed several times, ultimately landing before the Supreme Court of the United States. The Supreme Court agreed with the nondebtor party, holding that the bankruptcy court had no jurisdiction to hear the contract suit, and that Congress's broad grant of jurisdiction to bankruptcy courts violated the separation of powers doctrine by conferring extended jurisdiction on a court that did not have a lifetime appointment and the other protections given an Article III judge.[1]

Eventually, a new system was implemented under which bankruptcy courts can hear and make ultimate decisions about cases involving core[2] bankruptcy issues but must have the federal district courts review any decision that the bankruptcy courts make that are outside that core. These decisions outside the core (merely related to the bankruptcy case over which the bankruptcy court presides) will be reviewed by the district court unless the parties agree that the bankruptcy court can make final decisions in these matters. In fact, bankruptcy judges are now entirely adjuncts to the district court. They have

1. As an aside, Article I judges, unlike Article III judges, are not entitled to lifetime appointment or to protection against a decrease in salary.

2. Core issues are issues that pertain directly to bankruptcy law and require an interpretation of the Bankruptcy Code, as distinguished from, for example, a case in which one of the parties is in bankruptcy but the litigation deals with a contract dispute.

no original jurisdiction. All jurisdiction vests in the district courts under 28 U.S.C. §1334, and the district courts have the power to refer core matters to the bankruptcy court under 28 U.S.C. §157(a). The district courts retain complete control over the reference, although as a practical matter, every district court in the nation has enacted a local rule that automatically refers all bankruptcy cases to the bankruptcy court.

The decision in Northern Pipeline was revisited in perhaps the most factually interesting bankruptcy jurisdiction case in history, Stern v. Marshall, 564 U.S. 462 (2011). In this case, the U.S. Supreme Court had to decide if the bankruptcy court in the case of Anna Nicole Smith (a former Playboy bunny) could decide a case by Smith alleging that her stepson committed tortious interference against her. The bankruptcy court decided the case, but thereafter, the Supreme Court found that Anna Nicole's bankruptcy judge did not have the right, under the U.S. Constitution, to enter final judgment on a claim that doesn't fall under the Bankruptcy Code's definition of a core bankruptcy issue and isn't part of the bankruptcy estate's claims process.

The implication from Stern was that bankruptcy courts lack the ability to enter final judgments over noncore proceedings. Indeed, in Executive Benefits Insurance Agency v. Arkison, the Court declared that a bankruptcy court acted correctly when it issued proposed findings of fact and conclusions of law over a noncore matter, and then the district court conducted de novo review. (*See* 573 U.S. 25 (2014).)

However, the Court's latest decision seems to allow bankruptcy courts to enter final judgments over noncore proceedings as long as the parties consent to the bankruptcy court's jurisdiction. The Court, in Wellness International Network, Ltd. v. Sharif, held that bankruptcy courts do not violate the structure of Article III by entering final judgments over noncore proceedings. (*See* 575 U.S. 665 (2015).) Justice Sotomayor reasoned that Stern hinged on the issue of consent. In Stern, Anna Nicole Smith's stepson did not consent to jurisdiction in the action for tortious interference. In contrast, in Sharif, the Court said that the debtor implied consent to bankruptcy court jurisdiction by participating in the creditor's action for a declaratory judgment that the debtor was hiding assets, an action the majority considered to be a noncore proceeding. At last, it appears that bankruptcy courts have power to enter final judgments over noncore proceedings, so long as there is consent, either express or implied.

QUESTION 1. The bankruptcy courts' jurisdiction:

1. was limited after the case of Northern Pipeline Construction Co. v. Marathon Pipe Line Co.
2. only allows the court to hear core proceedings.
3. requires the federal district courts to review the bankruptcy courts' decisions on all matters.

4. requires the federal district courts to review the bankruptcy courts' decisions on all noncore matters, unless parties consent to bankruptcy court jurisdiction.

A. 1 and 2 only.
B. All of the above.
C. 1 only.
D. 1 and 4 only.

ANALYSIS. As set forth previously, choice **1** is true. The court's jurisdiction was limited after the Supreme Court decided the Northern Pipeline case. The rest of the answers are harder to parse through. In this problem, it is easier to find the correct answers than to eliminate the wrong ones. Choice **4** is also correct. What happens after Sharif is that bankruptcy courts may make final judgments on noncore matters with the parties' consent, but otherwise district courts oversee and check decisions on noncore matters. However, the district courts are not—as is stated in **3**—required to review all of the bankruptcy courts' decisions. Nor can the bankruptcy courts hear just core matters, as is stated in **2**. They can hear noncore matters but cannot make final decision on those matters, unless the parties consent. Thus, the correct answers are **1** and **4**, making **D** the correct answer.

QUESTION 2. Bankruptcy judges are not appointed for life, and instead serve terms of 14 years, because:

A. they have less education than federal district and circuit court judges.
B. they have less status than other federal judges.
C. they are elected like many state court judges.
D. although they are federal judges, they are appointed under Article I, not Article III, of the U.S. Constitution.

ANALYSIS. None of these statements is true except **D**. There is real magic in Article III, which provides lifetime appointment and a promise of no diminution in salary, privileges thought to provide complete impartiality and fairness to litigants. Bankruptcy judges are not appointed under Article III,[3] do not get lifetime appointment, and thus have more limited jurisdiction. They are not less qualified or of lower status than other federal judges—they are simply more specialized and appointed under a different part of the Constitution. As far as where the 14-year appointments came from, when Congress was passing the Code in 1978, neither the Republicans nor the Democrats knew who would be president when it came time to reappoint the bankruptcy judges,

3. They are appointed by the Federal Circuit Courts of Appeals.

and neither side wanted the other to be able to appoint more than 200 federal judges. Someone asked how long the U.S. district court judges usually served and the research showed that the average term was 14 years. Thus, Congress picked a term of 14 years. We bet you thought the process would be more scientific than that!

C. Appeals from the Bankruptcy Court

Bankruptcy courts are trial courts and are part of the federal judicial system.[4] Once a bankruptcy court hears an issue and enters a final order, the losing party can appeal the decision. Normally, a federal district court in the jurisdiction in which the bankruptcy court sits hears this appeal. This is an odd system, to be sure, as you then have a trial court hearing an appeal from another trial court. To make it even odder, the appeal is coming from what is essentially a court of the same level, given that district courts have referred bankruptcy cases to their sister courts, which are not lower in status.

Because the review given by the district courts at this first level of appeal was not always a true review but was sometimes a rubber stamp, some circuits now offer appellants an alternative forum for the first level of appeal.[5] These are called bankruptcy appellate panels, or BAPs, and are available only in the First, Sixth, Eighth, Ninth, and Tenth Circuits. Bankruptcy judges from around these circuits sit on the BAPs in groups of three. They hear cases decided by other bankruptcy judges in their circuits. Both of us teach in circuits that have a BAP, and we can see the benefits of an appeal to a bench that is knowledgeable on bankruptcy matters. Yet, the system has not been adopted nationwide, and most bankruptcy court decisions are still reviewed by district courts.

Appeals can go from the bankruptcy court to either the district court, the BAP, or in some cases, directly to the Federal Circuit Court of Appeals. This is a recent change brought on by the 2005 amendments.

Under prior law, appeals from decisions rendered by the bankruptcy court were always heard by either the district court or a BAP. Requiring two levels of appeal in every case added costs to all appeals. Additionally, decisions rendered by a district court as well as a BAP are generally not binding and lack stare decisis value. To address these problems, the 2005 law amended §158(d) of Title 28 to establish the possibility of a direct appeal to the circuit courts of appeals, through a two-step certification process. As you'll see, however, only

4. The bankruptcy courts hear both whole bankruptcy cases that can have many parts, as well as complaints filed within bankruptcy cases, which are adversary proceedings.

5. It is not hard to see why. Consider what it is like to send a case on appeal from a very specialized court to a very general court with little familiarity with the subject matter. What kind of review will the district court generally do? After all, if a district court judge had a bankruptcy question, whom would he or she ask for help?

a small percentage of cases will qualify for a direct appeal to the federal court of appeals.

The first step is a certification by the bankruptcy court, district court, or BAP (acting on its own motion, on the request of a party, or the appellants and appellees acting jointly). The certification must be issued by the lower court if (1) the bankruptcy court, district court, or BAP determines that one or more of certain specified standards are met; or (2) a majority in number of the appellants and a majority in number of the appellees request certification and represent that one or more of the standards are met. The second step is authorization by the circuit court of appeals. Jurisdiction for the direct appeal is present only if the court of appeals authorizes the direct appeal.

This procedure is intended to be used to settle unresolved questions of law where there is a need to establish clear binding precedent at the court of appeals level, where the matter is one of public importance, where there is a need to resolve conflicting decisions on a question of law, or where an immediate appeal may materially advance the progress of the case or proceeding. The courts of appeals are encouraged to authorize direct appeals only in these circumstances.

Although some cases might come up that justify certification, even when binding precedent already exists on the issue, it is anticipated that this procedure will rarely be used where the matter can appropriately be resolved initially by district court judges or BAPs.

QUESTION 3. Bankruptcy court decisions are initially appealed to:

A. the federal district court in the district in which the bankruptcy court sits.
B. the federal circuit court for the same circuit in which the bankruptcy court sits.
C. a BAP, which comprises other bankruptcy judges within the same federal circuit as the bankruptcy court from which the decision is being appealed.
D. either A, B, or C above, depending on the circumstances.

ANALYSIS. Under the prior law, the first level of appeal from the bankruptcy court was either to the BAP or to the federal district court, and those options remain under the 2005 amendments. Not all circuits have a BAP, but those which do offer appellants a better chance at a real review than those that offer appeals only to the federal district court. Additionally, the 2005 amendments allow direct appeals to the appropriate court of appeals under certain circumstances, which are described in 28 U.S.C. §158. Therefore, **D** is the correct answer.

D. Preemption and the Relationship Between Federal Bankruptcy Law and State Law

Throughout the Federal Bankruptcy Code, the drafters refer to applicable non-bankruptcy law, by which they mean state law.[6] But as you will see, federal law on the subject of bankruptcy law always preempts or beats state law on the same subject. In many cases, though, the Bankruptcy Code defers to state law in defining certain concepts. What constitutes a property interest is one thing that is defined by looking to state law, as well as the definition of fraud. There are many other areas in which the Bankruptcy Code borrows definitions and law from state law as well.

E. The Court's Equity Power Under §105(a)

Bankruptcy courts are courts of equity, which means that throughout a bankruptcy case, the court is charged with doing what is in the best interest of everyone affected by the case, according to the spirit of the entire Bankruptcy Code. To that end, §105(a) states that "the court may issue any order, process, or judgment that is necessary or appropriate to carry out the provisions" of the Bankruptcy Code. This may not sound radical, but the power given here is quite broad. Parties can ask for any imaginable relief from the court and cite §105(a) as the authority for the request. The court can grant the requested relief, as long as the court feels the relief promotes the purposes of the Code, and as long as the relief does not conflict directly with another provision of the Code.[7]

QUESTION 4. (CODE READER) Bankruptcy courts' equity powers, as described in §105 of the Bankruptcy Code:

1. are unlimited.
2. are most applicable in a Chapter 11 case, where the court is focused on helping the debtor to rehabilitate and reorganize its affairs.
3. cannot directly contradict another Bankruptcy Code provision.
4. can be invoked only upon the request of a party-in-interest in a case, not sua sponte.

---

6. The concept also encompasses tribal law.
7. The designation CODE READER means that you need to read §105(a) before attempting to answer this question.

A. 1, 2, and 4 only.
B. 2 and 3 only.
C. None of the above.
D. 3 only.

ANALYSIS. The bankruptcy courts' equity powers, as described in §105 of the Bankruptcy Code, are most applicable in Chapter 11, where the court is focused on helping the debtor to rehabilitate and reorganize its affairs. This section can certainly be used in all the chapters, but Chapter 11 is where you see §105 used most often. In a business context, many issues come up that are not addressed explicitly in the Code or the case law interpreting it. These areas, about which the Code is silent, are fertile ground for §105(a). A common §105(a) request is that the court stay litigation against the owner of a company in bankruptcy, even though the owner is not himself in bankruptcy, so that the person who is running the debtor company (and this person's valuable time) is not monopolized by the pending litigation at the expense of the reorganization process. This is called a co-debtor stay. Thus, **2** is correct. Choice **3** is correct as well, as is stated previously. The judge is free to improvise on issues on which the Code is silent, but can't conflict with the Code regarding issues on which Congress has explicitly spoken. Thus, the answer is **B.**

As for the statement contained in **4**, the Code does not specifically answer the question, but by now you should have some instinct about which answer is correct. Section 105(a) is all about fairness and equity. Would it make sense for the judge to have to wait for someone to ask for something, if it was clear that it needed to be done? We think not. **4** is incorrect, so the correct answer here is **B**, choices **2** and **3** only.

F. Sovereign Immunity of States and Tribes

Until approximately 25 years ago, states regularly participated in bankruptcy proceedings by filing proofs of claim,[8] filing and responding to motions and complaints, and appearing on various issues. In 1996, however, the U.S. Supreme Court decided a case that had nothing to do with bankruptcy, but that nevertheless changed the practice of bankruptcy in drastic ways. In Seminole Tribe v. Florida, 517 U.S. 44 (1996), the Seminole Tribe sued Florida in federal court over noncompliance with a state statute requiring good faith in negotiating the terms of a gaming agreement. The tribe sued the state of Florida pursuant to the Indian Commerce Clause found in Article I of the

8. A proof of claim is a pleading signed by a creditor under oath, indicating how much money the debtor owes the creditor and how the debt arose.

Constitution, and the state of Florida defended by saying that federal courts have limited powers over states under the Eleventh Amendment, which, the state argued, takes precedence over the Article I powers.

The Supreme Court ultimately held that the tribe could not sue the state of Florida in federal court because that would violate the Eleventh Amendment prohibition against suing states in federal court against their will. While they were at it, the Supreme Court noted that it did not believe that its ruling would affect the other Article I powers because states are not regularly sued in federal court under the other Article I powers, such as bankruptcy. As it turns out, this statement was untrue by a long shot, as states are involved in many bankruptcy cases every year. Congress even contemplated this problem and drafted Code §106, which states that sovereign immunity is abrogated[9] for many Bankruptcy Code purposes.

Nevertheless, since the Seminole Tribe case, states have been attempting to ignore bankruptcy cases and to exercise their collection rights outside bankruptcy. Bankruptcy courts, on the other hand, have been struggling to figure out which actions they can take that might affect a state, and which they must not take.

In 2006, the Supreme Court provided some relief from the sovereign immunity chaos. In a 5 to 4 decision, the Supreme Court held in Central Virginia Community College v. Katz that a bankruptcy court had jurisdiction to hear a trustee's adversary proceeding to avoid a debtor's transfer to a state agency. The majority opinion (written by Justice Stevens) specifically stated that the Court was not holding that sovereign immunity is abrogated by the Bankruptcy Clause. Rather, the Court was merely ratifying the Bankruptcy Clause, which says that the states had "acquiesced in a subordination of whatever sovereign immunity they might otherwise have asserted in proceedings necessary to effectuate the in rem jurisdiction of the bankruptcy courts." Thus, bankruptcy courts apparently have always had jurisdiction to hear at least one type of suit against a state, an avoidance action (the subject of Chapter 12 of this guide).

The Katz case came from the Sixth Circuit Court of Appeals, which affirmed a bankruptcy court's denial of a motion to dismiss filed by Central Virginia Community College. The debtor had paid invoices issued by a college bookstore, and the Chapter 7 trustee attempted to avoid those transfers. Central Virginia moved to dismiss based on sovereign immunity, stating that a trustee was barred from bringing an avoidance action against an agency of the Commonwealth of Virginia.

As set out previously, the Court in Seminole Tribe held that the Eleventh Amendment prevented Congress from authorizing an Indian tribe to sue a

9. This simply means that sovereign immunity cannot be used or alleged by states in bankruptcy proceedings because it does not apply.

state to enforce legislation enacted under the Indian Commerce Clause. The dicta in the Seminole Tribe case suggested that this might also be true with the Bankruptcy Clause.

The Katz case clarifies that states agreed to a subordination of their rights at the time the Bankruptcy Clause was ratified. To reach this conclusion, the majority examined the history of the colonial period and years leading to the Constitutional Convention. During the colonial days and the period of the Articles of Confederation, debtors were subject to various bankruptcy laws adopted by the separate states. A debtor who turned over all of his or her assets to a trustee in one state and received a discharge would still be subject to the claims of creditors under another state's bankruptcy laws. Thus, the delegates to the Constitutional Convention thought that fairness dictated that Congress should be provided with the authority to pass uniform federal bankruptcy laws. The majority further explained that bankruptcy jurisdiction is in rem. Courts have traditionally understood this power to include orders to avoid transfers of the debtor's property.

According to the Katz court, the question is not whether the in rem jurisdiction to avoid transfers of the debtor's property abrogates a state's immunity from actions to avoid preferences, but rather whether such avoidance actions are within the scope of Congress' power to enact laws on the subject of bankruptcy. The majority held that because the states did not object to the Bankruptcy Clause at the time of its adoption (there was little or no debate), and in effect agreed to subordination of their rights by the ratification of the Bankruptcy Clause, bankruptcy courts have jurisdiction to hear avoidance actions against states or their agencies.

The minority opinion, written by Justice Thomas and joined by Chief Justice Roberts and Justices Scalia and Kennedy, found that the majority "greatly exaggerates the depth of the framers' fervor to enact a National bankruptcy regime." In addition, the minority stated that "[n]othing in the text of the Bankruptcy Clause suggests an abrogation or limitation of the state's sovereign immunity."

The holding in Katz opens the door for avoidance actions to be brought against state governments or state agencies. Moreover, it closes the door on a tumultuous time in bankruptcy history, in which some parties to the case (namely states) were allowed to go AWOL on the system. Thank goodness this period of confusion is over. Very few people in the bankruptcy world believed that the Supreme Court meant to exclude states from the bankruptcy process when it wrote Seminole Tribe. Yet the Seminole Tribe opinion certainly suggested that they did. Katz cleared this up. States can be sued in bankruptcy courts under the courts' in rem powers.

QUESTION 5. (CODE READER) After the Seminole Tribe decision and before the Katz case, §106 of the Bankruptcy Code, which purports to waive all sovereign immunity claims of states in federal bankruptcy proceedings, was considered jurisprudentially problematic because:

A. it is not well written.
B. Congress recently revoked it.
C. Congress arguably had no power to enact §106.
D. it conflicts directly with the policies of the Bankruptcy Code.

ANALYSIS. Answer **A** is incorrect. It is not because §106 of the Bankruptcy Code is not well written that it is ineffective. In fact, it reads quite well. The problem, however, is that according to sovereign immunity cases between Seminole Tribe and Katz, Congress arguably had no power to enact §106. As a result, the correct answer is **C. B** is incorrect because Congress has not revoked it, and **D** is certainly incorrect because §106 does not conflict directly with the policies of the Bankruptcy Code. Rather, §106 is consistent with the provisions of the Bankruptcy Code. What §106 is potentially inconsistent with, however, is the notion that states' rights cannot be affected in federal courts without their approval. As a result, the correct answer is **C**. Nevertheless, Katz clarifies that states can be sued in bankruptcy court.

Martin's and Keating's Picks

1. Question 1 **D**
2. Question 2 **D**
3. Question 3 **D**
4. Question 4 **B**
5. Question 5 **C**

6

Case Administration and Structure of the Code

OVERVIEW

A. Changes in Case Administration Under the 2005 Amendments
   1. More documents
      a. Overview
      b. The details
   2. New attorney obligations
   3. The creditors' meeting
B. Basic Chapter 7 Administration
C. Basic Chapter 13 Administration
D. Basic Chapter 11 Administration
E. The Structure of the Code
F. The Closer: Chapters 4, 5, and 6
Martin's and Keating's Picks

This section briefly describes some nuts and bolts about bankruptcy proceedings,[1] as well as the bankruptcy court system. This brief discussion will help you understand the rest of the material. Each bankruptcy court has its own clerk's office and its own courtrooms. It operates as a separate federal court. A case is initiated by filing a bankruptcy petition with the clerk's office that contains very basic information about the debtor. Once this is filed, all collection actions against the debtor are automatically stayed.[2]

Bankruptcy has always involved a very long list of paperwork and disclosures. Clients often wonder why they need to describe their assets, their liabilities, and their financial histories in such great detail. I like to explain to them that the seemingly endless disclosures are something they must give

1. A bankruptcy proceeding is a whole bankruptcy case, as opposed to a piece of litigation within a bankruptcy proceeding, which is called an adversary proceeding.
2. There are exceptions if the debtor has already filed a bankruptcy case that has been dismissed in the not-so-distant past. *See* Chapter 7, part B of this guide.

in exchange for their bankruptcy discharge (and the other benefits of bankruptcy). The main thing for a client to know is that the disclosures must be completely truthful. The penalties for lying are steep and include jail time. This is how the system (a generally liberal system at that) is policed. The changes to bankruptcy reform, enacted in 2005, contained several new entry barriers for debtors. Most of them complicate the system and thus deter bankruptcy filings. Some people say this was part of the purpose of the bankruptcy reform of 2005.

A. Changes in Case Administration Under the 2005 Amendments

1. *More documents*

a. Overview While debtors have always had to produce a lot of documents and disclosures to file for bankruptcy, the standards are higher under the 2005 amendments, and there is much more to keep track of. Detailed reports on assets and liabilities, security interests, transfers, and income all must be produced with every petition. The means test contained in §707(b)(2) adds another layer of complexity, as it requires verified information about the debtor's income and expenses for the six months before the filing. The 2005 amendments also require the debtor's attorney to certify that he or she has independently made an investigation into the detailed disclosures provided by the debtor. (*See* 11 U.S.C. §707(b)(4)(C) and (D).)

b. The details Besides all the extra paperwork, in the 2005 amendments Congress made the overall process of filing for bankruptcy more arduous. First, all individual debtors must complete credit counseling (actually called "credit briefing" in the Code) in the 180 days before bankruptcy as a condition of eligibility for bankruptcy relief. (*See* 11 U.S.C. §109(h)(1).) Exceptions may be allowed if access to such counseling is not readily available or if the debtor is incapacitated or away on military duty. There are some other exceptions to the credit briefing requirement as well, but it is by far easier to get the credit counseling than to be excused from getting it.

Next, as always, the debtor files his or her petition instituting the case, which contains basic information about the debtor and the debtor's assets and liabilities. This two-page petition also states that the debtor is signing his or her bankruptcy paperwork under penalty of perjury. The petition instituting the case must normally be accompanied by a filing fee, although people whose income is less than 105 percent of the official poverty line can have the filing fee waived. (*See* 28 U.S.C. §1930(f)(1).) This was new in most jurisdictions as a result of the 2005 amendments and is one way in which bankruptcy reform actually reduced barriers to filing. Since bankruptcy is primarily a middle-class phenomenon, however, this affects only those poor enough to take advantage of it.

Although the debtor technically has 14 days to file them, the petition is often accompanied by the granddaddy of all disclosures, the debtor's schedules of assets and liabilities and statement of affairs. All the disclosures are designed to provide the trustee and the creditors with a full picture of the debtor's financial condition. The schedules tell all about each and every asset (with its value) and each and every debt (with the address of the creditor and the account number) of the debtor. This includes all contingent and unliquidated debts as well. The schedules also describe the debtor's income and expenses. The schedules are in essence a snapshot of the debtor's exact financial condition as of the time of the bankruptcy filing.

The statement of affairs, on the other hand, tells the story of how the debtor got into this mess in the first place. It asks the debtor to disclose the debtor's income over the past two years, and everything else that happened to the debtor financially over various periods of time. Were there fires, foreclosures, repossessions, thefts? Did the debtor close any bank accounts? Did the debtor make any payments to creditors over certain amounts that could constitute preferences? Did the debtor give large gifts? The statement of affairs is not a snapshot but a look back over the past two years to determine what happened to the debtor and his or her money.

The 2005 amendments added more paperwork for the debtor and the debtor's attorney in every bankruptcy case. The debtor must now gather and produce pay stubs, tax returns, old bills with creditors' exact addresses (one could get some of this information on the Internet in the past), checkbooks, old credit card bills, and endless other documentation listed in the next paragraph. The new law also put additional pressure on debtors' attorneys to verify the accuracy of all of the disclosures made by the debtor in his or her bankruptcy. A lawyer who fails to correctly transcribe the values and other information on these documents can be forced to forfeit his or her fees, or, worse yet, can be subject to various sanctions. (*See* 11 U.S.C. §§526, 707(b).)

A failure to produce all the correct paperwork can result in dismissal of a debtor's case. Specifically, if all of the paperwork requirements are not complied with by Day 45 of the case, dismissal of the case is deemed automatic, although no one seems to know quite how that will work.[3]

3. Adding to the confusion, the bankruptcy court has discretion to not dismiss cases based on the debtor's failure to file requisite financial disclosures prior to expiration of the 45-day statutory deadline, apparently taking the "automatic" out of this so-called automatic dismissal. This discretion can be granted whenever a court reasonably determines that there is no continuing need for this information, or that waiver of the filing requirement is necessary to prevent automatic dismissal pursuant to statute from furthering a debtor's abusive conduct. *See* 11 U.S.C. §521(a)(1)(B), (i)(1); In re Warren, 568 F.3d 1113 (9th Cir. 2009).

Here are the specifics of what must be produced and when:

- Tax returns for the most recent year. (*See* 11 U.S.C. §521(e)(2)(A)(I).) This can be a major problem where spouses are separated or divorced and the nondebtor spouse has possession of the tax return.
- A certificate of credit counseling (this is actually called a credit briefing in §109(h)(1)). (*See* 11 U.S.C. §521(b)(1).)[4]
- A copy of the budget plan developed during the credit briefing. (*See* 11 U.S.C. §521(b)(2).)
- Copies of all payment advices (e.g., pay stubs) from employers received within 60 days of filing. (*See* 11 U.S.C. §521(a)(1)(b)(iv).)
- An itemized statement of monthly net income and any anticipated increases in income or expenses. (*See* 11 U.S.C. §521(a)(1)(B)(v), (vi).)
- With the statement of the debtor's financial affairs, if §342(b) applies, debtor must file a certificate of either (i) an attorney that delivered the appropriate notice of §342(b), or (ii) of the debtor stating that such notice was received and read by the debtor in case no attorney was indicated and no bankruptcy petition preparer signed the petition. (*See* 11 U.S.C. §521(a)(1)(B)(iii).)
- A statement of intention with respect to property securing consumer debts. (*See* 11 U.S.C. §521(a)(2).)
- A record of any interest that a debtor has in an educational individual retirement account or under a qualified state tuition program. (*See* 11 U.S.C. §521(c).)
- On request, the debtor must file (1) each tax return for tax years ending while the case is pending; (2) returns filed for tax years preceding the filing that are filed while the case is pending; (3) any amendments to returns. (*See* 11 U.S.C. §521(f).)
- On the request of the U.S. Trustee or the case trustee, the debtor must provide photo identification that establishes the identity of the debtor. (*See* 11 U.S.C. §521(h).)

2. *New attorney obligations*

Amended §526(a)(4) limits the advice an attorney can give to a client regarding planning the bankruptcy case. For example, the attorney may not counsel the debtor to take on new debt in contemplation of bankruptcy. In 2010, this provision withstood a First Amendment challenge when the Supreme Court interpreted the phrase "in contemplation of" bankruptcy narrowly. Under a narrow construction, the Court held, the provision prohibits attorneys from advising debtors to incur additional debt when the motivation for doing so is to load up on debt expecting that the debtor will file for bankruptcy and have

4. The Bankruptcy Code does not explicitly require the debtor to file the certificate regarding the credit counseling or briefing with the petition. Section 521(b)(1) only says the certificate ultimately must be filed. Section 109(h) requires that the briefing be accomplished within 180 days before the filing. However, a bankruptcy rule seems to require the debtor to file the certificate proving that such briefing has been accomplished, with the petition.

the debt discharged. That narrow interpretation, however, allows attorneys to advise debtors to incur additional debts "for a valid purpose," such as avoiding the need to file bankruptcy. *See* Milavetz, Gallop & Milavetz, P.A. v. United States, 559 U.S. 229 (2010).

Another attorney duty involves ensuring that a client is eligible for Chapter 7. If a debtor filed a Chapter 7 and a court later finds that doing so was an abuse under the means test, §707(b)(4) authorizes the court to grant attorneys' fees to the trustee or creditor who brought the motion. Under the test, the court is directed to award such fees only if it finds that the debtor's attorney violated Rule 9011 (the Bankruptcy Rule corollary to Rule 11). Rule 9011 requires that petitions be filed only upon reasonable inquiry into the facts of the case. Rule 9011 also requires that the legal contentions implied by the petition be warranted by existing law or by a nonfrivolous extension of the law. This is a high standard for imposing fees, but some attorneys may decide the risks are high enough that they should steer clients towards Chapter 13 cases instead. Section 707(b)(5) seems to impose a Rule 9011 standard on creditors and trustees bringing unsuccessful motions to dismiss under the means test, but the language is so garbled it is hard to see how it would work.

3. *The creditors' meeting*

Not too long after the debtor files his or her petition instituting the bankruptcy case, he or she is required to appear at a meeting called a "341 meeting," or first meeting of creditors, where creditors can come and ask questions of the debtor. The meeting is named after the Bankruptcy Code section that mandates the meeting and requires the debtor to attend. Often, none of the creditors show up because they gain no better repayment rights for attending— it is an informational session only. The Chapter 7 trustee runs the meeting by asking the debtor pointed questions about the disclosures made in the statement of affairs and the schedules of assets and liabilities that each debtor has (hopefully) filed. If any creditors do attend the meeting, they also are free to ask the debtor questions.

B. Basic Chapter 7 Administration

In a Chapter 7 case, the Chapter 7 trustee runs the 341 meeting.[5] After the meeting, the trustee in a Chapter 7 case will set out to try to find assets to distribute to creditors, as he or she is a fiduciary for the creditors and is charged with finding whatever might be available for distribution to creditors. The

5. Technically, the first trustee appointed in the case is called the interim trustee and is just the temporary trustee. Creditors have the right to have someone other than the interim trustee appointed as the permanent trustee in the case. In practice, it is very rare for the interim trustee not to be appointed as the permanent trustee.

trustee is aided in the search by the schedules of assets and liabilities and the statement of financial affairs filed by the debtor and by questions that were asked at the 341 meeting. If there is nothing to distribute (what we call a no-asset case), which often happens, the case will be finished within three months of the filing, the debtor will be discharged from most debts, and the case will be closed.

If there are assets to distribute, the case can go on for several months or even years, although the debtor's discharge should still take just three months, assuming that no unusual problems arise. The discharge is discussed further in Chapter 13.

C. Basic Chapter 13 Administration

In a Chapter 13 case, the 341 meeting is run by the Chapter 13 Trustee's Office. The Chapter 13 trustee is often a standing trustee, meaning that the same person is the trustee for every Chapter 13 case within the district. Most of the questions in a Chapter 13, 341 meeting center on income and expenses, the assets, and whether the repayment plan is feasible. The 341 meeting takes much longer in a Chapter 13 case and is more detailed than in a Chapter 7.

After the 341 meeting, the trustee will set out to determine if the Chapter 13 plan that the debtor has proposed meets the requirements of the Code. If it does, the trustee will allow the plan to go forward and be approved or confirmed by the court. If there are problems, the trustee might object to confirmation of the plan. If the plan is not ultimately approved, the case will be dismissed. This means that the debtor will no longer be in bankruptcy and will have lost his or her filing fee. The parties will be back where they started from under state law.

D. Basic Chapter 11 Administration

In a Chapter 11 case, a person from the United States Trustee Program runs the 341 meeting. The U.S. Trustee Program is an arm of the Department of Justice, and its job is to oversee the procedures, as well as the attorneys' fees, in all cases, but particularly Chapter 11 cases. The U.S. Trustee is charged with ensuring that lawyers and trustees are properly using the bankruptcy system. This is done by supervising the debtors and the trustees in a large variety of tasks.[6]

The U.S. Trustee Program is a totally different office than that of the Chapter 13 Trustee's Office and is staffed with entirely different people. The

6. *See* 28 U.S.C. §586.

attorneys in the U.S. Trustee Program are often Assistant U.S. Trustees because there are only 21 U.S. Trustees representing 21 regional offices throughout the U.S., but there are many more bankruptcy districts. (*See* 28 U.S.C. §581.)

The duties of United States Trustees were expanded under the 2005 Code amendments. These duties are set out in §586. They now include appointing case trustees under Chapters 7 and 11, performing general monitoring of cases and attorneys' fees, appointing creditors' committees in Chapter 11 cases, monitoring overall abuse in the consumer bankruptcy system, certifying credit counseling agencies, and approving debtor education programs.

E. The Structure of the Code

One thing you should notice about the Code's structure is that its Code sections are located in mostly odd-numbered chapters, starting with Chapter 1, which contains definitions, the sovereign immunity section, the equity powers section, and some other preliminary things. These are the topics we covered first and can be broadly characterized as the General Provisions.[7] Case administration issues, like the ones discussed here, are covered in the Code sections in the 300 series. Examples are §§341, 362, etc. In the next seven chapters, Chapters 7 through 13, we will cover the topics found in the 500 series of the Code. These Code sections articulate the general relationships between creditors, the debtor, and the estate in all types of cases under the Code. These sections include §§507 (priorities); 541 (the estate); and 544, 547, and 548 (the avoiding powers); as well as many others.

Thereafter, the Code is structured around the different kinds of bankruptcy, most notably around Chapters 7, 13, and 11, but also Chapters 9 and 12. As you might have guessed, the 700 series of Code sections cover Chapter 7 concepts, the 1300 series addresses Chapter 13 concepts, and the 1100 series covers Chapter 11 concepts. We have not mentioned where to find provisions on Chapter 12 and Chapter 9, but we imagine that you would know where to find these.

F. The Closer: Chapters 4, 5, and 6

For this Closer, you will be doing something somewhat unusual. You should pick a beginning of a sentence from the left-hand column and combine it with one of the sentence endings found in the right-hand column in order to come up with four correct statements of the law abstracted from Chapters 4, 5, and 6.

7. These are the names given to each chapter in the Bankruptcy Code.

1. One of the big benefits of bankruptcy for the debtor is	the court can enter any order consistent with the policies of Chapter 11 as long as it is not inconsistent with any particular provisions of the Code.
2. The reason we have specialized bankruptcy courts is	it gets most of a debtor's litigation into one place.
3. The big brouhaha about bankruptcy court jurisdiction results from the fact that	bankruptcy courts could become courts of general jurisdiction with broad powers.
4. The thing about bankruptcy courts' equity powers is	bankruptcy is a detailed and complex process that requires special expertise.

ANALYSIS. The best way to answer a complex question like this is to see if you can pick one combination that you are certain is correct and then match those two answers together, leaving fewer choices for the remaining three. Many of the answers on the right-hand side could be benefits to the bankruptcy debtor, so you should leave that one alone to start. Unfortunately, even choice **3** on the left-hand side, the one about bankruptcy court jurisdiction, could be answered through several of the sentence endings found in the right-hand column. Probably the easiest sentence fragment to start with is the one describing the courts' equity powers. One of the answers very closely describes what you have learned about the §105 equity powers— namely, that a court can enter any order consistent with the policies of Chapter 11, but not inconsistent with any particular Code provision. Thus, one complete sentence is that the thing about the bankruptcy court's equity powers is that the court can enter any order consistent with the policies of Chapter 11 but not inconsistent with any particular Code provision. So that eliminates those two answers from consideration. That did not require very much analysis, as that is the exact same standard set out in the materials in Chapter 5.

Next, you should probably try to match up the second half of the sentence for choice **2** (the reasons why we have specialized bankruptcy courts). This is not because bankruptcy courts may become courts of general jurisdiction. In fact, this is a fear about bankruptcy court jurisdiction resulting from the possibility that jurisdiction can be too broad. The reason we have specialized bankruptcy courts is because bankruptcy is a detailed and complex process that requires special expertise. Now we have two of the possible four answers eliminated and we're left with only two choices for each. Choice **3**, the big brouhaha about bankruptcy court jurisdiction results from the fact that bankruptcy courts may become courts of general jurisdiction with broad powers. So, that is the correct sentence completion for choice **3**. People in the legal system are concerned that a bankruptcy court, which has very specialized rights and powers, will become a court of general jurisdiction (with broad powers), hearing a broader range of cases than originally contemplated and eschewing their rightful place as the specialized court for which it was designed.

This leaves, for the last answer, the following sentence completion: One of the biggest benefits of bankruptcy for the debtor is that this gets most of the litigation into one place. It would certainly be handy if a debtor that is subject to a lot of litigation could have it all heard in one place. As we saw in connection with the jurisdictional materials in this guide, not all of the debtor's litigation can be placed in one place, as some of it may be outside the court's jurisdiction. On the other hand, many of the matters to which the debtor is a party can be resolved within the bankruptcy court process, as many of these matters deal with debt collection and things that are specifically within the court's jurisdiction. As this question showed, there are many complex nuances surrounding bankruptcy court jurisdiction and the breadth of the courts' powers. We hope that you found this question helpful and not too confusing.

Martin's and Keating's Picks

The Closer: Chapters 4, 5, and 6 (see above)

7

The Automatic Stay

OVERVIEW

A. Exceptions to the Automatic Stay

B. Multiple Filing Cases: When the Stay Is Not So "Automatic"

1. One prior dismissed case
2. Two or more dismissed cases
3. Extending the 30-day stay under §362(c)(3)
4. Obtaining a stay under §362(c)(4)
5. Which stay does the repeat filer NOT get?

C. Relief from the Automatic Stay

D. The Closer: Chapter 7

Martin's and Keating's Picks

A bankruptcy filing dramatically changes the landscape for collecting creditors. Nonbankruptcy state law collection procedures are an individual effort, with each man or woman for himself or herself to see who can execute on valuable assets first. By comparison, bankruptcy is a collective process. Its goals include equality of distribution to creditors and providing the debtor a breathing spell from collection efforts.

The breathing spell is accomplished through the equivalent of an immediate court order or injunction, effective as soon as the debtor files his or her bankruptcy petition, enjoining all collection efforts against the debtor or the debtor's property, regardless of where it is located. This order imposes by law what is called the automatic stay, which is codified in §362 of the Bankruptcy Code. Section 362(a) outlines all of the different activities that are stayed by the bankruptcy filing. They include any attempt to collect on a pre-petition debt,[1] any continuing lawsuit to collect a debt, any repossession of a debtor's assets, any attempt to exercise control over property of the debtor's estate

1. Although this is a bit of a generalization, all types of bankruptcy tend to clean up or discharge only debts that were incurred before the bankruptcy was filed. As one would expect, debts incurred after the bankruptcy are the debtor's full responsibility and are generally not affected by the bankruptcy in any way.

(defined very broadly, as discussed in Chapter 8), any attempt to perfect a security interest, and pretty much anything else you can think of that would allow a creditor to improve its own position against the debtor compared to other creditors. The stay continues in place until the bankruptcy proceeding is closed or terminated, or until a creditor gets the stay lifted, in order to pursue its own particular debt. Section 362(a) is easy to read, and you should read it now before trying the problems in this chapter.

QUESTION 1. Which of these is NOT one of the purposes of the automatic stay imposed by §362?

A. Protection of the debtor's estate from dismemberment.
B. Promotion of equality of treatment among creditors.
C. Keeping creditors from recovering on their claims.
D. Protection of estate property so that creditors can be paid on their claims.

ANALYSIS. This question helps explain the temporary nature of the automatic stay, as well as the purposes of the stay. The answer is **C.** The purpose of the stay is not to keep creditors from collecting. In fact, the idea behind the stay is that if individual creditors are precluded from dismembering the estate, the estate can be sold for the benefit of all creditors in an orderly fashion rather than in a piecemeal way. **A** is certainly true. The stay is in place so that the estate will not be disturbed in an inefficient way. **B** is also true, as noted in the text previously. **D** is also true because creditors on the whole stand a better chance of being paid if a previous creditor, who just happened to be quicker to execute, has not already grabbed the assets in satisfaction of that creditor's individual claim.

A. Exceptions to the Automatic Stay

Section 362(b) outlines the exceptions to the automatic stay. Criminal suits are not stayed, nor are suits to determine or modify paternity or marital support, or to collect marital support. Actions by governmental units to enforce police powers also are not stayed. These are actions taken by state, local, federal, or tribal governments to protect the health and welfare of citizens. Examples include actions taken to stop a company from polluting or to stop ongoing dangerous activity. Be careful here, however. Actions by governmental units merely to collect debts are stayed, and the line is hard to draw. Suffice it to say that all collection suits must stop after a bankruptcy case is filed, even if the plaintiff is a governmental body. Suits designed to stop a real danger to the public, if brought by a government body, are not stayed.

QUESTION 2. (CODE READER) Which of these actions on the part of a creditor would not violate the automatic stay imposed by §362(a)?

A. A secured creditor repossessing its collateral after a bankruptcy filing.
B. A secured creditor selling collateral it had already collected pre-petition.
C. A parent suing for paternity post-petition.
D. A state collecting income taxes.

ANALYSIS. The best answer is **C.** A parent may sue or continue to sue for paternity, despite the debtor-defendant's bankruptcy. The statute says this in very clear language in §362(b)(2)(A)(i). The statute forbids the actions outlined in **A** and **B. A** is wrong because a secured creditor may not repossess collateral after a bankruptcy filing. *See* §362(a)(3), which specifically forbids anyone from taking acts to obtain possession of property of the estate. **B** is somewhat more difficult because people seem to forget that if a secured creditor takes or repossesses property pre-petition, the Code does not allow it to sell that property post-petition while the debtor still has an ownership interest in it because it is still part of the bankruptcy estate. As will become clearer after reading the next section, the debtor's bankruptcy estate still has an interest in the repossessed property as long as the creditor has not yet sold the property, and thus the creditor would violate the stay by selling this repossessed stuff post-petition. (*See* Knaus v. Concordia Lumber Co., Inc., 889 F.2d 773 (8th Cir. 1989); *see also* §362(a)(5), which forbids a creditor from enforcing a lien against property of the debtor's estate.) Finally, **D** may be incorrect if the state's action is just a garden-variety collection action. A suit to collect taxes certainly does not fall within the police powers exception because it is not a suit to stop imminent danger to the public; rather, it is a mere action to collect on a debt. However, under certain circumstances, a state may retain an income tax refund in collection of income taxes due, if both the refund and liability relate to a taxable period that ended before the date of the order for relief. (*See* §362(b)(26).)

QUESTION 3. (CODE READER) Which of the following is stayed by §362(a)?

A. An action for child support.
B. An action to stop chemical pollutants from damaging a bridge in a medium-sized town.
C. An action by a state to collect a fine.
D. A criminal prosecution.

ANALYSIS. Perhaps this is redundant, but the answer is **C**, an action by a state to collect a fine. This correct answer can be reached most easily by process of elimination. Look over the choices. The criminal suit is most obviously not stayed. This of course assumes that it actually is a criminal action and not just a suit to try to collect a fine from the debtor, such as a small fine that could be paid by a debtor to settle a bad check charge, with no real risk of jail time. That may not be a true criminal action. But assuming that the suit is what it says it is, then the criminal prosecution described in **D** is not stayed, so **D** is not the correct answer. **A** is also incorrect as it is clear from §362(b)(2)(A) that child support actions are not stayed at all. The statute uses the words "domestic support obligation" in §101(14A), and this includes child support, so this action is not stayed. Assuming destruction of this bridge would harm the public, and assuming that a municipality is bringing the suit, **B** also is not stayed. **B** describes a quintessential exercise of a state's police power, something that is not stayed by a bankruptcy filing. The correct answer, **C**, describes quintessential debt collection, which is always stayed regardless of who is doing it.

A bit more about the stay and marital obligations, support, divorce, and so on: The 2005 amendments modified the Code to allow many more family-related lawsuits to go forward, despite the bankruptcy of one party or spouse. For example, the following types of lawsuits are not subject to the automatic stay:

- suits to establish paternity,
- suits to modify an order for support,
- suits to modify custody or visitation rights,
- suits to dissolve a marriage (unless there is a property settlement award involved, then the action is stayed), or
- suits to determine if there has been domestic violence.

A trustee or nondebtor spouse also can continue to collect support obligations from the debtor, at least from property that is not property of the estate (the subject of the next chapter). A debtor who is not current on his or her domestic support obligations, as defined in §101(14A), can have a professional or driver's license revoked, can be reported to a credit reporting agency, can have a tax refund intercepted, and can even have his or her bankruptcy discharge denied.

QUESTION 4. (CODE READER) Joe Smith, an individual debtor, files Chapter 7 bankruptcy at a time when he owes $1,000 to Caroline Regan, a neighbor of his who lent Joe the money a few months ago so that Joe could take his family on a trip. Caroline gets a state-court judgment on her claim and then garnishes Joe's paycheck, which represents only postpetition wages that were earned by Joe. If this garnishment occurred while Joe's automatic stay was still in effect, which of the following subsections of the Bankruptcy Code would NOT be relevant to the garnishment?

A. §362(a)(4)
B. §362(a)(5)
C. §362(a)(6)
D. All three of these subsections would be relevant to the garnishment.

ANALYSIS. This one is tricky because it requires that you understand the key principle behind the individual debtor's "fresh start" in a consumer bankruptcy. The key to the individual debtor's "fresh start" is that the debtor's post-petition wages are *not* property of the debtor's bankruptcy estate (*see* Chapter 8). Instead, those wages are considered by the Bankruptcy Code to be "property of the debtor." That means that §362(a)(4) is not relevant to this garnishment and that therefore **A** is the correct answer. The reason that §362(a)(4) is not relevant to this garnishment of the debtor's post-petition wages is the subsection refers to a stay of "any act to create, perfect, or enforce any lien against property of the estate." The garnishment here is an act to create the equivalent of a lien against "property of the debtor," but not "property of the estate." That means that §362(a)(5) is relevant to the garnishment because of its reference to creating a lien against "property of the debtor" that secures a pre-petition claim. Thus, choice **B** cannot be the correct answer. Similarly, choice **C** cannot be correct since §362(a)(6) stays any act to collect a pre-petition debt, which this garnishment attempts to do. Choice **D** is incorrect because, as explained above, §362(a)(4) and its prohibition of liens against property of the estate is *not* relevant to this garnishment of the debtor's post-petition wages.

QUESTION 5. Supplier has supplied yeast to Bakery for the last five years. Supplier delivers a supply of yeast on the first day of each month, and Bakery is supposed to pay Supplier within one week of delivery. Bakery files Chapter 11 bankruptcy at a time when Supplier has made the last two monthly yeast deliveries without getting paid. Bakery asks Supplier to deliver the current month's yeast supply shortly after Bakery's bankruptcy filing. Supplier tells Bakery that it will not make any new yeast deliveries unless Bakery first pays in full for the two pre-petition deliveries for which Bakery has still not paid. Has Supplier violated the automatic stay?

A. No, because sellers should always have the freedom to sell their goods to whomever they wish.
B. No, unless Bakery had offered to pay cash in advance for any post-petition deliveries that Supplier was willing to make.

C. Yes, because sellers such as Supplier are not allowed to discriminate against buyers who are in bankruptcy.

D. Yes, because Supplier's conditional refusal to deal with Bakery in this case amounted to an indirect act to collect a pre-petition debt from Bakery.

ANALYSIS. This question is a reminder of the tremendously broad scope of the automatic stay, particularly §362(a)(6). That subsection prohibits "any act" by a creditor to collect a pre-petition debt from the debtor. In this case, Supplier's refusal to deal with Bakery unless Bakery first paid the pre-petition debt that Bakery owed to Supplier was an act by Supplier to pressure Bakery into paying a pre-petition debt, contrary to §362(a)(6). Thus, **D** is the correct answer here. If Supplier had a general company policy of refusing to sell to buyers who were in bankruptcy no matter whether the buyer was willing to pay any pre-petition outstanding balances, such an unconditional refusal to deal would not be an automatic stay violation. Choice **C** is incorrect because the automatic stay says nothing about discriminating against debtors. Bankruptcy anti-discrimination rules are found in §525, and those rules are quite narrow in their scope. Answer **A** is incorrect because while it is true that sellers can sell to whomever they choose, sellers cannot use their leverage as key suppliers to coerce the debtor into paying a pre-petition debt. Choice **B** is incorrect because even if Bakery had not offered to pay cash in advance for post-petition deliveries, Supplier's conditional refusal to deal would still have been a stay violation.

QUESTION 6. Ricky Martin is thrilled beyond compare about the new addition to his home: a fabulous four-story graduated deck that hangs over the street and sidewalk in his swanky Beverly Hills neighborhood. The City is not so thrilled, and has brought an action against him alleging 11 counts of zoning violations. Disgusted with this as well as many other annoying things, including huge debts from an over-budget concert series, Ricky has filed a Chapter 7 petition. Which of the following statements is most correct, assuming all of the facts that follow were alleged and proven in court?

A. The City's action most likely is stayed because the City's primary goal is to improve economic conditions in Beverly Hills neighborhoods and protect resale values and other benefits for other residents.

B. The City's action is most likely not stayed because one of the City's goals is to collect sufficient fines from the suit to redirect the road in front of Ricky's house.

C. The City's action is most likely not stayed because the City's goal is to improve economic conditions in Beverly Hills neighborhoods and protect resale values and other benefits for other residents.

D. The City's action is most likely stayed because the purpose of the suit is to keep people from being injured by the addition, which extends over the sidewalk.

ANALYSIS. This problem demonstrates how hard it can be to prove another person's motivations in a lawsuit. However, you are asked in the problem to just assume that these are the facts that the court hears in the trial on this issue. The issue is whether the City's suit is really one to protect the safety of the public. If it is, then the suit is not stayed. If the suit's real purpose is not to protect the public, but some form of financial gain, then the suit is stayed. The question is complicated because it requires you to determine whether the goal in each option is consistent with the purpose of the exemption from the stay.

Start with **A**. This option says that the action is stayed because the purpose of it is to improve economic conditions for the neighborhood. This answer is correct then, because unless physical safety is at risk, the suit is stayed. **A** is still in the running. Because **C** is almost the same option (it contains the same goal but an opposite result), let's skip to it. In **C**, the same goal is given but the choice says the suit is not stayed. This is wrong. If safety is not at risk, then the suit is stayed.

In **B**, the reason for the suit is to raise money for the City, and the answer says that because of this reason, the suit is not stayed. Lights should turn on! This is exactly the kind of thing that is stayed. This is just a money fine. No one will be hurt if the City does not collect.

Now, moving on to **D**, it clearly contains the only facts that could suggest that the suit is not stayed, right? It says that the City's purpose in the suit is to protect the public from injury. This strongly suggests that the suit is not stayed. The only problem is that this option draws the wrong conclusion, and states that because safety is the City's motivation, the suit is stayed. **A** is the correct answer, and is in fact the only correct answer. So, even though this was a tough question, you were not required to pick the better of two right answers.

QUESTION 7. (CODE READER) Danny Debtor files Chapter 7 bankruptcy and then, shortly after filing, he buys on unsecured credit a new laptop computer from the Apple Store before he receives his Chapter 7 bankruptcy discharge. Debtor fails to make his first payment to the Apple Store, and that payment was due prior to Debtor receiving his discharge in his Chapter 7 case. Also before Debtor's discharge, the

Apple Store gets a judgment for Debtor's missed payment and begins garnishing Debtor's post-petition wages. Has the Apple Store violated the automatic stay with its garnishment of Debtor's post-petition wages prior to Debtor's discharge?

A. Yes, because it is an enforcement against Debtor of a money judgment while Debtor is still in bankruptcy.
B. Yes, because it is an enforcement of a lien against property of Debtor.
C. No, because the garnishment is based on a post-petition debt rather than a pre-petition debt.
D. No, but it would be if Debtor had purchased the laptop on secured credit rather than unsecured credit.

ANALYSIS. This question is a good reminder that as broad as §362(a)'s scope is, that scope is still not unlimited. As a general matter, the focus of the various subsections of §362(a) is on stopping actions by creditors that are based on pre-petition debts to the debtor and on actions against property of the estate. This garnishment by the Apple Store fits neither of those categories. The debt that underlies the garnishment is based on a post-petition debt, not a pre-petition debt. And the property of Debtor that is being garnished is Debtor's post-petition wages, which are not property of the estate. Therefore, the correct answer here is **C**. Choice **A** is incorrect because, as just noted above, not every enforcement against Debtor of a money judgment while Debtor is still in bankruptcy is necessarily a violation of the automatic stay. Choice **B** is incorrect because even if a garnishment is considered to be the enforcement of a lien against Debtor's post-petition income, as long as the debt is a post-petition debt and the lien is not against property of the estate, that enforcement does not fall within the scope of the automatic stay. Finally, Choice **D** is wrong because even if Debtor had purchased the laptop post-petition on secured credit, that would not cause the Apple Store's post-petition garnishment to be a violation of the stay.

B. Multiple Filing Cases: When the Stay Is Not So "Automatic"

Remember that automatic stay you just learned about? Sometimes it is not so "automatic." One of the true beauties of bankruptcy has always been that once you file for it, an automatic stay goes into effect immediately, staying all collection efforts. Under the 2005 amendments, some debtors are not entitled to a full automatic stay upon the filing of a case.

If there are past bankruptcies, the debtor's attorney will need to know if any past cases were dismissed during the year before this petition will be filed. If there are cases that have been dismissed during this one-year period, either voluntarily or involuntarily, the stay (as we know it) may not go into effect under §362(c)(3) and (c)(4).

Thus, closing a case because of the entry of a discharge will not affect the stay, although it might preclude one from obtaining another discharge. The bottom line, as set out in the following paragraphs, is whether the new case was filed in good faith. The presumption is that it was not.

1. *One prior dismissed case*

Section 362(c)(3) states that if the debtor has one prior dismissed case within a year, then the debtor gets the stay for just 30 days, except as extended by the court. However, if a person files a Chapter 7 that is dismissed under the means test, the subsequent Chapter 13 case is not affected. The debtor gets the full stay as before. However, if the first case was a Chapter 7, 11, or 13, and was dismissed for some other reason, the second case will be entitled to just a 30-day stay automatically. If the debtor wants the stay extended, he or she will need to work through the presumption discussed below and move to have the stay extended.

2. *Two or more dismissed cases*

Section 362(c)(4) states that if the debtor has two or more dismissed cases within the year, the stay does not go into effect at all.

3. *Extending the 30-day stay under §362(c)(3)*

A request to extend the stay is made by motion, and the standard is whether the new case has been filed in good faith. Naturally, the motion must be filed while the stay is still in effect. It is good practice to file a motion to extend the stay with the bankruptcy petition, if one is needed, although the Code does not require this.

Section 362(c)(3) creates a presumption that the new case was not filed in good faith in certain cases, which the debtor must then rebut. The presumption arises if:

the debtor failed to amend the petition or other documents as required by the Code or the court, except through inadvertence or negligence, or

the debtor failed to provide adequate protection as ordered by the court (presumably this does not refer to pre-petition adequate protection, just that ordered by the court), or

the debtor failed to perform the plan.

Although the statute does not say this, common sense suggests that if the debtor had medical or other reasons for failing in the prior case, or if the debtor's income dropped precipitously or if some other unforeseen event caused the debtor to be unable to continue with the prior case as planned, the presumption would not arise. If no presumption arises, then the debtor can get the stay extended by proving by a preponderance of evidence that the case was filed in good faith. If the presumption does arise, good faith must be proven by clear and convincing evidence, at least according to some courts. How is the presumption rebutted? Normally, by proving good faith, as that standard would be proven under the Chapter 13 plan good faith standard, or perhaps by looking at the standard for converting or dismissing a case under Chapter 13 under §1307. Congress did not set out the standard for good faith under §362(c)(3), so we need to borrow a test for good faith contained in another part of the Code or some other law. Here is a summary of one court's incarnation of this thoroughly confusing test.

In In re Charles, 334 B.R. 207 (Bankr. S.D. Tex. 2005), the court adopted a three-part analysis for considering motions to extend the stay under §362(c)(3). The first step is to determine whether a presumption exists that the case was filed not in good faith. The court in Charles held that the party opposing the stay extension has the burden to prove, by a preponderance of the evidence, that more than one previous case was pending during the prior year as provided in §362(c)(3)(C)(i)(I) or that one of the factors set forth in §362(c)(3)(C)(i)(II) has triggered a bad faith presumption. As for whether there has been a change in circumstances or other reason to believe that the current case will result in discharge as provided in §362(c)(3)(C)(i)(III), the Charles court found that the burden rests with the debtor (or party in interest seeking the stay extension).

Because the bad faith presumption did arise in this case, the court stated that it must next consider whether the case was filed in good faith under both "objective" and "subjective" standards. In analyzing "objective" good faith, the court stated that it first considers whether the case is likely to result in discharge. If the debtor satisfies this objective test, then the court shall consider whether "subjective" good faith exists, by applying a totality of circumstances test which considers factors such as (1) the nature of the debt held by the affected creditor; (2) the nature of the collateral held by the creditor; (3) eve-of-bankruptcy purchases; (4) the debtor's conduct in the present case; (5) reasons why the debtor wishes to extend the stay; and (6) any other unique circumstances.

In this case, the court found that the debtor's Chapter 13 plan was likely to be confirmed and that the case would result in discharge, primarily because the debtor had proposed that her plan payments be made through an automatic debit on a joint checking account with her daughter. Additionally, the court was satisfied that "subjective" good faith was present.[2]

---

2. Although one hopes for simplification of this multi-step process, more than ten years after Charles, some courts continue to apply "the Charles factors" with only slight modification. Rather than referring to an "objective" good faith test that, if successful, is followed by the six-factor "subjective" good faith test, the courts now formulate the test as one eight-factor test. The first two factors are basically the old objective test: (1) whether the creditors consent to the stay extension, and (2) whether the case is likely to result in discharge. These are threshold factors. If at least one creditor opposes the extension, and if the case is likely to result in discharge, then the court proceeds to balance the six factors that Charles termed the "subjective" test. *See, e.g.*, In re Acosta, 540 B.R. 308 (Bankr. S.D. Tex. 2015).

4. *Obtaining a stay under §362(c)(4)*

If the debtor has more than one prior case, then no stay will go into effect on a subsequent bankruptcy case. So how does such a debtor apply for a stay? The debtor will need to seek an emergency stay to stop a foreclosure or whatever the situation calls for. The prior cases create a presumption that the new case was filed in bad faith, which the debtor must now rebut. The debtor does this in much the same way discussed above, although for a person with two prior bankruptcies or more, this will be harder to do. The court has a lot of flexibility in fashioning the stay. The court can have the stay imposed on all or just some creditors, and can impose additional conditions or limitations as well.

5. *Which stay does the repeat filer NOT get?*

As it turns out, the language of §362(c)(3) is very narrow. It says that if there is a prior case (as we discussed previously), the stay under §362(a) (that very broad stay you just learned about):

> with respect to any action taken with respect to a debt or property securing such debt or with respect to any lease shall terminate with respect to the debtor on the 30th day after the filing of the case.

Compare this with the broad and inclusive language of §362(a), which—through all of its enumerated parts—essentially stays virtually all imaginable collection efforts against the debtor, the debtor's property, or the estate's property. This language of §§362(a) and 362(c)(3)(A) could not be any more different.

As many courts have noted, if Congress had intended for §362(c)(3)(A) to terminate all provisions of the automatic stay after a repeat filing, it could have clearly said so, as it did in §362(c)(4)(A)(i). Instead, Congress chose to describe the termination of the stay quite differently, and because Congress, in terminating aspects of the automatic stay in §362(c)(3)(A), chose language that is so vastly different than the straightforward language it used in §362(c)(4)(A)(i), §362(c)(3)(A) is not as broad as §362(c)(4)(A)(i). This means that all of the protections of the automatic stay are not eliminated by §362(c)(3)(A).

Rather, the stay that is lost under §362(c)(3), for cases with one prior case within the year, is only the stay applicable to the debtor (not the debtor's property), and even then, only to state court actions taken before the debtor filed the bankruptcy. This means that the creditors can harass and otherwise ignore the stay as to the debtor in a repeat filing case, and perhaps can get possession of secured property, but can in no way touch estate property. Thus, the stay is the same as always (broad) as to estate property.

QUESTION 8. Which of the following statements are correct under §362(c)(3)?

1. The debtor is not permitted to file more than one bankruptcy case within the same year.
2. The debtor who files more than one case within a year may not get the full benefit of the automatic stay imposed by §362(a).
3. The fact that a debtor has filed more than one bankruptcy case within a year does not necessarily mean that the debtor will not receive the full benefit of the automatic stay imposed by §362(a) in the future case or cases.
4. Section 362(c)(3) can cause the whole stay imposed by §362(a) to disappear, under certain facts.

A. Choice 1.
B. Choices 1 and 3.
C. Choices 2 and 3.
D. All of the above.

ANALYSIS. Going through the numeric choices, statement **1** is not correct, but this is a bit tricky. Congress wrote §362(c) to discourage repeat filings. The section does not, however, limit the number of bankruptcy cases a person can file. The debtor can file as many cases as he or she chooses. The ramification of these repeat filings is that the debtor may not get the full benefit of the automatic stay imposed by §362(a) if more than one case is filed. This is not, however, a prohibition against filing more than one case.

Statement **2** is correct. The debtor may not get the full benefit of the stay in subsequent cases. In a sense, one rarely gets the full benefit of the stay, because in many cases the debtor will need to file a motion to get the stay extended, which will require procedural effort, if nothing else. Although it seems to say the opposite of statement **2**, statement **3** is also correct. The debtor can move to have the full automatic stay re-imposed in a subsequent case, giving the debtor the full benefit of §362(a). Statement **4** is incorrect. As discussed previously, the automatic stay imposed by §362(a) is very broad, staying all collection efforts, all attempts to obtain a security interest or to obtain possession of property of the debtor or the estate, and all attempts to collect a pre-petition debt. The stay that is lost in multiple filing cases, after 30 days or else from the inception of the case, is only part of the stay, namely, the stay of actions commenced before the debtor's new case, and the stay of collections from secured property affected by those actions. Thus, the correct answer is choice **C**.

Keep in mind that in a case under §362(c)(4), for those with more than one prior case within the past year, the result is very different. The entire stay imposed by §362(a) fails to go into effect unless the court imposes one.

C. Relief from the Automatic Stay

Sometimes creditors are able to have the automatic stay removed or lifted so they can exercise their state court collection rights, just as if there was no bankruptcy. With some exceptions that are not important here, this right is only granted to secured creditors who can prove certain elements. These elements essentially show that the moving creditor is more entitled to the collateral than the debtor and the other creditors.

If a secured creditor can prove either: (1) "cause" to lift the stay, which typically boils down to proving that its position in the collateral is at risk (what the Code calls a "lack of adequate protection");[3] or (2) that (a) the debtor has no equity in the collateral,[4] and (b) the collateral is not necessary to an effective reorganization, then the court will allow the creditor to take back its collateral. In a Chapter 7 bankruptcy, the most common situation in which the stay will be lifted is one in which a secured creditor is "under-secured." For example, if a secured creditor is owed $10,000 and the automobile that is the collateral is worth only $8,000, the stay will usually be lifted, and the secured party will be allowed to repossess the auto and sell it to satisfy at least part of its debt. You can probably see in this case that there is no value in the car for the estate because the debtor has no equity in the auto. Thus, it makes sense to give it back to the creditor.

At least in a Chapter 7 case, the car is not necessary to an effective reorganization because the case is a liquidation and there is no reorganization, so the second test is met. Because the debtor is still driving the car and it is still depreciating, and because the debtor is not making the payments on it, the first test is likely to be met as well. The creditor's position is deteriorating, and is thus not adequately protected.

We will be discussing relief from the automatic stay in greater detail in our discussions of Chapter 11 (*see* Chapter 30 of this guide), where the concept is far more critical to the success of the case. A Chapter 7 debtor who is behind on his or her obligations to secured creditors will find very little relief under a Chapter 7 case. If a Chapter 7 case is filed in a situation in which the mortgage is past due (or in arrears), the creditor will probably succeed in getting the stay lifted. If not, the case will be over in just three short months, after which time the automatic stay will disappear, leaving the creditor free to foreclose.

Again, Chapter 7 does not help debtors who are behind on their obligations to secured creditors. There is no plan in a Chapter 7 case, and thus no time during which the debtor can make up for the past due payments.

3. Just so you know, a lack of adequate protection is just one form of "cause," but is certainly the most common form of cause. Another form of lack of adequate protection, and also cause, would be a failure of the debtor to maintain insurance on the collateral.

4. This means that the outstanding loan balance on the property exceeds the value of the collateral or is exactly equal to its value, leaving the debtor with no equity in the collateral.

Practically speaking, a debtor who is behind on the home mortgage will not be allowed to keep the home unless the arrears (those past due amounts) are made up or cured within a very short period of time after the filing. Thus, most Chapter 7 debtors who are homeowners are current on their mortgage and should keep it that way.

D. The Closer: Chapter 7

Merry Mack Home Mortgage Company has just moved to lift the stay in the case of Joe and Monica Mooney. Joe and Monica are in a Chapter 7 proceeding, which they filed about a month ago. The court is currently considering Merry Mack's motion to lift the stay. Assuming all of the following four things are true, which facts are relevant to the court?

1. The Mooneys are way behind on their payments.
2. The Mooneys' home is worth $100,000 and their loan is $120,000.
3. The Mooneys have been renting the home, in violation of the loan agreement.
4. The Mooneys have placed significant improvements on the home, thus building up their equity in the home.

A. All of the above.
B. 1, 2, and 3, only.
C. 2, 3, and 4, only.
D. Just 1 and 2.

ANALYSIS. This question asks you to imagine what the court would consider relevant under §362(d), the standard set out earlier. The big problem for bankruptcy debtors in Chapter 7 is that there is no plan through which they can cure home mortgage payments. Choice **1** states that the Mooneys are way behind on their home mortgage, and this is unquestionably relevant to the court's determination. In a Chapter 7, it is absolutely critical that the Mooneys remain current or get current as quickly as possible or they will not be able to keep their home. Choice **2** is also relevant. It appears that under §362(d)(2), the debtor has no equity in the property. Here, the debtor is not reorganizing, so the part of the standard discussing whether the property is necessary to an effective reorganization is essentially irrelevant. Thus, choices **1** and **2** are both relevant.

Choice **3** is also relevant because the debtor is in violation of the loan agreement. As you will learn in later chapters of this guide, the fact that the debtors have rented out their home, in violation of the loan agreement, could make Merry Mack lack adequate protection. Why? Because the bank has asked the debtor not to do that, perhaps because renting the property could reduce its value. It is not necessarily clear whether **3** would be relevant to the court, because it's not clear whether it would actually make Merry Mack lack adequate protection. The fact in and of itself, however, could be relevant to the court. Choice **4**, however, is not relevant. You are asked to assume here that all of the facts are true, and choice **2** indicates that the home loan is under water, meaning that the debtor has no equity in it and the bank's loan is partially undersecured. As a result of this, it doesn't matter whether improvements were made on the property because the debtor still has no equity on the property. Consequently, the correct answer is **B** and the other answers are incorrect. As stated in the text above, you will learn a great deal more about relief from the stay when we study this subject matter in the context of Chapter 11.

Just so you know, the automatic stay only lasts for approximately 90 days in a Chapter 7 anyway, so many courts will simply wait until the 90 days are over and at that time the lender will clearly be free to foreclose on this mortgage. You might be assuming at this point that Chapter 7, then, never provides any benefit to a homeowner. This is not correct, but what is true is that if a debtor in Chapter 7 wants to avail himself or herself of a Chapter 7 bankruptcy, he or she should be current on the mortgage. As long as the debtor is current on the mortgage, the mortgage company will not have a right to sell the home simply because the debtor filed for bankruptcy. We will discuss this subject matter a bit more in another context when we reach Chapter 16, dealing with keeping secured property while in Chapter 7.

Martin's and Keating's Picks

1. Question 1	**C**
2. Question 2	**C**
3. Question 3	**C**
4. Question 4	**A**
5. Question 5	**D**
6. Question 6	**A**
7. Question 7	**C**
8. Question 8	**C**
The Closer: Chapter 7	**B**

8

Property of the Debtor's Estate

OVERVIEW

A. Breadth of the Estate

B. Legal and Equitable Interests in Property

C. Retirement Funds

D. Post-Petition Assets

  1. Chapter 7 post-petition assets

  2. Post-petition assets in a Chapter 13 or a Chapter 11 case

Martin's and Keating's Picks

A. Breadth of the Estate

When a bankruptcy case is filed, all of the debtor's property as of the filing date, wherever located, and by whomever held, forms an estate for the benefit of creditors. Virtually every possible interest of the debtor in property, whether it is a contingent interest, a partial interest, a legal interest, or an equitable interest, goes into this estate under §541(a). This applies to property owned or interests held as of the filing. In contrast, at least in a Chapter 7 case, most post-filing assets do not come into the estate, as explained in the following paragraphs.

One of us likes to hold up a huge bag in front of the class and explain that almost every possible kind of interest that the debtor has in anything at all will go into the bag. Although many things will later come back out of the bag, due to the debtor's exemptions, security interests of secured creditors, and other things, the estate initially contains every imaginable interest of the debtor in property in which the debtor has rights, as of the time the bankruptcy case is filed. The important thing is that absolutely everything in which the debtor has any rights must be disclosed in the bankruptcy paperwork, and almost all assets come into the estate, at least initially. You should read §541(a) now.

QUESTION 1. The best way to describe the way the Bankruptcy Code defines a debtor's estate is that:

A. it includes all of the debtor's equitable interests in property.
B. it includes all of the debtor's legal rights in property.
C. it includes contingent property that might come into the debtor's estate in the future.
D. it is one of the broadest possible notions of property that one could conjure up.

ANALYSIS. The answer here is **D**, even though a few things are excluded from the debtor's estate (such as spendthrift trusts, certain employee benefit plans, and certain accounts designated for educational purposes), which are listed in §541(b). Overall, the estate is broadly defined. If the debtor has an interest in a possible lawsuit, but no one has sued anyone and the debtor is not even sure that he will even pursue the claim, the potential lawsuit goes into the estate and should be listed on the schedules of assets and liabilities. If the debtor buys a lottery ticket pre-petition and may win the jackpot, even though it seems silly, the potential embedded in that lottery ticket belongs to the estate. The ticket was purchased pre-petition with pre-petition assets. If the debtor were to win, the creditors would get the proceeds, assuming that they were not exempt.

B. Legal and Equitable Interests in Property

Although everything in which the debtor has any interest of any kind must be disclosed in the bankruptcy case, this does not mean that the trustee will necessarily take these assets. Let's say that the debtor is holding a bank account, in his name and his grandmother's name jointly, for the sole benefit of his grandmother. It's all her money; none of it is his. The debtor's interest in the account, though it is only a legal interest, is part of his bankruptcy estate. This asset absolutely must be listed on the debtor's bankruptcy schedules anyway. The trustee will not take this money to pay creditors because the debtor's interest in the bank account is solely a legal interest. The trustee will not take the grandmother's money, but this account must be disclosed nevertheless. The idea is that the trustee has a right to examine these items and make sure that the debtor is accurately determining whose money is in the account, and also telling the truth about the facts.

QUESTION 2. When the Bankruptcy Code defines the debtor's estate to include all of the debtor's interests in property, whether legal or equitable, what does it mean by equitable interests?

A. Something that is titled in someone else's name but that the debtor actually uses and pays for.
B. Something that is titled in the debtor's name but actually is owned or belongs to someone else.
C. Something that the debtor is holding for another person.
D. Something that someone else is holding for the debtor.

ANALYSIS. The answer is **A**. An equitable interest is something that is not in the debtor's name but the debtor is the equitable owner. An example would be where a daughter purchases a car and takes out a car loan for her father, who is unable to qualify for the loan. He pays for the car and it is his but it is in his daughter's name. An equitable interest is something that the debtor in fact pays for and enjoys the ownership rights of.

B describes a legal interest, which is merely a legal title with no rights of ownership, which is what the debtor's interest would be in the previously-discussed grandmother example. The property mentioned in **B** is something the debtor owns a legal interest in but not an equitable interest. It comes into the estate but there is no value there for the trustee or the creditors because someone else has the valuable rights in the property.

As far as **C** and **D** are concerned, these are not equitable interests. These assets still must be disclosed because they are examples of property that are in the possession of someone other than their owner. As you probably remember from your first-year property class, possession itself often has little to do with ownership, legal and equitable rights, or anything else relevant in the law. It is just a physical place. Thus, the answer is **A**.

QUESTION 3. Jeanette buys a new car on credit with no money down. Finance Corp loans her the $30,000 required to purchase the new car with a 72-month repayment plan. Three months after buying the new car, Jeanette files a Chapter 7 bankruptcy. Up until the bankruptcy filing, Jeannette has not missed any payments on the car. At the time of the bankruptcy, the car's value is just $25,000 but Jeanette owes $29,000 on the loan to Finance Corp. When Jeanette files her bankruptcy, will her car become property of the estate?

A. Yes, unless her state's exemptions cover this car.
B. Yes, whether or not her state's exemptions cover this car.

C. No, because the car has no value to the estate.
D. No, because Jeanette has neither a legal nor an equitable interest in the car at this point.

ANALYSIS. The correct answer is **B**. Answer **A** sounds plausible because what comes in as property of the estate may ultimately be taken out of the estate if the debtor has an applicable exemption, including under state law. However, there are at least two separate reasons why **A** is not the correct answer here. First, when Jeanette files her bankruptcy, the car clearly is property of the estate whether or not Jeanette chooses to exempt the car during the case. Second, even if Jeanette's state has a car exemption, it's not going to matter to Jeanette because she has no equity in the car. The secured creditor's lien in the car will come ahead of the debtor's exemption in the car, and in this case the secured creditor's lien fully covers the value of the car.

Answer **C** is tempting because it is true that this car will have no value to the estate. Yet the lack of value to the estate in a particular piece of property does not stop that property from being property of the estate. It means that the trustee in bankruptcy will likely choose to abandon the property under §554, but the property is still property of the estate at the time of the debtor's bankruptcy filing. Choice **D** is wrong because it is a false statement: Jeanette has both a legal and an equitable interest in the car at this point. She has a legal interest because she is the titleholder of the car; she has an equitable interest because she still has the right to use and enjoy the car. Due to Jeanette's legal and equitable interests in the car at the time she files bankruptcy, answer **B** is correct, since (as explained above) it doesn't matter whether her state's exemptions cover this car.

C. Retirement Funds

The 2005 amendments added significant protection for the retirement funds of bankruptcy debtors. As a conceptual matter, do you think that retirement funds, earned before a debtor's bankruptcy filing, fall within the estate? Surely they do. On the other hand, some retirement funds are necessary to protect a person in old age, right? Thus, these funds fall within the definition of pre-petition assets, and form part of an individual's bankruptcy estate. Nevertheless, there may be policy reasons to exclude them from the estate.

The amended Code specifically excludes from the estate all employee contributions to any ERISA-qualified employment plan, deferred compensation plan, tax-deferred annuity, or health insurance plan. The 2005 amendments also exclude certain educational accounts for the debtor's children and grandchildren. (*See* §541(b)(5) & (6).) This is true even if the accounts are held in the debtor's name and the debtor has a right to withdraw the funds. (*See Id.*)

To be more specific, under §541(b)(5)-(8), the following are now completely excluded from the debtor's estate, meaning that there is no need to exempt these assets to keep them free of creditor claims:

> (5) Funds placed in an individual retirement account (as defined in section 530(b)(1) of the Internal Revenue Code of 1986 ("The IRC")) made at least one year prior to the bankruptcy filing, but only if the designated beneficiary is a child, stepchild or grandchild of the debtor for the taxable year in which the funds were contributed, and if other limitations imposed by the Internal Revenue Service regarding the amount of these benefits are met. For amounts placed in the account between 365 days and 720 before the filing, only 50% of these amounts are excluded from the estate, up to a total amount excluded of $8,575.
>
> (6) Funds used to purchase tuition credits under section 529 of the IRC, as long as the relevant tax limitations as to amount and beneficiary are met, made at least one year prior to the filing, except that for amounts placed in the account between 365 days and 720 before the filing, only 50% of these amounts are excluded from the estate, up to a total amount excluded of $8,575.
>
> (7) Amounts withheld by an employer from the wages of employees, for contributions to employee benefit plans under ERISA, or deferred compensation plans under section 403(b) of the IRC, or to a health insurance plan regulated by the state.
>
> Or amounts received by an employer from an employee as contributed to an employee benefit plan under ERISA or under section 414(d) of the IRC, a deferred compensation plan under section 457 of the IRC, or a tax-deferred annuity under section 403(b), or to a health insurance plan regulated by the state.

As we describe later in Chapter 9 on exemptions, there is another big change protecting retirement funds. Some people hold their retirement funds in Individual Retirement Accounts (IRAs), which are considerably more flexible than the ERISA-qualified funds we just mentioned in the last paragraph. Before you read on, think about what it means for an asset to be outside the debtor's estate. It means that the debtor needs not use up his or her exemptions to save the asset. Rather, the asset does not come into the estate at all.

In addition to those retirement funds that are exempt from the estate because they are held in ERISA-qualified pension plans, for example, Congress has vastly improved a bankruptcy debtor's ability to protect other retirement funds, namely those held in IRAs. IRAs are now exempt (they come into the estate but come back out as exempt property) for up to $1,711,975 per person. No, this is not a typo. Not only that, but the court can allow a debtor to exempt more than the $1,711,975 if it deems the $1,711,975 insufficient for the debtor's needs. (*See* 11 U.S.C. §522(n).)

Given that more than one-half of all the people in the United States do not have one dime in any form of retirement fund, these provisions chalk one up for the rich and bankrupt.

D. Post-Petition Assets

1. *Chapter 7 post-petition assets*

In a Chapter 7 case, property that the debtor obtains after the case is filed does not become part of the debtor's estate. Rather than estate property, this is what we think of as fresh start property, property that the debtor may keep as part of his or her fresh start. One very important rule is that all of the debtor's wages in a Chapter 7 case earned after the case is filed are his or hers to keep and do not become part of the debtor's estate. By the way, this is not true in a Chapter 11 or a Chapter 13 case. There are a couple of significant exceptions to this rule about property that the debtor obtains after the bankruptcy, or post-petition. If a debtor inherits money or property within six months after the bankruptcy filing, then this inheritance does become part of the estate. (*See* §541(a)(5)(A).) Also, if any pre-petition asset that is part of the estate earns income, profits, or proceeds after the filing, all of those come into the estate as well, even though post-petition assets generally do not.

Marital property settlements that the debtor receives post-petition, resulting from a pre-petition divorce, also form part of the estate (*see* §541(a)(5)(B)), as do (as stated before) the proceeds and products of pre-petition property that the debtor does not receive until post-petition. (*See* §541(a)(6).) Tax refunds for the prior year also become part of the estate, even if the debtor has not yet filed a return by the time of the bankruptcy.

QUESTION 4. Carol Myers owned 100 shares of GM stock when she filed her bankruptcy petition, along with her home and a small rental property. Before filing for bankruptcy, she also had been in a car accident, which left her with a sore left shoulder. She filed for bankruptcy under Chapter 7 because she could no longer pay her bills after the accident. Her father felt so sorry for her after hearing this news of her bankruptcy that he gave her 100 shares in Home Depot. Which of the following assets do not go into Carol's Chapter 7 bankruptcy estate?

A. The income from her rental property.
B. Her post-petition dividends from her Home Depot stock.
C. Her post-petition dividends from her GM stock.
D. Her settlement with the guy who hit her in her car.

ANALYSIS. This may seem easy, but students find it hard at times to tell the difference between purely post-petition assets, such as the shares of stock Carol's father gave her, and proceeds from existing pre-petition assets, such as the rent or the dividends from her GM stock. Here, the rent comes directly from a pre-petition asset, so of course it is part of the bankruptcy estate. The dividends from her GM stock are also proceeds of a pre-petition asset, even though Carol receives them post-petition. Finally, as we discussed briefly above, when Carol filed for bankruptcy, the proceeds of her pre-petition accident became part of her bankruptcy estate, solely because the accident happened pre-petition. Thus, the correct answer is **B**, because her father gave her the stock post-petition and its proceeds would also be post-petition assets.

QUESTION 5. (CODE READER) Charles is forced to file Chapter 7 bankruptcy when he loses his job due to layoffs in his manufacturing industry. Charles' grandmother dies 168 days after Charles files his bankruptcy petition. Three weeks after his grandmother's death and 189 days after Charles' bankruptcy filing, the executor of his grandmother's estate reads the will, which provides that Charles has inherited $300,000. Charles is surprised because he had known nothing about this pending inheritance. A month after the reading of the will, Charles receives the money. When Charles receives the $300,000, will that money become property of his bankruptcy estate?

A. No, because Charles did not receive the money until more than 180 days after he filed bankruptcy.
B. No, because Charles had no idea that he was entitled to the money until more than 180 days after he filed bankruptcy.
C. No, because the executor did not read the will until more than 180 days after Charles filed bankruptcy.
D. Yes, because Charles become entitled to acquire the money within 180 days after he filed for bankruptcy, even though he was unaware of that fact until after 180 days.

ANALYSIS. The key to getting the right answer on this one is to read the Code language very closely. Section 541(a)(5) brings into the debtor's bankruptcy estate any bequest or inheritance that the debtor "acquires or becomes entitled to acquire within 180 days after" the date of the debtor's bankruptcy filing. The key measuring point, then, is not when the debtor actually acquires such interest. If that were the key date, then answer **A** would be the correct answer here, since that answer focuses on when Charles received the bequest money. Given the language of the statute, though, we know that **A** is wrong and that the correct answer must be **D**. Once Charles' grandmother died, that is when he became "entitled to acquire" the inheritance money. The reading of the will and the disbursing of the funds still had to happen, but Charles' legal entitlement was fixed before the 180 days had expired. That is why **C** is also wrong, and **B** is similarly wrong because Charles' state of knowledge about the inheritance is not relevant under the statutory language.

2. *Post-petition assets in a Chapter 13 or a Chapter 11 case*

In a Chapter 13 or a Chapter 11 case, post-petition assets that are received or obtained by the debtor during the case do become part of the estate. For example, in a Chapter 13 case, the debtor's post-petition income not only becomes part of the estate, but is usually the asset through which the plan payments will be made. This is incredibly sensible, as the debts ordinarily will be paid over time, from post-petition assets. Conversely, other assets the debtor obtains during the case, such as gifts and other cash or property, also become part of the Chapter 13 estate and thus must be contributed to the plan. In a Chapter 11 case, post-petition assets acquired during the case also become part of the estate. As a Chapter 11 is a repayment case, this makes sense and should be easy to remember. After all, the debtor in a Chapter 11 case usually uses his or her future income and profits to fund the plan.

Martin's and Keating's Picks

1. Question 1 **D**
2. Question 2 **A**
3. Question 3 **B**
4. Question 4 **B**
5. Question 5 **D**

9

Exemptions in Bankruptcy

OVERVIEW

A. State Versus Federal Exemption Schemes

B. New Limitations on the Homestead Exemption

C. Exemptions for Individual Retirement Accounts

D. The Valuation of Exempt Property

E. Voiding Involuntary Liens, and Nonpossessory, Non-Purchase-Money Security Interests That Interfere With an Exemption

F. The Closer: Chapters 8 and 9

Martin's and Keating's Picks

Every bankruptcy debtor gets to keep some of his or her property, even though he or she has bilked creditors. You might ask yourself, "Why have we developed a system that allows bankruptcy debtors to keep a significant amount of their property, despite a stack of unpaid bills?" The federal and state exemptions schemes allow people to keep enough assets to survive, and some provide much more than that. The theme of exemption law is that people who are over-indebted can still live inside, drive a car, and wear their clothes, without fear that a creditor will try to take these necessities. If we allowed creditors to take all of a debtor's possessions, it would be difficult (if not impossible) to get a fresh start.

In Chapter 7 cases, the exemptions determine which property the debtor can keep and which assets must instead be given to the trustee for sale and distribution of the proceeds to creditors. In a Chapter 13, the debtor generally will not need to sell the nonexempt assets. Instead, the exemption calculations will be used to determine the minimum amount the debtor must distribute under the plan to unsecured creditors, because the best interest test requires that the debtor pay creditors at least what they would have received in a Chapter 7 case, from the sale of the nonexempt assets. Most Chapter 11 cases are business reorganizations, and because corporations and limited liability corporations (LLCs) are not entitled to exemptions, the exemptions often play no part in a Chapter 11. If an individual were to file a Chapter 11 case, however, perhaps because the person is over the Chapter 13 debt limits, the exemptions would be used in the individual Chapter 11 case in exactly the same way as in a Chapter 13 case, to measure the minimum amount the debtor must pay to unsecured creditors. The exemptions provide a specific item-by-item list of exactly what a debtor can and cannot keep once he or she is in bankruptcy, free from creditor claims. Because the exemptions are in specific items of property, not in just whatever items the debtor has, the debtor sometimes must choose between various items, much like ordering off a menu in a Chinese restaurant—one from category A and one from category B, and so forth.

A. State Versus Federal Exemption Schemes

All jurisdictions have state exemptions that can be used in bankruptcy as well as outside bankruptcy.[1] Some states also allow a debtor to choose between either these state law exemptions or the federal exemption scheme contained in the Bankruptcy Code. For those debtors who get to choose between the federal and the state schemes, the choice will be made based on the type of assets the debtor has. One scheme may be great for one person but horrible for another.

The federal exemptions are probably average in generosity, as compared to the various state exemptions. As you can see in Table 9.1, the main benefit that the federal set of exemptions provides is a free or wildcard category, which allows a debtor to protect absolutely anything, including cash or investments. We call this the wildcard or the pour-over exemption. It is called the wildcard exemption because it can be used for anything, like a wild card in a game of cards. It is called the pour-over exemption because a very substantial portion of this exemption comes from the unused homestead exemption, or amounts that pour-over from the homestead exemption. States rarely offer generous wildcard exemptions and thus the federal system is often better for debtors with cash assets.[2]

Married couples may double all of the federal exemptions to get a mathematically doubled exemption limit. If you see a problem involving a couple, it is best to immediately create a chart that doubles your exemptions so you don't forget this as you work through the problem. Also, do not forget that any wildcard or pour-over exemption also doubles.

Although there are more, the most commonly used federal exemptions are listed in the following table. Keep in mind that these numbers are adjusted upward for inflation and may have changed since this book was printed.

1. In some states, such as Delaware, these are extremely minimal, allowing the debtor to keep just a few items, and almost nothing of value.
2. By this we mean cash, savings accounts, stock accounts, money market accounts, and other investments, and anything else that can be liquidated quickly in an established market.

Table 9.1

Description of the Asset	*Amount of Asset Protection**	*Bankruptcy Code Section*
Homestead		
and personal property that the debtor uses as a residence, including a mobile home	Up to $31,575	11 U.S.C. §522(d)(1)
Motor Vehicle		
Debtor's interest in one motor vehicle	Up to $5,025	11 U.S.C. §522(d)(2)
Household Goods		
Debtor's interest in household: furnishings, goods, clothing, musical instruments, etc.	Up to $800 per item; $16,850 in total	11 U.S.C. §522(d)(3)
Jewelry		
Held by the debtor or the dependent of the debtor	Up to $2,125	11 U.S.C. §522(d)(4)
Wildcard		
A debtor may use this for anything; additional homestead exemption if the homestead is not completely used	Up to $1,675 for any item, plus up to $15,800 for any unused portion of a homestead exemption	11 U.S.C. §522(d)(5)

*These numbers are adjusted every three years based upon changes in the Consumer Price Index. These are the numbers effective April 1, 2025. They may not be the correct ones at the time you pick up this book, so check your Code to be sure.

Only approximately 16 states allow bankruptcy debtors to use the federal exemptions. Moreover, each state's own exemptions emphasize more protection for some things than others. These state exemptions can have massive benefits, or they can provide almost no relief at all. The variation between jurisdictions can be so extreme that some debtors deliberately move to a jurisdiction to get that state's exemption. The 2005 amendments limit this ability but do not eliminate it, as we will soon see. Several states have unlimited homestead exemptions, including Texas and Florida. If you lived in Texas and had a $10 million home paid off, you could keep the home and file for bankruptcy. Creditors would not get any of the value of the home. The same is true in Florida; however, the state exemptions allow a person only $1,000 worth of assets other than a home. This is very difficult for non-homeowners and would not even allow people with homes to furnish them. Moreover, Florida has opted out of the federal exemptions scheme and, as a result, debtors in Florida can only use the state exemptions. Clearly, debtors who live in states in which they can choose their exemption scheme have more options and flexibility.

In New Mexico, for example, a debtor may choose to protect his or her assets under either the state or the federal exemption scheme. You must, however, pick one scheme or the other.[3] For example, a debtor could not use the homestead exemption from New Mexico and combine it with the federal jewelry exemption. In those states that allow a choice of exemptions, making the choice is an important strategic decision. This is also an area frequently tested on exams. The best way to tell which exemption scheme is best for a debtor is to take the debtor through both exemption sets completely, and then see which scheme allows the debtor to keep the largest amount of assets. You will be practicing this task shortly. In the end, like most other legal decisions, it is the debtor's decision as to which set of exemptions to adopt, but it is very important for the attorney to provide accurate information on what would happen under each option.

IMPORTANT NOTE: The questions in this chapter follow a different format from the others you have seen so far. Some of these questions will take a bit longer to answer, but will give you much more realistic practice in handling complex exemptions questions. For questions 1 and 3, you will need to try to answer the question asked in each of the four parts (A, B, C, and D) before moving on to read the analysis. We suggest you do this in columns on a separate piece of paper before reading the answer. Otherwise, the numbers get too confusing. Reading about the calculations without trying to do your own will do nothing but confuse you. Out of these two questions, you will receive as much practice calculating exemptions as you would get from eight separate multiple choice questions but with far less reading.

ANOTHER IMPORTANT NOTE: Try to remember two things. First, sometimes an item is only partially exempt under a particular category but can be fully exempted with the help of the wildcard or pour-over exemption. Second (and we know this sounds elementary), the debtor only can use the exemption or part of the exemption for which he or she actually owns property. You cannot determine the amount of a person's exempt property merely by totaling the exemption list. No one has assets in all these categories, or in these exact amounts.[4]

QUESTION 1. Assume a state's exemptions are as follows: Homestead—$40,000, Motor Vehicle—$7,000, Household Furnishings—No Limit, Jewelry—$2,500, Wildcard—$500 or $2,000 (if the debtor did not use any of the homestead). The state has not opted out of the federal

---

3. No jurisdictions currently allow a debtor to pick and choose which portions of which exemptions they would like to adopt.

4. In other words, let's say you live in a state where you have to use the state exemptions even in bankruptcy and where the auto exemption is $4,000. If your car is worth just $500, no one is going to pay you the other $3,500 that the exemption would allow if you had a better car. You can only exempt $500 because that is all that you have.

exemption scheme. Based solely on the following set of details, determine which set of exemptions a debtor should use: the federal system or the state exemption system. **NOTE:** There are four questions in one here. Good luck!

A. A single debtor who has $18,000 worth of equity in her home, $1,000 worth of equity in a motor vehicle, $35,000 in miscellaneous furniture and household goods, $1,100 in jewelry, and no cash.

B. Joint debtors who have $20,000 worth of equity in their home, two motor vehicles with $2,000 worth of equity each, $5,000 in furniture, a $1,000 wedding ring, and $25,000 in cash.

C. A single debtor who rents an apartment, has a vehicle with $19,000 in equity, $8,000 in furniture and household goods, no jewelry, and no cash.

D. Joint debtors who have $80,000 worth of equity in their home, two motor vehicles with $2,700 worth of equity each, $15,000 in household goods, a $400 wedding ring, and $900 in cash.

ANALYSIS. **(A) State.** The debtor in question **A** would do best under the state exemptions because of the large amount of value in household goods. The miscellaneous household goods can all be exempted under the state exemptions. In this case, the debtor would be allowed to keep all of the $35,000 in furnishings. The other assets would have been exempt under either scheme. But if the debtor had filed under the federal exemption scheme, she would have only been able to keep $32,130 of the household goods—$16,850 from the household goods exemption and $15,250 from the wildcard exemption, which has two parts here; $13,575 that was unused from the homestead exemption; and then the $1,675 in wildcard exemption that every debtor gets, regardless of use of the homestead exemption. If an attorney picked the wrong exemptions, this would have cost the debtor valuable assets, namely $2,870 in household goods. Go back and do the math yourself and see if you come up with the same numbers we did.

(B) Federal. These debtors would do best under the federal set of exemptions because of the large amount of cash they wish to exempt. Because this is a joint debtor situation, the debtors can double their exemptions. Their homestead coverage under the federal exemptions would protect them up to $63,150 (i.e., $31,575 times two people), so their $20,000 of equity would be protected. They also have $43,150 left from their homestead exemption and, jointly, $3,350 in the wildcard exemption everyone gets regardless of what's left from the homestead exemption. Remember, you can only use $15,800 of the homestead exemption per person for the pour-over, or just $31,600 total—not the whole $43,150 in unused exemption from their equity in the house. These two numbers get them to $34,950, under 11 U.S.C. §522(d)(5), so they can use that to save all of their cash. Their motor vehicle, personal property, and jewelry would also be protected under the federal exemption. If the debtors used the state exemption scheme, they would have only been able to keep $1,000 of their cash. The debtors get a wildcard exemption of $500 each, in any case, and up to $2,000 each (or $4,000 total) if they have no homestead. Once they use one dollar's worth of equity for a homestead under the state exemptions, however, the wildcard exemption under state law drops to $500 per person. If an attorney had chosen the state scheme instead, he or she would have made a roughly $24,000 mistake.

(C) Federal. This debtor would do best under the federal set of exemptions because the wildcard exemption will help the debtor save the extra equity in his vehicle. The debtor's household goods, jewelry, and cash all fit within both the state and federal exemptions, and the debtor has no homestead, so if he chooses the federal scheme, he also has the full wildcard or pour-over exemption left to spend as he chooses, which is $15,800 plus $1,675 for a total of $17,475. Under the federal exemptions, the debtor can use this $17,475 however he chooses. The debtor can also stack the exemptions, meaning he can use the wildcard in conjunction with other more specific exemptions. Thus, this debtor can use the $5,025 from the motor vehicle exemption and then use the pour-over exemption to cover the remaining equity in the car since these two exemptions stack to a total of $22,500. If the debtor had relied on the state exemptions, he would only have been able to exempt the $7,000 from the motor vehicle exemption and $2,000 from the wildcard provision.[5] Clearly, under the state exemption scheme, the trustee would have sold the vehicle and just given the debtor the exemption amount of $9,000.

This one is very tricky, because on its face, it looks like the vehicle exemption is larger under the state exemptions. The federal wildcard exemption, however, can be used for anything at all. Thus, if the debtor has extra equity in anything, including a car or something else that is already on the list, those things can be saved through the use of the generous federal wildcard exemption. In this case, if the debtor had used the state scheme, it would have been a $10,000 mistake.

(D) State. These debtors would do best under the state set of exemptions because of the large equity in their home. The debtors' furnishings, motor vehicle, and jewelry are all completely covered under both the state and federal exemptions. Under the state exemptions, joint debtors may exempt $80,000 in equity ($40,000 per debtor) in a home. On the other hand, the federal exemptions would only exempt $63,150 in equity under the homestead exemption, plus an extra $1,675 per person for either the equity in the home or the cash, which leaves a total uncovered amount of $14,400.

Summary. As you can see, a simple mistake here or there can cost a debtor thousands of dollars. For an attorney in an exemption election state,

5. Note that the wildcard exemption is bigger under state law for this debtor because the debtor does not own a home.

it is important to calculate both exemption schemes completely to make sure nothing is overlooked.

B. New Limitations on the Homestead Exemption

Much of this country's personal wealth is held in homesteads. As discussed previously, some states allow unlimited homestead exemptions and others have virtually no homestead protection. This fact has troubled some lawmakers for years, and the debates leading up to the 2005 amendments reflected a desire by some lawmakers to crack down on the unlimited exemptions. An amendment was proposed that would have limited the homestead exemption to $250,000 per person.

While that particular amendment did not pass, the 2005 amendments do limit the amount of money a debtor can convert into home equity in the years leading up to his or her bankruptcy. The homestead exemption is reduced by an amount attributable to otherwise nonexempt property that the debtor disposed of with intent to delay, hinder, or defraud creditors. This provision applies to all property converted from nonexempt to exempt property during the ten years before the bankruptcy with the intent to hinder, delay, or defraud creditors. (*See* 11 U.S.C. §522(o).) Thus, there now is a $214,000 cap on the homestead exemption for some people, namely those who commit certain unethical acts, such as fraud, securities crimes, fraud in the fiduciary capacity, and other unethical acts. (*See* 11 U.S.C. §522(q).)

The 2005 amendments also limit the ability of people to move to get better exemptions. In one of the more confusing provisions of those amendments, §522(b)(3) states that a debtor's exemptions for bankruptcy are those from the state where the debtor resided during the 730 days before the bankruptcy case. (That's two years, right?) But what if the debtor moved during that time and thus lived in more than one place? If the debtor did not live in the same place for the full 730 days before the bankruptcy, you look back to the 180 days before the 730 days and that state's exemptions apply. Admittedly, that's pretty weird. The debtor can still plan the whole thing to get better exemptions through moving; it just takes a bit more money and planning, something that will be easier for rich people than for poor people.

The 2005 amendments for choosing the exemptions are unworkable, particularly when applied to the homestead exemption. In many states, a homestead exemption for that state can be used only for a home located in that state. This means it won't do a debtor much good to use his or her Minnesota exemptions if he or she now lives in Florida. If the debtor were living in more than one place two and one-half years before the filing, the question will be which of the places constituted the debtor's domicile. Keep in mind that none of this has anything to do with venue, which determines where the debtor must reside to file his or her petition. The rules for that remain the same. The debtor must live in a state for 180 days to file for bankruptcy in that state.

QUESTION 2. Kip Clausen was sick of cold Philadelphia winters, so he decided to sell his unencumbered $300,000 home in Pennsylvania and move to Florida to live with his Auntie and fulfill his dream of becoming a rock star in Miami's hot South Beach. He had lived in Philadelphia for most of his adult life. After the move, Kip lived with Auntie for just over a year when their relationship soured. He was having difficulty breaking into the rock scene and she felt he needed a real job. Kip then decided to pursue his dream: He bought an apartment in South Beach and spent the rest of the proceeds from his Philadelphia home to buy a share in a hot new club, where he could practice his act.

Within six months, Kip is broke, the club has closed down, and his only asset is the apartment, worth approximately $350,000 now due to fabulous appreciation. Pennsylvania has no state homestead exemption for Kip, a single man, although it does allow debtors to use the federal exemption scheme. Kip wants to file a Chapter 7 in Florida, which has an unlimited homestead exemption. It has been 22 and one-half months since he moved from Pennsylvania to Florida. Will his Chapter 7 filing save his new home?

A. Yes, because Kip had a legitimate right to save his Pennsylvania home under the Pennsylvania homestead exemptions.
B. Yes, because now that Kip owns a home in Florida, he is entitled to use the unlimited Florida homestead exemption.
C. Yes, because Kip has lived in Florida for most of the past two years, so he can use Florida's homestead exemption.
D. No, because Kip lived in Pennsylvania during the six months before the two years preceding his bankruptcy filing, so he can now only use the Pennsylvania exemptions.

ANALYSIS. The correct answer here is **D. A** is false. Kip has no right to keep his home under Pennsylvania law. It would have been sold by the trustee in a Chapter 7 case because it was not exempt. **B** is also incorrect. Owning a home in Florida by no means permits Kip to avail himself of the Florida exemptions. Rather, Kip must live in Florida for two full years to use the Florida exemptions. Even **C**, which seems intuitively sensible, at least more so than choice **D**, is incorrect. Kip is short a month and a half and the law requires Kip to live in Florida for the full two years before his filing. Because he did not live in any one state for the full two years before his bankruptcy filing, the law looks to where he lived during the six months before the past two years. Here that is Pennsylvania, and Pennsylvania exemption law provides him no relief. His trustee can sell his house if he files right now.

This situation creates an opportunity to either use creative lawyering skills or to commit malpractice. Do you see it? What is your best advice for Kip? If he waits just one and a half more months to file, he can use Florida's exemptions and save the house. As he seems to be in no huge rush, this is what he should do.

C. Exemptions for Individual Retirement Accounts

In the 2005 amendments, Congress created a new class of exemptions related to retirement plans. Now the following are exempt under the federal exemptions scheme:

- Retirement funds held in a tax-exempt account under §§401, 403, 408, 408A, 414, 457, or 501(a) of the IRC. (*See* 11 U.S.C. §522(b)(3)(C).)
- Retirement funds to the extent that those funds are exempt from taxation under these same sections. (*See* 11 U.S.C. §522(d)(12).)

This created a new federalized exemption scheme for a long list of retirement-type assets, available even in opt-out states: qualified, employee-sponsored and defined-contribution plans (e.g., 401(k) plans), 403(b) plans (qualified annuity plans established by an employer for an employee under IRC §§404(a)(2) or 501(c)(3), which may be thought of as 401(k)s for the non-profit sector), Individual Retirement Accounts (IRAs), Simplified Employee Pensions (SEPs), and Savings Incentive Match Plans for Employees (SIMPLEs) (which are not eligible for rollovers because they are excluded from the definition of eligible retirement plan), Roth IRAs, other retirement plans for controlled groups of employees (predecessor employers, partnerships, proprietorships, governments, churches), and eligible deferred compensation plans established and maintained by eligible employers.

This was a tremendous boon for the wealthy and middle class and a huge change in the law. Interestingly, only IRAs (and Roth IRAs) are limited at all in amount, and those are limited to $1,711,975per person. Even then, the court can increase the amount allowed if it finds that the "interests of justice so require."

This was a huge change from prior federal exemption law, under which there was no federal exemption whatsoever for funds held in any of these accounts.

NOTE: Again, even debtors who choose the state exemption scheme get the $1,711,975 (or greater) exemption in IRAs because the provision is found in §522(n) rather than the election section, §522(d).

Also, don't forget that ERISA-qualified pension plans do not come into the estate at all and are thus preserved for the debtor in an unlimited amount. As a policy matter, is Congress creating incentives for people to save for their retirement, or simply favoring the rich?

D. The Valuation of Exempt Property

Exemptions are based on a mathematical limit that a debtor is allowed to keep. Given the importance of valuation in determining whether a debtor can keep certain property, you might wonder who determines the value of the debtor's property. The debtor is the one who determines what he or she feels the property is worth.[6] The valuation numbers that the debtor chooses go directly into the schedules, which become public record. Not only is this document available to the public, it is also scrutinized extensively by the trustee in the case, and possibly by creditors as well.

A debtor can use many different methods for this exemption valuation. Each type of property requires a little different method of valuation. For the most part, homes require a recent appraisal, a study of comparable homes in the area, or some other recent approximation of home values in the area. Debtors should not rely on property tax assessments to approximate the value of their homes. Property tax valuations are almost always low and, if disclosed as the source of the valuation,[7] may draw an objection from the trustee or the debtor's creditors.

The valuation of a vehicle is much more straightforward because of the ease and availability of book evaluations. These can be found by referencing the Kelly Blue Book (http://www.kbb.com), NADA (http://www.nada.com), and other similar sources. It is very easy for a debtor's attorney to plug in the year, make, model, and options of the debtor's vehicle and determine the appropriate value to use. There is, however, significant controversy over whether a debtor should use the wholesale or retail values for his or her valuation in a Chapter 7 case. Some courts have interpreted the value to be an average of the two. Under a simple Chapter 7 bankruptcy, it is unlikely that a major valuation concern would arise over which value the debtor should have chosen, unless the values are significantly different. Valuation conflicts like

6. The 2005 Amendments can be read to require attorneys to perform their own research and requires them to oversee this valuation process, something that will drastically increase the cost of bankruptcy services and may even cause some attorneys to stop offering bankruptcy services. For example, see In re Clink, 770 F. 3d 719 (5th Cir. 2014). The court sanctioned an attorney under 707(b)(4)(C) and (D) for signing a petition and falsely certifying "that the attorney has no knowledge after an inquiry that the information in the schedules filed . . . is incorrect." The attorney there counseled the debtor to not list her horses on the petition and submitted a petition that was different than the one the debtor signed.

7. The trustee will want to know where the values on the schedules came from.

this occur much more frequently during the plan calculations in Chapter 13 bankruptcies because they have more of an impact on the outcome of the case.

When it comes to the valuation of personal property, the debtor is given more slack. Because it would be totally inefficient to require a debtor to obtain an appraisal on all of his or her property, the court typically accepts the debtor's personal approximation of the value of his or her personal property. When calculating the value of a debtor's property, the debtor should use a value that would reflect the item's current market price, if the item were sold on the used goods market. This essentially means a garage sale. It is a common mistake for debtors to approximate the value of their property at what they paid for it, or significantly close to it. For example, if a debtor bought a $2,000 couch five years ago it would be difficult to sell it today at $1,500. It is important to make sure the debtors understand the valuation of personal property should be at used or "garage sale" numbers. This valuation process may have a direct effect on just how much property the debtor can protect. Although the debtor is allowed some slack, if a valuation seems inappropriate, the trustee may object to it. He or she will investigate the matter and determine whether the sale of any items over the exemptions would provide any significant amount of money to the creditors. When the trustee makes this decision, he or she takes into account the cost of sale in determining what the net benefit to creditors would be.

A debtor's attorney tries his or her best to place as much of the debtor's property into these exemption categories. This can be visualized by characterizing each exemption as being a very large plastic bin. Each plastic bin represents one category of an exemption. For example, there will be one very large bin for cars, another for the debtor's clothing, another for the debtor's cash, and so on. In this visualization, the debtor's attorney has the task of placing as much property in each bin as possible.

On the other hand, trustee and creditor attorneys try their best to prevent as much of the debtor's property from getting into these exemption categories. The more property they can keep out of the bins, the more that goes into their clients' (or in the case of trustees, their beneficiaries') pockets. Using these visualizations, a creditor's attorneys can be seen as following the debtor's attorney around to make sure everything in each bin belongs there and the mathematical limit for each box is not exceeded. The more property that finds its way into the bins, the less there is to distribute to the creditors. The most common way to try and gain more money for the creditors is to object to valuation in hopes that it will be re-evaluated at a value high enough to justify its sale and distribution, or in hopes that the debtor might borrow money to buy the nonexempt portion, which can then be distributed to creditors.

Valuation of exempt property is a common area of dispute. The trustee often asks how the debtor arrived at the value numbers in the paperwork during the Section 341 meeting discussed in Chapter 6. If the trustee believes the debtor has undervalued an object, he or she can do more research into the valuation or require the debtor to prove the value. The most common way to resolve a valuation dispute is by simply performing an appraisal. Most objections will arise only when the asset will create a meaningful distribution for creditors.

QUESTION 3. Assume the debtor lives in a state where the state exemptions are minimal and that use of the federal exemptions is permitted and would yield more for the debtor than the state exemptions in all four of these examples. For each of the following debtors, determine how much of his or her property you can exempt under the federal exemptions and how much would be available to his or her creditors. For simplicity's sake, do not include the cost of sale or the trustee's fee in any calculations. Again, do each part separately (A, B, C, and D). There are four separate questions here.

A. An individual debtor who has $40,000 in equity in his home, $5,900 equity in his car, a $2,000 big-screen TV, $500 in clothing, $5,000 in household items (no single item more than $800), no jewelry, and $1,000 in stocks.

B. An individual debtor who has $10,000 in equity in her home, $1,000 equity in her car, $2,000 in household items (no single item more than $800), $5,000 in jewelry, and $500 cash.

C. Joint debtors who have $67,000 in equity in their home, $2,000 equity in one car, and $6,000 equity in another car, $15,000 in household items (no single item more than $800), $2,000 in jewelry, and $4,000 in a savings account.

D. Joint debtors who rent their home, have $1,000 equity in one car and no equity in the other, $7,500 in household items (no single item more than $800), $500 in jewelry, and $25,000 in cash.

ANALYSIS. **(A) About $9,825 for creditors.** Beginning with the home, an individual debtor can exempt up to $31,575 of the equity in his home. In this example, the debtor can only protect $31,575 of the total $40,000 in equity, which would provide $12,100 of remaining value for the creditors from the home equity, unless the debtor also wants to use his general wildcard exemption of $1,675 for this asset too, but let's assume not and keep going. Moving to the equity in the car, the debtor can only exempt $5,025, but the debtor can also use the $1,675 general wildcard exemption. Opting to use that here would save the car with $200 left over. Assuming the debtor does this, creditors get nothing from the car. The big-screen TV would fall under the household goods exemption, but because you can only exempt up to $800 of any single item, another $1,200 would go to his creditors. This, of course, assumes that the items in the problem have been valued at garage-sale prices, which might be unrealistic for this big-screen TV!

The clothing and household items would all fit within the exemptions. The debtor is allowed $16,850 in total, so if you subtract the $800 used for the TV, the $500 for the clothing, and the $5,000 left in miscellaneous household items, that still leaves the debtor plenty of room. Unfortunately, the leftover exemption cannot be applied to another area. Finally, since we assumed the debtor would use the general wildcard exemption of $1,675 to save the car, there is only $800 left to apply to the $1,000 worth of stock. That leaves creditors with $200. Perhaps the debtor would use the general wildcard exemption to save the stock and not the car (or to apply it to the house or television) but that of course is the debtor's decision, not the attorney's. Again, the debtor can't use the leftovers from the home to augment (d)(5)'s wildcard because he used up the whole exemption on his house. Adding together the $8,425 in home equity, the $1,200 from the big-screen TV, and the $200 in stocks, creditors in this case could realize $9,825 from this debtor's assets. This is a rare case in which the creditors would receive a substantial amount of money. The cost of sale and the trustee's fee (which varies per district and varies per total amount distributed to the creditors) would still be deducted from this $9,825 amount.

(B) $0. Beginning with the home, an individual debtor can exempt up to $31,575 of the equity in a home. In this example the debtor has more than enough to protect her homestead, and this leaves $21,575 of the homestead exemption unused. Up to $15,800 of this amount can be used to exempt something later under the wildcard exemption. The $1,000 equity in her vehicle is also well under the $5,025 vehicle exemption, but the debtor cannot apply the extra $4,025 to another area. Only the wildcard exemption works in that way. The $2,000 is also well under the $16,850 total exemption for household goods but also cannot be applied to another area.

The jewelry is where this debtor begins to look as though she has a problem. The federal exemption for jewelry is only $2,125. This means that $2,875 is not exempted and could possibly be available to creditors. Because the debtor did not use the whole homestead exemption, however, the debtor has the usual $1,675 available, plus $15,800 pour-over from the unused homestead exemption ($21,575 was unused from the homestead exemption, but only $15,800 can pour over), for a total of $17,475 to use however she'd like, which is more than enough to cover the $2,875 overage in her jewelry, as well as the $500 in cash. This is a more realistic example of your normal bankruptcy debtor with little or no distribution to the creditors.

(C) $5,475 for creditors. Beginning with the home, joint debtors can exempt up to $63,150 ($31,575 for each of them) in equity in their home. In this example, the debtors can only protect $63,150, which would leave $3,850 in equity for their creditors. Moving to the equity in the car, the debtors can only exempt $5,025 per vehicle. In this case, the one car is covered under the exemption but the other is over by $975, which is at least theoretically available to creditors. They used their entire homestead exemption, so their wildcard exemption is just $1,675 per person, or $3,350. This could be used to save the second car, and we'll assume for now that this is what they choose to do. As for the household items, joint debtors can use up to $16,850 per person (or $33,700 in total) as long as no single item is more than $800. In this case they can exempt all of their $15,000 worth of household items but the exemption left over cannot be used in another place. Joint debtors can exempt $2,125 each in jewelry, so combined, they can exempt $4,250 in total, which is more than the $2,000 they have.

Finally, they have $2,375 remaining from their wild card to use to save that much cash from the $4,000 in their savings account, so creditors will get the $1,625 remaining in the bank account. It may have been better for these debtors to try to save more of the cash rather than the second car, but this is their decision and this is part of the purpose of the wildcard exemptions. This example shows that even if it is clear which exemption scheme to use, any scheme can be used in different ways, to the debtor's benefit or detriment.

In real life, these debtors would most likely use the couple's combined wildcard of $3,350 to save the house, by applying this wildcard to the $3,850 in shortage and then ponying up $500 in cash to the trustee. If they could keep their house, they would likely be happy to let the rest of this stuff go. Though the decision is up to them, it is nice to know that this can be done. Dollars are dollars. As long as creditors are in the same position, this is an acceptable way to save the home.

(D) $0. Because these joint debtors rent their home, they do not have to use any of their homestead exemption. This means that the individual wildcard exemptions can be completely used. The debtors' $1,000 worth of equity in their car falls well under the $5,025 exemption limit, so nothing would be distributed to their creditors but the unused portion could not be applied to another area. The $7,500 in household items would be treated in a similar fashion because they are well under the $33,700 maximum household item exemption ($16,850 each). The jewelry would also fall under the $4,250 exemption ($2,125 each), so nothing from here would be distributed to their creditors. As for the cash, the debtors must rely completely on the wildcard. The wildcard allows $15,800 per debtor from the leftover homestead, plus the $1,675 each that everyone gets regardless of use of the homestead exemption, for a total of $34,000. Wow! This protects all of the cash too. The creditors in this case would get nothing.

Summary. These examples show how exemption calculations are performed. As a general rule, the federal exemptions are good for those individuals with lots of cash or special items that fall outside other categories. Most other jurisdictions do not have wildcard provisions as large as the federal exemptions provide. You can also see from these examples that, as a debtor's attorney, an error in what you can and cannot exempt could mean more money to the creditors and less to your debtor. For this reason, it is imperative that anyone performing these calculations do so carefully and have them checked.

E. Voiding Involuntary Liens, and Nonpossessory, Non-Purchase-Money Security Interests That Interfere With an Exemption

Under §522(f) of the Code, the debtor can avoid involuntary liens that interfere with or impair one of the debtor's exemptions. You may recall that a judgment lien creditor (also called an involuntary lien creditor) becomes secured by getting a judgment against the debtor and then executing on certain property. You'll also recall that the debtor is allowed to exempt certain property from execution under state law. The creditor cannot touch these items, as they are exempt from state execution.

This theme continues in bankruptcy. Any property that the debtor has claimed as exempt under either the state or the federal exemption scheme cannot be impaired or interfered with by an involuntary lien. If there is a judgment lien on property in which the debtor claims an exemption, the debtor can move to have the involuntary lien avoided, which will turn the judgment lienholder back into an unsecured creditor.

Before getting into the specifics of avoiding such a lien, think a bit about this. If a debtor owns a home that has a voluntary mortgage lien on it, this lien will not be affected by the debtor's exemptions. Voluntary secured creditors come ahead of the debtor's exemptions in particular property. If the debtor grants a security interest to a creditor in the house or the car, this must always be satisfied first, so the exemptions are not relevant to secured creditor treatment. After the secured parties' rights, which are in first position, the exemptions come next, followed by the claims of executing creditors.

Let's look at an example outside of bankruptcy. Say that a person owns a home worth $200,000 in Arizona. Let's also say that the state homestead exemption is $40,000 per person. The debtor also owes $150,000 on the house to the mortgage holder. Jerry Judgment Creditor obtains a $20,000 judgment against the debtor and forces the sale of the home. The first party entitled to payment is the mortgage holder, who either takes $150,000 or keeps its lien. The second to be paid out of the sale is the debtor, who gets $40,000 for the state law exemption. Finally, though there is only $10,000 left, this goes to the judgment holder, who is paid half of his debt.

Let's look at another quick example, this time in a bankruptcy context. James owns a car that is worth $8,000. He owes $2,000 on the car to the secured party who lent him the money to buy it. Visa obtained a judgment against James for $5,000 and executed on the car by having the sheriff remove it from James's driveway in the middle of the night. The next day, James filed for Chapter 7 bankruptcy and thereafter moved under §522(f) to avoid Visa's involuntary judgment lien on the car. James chose the federal exemptions in his bankruptcy. Can Visa's lien be avoided, and if so, to what extent? While the Code section itself seems to suggest that if a judicial lien impairs an exemption at all, it can be avoided in toto, cases have held that a judicial lien that only partially impairs an exemption is only partially avoidable. In this case, the voluntary secured lender has the first dibs on the car for $2,000; then the debtor's exemption must come out. That leaves only $2,225 in value left for Visa, but that part of the lien stays in place. The lien is not avoided completely, but only to the extent that it impairs an exemption.

In addition to judicial liens, the debtor can also avoid non-purchase-money, nonpossessory security interests in household furnishings, household goods, wearing apparel, appliances, books, animals, crops, musical instruments, or jewelry that are held primarily for the personal, family, or household use of the debtor or a dependent. These are non-purchase-money voluntary liens, meaning that the security interest secures debt that was not incurred to buy these items of collateral. Rather, the items were pledged to secure a later loan or debt. Non-purchase-money, nonpossessory, security interests in worthless household goods are often taken by payday loan companies and other subprime lenders as leverage against consumer debtors rather than as collateral that the lenders actually intend to sell. In any event, the security interests are avoidable in bankruptcy, just like judicial liens, so long as the security interest impairs an exemption.

Just so you know, the 2005 amendments limit the debtor's ability to avoid liens on household goods to a very specific list of goods. Specifically, the definition for "household goods" in §522(f)(4)(A) identifies the types of qualifying goods and limits the quantity of certain items, such as appliances, one radio, one television, one VCR (while the Bankruptcy Code exemption dollar amounts are automatically updated every three years, you can see that the specific electronic items listed in the Code are clearly not updated!), linens, china, crockery, kitchenware, and so on. Additionally, §522(f)(4)(B) excludes certain items, such as artwork and types of motor vehicles, and limits the aggregate value of other types of goods.

QUESTION 4. Janet Ryan is a lawyer who does personal-injury plaintiff's work. In a somewhat ironic twist of fate, Janet was in a car accident that was caused by her negligence. The driver of the other car was seriously injured and received a $100,000 personal-injury judgment against Janet. Worse yet for Janet, she did not have liability insurance for automobile accidents. Janet owns a home that has a current market value of $250,000. Big Bank has a mortgage loan against Janet's home for $200,000. In Janet's state, the homestead exemption is $30,000. When Janet is unable to pay the $100,000 judgment, the other driver gets a judicial lien on Janet's house for the amount of the judgment. Janet then decides to file Chapter 7 bankruptcy. Assuming that Janet uses her state's exemptions in bankruptcy, what will be the value of her accident victim's judicial lien on Janet's home after the judicial lien is avoided to the extent allowable under the Bankruptcy Code?

A. $20,000.
B. $30,000.
C. $50,000.
D. $100,000.

ANALYSIS. The correct answer is **A**. The first issue to note here is that Big Bank's mortgage will come ahead of the accident victim's judicial lien whether Janet is in bankruptcy or outside of bankruptcy. Therefore, choice **D** must be incorrect because that answer assumes that the victim's judicial lien comes ahead of Big Bank's mortgage. The next point to see here is that Janet's exemption will come ahead of the victim's judicial lien outside of bankruptcy. Section 522(f)(1)(A)'s lien-avoidance provision will provide for that same result inside of bankruptcy. This means that **C** has to be wrong because **C** assumes that the accident victim's judicial lien would capture all of Janet's potential equity, even that part which is covered by Janet's $30,000 exemption. Answer **B** is wrong because it gives us the amount of Janet's equity that she gets to keep rather than the value of the accident victim's judicial lien, which is what the question asks for. To calculate the value of the accident victim's judicial lien, we take the value of the home ($250,000) minus Big Bank's mortgage ($200,000) minus Janet's exemption in her home ($30,000). That leaves us with $20,000, which is choice **A**.

F. The Closer: Chapters 8 and 9

You represent Honey Halliburton, who has lent money to Fred Friton, who owns a brokerage house in Albuquerque. The money was used to buy a beautiful oceangoing yacht in which Honey took a security interest. Fred has fallen on hard times and has decided to file a Chapter 7 bankruptcy petition. As a diligent lawyer for Honey, you have gone down to the bankruptcy court to review Fred's bankruptcy petition, statement of affairs, and schedules of assets and liabilities. Lo and behold, you have discovered that the yacht on which Honey holds a security interest was not listed anywhere on Fred's petition or statement or schedules. Essentially, this means that Fred failed to list the yacht as one of his assets on his Schedule B, and also failed to list the yacht as exempt property on Schedule C. Honey is not interested in getting involved in the bankruptcy case. All she wants is to get back her yacht. What is your best move on behalf of Honey?

A. Object to Fred's bankruptcy case on the basis that he is ineligible because he is a stockbroker.
B. Don't worry about the bankruptcy, because Fred has failed to list the assets as part of his estate, and instead, simply help Honey repossess the yacht.
C. Just to be safe, request that the bankruptcy court lift the stay to allow Honey to repossess the yacht.
D. Do what is suggested in C, but also file a complaint objecting to Fred's discharge, on the basis that he has hidden assets from the bankruptcy court.

ANALYSIS. Perhaps it is too early to even be discussing the options set out in choice **D**, namely that Honey objects to Fred's entire discharge under §727 of the Bankruptcy Code, because he has filed false documents with the court. In any event, Honey has indicated that all she wants is the yacht, so perhaps it is not necessary to discuss the ins and outs of this subject matter at this time. If all that Honey really wants is the yacht, she doesn't care much about the bankruptcy, then what you need is relief from the automatic stay, as suggested in choice **C**. What about just doing what is suggested in choice **B**, namely, repossessing the collateral because it appears that the debtor has admitted that it is not part of his estate? This would clearly be a risky move, as it is not true that this asset is not part of Fred's estate simply because he failed to list it on his petition. We have not seen cases discussing this issue, but we feel certain that if a debtor were in bankruptcy and a creditor knew that, the creditor could not repossess the collateral even if that collateral was not listed anywhere on the debtor's disclosure documents. Thus, we believe that **C** is a better answer than **B**.

What about choice **A**? Should you object to the case because Fred is ineligible given that he is a stockbroker? First, the question does not necessarily say that Fred is a stockbroker himself, it simply says that he owns a brokerage firm. More important, however, this answer is incorrect because it does not achieve Honey's goal, namely the goal of getting back the yacht. Choice **A** simply suggests that you object to the case based on Fred's ineligibility, which will do nothing to return the yacht. The fact is that choice **D**, objecting to Fred's discharge, as well as moving to lift the stay, will probably produce the yacht more quickly than simply moving to lift the stay. It is a very serious matter not to list assets on the petition; we will discuss this matter further in Chapter 13 of this guide. Thus, we believe that the correct answer is **C**, but choice **D** is also a very good answer.

Martin's and Keating's Picks

1. Question 1	(see text)
2. Question 2	**D**
3. Question 3	(see text)
4. Question 4	**A**
The Closer: Chapters 8–9	**C or D**

10

Priorities

OVERVIEW

Martin's and Keating's Picks

Despite the Bankruptcy Code's emphasis on equality of treatment, some claims are paid ahead of other claims, even among unsecured creditors. This is accomplished through the Bankruptcy Code's priority scheme, which is set out in §507(a) of the Code, and to which you should now turn. You cannot answer some of the questions below without reading your Code. These questions are designated with the phrase CODE READER.

The priority scheme is the Bankruptcy Code's most flagrant social engineering provision. As a society, we believe that some creditor claims are more important than others. We purposely give preference to those whom we feel need preference, as well as some who have simply asked for special treatment. While the claims that have priority under §507 are presumably those debts that society places the most value on and most wishes to be paid, some creditors have found their way into the section merely by successfully lobbying Congress. Priorities are important in every type of bankruptcy case. In a straight Chapter 7 liquidation, §507 tells the trustee which creditors to pay first out of the proceeds of any sales. In a Chapter 13 case, all priority claims (meaning those entitled to priority under §507(a)) must be paid in full under the Chapter 13 plan. In a Chapter 11 case, all priority claims must be paid in full under the plan, but most must actually be paid much earlier, shortly after the court approves the reorganization plan. The way that §507 works is that each category of claim that is entitled to special priority is listed in the section in the order of priority that the claims are paid. Thus, because domestic support obligations are in §507(a)(1), they come ahead of recent taxes, which are found in §507(a)(8). Employee wage claims, which are found in §507(a)(3), obviously come ahead of taxes but behind domestic support obligations. Priority claims in higher categories must be paid in full before the next category of priority claim gets anything at all.

IMPORTANT: Note that the section applies only to unsecured claims, meaning those without collateral securing them. Secured claims are not included because secured parties are protected by their collateral, at least up to the value of the collateral securing their claims. Secured creditors may be able to get back their collateral, or, if the trustee sells it, will be paid first out of the proceeds.[1] In effect, property encumbered by a security interest or lien is not available to pay unsecured creditors, except to the extent that the debtor has equity in the property that is not exempt.

Unsecured claims entitled to priority are called priority claims. As described previously, §507 ranks these special types of unsecured claims, and provides that they are paid ahead of other unsecured claims that are not entitled to priority. Unsecured claims not entitled to priority are called general unsecured claims or just general claims.

QUESTION 1. (CODE READER) Which of these has the highest priority in any form of bankruptcy?

A. A claim for taxes.
B. A claim for post-petition attorneys' fees under §503(b).
C. A fully secured claim.
D. A claim for pre-petition attorneys' fees.

ANALYSIS. Once one starts to sort out the unsecured claims, the post-petition attorneys' fees mentioned in **B** are in second position under §§507(a)(2) and 503(b), and even then, second only to domestic support obligations, which are not always due. Next in line within the unsecured creditors mentioned here are the taxes described in **A**, which are a §507(a)(8) claim and thus eighth in line among the unsecured priority claims. Notice how we keep talking about the ranks of creditors among the unsecured claims. We want to make sure you never forget that secured claims beat out all of these claims, for the most part. Remember that there are two general types of claims, secured and unsecured, and secured is better. Thus, the correct answer is **C**.

HINT: The priority claims are at the top of the heap of the unsecured claims, but if all of the property of the estate has been pledged to the secured creditor or a group of secured creditors, the priority claims are at the top of a heap of nothing. They do not get paid.

As for **D**, attorneys who work on bankruptcies pre-petition are in a precarious position. To get high-priority treatment under §507(a), the only category of the priority claims that the attorneys' fees could even arguably fall into, the attorney must do something in the case to benefit the estate and its

1. They also may be paid in full by the debtor under the normal payment terms; or, in a reorganization-style case like a Chapter 13 or a Chapter 11, they'll be paid under the plan.

creditors. Post-petition work of the trustee and the trustee's attorney qualifies, but the Chapter 7 debtor's attorney, be it pre-petition or post-petition, is not entitled to administrative priority treatment. Thus, the claims in **D** get no priority treatment at all. They are general unsecured claims, which is why all attorneys doing Chapter 7 cases should get paid through an up-front retainer, before the bankruptcy case is filed.

Many nonlawyers and lawyers alike are shocked to hear that out of all the claims entitled to priority under §507 (which include claims for deposits in a limited amount, child support and alimony, taxes within certain periods, and people who have done business with a company while it was in financial trouble),[2] the attorneys and trustees who work on the post-petition case are near the front of the line to be paid. Unfair and self-serving, perhaps, but think about how many trustees and attorneys would participate in the administration of bankruptcy cases if they could not get paid for their services. Maybe it is not quite as unfair as it seems.

The priority scheme goes against the basic principle of equality of distribution underlying the Code. There is a reason for this exception to the equality principle, however. As a society, we consider some types of debts more entitled to repayment than others. For example, we believe that child support payments should have priority over some other claims, and also that tax claims should have priority over some other claims.

QUESTION 2. The Bankruptcy Code's priority scheme is designed to reflect:

A. the interests of those special interest groups who lobbied Congress the year §507 was enacted.
B. the interests of society as a whole, by giving special treatment to those who we feel are most entitled to it under our societal norms and values.
C. the judgments of those who have worked in the bankruptcy system over the years and who know who needs help the most.
D. all of the above.

ANALYSIS. The answer is **D**. This question is included to let you know that the priority scheme was not handed down from above in one organized swoop. Many hands drafted these provisions. Initially, the folks mentioned in **C**, who are most familiar with the system and its nuances, wrote them. These priority provisions were then tinkered with extensively by the people mentioned in **A**, which is the only explanation we can give for why grain sellers

2. This is something we would like to encourage as a society.

and fishermen get special treatment in §507(a)(6), over other food producers. Go figure. Finally, as set out previously, the system is designed by all of these people to protect the interest of society as a whole, and with a few odd exceptions, it seems to do a decent job of it.

In examining all the parts of §507, one can see that the reasons for the special treatment vary. In the case of child support, the recipient is not a good risk spreader as the child support could be one of few sources of income for the child. Another person is relying on the payment, perhaps for survival. Taxes are given special treatment because if they remain unpaid, then the public has to make up for the difference. However, taxes are not as special as one might think. The authorities still must comply with the automatic stay, and the period during which the taxes are entitled to priority treatment can be quite short. For example, income taxes generally have priority for only the past three taxable years, and property taxes have priority only for one year. By limiting the period of priority, the Code drafters are rewarding diligent collection efforts and discouraging the alternative behavior of allowing governments to sit on their collection rights.

QUESTION 3. (CODE READER) Which of these statements is false?

1. All taxes described within §507(a)(8) share proceeds of a bankruptcy sale pro rata.
2. Section 507(a)(8)(A) taxes get paid first, then §507(a)(8)(B), then §509(A)(8)(C), and so on.
3. Income taxes always have priority status in a bankruptcy.
4. Trust fund taxes, which the debtor has collected or withheld from employees, always have priority in a bankruptcy.

A. 1, 2, and 3.
B. 2 and 3.
C. 3 and 4.
D. None of the above.

ANALYSIS. Choice **1** is true, which means that **2** must be false, as these statements are opposites. The Code itself does not come right out and say this point blank, but by implication all of the taxes have eighth priority, so they share pro rata. We always wish the Code was better written and clearer, but it is not, so we live with it. An annotated Code can be your best defense. Mine clearly states that the taxes share pro rata, in the notes following the section. Choice **3** is incorrect because, as stated in the text, income taxes only have priority for about three years. We say "about" because the Code, quite confusingly, gives priority status to all income taxes for which a return was last due within three years of the filing of the petition. Most personal income taxes are due on April 15 of the upcoming year. Thus, for example, a tax for the year 2021 would be due on April 15, 2022. This essentially gives most income taxes priority for a period of three years, but an additional three months' worth might get priority depending on the time of year the bankruptcy case is filed. This may be more than you want to know at this point. Our main goal here is to make sure you know that there is a time limit on many taxes and if they are not collected diligently, they may become general unsecured claims.

Just so you know, though, not all taxes lose their priority status over time. For example, assume the debtor runs a business and is required to withhold certain amounts from her employees' paychecks under federal Social Security and other law. She withdraws the required amount but does not remit the withheld funds to the IRS because she hits an unexpected financial bump and ends up in bankruptcy. Whether she runs a sole proprietorship or a corporation, she is personally liable forever for those withheld funds, which are referred to as trust fund taxes. Additionally, these taxes get priority status in bankruptcy under §507(a)(8)(C).

Thus, **1** and **4** are true, **2** and **3** are false, and **B** is the correct answer.

QUESTION 4. (CODE READER) Which of these creditor claims are not entitled to priority treatment under the Bankruptcy Code?

A. Domestic support obligations.
B. Student loans.
C. Back taxes.
D. Grain sellers.

ANALYSIS. If you looked in your Code, you learned that the answer is **B**. Remember that priority status just means that a debt is close to the front of the line for payment, that's all. There are no guarantees of payment. Soon you will learn that many of the same debts that have priority status also get another perk. They are nondischargeable in a Chapter 7 bankruptcy, meaning that they will continue to be owed by the debtor even after the bankruptcy case is over. Priority status and nondischargeability status are two different things and are often confused. Try to pause and meditate over this difference, because most students tend to forget it.

Because student loans are nondischargeable under §523(a), along with most of the debts in §507(a), most students think that student loans get priority. They do not, however. Make a note to come back to this question once you have learned about nondischargeability in Chapter 13.

Now we are going to try some mathematical problems. Get out your calculator!

QUESTION 5. (CODE READER) Peter Perfect has hit rock bottom, filing for bankruptcy this past month. His Chapter 7 trustee has sold his only nonexempt asset, an old farmhouse, for $100,000. He owes his ex-wife $20,000 in past-due child support payments, in addition to owing $30,000 on his student loans, $10,000 in back federal income taxes for last year, and $10,000 for his county property taxes that were due two years ago. He owes his other, general unsecured creditors $100,000. What percentage distribution will his unsecured creditors get?

A. 30%
B. 50%
C. approximately 36%
D. approximately 40%

ANALYSIS. Now we are going to have some fun. Don't let the math scare you. One of us had math phobia as a college student. Now, problems like this are the best part of that co-author's job. She likes them because, unlike virtually all other parts of the law, there is a correct answer. As a student, this is rewarding because you can easily see whether you understand the concepts involved.

The first thing to do is determine which of these obligations have priority, because those will need to be paid first. Then you need to add the itemized claims that did not get priority to the unsecured creditor pool or class. Next you pay out the priority claims (subtract them from the total farm proceeds), and divide what is left by the amount of the unsecured claims. Voilà! That percentage amount is your unsecured creditor distribution. So let's go.

The ex-wife's debt is characterized as a domestic support obligation under the Code, so it gets priority under §507(a)(1). So far, $20,000 gets priority. The student loan does not get priority, as we just discussed, so we add the $30,000 for that to the general unsecured creditor class, which now is up to $130,000 in claims. The income taxes are from last year so they clearly get priority too, under §507(a)(8)(A). Now the priority claims class is up to $30,000.

What about the property taxes? Section 507(a)(8)(B) tells us that those get priority, but only for a year or so. These property taxes are from two years ago. Thus, they get added to the general unsecured class, which is now holding $140,000 in claims. We can stop briefly to check our work here. All of the claims against Peter total $170,000. We said there were $30,000 in the priority class, and $140,000 in the general unsecured (nonpriority) class, so it looks like we are all set so far.

Now deduct the $30,000 from the $100,000 and pay that to the wife and the IRS for the income taxes. We are left with $70,000 in proceeds to pay off $140,000. No calculator needed here, as the math works out to exactly 50 percent. The answer is **B**.

In your own mind now, calculate the amount that each of the unsecured creditors gets. Piece of cake, right? The student loan company gets $15,000 for its $30,000 claim, the county gets $5,000 for its $10,000 property tax claim, and the other unsecured creditors also each get one-half of what each is owed. As a preview of what is to come, the unnamed unsecured creditors will have the rest of their debts discharged, as will the county for the remainder of the old property tax claims. The debtor will continue to owe the rest of the student loan debt after his bankruptcy, however, because these debts are nondischargeable.

QUESTION 6. (CODE READER) The next three questions are all about Peter Ponzi, featured here. Peter Ponzi is in Chapter 7 and is knee deep in debt from his failed e-business. His assets are probably worth less than $100,000, and he owes $40,000 in back income taxes and $100,000 in back trust fund taxes from his e-business failure. He also owes many deposits on back orders from customers that were never filled, as well as many past due bills to suppliers. Out of the creditors listed here, who will get the highest priority in his liquidation bankruptcy?

A. The trust fund taxes.
B. The income taxes.
C. The supplier claims.
D. The people who paid deposits.

ANALYSIS. This one involves poking through §507(a). The trust fund taxes and the income taxes are both in §507(a)(8), where they share pro rata. Since neither beats out the other, we assume those are not the correct answers. **C** is a red herring. Who are these suppliers? Unless Peter sells grain or fish through his e-business, there is no special treatment for suppliers. People who have paid deposits, however, get special treatment under §507(a)(6), at least up to a certain amount. Thus, **D** is the answer.

QUESTION 7. Once the property of Peter Ponzi is sold, the first one in line to be paid out of the ones listed below will be:

1. his bankruptcy attorney.
2. the bankruptcy trustee, for his commission.
3. the costs of sale.
4. the trust fund tax claims.

A. 1, 2, and 3 only.
B. All of the above.
C. 2 and 3 only.
D. Just 1 and 2.

ANALYSIS. As we've discussed, Peter's own attorney should have been paid up front. He gets no special treatment. Both **2** and **3** qualify as §507(a)(2) claims that get second priority treatment through this section and through §503(b), which pays those who have benefited the estate first, ahead of all other unsecured claims. Because these people and items get paid ahead of all taxes, the correct answer is **C**: **2** and **3** only. Peter will not be happy about this because he will remain liable for the trust fund taxes since these debts are not dischargeable.

QUESTION 8. (CODE READER) Marcia Masterpiece is an artist who paints portraits for a living. In a typical year, Marcia will paint about six portraits. She charges $20,000 for each portrait that she paints. The most recent portrait that she painted was for Bill Backus, a retired businessman. Unfortunately, two weeks after Marcia finished that painting, Bill filed for Chapter 7 bankruptcy without having paid Marcia any of the $20,000 that he now owed her. To what extent will Marcia have a priority claim for that $20,000 in Bill's bankruptcy?

A. Zero.
B. $20,000.
C. $15,150.
D. $4,850.

ANALYSIS. The correct answer here is **A**. This is one of those cases where the Code drafters might have been clearer than they were about the distinction between true employees and independent contractors. Even though §507(a)(4) does not state it in so many words, only true employees are entitled to a priority in the bankruptcy of their employer. On the other hand, most independent contractors are not entitled to a priority in the bankruptcy of a client as to money earned but not paid pre-petition. The only independent contractors that are entitled to a priority are sales people for whom at least 75 percent of their commissions during the previous year were earned from the client who is now in bankruptcy, *see* §507(a)(4)(B). That obviously does not apply to Marcia here, so she will simply have a general unsecured claim in Bill's bankruptcy. For that reason, all of the other choices must be incorrect.

QUESTION 9. (CODE READER) Frank Furman files Chapter 7 bankruptcy at a time when he owes $8,000 in unpaid child support to his ex-wife. Frank also has a number of other unsecured creditors whose claims are all nonpriority. When Frank's Chapter 7 trustee sells all of Frank's nonexempt assets, the trustee is able to collect a total of $11,000 for the estate. The trustee's own fees and expenses, which the bankruptcy court deems reasonable, amount to $6,000. How much will Frank's ex-wife receive from the trustee for the pre-petition child support?

A. Zero.
B. $8,000.
C. $5,000.
D. $6,000.

ANALYSIS. This one is tricky and requires a very close reading of the Code. Your first response is likely to be that Frank's ex-wife is entitled to the full $8,000 in unpaid pre-petition child support. After all, §507(a)(1) appears to give the first priority among unsecured claims to domestic support obligations such as this one. However, if you read that section closely, especially §507(a)(1)(C), you will realize that Congress built into this first priority a critical exception: the administrative expenses of the trustee. This exception makes sense. If Congress did not put the claims of the trustee first, then the trustee would simply refuse to do the work! You might ask, then why didn't Congress just make the trustee's claims the first priority? Good question, although the answer is probably a political one: It just sounds better to say that domestic support obligations are first.

In any event, what that means for this question is that the correct answer is **C**. That's because once the trustee gets paid the $6,000 in expenses, that leaves $5,000 to be distributed to Frank's ex-wife for past-due child support. You might try to argue that **B**, $8,000, is still the right answer since anything that Frank's trustee fails to pay now will still be owed by Frank because it will be nondischargeable. However, the question asks how much Frank's wife will receive "from the trustee." Therefore, anything that Frank's wife might receive later from Frank for this unpaid child support does not count for purposes of this question.

Martin's and Keating's Picks

1. Question 1 **C**
2. Question 2 **D**
3. Question 3 **B**
4. Question 4 **B**
5. Question 5 **B**
6. Question 6 **D**
7. Question 7 **C**
8. Question 8 **A**
9. Question 9 **C**

11

The Treatment of Secured Claims in Bankruptcy

OVERVIEW

A. Secured Credit in General
   1. Secured creditor remedies outside bankruptcy
   2. Secured creditor treatment in bankruptcy
B. The Comfort of Being Secured
C. Undersecured and Oversecured Creditors: Learning the Lingo
D. Practicing the Calculations
Martin's and Keating's Picks

We have just looked at the distinction between unsecured creditors with priority and unsecured creditors without priority. Another distinction, and a more important one, is the distinction between secured and unsecured (or general) creditors. While we discussed how secured creditors' rights differ from unsecured creditors' rights under state law in Chapters 1 and 2, it is now time to see how these rights differ under bankruptcy law.

A. Secured Credit in General

By now, you know that secured creditors are those who have liens on certain property, real or personal, of the debtor. Liens arise under state law, not under bankruptcy law, but the Bankruptcy Code recognizes them as property interests of the person holding the lien. The liens may arise as a result of (1) the judicial process in which a creditor gets a judgment, executes on the judgment, and has the sheriff levy on certain property of the debtor; (2) statutory or common law liens, which dictate that a lien arise because of the relationship of the parties (e.g., the lien that a landlord has on the personal property of the tenant that is on the premises); or (3) a voluntary act of the debtor (i.e., the debtor grants to a creditor a security interest in some of his or her property by creating a mortgage on real property or an Article 9 security interest on some of his or her personal property).

To be a voluntary secured creditor in a bankruptcy case, a creditor must comply with either Article 9 of the Uniform Commercial Code (UCC), which is state law, or with state real estate law. This law requires that the creditor have a contract granting it a security interest in certain property to secure repayment of the loan. This process is similar to granting a bank a mortgage on your home to secure your repayment of the loan. Usually, to be a secured creditor in a bankruptcy, the creditor also must do something to perfect this security interest.[1] Because the rules regarding secured creditor treatment in bankruptcy are most commonly used with respect to voluntary Article 9 security interests, the rest of this discussion focuses on voluntary security interests granted under Article 9 of the UCC.

1. *Secured creditor remedies outside bankruptcy*

When an Article 9 secured creditor's borrower is not in default and not in bankruptcy, the borrower pays the loan as promised. Eventually the creditor releases its security interest on the collateral and the debtor owns the property "free and clear," as we say. If the borrower does not pay the loan on time, and the loan instead goes into default, then the secured creditor has certain rights. These include the right to repossess its collateral, to sell the collateral to pay down the loan, and then to pursue the debtor for a deficiency judgment. A deficiency judgment is a judgment for the part of the loan that was not paid off from the sale of the collateral. The creditor is of course an unsecured creditor for this deficiency judgment because the collateral is already gone, right? There is no longer any collateral to cover the part of the loan that is still unpaid. If the creditor wants to get a judgment for this remaining debt, it will need to execute on other property of the debtor to be paid, just as any unsecured creditor would.

2. *Secured creditor treatment in bankruptcy*

This state law theme of being paid on default up to the value of the collateral, but not in excess of the value of the collateral, continues to some extent in the bankruptcy process. In a Chapter 7 case, if the debtor is a business and the business is now out of business, then the secured party can get the automatic stay lifted. That will enable the secured party to gain the right to

1. You need not be too concerned with exactly what this means. Generally, perfecting requires the creditor to give some sort of actual or constructive notice of the security interest to third parties. Frequently, this is accomplished by filing a form (hard copy or electronic) with the Secretary of State's office. What is most important for you to know about perfection for this course is that an unperfected security interest normally is treated as an unsecured claim in a bankruptcy. (*See* 11 U.S.C. §544(a)(1).) We'll cover this in more detail later.

repossess and sell its collateral in the same way it would repossess and sell outside bankruptcy. If the debtor is an individual Chapter 7 debtor, then a number of things could happen. First, the debtor may just keep paying the loan and the creditor will not be affected by the bankruptcy. The debtor could also reaffirm the debt or redeem the collateral, something you'll learn more about in Chapter 15. Alternatively, if the debtor is in default (behind on the payments), the secured creditor may get the stay lifted and again, gain the right to repossess and sell the collateral. If this happens, then the creditor is limited in its recovery to the value of its collateral. Once the creditor has sold the collateral, the deficiency claim becomes an unsecured claim in the bankruptcy, and in most Chapter 7 cases, the unsecured claim is simply discharged.[2] Thus, the secured creditor in a Chapter 7 liquidation can only be paid as much as its collateral is worth, unless there also is a distribution for unsecured creditors.

In a Chapter 13 or a Chapter 11 case, the secured party gets paid over time under the debtor's plan. Chapters 21, 34(E), and 37 of this guide describe this treatment in detail. The state law theme of being paid whatever can be realized from the collateral, and being an unsecured creditor for the rest, is continued for the most part in Chapter 13 and Chapter 11, although typically the collateral is never sold. As you will see, in both Chapter 11 and Chapter 13 cases, the amount a secured creditor is paid is usually tied to the value of its collateral, not the amount it is owed.[3] Thus, it is far better to be a secured creditor (as compared to an unsecured creditor) and also much better to be fully (as compared to only partially) secured.

B. The Comfort of Being Secured

Being a secured creditor in a bankruptcy—or outside a bankruptcy, for that matter—can be a comfortable place to be. It certainly beats the alternative, which is to be a general or an unsecured creditor, with no collateral from which to be paid if there is a default or a bankruptcy. In a sense, being secured can be like being at a cold concert or sporting event and having a warm blanket to cover you.

2. This assumes there are no assets to distribute to creditors, which is often (but not always) the case.
3. The debtor can sometimes pay the lesser of the loan amount or the value of the collateral. Home mortgages are one exception. Those generally must be paid in full, even if the home is worth less than the amount of the lender's loan. This was true under the prior law as well. Moreover, under the 2005 amendments, the debtor must pay car loans in full if incurred within two and a half years of the bankruptcy filing, and must pay all other secured loans in full if incurred within one year of the filing.

QUESTION 1. A creditor with an Article 9 security interest, whose borrower is in bankruptcy:

1. has a voluntary lien.
2. gets superior rights over unsecured creditors.
3. gets to repossess and sell its collateral despite the debtor's bankruptcy.
4. is referred to as a secured creditor in a bankruptcy case.

A. All of the above.
B. 1, 2, and 4.
C. 1 and 4 only.
D. 2 and 4 only.

ANALYSIS. A creditor with a security interest in bankruptcy has a voluntary lien, gets superior rights over unsecured creditors, and is referred to as a secured creditor in a bankruptcy case. Thus, the answer is **B**. Only statement **3** is incorrect. If the debtor had not filed a petition in bankruptcy, in most cases the secured creditor could repossess the property on which the security interest was given (the collateral), but as we have seen, the automatic stay will prevent the creditor from doing so after bankruptcy.

C. Undersecured and Oversecured Creditors: Learning the Lingo

To continue the previous analogy, the blanket could be too small to cover you. It's better than nothing, but does not keep you completely warm. This same thing can happen to a creditor who has collateral for its loan that is not worth enough to cover the loan. The creditor whose claim is bigger than the value of its collateral is called an undersecured creditor. Conversely, a creditor whose collateral value more than covers the amount due on their loan to the debtor is an oversecured creditor. The two are treated quite differently in bankruptcy. The oversecured creditor gets extra benefits not available to either undersecured or unsecured creditors, including interest that continues to accrue at the contract rate after the bankruptcy case has been filed.[4] The oversecured creditor can also recover attorneys' fees if the creditor must go to court to enforce its right to be paid. Essentially, the oversecured creditor's claim can grow during the case, just as it would if there were no bankruptcy (through the continuing accrual of interest and fees), whereas the unsecured

4. The debtor and the secured creditor are usually parties to a written loan contract that provides that interest will accrue at a certain interest rate and also that attorneys' fees will be charged to the debtor if the loan goes into default and the creditor has to hire an attorney to help collect the loan.

claim and the undersecured claim do not increase during the case. They stay the same. The way that secured claims are calculated is covered in §506 of the Code. Special rights granted to creditors that are oversecured are spelled out in §506(b).

Another thing about secured claims is that if they are undersecured, the claim ends up being split, for bankruptcy treatment purposes, into two parts. The part that is covered by the value of the collateral is treated as secured, and the part that is not covered is treated as unsecured. We call this bifurcation of the claim because it is split into two parts. The practical result is that the secured claim is really only as large as the value of the collateral. This concept is explained in §506(a). The secured creditor's claim is allowed in the amount of the value of the collateral, for the purposes of payment in bankruptcy. Whatever is left over of the claim is an unsecured claim. Let's try a few examples.

QUESTION 2. A secured creditor's claim is only secured under the definition in §506(a):

1. if it has collateral.
2. if it perfected its security interest.
3. if the creditor files a proof of claim and also claims in the proof of claim that it is secured.
4. to the extent of the value of its collateral.

A. 1 and 2 only.
B. 1 and 3 only.
C. All of the above.
D. 1, 2, and 4.

ANALYSIS. The answer here is **D**. Of course **1** has to be true because, by definition, one cannot be a secured creditor unless there is collateral for the loan. **2** is a little trickier. Under state law, a security interest must be perfected to give the secured party rights against most third parties, including the trustee in bankruptcy. This means that the trustee can avoid or eliminate any security interest that is not perfected. Practically speaking, this will turn the secured creditor into an unsecured creditor. Thus, **2** is correct.

Statement **3** is not true. The status of the claim filed will not be affected by the filing of a proof of claim, whether it overstates or understates the case. Secured claims are created under state law and they do not exist just because the creditor claims in its own self-serving proof of claim that it is secured. Nor is the reverse true. Filing a claim and not saying that it is secured when it actually is will not turn the claim into an unsecured claim. Filing a claim will not change the nature of the claim at all. If the claim is secured, it will remain so even if the proof of claim does not say that it is secured.

Finally, statement **4** is true with only the caveats set out in Chapter 21, which you will learn about later. This principle of the secured claim being no larger than the value of the collateral is the linchpin of valuing secured claims. They are only secured claims to the extent of the value of the collateral underlying them. If the loan in issue is for $10,000 but the collateral is only worth $5,000, the claim is secured in the amount of $5,000, pure and simple. The other part of the claim is an unsecured claim.

Let's try a review question now.

QUESTION 3. Brazen Bank holds a perfected security interest in Dominique's Boutique's entire inventory. The current inventory in stock is worth approximately $45,000. Brazen's loan balance is now $60,000, with interest still accruing. Which of these labels applies to Brazen?

1. Undersecured.
2. Oversecured.
3. Growing.
4. Bifurcated.

A. 1 and 4.
B. 1 and 3.
C. 2, 3, and 4.
D. 2 only.

ANALYSIS. Here we are practicing the new vocabulary that you just learned. The correct answer is **A**. From the discussion, you probably gathered that the creditor in the problem couldn't be both oversecured and undersecured, as these are mutually exclusive concepts. Thus, **1** and **2** cannot both be true. If Brazen is owed $60,000 but has collateral worth just $45,000, Brazen is underwater or undersecured. Thus, **1** is true and **2** is false. As for **3**, this is incorrect because the undersecured claim does not grow. It is not permitted under the rules to continue to accrue interest, so it will not grow. It will stay the same size. Finally, **4** is true because the undersecured claim will be split into two parts—the secured part and the unsecured part—and will thus be bifurcated. Quick! What is the size of each of the two parts of the bifurcated claim? Answer—$45,000 for the secured portion, and $15,000 for the unsecured portion.

D. Practicing the Calculations

As you will soon see, it is always good from the creditor's perspective to have more collateral than you need. Sometimes cases can drag on for some time.

This is particularly true in a Chapter 11 case. If the collateral value is high enough, the creditor can continue to charge interest during this delay and also collect reasonable attorneys' fees. We noted previously that the secured creditor's claim continues to accrue interest and attorneys' fees at the contract rate if it is oversecured. Section 506(b) makes it clear, however, that such post-petition interest and fees can accrue only for as long as there is still value left in the collateral.[5] In other words, once the claim equals the value of the collateral (remember that the claim continues to increase during the case for the oversecured creditor), all the fees and interest cease to accrue. They do not become part of an unsecured claim either. Timing issues can thus make for some tricky calculations.

QUESTION 4. John Carl Enterprises (JCE) owes First State Bank $450,000 at the time it files its Chapter 11 case. JCE has pledged an office building worth $500,000 as collateral for the loan. The loan agreement provides that interest will accrue on the loan at the rate of 12 percent per annum or 1 percent per month. Assuming that there are no attorneys' fees to add to this claim, and that the building neither appreciates nor depreciates in value, how long can this case go on (assuming no payments of any kind to First State Bank during the case) before this loan stops earning interest?

A. 5 months.
B. 9 months.
C. 11 months.
D. 18 months.

ANALYSIS. The answer is **C**, 11 months. How did we calculate this? We divided the equity in the building by the interest expenses each month. The loan is currently at $450,000, and the collateral is worth $500,000. This leaves $50,000 in equity that can be used to pay future interest. But interest is accruing at the rate of 1 percent, or $4,500, per month. After 11 months, this interest will equal $49,500. Yipes! If the case goes on for one year, not all that long in reality, then the loan will stop accruing interest after 11 months and a few days. This is an unrealistic problem because the creditor did not charge the debtor attorneys' fees. Thus, realistically, interest will actually be allowed on the claim for less than 11 months.

---

5. As we've discussed, any value in the collateral over and above the total secured creditor claims is called equity.

QUESTION 5. Use the same facts as in Question 4, but also assume that First State Bank has been spending approximately $2,500 per month on attorneys' fees in JCE's Chapter 11 case. Now how many months can pass before First State Bank's loan will stop accruing interest, and until it will need to begin paying its own attorneys' fees?

A. 6 months.
B. 8 months.
C. 7 months.
D. 11 months again.

ANALYSIS. OK, now this is not all that bad as far as math goes, right? Instead of dividing the remaining equity in the building, the $50,000, by $4,500 a month for just the interest, you now add to those payments $2,500 a month for attorneys' fees, for a total cost of $7,000 a month. When this is done, it turns out that the equity is eaten up after just over 7 months. So the answer is **C.** This assumes that the attorneys' fees are reasonable, which §506(a) requires for the creditor to recover the fees from the debtor.

Martin's and Keating's Picks

1. Question 1 **B**
2. Question 2 **D**
3. Question 3 **A**
4. Question 4 **C**
5. Question 5 **C**

12

The Avoiding Powers

OVERVIEW

A. Preferential Transfers
   1. Preferential payments and transfers in consumer bankruptcy cases
   2. Defenses to preference actions
   3. Ordinary course of business defense
   4. The new value exception to the preference statute
   5. The substantially contemporaneous exchange for new value exception
   6. Setoff preferences

B. Avoiding Fraudulent Transfers Under the Bankruptcy Code

C. Avoidance of Unperfected Security Interests Under the Trustee's Strong-Arm Powers Contained in §544(a)

D. The Closer: Chapter 12

Martin's and Keating's Picks

One goal of a bankruptcy is the orderly distribution of the debtor's assets among the debtor's creditors. The debtor, however, may attempt to frustrate this goal by transferring property before the bankruptcy to favored creditors. Many transfers on the eve of bankruptcy are perfectly proper and will be recognized in the bankruptcy proceedings as legitimate. Some, however, are deemed by the Code to be improper and can be avoided by a trustee or a debtor-in-possession.

Trustees and debtors-in-possession have almost magical powers to bring certain property that has been transferred away before a debtor's bankruptcy back into the debtor's estate. These powers are called the avoiding powers. There are many avoiding powers, but we'll focus on just the main ones.[1] Avoiding powers play an important role in most Chapter 11 cases and in some Chapter 7 and Chapter 13 cases. Some teachers teach a great deal in this area,

1. The other avoiding powers include avoiding statutory liens that become effective against the debtor on bankruptcy or insolvency, or statutory liens by landlords for past due rent (11 U.S.C. §545), avoidance of certain post-petition transfers (11 U.S.C. §549), and avoiding certain setoffs (11 U.S.C. §553). We are skipping over these because they are rarely taught in a beginning bankruptcy class.

and others tread lightly over the area. The three most commonly avoided types of transfers are preferential transfers, fraudulent transfers, and transfers of security interests that were not perfected at the time a bankruptcy case was filed. When the debtor makes an impermissible transfer like this, within the particular time set by the Code in each case, the trustee or the debtor-in-possession can avoid or undo the transfer and thus bring the property or its value back into the debtor's estate for the benefit of all creditors. The policy behind reversing these transfers of property is equality of treatment between creditors. Avoidance of such transfers softens the transition between the prepetition period, during which some creditors may have improved their position by accepting property from the debtor or using the state court collection processes and the debtor's bankruptcy. In some cases, a creditor may have executed on property immediately before the bankruptcy. In other cases, the debtor may simply have transferred property or payments to a creditor, either to keep creditors from taking action or just because the debtor wants to pay one creditor over another. Sometimes the debtor gives away property to avoid having to give it to creditors. At other times, a debtor may simply sell something for less than its fair value. All of these transfers of property are subject to avoidance if certain elements are met. The "transfer" in these cases may be the payment of money or the transfer of ownership in property. It also may be the creation of a security interest, under Article 9 of the Uniform Commercial Code (UCC) or real property law. Thus, if a debtor gives a mortgage on his or her house, this constitutes a transfer for the purposes of the avoidance powers.

A. Preferential Transfers

One of us always begins our coverage of preference law with the following limerick:

What is a preference? It's now time to learn it,
This won't be easy and you'll have to earn it,
While exceptions abound,
Here's the one rule I've found:
"If Debtor does you a favor, then you must return it!"

What is a "preferential transfer"? Many of us make them at the end of each month when the balance in our checking account is insufficient to pay all of our bills. We pay the electric company in full because we are already a month overdue and we are afraid that they will turn off the electricity if we don't. We also pay something on our credit cards, and we make our mortgage or rent payment. We don't, however, pay the vet's bill for shots she gave our dog or the dentist's bill, because we know they will not do anything except send us a new bill next month, perhaps tacking on an interest charge. These payments are all preferential transfers in the broad sense of that term. Some creditors have been "preferred" over others. Some got paid; some did not. Outside of bankruptcy, there is no law prohibiting these transfers. Indeed, there is absolutely nothing morally wrong with paying some creditors but not others. Even in bankruptcy, as we shall see, there is nothing immoral about what the debtor has done. These payments may need to be undone, however, to treat creditors equally.

For example, assume that Trah Derf owns a small construction company that is having financial difficulties. Trah decides that he will file a Chapter 7 bankruptcy at the end of the month. In the middle of the month he receives a payment of $50,000 for work that he has completed. At the time, he has a number of creditors, subcontractors, and suppliers, none of whom have liens, to whom he owes a total of $200,000. He owes one of these, a lumberyard, $50,000. Because the owners of the lumberyard have always been willing to extend him credit and do other favors for him, he pays the entire $50,000 to them. A couple of weeks later, he files his bankruptcy petition. Trah has frustrated the concept of equal payment. If he had kept the $50,000 and listed it as one of his assets, it would have been split among all of his creditors and each (including the lumberyard) would have been paid 25 cents on the dollar. The lumberyard, instead of getting $50,000, would have gotten $12,500. As you might guess, the Bankruptcy Code unwinds this kind of preferential transfer, and the trustee will probably be able to get back the $50,000 from the lumberyard.

Section 547(b) contains the elements of an avoidable preferential transfer, and requires (1) a transfer (2) of property of the debtor (3) on account of an antecedent debt (4) made within 90 days before the filing (one year for transfers to insiders such as family members) (5) while the debtor was insolvent. To be avoidable, the transfer also must allow the creditor to receive more than it would have received in a Chapter 7 case.[2]

Why is insolvency required for a transfer to be a preference? Perhaps it is because at the time of insolvency, even if it precedes the bankruptcy filing, the policy of equality of treatment among creditors kicks in. More importantly, if the debtor is not insolvent at the time of a purportedly preferential transfer, there is no harm to other creditors because the remaining property should be sufficient to cover all creditors' claims.

The policy reasons behind preference avoidance should now be clear, and they should help you remember the rule. Bring back the transferred property and allow it to be distributed among creditors equally, or at least according to the priority scheme.[3]

---

2. This last element means that if a bank lends money and takes back a security interest for the new debt, there is no preference through the grant of the security interest. That is because in a Chapter 7 bankruptcy of the debtor, the bank would recover from the collateral and thus would be no better or worse off as a result of the transfer.

3. When the property transferred is a security interest collateralizing an old or antecedent debt rather than a new one, avoiding the transfer can change the entire course of the case.

One issue that bears mention when discussing the elements of an avoidable preference is the timing of the transfer. If the transfer consists of a payment in cash, there is usually little or no question about when the transfer is made. If the transfer, however, is the transfer of a security interest from the debtor to the creditor, things get a little more complicated. That is because the transfer of a security interest in effect involves two stages: attachment, which is when the transfer of the security interest becomes effective between the debtor and the creditor; and perfection, which is when the transfer of the security also becomes effective as against third parties, such as other creditors or the trustee in the debtor's bankruptcy.

To clarify the rules in this area, the drafters of the Bankruptcy Code included §547(e)(2), which tells us when a transfer takes place for preference purposes. In effect, that subsection tells us that when the transfer is of a security interest, the transfer takes place for preference purposes at the time of attachment as long as the security interest is perfected within 30 days of attachment. If perfection is delayed for more than 30 days following attachment, then the transfer of the security interest takes place at the time of perfection. Finally, if there is no perfection by the later of the commencement of the bankruptcy case or 30 days following attachment, then the transfer of the security interest is deemed to take place immediately before the bankruptcy filing.

If these rules seem confusing in the abstract, consider how they work in practice by doing the questions that follow.

QUESTION 1. Debtor Corp wants to borrow $50,000 from Big Bank on an unsecured basis. Big Bank refuses to loan to Debtor Corp on an unsecured basis, so Debtor Corp instead offers Big Bank a security interest in Debtor Corp's $100,000 worth of equipment to secure the $50,000 loan. On June 1, Big Bank lends the money and Debtor Corp simultaneously grants Big Bank the security interest in its equipment. On June 20, Big Bank files a financing statement and perfects the security interest. On July 15, Debtor Corp files Chapter 7 bankruptcy. Will Debtor Corp's transfer of the security interest to Big Bank be avoidable as a preference by the Chapter 7 trustee?

A. Yes, because the transfer took place on June 20 when Big Bank perfected the security interest and that makes the transfer on account of an antecedent debt.

B. Yes, because the collateral here was worth twice as much as the loan, which means that the transfer of the security interest made Big Bank much better off than it would be otherwise in Debtor Corp's Chapter 7 bankruptcy case.

C. No, because the transfer of a security interest always takes place at the time of attachment, and in this case that means that the transfer was not on account of an antecedent debt.

D. No, because under the facts of this particular case the transfer of the security interest took place at the time of attachment, and therefore the transfer was not on account of an antecedent debt.

ANALYSIS. The correct answer is **D**. As we explain above, §547(e)(2) says that for preference purposes, the transfer of a security interest takes place at the time of attachment as long as perfection follows within 30 days. That was the case here since attachment took place on June 1 and perfection took place on June 20. That means that the transfer of the security interest took place on June 1, which was the same day that Big Bank extended credit. Therefore, the transfer was not on account of an antecedent debt. Choice **C** is wrong because the transfer of a security interest does not always take place at the time of attachment. It depends on when perfection takes place relative to the date of attachment. Answer **A** is wrong because it incorrectly dates the time of transfer as the date of perfection rather than attachment. Choice **B** is wrong because the fact that Big Bank is oversecured does not necessarily make the transfer of the security interest a preference.

QUESTION 2. Same facts as Question 1, but now assume that the loan was made on May 25 rather than June 1. Assume that the other dates remain the same: attachment on June 1, perfection on June 20, and Debtor's bankruptcy filing on July 15. Will Debtor Corp's transfer of the security interest to Big Bank be avoidable as a preference by the Chapter 7 trustee?

A. Yes, because now the transfer of the security interest is on account of an antecedent debt.
B. No, because perfection still took place within 30 days of attachment as required by §547(e)(2).
C. No, because perfection still took place within 30 days of when the loan was made as required by §547(e)(2).
D. No, because attachment still took place within 30 days of when the loan was made as required by §547(e)(2).

ANALYSIS. The correct answer is **A**. Even though Big Bank continues to qualify for the 30-day "grace period" that §547(e)(2) offers between attachment and perfection, the only effect of meeting that grace period is to establish the date of transfer of the security interest as the date of attachment rather than perfection. So the date of transfer here is still June 1, the date of attachment. However, the extension of credit now takes place on May 25, which is prior to the date of transfer. That means that this transfer of a security interest was on account of an antecedent debt and thus amounts to a preference, assuming that all of the other elements of a preference have been met. That is why **B** is incorrect. **C** and **D** are incorrect because they both misidentify the two events that are covered by the 30-day grace period of §547(e)(2).

QUESTION 3. Same facts as Question 1, but now assuming the following about the dates of the relevant events: the loan is made and attachment occurs both on June 1; perfection occurs on July 7; and Debtor Corp files bankruptcy on July 15. Will Debtor Corp's transfer of the security interest to Big Bank be avoidable as a preference by the Chapter 7 trustee?

A. Yes, because anytime there is a delay between attachment and perfection within 90 days before a debtor's bankruptcy, that transfer will amount to an avoidable preference.
B. Yes, because perfection in this case took place more than 30 days following attachment.
C. No, because the loan and the attachment of the security interest both took place on the same day and therefore the transfer of the security interest was not on account of an antecedent debt.
D. No, because the transfer of a security interest is only a preference when the loan is originally an unsecured loan that later becomes secured with the transfer of the security interest.

ANALYSIS. The correct answer is **B**. Now that the date of perfection is more than 30 days following the date of attachment, §547(e)(2) tells us that the date of transfer of the security interest is the date of perfection, which is July 7. That date makes the transfer of the security interest "on account of an antecedent debt" and therefore a preference, assuming that all of the other elements of a preference have been met here. Choice **A** is wrong because it ignores the possibility of a delayed perfection falling within the 30-day grace period of §547(e)(2). Answer **C** is incorrect because it wrongly assumes that the date of the transfer of the security interest in this case was the date of attachment rather than the date of perfection. Choice **D** is wrong because it is possible for the transfer of a security interest to be avoidable as a preference even when the loan to the debtor is a secured loan from the beginning, as long as there is more than a 30-day delay between attachment and perfection, as in this case.

QUESTION 4. Don's Auto is way behind on its payments to Karl's Parts, which has recently insisted that Don's come current on its account, or it will obtain a judgment and execute. Don's can't come current, so instead it grants a perfected security interest to Karl's in all of its parts (its inventory) to secure the past-due amounts. Two months later, under the crush of other debt problems, Don's files a Chapter 11 petition and moves to avoid the security interest. Is the transfer of this security interest to Karl's an avoidable preferential transfer?

A. Yes, as long as the debtor was insolvent at the time the creation of the security interest was made or as long as no one proved otherwise.
B. Yes, on just the facts given.
C. No, because the security interest was granted in exchange for a new loan rather than on account of an antecedent debt.
D. No, because the debtor is the one who made the transfer, and it would be unfair to allow the same party to now avoid the transfer.

ANALYSIS. **A** is the correct answer because the facts bear out all of the required elements except for insolvency. **B** is incorrect, as one cannot conclude that this transfer is avoidable unless you also assume that the debtor was insolvent at the time the transfer was made. Although the debtor is presumed to be insolvent for the 90 days preceding the bankruptcy filing, the presumption can be rebutted, which is why **B** is less correct than **A**. The facts in this problem do not tell us anything about insolvency or about who proved what on the issue. **A** is completely correct, and **B** may or may not be, depending on these missing facts. Going through the other elements for practice, the transfer was made to secure an antecedent debt, within 90 days of the filing, and allowed the creditor to get more than it would have received in a Chapter 7 case. Thus, it is avoidable.

The facts set out in choice **C** are inconsistent with the facts in the problem, which states clearly that this security interest is being granted to secure the old or antecedent debt, rather than any new credit.

D is also untrue but is worth some discussion. When there is a debtor-in-possession rather than a trustee, which is usually the case in a Chapter 11 case like this, the debtor-in-possession acts as a fiduciary for the creditors and is charged with the duty of avoiding preferences if doing so will benefit the creditors. Thus, the debtor is the one that would bring an avoidance action like this, as odd as that seems, in light of the fact that the debtor is the one that made the transfer. As the next question demonstrates, the debtor may well want the transfer avoided. Indeed, from a practical standpoint the avoidance of preferential transfers is most important in Chapter 11 cases.

QUESTION 5. In Question 4, what effect would it have on the case if the inventory was the only unencumbered asset in the case before this transfer, it was worth $100,000, Karl's was owed $100,000, and unsecured debts totaled $400,000 without Karl's, who is now secured? Also assume that administrative claims for post-petition expenses and legal fees total $25,000 in the case. Being unsure whether the debtor will have other assets to distribute to creditors from its future profits, avoidance of the Karl's preference alone will:

1. provide funds from which Don's can pay its bankruptcy counsel, who might otherwise go unpaid.
2. create a distribution to unsecured creditors of approximately 20 percent.
3. create a distribution to unsecured creditors of approximately 15 percent.
4. practically speaking, give Don's a chance to reorganize whereas before it really had none.

A. 1, 2, and 4.
B. 1 and 3.
C. 1 and 4.
D. 1, 3, and 4.

ANALYSIS. Let's do the math first and then talk policy. This problem demonstrates how important avoidance of preferential transfers can be. If the transfer is not avoided, Karl's gets paid in full, and the lawyer does not get paid, nor does any other creditor in the case. This is certainly true unless the debtor can raise other money from its operations to fund a plan and to pay a distribution to creditors. If the transfer is avoided, everything changes. Karl's, rather than getting paid from the sale of the inventory in which it holds a lien, just becomes an unsecured creditor for the same $100,000 it was owed before. It no longer is secured, making the unsecured creditor class $500,000.

If it were necessary to sell the inventory to pay creditors, rather than paying creditors from future operations, the administrative claims would get paid first, $25,000, which would pay them in full. The $500,000 in unsecured claims would share the other $75,000, causing them to get a 15 percent distribution. The general unsecured creditors would have received a 20 percent distribution ($100,000 divided by $500,000) if there had been no administrative priority claims, but because there are such claims, **1** and **3** are true and **2** is incorrect. This means that the answer has to be either **B** or **D** depending on whether **4** is true.

Is **4** true? It would seem so. Without unencumbered assets, no attorney or other professional will take a Chapter 11 case. There has to be a decent prospect of payment, from a source other than speculative future operations, to make the case worthwhile. This may sound coldhearted, but it is a fact.

Chapter 11 cases are contingency fee cases if there is no retainer and there are no unencumbered assets. Moreover, there is very little chance of actually staying in operation and reorganizing if there are no assets from which to raise cash to get stabilized. The debtor may need at least a few assets to pledge as collateral for new loans. Thus, the correct answer is **D**: choices **1**, **3**, and **4**. As this example suggests, the avoidance powers can raise money that is critical for operations in a Chapter 11 case.

1. Preferential payments and transfers in consumer bankruptcy cases

In Chapter 7 and 13 cases, preferential transfers can be avoided, but this often makes less difference in the case than it does in a Chapter 11. This is because payments made during the preference period tend to be smaller and thus have less of an impact on the case when they are recovered.

At times, however, preferences do play an important part in consumer bankruptcy cases. You might recall from our prior discussion that transfers to insiders can be avoided for a full year, rather than the usual 90 days for other transfers. The word insider is defined in §101(5) of the Code and includes family members. In many consumer cases, the insider in question is a family member. For example, a mother might lend a child money to buy a car, and the child may pay the loan back over time.

Payments to insiders are avoidable by a trustee for a full year because, as the theory goes, an insider is more likely to be aware of the debtor's failing financial condition and thus to decide to lend the money and take the risk anyway, perhaps thinking that he or she can be paid back any time. Insiders are also more likely to be preferred by the debtor. Sometimes we may even question the motivation of the so-called loan, assuming on some subconscious level that Mom really meant to make a gift here, right?

QUESTION 6. Kate borrowed money from Mom to buy a car for cash. Mom did not take back a security interest in the car. Kate has paid Mom $200 a month for the past 12 months. How much of these payments can be avoided as a preference, if any?

A. $1,200.
B. $3,600.
C. $600.
D. $2,400.

ANALYSIS. The answer here is all of the payments, or the full $200×12, or **D**, $2,400. Note that if Mom had just taken a security interest in the car at the time she lent the money, the transfer could not be avoided. We'll discuss this more in detail in the following paragraphs, but if Mom were secured, she'd get paid in full in a Chapter 7 and thus, she would not be getting more here than she would get in a Chapter 7. Thus, this element would not be present, and the transfer would not be avoidable.

Note also that based on the discussion that follows, Mom may have a good argument that this situation falls within one of the exceptions to the preference laws and thus is not recoverable by the trustee.

2. *Defenses to preference actions*

There are a few defenses to preferential transfer avoidance, which means that in some situations, the preference elements are all met, but the payee can assert a defense that will keep the trustee from recovering the preferential transfer.

3. *Ordinary course of business defense*

Our Question 6, involving Mom and Kate, implicated the most common defense to the preference laws, as well as one of the most litigated areas in avoidance powers laws in general, namely the ordinary course of business defense to the preference statute.

The Code states, in so many words, that paying your monthly bills in the ordinary course of your affairs— such as the rent, the mortgage, the electric bill, or the installment on the furniture loan— falls within an exception to the preference laws. (*See* 11 U.S.C. §547(c)(2).) Payments of regular monthly bills are the quintessential ordinary course payments, although other payments sometimes qualify as well. In a sense, most of these debts are antecedent or old.[4] The key, however, is that they are being paid off regularly, and they're not past due. Payments on past due bills, or bills that have become old, are always preferences. This exception recognizes that some payments just don't qualify as old or past due, even if the underlying debt is technically antecedent.

The Mom and Kate problem certainly seems to fall in that category, assuming Kate was diligent about making her payments to Mom at more or less the same time each month, although frankly, we've never seen the ordinary course defense asserted in a family case. Most of the time, this defense is used in a business context. Under the pre-2005 law, this defense could only be asserted if the payments were made within the ordinary course of business between the parties, as well as the ordinary course within the industry.

Under the current §547(c)(2), a transaction fits within the ordinary course exception to the preferences statute if the payment was made by the debtor either within the ordinary course of business between the parties or within ordinary business terms within the industry. The defendant need not prove both of these two elements, thus making more transactions subject to the exception. Thus, while it would not have worked before the 2005 amendments, under the current law, the payments Kate made to Mom would likely fall within the ordinary course of business exception to the preference statute.

4. Think about it. The mortgage may have been taken out a long time ago.

4. *The new value exception to the preference statute*

Another exception to the preference laws is called the new value exception, which is contained in §547(c)(3). This exception allows a creditor who has extended credit, after receiving a preferential payment, to deduct the amount of the new credit or new value from the preference received. Assume that Joann's Beauty Salon paid her supplier $1,000 during the preference period and the bills she paid were past due. After Joann's made that payment, however, the supplier delivered an additional $500 worth of merchandise to Joann's on credit. The new value exception would net out these amounts and cause a court to conclude that the supplier received a preferential payment of $500 and should return that amount to the estate. This is the amount by which the supplier's position was improved during the preference period. Another way of looking at it is as if the last $500 in shipments were cash deals, for which the supplier was previously paid through the $1,000 payment. This may just confuse things for you, but hopefully you get the general drift.

Was it still worth it for the supplier to ship the last $500? Yes, we think so. Either way, the supplier would have to either pay back the $1,000, or pay back $500 plus the $500 in supplies. At least under the second scenario, involving the supplies, the supplier can get the profits from the sale of those goods and not just be out the whole $1,000. The exception encourages businesses to continue to deal with distressed companies, by giving them credit for any value they add to the estate during the preference period.

Despite this incentive, note how preference law is not fair at all to the one who received the transfer and then must return the transfer to the trustee. After all, this supplier was owed the $1,000! Why should she have to pay this money back just because her customer always paid late? This unfairness is not relevant, however, as lack of fairness is no defense to a preference.

5. *The substantially contemporaneous exchange for new value exception*

This exception, the contemporaneous exchange for new value exception, found in §547(c)(1), is almost superfluous because it negates one of the elements of preference law. A preference is only a preference if it is a payment made on account of an antecedent debt. If the payment is being made contemporaneously with receipt of the good or services the debtor is buying, this is not a payment made on account of an antecedent debt.

The real reason why the exception appears in the Code is that the exchange need not be precisely contemporaneous but can be just substantially contemporaneous. Thus, you could have a contemporaneous exchange for new value even though the debtor did not hand over a payment at the very moment that its supplier gave it the goods. Emphasize the word substantially, and you'll get the picture.

QUESTION 7. You own Max Videos, which owes quite a bit to Video Warehouse, the prime supplier of Max. Video Warehouse insists that you come current immediately and also start paying cash on delivery (COD) in the future. You have no choice but to comply, so on January 1, you pay the outstanding bill of $1,600, which covers about four months of videos. In January and February, you also order two new shipments of videos and pay $400 each for those, paying COD as Video Warehouse has insisted. By March 28, Max is dead on its feet, and you close it down.

Thereafter, creditors put Max into involuntary Chapter 7 and the trustee moves to avoid the payments to Video Warehouse during the 90 days before the filing. Can the trustee recover any of these payments under §547?

A. Yes, the trustee can recover a total of $2,400.
B. The trustee can recover $800 for the two COD payments, but not the other $1,600 because this was a payment made in the ordinary course of business.
C. The trustee cannot recover anything.
D. The trustee can get the $1,600 but not the $800, because the $800 comprises contemporaneous exchanges for new value.

ANALYSIS. **D** is correct. The $1,600 was not paid in the ordinary course of business. To the contrary, this was a classic "catch-up" payment, made within the 90 days before a bankruptcy. The $800, however, comprised contemporaneous exchanges for new value, which is true of any COD payment. The debtor exchanged the goods for the cash, all at once, right then and there. This is quintessential contemporaneous exchange, as are payments by wire transfers sent when the goods are received. A payment made by mail, right after receipt of the goods, presents a closer case but probably is not a contemporaneous exchange. Thus, **D** is the correct answer.

QUESTION 8. **(CODE READER)** On January 1, Debtor borrowed $5,000 from Crul, giving to Crul a security interest in her automobile. Crul perfected its security interest under state law on March 1. On May 1, Debtor filed a Chapter 7 petition in bankruptcy. Under §547, which of the following is true?

A. The trustee cannot avoid Crul's security interest because it was beyond the 90-day period.
B. The trustee cannot avoid Crul's security interest because it was not for an antecedent debt.

C. The trustee cannot avoid Crul's security interest because the creation of a security interest is not a transfer of property.
D. The trustee can avoid Crul's security interest if Debtor was insolvent in March.

ANALYSIS. **C** is definitely not the correct answer because, as mentioned above, the creation of a security interest is a transfer. **A** and **B** depend on when the transfer occurred. Logically, it can be argued that the transfer was on January 1, hence outside of the 90-day period. However, the Bankruptcy Code says that a transfer occurs when the security interest is perfected. Here, that was on March 1, and thus it is within the 90-day period and **A** is incorrect. Also, the transfer that occurred on March 1 was for a debt incurred on January 1, and thus it was to secure an antecedent debt. That leaves **D**, which turns out to be a correct answer.

6. *Setoff preferences*

Section 553(a) generally respects a creditor's nonbankruptcy setoff rights subject to a few exceptions. Under nonbankruptcy law, a valid setoff requires mutuality of obligations, maturity of obligations, and some act of setoff. A setoff can arise in many contexts, but certainly one of the most common is where a debtor takes out a loan from the same bank where the debtor has a bank account. In that situation, the debtor's bank account is really just a debt that the bank owes to the debtor to the extent of the funds in the debtor's account.

So, for example, imagine that the debtor owes $5,000 to the bank but also has $2,000 in a bank account at the same bank. If the $5,000 loan comes due and the debtor fails to pay it, the bank will (absent some contractual or statutory provision that forbids it) set off the $2,000 in the debtor's bank account and apply it towards the $5,000 that the debtor owes the bank. The debtor will then owe the bank just $3,000 but will have zero funds remaining in its bank account.

There are two important exceptions to a creditor's right to exercise its state-law right of setoff once the debtor is bankruptcy. You might think of both of these exceptions as situations in which the creditor has created the equivalent to a "preference" in favor of that creditor during the 90 days before the debtor filed bankruptcy. Both exceptions under §553(a) require as one element that the debtor was insolvent at the time of the setoff preference, but §553(e) creates a rebuttable presumption that the debtor was insolvent during the 90 days before filing bankruptcy.

The first exception, §553(a)(3), reduces the creditor's setoff right in bankruptcy to the extent that the creditor's obligation to the debtor was incurred within 90 days prior to filling for the purposes of obtaining a right to setoff. So §553(a)(3) covers the not uncommon case where the bank in our hypothetical demands that the debtor keep a compensating balance in the debtor's account, and the bank's demand is made within 90 days prior to the debtor's bankruptcy.

Imagine in our hypothetical above that 50 days before the debtor filed for bankruptcy, the debtor's bank account was empty and the bank demanded that the debtor must deposit and maintain a balance of at least $4,000. In that situation, when the debtor files for bankruptcy, the bank would not be able to set off the $4,000 that the debtor deposited in response to the bank's demand on Day 50 before the debtor's filing.

Section 553(a)(2)(B) is the second exception to a creditor's state-law setoff right that takes the form of a preference in favor of the creditor. That subsection reduces a creditor's setoff right to the extent the creditor purchased its claim against the debtor from some other creditor of the debtor within 90 days before the debtor's filing. Suppose, for example, the debtor owed the bank $5,000 but the debtor also had $10,000 in their bank account. Then, however, within 90 days before the debtor's bankruptcy, the bank purchased a third-party creditor's claim of $3,000 against the debtor. In that case, once the debtor filed for bankruptcy, the bank would attempt to assert an $8,000 setoff right against the debtor. However, due to the §553(a)(2)(B) exception, the bank would merely have a $5,000 setoff claim against the debtor rather than an $8,000 setoff claim. In other words, the bank would be precluded from using the $3,000 purchased claim to set off any funds in the debtor's bank account.

Please keep in mind that no matter what right of setoff a creditor has, the creditor cannot exercise it against the debtor following the debtor's bankruptcy filing without first getting lift of the automatic stay from the bankruptcy court. That restriction comes from §362(a)(7)'s specific prohibition against post-petition acts of setoff. However, the Supreme Court in Citizens Bank of Maryland v. Strumpf held that a bank could "freeze" a debtor's bank account post-petition while the bank is seeking a lift of stay to exercise an otherwise valid right to set off against the account.

That way, even before the bankruptcy court has an opportunity to hear the bank's lift of stay motion to allow the setoff, the bank can at least prevent the debtor from withdrawing the funds from the debtor's account. Those funds, after all, represent the bank's cash collateral, at least to the extent that the bank has a valid right of setoff against them. Without the bank's right to freeze the debtor's account pending a court hearing on the lift of stay motion, the debtor might remove all the money from its account and spend it before the bank can get adequate protection for its cash collateral interest.

QUESTION 9. (CODE READER) Debtor Corporation ("Debtor") owes Bank $1.275 million on an unsecured term loan that is due in six months. Debtor has a bank account at Bank into which Debtor had deposited $300,000 eight months earlier when Debtor first opened the account. Four weeks ago, Bank told Debtor that Debtor was now required to keep a balance of at least $450,000 in Debtor's bank account at all times.

Debtor then put an additional $450,000 in the account to bring the total to $750,000. Debtor is about to file Chapter 11 bankruptcy today, with no activity in the account since the $450,000 deposit. Debtor's bank account currently shows a $750,000 balance and Debtor still owes Bank $1.275 million on the term loan that is due in six months. Assume that Debtor was insolvent in the 90 days before it filed Chapter 11. What is the extent of Bank's setoff right against Debtor once Debtor files its Chapter 11 petition (assuming that Bank first gets any necessary court permission to exercise such a setoff right post-petition)?

A. $300,000
B. $450,000
C. $750,000
D. $1.275 million

ANALYSIS. As noted above, §553(a) of the Bankruptcy Code allows a creditor to retain whatever pre-petition setoff right that it had against a debtor, subject to the automatic stay of §362(a) and some special rules limiting setoff rights that are found in §553(a). One of those setoff limitations is §553(a)(3), which reduces a setoff right that a creditor could otherwise exercise in bankruptcy to the extent that the creditor required a compensating balance from the debtor in the 90 days prior to the debtor's bankruptcy filing while the debtor was insolvent. In this case, Bank's demand that Debtor keep a $450,000 compensating balance occurred four weeks before Debtor filed for bankruptcy and that is when Debtor deposited an additional $450,000 into its account. Therefore, Bank's setoff right, which would otherwise be for the full $750,000 in Debtor's account, is now reduced to $300,000 due to the operation of §553(a)(3), which would disallow Bank's setoff as to the $450,000 that was required by Bank and incurred within 90 days of Debtor's filing. Therefore, the correct answer is **A.**

QUESTION 10. (CODE READER) Debtor Corporation ("Debtor") owes Bank $500,000 on an unsecured term loan that is due in six months. Debtor has a bank account at Bank into which Debtor had deposited $700,000 eight months earlier when Debtor first opened the account. Four months ago, Bank purchased a $50,000 claim from a different unsecured creditor of Debtor. Two months ago, Bank purchased a $125,000 claim from yet another unsecured creditor of Debtor. Debtor is about to file Chapter 11 bankruptcy today, with no activity in the account since the $700,000 deposit. Debtor's bank account currently shows a $700,000 balance and Debtor now owes Bank a total of $675,000, which includes the two claims against Debtor that Bank purchased from third-party creditors. Assume that Debtor was insolvent in the 90 days before it filed Chapter 11. What is the extent of Bank's setoff right against Debtor once Debtor files its Chapter 11 petition (assuming that Bank first gets any necessary court permission to exercise such a setoff right post-petition)?

A. $675,000
B. $500,000
C. $550,000
D. $625,000

ANALYSIS. This question tests your knowledge of §553(a)(2). That subsection, you will recall from the discussion above, prohibits a creditor from exercising a post-petition setoff right that otherwise existed under nonbankruptcy law to the extent that the claim against the debtor was transferred by a different creditor of the debtor within 90 days before Debtor's bankruptcy filing. Here there were two transferred claims, but only one of them— the $125,000 claim— was transferred during the 90-day prohibited window. Therefore, Bank in this case should be able to set off its original loan of $500,000 as well as the $50,000 claim that it purchased four months before Debtor's bankruptcy filing. That means that **C** is the right answer here, since Bank can set off $550,000 against the $700,000 that is now in Debtor's account. Choice **A** wrongly assumes that both of the transferred claims that Bank received are eligible for setoff in Debtor's bankruptcy. Choice **B** wrongfully assumes that neither transfer is eligible for setoff, and **D** incorrectly assumes that the $125,000 transferred claim is eligible for setoff but the $50,000 claim is not.

B. Avoiding Fraudulent Transfers Under the Bankruptcy Code

As you know, all states have laws allowing harmed creditors to avoid fraudulent transfers. Most of these state laws allow the reversal of such transfers for a period of six years after the transfer is made. Under §544(b)(1), the trustee may attack a transfer by the debtor as fraudulent under the state law if there is a creditor with an unsecured claim existing at the time the petition is filed, who had the right to avoid the transfer under the state law.

Among the trustee's (or the debtor-in-possession's) avoidance powers is a federal version of fraudulent transfer law. Section 548 of the Bankruptcy Code allows the trustee or the debtor-in-possession to set aside a fraudulent transfer made by the debtor, while the debtor was insolvent or that caused the debtor to become insolvent, within one year before the debtor's bankruptcy filing. Like state law, §548 allows transfers to be avoided for both actual fraud (transfers made with actual intent to hinder, delay, or defraud creditors) as well as constructive fraud (transfers for less than fair value that leave the debtor insolvent). Once a transfer has been avoided, the person who received the transfer (either directly or indirectly) is liable to the trustee for return of the property in question. (*See* 11 U.S.C. §550.) You should also know that engaging in a fraudulent transfer before a bankruptcy could cause a Chapter 7 debtor to lose his or her entire bankruptcy discharge, a topic taken up in a later chapter of this guide. (*See* 11 U.S.C. §727(a)(2).)

The policy behind §548 is clear. A person cannot give away property or sell it for less than it is worth, if doing so will harm her creditors by leaving them with fewer assets than are necessary to pay their claims. It is easy to see why we undo a debtor's transfer when the transfer was made to purposely avoid the claims of creditors. It is much harder to understand why we undo sales for less than fair value. Consider this example.

Let's say Sarah needs groceries so she sells her brand new computer/DVD entertainment center (which she bought for $5,000) to her friend for $1,000. The friend is trying to help and does not even really want the system. If Sarah later goes into Chapter 7 or Chapter 13, her trustee can probably avoid the transfer and bring the system back into the estate for sale and then distribution to creditors. What does it mean to avoid the transfer? It means that the friend will have to give back the system, although the friend can at least require the trustee to reimburse her for the $1,000 purchase price that she paid to Sarah. (*See* §548(c).) WOW! This really makes you wonder about deals you enter into for used goods that seem too good to be true.

This conclusion assumes two things: first, that the system is worth more than $1,000, which may not be the case; and second, that the system would not have been exempt in Sarah's bankruptcy. If it would have been, then the transfer did not harm creditors, and she is free to transfer it to whomever she chooses.

QUESTION 11. On December 1, the debtor, whose gross annual income for the year was $75,000, made a gift of 100 acres of farmland he owned to Cyclops Charitable Trust, a charity that was tax exempt under federal law. Cyclops intended to use the property to construct a treatment center for abused dogs and cats. The land was worth $100,000. On March 1, the debtor filed a petition in bankruptcy. Which of these statements is accurate?

A. If the debtor had no actual intent to defraud his creditors, the gift of the farm cannot be a fraudulent transfer.

B. The gift is fraudulent unless the debtor can prove that he was not insolvent and did not become insolvent as a result of the gift on December 1.

C. The gift is not fraudulent unless the trustee can show that the debtor was insolvent on December 1 or became insolvent as a result of the gift.
D. The gift was not a fraudulent transfer because the debtor owed no obligation to Cyclops and hence it was not for an antecedent debt.

ANALYSIS. **A** is incorrect. A transfer for less than fair consideration is a fraudulent transfer irrespective of the motive or intent of the transferor. Because this was a transfer for less than fair consideration, it is constructively fraudulent if the debtor was insolvent at the time of, or as a result of, the transfer. **D** is also incorrect. It confuses preferential transfers with fraudulent transfers. (This one also confused a couple of bankruptcy professors, on whom this question was tested.) The correct answer is **C**. Unlike the section on preferential transfers, there is no presumption of insolvency when the trustee is attacking a transfer under the fraudulent transfer section. If insolvency is proved, the Cyclops Charitable Trust is out of luck and must give the land to the trustee.

Another small point: Section 548(a)(2) provides an exemption for gifts to charitable organizations, but the exemption is not applicable here because the gift must be no more than 15 percent of the debtor's annual income.

C. Avoidance of Unperfected Security Interests Under the Trustee's Strong-Arm Powers Contained in §544(a)

Virtually all bankruptcy attorneys, as well as quite a few other attorneys, know that unperfected security interests can be avoided in bankruptcy. When this happens, the previously secured creditor is turned into a general unsecured creditor. The security interest is, in essence, returned to the estate, and the property is now unencumbered and its value can be distributed to unsecured creditors.

You'll recall from your Secured Transactions class that when determining the priority of claims between two secured creditors, one that has perfected its security interest has priority over one who has not perfected. Moreover, the judgment lien creditor also has priority over the unperfected voluntary security interest, which is why perfection is important to maintaining one's position.

Outside bankruptcy, the fact that a secured party has failed to perfect does not wipe out the security interest completely. Rather, the secured party still has the rights of a secured party as against the debtor and can repossess its collateral and sell it to realize on the creditor's claim.[5]

The priority themes contained in Article 9 of the UCC are continued in the Bankruptcy Code, although the avoidance powers go a step further and allow the trustee to wipe out the unperfected security interest entirely rather than letting it linger around in its low-priority state. The reason? Because we hate secret liens and fear that they could mislead creditors into thinking the debtor has more unencumbered assets from which to pay creditors than the debtor actually has.

The policies here are obvious, but the Code reaches this result in a way that is probably more complex than it needs to be. Following the theme of Article 9, the Code gives the trustee the rights of a hypothetical judgment lien creditor. (*See* 11 U.S.C. §544(a).) Because lien creditors beat out unperfected security interests under Article 9, the trustee can beat out an unperfected security interest. We call these avoidance powers the trustee's strong-arm powers, although we are not sure why.

For those not familiar with secured transactions, we think it is enough to just remember that the trustee has the right to avoid unperfected security interests under §544(a) and leave the hypothetical lien creditor status out of it.

D. The Closer: Chapter 12

Bank One gets attachment of a security interest from Debtor Corp in accounts worth $100,000 on March 1 to secure a new loan under a line of credit that Bank One made available to Debtor Corp on that same day. Bank One never perfected this security interest before Debtor Corp filed Chapter 11 bankruptcy on March 15 of that same year. Once Bank One realizes that Debtor Corp has filed for bankruptcy, Bank One files its financing statement on March 19 and perfects its pre-petition security interest. Can the trustee or debtor-in-possession avoid the transfer of this security interest to Bank One?

A. Yes, using either the trustee's §544(a) strong-arm powers or the trustee's §547(b) preference-avoiding powers.

B. No, neither under the trustee's §544(a) strong-arm powers nor the trustee's §547(b) preference-avoiding powers.

5. This is true, assuming no senior lienholder's rights are impaired.

C. Yes, under the trustee's §544(a) strong-arm powers but not under the trustee's §547(b) preference-avoiding powers.
D. **Yes,** under the trustee's §547(b) preference-avoiding powers but not under the trustee's §544(a) strong-arm powers.

ANALYSIS. This is a very tricky one. The correct answer is **C**. The key to this question is realizing that the 30-day grace period between attachment and perfection that is given in §547(e)(2) is only effective as against the trustee's preference-avoiding powers but does not operate to save an unperfected secured creditor from the trustee's §544(a) strong-arm powers. In this case, Bank One does qualify for the grace period of §547(e)(2) even though its perfection occurs post-petition, since the perfection is still within 30 days of attachment. That means that for preference purposes, the timing of the transfer of Bank One's security interest is the date of attachment, March 1, the same date as the loan was made. Therefore, the transfer of that security interest is not on account of an antecedent debt and therefore is not a preference. However, Bank One's security interest is still an unperfected security interest at the time of Debtor Corp's Chapter 11 filing. Therefore, the trustee or debtor-in-possession can avoid that unperfected security interest and transform Bank One into an unsecured creditor in this case. That's because the trustee's §544(a) strong-arm powers are not affected by the grace period given to late-perfecting secured creditors under §547(e)(2). All of the other three answers are wrong for the reasons just given.

Martin's and Keating's Picks

1. Question 1	D
2. Question 2	A
3. Question 3	B
4. Question 4	A
5. Question 5	D
6. Question 6	D
7. Question 7	D
8. Question 8	D
9. Question 9	A
10. Question 10	C
11. Question 11	C
The Closer	C

13

The General Bankruptcy Discharge

OVERVIEW

A. The Policy Behind Discharge for Individual Debtors
B. The Timing of the Discharge
C. The Scope of the Discharge
   1. Only pre-petition debts are discharged
   2. Only claims are discharged
   3. Not all debtors get a discharge
   4. Some debts are not entitled to discharge

Most individual debtors file a bankruptcy petition under either Chapter 7 or 13.[1] For these debtors, the whole purpose of the bankruptcy is to obtain a discharge. The bankruptcy discharge frees the debtor from the legal obligation to pay discharged debts and creditors are forever barred from collecting those discharged debts because §524(a)(2) contains a permanent injunction against collection.

A. The Policy Behind Discharge for Individual Debtors

In Local Loan v. Hunt, 292 U.S. 234 (1934),[2] the U.S. Supreme Court explained the policy behind this incredibly important aspect of bankruptcy law:

1. Individuals also can file cases under Chapter 12 if they are family farmers, or under Chapter 11. One reason individuals use Chapter 11 is that they are over the Chapter 13 debt limits.
2. Authors Charles Tabb and Ralph Brubaker claim that this is the most cited bankruptcy case in history, suggesting the overall importance of the fresh start doctrine to U.S. bankruptcy policy. *See* Charles Tabb & Ralph Brubaker, Bankruptcy Law: Principles, Policies, and Practice (2015).

> One of the primary purposes of the bankruptcy act is to "relieve the honest debtor from the weight of oppressive indebtedness, and permit him to start afresh free from the obligations and responsibilities consequent upon business misfortunes." This purpose of the act has been again and again emphasized by the courts as being of public as well as private interest, in that it gives to the honest but unfortunate debtor . . . a new opportunity in life and a clear field for future effort, unhampered by the pressure and discouragement of preexisting debt.

This policy is a unique American phenomenon. Note the emphasis in this landmark case on a "clear field for future effort." The theory is that American capitalism is best served by making sure that people are motivated to make money, and free to spend and fuel the economy in the future.

Many bankruptcy professors are still unclear how the 2005 amendments fit into this philosophy. Do we no longer care about fueling the economy? Are we saying that people are using too much credit? When we limit access to the bankruptcy system through bankruptcy reform, are our motivations in bankruptcy reform moral or economic? These questions are rhetorical, of course, and perhaps time will help answer them.

B. The Timing of the Discharge

The discharge is handled differently in Chapter 7 and Chapter 13 cases. In a Chapter 7 case, the discharge happens more or less automatically, at the end of the case. This takes approximately 90 days from the date of the filing. The discharge is dependent on the debtor surrendering all of his or her nonexempt property to the trustee, and also being completely honest in the bankruptcy paperwork, among other things.

In a Chapter 13 case, as well as a Chapter 12 case, the debtor usually does not receive a discharge until he or she has completed all of the plan payments and other obligations.[3] This means that it takes three to five years to obtain a Chapter 13 discharge. If the plan is never finished, the payments are essentially lost. In a Chapter 11 case, most debts are discharged on confirmation or approval of the plan, not on completion of all plan payments. Under the 2005 amendments, this is not the case in Chapter 11 cases filed by individual debtors. Individual debtors now receive their discharge only after making their plan payments in both Chapter 13 and Chapter 11 cases.

---

3. Section 1328(b) does allow a Chapter 13 debtor to obtain a discharge even without completing a plan, where the debtor has met with circumstances for which she should not be held accountable, has paid creditors at least as much as they would receive in a Chapter 7 case, and modification of the plan is not practicable. These facts could result in a Chapter 7-style discharge, but if secured property was not yet paid for, could also result in loss of that property (*see* 11 U.S.C. §1328(b)).

C. The Scope of the Discharge

Various bankruptcy provisions limit the scope of the debtor's discharge, all of which are discussed below and in the coming chapters.

1. *Only pre-petition debts are discharged*

For the most part, only debts that arose before the bankruptcy are discharged, as bankruptcy is only designed to clear up the debtor's pre-filing obligations. This makes sense. The debtor will list all of his or her pre-filing debts in the schedules of assets and liabilities and the statement of affairs. The creditors listed in this paperwork will receive notice of the bankruptcy case and thus due process in the case. The debtor is expected to pay any debts that arise after the filing, just like a person who is not in bankruptcy. Naturally, these post-petition creditors will not be listed on the bankruptcy paperwork and will not receive notice of the case.

Assume that a debtor files a Chapter 7 case in the morning and in the afternoon takes out a new car loan. Will the new car loan be discharged? Absolutely not. The auto lender will probably have a security interest on it that will allow the creditor to take the car back if the payments are not made. Moreover, the debtor will always owe the entire debt, not just the secured part, because the car was purchased after the filing. This would be a post-filing debt, for which the debtor will be liable and on which the filing will have no impact whatsoever.

These rules are modified slightly in Chapter 13 and Chapter 11 cases. As a result, some post-petition debts are sometimes included in the discharge in these other types of cases. In a Chapter 11 case, the confirmation order discharges all preconfirmation debts, some of which will be incurred during the case. (*See* 11 U.S.C. §1141(d).) In a Chapter 13 case, all debts dealt with in the plan are discharged, and while most of those will be pre-bankruptcy claims, it is possible that some will be from the post-petition period. (*See* 11 U.S.C. §1305.)

2. *Only claims are discharged*

To be discharged, a debt must have risen to the legal level of a claim, as that word is described in §101(5). The definition of a claim is pretty broad, however, and most things that you might think are not yet claims, and should not be listed on the bankruptcy paperwork, probably are claims. Thus, most of these things can be discharged in bankruptcy. For example, if the debtor was in a car accident and it is not even clear whose fault it is, and no suit has been filed, the debtor should list the other party to the accident in his or her bankruptcy schedules. If it turns out, long after the bankruptcy case is over, that the debtor is liable for the accident in a negligence suit, the debt would be discharged in the bankruptcy even if the debt was never liquidated, as long as the potential creditor was listed on the bankruptcy paperwork and so long as there was no distribution in the case. The timing of this situation confuses students, who often disbelieve that this debt would be discharged. It is true, however, given the broad definition of "claim" found in §101(5). This issue is discussed in detail in Chapter 32.

3. *Not all debtors get a discharge*

Additionally, as you'll see in greater detail in Chapter 15 of this guide, some individual debtors are not entitled to a discharge at all. Thinking back to what you read in Local Loan v. Hunt, bankruptcy discharges are for honest but unfortunate debtors. The right to a discharge comes with obligations on the part of the debtor— to be honest in the case, to turn over nonexempt assets rather than trying to hide them, and to disclose absolutely everything that the bankruptcy paperwork requires. These obligations are not taken lightly. Failure to comply will result in denial of the entire discharge. Hiding assets and lying in the case are obvious reasons to deny a debtor a discharge, but a discharge can also be denied for less obvious behavior such as making a fraudulent transfer right before the case, not keeping records, or losing money without explanation.

Corporations, partnerships, and limited liability companies do not get a discharge in Chapter 7. Thinking back once again to Local Loan v. Hunt, individual debtors (meaning people) need a discharge to continue their lives, unhampered by past debt and hopefully in better financial health in the future. Artificial or legal entities, corporations, partnerships, and limited liability companies, do not need a discharge in Chapter 7. They can just disappear. They do not have lives to continue into the future and can instead just be dissolved. Thus, in outlining all of the reasons why a debtor might be denied a general discharge, §727(a)(1) provides that the debtor shall obtain a discharge unless "the debtor is not an individual."

4. *Some debts are not entitled to discharge*

A debtor can receive a general discharge but still be left with some debts after the bankruptcy. Some of these debts are excepted from discharge because society has decided that these are the types of debts that people should be obligated to pay, no matter what. (*See generally* 11 U.S.C. §523(a).) These nondischargeable debts include alimony and child support, debts for recent taxes and some other taxes regardless of age, debts resulting from criminal restitution claims, debts arising while driving under the influence of alcohol, and student loans. These types of debts are not discharged in a case under Chapter 7, Chapter 13, Chapter 12, or Chapter 11.

In a Chapter 7 case, as well as a case filed by an individual under Chapter 11 or 12, there are many other debts that are not discharged.

Nondischargeable debts include debts incurred by fraud, debts for luxury goods purchased within 60 days of the filing,[4] certain property settlement debts owed to spouses, debts neither listed nor scheduled in the bankruptcy paperwork, debts for fraud or defalcation while acting in a fiduciary capacity, and debts arising from embezzlement or larceny.

It is incredibly interesting that debts for this long list of naughty deeds do get discharged in a Chapter 13 case. The bankruptcy discharge is far broader in a Chapter 13 than in these other chapters because Congress wanted to create incentives for people to try to pay back as much debt as they could through a Chapter 13. (*See* 11 U.S.C. §1328.) This was done to encourage people to file a Chapter 13 rather than simply filing a Chapter 7 liquidation and immediately discharging most debts.

Finally, under §524(c), a debtor can choose to waive his or her discharge of a particular debt by reaffirming that debt. Reaffirmation involves promising to pay back a debt that would otherwise be discharged in bankruptcy through a formal court-supervised process. Both secured and unsecured debts can be reaffirmed, though it is usually not advisable to reaffirm unsecured debts. In some jurisdictions, even secured debts should not be reaffirmed, as we will discuss further in Chapter 16.

Just so you know, in addition to the formal reaffirmation process, which has significant disadvantages, the debtor can also choose to voluntarily repay any debt that would otherwise be discharged in bankruptcy, without entering the formal reaffirmation process. (*See* 11 U.S.C. §524(f).) This is not unfair preferential treatment and is not frowned on in the Code. In many situations, it is preferable to formal reaffirmation. All of this is discussed further in Chapters 14, 15, and 16 ahead.

4. There is a presumption that such debts are nondischargeable on the basis of fraud, but the presumption can be rebutted. (*See* 11 U.S.C. §523(a)(2)(C).)

14

Exceptions to Discharge Under §523

OVERVIEW
A. Taxes
B. Exceptions to Discharge Based on Fraud
  1. Objections based on actual fraud
  2. Fraud based on the use of a false financial statement
  3. A presumption of fraud for charging luxury goods or taking cash advances within 60 days of the filing
C. Objections to Discharge Based on Fraud in the Fiduciary Capacity, Embezzlement, or Larceny
  1. Fraud in the fiduciary capacity and embezzlement
  2. Larceny
D. Forgetting or Simply Failing to List a Creditor on the Bankruptcy Paperwork
E. Domestic Support Obligations Under §523(a)(5) and §523(a)(15)
  1. The difference between support obligations and property settlement obligations in bankruptcy
  2. Marital obligations and the automatic stay
  3. Two additional reasons why it matters whether a debt is support or a mere property settlement debt
F. Intentional Torts and Debts Stemming from Driving Under the Influence of Alcohol
G. Student Loans
H. Conclusion
Martin's and Keating's Picks

As discussed previously, the primary and often the only reason that a debtor files a bankruptcy petition is because he or she wants to be discharged from debts. In most cases, the discharge is pretty much automatic. But, as you probably have guessed, it isn't that simple in some cases. Not all debts are discharged because there are exceptions to the dischargeability of debts.[1] This chapter deals with those debts that are not dischargeable.

The Bankruptcy Code is policy-driven law. As discussed in Chapter 13, the Code gives debtors a "fresh start" through a broad discharge of various debts and obligations. Section 523 contains exceptions to the discharge, based on countervailing policy considerations designed to protect the interests of certain creditors. While the bulk of the Code gives the debtor an opportunity to erase or discharge most debts, §523 limits the type of debts that can be discharged. Most of these exceptions to discharge are found in subsection (a) of §523. You should read §523(a) now. Although the section lists 18 categories of debts that are nondischargeable, your class (as well as this book) will discuss only the most common exceptions to discharge. Try not to confuse the issue discussed here (nondischargeability, and the exceptions to discharge for particular debts), with objections to discharge, a phrase that refers to the process of objecting to a debtor's entire bankruptcy discharge, which is the subject of the next chapter.

A. Taxes

Section 523(a)(1)(A-C) makes virtually all taxes that are entitled to priority under §507(a) nondischargeable. This is true under all chapters and cases filed under the Bankruptcy Code. As we covered §507(a) in some detail in Chapter 10, we won't revisit that territory here. The key to determining whether taxes are entitled to priority, and are thus nondischargeable, is determining what type of taxes they are and when a return was due for them.

Because all priority taxes are nondischargeable in a Chapter 7 case, suffice it to say that a debtor with major tax problems will rarely gain relief. Although the same taxes are also nondischargeable in a Chapter 13 case, Chapter 13 does provide some relief for taxes because they can be satisfied over the life of the plan. More importantly, once a Chapter 13 case is filed, the taxes stop accruing interest, which can be a great help and thus a powerful incentive to file.

In a Chapter 7 case, if the debtor's taxes are large and recent, filing a bankruptcy case will provide very little help. In some ways, this is similar to situations in which a debtor wants to file for Chapter 7 because he or she is behind on a mortgage. The case will ultimately accomplish little for the debtor.

---

1. Some debts, such as taxes and domestic support obligations, are not discharged because they are societal priorities. In other cases, the trustee or one of the creditors may object to the debtor's entire bankruptcy discharge based on some unsavory behavior on the part of the debtor. Indeed, certain conduct by the debtor may lead to a dismissal of the bankruptcy proceeding, leaving the debtor without a discharge and in the same position as before the filing, and perhaps in an even worse position. This is the subject of Chapter 15 of this guide.

B. Exceptions to Discharge Based on Fraud

Under §523(a)(2), a debtor who obtains credit through fraudulent means is not to be permitted to discharge the resulting debt in a Chapter 7 case. The goals of Congress in drafting the three fraud-based exceptions to discharge include protecting the defrauded creditor and not rewarding fraudulent behavior on the part of the debtor.

1. *Objections based on actual fraud*

Section 523(a)(2)(A) makes debts obtained through actual fraud nondischargeable. Actual fraud is proven by establishing the elements of common law fraud, which always requires the objecting creditor to prove actual intent to defraud. One example of such a test for actual fraud[2] requires that the objecting creditor prove these six elements: (1) the debtor made a representation; (2) the representation was false; (3) the debtor knew it was false at the time it was made; (4) the representation was made with the intent to deceive the creditor; (5) the creditor actually and justifiably relied upon the representation; and (6) the creditor sustained a loss or was damaged as a proximate result of the false representation. (*See* Fowler Bros. v. Young (In re Young), 91 F.3d 1367, 1373 (10th Cir. 1996).) For reasons that will become apparent in a moment, this exception to the dischargeability of debts is known as the actual fraud exception to discharge.

QUESTION 1. Sarah Sellers sold her home to Bernie and Bernice Buyers. In connection with the sale, she gave them a warranty deed. In the state in which this home is located, a warranty deed is essentially a warranty or promise that the property being transferred is free and clear of all liens and encumbrances. As it turned out, there was a huge mortgage on the property and the Buyers sued Sarah in state court to recover for this transgression. Sarah ended up in Chapter 7 bankruptcy, where the Buyers objected to the discharge of her debt on the basis of fraud. The Buyers will likely recover in the case only if:

A. Sarah knowingly gave them the warranty deed.
B. Sarah knew the legal meaning of the warranty deed and knew there was a mortgage on the property.
C. Sarah knew of the mortgage when she sold the Buyers the property.
D. the Buyers knew of the mortgage when Sarah sold them the property.

2. The elements of common law fraud vary from state to state. Using the state definition for fraud is one example of a case in which the Bankruptcy Code borrows from or defers to state law.

ANALYSIS. If the Buyers knew about the mortgage, they could not sue Sarah for fraud, so we can eliminate **D** right away. As for the others, think back to the requirements for nondischargeability. There must be intent to defraud, meaning an actual intent and not some sort of presumed intent, recklessness, or negligence. Just because Sarah knew about the mortgage does not prove that she intended to defraud the buyers. That is what title insurance is for. Thus, **C** alone is incorrect. Moreover, even if she knowingly gave them the warranty deed, this does not prove actual intent either. The only fact offered here that would prove an actual intent to defraud is that Sarah knew what it meant to give the warranty deed, namely that she knew when she gave it to them that she was promising them that there were no mortgages or other liens on the property. Even then, to be liable for fraud, Sarah would also need to be aware of the existing mortgage. Thus, the correct answer is **B**.

2. Fraud based on the use of a false financial statement

Section 523(a)(2)(B) makes debts obtained through the use of a false financial statement nondischargeable. You might wonder why a case like that would require its own separate test, as this still sounds like fraud and could be covered under the provisions of §523(a)(2)(A) discussed previously. The reason for this separate provision is that debtors fill out financial statements to get loans all the time, and in some cases, the creditors help them fill out the forms. The debtors do not always understand the forms, and the creditors do not always rely on the information contained in them. To deal with these special cases, Congress came up with a different rule.

To establish nondischargeability under this subsection, there must be a writing pertaining to the debtor's financial condition, and the writing must be materially false, meaning, "the document must not only be erroneous, but rather contain information which renders the document substantially inaccurate." (*See* Miller v. Boles (In re Boles), 150 B.R. 733, 740 (Bankr. W.D. Mo. 1993).) In essence, the false information must bear on an "important or substantial truth." (*See* First Interstate Bank v. Greene, 96 B.R. 279, 283 (BAP 9th Cir. 1989).) Finally, and perhaps most importantly, the creditor must rely on the false or inaccurate information to his or her detriment. Thus, there are three essential elements to this exception to discharge: (1) there must be a writing pertaining to the debtor's financial condition; (2) the writing must contain a material misrepresentation; and (3) the creditor must rely on the misrepresentation in the writing to his or her detriment.

QUESTION 2. Capitol Finance helped the Petersons fill out their application for a line of credit loan. When the application asked the Petersons to value their furnishings, Capitol told them that it is standard in the industry to use one-third of the value of their home as the value of the furnishings. They did as instructed, placing $30,000 in that space, although they probably paid around $15,000 for the furnishings. The Petersons later lost their jobs and filed a Chapter 7 case. On the advice of their attorney, they valued their furnishings on their bankruptcy schedules at garage-sale prices, a total of about $5,000. Capitol objected to the dischargeability of their debt based on the funny numbers found in the loan application. What is the likely result?

A. The Petersons will succeed because they did not have actual intent to defraud anyone, thus defeating a claim for actual fraud, and because Capitol did not rely on the false financial statement.
B. The Petersons will succeed because they were told to lie on the application.
C. Capitol will succeed, because regardless of the reason, the Petersons falsified the financial statement.
D. Capitol will prevail because it relied on the false financial statement to its detriment.

ANALYSIS. This question assumes that Capitol is requesting nondischargeability based on both actual fraud and the use of a false financial statement. The false financial statement ground will not work for Capitol under these facts, because Capitol certainly did not rely on this part of the financial statement in making this loan. If what the loan officer said is true, then every application values furnishings at one-third of the value of the home. Moreover, the loan officer seemed to know that this was not the actual value of the Peterson's furnishings, so he could not honestly say he relied on the financial statement. This makes **D** incorrect. **C** is incorrect because falsity is not enough. Under the false financial statement test, you need reliance as well, which is missing here, and under the actual fraud test, you need intent to defraud. Both are missing here. Of the two remaining answers, **B** is not as specific as **A**, and is thus not as good an answer. Yes, the debtors were told to use a formula to value their personal property on their loan agreement, but that fact alone does not prove or disprove Capitol's case. The statements in **A** go to the heart of Capitol's case and thus **A** is the best answer.

3. *A presumption of fraud for charging luxury goods or taking cash advances within 60 days of the filing*

Section 523(a)(2)(C) states that debts incurred within 90 days of the bankruptcy filing—to buy luxury goods or services under an open-ended plan (which includes a credit card)—is presumed to be nondischargeable on the basis of fraud. This is sometimes called the presumptive fraud section. The theory behind this fraud-based objection to discharge is that a debtor who goes out and loads up on luxury goods right before filing for bankruptcy was or should have been aware of his or her dire financial condition, and probably had no intention of paying back the debt anyway. Thus, Code policy assumes that the person never intended to pay back the debt and excepts it from discharge on that basis: as a form of fraud on the creditor. As a result, the debtor should be required to pay the debt back after the bankruptcy is completed.

The phrase "luxury goods or services" is not defined in the Bankruptcy Code but essentially means goods not necessary to support the debtor or the debtor's dependents. As you can well imagine, interpreting this phrase involves a great deal of discretion on the part of the judge. Is a computer a luxury good? Does it depend what you do for a living? How about food or a mastectomy? What about a new suit or underwear?

This same section (§523(a)(2)(C)) presumes that all cash advances aggregating more than $1,250 from a single creditor taken out within the 70 days before a bankruptcy filing are also nondischargeable on the basis of fraud, under the same logic. The debtor took the cash with full knowledge of his or her financial condition and with no intention to pay the debt back. Note that balance transfers (meaning transfers from one credit card to another), which credit card companies sometimes characterize as cash advances in their own bookkeeping, do not constitute cash advances for the purposes of this section.

An important limitation on this objection to discharge is that no creditor can object under this section unless it is owed more than $900 total "for luxury goods or services" or $1,250 for cash advances. Thus, if the debtor charges $700 worth of designer candles during the 90 days before his or her bankruptcy filing, and then gets a cash advance from a different creditor of $1,000 to pay his or her mortgage, either creditor could rely on the actual fraud exception (the one we talked about earlier), but neither could use the presumptive fraud section. Neither creditor is owed enough for luxury goods or services.

On the other hand, if the debtor charges $950 to his or her MasterCard for jewelry and then charges another $1,000 to the same card for designer houseplants, MasterCard could rely on the luxury goods exception. Just remember also that the debtor can rebut the presumption of fraud under this section by proving that he or she did not contemplate bankruptcy at the time of the charges or by proving that the goods are not luxury goods.

QUESTION 3. Jerry Jones works in a sporting goods store and also teaches surfing on the side. Within 90 days of his Chapter 7 case, he charged the following items to his Visa card:

$400 in food,
$400 in surfing equipment,
$350 for a new TV and a DVD player.

If Visa objects to the dischargeability of its debt based on the presumption of fraud for purchases of luxury goods, what will be the result?

A. Visa will win because it is clear that Jerry had no intention of paying Visa back for these items.
B. Visa will succeed in getting its debt deemed nondischargeable for the TV and DVD player, but not for the food or the surfing equipment.
C. Visa will succeed in getting its debt deemed nondischargeable for the TV and DVD player, as well as the surfing equipment, but not for the food.
D. Visa will not succeed in its objection because the amounts charged for luxury goods do not exceed $900.

ANALYSIS. If **A** were true, Visa would have a good claim under the actual fraud exception to discharge. If Jerry really had no intention of paying back any of this debt, the debt would qualify as debt incurred through actual fraud, which is why clients should be told not to use their credit cards, even for food, once they have decided to file for bankruptcy. Here, though, the facts do not suggest that Jerry knew he would not pay back the debt when he took it out. The problem also states that Visa is basing its objection on the luxury goods presumption.

B and **C** are both very tempting answers and allow us to explore the slippery issue of which items are luxury goods and which are not. Food is not a luxury good, at least not as a general matter, so these amounts would not help establish Visa's case under §523(a)(2)(C). The TV and DVD player, at the other end of the spectrum, seem to be luxury items to me, although every court is different. In one strange case, a court found $1,100 worth of collector Barbie Dolls to not qualify as luxury goods. (*See* Sears, Roebuck & Co. v. Johannsen (In re Johannsen), 160 B.R. 328 (Bankr. W.D. Wis. 1993).)

Whether the surfing equipment would constitute luxury goods depends, we suppose, on whether the court finds that the debtor needs the equipment to teach surfing. We would think that if he did not, these would clearly be luxury goods, but if he did need them to make money, a court could easily say they were not luxury goods.

We don't need to decide this issue to answer this question, because **D** is the correct answer. Once the food is subtracted from the tab, there are insufficient charges left as potential luxury goods to meet the §523(a)(A)(C) threshold amount of $900. Tricky.

IMPORTANT TIP: Keep in mind that this test merely creates a presumption that the luxury goods charged or the cash advances taken were charged with no intent to pay back the debt and thus were charged through fraudulent means. The debtor can rebut this presumption, essentially by proving that he or she had no intention of filing for bankruptcy at the time of the charge and had some reasonable belief that he or she could pay back the debt.

C. Objections to Discharge Based on Fraud in the Fiduciary Capacity, Embezzlement, or Larceny

Section 523(a)(4) augments §523(a)(2)(A), by not discharging debts incurred "for fraud or defalcation while acting in a fiduciary capacity, embezzlement, or larceny."

1. Fraud in the fiduciary capacity and embezzlement

The fraud referred to in this section is different from that covered in §523(a). It deals not with the actual fraud or the debtor's purchases of luxury goods or services, but instead with fraud within a fiduciary relationship. It makes nondischargeable debts for fraud in the context of a unique position of trust and power.

QUESTION 4. Kim Cook hired Jose Garcia as her attorney to help her become the conservator of her nephew's assets after his father was killed in a motorcycle accident. Jose accomplished Kim's goal, and she became Will's conservator. Eventually, unbeknownst to Jose, Kim absconded with all of Will's money. Jose was sued by Will and eventually filed a Chapter 7 bankruptcy case. Will filed a complaint requesting that his debt be deemed nondischargeable on the basis of fraud in the fiduciary capacity. From what you have been told here, is the debt to Will nondischargeable?

A. Yes, because Jose was Will's fiduciary and Jose committed fraud by allowing Kim to take Will's money.
B. No, because although Jose was Will's fiduciary, Jose didn't know about the stolen funds and therefore cannot be liable for fraud in the fiduciary capacity.
C. No, for two reasons; first, because Jose did not commit fraud and, second, because Jose was not Will's fiduciary.
D. Yes, because even if Jose did not know Kim was using or taking Will's money, he should have been watching the funds for Will.

ANALYSIS. The key to understanding the fiduciary capacity objection to dischargeability is knowing how to recognize a fiduciary relationship. Here, it may seem obvious that Jose's legal relationship is with Kim, and not Will, but this issue continues to be litigated. Although Kim is Will's fiduciary and Jose is Kim's fiduciary, Jose is not Will's fiduciary, and thus owes no fiduciary duties to Will. Thus, both **A** and **B** are incorrect. If Jose were aware of the embezzlement or theft, then he may have a duty to tell Will. Under these facts, however, this does not appear to be the case. Without actual knowledge of the problem, Jose is under no duty to Will, and certainly had no obligation to watch the money for Will. Thus, **D** is also incorrect. The correct answer is **C**.

By the way, if Kim were the one in bankruptcy, Will could surely have her obligations to him deemed nondischargeable, either under the embezzlement part of §523(a)(4), or under the part dealing with fraud in the fiduciary capacity.

2. Larceny

Another debt not discharged in bankruptcy is one resulting from larceny. The question then becomes, what is larceny?

QUESTION 5. Roy West owns a pottery gallery in Santa Fe, New Mexico. Rosa Ramon has consigned four authentic Native American pots to Roy for sale in his store, meaning that she still owns the pots, and once he sells them, he is to remit the proceeds of the sale to Rosa. Roy sold all four pots, and due to his dire financial circumstances, filed for bankruptcy before he had paid Rosa. Rosa sued Roy in bankruptcy court, claiming that her debt was nondischargeable as a result of larceny. Is Roy likely to escape liability to Rosa?

A. Yes, because at the time Roy received the goods from Rosa, they were procured legally.
B. No, because Roy intentionally sold the pots.
C. Yes, because at the time Roy sold the pots, he planned to pay Rosa; it just did not work out that way.
D. No, because at the time he sold the pots, Roy knew or should have known that he would not be able to pay Rosa for them, so he should have returned them to her.

ANALYSIS. This question is unanswerable without a careful consideration of the larceny statutes in the jurisdiction and of the cases interpreting it. You may be scratching your head and wondering whether you have to be a criminal lawyer to understand this exemption. The answer is no, but you will have to learn about larceny if this exemption comes up.

In some jurisdictions, larceny may require that the goods be taken involuntarily. In those states, **A** is a correct answer. In some jurisdictions, even though the goods were originally obtained legally, the sale of bailed goods with intent to keep the money may constitute larceny. Some larceny statutes may require criminal intent at the time that the consigned goods are sold. In those states, **C** is a correct answer. **D** would be correct in those states that look to the consignor's intent at the time the consignor received the goods. The point is that here, as in many other places, the Bankruptcy Code requires you to look to state law to solve problems.

For example, in New Mexico and many other states, larceny requires that a person procure goods through unlawful means. Unfortunately for Rosa, she gave the pots to Roy to sell, so this element is not met. The correct answer, under New Mexico law, is **A**.

Note that doing some intermediate act intentionally but meaning no harm will rarely cause a debt to be deemed nondischargeable. Thus, **B** is not relevant. This is not like intentional torts, although we will be discussing those shortly. For most of the exceptions we've discussed so far, the debtor needs the intent to do evil to have his or her discharge limited.

D. Forgetting or Simply Failing to List a Creditor on the Bankruptcy Paperwork

Just as §523 seeks to prevent fraudulent behavior from reaping the benefits of a fresh start, the section also seeks to protect uninformed and unaware creditors. Specifically, the debtor's bankruptcy petition and accompanying documents, and the notices that are sent based upon the information contained in these documents, are designed to put all creditors on notice that a bankruptcy has been filed. This notice serves many practical purposes and one purpose required by the United States Constitution. Practically speaking, the notice tells creditors who receive it to stop all collection activity pursuant to §362(a), informs them to file a proof of claim if there are assets to distribute in the case, and informs them of the deadline to object to the dischargeability of their debt or to the debtor's entire discharge. By providing these deadlines and this general notice of the case, the creditor has received the procedural due process required by the U.S. Constitution when a person's property (their right to recover their debt) is taken from him or her.

Win or lose, object or not, the creditor has received all the due process necessary by law if he or she has been listed on the petition and has received notice of the debtor's bankruptcy filing. On the other hand, §523(a)(3) provides that debts that are not listed on the schedules of assets and liabilities ("neither listed nor scheduled," as the statute states) are not dischargeable. The theory here is that by not listing the debt on the petition, the debtor has taken away the creditor's due process in the case by eliminating notice of the bankruptcy, the opportunity to object to the discharge of the debt, and the opportunity to file a claim. The practical result of such an omission is that the unlisted debt will not be discharged in or otherwise affected by the bankruptcy.

Unlike the actual fraud exception, there is no mental intent requirement under §523(a)(3). Whether the debtor purposely sought to leave a creditor off his or her schedules or whether the debtor just forgot, if the creditor and the debt are not on the schedule, that debt will not be discharged. The only way a debtor can get around this requirement is by proving the creditor had notice or actual knowledge of the bankruptcy case and, with this knowledge, could have filed a proof of claim.[3]

E. Domestic Support Obligations Under §523(a)(5) and §523(a)(15)

Section 523(a)(5) provides that debts for domestic support obligations are not dischargeable in any type of bankruptcy. Section 523 recognizes that a debtor may have obligations to former spouses or children that would, if discharged, have the effect of forcing these "creditors" onto public assistance or into poverty.

As is true in many separation agreements, property settlements are distinguished from and treated differently than debts for support. The dischargeability of property settlement debts in a Chapter 7 case is covered in §523(a)(15), which used to awkwardly balance the hardship that discharging the debt would have on the nondebtor spouse, against the hardship the debtor would endure if the debt is not discharged. As the legislative history of this former statute explained, the "benefits of the debtor's discharge should be sacrificed only if there would be substantial detriment to the nondebtor spouse that outweighs the debtor's need for a fresh start." (*See* 140 Cong. Rec. H. 10752-1 (daily ed. Oct. 4, 1994).)

The 2005 amendments eliminated this very odd and unworkable test and made property settlement obligations arising out of a marital settlement agreement nondischargeable as well, at least for Chapter 7 bankruptcy cases filed on or after October 17, 2006.

1. *The difference between support obligations and property settlement obligations in bankruptcy*

Domestic support obligations flowing from a divorce are defined in the Bankruptcy Code as any debt that accrues before, on, or after the filing of the bankruptcy petition, including interest due under nonbankruptcy law, owed to a spouse, former spouse, child of the debtor, or such child's parent, legal

3. Some courts have held that if the error is inadvertent and there were no assets to distribute in the case in any event, the debt can be discharged because the failure to list the creditor was a harmless error. The logic is that the creditor would not have received a distribution in any event. This reasoning never applies to exceptions to discharge, which are always preserved if a creditor is left off the petition. Moreover, even for garden-variety claims, a careful lawyer will not rely on these harmless error cases, and will list every debt so that the debtor can get the broadest discharge possible. Intentionally leaving debts off the petition and schedules can cause other problems as well, including objections to the debtor's general discharge under §727(a)(4), covered in Chapter 15.

guardian, or responsible relative. Some of these terms remain undefined in the Code, but the clear intent of Congress is to broaden the possible holders of domestic support obligations to include nonmarried parents of a child of the debtor, as well as various responsible persons and legal guardians. The obligations covered include those for alimony, maintenance, and support, as established in a divorce decree, a separation agreement, a property settlement agreement, or a court order. The claims covered by the definition include those for support held by governmental entities. (*See* 11 U.S.C. §101(14A).) Debts that fall into the category of a domestic support obligation are not dischargeable in a bankruptcy of any kind.

Marital property settlements, on the other hand, are treated differently in some cases, so the distinction can be critical. Debts arising from property settlement agreements are not dischargeable in Chapter 7 but are dischargeable in Chapter 13, assuming the debtor makes the required plan payments. Domestic support obligations have first priority in a Chapter 7 case, whereas property settlement claims have no special priority at all.

Because of this and a few other differences in treatment between the two types of claims, you need to be able to distinguish between support and property settlement obligations. While most people think of a property settlement as an agreement to split up property, for many couples the property settlement part of the divorce also includes promises by one spouse to pay certain debts the couple incurred during the marriage. Generally speaking, promises to pay the mortgage, the car payment, the credit card bills, and other debts to third parties are part of a property settlement.

Because support payments are never dischargeable in any bankruptcy, every creditor receiving payments under a marital settlement agreement hopes that they will be characterized as support payments. On the other hand, many bankruptcy debtors will try to argue the opposite, hoping to turn all obligations into potentially dischargeable property settlement debts. The bankruptcy court will look beyond the names given to obligations in the agreement itself to see what the payments are actually for. The names given to the obligations in the agreement are a starting point for analyzing the nature of the payments but will not determine, in and of themselves, whether a debt is dischargeable.

QUESTION 6. Carol Cole and Bud Winter just separated. He wants to keep their house and she couldn't care less about the house. It has no mortgage and is worth $100,000. The couple lives in Texas, and they have nothing else to speak of. He promises in the very amicable divorce to pay her $50,000 over five years, in equal monthly installments. In the agreement, there is no explanation of what the payment is for, but the agreement does provide that Bud gets the house. Bud then falls on tough times and ends up in bankruptcy. How would you characterize his obligation to pay her the $50,000, given only what you have been told?

A. Clearly as support, because she is getting paid $50,000 over five years.
B. Probably as support, because this is a payment over time and that is usually an indicia of support, particularly if the payments were to be made monthly.
C. Probably as a property settlement, because Carol is getting paid exactly half of the value of the assets they owned together.
D. Unquestionably a property settlement, because Carol is getting paid exactly half of the value of the assets they owned together.

ANALYSIS. Be careful about being too sure of anything in this area, as there will often be facts that could lead one in either direction. The agreement is poorly written and leaves a great deal up to chance. Given what you know, however, the best answer is **C**, because it really does look like a payment for half the value of the house that Bud is keeping. **A** and **B** are both incorrect, although **A** is the worst answer because it is definitely incorrect. These payments do not look much like support. Although monthly payments often look more like support than yearly payments, the lump sum — equal to half the house — is set out in the agreement. It looks like a property settlement but we cannot be certain of how a court would rule, so **C** is better than **D**.

How can you tell if a payment is a support obligation or part of a property settlement? Obviously, if the agreement says that John will pay Jenny $500 in child support, then that debt is child support and will not be affected in any way by John's bankruptcy. On the other hand, if the agreement says John will pay all of the couple's credit card debt, any court in the world would say that is just a property settlement obligation. We say "just" not to be disparaging but to hammer home how much more important support obligations are and the better treatment they receive in bankruptcy.

Many situations are far less clear. What if the agreement says "instead of child support, John will make the house payment and the payments on the car Jenny drives"? How would this be interpreted, compared to language stating that John will make these payments "in lieu of child support"? The court in these instances will need to determine the intent of the parties at the time the agreement was entered into, assuming that the agreement is ambiguous.

QUESTION 7. Clyde and Carol have two children, ages five and two, and their marital settlement agreement provides as follows:

Clyde will pay the house payment for the house in which Carol and the children live and will also make the payments on Carol's car.

Clyde will make the payments on Carol's car and the house, and will pay no child support and no alimony.

Given what you know, which of these additional facts would make it most likely that these obligations would be found to be support obligations rather than property settlement obligations?

A. Both the house and the car will be paid off within five years.
B. The agreement provides that Clyde will pay the house payment and a reasonable car payment until the time that the youngest child turns 18.
C. The reason for the divorce was Clyde's infidelity, and Clyde remarried the day after his divorce from Carol became final. Carol remarried a week later.
D. Carol gave up all rights to the couple's savings account of $200,000 in return for this deal so that Clyde could start a new business.

ANALYSIS. This is a very tough question with two possibly good answers. First, we'll eliminate the obviously incorrect ones. The distinction we are learning here is between property settlements and support obligations. **D** seems realistic because maybe Carol would do this deal, but that is not what you were asked. **D** is a property settlement because Carol is essentially loaning money to Clyde and then being paid back through his making the house and car payments. **C** is also incorrect. The fact that they both remarried would not seem to shed any light on the nature of the payments. Indeed, it might indicate that Carol wanted to receive specified payments each month that were not tied to the vagaries of child support.

A is incorrect, but only because the five-year payment term seems unrelated to anything else in the couple's lives. It just doesn't prove a case one way or another. Compare that to **B**, the correct answer. Suddenly, this looks like child support because Clyde is to provide this financial assistance to Carol until the kids are of legal age. The payments are tied in time (temporally) to the children's emancipation, a very helpful fact if Carol is trying to prove that this is support.

Here is a quick review question before we move on.

QUESTION 8. Assuming we represent Carol, why do we care if these payments are characterized as support or property settlement obligations?

A. Support payments are more important to society.
B. Support payments can be enforced criminally.
C. This characterization as support would definitely make this debt nondischargeable in all forms of bankruptcy.
D. It is easier to collect support than property settlement debt in state court.

ANALYSIS. The correct answer is **C**, as this is a discussion about dischargeability. We care because support obligations have to be paid and are not dischargeable in bankruptcy. Most of the other answers are correct, but what we are concerned about in this discussion is whether a debt can be discharged in bankruptcy.

2. Marital obligations and the automatic stay

The distinction between support and property settlements is also important in determining which state court actions are stayed by a bankruptcy filing. Actions to determine or collect alimony, maintenance, or support are not stayed at all under §362(b). Actions to either establish or collect a property settlement obligation are stayed. Practically speaking, once again, if you are not absolutely sure you are talking about support, it is safest to request relief from the automatic stay before proceeding against the debtor in state court.

QUESTION 9. In the previous questions about Carol and Clyde (Questions 7 and 8), Carol's attorney should take what course of action, if any, to protect her rights?

A. Take no action, as it is apparent that the debts are support obligations that will not be discharged in bankruptcy, and it would be best to save Carol's money.
B. Sue Clyde in state court to collect these amounts.
C. Request that the bankruptcy court find these debts to be support obligations and thus nondischargeable obligations.
D. Ask Carol which of these options she prefers.

ANALYSIS. We're all for empowering a client, but the legal answer here is clear enough to make this a decision for the attorney, rather than the client. It is unclear whether the debts in this question are property settlement debts or support debts. Given this lack of certainty, it would be crazy to rely on the fact that these are clearly support obligations and do nothing. If it turns out that these are not support, then by default, these debts will be classified as property settlement debts. As such, they will be discharged for failure to object to their dischargeability. Thus, **A** is incorrect. **B** is incorrect because suits to collect a property settlement are stayed and thus suing Clyde in state court would risk subjecting Carol to sanctions for violating the automatic stay, if the debt is found not to be support. **D** is a plausible answer, but since **A** and **B** are clearly wrong, it is questionable whether they should even be presented to Carol as options. This leaves **C** as the correct answer. The only safe thing to do, given the uncertainty, is to ask the bankruptcy court for a determination of the type of debt, while asking that the debt not be discharged in any case. Of course, you can take this action only with the client's consent.

3. *Two additional reasons why it matters whether a debt is support or a mere property settlement debt*

If you need two additional reasons to learn the distinction between a support obligation and a property settlement, here they are: (1) support obligations have priority status under §507(a)(8), whereas property settlement obligations have no priority status; and (2) property settlement obligations are always dischargeable in a Chapter 13 case, whereas support obligations never are.

F. Intentional Torts and Debts Stemming from Driving Under the Influence of Alcohol

For policy reasons, debts for intentional torts, such as battery, assault, and so forth, as well as debts for judgments resulting from driving while under the influence of alcohol (DWI) are not dischargeable. (*See* §523(a)(6) and (9).) These sections are expressions by Congress that a debtor will not be excused from liability for behavior, whether intentional or not, that society abhors. Interestingly, as you will see in the discussions of the super-discharge in the Chapter 13 materials, intentional tort debts are dischargeable in a Chapter 13 case. DWI debts, however, are not, again reflecting the seriousness of such obligations.

QUESTION 10. Dave Debtor hit Pam Pedestrian with his car. Which facts would suggest that Pam's claim is not dischargeable in Dave's subsequent Chapter 7 case?

1. He was not carrying comprehensive liability insurance at the time.
2. He had inadvertently run a red light when she darted in front of his car and was hit.
3. He hit her on purpose.
4. He was drunk when he hit her.

A. All of the above.
B. Either 1, 3, or 4.
C. Either 3 or 4.
D. Either 2 or 3.

ANALYSIS. Both **3** and **4** seem to clearly establish nondischargeability. Debts resulting from drunk driving are not dischargeable in either a Chapter 7 or a Chapter 13 case. If he hit her on purpose, this would be an intentional tort, which would not be dischargeable in a Chapter 7 case. Thus, both **3** and **4** establish nondischargeability. Choice **2** suggests that the contact with Pam resulted from negligence, and negligence claims are always dischargeable, so **2** is incorrect. The tough question here is whether failing to carry liability insurance could itself rise to the level of an intentional act that could cause the debt to be nondischargeable. While one textbook editor has raised the question of whether a failure of a doctor to carry malpractice insurance could result in a nondischargeable debt (Charles Tabb and Ralph Brubaker, supra Chapter 13 note 2, at 541), We doubt whether the failure to carry auto insurance for this accident would result in a finding of intentional tort. Thus, the best answer is C: either **3** or **4**.

G. Student Loans

Student loan obligations are not dischargeable except in very rare situations. A student loan is a general unsecured debt, and it is not entitled to priority. However, based on the fear that a student will receive the benefit of an education, and then file for bankruptcy, Congress made student loans nondischargeable. This exception to discharge also helps ensure that there will be more funds available to be used to educate future generations of students.

While generally disallowing the discharge of student loans, Congress also recognized that in rare situations, it might be necessary to allow student loans to be discharged. Section 523(a)(8) provides that student loans may be discharged if the debtor has suffered "undue hardship." Unfortunately, the Bankruptcy Code does not define "undue hardship," so each court has developed its own interpretation of the undue hardship test. As an example, the Second Circuit's test requires that the debtor prove three things: (1) that the student cannot meet his or her current expenses; (2) that this financial condition is likely to endure; and (3) that the student has made an effort to pay back the loan in issue. (*See* Brunner v. New York State Higher Education Services Corp., 831 F.2d 395 (2d Cir. 1987).) Some courts use much longer and more complex tests. (*See* Educational Credit Mgmt. Corp. v. Jesperson, 571 F.3d 775 (8th Cir. 2009).) Indicia of undue hardship include permanent disabilities, inability to find work, and other permanent problems. The test is extremely difficult to meet in most districts, which is what Congress intended.

Unlike with most other objections to the dischargeability of a debt, which are instituted by creditors, the debtor requests that the student loans be discharged by way of complaint. Thus, the debtor has the burden of proving that he or she meets the undue hardship standard. Assume the debtor in Question 11 lives in a jurisdiction that follows Brunner.

QUESTION 11. Barbara Backman just broke her back and as result, lost her job as an auditor at a Big Four accounting firm. Not too long thereafter, she fell behind on her mortgage and had her condo foreclosed. Her doctor predicts that she will be laid up for at least another six months. She is now in Chapter 7 and has moved to discharge her substantial student loans under the "undue hardship" test. She has been diligently paying on the student loans for four years. Will she likely succeed in discharging her student loans?

A. Yes, because Barbara has been diligently trying to pay back the loans.
B. No, because her injury is not permanent.
C. Yes, because she has suffered extreme hardship by losing her job and her home.
D. Yes, because she is unable to pay back the loan and also meet her expenses with her meager disability payments.

ANALYSIS. This question helps you learn the elements of this exception. At least under the Brunner test outlined previously, Barbara must meet all of the elements to have her debt discharged. Just trying her best to repay the loan will not do the trick (**A**), nor will she win the day by proving that she has endured all manner of catastrophe (**C**). Finally, she apparently can show that she cannot pay her loans and her current expenses (**D**), but this, too, is insufficient to establish that she is entitled to discharge her student loans. Because her injury is temporary and because she has a good education, it is unlikely that she can prove that her financial hardship is likely to continue indefinitely. Thus, the answer is **B**, and she is unlikely to be able to discharge this debt.

H. Conclusion

To finish this long and complicated chapter, we offer two review questions.

QUESTION 12. A stabbing victim is most likely to have his debt deemed nondischargeable under which exception to discharge?

A. Fraud
B. Breach of fiduciary duty
C. Intentional tort
D. Larceny

ANALYSIS. OK, so this is a bit of a softball, but we are amazed that most of our students do not recognize that stabbing is civil assault, and thus an intentional tort. The answer is **C**. We hope you got it!

QUESTION 13. Two months before filing for bankruptcy, John purchased a giant-screen TV as part of an agreement with his former spouse, Jan. The agreement was made a year earlier when the two divorced and provided that Jan would forgo alimony payments in exchange for the brand new TV John was to buy. The TV cost $2,000, and John charged it to his Visa card. John decided to keep the TV, and in preparing to file for bankruptcy, decided not to mention the purchase in his petition. The credit card company, his former wife, and the trustee all object to the discharge of the $2,000 in debt. Who is likely to prevail? You can pick more than one.

- **A.** The former spouse. Under §523(a)(5) this debt is in lieu of support.
- **B.** The credit card company. Under §523(a)(2)(C), this purchase is for a luxury good. As such, the $2,000 cannot be discharged.
- **C.** The trustee. Under §523(a)(3), because the debtor did not list this debt on his petition, the debt cannot be discharged

---

ANALYSIS. The question here is who is entitled to be paid as a result of this purchase. Jan is owed the equivalent of the TV, but need not get the actual TV. If the TV was really promised in lieu of alimony, then she should be paid with either the TV or its value in cash. **C** is incorrect because, even if this were left off the petition, it would be the credit card company that would obtain the payment and would file the nondischargeability petition, not the trustee. **B** seems true enough, assuming this is a luxury good, which it appears to be. **A** and **B** are both correct and **C** is incorrect.

Martin's and Keating's Picks

1. Question 1 **B**
2. Question 2 **A**
3. Question 3 **D**
4. Question 4 **C**
5. Question 5 **A**
6. Question 6 **C**
7. Question 7 **B**

8. Question 8	**C**
9. Question 9	**C**
10. Question 10	**C**
11. Question 11	**B**
12. Question 12	**C**
13. Question 13	**A and B**

15

Objections to the Debtor's General Discharge

OVERVIEW

A. A Knowing and Fraudulent False Oath in or in Connection with a Bankruptcy Case
B. Inexplicable Loss of Money
C. Concealment, Loss, Destruction, Falsification, or Mutilation of Records, or a Failure to Keep Records
D. Transfers Made with Intent to Hinder, Delay, or Defraud Creditors
E. Prior Discharge Within Past Eight (or Six) Years
F. Failure to Complete the Debt Management Course Under §727(a)(11)
G. The Closer: Chapters 13, 14, and 15 (CODE READER)
Martin's and Keating's Picks

Like §523(a) discussed earlier, §727 is used to limit the debtor's discharge. Compared to the limited objections reviewed in the last chapter, which pertain to objections to the dischargeability of just one debt, this chapter discusses a far greater threat to the debtor's entire bankruptcy case, namely objections to the debtor's general discharge. In some ways, comparing §523 objections to §727 objections is like comparing a misdemeanor to a felony. To bring an objection to the debtor's general or global discharge, you have to really mean business.

Moreover, the debtor must have done something that society really abhors. While some of the §523 objections are for bad deeds, such as fraud or intentional torts, many simply protect debts that we as a society want to protect. No bad deed is required. By comparison, §727 almost always requires a very bad act, such as hiding assets, lying in your bankruptcy case, "losing" a boatload of assets, or destroying your business records. A debtor's entire discharge can be denied only if the debtor essentially thumbs his or her nose at the whole system or comes off as totally dishonest. Because it is easy to confuse the two sections, we call objections to the discharge of a particular debt objections to dischargeability (referring to the debt), and call objections to the general discharge objections to discharge (referring to the debtor him- or herself). If an objection to discharge is successful, none of the debtor's debts get discharged. From the debtor's standpoint, the entire case is a waste. Indeed, the debtor will be worse off because all of the debtor's nonexempt property will be gone, and the debtor will still owe all of the debts that weren't paid by the trustee.

The justification for the Code's objections to the general discharge and the fairly severe punishment for noncompliance is that the bankruptcy system requires complete and total honesty and disclosure in order to work. Honesty and full disclosure are the two ethical and practical pillars of the system. These overlapping obligations are required of every debtor in exchange for the fresh start. The debtor who hides assets or is dishonest about material obligations is not entitled to a bankruptcy discharge. And, because getting a discharge is the raison d'être of every debtor's entire case, denying a debtor a discharge is tantamount to taking away the entire benefit of the debtor's bankruptcy case. Section 727(a) contains more than ten grounds for denying a debtor a general discharge. This book will cover the five most common grounds only.[1] These are also the grounds that are covered in most bankruptcy textbooks.

A. A Knowing and Fraudulent False Oath in or in Connection with a Bankruptcy Case

Section 727(a)(4) contains one of the commonly used objections to discharge.[2] Under this section, a discharge can be denied if a debtor makes a "knowing and fraudulent false oath in or in connection with the case." The creditor objecting to discharge must prove that the false oath was made in the case, not before the case or in some other capacity. This objection goes to the very heart of the honesty and disclosure requirements. The false oath requirement refers to a statement made under oath, most commonly either in the written bankruptcy disclosure documents (the petition, the statement of affairs, or the schedules of assets and liabilities), or at the creditors' meeting or another bankruptcy court hearing or deposition. The statement must be false, of course, and the debtor must make the oath knowing that it is false. The additional requirement that the oath be fraudulent essentially imposes a materiality requirement. Thus,

1. If the debtor is not an individual, then the debtor does not get a discharge. This means that corporations in a Chapter 7 case do not get a discharge, nor do they need one. They can just cease to exist. Other grounds to deny a discharge include that the debtor presented a false claim, withheld books and records from the trustee or the court, refused to obey an order of the court, invoked the Fifth Amendment against self-incrimination and refused to testify about a material matter even after being granted immunity, or committed any of these acts in a prior bankruptcy case.

2. Don't be misled into thinking that general (or global) discharges are commonly denied, however. Probably less than one-tenth of one percent of all debtors have their global discharge denied.

the creditor must prove that the debtor made (1) a false oath; (2) knowingly; (3) that is material enough to be fraudulent; and (4) that was made in, or in connection with, the case.

QUESTION 1. Peter Pocket has made various errors and omissions during his bankruptcy case. Which of them is most likely to cause his general or global discharge to be denied?

A. Peter listed his home's value at $150,000 but he actually thinks it might be worth more like $200,000.
B. Peter did not disclose the debt he owes to his cable company because he does not want the company to know that he is in bankruptcy.
C. Peter inadvertently failed to disclose that he thinks one of his employees stole money from him and someday hopes to sue the guy for $50,000.
D. Peter did not list an interest in a partnership he owns that is expected to make a great deal of money in the future, but has not made a profit or a distribution so far.

ANALYSIS. Peter does have some problems here, and should not have done any of these things. The question is whether any of these is sufficient to deny his entire bankruptcy discharge. Start any question asking about what is most likely by eliminating the wrong answers. Which of these seem the least problematic?

Be sure and read every word of each answer here. Because the employee suit was left off the petition inadvertently, this is a close case between the cable company nondisclosure and the nondisclosure about the employee suit. The employee suit omission could never be used to deny Peter's discharge because the lack of disclosure was not done knowingly. No mistake, however stupid, can result in the denial of a discharge, if the court determines that it was an honest mistake.

The failure to list the cable company is clearly a knowing false oath, and despite what many debtors believe, the bankruptcy paperwork requires a debtor to disclose all debts to all people, with no exceptions. And, as you learned in the last chapter, this debt to the cable company will not be discharged, and the debtor will be required to pay it despite the bankruptcy under §523(a)(3) because the cable company did not receive notice of the bankruptcy case. On the other hand, what's the big deal? This omission is unlikely to result in denial of the debtor's general discharge because the omission or nondisclosure is not material. Despite this conclusion, it is not a good idea to leave debts off the bankruptcy petition.

It is also unlikely that choice **A**, the undervaluation of the home, would result in denial of Peter's discharge, although the reasons are less obvious.

Knowingly leaving assets off the disclosures is likely to result in denial of a general discharge. However, undervaluing assets, even if done on purpose, rarely results in denial of a discharge. If this were done repeatedly, with many items of the debtor's property, it could result in denial of a discharge, but this would be rare. The reason is that once an asset is listed on the paperwork, the trustee is on notice of its existence. He can question the debtor at the §341 meeting, test the values given against the marketplace, and reach his own conclusions about the value of the item. Remember why the trustee cares about the value of an item. If he thinks it is worth more than what the debtor has claimed it is worth, and that it is worth more than the debtor's allowed exemption in the item, he can sell it and distribute the difference between the exempt amount and the value realized. What is most important is that the asset be disclosed, at least for §727 purposes. A debtor has every incentive to use realistic values on his or her petition because doing otherwise will cause the trustee to look into the value of the item and might eventually result in loss of the item. Once the asset is disclosed, however, undervaluation will rarely result in denial of a discharge.

All that is left, then, is failure to disclose the interest in the partnership, so the correct answer is **D**. If any of these nondisclosures were fatal to Peter's discharge, this would be the one. It looks like he left this property interest off his disclosures knowingly, although that is somewhat unclear. If not, no problem. This example drives home how important it is for the lawyer to ask thorough and pointed questions. If the lawyer did this, this partnership interest should have come up in conversation, and possibly would have been disclosed. Many discharges have been denied for failure to list interests in partnerships and corporations, although the case against Peter would be far stronger if he had failed to list an interest that was currently yielding a profit.

B. Inexplicable Loss of Money

One ground for denial of a discharge is that the debtor has failed to explain satisfactorily a "loss of assets or deficiency of assets to meet the debtor's liabilities." (*See* §727(a)(5).) In essence, this means that the debtor has failed to explain what happened to income or property that he or she seemed to have before the financial trouble began. In one case, $90,000 went missing, and the debtor claimed to have spent it on "wine, women, and song."[3] In another case, a person just lost $20,000. Although he was a big spender and said he carries huge amounts of cash, the court found denial of a discharge justified, given that he had no explanation for where the $20,000 went.[4]

---

3. The court found the story incredulous and denied the debtor's discharge. In re Bahre, 23 B.R. 460 (Bankr. Conn. 1982).
4. In re Reed, 700 F.2d 986 (5th Cir. 1983).

QUESTION 2. The likely rationale for this ground for denial of a discharge is that:

A. people should be more careful with money.
B. the lost money is probably under the mattress.
C. people should be rewarded for keeping good records.
D. bankruptcy is a privilege enjoyed only by those who have learned to deal wisely with money.

ANALYSIS. **A**, **C**, and **D** are variations on the same theme and all are wrong. As a general matter, bankruptcy is available to people who have done really stupid things with money. Frankly, it's there for those who have made mistakes, as well as those who have suffered misfortune. As we previously mentioned, it is for the "honest but unfortunate debtor" (Local Loan v. Hunt, 292 U.S. 234 (1934)). The only explanation for this rule, that you cannot get a bankruptcy discharge if you have inexplicably lost a great deal of money, is that you still have it somewhere. Thus, the correct answer is **B**.

C. Concealment, Loss, Destruction, Falsification, or Mutilation of Records, or a Failure to Keep Records

Section 727(a)(3) makes it grounds for denial of a general discharge to destroy, mutilate, conceal, falsify, or even lose financial records. It is easy to see why a bankruptcy debtor cannot receive a discharge if he or she destroys or hides records. It is a little harder to understand why people are punished for losing their records. The justification for this rule is that every bankruptcy trustee has a right to examine the financial records of his or her debtor, which can only be done if these records are kept and available. There is also a suspicion that if people do not safeguard these records, for whatever reason, they may be trying to hide something. In one famous case, a debtor who lacked candor in the court's eyes claimed that the rubbish man must have taken all his business records, which he was storing in the garage near his trashcan (In re Harron, 31 B.R. 466 (Bankr. D. Conn. 1983)).

Section 727(a)(3) also provides that a failure to keep records can be a ground for denying a discharge. A court is most likely to deny a discharge based on a failure to keep records when there is evidence that the failure was intentional and in contemplation of bankruptcy. Practically speaking, though, courts have held that the record-keeping requirement essentially applies only to businesspeople, and not to the average consumer. The Code itself does not say this, but courts have interpreted the section in this way, perhaps in recognition that average people are not always organized— at least one of the co-authors of this book included!

D. Transfers Made with Intent to Hinder, Delay, or Defraud Creditors

From the state law chapters of this guide, you learned that people are not necessarily free to transfer (or give away) their assets, particularly if doing so will make them insolvent or if they are giving away assets to avoid creditor claims. You learned that a transfer could be a fraudulent transfer and could be avoidable or reversible, if the debtor intended to hinder, delay, or defraud creditors, or even if there were no such intent but the debtor transferred an asset to another person for less than equivalent or fair value. Outright gifts can be undone in this way, as can sales of assets for less than the market value of the item sold.

Fraudulent transfer law stands in odd juxtaposition with another area of debtor-creditor law, referred to as pre-bankruptcy planning. Pre-bankruptcy planning is the process by which a person who is contemplating bankruptcy determines whether he or she is holding assets in a way that takes best advantage of the exemptions allowed under the Bankruptcy Code. For example, let's say that Susie lives in Florida, where she is allowed (both inside and outside bankruptcy) to exempt all the equity or value in a home of any value. Florida does not allow a person to keep any cash from the reach of creditors, however, and Susie has a bank account with $20,000 in it. Susie decides to use the $20,000 in cash to pay down her home mortgage. Now the $20,000 has been converted to home equity, which is exempt. One result of this transaction is that the debtor does not lose the $20,000. The other result is that creditors do not get the $20,000 in her bankruptcy. On its face, this example seems to be a clear fraudulent transfer, since Susie obviously had the actual intent to defraud her creditors when she made the transfer, which was designed to keep her creditors from getting the $20,000. Confusingly, the legislative history of the Bankruptcy Code seems to allow a reasonable amount of pre-bankruptcy planning. In fact, the legislative history goes so far as to say that:

> As under current law, the debtor will be permitted to convert nonexempt property into exempt property before filing a bankruptcy petition. The practice is not fraudulent as to creditors, and permits the debtor to make full use of the exemptions to which he is entitled under the law.[5]

5. H.R. Rep. No. 595, 95th Cong., 1st Sess. 361 (1977).

Some courts have found, however, that the phrase "as under current law," means that if the debtor intends to hinder, delay, or defraud creditors through the transfer, the transfer can be undone despite this language in the legislative history.

In addition to these conflicting signals in these two related areas of the law, a third area of the law draws on the other two and adds to the confusion. Section 727(a)(2) states that a debtor can be denied a general discharge if he or she transfers property of the estate, within a year before the filing or after the filing, "with intent to hinder, delay or defraud a creditor or officer of the court." This is a very serious punishment! Having a transfer reversed or avoided is one thing. Losing one's entire bankruptcy discharge is quite another. Some courts continue to hold that pre-bankruptcy planning is acceptable if it is within reason, while others deny an entire bankruptcy discharge for relatively small transfers done in the spirit of pre-bankruptcy planning.

Some scholars suggest that what matters most is the size of the transfer. In one case, the court denied a discharge for transfers of $700,000 made by a doctor who admitted that he transferred the assets to keep them from creditors. (*See* In re Tveten, 848 F.2d 871 (8th Cir. 1988).) The same court let the discharge go through for farmers who transferred $31,000 for essentially the same reasons. (*See* In re Hanson, 848 F.2d 866 (8th Cir. 1988).) Oddly, another doctor was allowed his discharge after transferring $400,000. (*See* In re Johnson, 880 F.2d 78 (8th Cir. 1989).) These cases certainly do not elucidate the extent to which a debtor can engage in pre-bankruptcy planning.

One thing that is clear in this whole mess, however, is that a debtor needs fraudulent intent in order to be denied a discharge under §727(a)(2). It is not enough to simply transfer assets for less than their fair market value.

QUESTION 3. Don Martin always gives each of his five children $10,000 a year, as part of his overall estate planning. His children have come to rely on these gifts, some of which they use to visit dear old dad. This past year, these gifts, along with large losses in the stock market, caused Don to hit rock bottom. Six months after his last set of gifts, he files for Chapter 7. Can Don's discharge be denied as a result of these gifts?

A. Yes, because the gifts made him insolvent.
B. Yes, because he got nothing in return for the gifts, except a few extra visits with the grandkids.
C. No, because the gifts were not made in an effort to avoid paying creditors.
D. No, because the gifts were part of plan that has been going on for years, and there is no reason why this year should be any different.

ANALYSIS. This one is not too difficult if you refer back to the language of the statute. Although gifts by an insolvent debtor can be recovered by a trustee as a fraudulent transfer, insolvency is irrelevant under the test contained in §727 (a)(2), so **A** is incorrect. Whether he received fair value is also irrelevant as the test here is the actual fraud test in fraudulent transfer law, not any form of constructive fraud. That means that **B** is also incorrect. **C** and **D** are both plausible answers along the same theme, but one is better because it is more specific. The best answer is **C**. Specifically, from what we can tell here, the transfers were not made to keep assets out of creditors' hands but to give the assets to the kids. **D** is proof of **C**, and it is quite good proof that this is not a sudden plan to bilk creditors.

Still, you should find this area a bit slippery. Wasn't Don's overall long-term plan to keep his money in the family and out of the hands of all creditors, including future nursing homes, perhaps? While we hope you learned from the question, doesn't this area of the law just encourage one to lie about the real reasons for doing things?

Let's practice another question.

QUESTION 4. Penny Philanthropist lives on 500 acres of beautiful woodlands, worth approximately $750,000. As it turns out, her land constitutes some of the last habitat for the spotted owl. To pay medical expenses for her sick mother, she obtained a signature (unsecured) loan from her favorite banker at Best Bank for $400,000. She has no income and is beside herself, as Best Bank has obtained a judgment and is threatening to execute on her land. With the endangered birds in mind, she transfers the land and home, by quitclaim deed, to the Nature Conservancy, so that Best Bank cannot take it. After all, she is not sure the bank will protect the birds, and they could become extinct. Not too long thereafter, she files a Chapter 7 bankruptcy petition. Best Bank has objected to her discharge on a number of grounds, including §727(a)(2). Have the elements of §727(a)(2) been met?

A. No, because her only goal was to protect the birds, a laudatory goal.
B. No, because she borrowed the money for a good cause, to help her mother.
C. Yes, because she transferred the land so Best Bank could not have it.
D. No, because Best Bank is equitably estopped from bringing an action against her under these facts.

ANALYSIS. It is not easy to know what to eliminate first here. We suggest you go back to the statutory language. What do you need? A transfer, with intent to delay, hinder, or defraud creditors. Do you have that? **A** says that her only goal was to protect the birds, but is that true? Doesn't she have two goals, or at least one compound goal, namely to protect the birds by keeping the land from Best Bank? **A** is only partially true, as a factual matter. It is not the best answer. **B**, although it pulls at our heartstrings, is absolutely irrelevant to the question, which asks if the elements are met. **D** is also wrong. The question asks if the elements are met, and if there was such an estoppel argument, which there is not, it would not be relevant to whether the underlying elements of the test were met. Here, the answer is **C**, and under the test, Penny can have her discharge denied for her noble efforts.

If nothing else, this example should help you remember this rule easily. Seemingly harsh or unfair results often have that effect on learning. Without taking way too much from that benefit, we will admit that bankruptcy courts are courts of equity. Thus, it is possible that the court will not deny Penny her discharge but will instead just undo the transfer so that Best Bank will not lose its rights in the property. Do keep in mind, however, that just because a transfer can be undone does not mean that a debtor won't lose her discharge as a result of the transfer. All fraudulent transfers can be undone. The loss of a discharge is a different and tougher remedy for the creditor.

QUESTION 5. (CODE READER) Shannon Sharp is a single mom whose only child is Charlie, who is now 30 years old. Charlie is planning to ask his long-time girlfriend, Jane, if she would marry him. Shannon is excited for Charlie and is very fond of Jane. Shannon's only piece of jewelry is the engagement ring that her grandmother left to her, and the ring is worth about $4,000. Shannon is planning to file Chapter 7 bankruptcy next week because her former business partner, Barbara Reed, got a judgment against Shannon a few days ago for $200,000 in a breach of contract dispute. Charlie doesn't know about his mom's planned bankruptcy when he asks her if he can give the engagement ring to Jane tonight when he proposes to her. Shannon tells him yes for two reasons: first, because she really does like Jane; and second, because she would like nothing better than to keep Barbara from getting that ring when Shannon files for bankruptcy next week. Unbeknownst to Shannon, her state has a $5,000 exemption for jewelry. After Shannon files for bankruptcy next week and all of these facts come to light, should the court deny Shannon's Chapter 7 discharge?

A. Yes, because Shannon permitted Charlie to transfer the ring while Shannon had the intent to hinder, delay, or defraud Barbara.

B. No, because Shannon did not actually transfer the ring herself.

C. No, because a big part of Shannon's motivation for allowing Charlie to transfer the ring had nothing to do with defrauding Barbara.

D. No, because Shannon would have been able to fully exempt the ring anyway in bankruptcy, so Barbara was not hurt by the transfer.

ANALYSIS. The correct answer is **A**. Before we explain why, let us walk through each of the three wrong answers to see why they are wrong. Choice **B** is wrong because the language of §727(a)(2) is clear that it is enough that the debtor "permitted" property of the debtor to be transferred with the requisite intent in order for that subsection to be satisfied; the debtor herself does not have to do the transferring. Answer **C** is wrong because it doesn't matter whether the debtor has other reasons for wanting to make the fraudulent transfer as long as one of the debtor's intentions in making or permitting the transfer is to hinder, delay, or defraud creditors. Choice **D** is wrong because the language of §727(a)(2) simply requires that the property transferred be "property of the debtor." It does not say that the property must be "nonexempt." Even still, it might seem that a debtor's transfer of exempt property will never hurt creditors. However, whenever a debtor transfers exempt property for nothing or for less than fair value, that means that the debtor is now in a position to convert nonexempt property into property that will qualify for the exemption category of the exempt property that was given away. In that way, creditors can indeed be adversely affected by a debtor's give-away of exempt property. Now that you recognize why all three of the other choices are wrong, you can see why **A** is the correct answer.

E. Prior Chapter 7 Discharge Within Past Eight (or Six) Years

You'll often hear people say that you can only file for bankruptcy once every six, seven, or eight years.[6] Actually, you can file as often as you like, but if you received a Chapter 7 discharge during the past eight years, you cannot receive another one. Because the discharge is the main purpose of the case, the common lore is more or less true. A discharge is available only once every eight years in a Chapter 7 or a Chapter 11 case. *See* §727(a)(8). In a Chapter 13 or a Chapter 12 case, the period is six years. Moreover, in a Chapter 12 or 13 case, a debtor may be able to get a second discharge within the six-year period, if he or she paid 100 percent of the allowed unsecured claims in the prior case (not much of a discharge) or if the debtor paid 70 percent or more of such claims, used his or her best efforts to pay creditors in the prior case, and proposed the prior plan in good faith. (*See* 11 U.S.C. §727(a)(9).)

Other than the failure to attend the debt management course mentioned in the next section, the eight-year bar to a discharge is the only ground for

6. Some people incorrectly claim that you can only file once every six years, which was the rule from 1978 until 2005. Others claim that you can only file once every seven years, which was the rule under the old Bankruptcy Act.

denial of a global discharge that does not involve a bad deed. There are no lies, no hidden assets, no evil intentions required. For whatever reason, Congress merely decided that bankruptcy was something one could only avail oneself of once in a while.

The eight-year rule has an interesting effect. Some lenders, especially used car dealers and small loan lenders, jump at the chance to lend to someone who has just filed a bankruptcy petition because they know the debtor cannot get a discharge for eight years. Have you seen advertisements that offer loans to debtors who have filed a bankruptcy petition? This is the reason! Discover Credit Cards even sends debtors a congratulatory greeting card on their discharge, made especially for Discover by Hallmark! Who knew bankruptcy debtors could be such good credit risks?

F. Failure to Complete the Debt Management Course Under §727(a)(11)

Section 727(a)(11) now requires the debtor to complete an instructional course regarding personal financial management before receiving a discharge under Chapter 7. What is it? It is unclear exactly what such a course must entail, but clear that this is a more extensive course than the credit briefing required under §109(h)(1). It also appears there are no hardship exceptions to completion of the debt management course.

G. The Closer: Chapters 13, 14, and 15 (CODE READER)

You're working as a clerk for a law firm that does not know much about bankruptcy. The Boss, who specializes in construction litigation, has asked you to look through some files and tell him whether or not certain ***debts*** will be discharged (under §523) or whether certain ***debtors*** will receive a general discharge (under §727) in each case. He has asked you to put the files in order, with the ones most likely to be discharged or to receive a discharge on top and the ones in which the claims or the debtors are least likely to be discharged on the bottom, with the uncertain cases in between. He has also asked you to write the Code section on which you base your conclusion on the outside of each file. All of the cases are Chapter 7 cases. The files are as follows:

1. The general discharge of McCafferty Corporation.
2. The general discharge of a debtor whose ex-wife has objected to his bankruptcy discharge on the basis that he is hiding things.
3. The discharge of an allowed secured claim of a lender holding a purchase money security interest in a refrigerator.
4. The discharge of claims for deposits held by customers of an individual debtor who does construction work.

The files should be in the following order (from top to bottom):

A. 1, 2, 3, 4.
B. 1, 4, 2, 3.
C. 4, 3, 2, 1.
D. 4, 3, with 1 and 2 tied.

ANALYSIS. We need to go through these one by one, as this is a complicated question. Starting with **1**, McCafferty Corporation cannot receive the discharge pursuant to the provisions of §727(a)(1). As a result, this file should go on the bottom of the pile with 727(a)(1) written on top. Corporations do not receive Chapter 7 discharges, as the Code provides that the court should not grant a discharge unless the debtor is an individual. Looking at **2**, the case in which the ex-wife has objected to her husband's discharge based on the fact that he is hiding things, there is a real possibility that the debtor could lose his entire discharge if the claims made in this particular case are proven. The relevant Code section is 727(a)(4), which would deny the debtor his entire discharge, if proven. Consequently, this one should go in the middle of the pile for now. It is not clear that this gentleman will lose his discharge, but it's possible that he might.

Looking at **3**, the claims for the lender who holds a purchase money security interest on the refrigerator, this claim should go very close to the bottom of the list, as there is no chance that the lender who holds an allowed secured claim on the refrigerator is going to lose its secured claim in the bankruptcy. Secured claims do not get discharged in bankruptcy, and probably the most relevant Code section for this principle is 507(a). Both **1** and **2** will never be discharged and appear to be tied for the bottom of the pile.

Now let's look at the claims for the deposits of customers of the individual debtor who does construction. If you look at §§523 and 727, you will see that there is no special nondischargeability status given to claims like this. Consequently, it is very likely that these claims will be discharged and choice 4 should be at the top of the pile. The fact that deposit claims get special priority under §507(a)(6) may have confused you. However, this is not the same as being nondischargeable. Thus, the correct answer is **D**.

Martin's and Keating's Picks

1. Question 1	**D**
2. Question 2	**B**
3. Question 3	**C**
4. Question 4	**C**
5. Question 5	**A**
The Closer: Chapters 13, 14, and 15	**D**

16

Keeping Secured Property in a Chapter 7 Case

OVERVIEW

A. Redemption

B. Reaffirmation: When Is It Necessary or Advisable?

1. General principles of reaffirmation
2. The formal requirements of reaffirmation
3. When is reaffirmation necessary? The "keep and pay" option

C. The Closer: Chapter 16

Martin's and Keating's Picks

As we have said before, Chapter 7 rarely cures problems flowing from drastically past-due payments to secured creditors. Chapter 13 offers much better options for dealing with past-due secured debt on property that the debtor would like to keep.

In a Chapter 7 case, however, the debtor does have at least two — and in some jurisdictions, three — options for keeping property that is the subject of a security interest. The three options are: (1) redemption (essentially paying the value of the property in cash to the secured party and thus extinguishing the security interest); (2) reaffirmation (essentially agreeing to honor the original loan agreement and pay off the whole loan as promised, including interest and penalties that are due, despite the bankruptcy);[1] or (3) simply keeping the payments current without agreeing to all of the loan conditions. The first two options are specifically allowed in the Code and the third (which is sometimes called "keep and pay," "ride through," or the "fourth option")[2] is court-created.

1. Reaffirmation essentially allows the debtor and the creditor to work out new terms if they choose. In our experience, most creditors simply ask the debtor to sign the prior loan agreement again.

2. It is actually called the fourth, not the third, option, because another option for dealing with secured debt is to give back the collateral. Because that is the third option (one we would not highlight in a discussion of how to keep the collateral), keeping the payments current and not signing a reaffirmation agreement is called the fourth option.

Some jurisdictions allow only the first two options. Moreover, the 2005 amendments attempted to eliminate the so-called fourth option, although it is not clear that this goal was accomplished.

A. Redemption

The first option we'll discuss is redemption. The name of this remedy has religious connotations and sounds so cleansing, but actually, all redemption means is that if the debtor has cash, the debtor can buy the secured property out from under the security interest for the lesser of the loan amount or the value of the property. This option is available to the debtor for any property used for personal, farm, or household purposes. The debtor must pay the redemption price in cash up front, however—a large disincentive for most cash-starved debtors.

The big benefit, if the debtor can come up with the cash, is being able to buy the property at a discount because it has depreciated. Needless to say, redemption is most helpful when the value of the property is far less than the loan amount. Redemption allows the debtor to buy depreciated property at a deep discount as compared to what he or she would otherwise pay over time to keep the property. If the property has not depreciated and the loan amount is lower than the value of the property, then there is little benefit to redemption.[3]

QUESTION 1. You just bought a huge stereo/TV entertainment center and charged it. It cost $5,000. You made a payment but then fell behind, and interest continued to accrue. The balance is now $5,300. The store you bought it from will give you $1,800 for it. There are no other offers on it. The big advantage of redemption to you is:

A. you will not have to pay the secured creditor.
B. you can give the stereo/TV back without any repercussions.
C. you can get an entertainment center for $1,800, even though the current balance on that entertainment center is $5,300.
D. you can pay for the system in regular monthly installments and then give it up later if you don't want it anymore, and not have to pay the deficiency.

ANALYSIS. The answer is **C** as discussed below, but let's see why the others are wrong. **A** is not the answer. **A** is never the answer. Secured creditors

3. If the redeemed property is worth less than the claim amount, the rest of the secured party's claim becomes an unsecured claim, which is entitled to an unsecured distribution if there is one.

are special. They are formidable. They have property interests. They always must be paid. The questions are always when and how much, unless the debtor chooses to give back the collateral. That is the option offered in **B**. The statement made in **B** is 100 percent true, if stated by itself, without the prefix to the question. A debtor is always free to give the property back in a Chapter 7 case and not have to pay the huge deficiency of $3,500. This really is a huge benefit, because despite what many people seem to think, giving back the property outside bankruptcy will not extinguish the debt and the debtor will still have to pay the rest. In bankruptcy, the deficiency gets discharged after it is paid at the rate of other unsecured creditors in the case, which is usually zero. Choice **B** is still incorrect, however, because this is not a benefit of redemption. In fact, this option has nothing to do with redemption.

D also has nothing to do with redemption. Choice **D** is the big benefit of the "fourth option," or the "keep and pay" option. You can keep the secured creditor's collateral and give it back later, without having to pay the deficiency.

The answer is choice **C** and it is quite a big advantage. Redemption allows you to get the entertainment center for its current value, $1,800.

QUESTION 2. What is the biggest disadvantage to redemption?

A. Some courts do not allow it.
B. Most debtors have no cash with which to redeem, and the cash must be paid now.
C. The debtor has to pay full price for the property being redeemed.
D. It requires the debtor to commit to making payments far into the future.

ANALYSIS. The clear winner here is **B**. Think about it. How many bankruptcy debtors have enough cash to come up with the value of their property? Unless it is extremely low in value, as is often the case with furniture, for example, most debtors can't afford to pay even the value of their collateral. Coming up with this cash is the biggest disadvantage of redemption because to redeem, the debtor has to pay the whole amount due in cash immediately. That's the trade-off for being allowed to pay what is in most cases a greatly reduced price for the goods.

C is incorrect. At least in most cases, the beauty of redemption is that the debtor does not have to pay the full price for the goods. Redemption allows the debtor to purchase the property for the lesser of the value or the loan amount. Most things depreciate, allowing for a big discount. Again, although most people don't have the cash to redeem, if they can come up with the cash, the beauty is in not having to pay full price.

A is incorrect because the Bankruptcy Code requires courts to allow redemption. Not all courts permit "ride through" or "keep and pay," an option we'll be discussing later, but §722 states explicitly that the debtor may redeem property by "paying the holder of such lien the allowed secured claim of such holder" (11 U.S.C. §722). You'll recall from Chapter 11 that an allowed secured claim is defined to be only as large as the value of the collateral. Thus, all courts are required to allow redemption.

D is also wrong because all the payments are made up front. There are no payments into the future. This option alludes to the huge disadvantage of the reaffirmation option, which we will discuss shortly.

QUESTION 3. Both Jack and John bought beautiful customized, decked-out Chevy Camaros from a local dealer 10 years ago for $16,000. John abused the car and it is now worth $6,000. Jack took amazing care of his and his is now worth $10,000. They are both now in Chapter 7 and would like to redeem their vehicles. How much will this cost?

A. It will cost each $10,000, the value of a well-taken-care-of car.
B. It will cost Jack $10,000 and John $6,000.
C. It will cost each $6,000.
D. Neither can redeem.

ANALYSIS. The answer here is **B**, because each of the two gentlemen must pay the value of his own car to redeem. Now, this could strike you as a bit unfair. In fact, it seems downright criminal on some level that the person who failed to take good care of someone else's collateral can now turn around and buy it for less as a result of not taking care of it. It almost makes you wonder if the creditor might have some other recourse against Jack, an issue discussed in Chapter 21, Question 7.

It also seems a bit unfair towards John, right? Now he has to pay almost twice as much because he did take care of the car. Although it may seem unfair, do you think it really is? On at least one level it is perfectly fair. While John is paying more, he is also getting a better car that is worth what he is paying for it. Each is paying the value of what he is getting in return.

Another requirement for a debtor who wishes to exercise redemption rights under §722 is that either the debtor must exempt the property the debtor seeks to redeem or the trustee must abandon that property. The trustee will only abandon the property if there is no value in the property for the estate. For example, imagine that the property is worth $5,000 but a purchase-money secured lender is still owed $7,000 against the property. In that case, the trustee would abandon the property under §554 because the debtor has no equity in the property for the estate to inherit.

By contrast, imagine a case where the property is worth $7,000 but the secured lender is owed just $5,000. In that case, the trustee would not abandon the property in which the debtor has $2,000 worth of equity that the trustee might be able to sell for the benefit of the estate. However, in this second case, perhaps the debtor has an exemption that it can claim in the $2,000 of equity. If the debtor did have such an exemption and exempted its $2,000 in equity, then the debtor would be eligible to redeem the property by paying $5,000 to the secured lender.

Suppose that in the second situation, where the property was worth $7,000 and the secured creditor was owed just $5,000, the property was not subject to an exemption for the debtor. Could the debtor still redeem the property under §722? Yes, but only if the debtor had enough cash to "buy" the $2,000 of equity back from the estate by paying that amount to the trustee, and then paying $5,000 to the secured creditor to redeem the remainder.

QUESTION 4. Debbie Debtor buys a new car on secured credit from Car Dealer. The car costs $28,000 brand-new but is now worth just $17,000 one year following her purchase. Debbie lives in a state that has a $5,000 automobile exemption. Car Dealer is still owed $21,000 on the car loan. If Debbie files Chapter 7 bankruptcy today, will she be able to redeem her car?

A. Yes, for $12,000 after she exempts the car to the extent of $5,000.
B. Yes, for $17,000 after the trustee abandons the car.
C. Yes, for $21,000 after the trustee abandons the car.
D. No, because this car is too valuable for the trustee to abandon, and Debbie's exemption isn't large enough to cover the value of the car.

ANALYSIS. The correct answer is **B**. Before we see why that is the right answer, let's eliminate the other three choices first. The reason that **A** is wrong is that Debbie's exemption under state law is subordinate to her secured creditor's claim, which in this case covers the entire value of her car. Nor is this a case where §522(f)'s lien-avoidance provision will come to the rescue because Car Dealer's secured loan is a purchase-money loan and a car does not fit within the relevant category of §522(f)(1)(B) goods anyway. Answer **C** is wrong because after the trustee abandons Debbie's car, Debbie will only have to pay the current value of the car to redeem it under §722 rather than the full amount still owing to her secured creditor. Choice **D** is wrong because no matter how valuable the car is, the trustee only inherits whatever equity that the debtor has in the car, which is zero in this case due to the secured creditor's claim. Therefore, the trustee will indeed abandon the car here under §554 as having "inconsequential value and benefit to the estate." Answer **B** is correct because after the trustee abandons the car, Debbie will simply need to pay $17,000, the current value of the car, to Car Dealer in order to redeem the car.

QUESTION 5. Same facts as Question 4, except now assume that the car's value at the time of Debbie's Chapter 7 filing is $23,000 rather than $17,000. Now will Debbie be able to redeem her car in bankruptcy?

A. Yes, for $23,000 after the trustee abandons the car.
B. Yes, for $23,000 after Debbie exempts her equity in the car.
C. Yes, for $21,000 after the trustee abandons the car.
D. Yes, for $21,000 after Debbie exempts her equity in the car.

ANALYSIS. The correct answer is **D**. Remember that a debtor's exemption is always subordinate to a secured creditor's claim on the exempt property. In this case, the property is worth $23,000 and the secured creditor is owed $21,000, so that means that Debbie has $2,000 worth of equity in the car when she files her Chapter 7 bankruptcy. Because Debbie's state has a $5,000 automobile exemption, she can fully exempt her $2,000 equity in the car and qualify for the right to redeem the car. In order to redeem the car, she would pay Car Dealer the amount of its allowed secured claim, which here is $21,000, the remaining balance on the loan. Choice **A** is wrong for two reasons: first, because the trustee would not abandon Debbie's car given that Debbie has $2,000 worth of equity in the car that she must use her exemptions on; and second, because Debbie would only need to pay Car Dealer the amount of Car Dealer's allowed secured claim, which is $21,000 rather than $23,000. Answer **B** is wrong because it says that Debbie must pay $23,000 rather than $21,000 to redeem. And **C** is wrong because it says that the trustee would abandon the car.

QUESTION 6. Same facts as Question 4, except now assume that the car's value at the time of Debbie's Chapter 7 filing is $27,000 rather than $23,000. Now will Debbie be able to redeem her car in bankruptcy?

A. No, because she can no longer exempt the car, and the trustee will not abandon the car.
B. Yes, for $22,000 after she exempts her equity in the car.
C. Yes, for $21,000 after the trustee abandons the car.
D. Yes, for $21,000, but only after she exempts the car and pays the trustee $1,000 to buy back the remaining equity in the car to which the estate would otherwise be entitled.

ANALYSIS. This is a tricky one. The correct answer is **D**, but let's walk through the other choices first. Answer **A** is a reasonable choice (but not the best answer, see below) since it is true that Debbie can no longer fully exempt her equity in this car, which is now $6,000 (the difference between the car's current value of $27,000 and the $21,000 which Car Dealer is still owed on the car loan). It is also true that the trustee will not abandon this car because even after Debbie exercises her $5,000 exemption in the car, there is still $1,000 worth of value remaining beyond her exemption that her bankruptcy estate would inherit from her. Choice **B** is wrong because even though the difference between the car's value and her $5,000 exemption is $22,000, her cost of redemption (which is paid to the secured creditor) should still not exceed what the secured creditor is owed, which here is only $21,000. Answer **C** is wrong because as explained above, the trustee will not abandon the car here when there is $1,000 of equity in the car for the estate even after subtracting the secured creditor's claim and the debtor's exemption from the current value of the car. That leaves **D**, which is the best answer even though you won't see a specific reference in §722 to this situation. What is happening here is that the debtor is paying the trustee the value of the equity that the estate would otherwise inherit from the property that the debtor wishes to redeem. The trustee would be happy to get the $1,000 directly from the debtor rather than doing a sale of the car to a third party for $27,000 and then having to distribute the first $21,000 to the secured creditor and the second $5,000 to the debtor.

B. Reaffirmation: When Is It Necessary or Advisable?

Reaffirmation is another option for keeping collateral subject to a security interest. Just so you know, unsecured debts can be reaffirmed as well, although this is seldom a good idea.

1. General principles of reaffirmation

Reaffirmation is a process by which the debtor agrees to pay a loan or debt, rather than having it discharged in his or her bankruptcy case. In essence, it is a voluntary waiver of the discharge of a particular debt. At its most basic, a reaffirmation agreement is an agreement between the debtor and the creditor that a debt that otherwise would be discharged will be repaid. The agreement can contain new terms of repayment but most that we have seen simply restate the original loan terms and ask the debtor to agree to pay as originally agreed, with all interest, fees, due dates, and so on.

2. The formal requirements of reaffirmation

Section 524 contains the rules for reaffirmation, which require that reaffirmation occur before the discharge in the case, that a written reaffirmation agreement be filed with the court, that the debtor's attorney certify that the reaffirmation will not impose an undue hardship on the debtor, that the agreement state clearly that reaffirmation is not required and is voluntary on the part of the debtor, and also that the debtor be given 60 days to revoke the reaffirmation agreement. If the debt is unsecured, the attorney also must certify that reaffirmation is in the debtor's best interest. These rules are stringent because in the past, some creditors have abused the reaffirmation process, by trying to cajole the debtor into reaffirming, and by trying to achieve reaffirmation without the court's knowledge or blessing.

The requirement that a debtor who is represented by counsel have counsel certify that the reaffirmation does not impose an undue hardship on the debtor is designed to make lawyers think first before condoning reaffirmation. Any reaffirmation will impair the fresh start, and it is a big deal to sign a certification making this statement. This is particularly true if the debt being reaffirmed is unsecured, in which case the attorney must find the agreement to be in the debtor's best interest. In cases in which an attorney does not represent the debtor, the court itself sets a hearing to decide whether to approve the agreement. The agreement will be approved only if the court finds that the agreement will not be an undue hardship for the debtor and also finds it to be in the debtor's best interest to sign the agreement.

Some courts allow unrepresented debtors to file reaffirmation agreements pro se, so that the court can make the determination about whether the agreement creates an undue hardship for the debtor.

Section 524(k), (l), and (m) now contain a tremendous number of conditions for reaffirmation. The creditor seeking to have his or her debts reaffirmed must now give long "truth-in-lending" type disclosures to the debtor before procuring the reaffirmation agreement. Like most long disclosures, these are not likely to be read and thus will be unlikely to curb abuses.

In a famous case involving Sears, it was discovered that Sears was deliberately not filing reaffirmation agreements with the court because it feared that the court would not approve the agreements (In re Latanowitch, 207 B.R. 326 (Bankr. D. Mass. 1997)). In a two-year period, in the District of Massachusetts alone, Sears knowingly failed to file reaffirmation agreements that it had solicited from unrepresented debtors in over 2,700 cases. This case and its progeny cost Sears over $400 million in settlements, highlighting the importance of following the reaffirmation rules.

3. *When is reaffirmation necessary? The "keep and pay" option*

Many creditors send reaffirmation agreements to debtors, or if the debtors are represented, to their counsel. A surprisingly large number of reaffirmation agreements are executed. Why? According to Professors Charles Tabb and Ralph Brubaker, there are four main reasons: (1) to allow the debtor to keep collateral that the creditor could otherwise repossess without the agreement; (2) to settle litigation; (3) to protect a co-obligor on the debt (such as a guarantor); or (4) for personal reasons, such as to preserve a personal relationship with a creditor.[4] An additional reason is that, in some jurisdictions and under some readings of the Code, the Bankruptcy Court requires the debtor to sign the agreement in order to keep the secured party's collateral.

Keeping the property while continuing to make payments without signing a reaffirmation agreement is the "ride through" or "keep and pay" option. The Code itself now purports to eliminate the "keep and pay" option. However, even if the Code itself no longer allows "ride through" (a fact that is still unclear), the creditor can agree to allow the debtor to simply continue paying on the loan as promised without a reaffirmation agreement. Of course, the creditor would almost always prefer to get a formal reaffirmation agreement but may be willing to accept payments without such an agreement.

The debtor need not reaffirm a real estate loan but can instead "keep and pay." Sections 521(a)(6) and 362(h) refer specifically to personal property loans, and section 524(j) seems to contemplate "ride through" on real estate loans. A recent bankruptcy case holding that a debtor can "ride through" on a real estate loan and need not reaffirm is In re Law, 421 B.R. 735 (Bankr. W.D. Pa. 2010). *See also* In re Hart, 402 B.R. 78 (Bankr. D. Del. 2009) and In re Bennet, 2006 WL 1540842 (Bankr. M.D.N.C. 2006).

Congress wanted to eliminate "ride through" or "keep and pay" because it was seen as unfair to allow the debtor to keep collateral while it depreciates without deciding whether to pay the debt off or not. It leaves the risk of depreciation with the secured party while the debtor enjoys the collateral. Even if courts ultimately decide to eliminate it for personal property, please remember that "keep and pay" is still available for real estate collateral because the 2005 Code amendments purporting to limit the fourth option apply only to personal property. (*See* 11 U.S.C. §521(a)(6).)

QUESTION 7. The biggest disadvantage to reaffirmation is that:

A. it makes the debtor look silly.
B. it makes the debtor's attorney look irresponsible.
C. it requires that the debtor pay back a debt that would otherwise be dischargeable.
D. it allows the debtor to keep property that he or she would otherwise have to return to the creditor.

ANALYSIS. The answer here is **C**: reaffirmation would require the debtor to pay back a debt that would otherwise be discharged. In the case of unsecured debt, it is hard to justify such a decision and courts seriously frown on such

4. Tabb and Brubaker, Bankruptcy Law Principles, Policies, and Practices (Lexis Nexis 2015).

reaffirmations. The debtor can always voluntarily repay whatever debts he or she chooses to repay without formally reaffirming, which should take care of mending personal relationships. The debtor can even promise to pay the debt in writing but not file it with the court, which would make the promise a moral one, but not a legally binding one. This is more comfortable for the attorney because it eliminates the lawyer's need to certify that the reaffirmation is in the debtor's best interest. (*See* 11 U.S.C. §524(d)(2).)

While no reaffirmation agreement makes the debtor look irresponsible (after all, most debtors do not even understand the agreements that creditors send), they can make the lawyer look bad. Thus, **A** is incorrect and **B** (it makes the lawyer look irresponsible) is true, but is simply not as large a disadvantage as **C** (the debtor now has to pay back the whole debt). **D** says that the biggest disadvantage to reaffirmation is that it "allows the debtor to keep property that he or she would otherwise have to return to the creditor." We hope that you were able to eliminate **D** rather promptly. If it were necessary for the debtor to reaffirm in order to keep the collateral, getting to keep the collateral would be an advantage, not a disadvantage, to reaffirmation. Do keep in mind that **D** is not even accurate in some places. It is not always necessary to reaffirm to keep a creditor's collateral. In some jurisdictions it is enough to just keep the payments current.

QUESTION 8. The most compelling reason to think that the "keep and pay" option is unfair to the secured creditor is that:

A. the court might never find out about the arrangement.
B. the creditor could receive the goods back long after the bankruptcy case is over, and after the collateral is greatly depreciated, and be unable at that time to pursue its deficiency claim.
C. the creditor might prefer repossession.
D. the creditor will not know its rights up front.

ANALYSIS. This question requires you to pick the best answer among a few that could be correct. It is easiest to find bad answers and eliminate them first here. **A** seems to be the worst answer. What difference does it make if the court knows about the arrangement? It is in the debtor's best interest to get to keep the collateral as long as he or she wants to, without making a commitment to reaffirm, and without having to worry about a future deficiency claim. It doesn't seem that the court in a Chapter 7 case has much interest in that issue. The court is there to protect the debtor in a reaffirmation context and such protection is not needed in a "keep and pay" scenario.

C is also not too relevant, but we guess it could be correct. The decision about what to do about the collateral is generally the debtor's decision to make here. The creditor may prefer repossession but that's not the best reason why "keep and pay" is unfair. The best answer is **B**. What if the collateral really depreciates while the debtor is using it and then the debtor decides to return it? As a general policy matter, many people think we should require bankruptcy debtors to either pay for collateral up front (redemption) or to commit to paying it over time (such as in a Chapter 13 plan). This option leaves all of the risk of depreciation with the creditor. **D** is also a good answer but does not seem to be as much of a fairness issue as the depreciation issue. If you chose either **B** or **D**, you probably understand this quite well.

C. The Closer: Chapter 16

This section contains a series of three closers, drawn from this chapter as well as Chapter 9, which covers exemptions. Sometimes bankruptcy topics intersect in mysterious ways, and this section demonstrates this fact. You may need to briefly look back to Chapter 9. Good luck!

(1) Fred loaned Nathalie $10,000, interest-free, and Nathalie agreed to pay the loan back at $1,000 a month. The payments were to start in September of 2025. At the time of the loan, Fred took a security interest in Nathalie's new giant-screen television, which she had purchased from Ballio's on her credit card. She paid $5,600 for the television, and Ballio's now says it would pay $3,200 for it if it were to buy it used. Nathalie has made no payments to Fred and Fred just found out that she has filed a Chapter 7 bankruptcy. If you are representing Nathalie, which of the following would be most beneficial for her, assuming she wants to keep the TV?

A. Tell her it is most beneficial to give it to Fred in satisfaction of his debt. No one who is in bankruptcy needs a giant-screen TV and it is not exempt anyway.
B. Tell her to redeem the TV by paying Fred $3,200 in cash, assuming she has that cash available to her.
C. Tell her to reaffirm the debt to Fred and agree to pay him the $10,000 because this is probably the only way to get to keep the TV.
D. Tell her to avoid the lien on the TV under §522(f), with your help, assuming she meets all of the requirements.

ANALYSIS. This question could be used to test exemptions, redemption, and reaffirmation, not to mention client counseling and ethics. Your client has told you that she wants the TV. Is it your place to tell her that she does not deserve it? That she does not need it? Some would say yes and some would say no. But the question does not tell us whether or not the TV is exempt, so **A** is incorrect. This choice says the TV is not exempt, but if it is fully encumbered and the lien cannot be avoided, there is no need to exempt it. There is no equity.

B sounds like a good answer — better than the last one, at least. It accurately describes the financial ramifications of redemption. Nathalie would need to pay the fair market value for the TV in immediate cash and that would allow her to keep the TV. **B** says she has the cash. If this property were redeemed, Fred would get an unsecured claim in her bankruptcy for the $6,400. **B** is a good answer, although a better one is still to come.

We hope nobody chose **C**. Reaffirmation is almost always lame-brained, and here it is beyond silly. Who would pay $10,000 for a $3,200 TV? Lots of clients will try, believe me. Why? They have no cash to redeem and they are convinced they will never be offered another nice thing for the rest of their lives. To allow redemption, you, the lawyer, have to sign papers saying this will not be a burden to your client! DON'T DO IT!

The monkey wrench in the question is choice **D**. Lien avoidance will allow the debtor to keep a piece of personal property used primarily for personal, farm, or household use, if the property would be exempt and if the lien interferes with the exemption. We do not know if the property is fully exempt, but if it is, as choice **D** states (that all of the requirements of lien avoidance are met), then it is far more beneficial to Nathalie to avoid the lien under §522(f). She would get to keep the TV and would not have to pay Fred anything for it. Poor Fred! The correct answer here is **D**.

(2) (CODE READER, §522(f).)

Nathalie can only avoid this lien if:

A. the TV is not a luxury item.
B. Fred consents to having his lien avoided.
C. the TV is used for business purposes.
D. the TV is exempt.

ANALYSIS. Read §522(f). Liens that interfere with an exemption (property that is fully exempt), can be avoided if the property is used primarily for personal, farm, or household use. Luxury has nothing to do with it, nor do we need Fred's consent. Few liens could be avoided if we did. Thus, the answer is **D**.

(3) Very few security interests in TVs can be avoided. Why is this one different from most?

A. Fred, the secured party here, is an individual rather than a store.
B. Fred's lien is not a purchase money security interest.
C. This TV is used primarily for household use and most are used in businesses.
D. This TV is exempt.

ANALYSIS. Only nonpossessory, non-purchase-money security interests in household goods can be avoided. We find it fairly unlikely that there are many non-purchase-money security interests in TVs out there. We would imagine that most of the liens in TVs arise out of their purchase. Thus, the answer is **B**. As for **A**, it matters not that Fred is an individual, except as it bears on the fact that he does not normally sell TVs (*see* prior sentence). We couldn't guess whether most TVs are exempt, so **D** is not a great answer, and **C**? Don't forget to use your common sense. The statement in **C** is incorrect, right? Most TVs are not used in business. The correct answer is **B**.

Martin's and Keating's Picks

1. Question 1	**C**
2. Question 2	**B**
3. Question 3	**B**
4. Question 4	**B**
5. Question 5	**D**
6. Question 6	**D**
7. Question 7	**C**
8. Question 8	**B**

The Closer: Chapter 16

Question 1	**D**
Question 2	**D**
Question 3	**B**

17

Dismissal

OVERVIEW
A. Dismissal for Failure to Cooperate in the Case
B. Dismissal Under the Means Test: The New Issue in Consumer Bankruptcy
C. Dismissal for Abuse of Chapter 7: The Old Standard and the New Means Test
   1. The old test
   2. The new test for abuse under §707(b): The means test
      a. Income
      b. Allowable expenses
      c. Figuring out what's left
      d. How can the debtor rebut the presumption?
Martin's and Keating's Picks

While one alternative to getting a bankruptcy discharge is having a debtor's global discharge denied under §727 (or having an individual debt deemed nondischargeable), and another is having a debtor's discharge limited in some piecemeal ways under §523(a), yet another alternative to discharge is having the case dismissed under §707.

A. Dismissal for Failure to Cooperate in the Case

Again, the debtor is usually free to dismiss his or her own case, as long as doing so will not harm creditors.[1] A debtor might choose to do so because he or she can now, unexpectedly, sell his or her assets for more than the existing debts.

1. If the debtor is dismissing his or her case because he or she hid assets and got caught, or because other assets were discovered that could be used to pay creditors, most courts will not allow a voluntary dismissal.

More likely though, if dismissal is sought, it is the case trustee who is requesting dismissal, because the debtor has failed to do what is required during the bankruptcy proceeding. The debtor is required to appear at the Section 341 hearing and to accurately fill out the disclosure documents (discussed more fully in Chapter 6), to get a discharge. There are no exceptions as this is the price the debtor pays for the discharge.

Most trustee-generated dismissal motions request dismissal because the debtor has failed to file the disclosure documents in the case, to appear at the §341 hearing, to produce requested information or documents to the trustee, or to comply with an order of the court in the case. If the case gets dismissed, the case disappears and the debtor gets no benefit from it.

QUESTION 1. Appearing at a §341 First Meeting of Creditors:

1. is required of all debtors who would like to obtain a bankruptcy discharge.
2. is required unless the debtor has a good excuse for not attending the meeting.
3. allows creditors to question the debtor about how he or she got into this mess.
4. is required of all creditors who would like to have their claims paid.

A. 1 and 2 only.
B. 1 and 3 only.
C. 3 and 4 only.
D. All of the above.

ANALYSIS. Most debtors in bankruptcy are looking for just one thing, a discharge. **1** is correct, namely that a debtor must appear at this meeting if he is to have his claims discharged. In one case involving a missing debtor, as well as one involving an agoraphobic,[2] the courts required attendance at the meeting, regardless of the hardship it would impose on the debtor, because this is one of the rules of the game. It goes along with full disclosure. Thus, statement **2** is incorrect. **3** is a correct statement, however, as this is the purpose of the §341 meeting, to allow creditors to ask questions. For the most part, creditors do not go to this meeting, but that doesn't change the obligations here. **4** is incorrect (and even off the wall in some respects). In most consumer cases, claims will not be paid, but discharged instead, because there are no nonexempt assets from which to pay claims. Even where there are assets, however,

2. A person who fears open spaces, or contact with the outside world, who does not normally leave the house.

payment bears no relationship to attending this meeting. Thus, the correct answer is **B**: choices **1** and **3**.

As set out in Chapter 6, failure to produce all the correct paperwork can result in dismissal of a debtor's case. Specifically, if all of the paperwork requirements are not complied with by day 45 of the case, dismissal of the case is deemed automatic. Here are the specifics:

- Tax returns for the most recent year. (*See* 11 U.S.C. §521(e)(2)(A)(I).) This can be a major problem where spouses are separated or divorced and the nondebtor spouse has possession of the tax return.
- A certificate of credit counseling (this is actually called a credit briefing in §109(h)(1)). (*See* 11 U.S.C. §521(b)(1).)
- A copy of the budget plan developed during the credit briefing. (*See* 11 U.S.C. §521(b)(2).)
- Copies of all payment advices (e.g., pay stubs) from employers received within 60 days of filing. (*See* 11 U.S.C. §521(a)(1)(B)(iv).)
- An itemized statement of monthly net income and any anticipated increases in income or expenses. (*See* 11 U.S.C. §521(a)(1)(B)(v), (vi).)
- With the statement of the debtor's financial affairs, if §342(b) applies, debtor must file a certificate of either (i) an attorney that delivered the appropriate notice of §342(b) or (ii) the debtor stating that such notice was received and read by the debtor in case no attorney was indicated and no bankruptcy petition preparer signed the petition. (*See* 11 U.S.C. §521(a)(1)(B)(iii).)
- A statement of intention with respect to property securing consumer debts. (*See* 11 U.S.C. §521(a)(2).)
- A record of any interest that a debtor has in an educational individual retirement account or under a qualified state tuition program. (*See* 11 U.S.C. §521(c).)
- On request, the debtor must file (1) each tax return for tax years ending while the case is pending; (2) returns filed for tax years preceding the filing that are filed while the case is pending; (3) any amendments to returns. (*See* 11 U.S.C. §521(f).)
- On the request of the U.S. Trustee or the case trustee, the debtor must provide photo identification that establishes the identity of the debtor. (*See* 11 U.S.C. §521(h).)

Automatic dismissal has caused confusion among the judges, who are not sure how to accomplish this automatic dismissal. One felt motivated to write a Dr. Seuss-style poem expressing his exasperation about what to do if a debtor did not comply with the paperwork requirements but no one in the case objected. As Judge Cristol of the Southern District of Florida asked:

> I do not like dismissal automatic,
> It seems to me to be traumatic.
> I do not like it in this case,
> I do not like it any place.
> As a judge I am most keen
> to understand, What does it mean?

How can any person know
what the docket does not show?

The puzzle of 521(i) leads Judge Cristol to further plead:

What does automatic dismissal mean?
And by what means can it be seen?
Are we only left to guess?
Oh please Congress, fix this mess!
Until it's fixed what should I do?
How can I explain this mess to you?[3]

B. Dismissal Under the Means Test: The New Issue in Consumer Bankruptcy

The heart of the 2005 bankruptcy amendments is the "means test" added by Congress to force more people to file Chapter 13 bankruptcies rather than allow most to simply discharge their debts in a Chapter 7 case.[4]

One of us always begins coverage of the means test with the following limerick:

Law school seemed perfect for me,
With my English and History degree,
But the "means test" has shown,
What I've always known,
I should not have dropped Calculus Three

C. Dismissal for Abuse of Chapter 7: The Old Standard and the New Means Test

After the 1978 Bankruptcy Code came into being, some creditors began complaining that the new bankruptcy scheme was too lenient on debtors. Specifically, consumer credit companies complained that many debtors who could afford to pay back some of their debts in a Chapter 13 were instead filing Chapter 7 cases and simply discharging their debts.

3. In re Riddle, 344 B.R. 702 (Bankr. S.D. Fla. 2006).
4. The authors thank Professor Jason Kilborn for providing much of the text and many of the questions for this section.

1. *The old test*

The original Code had no requirement that a Chapter 7 debtor be unable to pay some debts under a Chapter 13 plan. In fact, the spirit of the Code was that the debtor could freely choose between a payment plan under Chapter 13 or a straight liquidation under Chapter 7.

Congress responded to the pressure from the consumer credit industry by adding §707(b) to the Code. The pre-October 17, 2005 version of the Bankruptcy Code ominously and somewhat vaguely states that the court may dismiss a case filed by an individual under Chapter 7 if the individual has primarily consumer debts and if the court finds that "the granting of relief would be a substantial abuse of the provisions of this Chapter."

Interesting, but what does it mean? After several years of interpreting this language, courts had developed two schools of thought to determine if a Chapter 7 case is a "substantial abuse" under the prior §707(b). Both tests recognize that, based on the section's legislative history, the primary abuse Congress is talking about here is being able to afford to pay back some of one's debts.

The test is misnamed, which confuses people. The name implies that the debtor has done something evil in the heart, not simply chosen a liquidation case over a repayment plan. Yet even under the old law, substantial abuse simply meant the debtor had an ability to pay back some of his or her debts.

Before October 17, 2005, the test for dismissal of a Chapter 7 case was called the "substantial abuse" test. Because this test was broad and vague, it naturally left a lot up to the court's discretion. A very large part of this test (which is still in existence but no longer the primary abuse test under §707(b)) depends on whether the debtor could afford to pay back some of his or her debts. Thus, an abusive case has always been understood to mean a case that was filed as a Chapter 7 (liquidation and easy discharge) case but really should be a Chapter 13 payment plan case.

2. *The new test for abuse under §707(b): The means test*

The new abuse test became effective on October 17, 2005. Congress decided that a significant goal of bankruptcy reform would be to make people who can afford to do a repayment plan do one, rather than allowing debtors to do an easy Chapter 7 case.

The old test presumed that the debtor was the best person to decide what kind of bankruptcy case to file, and that debtors should not be forced to do repayment plans against their will. Part of the reason for this rationale is that most Chapter 13 cases fail anyway because of the long time commitment needed to actually complete a payment plan and get a discharge.

The new law removes the presumption in favor of the debtor's choice of bankruptcy type and changes the name of the test from "substantial abuse" to just plain "abuse." It also sets forth one of the most complex mathematical tests imaginable to determine whether there is "abuse."

Again, the idea is that a Chapter 7 case is an abuse, and should be dismissed or converted to a Chapter 13, if the debtor can afford to pay back some of his or her creditors. The new test is called the means test. This is probably the most famous part of the 2005 bankruptcy reform bill.

NOTE: Before we get into the ins and outs of the means test, you should know that a court or the U.S. Trustee can always bring a motion for general abuse of Chapter 7 under a test called the totality of the circumstances test or the general abuse test. Again, the primary fact indicating that there is abuse under this test is that the debtor has income over and above his or her reasonable expenses, sufficient to pay a Chapter 13 plan. This is no different from prior law. This test is used when the debtor has done something to make the court, or the U.S. Trustee, think that the case should not go forward. This original basis for dismissal of a Chapter 7 case is not available to other parties in the case, like creditors, and is not likely to be used much now that the means test has been passed.

ANOTHER NOTE: All abuse motions under §707(b) — under the old or the new test — can be brought only against people whose debts are primarily consumer debts. Wealthier consumers with lots of business debts are not covered by the means test at all.

Under the 2005 law, the main ground for dismissal for abuse under §707(b) is the means test. This test can be used by any creditor in the case or the case trustee, not just the court or the U.S. Trustee.

To determine if a debtor can afford to pay some of his or her debts and has thus filed a Chapter 7 case that is an abuse of a Chapter 7, one must:

1. Calculate the debtor's current monthly income.
2. Deduct some allowable expenses.
3. See what is left.
4. In some cases, compare what is left to how much the debtor owes creditors.

In sum, then, think of it like this:

Current monthly income – allowable expenses = money left for creditors

a. Income We start by trying to calculate what the 2005 law calls the debtor's "current monthly income." If the debtor's current monthly income (defined in the next section of this chapter) from all sources (including regular gifts from family members) is below the median income for a family of that size in the debtor's state, no one can assert the means test. Only judges and the U.S. Trustee's Office can assert the general abuse test we discussed briefly before.

What income? The definition of current monthly income is not the debtor's actual current income, but a monthly average of the income the debtor has received over the past six months. Never mind that the debtor might not be making this amount now. This is the number from which the debtor's expenses will be deducted to see if the debtor is required to file a Chapter 13 repayment plan or can instead choose to discharge most of his or her debts.

Calculating this income figure can be quite complex. You include the debtor's income (and that of any non-separated spouse, even if the case is not a joint case). You also include regular contributions that anyone else makes to cover household expenses. Social Security payments are not included, however, nor are victim's compensation payments. Therefore, older people on limited incomes primarily from Social Security are not affected by the means test at all. But they are, of course, affected by the other changes to the Code covered in this book, just like everyone else.

This current monthly income calculation is a very important number. Why? As just set out, if the debtor's "current monthly income" times 12 is below the median annual income for a family of the debtor's household size in the debtor's state, no one can assert the means test. This is critical.

If 12 times the debtor's current monthly income is less than the relevant median annual income, the means test is over, and no one can claim presumptive abuse. And, as set out previously, only the judge and the U.S. Trustee's Office can assert the general abuse part of the test.

Median incomes for families of various sizes in all the different states are surveyed periodically by the Bureau of the Census. Because the Census does not compile income figures by household size and state every year, the current figures have to be extrapolated from the most recent year that the Census published such figures. The U.S. Trustee's office publishes an updated list each year on its website, http://www.usdoj.gov/ust/eo/bapcpa/meanstesting.htm. Because the U.S. Trustee is responsible for monitoring the means test, it makes sense to use the figures that the U.S. Trustee's office publishes, even though other figures are also available.

b. Allowable expenses If 12 times the debtor's current monthly income is higher than the median annual income for the debtor's household size in the debtor's state, the debtor fails this first median income safe harbor and must continue with the means test itself. Now one must figure out which allowable expenses the debtor can deduct from his or her family income under the 2005 means test.

NOTE ABOUT SOMETHING FUNKY IN THE MEANS TEST: Unlike the safe harbor test for median income, when calculating expenses in an individual (non-joint) case, the debtor's spouse's income is only considered in the means test to the extent used to cover household expenses. We (and most bankruptcy scholars) believe this is a correct interpretation of the impact of a spouse's income on the expense part of the means test, although we have no idea how — practically speaking — one can actually tell how much of a spouse's income is used to cover household expenses. What if a couple saves one salary and spends the other one? We do not know the answer to these practical questions and can only wrestle, along with the rest of you, with §§101(10A)(B) and 707(b)(7).

Now, back to the basics.

Most of the allowable expenses for the means test are taken from the IRS collection standards. What are these? The IRS has developed living expense standards that are used by agents when working out payment plans with taxpayers for overdue taxes. To find these, go to https://www.irs.gov/Businesses/Small-Businesses-&-Self-Employed/Collection-Financial-Standards. You will see there that the IRS disclaims any responsibility for use of its figures in bankruptcy cases. So what is one to do? Once again, the U.S. Trustee's office publishes a parallel list of expense guidelines that mirror the IRS guidelines, with a few very small differences applicable only in consumer bankruptcy cases. For a discussion of the differences and the current figures, go to http://www.usdoj.gov/ust/eo/bapcpa/meanstesting.htm.

The first major deduction is a lump sum for **food, clothing, personal care**, and **entertainment**. The debtor can put into his or her budget the full amount allowed for these items by the IRS, even if they do not normally spend that much. The debtor can actually spend 5 percent more than these guidelines permit for food and clothing, if he or she demonstrates that these expenses are reasonably necessary (the extra 5 percent amount is calculated and published on the U.S. Trustee's website).

For **rental housing, utilities,** and **transportation expenses,** the IRS allows debtors to deduct only their actual expenses, even if they are less than the published expense allowance. In bankruptcy cases, in contrast, the law and developing practice seem to allow debtors to include in their budget the entire relevant expense allowances as published by the U.S. Trustee's office.

NOTE: Secured debts, such as mortgage payments and secured car loan payments, are accounted for separately, with a full allowance for deductions for secured debt payments. As a result, a debtor with a large car payment or home mortgage need not fit those expenses anywhere within the IRS guidelines.

The means test also allows for two groups of other miscellaneous types of deductions. First, the IRS guidelines allow the debtor to deduct his or her actual "other necessary expenses" for things like taxes, health and life insurance, child care, and court-ordered payments (such as child support and alimony). The means test incorporates this allowance exactly as the IRS applies it; thus, the debtor can deduct his or her actual expenses for such things. Second, the Bankruptcy Code separately identifies a few other expenses that can be deducted in the means test, including:

- Extra home energy costs not covered under the IRS guidelines.
- The actual monthly expenses of caring for ill, elderly, or disabled members of the debtor's immediate family or household.
- Actual monthly private or public elementary or secondary school expenses (up to $1,500 per year per minor child).

- The actual monthly expenses of administering a Chapter 13 case (a complex calculation of the percentage, from tables published on the U.S. Trustee's website, of the debtor's plan payments that would go to the trustee if the debtor were to do a hypothetical Chapter 13 payment plan).

Next, the debtor can deduct 1/60th of the amount of all allowed secured claims that are scheduled by contract to come due within the next five years, as well as 1/60th of the total priority unsecured debts, that is, tax and child support arrears and other unsecured claims entitled to special treatment under the Bankruptcy Code, which we talked about in Chapter 10.

Finally, the debtor can deduct continuing charitable contributions of up to 15 percent of the debtor's gross income. That is a lot; however, it looks as though those need to be contributions that the debtor was making before seeking bankruptcy, not just a new way to avoid paying creditors.

c. Figuring out what's left

LESS THAN $171.25 LEFT: NO PAYMENT PLAN REQUIRED

Whether a person has to pay a payment plan depends on this last step, determining if any money is left at the end of the month, after taking the current monthly income and deducting all of the expenses we just ran through.

If what is left is less than $171.25 per month, the debtor has passed the means test. There is no presumption of abuse. The debtor can proceed with a Chapter 7 case.

As you can see, there are an enormous number of deductions for secured claims, priority taxes and support, charities, and so on, making it pretty easy on some level to get out of paying a Chapter 13 plan. Surely this cannot be what was intended.

BETWEEN $171.25 AND $285.83 LEFT PER MONTH: A FIVE-YEAR PAYMENT PLAN REQUIRED IF THE PLAN WOULD PAY AT LEAST A 25 PERCENT DISTRIBUTION ON UNSECURED CLAIMS

If what is left is between $171.25 and $285.83, and if this amount times 60 is not enough to pay at least 25 percent of all of the debtor's general unsecured claims over five years, then the debtor has again passed the means test and there is no presumption of abuse.

Now obviously, for this part of the test, the more debt the debtor has, the less likely that he or she will be required by law to pay a repayment plan.

For example, if a person had $41,100 in debts and $171.25 left per month, the person would have to do a Chapter 13 payment plan. That's because 60 times $171.25 equals $10,275, and 25 percent of $41,000 is $10,275. In other words, this debtor's monthly disposable income over five years could pay 25 percent of this debtor's general unsecured claims. If the debtor's debts were just one dollar more, say $41,101, no payment plan would be needed. That's because with that one extra dollar, this debtor's five-year disposable income would now fall just short of the 25 percent line. At this point, you might be saying, "How random!" But then again, you need to keep in mind that the law is often forced to draw arbitrary lines outside of bankruptcy as well. This part of the test also seems to favor people who have larger debts, thus rewarding profligate spenders over frugal ones. Of course, that is equally true in a Chapter 7 case even aside from the means test: the most profligate pre-petition spenders get to discharge the greatest amount of debt, while more frugal debtors will get a lesser discharge and thus a lesser benefit when they file Chapter 7 bankruptcy.

PAYMENT PLAN REQUIRED IF $285.83 OR MORE LEFT

If the debtor has $285.83 or more per month left over, after all of the allowed expenses are deducted, then he or she always flunks the means test. This means there is a presumption of abuse and a presumption that the debtor must do a Chapter 13 plan. This will need to be a five-year plan. The debtor cannot choose a three-year plan.

d. How can the debtor rebut the presumption? The only way to rebut the presumption of abuse created by the means test is for the debtor to swear to and document that there are "special circumstances" that would decrease the income or increase the expenses, so the debtor actually falls below the trigger points.

If the debtor has recently lost his or her job so the income for the six months prior to the filing was higher than the actual current income, we would think that would do the trick and would allow the debtor to avoid a payment plan, but this is left entirely to the discretion of the bankruptcy court. Until the many ambiguities in the 2005 law are resolved, however, we won't really know for sure how the presumption can be rebutted.

To allow you to read about the whole means test at once and without distraction, we have included all of the questions about the means test here at the end of the chapter. This is quite complex, so good luck!

QUESTION 2. Based on entries in the debtor's checkbook and bank statements, you have calculated the average of the debtor's actual net income from all sources over the past six months. The debtor assures you that these numbers represent every penny of income the debtor has earned from any source. You have multiplied this number by 12 and compared it to the appropriate median income table for your debtor's state, and it appears that median annual income for a family of the debtor's household size is several hundred dollars more than the number you have arrived at for your debtor. Can you forget about the means test and initiate a case under Chapter 7 for this debtor?

A. Yes, because if the debtor's current monthly income times 12 is less than the most recent annual median for the debtor's state and household size, the means test doesn't apply.
B. No, because the "median income" test just raises a presumption that the debtor passes the means test; I must nonetheless perform an actual calculation of expenses and disposable income.
C. No, because the debtor's checkbook and bank statements do not reflect the debtor's "current monthly income," as that phrase is used in the Bankruptcy Code's means test, despite the debtor's assurances.
D. Yes, because the "means test" is optional, and the local trustees and judges in our district have suggested that they intend to ignore it entirely.

ANALYSIS. The term "current monthly income" ("CMI") is misleading for a variety of reasons, including the issue tested in this question. Debtors might believe that their "income" is their take-home pay, as reflected in their actual net pay stubs and bank balances, but this is wrong.

CMI is gross income before any deductions for taxes, insurance, retirement, or any other of a variety of amounts withheld from the average person's paycheck. Most of these withheld amounts might well be properly deducted in determining the debtor's disposable income within the means test, but for this first part of the "median income" test, gross income is what we're after. The proper source of documentation for gross income is the debtor's "payment advices" or pay stubs from an employer, not bank statements and deposit tickets. Indeed, just looking at bank deposits, we can be relatively certain that this debtor has above-median income if after-tax income is only a few hundred dollars less than the median. Adding taxes and other paycheck withholdings back in will undoubtedly push this debtor's gross income well above the median. The information provided by the debtor is not CMI for another reason as well. It does not include (as far as we know) gifts or any other amounts received by the debtor's household, other than earned income. Thus, the correct answer is **C**.

Option **A** on its own contains a correct statement (at least as these provisions are being applied through the official forms) but it incorrectly states the facts of this question. CMI describes gross (total, before-tax) income, whereas the hypothetical describes net (take-home) income deposited in bank accounts.

Option **B** is false. The median income test does not raise a presumption; it disposes of the issue. If the debtor's CMI is below the appropriate median, the means test does not apply at all to prevent the debtor from seeking relief under Chapter 7. This is not entirely clear from the law, but the official (mandatory) forms lead one to this conclusion. Indeed, empirical studies suggest that a great many debtors (perhaps the great majority) will be unaffected by the substance of the 2005 means test because they are below the median income, although even these debtors will suffer from the increased paperwork burdens and attorney expenses resulting from the recent reform.

Option **D** is also wrong. Congress devised the means test to reign in the discretion of local trustees and even judges. It is a mandatory gateway to bankruptcy relief through which all individuals with primarily consumer debts must pass, regardless of local preferences. If the presumption of abuse arises, not only the local trustees and courts, but also the U.S. Trustee or any creditor, can object to the debtor's petition for relief. If the local authorities disregard the test, the U.S. Trustee or creditors can be expected to appeal, and one would not expect any of the Circuit Courts of Appeals to countenance a local court's blatant disregard for the law. To be sure, local courts can liberally interpret the sort of "special circumstances" that might rebut the presumption of abuse, but the means test cannot be simply ignored if it applies.

QUESTION 3. Your review of proper documentation of the debtor's total income from all sources over the past six months reveals the following: Last year, the debtor's total annual income was $60,000. This year, the debtor had been earning $5,000 per month for the fifth and sixth months preceding the current month, but the debtor lost her job and was unemployed for the next three months, in which she had no income at all (the fourth, third, and second months preceding the current month). This last month, the debtor earned $8,000 from her new job, and she expects to earn $8,000 per month for at least the next year. Now that her future looks brighter, the debtor wants to erase her old accumulated debts in a Chapter 7 to give herself a "fresh start." If median annual income for a household of the debtor's size in her state is $40,000, can this debtor forget about the means test?

A. No, because her current monthly income of $8,000 times 12 is far more than $40,000; she must proceed with the means test.
B. No, because her most current annual income is $60,000, far more than $40,000; she must proceed with the means test.
C. Yes, because her recent unemployment is a "special circumstance" that makes her automatically eligible for Chapter 7, despite her recently increased income.
D. Yes, because her $3,000 current monthly income times 12 is $36,000, just below the median.

ANALYSIS. Congress made some curious decisions about how to measure individual income in bankruptcy, as this problem illustrates. "Current monthly income" has nothing to do with how much income the debtor is earning right now or expects to earn in the near future, so option **A** is wrong. One would think that Congress would expect a payment plan from someone who expects to earn a $96,000 gross annual income for the foreseeable future, but this is not how the median income and means tests operate. Indeed, the debtor's substantial most current annual income is also irrelevant for this purpose, so option **B** is wrong, too.

Instead, "current monthly income" is an average of the debtor's last six months of income (actually an average of the debtor's income in the six months preceding the month in which the bankruptcy petition was filed). Here, the debtor earned $18,000 in the most recent six-month period, and dividing that number by 6 produces an average of $3,000 per month. This is the debtor's "current monthly income," and multiplying this number by 12 produces the presumptive annual income to be compared with the median annual income for the debtor's household size and state. Option **D** is correct. This debtor is exempted from the means test because her CMI times 12 is below median, despite her recent upturn in financial good fortune. Go figure.

Option **C** describes "special circumstances" improperly in at least three ways. First, if the debtor's CMI is below median, there is no need to refer to any special circumstances, as the debtor is not subject to the means test. Second, the fact that the debtor was unemployed recently is not particularly relevant to the question whether she can pay her debts now. If she were unemployed now, that might constitute special circumstances to allow her into Chapter 7 even if her CMI suggests (misleadingly) that she has more disposable income available than she actually does, but this is the opposite of the case in the hypothetical. Third, even if special circumstances were present and relevant in this case, special circumstances do not give rise to automatic waiver of the means test. The debtor must plead and document these circumstances to the court's satisfaction, and the court retains discretion to grant or deny an exemption from the "abuse" test.

QUESTION 4. In the preceding hypothetical, suppose you were to discover that the debtor is happily married and living with her spouse. You had thought the debtor was single because she was seeking an individual case, but the debtor explains that her spouse "doesn't need bankruptcy," so she is proceeding alone. If her spouse's average gross income over the past six months amounts to about $7,000 per month, does that change your answer as to whether she can ignore the means test?

A. No, because she is the only debtor in an individual case, only her income counts.

B. No, but only if her spouse contributes no income to household expenses.

C. Yes, but only if her spouse contributes enough income to household expenses to raise the debtor's CMI times 12 above the median.

D. Yes, because the two spouses' incomes together clearly push the debtor's CMI above the median.

ANALYSIS. Option **D** is the most correct. Although it is not clear that the debtor's non-filing spouse has a "current monthly income," it is clear that the income of a non-filing spouse is included in the median income test for complete exemption from the means test, under the income analysis part of the test. (If the spouses are separated, the non-filing spouse's income may be disregarded, but that is not the case here.) If the non-filing spouse's CMI is approximately \$7,000, that makes the joint CMI around \$10,000, which pushes the couple's annual gross income to \$120,000, or three times the median. Under these circumstances, the court or the U.S. Trustee might file a motion for abuse under §707(b) given the non-filing spouse's substantial income. Because this is an individual case and the debtor's CMI alone is below the applicable median, no party other than the court or the U.S. Trustee may file such a motion, but the 2005 law contains a number of provisions designed to encourage the U.S. Trustee to file such motions where appropriate. Creditors are prohibited from asserting abuse, given the debtor's small income, but the debtor's non-filing spouse's income should nonetheless be considered in light of the court's or U.S. Trustee's ability to assert abuse. The debtor may safely disregard the means test only if the debtor's and the debtor's non-filing spouse's combined CMI is less than the applicable median.

Options **A, B,** and **C** are thus close, but not completely accurate. With respect to creditors' ability to assert "abuse," the non-filing spouse's income is considered only to the extent that it is considered part of the debtor's CMI; that is, only to the extent the non-filing spouse's income is used to pay part or all of the debtor's household expenses. This is not an "all or nothing" question, as option **B** suggests. If her spouse uses income to pay some household expenses, only that income is considered part of the debtor's CMI. If her spouse contributed enough income to push the debtor's CMI above 1/12th of \$40,000, the debtor would fail the median income test in her own right, and any party, including a creditor, could assert "abuse," as option **C** suggests. Here, however, whether or not creditors might assert abuse given the use of the debtor's non-filing spouse's income, the debtor might in any event face an assertion of abuse from the court or U.S. Trustee based on her and her spouse's combined CMI. She should not ignore the means test, even if the law limits the number of parties that might assert abuse.

QUESTION 5. Debtor bought a car on credit from Dealer two years ago and granted Dealer a purchase-money security interest in the car. The purchase price for the car was originally \$30,000, but with interest and other finance charges, the contract calls for total payments of \$42,000 over the five-year life of the car loan. Debtor's loan agreement calls for 60 equal monthly payments of \$700, which Debtor has been making consistently over the past 24 months. You have checked the NADA valuation guide and found that a similar used car today would cost only $18,000, although Debtor still owes $25,200 over the next three years on the car loan. In calculating Debtor's disposable income for the means test, how much (if anything) can you deduct for Debtor's monthly car payment?

A. $700, the actual amount that Debtor has been paying each month, as required by the contract.
B. $420, the total amount due under the car loan contract over the next five years, $25,200, divided by 60.
C. $400, the IRS allowance for ownership expenses for one car in the debtor's region.
D. $300, the current replacement value of the car, $18,000, divided by 60.

ANALYSIS. Congress delivered a number of valuable benefits to car lenders in the 2005 amendments, and this problem illustrates some of those benefits. It also illustrates common mistakes in calculating payments on relatively short-term secured loans. The means test allows for deduction of all payments for allowed secured claims, apparently no matter how extravagant the expense. Thus, although the IRS expense guidelines list an allowance for car ownership, this allowance is inapplicable in bankruptcy if the debtor owns the car subject to a security interest; the entire allowed secured claim is an allowed expense, regardless of its size. Thus, option **C** is wrong.

Unlike most claims secured by collateral, the allowed secured claim for a consumer car loan secured by a purchase-money security interest less than 910 days old (approximately two and one-half years) is the entire amount contractually due, not the lesser of the value of the collateral or the amount due (as would generally be the case). Thus, option **D** is wrong. If the car had been purchased three years ago, **D** would accurately describe the debtor's obligations to the car lender.

Oddly enough, this is not the secured claim calculation used in the means test. Rather, regardless of when the car was purchased, allowable deductions for secured claims under the means test include the entire amount due, not the lesser of the value of the collateral or the amount due (as would normally be the case for typical unsecured claims). (*See* 11 U.S.C. §707(b)(2)(A)(iii).) This is an oddball result that creates an inaccurate calculation of what the debtor can afford to pay, but exasperatingly, this is apparently what §707(b)(2)(A) says!

The only remaining issue to flag (as if all that were not enough) is that the monthly means test deduction for such claims is not the amount that the debtor happens to be paying monthly now; option **A** is wrong. Rather, it is the total claim that will come due within the next 60 months (in this case, the entire claim) divided by 60. In other words, the total amount the debtor owes secured by the car is rescheduled over 60 months, rather than over the shorter remainder of the loan contract. Debtor's deduction for car payments is thus $25,200, the amount contractually due over the remaining 36 months of the loan contract, divided by 60, or $420. Thus, option **B** is correct.

QUESTION 6. Assume that the debtor in this question is an "above median" debtor who is therefore required to take the means test. You have determined that deducting all allowable expenses for the means test from the debtor's current monthly income leaves $225 per month "disposable" income. Can you seek Chapter 7 relief for this debtor, or may this debtor obtain bankruptcy relief only by completing a Chapter 13 payment plan?

A. Yes, I definitely can seek Chapter 7 relief, because the debtor's disposable income is less than $285.83 per month (less than $17,150 over a 60-month payment plan).
B. Yes, I can seek Chapter 7 relief, but only if the debtor's general unsecured debts total more than $54,000.
C. Yes, I can seek Chapter 7 relief, but only if all of the debtor's debts (secured and unsecured) total more than $54,000.
D. No, I cannot seek Chapter 7 relief, because the debtor's disposable income is not less than $171.25 per month (at least $10,275 over a 60-month plan).

ANALYSIS. This debtor falls in the middle ground between certain exclusion from and certain allowance of a Chapter 7 case (barring any grounds for a "general" or "totality of the circumstances" exclusion from Chapter 7). The debtor would be excluded from Chapter 7 by the means test if his disposable income was at least $285.83 per month, but this is not the only way to establish a presumed "abuse" of Chapter 7. Option **A** is thus too narrowly stated. By the same token, the debtor is not automatically excluded from Chapter 7 (presumed "abuse") if his disposable income exceeds $171.25 per month, so option **D** is too broad. Debtors with disposable income between $171.25 and $285.83 per month might be excluded from Chapter 7, but only if their disposable income is not less than 25 percent of their total general unsecured debts. Only general unsecured debts are considered here, as payments to secured and priority unsecured debts are already deducted in the means test itself, so option **C** is inaccurate. Option **B** is correct, because 60 times the debtor's disposable income of $225 equals $13,500, so this debtor can seek Chapter 7 relief only if $13,500 is less than 25 percent of his total general unsecured debt load; that is, only if his general unsecured debts exceed $54,000.

QUESTION 7. How would your answer to the preceding hypothetical change if the debtor's disposable income was $300 per month, but his general unsecured debts totaled $1 million?

A. This debtor cannot seek Chapter 7 relief absent documented "special circumstances" and a discretionary ruling by the judge that the presumption of "abuse" has been rebutted.
B. This debtor cannot seek Chapter 7 relief under any circumstances, as his monthly disposable income clearly exceeds the maximum amount allowed by the means test, $285.83.
C. This debtor can seek Chapter 7 relief, but only if the judge decides that $300 is so close to $285.83 that the debtor really should be allowed into Chapter 7 despite the means test.
D. This debtor can seek Chapter 7 relief because, although his income exceeds the means test threshold of $285.83, a 60-month plan would pay far less than 25 percent of his general unsecured debt (in this case, less than 2 percent).

ANALYSIS. To a very significant degree, the means test is hard and fast, but there is some small leeway. If the debtor's "disposable" income as calculated by the means test exceeds $285.83 per month, a presumption of abuse arises, and Chapter 7 is available only if the debtor can document "special circumstances" that convince the judge that the debtor's future disposable income will be less than the means test suggests (and less than $285.83) as a result of decreased income or increased expenses. Option **A** is correct. Option **C** overstates the extent of the court's discretion. Courts are not free to disregard the means test in "close enough" cases. If the court can find documented "special circumstances" to reduce the debtor's income or increase his expenses slightly, then the debtor's disposable income might fall below $285.83 and the presumption might not arise, but the courts cannot simply disregard presumed abuse. Option **B** overstates the case in the opposite direction. The means test is not absolute. Even for debtors with "excessive" disposable income, "special circumstances" might persuade the court that the means test has overstated the actual extent of the debtor's ability to pay, though this is entirely left to the discretion of each individual judge, at least until definitive case law begins to develop at the appellate level.

Option **D** is entirely wrong, and it illustrates the oddity of this test. The fact that this debtor could only pay less than 2 percent of his general unsecured debt over 60 months is irrelevant to the means test with this debtor's level of disposable income. The 25 percent analysis applies only to debtors with disposable income below $285.83 (and above $171.25). Even for debtors with only a few pennies more disposable income, an insignificant distribution to creditors is no basis for allowing a Chapter 7 and avoiding the expense and risk of a 60-month Chapter 13 plan. Congress's rationale appears to have been that $17,150 is always a meaningful distribution, regardless of the percent of unsecured debt that this amount might represent for any given debtor.

QUESTION 8. Darryl Debtor is single and just started a new job three months ago. The new job pays $55,000 per year. Debtor's previous job paid Debtor $45,000 per year. Debtor has had no interruptions in employment for the past three years. Debtor's outstanding nonpriority unsecured debts currently total $30,000, and they are primarily consumer debts. It is the first day of the month, and Debtor wants to know whether Debtor is eligible to file a Chapter 7 bankruptcy. The median income for a one-earner family in Debtor's state is $53,000. Debtor's monthly disposable income is $200. Will Debtor be eligible to file Chapter 7 bankruptcy if Debtor files today?

A. Yes, since Debtor would pass the means test even though Debtor would flunk the median test.
B. Yes, since Debtor would pass the median test, and that allows Debtor to avoid being subject to the means test.
C. No, since Debtor would flunk the means test, and that fact alone is enough to prevent Chapter 7 eligibility.
D. No, since Debtor would flunk the median test, and that fact alone is enough to prevent Chapter 7 eligibility.

ANALYSIS. The correct answer is **B**. Answering this question correctly requires that you understand two key concepts about the means test. First, if the debtor passes the median test, then the debtor will not have to pass the means test. Second, the median test is essentially a backward-looking test that focuses solely on the debtor's income for the past six months. In this case, Darryl Debtor was earning $55,000 per year for three of those six months, and $45,000 per year for the other three of those six months. Thus, his average annual salary for those three months was $50,000, which is below his state's median. An annual salary of $50,000 therefore puts Debtor below his state's median of $53,000 and allows him to pass the median test. Once he passes the median test, he does not have to take the means test in order to file Chapter 7 bankruptcy.

Choice **A** is incorrect because it wrongly suggests that Debtor has flunked the median test when in fact Debtor has passed the median test. Answer **C** is wrong because it says that flunking the means test is alone enough to prevent Chapter 7 eligibility. While Darryl Debtor would have flunked the means test if he had to take it (since his disposable income would allow him to pay 25% of his nonpriority unsecured debts in a five-year Chapter 13 plan), he doesn't even need to face the means test in this case. Choice **D** is wrong for two reasons: first, because it wrongly says that Debtor would flunk the median test here; and second, because it incorrectly states that flunking the median test is alone enough to prevent Chapter 7 eligibility. If a debtor flunks the median test, it simply means that the debtor must then pass the means test in order to be eligible to file Chapter 7 bankruptcy.

Martin's and Keating's Picks

1. Question 1 **B**
2. Question 2 **C**
3. Question 3 **D**
4. Question 4 **D**
5. Question 5 **B**
6. Question 6 **B**
7. Question 7 **A**
8. Question 8 **B**

18

Involuntary Bankruptcy

OVERVIEW

A. The Anatomy of an Involuntary Bankruptcy Case
B. The Closer: Chapters 17 and 18
Martin's and Keating's Picks

Whereas in many countries around the world, bankruptcy is something that you impose or force on a debtor; in the United States, the vast majority of all bankruptcy cases filed are voluntary cases instituted by the debtor. This is true of cases filed under all chapters of the Code.

A. The Anatomy of an Involuntary Bankruptcy Case

If creditors do wish to force a debtor into bankruptcy, it is generally required that three creditors, holding claims of at least $21,050 in the aggregate and holding noncontingent, undisputed claims petition the court. The court will allow the involuntary case to go forward only if it finds that the debtor is generally not paying debts as they come due, a test that has proven elusive over the years. Because this test is largely impossible to interpret, creditors take a big risk when filing an involuntary case.[1]

If the involuntary petition is dismissed by the court (other than with the consent of all petitioners and the debtor), the petitioners may be liable for damages under §303(i). If the court determines that the invalid petition was

1. 11 U.S.C. §303. Courts have had difficulty interpreting the meaning of this phrase. Does it mean that the debtor is generally not paying 100 percent of the debts, 50 percent of the debts, or perhaps failing to pay the long-term debts? What if the debtor is paying all debts but one, but the one not being paid is 400 times the size of all the others?

filed in good faith, damages are limited to the debtor's costs and reasonable attorney's fees. However, if the court determines that the petitioning creditors filed the petition in bad faith, they may be liable for any damages to the debtor that were proximately caused by the filing and even punitive damages if the court so determines. If the debtor has fewer than 12 total creditors—a test rarely met by any debtor—then just one creditor who meets the dollar and other eligibility requirements can file the petition for involuntary bankruptcy. Judges sometimes look askance at petitions filed by a single creditor, suspecting that these involve two-party disputes that are often best settled elsewhere. Some judges question the validity of all involuntary cases, as they are rarely properly filed and are somewhat inconsistent with the U.S. view of bankruptcy as a choice of the debtor, not creditors.

As set out previously, a debtor with 12 creditors or more (presumably most debtors), can only be forced into bankruptcy by three or more petitioning creditors with debts of $21,050 or more in the aggregate. Moreover, none of these petitioning creditors' claims can be the subject of a bona fide dispute under §303(b)(1). This is designed to keep people from throwing other people into bankruptcy just because the two have a disagreement about whether a debt is due.

Under the prior version of this statute, however, courts had interpreted this Code language in §303(b)(1) to mean that the petitioning creditor was ineligible to force a debtor into bankruptcy only if the debt was disputed on liability grounds, not because the two disagreed about the amount that was due. The 2005 Code amendments say that a petitioning creditor cannot have a debt that is in bona fide dispute as to the liability or the amount of the claim.

Do you think this will make it easier or harder to put someone into involuntary bankruptcy? Presumably, this will make it harder because the debtor can challenge the legitimacy of a creditor's status as a petitioning creditor merely by challenging the amount due.

QUESTION 1. In an involuntary bankruptcy proceeding, petitioning creditors are those who:

A. have disputed claims against the debtor.
B. are owed money by the debtor at the time of the petition.
C. sign the involuntary petition.
D. have been unpaid by the debtor at a time when other creditors have been paid.

ANALYSIS. C is the answer. Creditors with disputed claims do not qualify as petitioning creditors and thus should not file an involuntary petition, so **A** is incorrect. Both **B** and **D** simply describe what it means to be a creditor, not petitioning creditors. Petitioning creditors hire the attorney and sign the petition.

QUESTION 2. (CODE READER) Debtor Corp currently has a total of 17 creditors that are in the aggregate owed $62,000 in noncontingent, undisputed, unsecured claims. In addition, Supplier claims that Debtor Corp owes Supplier $20,000 for supplies that were delivered to but not paid for by Debtor Corp. Debtor Corp disputes the amount owed to Supplier, but not the existence of an unpaid, overdue debt to Supplier. Debtor Corp claims that it owes Supplier just $14,000, not $20,000. Three creditors each holding $3,000 noncontingent, undisputed, unsecured claims join forces with Supplier to try to force Debtor Corp into an involuntarily bankruptcy. Assume that the four creditors are proceeding in good faith and that they can readily demonstrate to the bankruptcy court that Debtor Corp is generally not paying its debts as they come due. When these four creditors file the involuntary petition, will Debtor Corp be able to have the petition dismissed?

A. Yes, because the four petitioning creditors fail to meet the minimum debt requirement of $21,050.
B. No, because even if we use the $14,000 amount that Debtor Corp admits that it owes to Supplier rather than the $20,000 figure that Supplier says that Debtor Corp owes Supplier, the four creditors would still exceed the minimum debt requirement of $21,050.
C. No, because the four petitioning creditors together are owed $29,000, which exceeds the minimum debt requirement of $21,050.
D. No, because even if we exclude Supplier's claim completely, Debtor Corp still owes $62,000 to its creditors, which well exceeds the minimum debt requirement of $21,050.

ANALYSIS. The correct answer is **A**. Before we explain why, let's take a look at the other three possibilities and see why each of them is wrong. Choice **B** is probably the most persuasive of the wrong answers. After all, both sides here admit that Debtor Corp owes at least $14,000 to Supplier. So why can't we just use that figure for purposes of meeting the $21,050 minimum amount for petitioning creditors? There are two reasons: first, because the language of §303(b)(1) says pretty clearly that we cannot use such a figure — it says that we cannot use claims that are subject to dispute even as to amount; and second, because this limitation against using claims about which the amount is disputed actually makes sense from a policy perspective. In a case like this one, Debtor Corp may be refusing to pay even the $14,000 that it admits it owes as leverage to get Supplier to agree that payment of $14,000 is payment in full for all of Debtor

Corp's outstanding obligations to Supplier. If Supplier's claim of $14,000 were allowed to count towards the $21,050 minimum, Debtor Corp might be pressured to pay that much to Supplier just to avoid the possibility of an involuntary bankruptcy and thereby lose its negotiating leverage with Supplier.

Choices **C** and **D** are easier to eliminate. We can eliminate **C** because that choice assumes that Supplier's disputed claim should count for the full $20,000 that Supplier argues for, when in fact the claim should not count at all for purposes of meeting the $21,050 minimum. Answer **D** is wrong because it assumes that the $21,050 minimum applies to the debtor's total outstanding debts rather than to the amount owed to the petitioning creditors. Choice **A** is correct because once we eliminate Supplier's claim from the mix, we are left with three creditors who are owed a total of $9,000, well short of the $21,050 in claims required of creditors who are petitioning for an involuntary bankruptcy filing.

QUESTION 3. (CODE READER) Debtor Corp is a small business that employs eight full-time staff members. Debtor Corp is having financial trouble and is generally not paying its debts as they come due. Debtor Corp currently has 14 creditors with noncontingent, undisputed, unsecured claims, including four employees who are each owed $12,000 in back wages. Two of those four employees file an involuntary petition to put Debtor Corp into bankruptcy. Should the two employees succeed in this petition?

A. No, because there needs to be at least three petitioning creditors given that there are 14 creditors in total.

B. No, because even though there only needs to be one petitioning creditor in this case, that petitioning creditor cannot be an employee of the debtor.

C. Yes, because two petitioning creditors are always enough as long as they meet the $21,050 minimum amount of claims.

D. Yes, because even though employees do not count towards the 12-creditor minimum mentioned in §303(b)(2), they should be able to count towards the petitioning creditor minimum in §303(b)(2).

ANALYSIS. This is a tricky one. It seems counterintuitive that employees would not count towards calculating whether a debtor has fewer than 12 total creditors (which determines whether one or three petitioning creditors is necessary), but then these same employees could count towards the minimum petitioning creditor requirement. That is what **D** is saying, and that is probably the right answer. Let's first look at and eliminate the other three answers. Choice **C** is a clear misstatement of the law because §303(b) says that as long as there are at least 12 qualifying creditors, then a minimum of three creditors must bring the involuntary petition. The number of creditors requirement and the minimum claims amount requirement are two separate and distinct requirements that each must be met for a successful involuntary petition.

Answer **A** is wrong because even though there are 14 creditors in total here, we cannot count the four employees towards the 12 minimum that would require three petitioning creditors under §303(b). Choice **B** is probably wrong for the same reason that **D** is probably right. The likely reason that the Code drafters did not want to include employees, insiders, or recipients of avoidable transfers towards the 12-creditor requirement is that all three categories of these creditors are presumed to be "friendly" creditors of the debtor. In other words, each of these three categories of creditors presumptively has a reason to want to keep the debtor out of bankruptcy. The drafters probably did not want to allow a debtor to insulate itself from an involuntary bankruptcy by having a number of friendly creditors that would push the total creditor number to 12 and thus require three petitioning creditors rather than just one to file an involuntary bankruptcy. Yet that same reason for not counting these friendly creditors towards the 12 minimum should arguably not apply when deciding whether any of these creditors can count as one of the necessary petitioning creditors for an involuntary bankruptcy. In other words, if even the debtor's presumptively friendly creditors are willing to petition for an involuntary bankruptcy against the debtor, that probably suggests that the bankruptcy is warranted. For that reason, **D** is likely the best answer.

QUESTION 4. (CODE READER) Same facts as Question 3, except now assume that the two employees who filed the involuntary petition have claims that are the subject of a bona fide dispute. As a result, the bankruptcy court dismisses the involuntary bankruptcy petition against Debtor Corp. Assuming that the two employees brought the involuntary petition in good faith, for which of the following categories of damages would the unsuccessful creditors be liable?

A. Costs and attorney's fees, damages proximately caused by the filing, and punitive damages.
B. Costs and attorney's fees.
C. Costs and attorney's fees, and punitive damages.
D. Costs and attorney's fees, and damages proximately caused by the filing.

ANALYSIS. If you recall the discussion earlier in this chapter, you will remember that §303(i) draws a big distinction between involuntary cases dismissed where the petitioners were found to be in good faith vs. involuntary cases dismissed where the petitioners were found to be in bad faith. If the unsuccessful petitioners are found to be in bad faith, then that opens the door to a wide array of damages for the debtor: not just costs and attorney's fees, but damages proximately caused and even punitive damages if the court deems it appropriate. In this case, however, where the unsuccessful petitioners are found to have filed the petition in good faith, then damages are limited to just the debtor's costs and attorney's fees. Therefore, the correct answer is **B**.

B. The Closer: Chapters 17 and 18

This Closer tests what you learned in Chapters 17 and 18, as well as back in Chapter 12, which covered avoidance powers. Again, the issues are beginning to intersect in less predictable ways as we learn more subject matter. Good luck!

You are an unsecured creditor and the largest supplier to Max Plumbing, Inc., the American Southwest's largest plumbing contractor. Lately, Max has been way behind in its payments, and you and the other unsecured creditors have been contemplating what to do. Recently, a few of you got together and decided to try to ride it out through the tough times, so that Max could get back on its feet. You have been contemplating taking a security interest in some of the equipment to secure your huge debt, which is now towering over $100,000 (basically, enough to put you under), and Max's management has more or less agreed. Just now, however, you saw Max's principal in the local bank. An officer said that Max had just pledged all of its assets to secure mostly past-due debts to the bank. You are furious. This was going to be your collateral if things did not work out.

What can and should you do?

A. Sue Max for conversion.
B. Avoid the preferential transfer to the bank under state law.
C. Put Max into involuntary bankruptcy (along with a couple of other creditors) and ask the trustee to avoid the preferential transfer of the security interest to the bank.
D. Put Max into involuntary bankruptcy and object to Max's discharge.

ANALYSIS. As far as we can tell, nothing has been converted here, so there is little point to doing what is suggested in choice **A**. The key here is that Max has given a valuable preferential transfer to the bank and your client needs to undo or reverse the transfer to have assets available to pay its claim. Because Max is behind on its payment to you and to other creditors (a fact that can be inferred from the discussions among creditors about the problem), you and two other creditors can put Max into involuntary bankruptcy and undo the transfer. You do need to put Max into bankruptcy first, as there are no state preference laws except as to certain payments to insiders under the Uniform Fraudulent Transfers Act. Thus, **B** is incorrect. **D** is incorrect because Max is a corporation, and it does not get a discharge or continue to exist after the case. Thus, there is no point to objecting to its discharge, and the answer is **C**.

Martin's and Keating's Picks

1. Question 1	**C**
2. Question 2	**A**
3. Question 3	**D**
4. Question 4	**B**
The Closer: Chapters 17 and 18	**C**

19

Overview of Chapter 13

This chapter provides an overview of Chapter 13. Don't get frustrated if you find it somewhat confusing and have many questions after you have read it. This is just a quick summary of Chapter 13, and what is mentioned here will be discussed in detail in later chapters of this guide.

As discussed earlier, consumer bankruptcies (as well as business bankruptcies) can be either "sell-out" or "pay-out" cases. Chapter 7 cases are sell-out cases, even though most debtors never need to actually sell anything because their assets are all exempt. The Chapter 7 model is based on the debtor selling all nonexempt assets (if there are any) and walking away. Chapter 13 cases, in contrast, are pay-out cases. Under the Chapter 13 model, the debtor typically does not sell his or her assets. Rather, the debtor can file a Chapter 13 and use his or her future income to pay back some debts over time and then, typically, discharge the rest.

If Chapter 7 is like a form of heaven — forgiveness of debt and starting a new life — then Chapter 13 could be seen as a form of purgatory. The debtor agrees to pay back at least some of his or her debts over time. The idea is that the debtor will propose a plan of repayment called a Chapter 13 plan, which will be approved by the court as long as it complies with a set of rules governed (not surprisingly) by Chapter 13 of the Bankruptcy Code.

Chapter 13 is for individuals only, not corporations or partnerships. Chapter 13 debtors must have regular income to qualify for Chapter 13, but this income can come from sources other than employment, including public benefits and even payments from other people. In other words, the income need not come from regular employment, despite the fact that Chapter 13 is sometimes called the "wage-earner" form of bankruptcy.

Chapter 13 plans are normally paid over three years, but some plans must be paid over five years, either because the Code requires it or because this is the only way the debtor can meet the Code requirements and still keep his or her house, car, etc. There are several good reasons for choosing Chapter 13 over Chapter 7, but the most common reason is that Chapter 13 allows the debtor to restructure secured debt that has become way past due and thus keep the house, the car, or whatever the secured property may be. You will recall that Chapter 7 accomplishes very little in such a situation, and thus, Chapter 13 may be the only way to save a house from foreclosure.

You'll also recall that post-petition wages do not become part of the bankruptcy estate in a Chapter 7 case. The Chapter 7 estate is comprised of the assets the debtor has an interest in at the time of the filing, and any income or proceeds flowing from those assets. In a Chapter 13 case, post-petition income, as well as other assets, become part of the estate. In fact, to qualify for a Chapter 13 plan, the debtor must have future disposable income over and above his or her current living expenses. This will be the money through which the debtor will pay his or her obligations contained in the Chapter 13 plan. If there is no extra income over and above the everyday living expenses, the debtor cannot get a Chapter 13 plan approved. It's just not going to happen.

All secured debts must be paid in full under a Chapter 13 plan but sometimes the debts are only considered secured debts up to the value of the collateral, so this is the amount that must be paid (the value of the collateral, not the amount of the debt), with interest, over the life of the plan.[1] Additionally, Chapter 13 requires that §507 priority debts also be paid in full, this time without interest. If there is insufficient disposable income to cover these claims, then there can be no Chapter 13 case. Also, the Chapter 13 trustee receives a percentage commission on every dollar that is paid through the case, so this must be paid for in the plan as well.

How much unsecured creditors must be paid in a Chapter 13 case depends on a few things. First, the debtor must contribute all of his or her "disposable income" to the plan. If the debtor has enough disposable income to pay the secured and priority debts, as well as the Chapter 13 trustee's fees, and there is still money left over, this must be paid to the unsecured creditors under the plan. However, after the 2005 amendments, above-median debtors will have their disposable income measured by the means test, at least initially. This creates some fairly bizarre results. See Chapter 23 for more information.

Additionally, in a Chapter 13 case, the debtor is not required to give up his or her nonexempt assets. The model is one of pay out, not sell out. Calculating the exemptions is still very important in a Chapter 13 because the debtor must pay the total value of all the nonexempt assets to creditors under the plan. In essence, the debtor is buying back the equity in the nonexempt assets by paying their value to the creditors who would realize that value on sale if the case were a Chapter 7. This means that if the debtor owns $10,000 in unencumbered, nonexempt assets, he or she must pay at least $10,000 to unsecured creditors under the plan. The plan also must be filed in good faith, a test with which you will become more familiar later. Finally, the Chapter 13 plan must be feasible to be approved.

---

1. In other words, with many secured debts, the debtor can pay just the value of the collateral, rather than the amount of the debt. Home mortgages are treated differently, and they generally must be paid in full, regardless of the value of the collateral. This is also true under the 2005 amendments of car loans taken out within 910 days (two and one-half years) of the filing and all other purchase money loans taken out within a year of the filing.

The debtor's goal in a Chapter 13 case is to get his or her plan approved or, as we say in the trade, "confirmed." A "confirmation hearing" is held by the court to decide whether to approve the plan. The Chapter 13 trustee, who will be the same person for many (if not all) Chapter 13 cases in the district,[2] will carefully review the plan, and perhaps suggest changes or question parts of it, such as the amount of disposable income that the debtor has. The bankruptcy judge is unlikely to approve a plan if there is a valid objection by the Chapter 13 trustee. If confirmation is approved and the plan goes through, the debtor must then make every payment. At the end, the debtor is discharged from any unsecured debts that were not paid under the plan.[3]

A great deal has changed about Chapter 13 since the first edition of the Glannon Guide to Bankruptcy was written. On October 17, 2005, Chapter 13 was changed from an entirely voluntary repayment plan option, used most often by people who had fallen behind on debts that were subject to a security interest, to one in which some people choose Chapter 13 because they cannot qualify for Chapter 7 under the means test. There always have been many good reasons to prefer a Chapter 13 case to a Chapter 7 case, but now some people will find their way to Chapter 13 because they have few other bankruptcy options.

This means some people will now choose Chapter 13 over no bankruptcy, because they are ineligible for Chapter 7 based on the means test. With this test came the notion that Chapter 13 was no longer a choice of the debtor in some cases but rather a decision made by the formula. Also, if a debtor is forced to use Chapter 13 rather than Chapter 7 under the means test, the debtor must do a five-year payment plan. In the past, all Chapter 13 debtors had a right to choose between a three-year plan and a five-year plan.

Along with these changes comes a much narrower discharge in Chapter 13 than was previously provided. Before these Code changes, the Chapter 13 discharge was broader and more lenient than a Chapter 7 discharge. Under the 2005 amendments, the discharge one receives in a Chapter 13 is very similar to the one received in a Chapter 7 case.

Another big change is that the debtor must pay the face value (not the stripped-down value) of more secured loans on personal property. This is because stripdown is available only for older loans now, as is described in more detail in Chapter 21.

---

2. In fact, in many bankruptcy districts, the Chapter 13 trustee is the same person in every case in the district. This person is then called the standing Chapter 13 trustee.

3. Usually, some debts do get discharged at this time, as it is unusual for a debtor to pay general unsecured creditors in full.

20

Chapter 13 Eligibility

OVERVIEW

Martin's and Keating's Picks

Section 109(e) states that Chapter 13 is available to individuals with regular income who owe noncontingent, liquidated, unsecured debts of $526,700 or less, and secured debts of $1,580,125 or less.[1] Stockbrokers are ineligible for Chapter 13, as are commodity brokers, but everyone else who meets these qualifications can file a Chapter 13 case. The debtor must receive credit briefing (also sometimes called credit counseling) before he or she can be eligible for Chapter 13, or for any other type of bankruptcy for that matter. (11 U.S.C. §109(h)(1))

The regular income requirement is quite flexible. The money does not need to be earned monthly, or even earned by the debtor. One recent case allowed the debtor's father to pay his plan. Public assistance benefits, as well as trust fund income, royalties, and similar earnings, also qualify as regular income.

QUESTION 1. Who among the following is clearly ineligible for a Chapter 13?

1. An oil well firefighter who fights four fires a year on average, earning $20,000 per fire.
2. A person on Social Security or other public benefits, but without a job.
3. A person who works on commission selling homes but has not sold a home for over a year.
4. A person whose girlfriend pays all of his bills, and who does not have a job.

1. This is as of April 1, 2022, and is revised periodically by the Judicial Conference of the United States. *See* 87 Fed. Reg. 6625 (Feb. 4, 2022).

A. 1, 2, and 3.
B. 2 and 4.
C. None of these people are clearly ineligible.
D. 3 only.

ANALYSIS. The correct answer is **C**, as none of these people is clearly ineligible for Chapter 13. If working four times a year were a reasonably accurate estimate of the debtor's work history, this alone would not disqualify the debtor. The debtor's income must be regular but need not be guaranteed. After all, anyone can be fired, right? Additionally, a person on Social Security or other public benefits[2] but without a job could have income considered regular, as could a person who works on a commission selling homes but who has not sold a home for over a year, or a person whose girlfriend or father pays all of his bills.

QUESTION 2. (CODE READER) Under §109(e), who among the following is clearly ineligible for Chapter 13?

1. A person with a $300,000 home and a $250,000 home mortgage, as well as an unexecuted $2 million tort judgment against her.
2. A person with a $300,000 home and a $250,000 home mortgage, as well as a potential $2 million disputed tort suit pending against her.
3. A person who is working now but is about to be fired, unbeknownst to her.
4. A person with a $1.8 million home mortgage but very little unsecured debt.

A. 1 and 2 only.
B. 1 only.
C. All of the above.
D. 1 and 4 only.

ANALYSIS. Like Question 1, this question is written in the negative and asks you to pick the persons who are clearly ineligible for Chapter 13. Thus, you are looking for people whose debt structures or income limitations put them outside the statutory parameters set out in §109(e).

Under §109(e), only an individual who owes, on the date of the filing of the petition, noncontingent, liquidated, unsecured debts of less than $526,700 and noncontingent, liquidated, secured debts of less than $1,580,125 may be a debtor under Chapter 13. The key to understanding this provision is

2. Just keep in mind that under welfare reform, many public benefits are only available for a total of five years per person.

recognizing that debts that are still disputed or contingent are not counted towards the debt totals for this purpose. Thus, the person described in **2** is not clearly ineligible because the pending tort suit is still contingent and the other debts fall well within the statutory debt limits.

Choice **3** is also incorrect because the eligibility statute requires a person with a current regular income but requires the debtor to make no guarantee about employment in the future. Thus, this debtor might actually be eligible for Chapter 13. This is a good thing, as few people could prove that they would absolutely be employed throughout the plan. Choice **4** is correct. This person seems to be ineligible for Chapter 13. The facts state that the debtor has a $1.8 million home mortgage. This is secured debt, which the statute says cannot exceed $1,580,125 if the debtor wishes to file a Chapter 13. While the house could be undersecured and thus some of the debt could actually be unsecured, home mortgages are treated differently than other secured debts in a Chapter 13, as you will see. Thus, the whole mortgage will be treated as secured.

The person described in choice **1** also seems to be ineligible. Thus, choice **1** is also correct, as this person has a $2 million tort judgment against her, which would be over the Chapter 13 unsecured debt limit. Also, note that if the $2 million tort judgment in choice **1** had been executed on, this would turn the tort debt into secured debt and put her over the secured debt limit as well. Thus, the best answer is **D**, which offers choices **1** and **4**.

ONE OTHER QUICK NOTE: Choice **1** does contain an ambiguity, as do most real-life bankruptcy situations. Choice **1** does not tell us if the tort suit is on appeal. Some courts would hold that if the case were on appeal, it would still be contingent and thus would not count in the eligibility calculations for Chapter 13. Thus, if the case were on appeal, then this person may not be clearly ineligible for Chapter 13. Ahhh . . . the plot thickens!

QUESTION 3. (CODE READER) Darcy Debtor has a regular income and lives in Florida. Her son, John, just graduated from medical school with $200,000 in student loans on which Darcy is the guarantor. Darcy also owes $400,000 on an unsecured loan that she took out for her small business, but that loan does not come due for another year. Darcy's bank has a $1.8 million mortgage on Darcy's $2 million primary residence, but Darcy's interest in her home is fully exempt under Florida law. Darcy has been struggling with her bills lately and would like to file a Chapter 13 bankruptcy. Will she be eligible to file?

A. No, because she exceeds the secured debt limit.
B. No, because she exceeds the unsecured debt limit.
C. No, because she exceeds both the secured and the unsecured debt limit.

D. Yes, because her complete exemption in her home means that she does not exceed the secured debt limit and her debt as a guarantor on her son's student loans does not count towards her unsecured debt.

ANALYSIS. The correct answer is **A**. As you may recall from Chapter 9, a debtor's exemption in property, even a home exemption, does not come ahead of a voluntary secured creditor such as a mortgage bank. Therefore, the fact that Darcy's home is "fully exempt" does not change the fact that she owes the mortgage bank $1.8 million, which exceeds the secured debt limit of $1,580,125 for Chapter 13 eligibility under §109(e). Choices **B** and **C** are both wrong because Darcy does not exceed the unsecured debt limit of $526,700 in this case. She does owe the $400,000 loan and that will count despite the fact that is not yet due. However, the $200,000 student loan that she is guaranteeing for her son, John, is still contingent for Darcy because John has not defaulted on it yet in order to trigger Darcy's liability as guarantor. Answer **D** correctly acknowledges this fact about Darcy's liability as guarantor. However, **D** is only half right because then it goes on to state incorrectly that Darcy's exemption in her home prevents the bank's secured debt from counting against Darcy's secured debt limit for Chapter 13 eligibility.

Martin's and Keating's Picks

1. Question 1 **D**
2. Question 2 **D**
3. Question 3 **A**

21

Secured Creditor Treatment Under Chapter 13

OVERVIEW

A. Treatment of Personal Property Loans and Other Secured Loans That Are Not Home Mortgages
   1. Bifurcation and "stripdown" or "cramdown"
   2. New limitations on stripdown
   3. Valuation
   4. The present value interest rate

B. Treatment of the Home Mortgage in Chapter 13

C. Recognizing When Stripdown Applies

D. A New Approach to Stripdown

Martin's and Keating's Picks

One of the most common reasons for a debtor to use Chapter 13, as opposed to Chapter 7, is to keep property subject to a security interest. You'll recall that in a Chapter 7 case, the only way to keep property subject to a security interest is to keep the payments to the secured creditor current or to pay the value of the collateral in immediate cash to the secured party.[1]

Both of these options are easier said than done. For many debtors, these options are not helpful. Few have the money to redeem the collateral by paying its cash value to the secured party. Moreover, many are already substantially behind on their payments and thus simply cannot stay current. Fortunately, Chapter 13 provides ready relief to those who are behind on their mortgage or car payments and would like to keep the property. Personal property, such as cars and many unattached mobile homes, is treated very differently than

1. Paying cash equal to the value of the collateral, all at once, is called redemption, as discussed more fully in Chapter 16 of this guide and also in §722 of the Code. Some courts also recognize the "keep and pay" option, also discussed in Chapter 16.

home mortgages, so it will be discussed here separately. As always, whether the secured property is personal or real estate, a home, or something else, secured debt is always treated more favorably than unsecured debt in recognition that security interests are property interests. This is true in a Chapter 13 as well, which contains very explicit requirements for the treatment of secured debt. Given these rules, and the fact that all secured debt must always be paid in full (at least up to the value of the collateral), with interest or something very much like interest, many Chapter 13 plans are structured around meeting these secured debt requirements. Because it is possible to propose a plan that makes no distribution to unsecured creditors, and because many debtors have no priority debts, some Chapter 13 plans do nothing more than pay secured creditors, along with debtor's attorneys' fees and Chapter 13 trustee's fees.

A. Treatment of Personal Property Loans and Other Secured Loans That Are Not Home Mortgages

As you will very shortly see, the debtor can drastically reduce the amount that he or she pays on some personal property loans, such as car loans and some mobile home loans, by just paying the value of the secured property, along with interest, over the life of the plan. In many ways, this is conceptually similar to a Chapter 7 redemption that can actually be paid over time. Like a Chapter 7 redemption, the debtor can pay less than the full amount of the debt. Chapter 13 has the added benefit of allowing that reduced amount to be paid in installments, rather than up front.

1. *Bifurcation and "stripdown" or "cramdown"*

Because many personal property items depreciate rapidly after they are purchased, they are often worth far less than the amount still owed on them. Because the debtor can sometimes reduce the debt to the amount of the value of the collateral, this makes Chapter 13 very beneficial. The authority for this is §506(a), which defines a secured debt as secured "to the extent of the value of such creditor's interest . . . in such property."

The process of reducing the loan to the value of the collateral is called, in bankruptcy parlance, the "stripdown" or "cramdown."[2] This literally just means reducing the claim to the value of the collateral under §506(a). The words "stripdown" or "cramdown" may not be official vocabulary words, but they describe a concept with which every bankruptcy attorney (and every

2. Note that stripdown or cramdown is used here as a noun.

bankruptcy professor) is familiar, namely the process of reducing a secured claim to the value of the collateral underlying it. The concept underlying these buzz words even has its own official WEST Key Number, number 51k3708.

As we will discuss shortly, the debtor's ability to "drastically reduce" the amount he or she pays for secured debt under this stripdown principle has been severely cut back. Now, stripdown applies only to car loans that are at least two and a half years old (the loan, not the car), and to loans on other things, including household goods, that were taken out at least one year prior to the filing.

A NOTE ABOUT TERMINOLOGY: We have always called this "cramdown," but have learned that many professors prefer "stripdown," because the word cramdown has another more official meaning that applies to forcing a Chapter 11 plan on a class of nonconsenting creditors. Purists feel it is inaccurate to use cramdown for the concept we describe here. We'll try to use stripdown instead, to eliminate student confusion, but cramdown is very commonly used in this way both in court opinions and in practice.[3]

Either way, whatever word you use, one of the biggest benefits of both Chapter 13 and Chapter 11 is the ability to "strip down"[4] the secured debt to just the value of the collateral. Stripdown is a very common testing area, and we suspect almost all bankruptcy exams contain at least some questions on the topic.

Traditionally, one could strip down all undersecured loans on personal property or investment real estate. One could not and still cannot strip down home mortgages. Now, Personal Property Purchase Money Security Interest (PMSI) loans in cars taken out within two and a half years of the filing and other PMSIs taken out within one year of the filing cannot be stripped down. For all of the following examples, assume the loans were taken out three years before the filing.

The example we use for the concept of stripdown is a car loan in which the loan is higher than the value of the car. You've often heard that once you drive a new car off the dealer's lot, it depreciates by some huge percentage, maybe even 50 percent. In other words, a person pays $20,000 but once it is on the street, the car is only worth $10,000. Probably the depreciation is not that drastic, but to be sure, the new car depreciates faster than the loan gets paid off. So for this example, assume that you buy a car for $20,000 on credit, and one year later the car is worth $15,000. For many cars, this is highly realistic. Also

3. *See, e.g.*, Lomas Mortgage, Inc. v. Louis, 82 F.3d 1, n.1 (1st Cir. 1996) ("The term 'strip down' is a colloquialism used to describe the process by which a secured creditor's lien is limited to the market value of its collateral. The term 'cram down' is also commonly used to describe this process.") *See, e.g.*, Till v. SCS Credit Corp., 124 S. Ct. 1951 (2004); In re Wilson, 174 B.R. 215, 218 n.2 (Bankr. S.D. Miss. 1994); In re Lutz, 164 B.R. 239, 241 (Bankr. W.D. Pa. 1994), rev'd on other grounds, 192 B.R. 107 (W.D. Pa. 1995)). Actually, as of 2003, the term "stripdown" was used for this purpose in 19 reported cases and "cramdown" in 152 reported cases.

4. Now the term is used as a verb, so it is two words rather than one.

assume that because you have paid a lot of interest at a high rate, the amount of the car loan is now $18,000. You have since fallen on tough times and now need to file for Chapter 13.

As in a Chapter 7 case, the secured party who gave you the car loan (assuming it was incurred more than 910 days before any bankruptcy filing) now has a claim that is bifurcated, or split into two parts. One part of the claim, the $15,000, is a secured claim (you'll recall from Chapter 11 of this guide that a secured claim is only as large as the value of the collateral supporting the claim), and the other part, the $5,000, becomes an unsecured claim. This unsecured part will be treated just like any other unsecured claim in the case. It does not matter that the $5,000 was once part of a secured claim. This procedure has allowed you to strip down your secured claim to $15,000, or the current value of your property.

Chapter 13 now considers your $15,000 secured debt and requires it to be paid in full. But what is meant by "paid in full"? Just the stripped-down amount. Payment of that will constitute payment in full of the secured claim. The secured part of the debt is "stripped down" from $20,000 to $15,000. Of course, the creditor has an additional claim (a bifurcated unsecured claim) for the other $5,000, but the debtor's plan does not have to provide that all of this will be paid. In some cases the plan may provide that only a small portion of it, or even none of it, will be paid. So long as the plan provides for payment of the secured part (the $15,000), the debtor can keep the car. This $15,000 can be paid off over the life of a three- to five-year plan with so much paid each week or month. As a result, the debtor may be able to keep the car, and indeed pay less for it than the original purchase price, under Chapter 13, whereas it is unlikely that the debtor could have come up with the $15,000 to redeem it under Chapter 7. The main thing to remember here is that paying the reduced or stripped-down[5] amount fulfills the Chapter 13 requirement that all secured claims be paid in full, because the size of the secured claim is defined as the value of the collateral in §506(a).[6]

Make sure that this makes sense to you before going on. The concept of bifurcation, or splitting the secured claim into two parts, is critical to understanding secured creditor treatment both in Chapter 13 and Chapter 11.

2. *New limitations on stripdown*

Again, under the 2005 amendments, only car loans that were taken out at least 910 days (approximately two and a half years) before a debtor's bankruptcy can be stripped down. This means that the loans that would have benefited the most from stripdown (those that are relatively recent and likely to be under

5. Now the term is being used as an adjective. It's a very flexible phrase.

6. This is true any time the collateral has depreciated below the amount of the loan. Otherwise the debtor must simply pay the loan amount.

water from quick, early depreciation) will now have to be paid at their full face amount.

This limitation on stripdown applies only to PMSIs. Having said that, think about what a PMSI is. It is a loan used to purchase the item that is the collateral for the loan. Most loans secured by personal property are loans that were taken out to purchase the items in question. If a loan is not a PMSI, there is no limitation on stripdown.

Stripdown of PMSI loans on things other than cars, such as household goods, also were cut way back under the 2005 amendments. For all personal property loans on things other than cars, only loans that are over one year old can be stripped down. (*See* 11 U.S.C. §1325(a); look at the dangling [and very lengthy!] sentence at the end of (a)(9).)

QUESTION 1. Mary Marks has the following property: a new living room set for which she owes $2,000 and is worth $600, a car on which she owes $5,000 and is worth $6,500, a computer set-up on which she owes $1,500 and is now worth $800, and a giant-screen TV for which she owes $4,000 and is worth $3,500. All loans were incurred three years before the filing. Which of these items is not subject to stripdown?

A. The TV.
B. The furniture.
C. The car.
D. They are all subject to stripdown because they are all personal property.

ANALYSIS. The answer is **C**. The car is not subject to stripdown because the car is oversecured. There is nothing to strip down because the value of the car has not dropped below the loan amount. Remember that stripdown or cramdown means to reduce the loan amount to the value of the collateral. If the loan balance is lower than the value of the collateral, the debtor has to pay the whole loan amount. **A** and **B** are both subject to stripdown, as they are both undersecured, and thus **D** (all of the above) is also incorrect.

QUESTION 2. Which of the creditors in the prior fact pattern is entitled to post-petition interest and attorneys' fees?

A. The one with the interest in the TV.
B. The one with the interest in the computer.
C. The one with the interest in the car.
D. All of the above.

ANALYSIS. This question reviews what you learned in Chapter 11 of this guide. Only an oversecured creditor is entitled to interest and attorneys' fees on its claim and thus the answer is the creditor with the interest in the car. Creditors **A** and **B** are both undersecured and thus incorrect, and **D** is incorrect for the same reason, which leaves answer **C**.

3. *Valuation*

We have assumed quite a few facts in the hypothetical, including the current value of the car that Mary Marks bought. Valuation is probably the most common factual dispute decided by bankruptcy courts. Valuation disputes come up in dealing with exemptions, redemption, stripdown, relief from the automatic stay, lien avoidance, the best interest of creditors test, Chapter 11 confirmation, and many other issues.

Valuation is often accomplished in large business cases, as well as in some consumer cases, through an appraisal of the property in question. Appraisals may vary greatly depending on the purpose of the valuation, as well as the assumptions made by the appraiser. When faced with more than one valuation, judges often favor the value given by the most credible appraiser. If both parties' appraisers are equally credible then the court will often just split the values down the middle. Normally, only business assets and real estate are appraised. Smaller items of personal property are rarely appraised due to the cost of an appraisal. When it comes to vehicles and mobile homes, most parties use Kelly's Blue Book, NADA, or another similar resource.

In Associates Commercial Corp. v. Rash, 520 U.S. 953 (1997), the U.S. Supreme Court decided whether the proper measure of value for stripdown purposes is the wholesale or the retail value, as both are offered by these blue book resources. After a long-standing split among the federal circuit courts about which of these two rules was preferable,[7] the U.S. Supreme Court followed neither approach, instead choosing the replacement value (a number somewhere in between wholesale and retail). The Supreme Court indicated in Rash that the proper value of a debtor's used personal property, for stripdown purposes, is the price at which the debtor could purchase a comparable used item.

Regardless of how value is determined, it is the single most important determination as to whether a debtor will be able to afford to pay the stripped-down value of a big-ticket item under his or her plan. Thus, as to any security interest that can be stripped down, the most critical question in the equation is the value of the collateral. (*See* Associates Commercial Corp. v. Rash, 520 U.S. 953 (1997).)

The 2005 amendments to the Bankruptcy Code codify Rash, by stating in §506(a)(2) that:

---

7. Because the valuation sets the amount that the debtor must repay the secured party, the wholesale value tended to be lower and thus favored the debtor, while the retail value tended to be higher and thus favored the secured party.

(2) If the debtor is an individual in a case under chapter 7 or 13, such value with respect to personal property securing an allowed claim shall be determined based on the replacement value of such property as of the date of the filing of the petition without deduction for costs of sale or marketing. With respect to property acquired for personal, family, or household purposes, replacement value shall mean the price a retail merchant would charge for property of that kind considering the age and condition of the property at the time value is determined.

QUESTION 3. The debtor is a dentist who owns his practice. He has filed a Chapter 13 bankruptcy and wishes to keep his dental chair, drills, and other equipment, all of which secure a debt of $40,000. In valuing the equipment for stripdown purposes, which of the following values is the court most likely to accept?

A. $35,000, because an expert testifies that is the wholesale value of similar new equipment.
B. $20,000, because an expert testifies that is what the equipment would bring at auction.
C. $30,000, because that is the amount that an expert testifies it would cost the dentist to purchase similar used equipment in the marketplace.
D. $40,000, because that is the amount an expert testifies it would cost the dentist to purchase similar new equipment.

ANALYSIS. **A** is incorrect for two reasons. Wholesale value is not the test, and the value should not be based on new equipment because the dental chair and other equipment will have depreciated. **D** is also incorrect. Although this is the replacement value in a sense, it would result in replacing the used equipment with new equipment. **B** seems like a reasonable approach to valuation, but it is not the test applied in the Rash case. **C** seems to be the best answer, because it appears to literally follow Rash. However, it is strange that **B** and **C** yield different results because both seem to go to the cost of replacing the equipment, and perhaps a court would split the difference. Although the Supreme Court has spoken on this issue, determining value in a specific case is still an unpredictable endeavor.

4. *The present value interest rate*

The other variable in determining the cost of paying off property that has been crammed down is the present value rate that the debtor will be required to pay. Section 1325(a)(5)(B)(ii) provides that the debtor must pay the full value, as of the effective date of the plan, of the allowed secured claim. This has been interpreted to mean that the creditor is entitled to the value of that claim as if it were being paid all at once on confirmation. Because the Code allows the payment over time, the debtor must compensate the creditor for the time value of money. A dollar paid a year from now is worth less than a dollar paid today. Thus, the debtor must pay the creditor for what the creditor loses in interest or other income by not receiving all of its money up front.

Practically speaking, we provide the secured party with the present value of its claim, and compensate it by assigning an interest rate to the debt. We somewhat cavalierly refer to this as the present value interest rate or simply the interest rate, but it is important to understand that it is not really interest. Rather, it is a payment to the secured party to provide it with the present value of its allowed secured claim.

Having said that, every court opinion on record discusses this concept in terms of "interest" and courts even use prevailing interest rates as a guide to determine what rate will fairly compensate a secured party for the time value of its money. Over the years, some courts have said that the proper rate is the prime rate plus an interest point or two.

Other courts have held that one must look to the rate this debtor would pay if he or she were looking to borrow money today and were not in bankruptcy. In 2004, the United States Supreme Court overruled case law using this standard and held that the rate to be applied in a stripdown is the prime interest rate, plus some added percentage points for a host of risk variables. (*See* Till v. SCS Credit Corp., 541 U.S. 465 (2004).) This issue is discussed with more precision in Chapter 36.

NOTE: The debtor can reduce the rate on a loan on personal property even if the loan's value cannot be stripped down. The ability to reduce the interest rate on a loan, as described in Till, applies even to loans for which the value cannot be stripped down. This means one can reduce the interest rate even on car loans taken out within two and a half years of the filing or other loans taken out within a year of the filing. This causes some attorneys to say things like "you can still strip down the rate, just not the value."

QUESTION 4. Debtor has filed a Chapter 13 petition. He owns an automobile that he purchased on credit three years ago. He wants to keep the car, but he owes $20,000 on the purchase price, which is secured by the car. The court has determined that the value of the auto is $15,000. To keep the car, Debtor's plan will have to provide for payments of:

A. a total of $15,000.
B. a total of $20,000.
C. $15,000 plus a market rate of interest on that amount over the length of the plan.
D. $15,000 plus interest at the contract rate specified in the loan agreement.

ANALYSIS. **A** is incorrect because he will have to pay the present value of $15,000, which is something more than that amount because it will be paid in the future. **B** is incorrect because the claim can be stripped down. Although a court might apply the interest rate specified in the original loan, this would be very unusual, so **D** is not the best answer. Hence, **C** is the best answer because it recognizes that although courts apply an interest rate, this will not necessarily be the rate specified in the loan agreement.

B. Treatment of the Home Mortgage in Chapter 13

The rules described previously for stripping down secured loans do not apply to home mortgages. The home mortgage industry convinced Congress in 1984 that if people were allowed to strip down their home mortgages, the entire home lending market would collapse. As a result, Congress passed §1322(b)(2), which states that a person may not modify or otherwise affect a secured loan on which the lender's only collateral is a home. We call this §1322's anti-modification clause.

Now many personal property loans also must be paid in full, as we discussed previously. This is because the 2005 amendments significantly curtail the debtor's right to strip down personal property loans as well, not just home mortgages.

In any event, as a result of special lobbying efforts by home mortgage lenders, home mortgages are paid under Chapter 13 (and also in cases filed by individuals under Chapter 11) in a totally different way than the stripdown approach. As you'll soon see, a home mortgage payment that is in default will always require a larger payment in Chapter 13 than the debtor was paying outside Chapter 13. As a result, feasibility (or ability to pay the plan) is often an issue. Many debtors cannot do what is required to cure the home mortgage, and thus cannot confirm or complete a plan.

Due to the anti-modification section for primary home loans, the debtor must continue to make the regular monthly payment to the lender and also pay off all of the arrears over the life of the plan. The math is often easier to calculate than with other secured creditors because there is no bifurcation and thus no stripdown. The debtor must, however, pay the present value of the arrears, so one must add present value interest to the arrears before dividing the arrears by the number of months of the plan and adding it to the regular monthly payment.

QUESTION 5. John Jet has been unemployed and, as a result, has fallen ten months behind on his home mortgage payment of $720 a month. He now has a job and would like to do a Chapter 13 plan over three years. The Code will permit this because his current monthly income is below the median in his state. He wants to know how large a payment he will need to allocate to the lender to be sure his plan is confirmable. None of these answers is perfect, but which is closest to the truth?

A. $220
B. $720
C. $960
D. $920

ANALYSIS. He always has to pay at least his regular monthly payment of $720 in a Chapter 13, so **A** is clearly incorrect. He is also behind and has to cure his total arrears, with present value interest added, over the life of his plan. Thus, $720, the amount of his regular payment alone, is also incorrect, making **B** wrong.

This leaves us with $920 and $960 as our viable choices. How far behind is he? $720 times 10 months = $7,200, correct? Split this by the number of months in his plan, 36, and you come up with $200 a month, in addition to his $720, or $920. This answer is offered in **D**, which is also wrong. Do you know why? Because he also has to pay present value interest to compensate the lender for not having the arrears cured right away (for the time value of money). Thus, while **C** will have a bit too much interest in it, it is closest to the correct answer and will clearly cover what is needed to pay the lender under the plan.

C. Recognizing When Stripdown Applies

You have now learned several complex rules for treating secured claims in a Chapter 13 case, each in a vacuum depending on the type of secured property that is at issue. You have learned that personal property loans can sometimes be stripped down but loans on real estate that is used as a principal residence cannot. Now we will describe a more global approach to determining which loans can be stripped down and which cannot.

D. A New Approach to Stripdown

Ask yourself three questions for each secured debt:

1. Is the loan undersecured (if not, no need to strip down)?
2. Is this the type of loan that can be stripped down (i.e., a personal property PMSI loan, not a home mortgage)?

3. Does the timing of the loan permit stripdown (i.e., is the loan old enough)?

To elaborate a bit, if the loan is oversecured, then stripdown will accomplish nothing for your client because the goal of stripdown is to lower the loan amount to the value of the collateral. If the collateral is worth more than the debt, there is nothing to strip down. As to the type of loan, personal property loans are candidates for stripdown but home mortgages are not. Finally, consider the timing. Recent PMSI loans (car loans taken out less than two and a half years before the filing and all other personal property loans taken out less than one year before the filing) for goods used by the debtor for personal use cannot be stripped down.

Now let's practice telling the difference.

QUESTION 6. The Lights own an unattached mobile home, on which they owe $31,000. They were approximately $10,000 behind on their payments and subject to a replevin action (like a foreclosure, but for personal property). They decided to file a Chapter 13 case to try and save the mobile home. The mobile home loan is three years old. The value of the mobile home is contested but the court decides that it is worth $9,000. The court sets the present value rate for this loan at 10 percent. The clients would like to do a five-year plan. Assuming the very unrealistic fact that the whole loan continues to earn interest at the simple rate of 10 percent per year throughout the whole loan, how much must the clients pay each month for the mobile home?[8]

A. $10,000, plus interest at 10 percent, divided by the number of months, 60.
B. Their regular payment, plus the amounts set out in A.
C. $9,000 plus 10 percent interest per year, for the life of the plan, which comes out to approximately $225 per month.
D. $9,000 plus 10 percent per year for the life of the plan, which comes out to approximately $350 per month.

ANALYSIS. If this were an attached mobile home, then this would be classified as real property that the debtor uses as a home, and **B** would be the correct answer. The Lights would need to pay their regular monthly payment each month, and would also have to cure the $10,000 in arrears by paying this amount with present value interest over the life of the plan. Thus, as we have

8. In real life, you will use an amortization table that you can easily find on the Internet to calculate your interest. We apologize to the accountants out there, but would like to teach this concept without requiring you to have a computer or an amortization calculator.

discussed, their monthly payment would go up, not down, if the mobile home were considered "real estate."

Because the problem states that the mobile home is unattached, our assumption would be that the mobile home is personal property and is thus subject to stripdown. Under the law of New Mexico (the state in which one of us lives), this is true. An unattached mobile home is personal property. Your own state law may be different, however, and state law governs this issue, so be careful. If the laws of New Mexico govern, what the Lights must pay is just the value of the mobile home, with present value interest. The value is $9,000, and to that we need to add the present value interest. Assuming we use a highly unrealistic and simplified interest calculation to understand the concept (admitting that this method is incorrect and will make accountants cringe), we can see that if the plan will go on for five years, we need to add 10 percent interest per year ($900) × 5 (or $4,500) to the $9,000, which will give us $13,500. We then divide that by 60 months and we get $225 per month. Thus, given this quirky way to calculate the interest (which makes the interest too high because it does not account for the drop in the principal over time), the answer is **C**.

D is incorrect, but by coincidence, this would be the correct answer if the debtor had chosen a three-year plan, and thus if you added three years' worth of the interest, that is $900 × 3 (or $3,600), to the $9,000 value you get $12,600 and then divided that by 36. **A** is also incorrect, for two reasons. **A** describes what it would take to cure a home mortgage, as if this were a security interest in real estate, but **A** does not include the regular monthly payment, so it is insufficient to pay what is required. Thus, the correct answer is **C**.

QUESTION 7. Refer back to Question 3 in Chapter 16, in which two different debtors each bought the same car from a dealer for $16,000 eight years ago, both tried to redeem the car in a Chapter 7 case, and both owed different amounts. The guy who did not take care of the car owed just $6,000 for his redemption, and the one who treated the car like gold had to pay $10,000. Assume that the one who beat up the car, Pete, never paid for the redemption in his Chapter 7 case and has converted his case to a Chapter 13. He now proposes to strip down the lien on the car and pay just the $6,000 with present value interest over three years. You represent his lender, who is furious beyond words about this nasty and unfair treatment. The client wants you to object vehemently to this treatment, and you have concluded that your best chance of getting paid a greater amount is through:

A. objecting to the concept of stripdown as unfair.
B. asking the court to use its equity powers under §105(a) and raise the stripdown value.
C. objecting to the dischargeability of the lender's debt under §523.
D. objecting to the value of the car, through an expert who can prove that the car is actually worth $8,000, not $6,000.

ANALYSIS. This question asks you to strategize about what type of objection might defeat this treatment, which certainly seems unfair, just as it did in the prior redemption question.

What should we eliminate first? **C** is a dead loser in this Chapter 13 bankruptcy. In Chapter 13, only certain debts are not discharged. *See* §§1328 and 523. This is none of those things. The lender would need to prove fraud, or perhaps an intentional tort, and even if the lender was able to do this, it would only make the debt nondischargeable. The lion's share of the debt would still be unsecured, albeit nondischargeable unsecured. Having collateral is the only way to make sure one gets paid anything, so **C** is incorrect.

Can you object to the stripdown on its own terms? No, so **A** is also incorrect. There is a very important rule to learn from this wrong answer. All that really matters for stripdown is the property's value. How it got that way makes no difference, unless the debtor very purposely trashed the property right before the case. This would be very difficult to prove in any case, and does not appear in the facts of this problem. Thus, **A** is also wrong. Remember that what matters for stripdown is the value of the collateral and that's it. The way that the value declined is not part of the stripdown analysis.

B is a huge long shot. Section 105 is constantly being used by debtors — often against creditor interests — to allow things that the Code does not specifically permit. The section can be used by the court any time the court feels that it is necessary to fulfill the particular purposes of the Code. Because this behavior on the part of the debtor creates the wrong incentives, allows assets to be wasted, and thus violates Code policy, perhaps the judge will make the debtor pay what would have been due if the car had been treated well. We still think this will fail.

Your best answer is clearly **D**. Stripdown or cramdown is all about value. If the value is higher, the debtor pays more.

Another option, one that is not listed in the possible answers, is to object to the Chapter 13 plan on the basis of a lack of good faith. Try turning to the factor test contained in Chapter 24. Can you find a factor that could support this objection?

QUESTION 8. Marilyn Marron has four loans to discuss with you, her attorney. She would like to know whether she will benefit by filing a Chapter 13 to deal with these loans. First, she has a loan out for her home on which she owes $200,000. The home is worth approximately $140,000, but unfortunately, she refinanced to consolidate a lot of credit card debts and the market later dropped in her neighborhood. Her monthly payment is $1,600, and she is six months behind on it. Next, she has a loan on a small house she bought ten years ago and now rents out. The tenants are behind on the rent, so she is four months behind on her payment of $600 per month. The little house is worth $50,000, and she owes about $55,000 on it. Her car loan is now five months behind as well. She bought the car last April for $10,000, but it is now worth just $4,000. Finally, she bought her mom a couch for Christmas two years ago and financed the purchase through a PMSI. She pays $400 a month for the couch. She figures the couch is worth about $600, and she still owes $2,000 on it. What will become of these loans in her Chapter 13 if she decides to do one?

A. All can be stripped down, which means she can pay just the value of each item.
B. None of these loans can be stripped down because all are oversecured.
C. Ms. Marron can strip down the car loan and the couch loan, but not the two real estate loans.
D. Ms. Marron cannot strip down the home loan or the car loan, but can strip down the loans for the rental property and for the couch.

ANALYSIS. The question here is which of these loans is undersecured, and also is of the type that can be stripped down. Then, assuming this type of loan can be stripped down, does the timing of the loan permit stripdown?

Discussing each option in the order set out in the suggested analysis here, **B** is incorrect because none of these loans is oversecured. All are undersecured. Go up and confirm that you understand this. If not, return to the text of Chapter 11 of this guide.

Second, **A** is incorrect because a home mortgage is not of the type that can be stripped down under §1322(b)(2). Note that it is undersecured, but it still cannot be stripped down. It is not of the correct type.

Choice **C** is incorrect because of the timing question. Both the car loan and the couch loan are of the type that could be stripped down (both are personal property loans), but the car loan is less than a year old. Thus, the car loan cannot be stripped down, and choice **C** is incorrect. What about the couch loan? It can and should be stripped down. For goodness' sake, what a sad loan to be paying off. This example demonstrates the purpose of stripdown. Don't make people pay back far more on a loan than the creditor could get if the creditor sold the collateral.

Choice **D** states that the rental property can be stripped down. But can it? Yes, as long as it is rental property purchased over a year ago. The prohibition against stripdown applies only to real estate used as a principal residence, so the debtor can most likely strip down both the couch and the rental property. Thus, as you may have guessed, choice **D** is the best answer.

QUESTION 9. (CODE READER) Elizabeth Richards owns and operates an unincorporated catering business. Elizabeth was ill for several months, which caused a drop in her business revenues, but now she is fully recovered. Elizabeth is behind on a number of debts and she would like to file a Chapter 13 bankruptcy to allow herself time to catch up financially.

Elizabeth owns two cars, each of which is subject to a purchase-money secured loan: a Honda Civic that she uses exclusively for her family and a Dodge Caravan that she uses exclusively for her catering business. She bought the Civic 36 months ago and currently owes $18,000 on that car, which is now worth $14,000. She bought the Caravan 24 months ago and currently owes $22,000 on that car, which is now worth $17,000. When Elizabeth files her Chapter 13, which of her two cars will be eligible for stripdown treatment in her plan?

A. Both cars.
B. Neither car.
C. The Civic but not the Caravan.
D. The Caravan but not the Civic.

ANALYSIS. The correct answer is **A**. Getting this question right requires a very close statutory reading of the "hanging paragraph" of §1325(a) that Congress added to the Code in 2005. Note first that Congress only prevented stripdown as to car loans that were taken out within the two-and-a-half years before the debtor files Chapter 13. So that means that the Civic is safe from stripdown based on timing alone. The Caravan loan, however, was taken out just two years before Elizabeth filed her Chapter 13 plan, which might make you think that it would not be eligible for stripdown due to the requirements of the "hanging paragraph." However, if you read the hanging paragraph closely you will see the anti-stripdown language applies only to purchase-money secured loans on cars that were "acquired for the personal use of the debtor." This Caravan was acquired by Elizabeth to be used in her catering business and therefore is not subject to the anti-stripdown language. Therefore, the Caravan loan can be stripped down just like the Civic loan, given that in both cases the outstanding loan amount exceeds the current value of the collateral. For that reason, all of the other three answers are incorrect.

Martin's and Keating's Picks

1. Question 1 **C**
2. Question 2 **C**
3. Question 3 **C**
4. Question 4 **C**
5. Question 5 **C**
6. Question 6 **C**
7. Question 7 **B**
8. Question 8 **D**
9. Question 9 **A**

22

The Treatment of Priority Claims in Chapter 13

OVERVIEW

A. The Closer: Chapters 19, 20, 21, and 22

Martin's and Keating's Picks

Section 1322(a)(2) provides that for a Chapter 13 plan to be confirmable, all claims entitled to priority under §507(a) must be paid in full under the plan. Thus, just as you saw that all secured claims (as they are defined in §506(a), up to the value of the collateral) must be paid in full under a Chapter 13 plan, the same is true of claims that have priority under §507(a). While priority claims also must be paid in full under a Chapter 13 plan, unlike secured claims, the holders of these priority claims are not entitled to present value interest on their claims.[1] Thus, to determine how much the debtor must pay each month to satisfy the claim in full, the debtor's attorney need only divide the allowed priority claims by the number of months in the plan.

So what are the priority claims in a Chapter 13 likely to be? While it is true that some Chapter 13 debtors run businesses and thus owe priority employee claims and perhaps claims to suppliers and deposit holders, most Chapter 13 debtors do not run businesses. The most common priority claims for your average debtor are likely to be past-due taxes and perhaps some past-due child support. The debtor's attorney also is typically paid through the Chapter 13

1. The Code section discussing priority treatment under Chapter 13 simply states that the plan must "provide for the full payment, in deferred cash payments, of all claims entitled to priority under §507 of this title, unless the holder of a particular claim agrees to a different treatment of such claim." The Code section dealing with secured creditor treatment, by comparison, states that with respect to each allowed secured claim provided for in the plan, the holder must agree to the plan, the debtor must surrender the collateral, or the plan must pay "the value, as of the effective date of the plan, of property to be distributed under the plan on account of such claims." As hard as it is to read, this last language has been interpreted to require that the debtor pay present value interest to the secured creditor to compensate the creditor for the time value of money. Because this language (value, as of the effective date of the plan) is not in the priority provision, paying a present value rate on priority claims is not required.

plan, and his or her fees are also priority claims. A debtor who has large tax liabilities can save a great deal on interest by filing a Chapter 13 case. As soon as the case is filed, both the interest and any penalties that would normally accrue outside bankruptcy cease.

We said previously that one must divide the allowed priority claims by the number of months to calculate this part of the plan payment. But how does one determine how much of the claim is allowed? Because many types of taxes get priority treatment only if they are recent, the issue of allowance comes up most often in that context. Not all taxes will need to be paid in full in every case. Remember the discussion of priority treatment in Chapter 10? Some taxes lose their priority status because they are too old. Others fall into categories that simply get less priority than others. Thus, you should never assume that all taxes are entitled to priority.

Another allowance issue comes up in the context of support payments under a marital settlement agreement. All past-due support payments must of course be paid in full under a Chapter 13 plan, but what about past-due property settlements? While property settlement agreements flowing from a marital settlement agreement do not get discharged in a Chapter 7, these claims do not get any special priority in either chapter, so they do not have to be paid in full under a Chapter 13 plan.[2]

QUESTION 1. For the past five years, Marlo Marks has run the hippest beauty salon in Austin (if you remember, Texas has an unlimited homestead exemption), but she recently ran into huge tax problems and the IRS threatened to shut her down. She is in your office and wants to know what a Chapter 13 case might do for her. She owns a great house on a lake that is worth approximately $250,000 and has no mortgage on it. She also owes $70,000 in withholding taxes, $50,000 in income taxes from her first year in business, and $25,000 from last year. Her other debts are pretty small and her salary right now is about $3,000 a month, net. What are her options?

1. Go into Chapter 13 and, to meet §1322(a)(3), pay the $145,000 over five years, for a monthly payment for just the priority taxes of $2,416.
2. Go into Chapter 13 and, to meet §1322(a)(3), pay the $95,000 over five years, for a monthly payment for just the priority taxes of $1,584.
3. Forget the bankruptcy and just refinance the house to pay the taxes due, which will be $95,000.
4. Forget the bankruptcy and just refinance the house to pay the taxes due, which will be $145,000.

---

2. We know that it is easy to confuse dischargeability with priority, but the rules for each are different, as this example shows.

A. 1.
B. 3.
C. 2 or 3.
D. 2 or 4.

ANALYSIS. The first step in answering this question is determining which of these tax obligations are actually entitled to priority treatment. In real life it can be hard to tell, but here, it has been made easy. Trust fund taxes are always entitled to priority, so the $70,000 must be paid. (*See* 11 U.S.C. §507(a)(8)(C).) These are funds that she, as the employer, withheld from her employees' paychecks and never remitted to the taxing authorities. They are held fictitiously in trust under the law (thus the name) because this is considered such a bad thing to do, as this was not Marlo's money.

The income taxes from her first year in business (which was five years ago) are too old to have priority. (*See* 11 U.S.C. §507(a)(8)(A)(i).) To get priority, they must be for a taxable year ending on or before the filing date on the petition (which is true here), but also be for a year "for which a return, if required, is last due . . . after three years before the date of the filing of the petition." These are much older. Even though Marlo does not have to pay these claims in full, because they are not priority claims, she may still need to pay a distribution on these taxes as unsecured claims (assuming she pays a distribution to her general unsecured creditors).

The $25,000, however, fits within the priority time frame set out in §507(a)(8)(1)(i), so this portion of the income taxes is entitled to be paid in full under the plan. That means that if Marlo files a Chapter 13 case, she needs to pay the total of all priority claims, the $70,000 plus the $25,000, for a total of $95,000, in full over the life of her plan. This would make choice **2** a viable option.

Choice **1** is incorrect because it requires Marlo to pay all $145,000 of the taxes (even the ones that are not entitled to priority) in full. Besides the fact that this is not required, the resulting payment number makes her budget way too tight, as she would then need to live off of a total of less than $600, not including the trustee's fee of 10 to 11 percent and her own attorneys' fees.

What about the possibility of refinancing and avoiding bankruptcy altogether? We like the idea, but what would be the financial benefits and detriments? First off, if there is no bankruptcy, the debtor would need to pay the whole $145,000 debt, not just the $95,000, right? The IRS has the legal right to all its funds outside bankruptcy, not just what it would get inside bankruptcy.[3] Thus, Marlo would need to borrow the whole $145,000. Over 20 years at 2007 interest rates, this would cost her approximately $1,200 a month, with interest, insurance, and tax escrows. If she really wants to avoid bankruptcy, this is

---

3. In reality, one could always try to settle for less than full payment, especially if the settlement was to be paid up front in cash. However, the IRS is under no obligation to accept less than the $145,000 unless there is a bankruptcy.

a good option, and would make **D** (**2** or **4**) the correct answer. If she does not care too much about the stigma of bankruptcy, and she can live on less than $1,400 a month,[4] she might be better off just doing the Chapter 13 and getting the taxes paid off in five, rather than 20, years. As **2** alone is not one of the answers offered, the best choice you have is **D**.

A NOTE ABOUT PRIORITY CLAIMS FOR DOMESTIC SUPPORT OBLIGATIONS: The definition of "domestic support obligations," which is one of the debts the debtor must pay in full in a Chapter 13 case under §1322(a), now includes support obligations arising before or after the case is filed, and also to various obligees, including "a spouse, former spouse, or child of the debtor or such child's parent, legal guardian, or responsible relative." This language clearly covers unmarried parents of children as well as many others not previously covered. Quite significantly, the phrase also applies to domestic support obligations owed to governmental units. (*See* 11 U.S.C. §101(14A).) These are acquired by assignment, and could be large enough to make a Chapter 13 plan infeasible.

A. The Closer: Chapters 19, 20, 21, and 22

Maria Marcos has an income of $1,400 from disability payments. She owns both a regular home, which has a $50,000 loan on it and a value of $40,000, as well as an RV-style mobile home that she inherited from her father. It is on wheels and sitting in her driveway. The mobile home has a $60,000 loan on it (taken out many years ago) and a value of $20,000. The regular payments on the mobile home are $600 a month and the regular monthly payments on the regular house are $500 a month. She is ten months behind on both loans. She also owes real estate taxes and income taxes from five years ago, for a total of $60,000. These taxes resulted from a dispute that her deceased father had about the ownership and income of certain land. None of these taxes has been reduced to a lien. Which of the following statements is correct based on the little that you have been told about Ms. Marcos's situation?

1. The debtor is ineligible for a Chapter 13 because she does not have a regular job.
2. Because the loan amount for the mobile home is bigger, the payment that the debtor would have to make on the mobile home would be

4. Don't forget the trustee's fees and her own attorneys' fees, which will make her total monthly plan payment more than $1,584.

larger in a Chapter 13 case than the payments she would need to make on her regular home.
3. The debtor has $60,000 in priority claims.
4. Because the debtor will need to pay off the mobile home in full during the three to five years that she is in Chapter 13, the payments on the mobile home will be larger than the payments on the regular home, which can be paid over a longer period of time under the original note.

A. All of the above.
B. 2 and 4 only.
C. None of the above.
D. 1 and 3 only.

ANALYSIS. As it turns out, all of the choices you were given (**1-4**) are incorrect. First of all, the debtor is not ineligible for Chapter 13 because she does not work. Her regular disability payments make her eligible for Chapter 13, as you learned in Chapter 20 of this guide. Any regular income is sufficient, even if it does not result from the debtor's employment. Choice **3** is also incorrect. The debtor does not have $60,000 in priority claims. According to §507(a)(8), old real estate taxes that have not been lien, and income taxes that are over three years old are not entitled to priority treatment under the Code.

The complicated parts of this question can be found in choices **2** and **4**. The difficulty here is that, although the debtor's loan on the mobile home is for $60,000, the mobile home is probably personal property (based upon the fact that it is an RV and on wheels) and, as a result, this loan can be stripped down to the value of the loan, or $20,000. Assuming that the debtor will be paying her Chapter 13 plan over 60 months or five years, she will need to pay the $20,000, plus present value interest. At 10 percent, this would mean adding another $10,000 or so (again, this is too much, but it is an estimation without a calculator) to the amount needed to be paid, for a total of $30,000, divided by 60 months and a monthly payment of $500.

If you look at the treatment of the regular home, on the other hand, §1322(b)(2) does not allow the debtor to strip down the home mortgage. Thus, even though the home is only worth $40,000, the debtor will still need to pay the full $50,000 to the creditor. This need not be done during the life of the plan, assuming that the home loan extends beyond that. Rather, the debtor can simply make the regular monthly payment of $500 a month and add to that the cure amount. In this particular case, the cure amount is 10 months × $500 = $5,000, plus present value interest on that particular amount of around $2,500 (or a slightly lesser amount), for a total of $7,500. This amount of default would require the debtor to pay $125 a month ($7,500 divided by 60 months) for the cure, plus the regular monthly payment of $500, for a monthly payment of $625 for the home mortgage lender over the five-year life of the plan.

Consequently, that means that the mobile home payment will be $500 a month, based on the stripdown value and based on the fact that it will be paid over the 60-month life of the plan, but the home mortgage will be $625 a month and will extend beyond the life of the plan. As a result of this, choice **2** is incorrect. It is not true that because the loan amount for the mobile home is bigger, the mobile home payment will be bigger under the plan. Nor is choice **4** true. The debtor will be paying off the home mortgage pursuant to §1322(b)(2) over the original note, whereas the debtor will be paying the mobile home off in full during the life of the plan. This does not necessarily mean that the payment will be larger on the mobile home. This somewhat unusual situation arises because the mobile home, a piece of personal property, can be stripped down to the value of the collateral, while the permanent home cannot. As a result, choice **4** is also incorrect, and the correct answer to this question is **C.**

Martin's and Keating's Picks

1. Question 1	**D**
The Closer: Chapters 19–22	**C**

23

The Disposable Income Test in Chapter 13

OVERVIEW

A. The Prior Disposable Income Test
B. The New Disposable Income Test
   1. Below-median-income debtors and the new disposable income test
   2. The debtor's budget and the status quo: Class issues
   3. Payments to 401(k) plans for below-median-income debtors
   4. Above-median-income debtors and the new disposable income test

Martin's and Keating's Picks

Section 1328(b)(1)(B) contains the Chapter 13 disposable income test, which is also sometimes called the best efforts test. This section requires the debtor to contribute all of his or her projected disposable income to the plan. (*See* 11 U.S.C. §1325(b).)

We hate to keep referring to prior law or the bankruptcy law before the 2005 amendments, but for the subject of the Chapter 13 disposable income test, this trip down memory lane is necessary. The prior or old test is used to measure disposable income for below-median-income debtors, and a new test is used for above-median-income debtors. This means we can still use the large body of interpretive case law developed over the past four decades for those below-median-income debtors, who, by the way, comprise the majority of bankruptcy debtors.

A. The Prior Disposable Income Test

The prior version of the Chapter 13 disposable income test became part of the Bankruptcy Code in 1984. At the time it was added, the "good faith" requirement was already in the Code, but there was no explicit requirement that the debtor use his or her income to pay as much as possible to creditors under the Chapter 13 plan. The disposable income test was added to the Code to ensure that all Chapter 13 debtors made as substantial an effort to pay creditors as possible.

Before 1984, some judges imputed into the good faith test a requirement that a debtor use all of his or her available income (after reasonable expenses) to pay creditors. The 1984 amendments made the requirements of Chapter 13 extra-clear. Use your available disposable income to pay your creditors, or your plan will not be confirmed.

How was disposable income calculated? By taking a debtor's "projected disposable income" and deducting the debtor's actual expenses, specifically those "reasonably necessary for the maintenance and support of the debtor and the debtor's dependents, including the debtor's business expenses." (*See* 11 U.S.C. §1325(b) (the pre-2005 version).)

Built into this test was the explicit ability for courts and trustees to challenge expenses as too extravagant, as being beyond what was necessary for the maintenance and support of the debtor and the debtor's dependents. This test still applies to the majority of Chapter 13 cases, namely those cases in which the debtor's current monthly income is below the median income in his or her state. This test raises some of the most interesting policy questions in bankruptcy law. What does a person really need? May a bankruptcy debtor maintain his or her current station in life while not paying his or her debts, even if the station is quite high? How much sacrifice is enough? Should the rich sacrifice more?

The 2005 amendments inserted a new disposable income test based upon the means test contained in §707(b). The new disposable income test applies only to above-median-income debtors. For below-median-income debtors, who will continue to be the majority of all Chapter 13 debtors, the old test still applies.

B. The New Disposable Income Test

The new disposable income test has, at least on its face, taken away some of the teeth of the prior test. It looks as though Congress had a less than clear understanding of the purposes and the functions of the prior disposable income test. Congress essentially imputed the "abuse test" (garnered from the means test) into the disposable income test. Because the means test reflects a financial fiction and does not measure a debtor's actual ability to pay creditors, its imputation into the disposable income test has left a wake of confusion.

Here is what appears clear. The court is now directed to apply the definition of "current monthly income" from the abuse test to set the debtor's income for the disposable income test. As you learned in Chapter 17, this is not the debtor's actual income, but instead an average of the debtor's past income for the six months before the debtor's bankruptcy petition. This number, because it is all about the debtor's past, and not necessarily about the future, can be easily manipulated by the timing of the petition. The resulting number could be more, but could also be far less, than the real income a debtor is earning while in Chapter 13. Does this make sense? It doesn't seem to.

The resulting number also does not change as the debtor's circumstances change, making it a poor fit for determining what the debtor can afford to pay creditors. Some debtors may be able to pay creditors much more than the formula suggests. When you deduct the allowed expense under the new test, more confusion arises because some of the expenses deducted under the means test are not actual expenses, but come off a chart of allowed expenses.

1. *Below-median-income debtors and the new disposable income test*

For those with current monthly income below the median (as calculated under the means test described in Chapter 17), the test works similarly to how it worked in the past (*see* §1325(b)(2)(A) and (B)), except that all the appropriate and necessary expenses are deducted from this artificial income we just talked about.

Studying the nuances of the old disposable income test (the one that now applies to only below-median-income debtors) is one of the most interesting endeavors in bankruptcy law. The inquiry poses the most fundamental questions about the human condition, namely "what does a person really need?" American materialism and consumerism, as well as relative wealth vis-à-vis the rest of the world, make the question even more interesting. Can you imagine foreign societies in which private schools, music lessons, and summer camp are considered necessities?

This topic raises two dueling questions. First, what should a person who has not paid his or her debts be allowed to spend money on — in other words, which expenses are really necessary within the meaning of the statutory language? At the same time, when a person is permitted, at least under present law, to choose between walking away from his or her debts and paying some of them off over time, how attractive should we make Chapter 13, to induce people to choose the repayment plan option? How stringent should we be, given that we would like to create an incentive for people to pay off at least some debts? You have heard that bankruptcy courts are courts of equity that have a great deal of discretion. In the extremely fact-based area of disposable income, in which the debtor's expenses are scrutinized and judged, judicial discretion is at an all-time high. One judge might find a $90 hair appointment outrageous, while another might find it a necessity. An animal lover might find pets to be a necessity, while another judge might find the debtor's food and vet bills inappropriate for a bankruptcy debtor.

For items that are obviously necessary, the issue becomes how much is reasonable to spend on food, medicine, car insurance, and so on. One Chapter 13 trustee told one of us that she considered $600 each month as per se reasonable for food for a family of four. However, some judges question the utility of per se budgets, claiming that there is no way to say that $700 or even $800 might not be reasonable in some situations, because the average family simply does not exist. Does the household have teenagers in it? Do the debtors have enough cash flow to take advantage of buying in bulk? Do they live in a remote area where food is expensive? Does the category "food" include toothpaste and toilet paper? Make-up for a teenage girl? What other expenses are reasonable? Is a $70 cable TV bill reasonable? One of us is a nonsubscriber and was surprised to learn that cable TV is generally a permissible expense for just about anyone.

QUESTION 1. Who is most likely to object to the debtor's expenses?

A. The judge, sua sponte.
B. The U.S. Trustee's Office.
C. An individual creditor.
D. The Chapter 13 trustee.

ANALYSIS. Keep in mind that the Chapter 13 trustee is the one who is charged with monitoring the debtor's expenses. Any expenses the Chapter 13 trustee can eliminate from the debtor's budget will immediately make assets available for distribution to the general unsecured creditors.[1] Because the Chapter 13 trustee is a fiduciary for all of the creditors, particularly the unsecured creditors, the correct answer is **D**.

Although the judge could raise an issue on his or her own, a lot of cases are assigned to each judge, and this is probably unlikely, so **A** is not the best answer. The U.S. Trustee, who is part of the U.S. Department of Justice, generally is not involved in Chapter 13 cases, except when it comes to monitoring attorneys' fees and attorney competence, so **B** is also incorrect. Finally, individual creditors are not very involved in most Chapter 13 cases, because most leave the objecting up to the Chapter 13 trustee. While **C** is a plausible answer, it is not the best answer. The question asks who is most likely to object, and the answer is the Chapter 13 trustee.

1. As we previously discussed, the plan will already have proposed that secured creditors and priority creditors be paid in full from other funds.

2. *The debtor's budget and the status quo: Class issues*

If a debtor is wealthier, meaning middle class or upper middle class, rather than lower middle class, some judges will scrutinize his or her expenses more. On the other hand, many court opinions on the subject of the disposable income (which is also called best efforts) test seem to allow the debtor to maintain the status quo. In other words, people who have always had high expenses will be allowed to continue to have high expenses, while really poor people will be allowed only the most basic expenses. For example, private school tuition has been found by some courts to be a reasonable and necessary expense as long as the cost is not excessive (whatever that means), and as long as the child has been attending the school for a considerable amount of time. (*See* In re Cleary, 357 B.R. 369 (Bankr. D.S.C. 2006); In re Nicola, 244 B.R. 795 (Bankr. N.D. Ill. 2000); and In re Burgos, 248 B.R. 446 (Bankr. M.D. Fla. 2000).) Other courts flatly disagree, finding private school to be a luxury and not a necessity. (*See* In re Nelson, 204 B.R. 497 (E.D. Tex. 1996).) One court held that the debtor could not continue to pay high veterinary bills for his elderly horses and dogs. Ouch! (*See* In the Matter of Wyant, 217 B.R. 585 (Bankr. D. Neb. 1988).) Braces, summer camp, and music and sports lessons for children have fueled similar debates. How much should children be required to pay for the sins (or credit indiscretions) of their parents? Can the children take piano lessons? Does it matter if they have always done so? What if they are gifted? Can they go to summer camp? Have a nose job? The list of variations on this question is endless.

QUESTION 2. Karla and Kyle Kordy have a current monthly income below the median in their state. They owe large sums to payday loan companies, rent-to-own agencies, credit card companies, and other subprime lenders,[2] resulting from a large bout of unemployment on Kyle's part. He is back at work now, and with their income they can afford to do a Chapter 13 plan that pays what is required to their home mortgage company, as well as the small amounts due for priority taxes. Based on their current expenses, they can only afford a 5 percent distribution to unsecured creditors. These expenses include violin lessons for Max and Abe, their two sons, ages 14 and 17, respectively. Abe is so talented that he has a chance to win a full scholarship at the Juilliard School. Max needs surgery on his nose, which is pressed to the right side and causing a slight breathing problem. Their health insurance company says this surgery is not covered because it is a preexisting condition, but the family found a wonderful doctor who agreed to take the $6,000 fee for the surgery

2. Subprime lenders loan money to people who presumably cannot get traditional loans at good rates. We call them "sub-prime" because they charge high interest rates (not the prime rate or anything close to that) to people who often have no other way to borrow.

over time, at a cost of $300 a month until paid. Can the payments for the surgery, as well as the violin lessons, continue post-petition?

A. Of course, because both are perfectly legitimate expenses.
B. The surgery is fine, but the violin lessons must cease.
C. The surgery can be had, but only Abe can continue the violin lessons, and even then, only because it could save the debtors money later by having his prestigious college education paid for through a scholarship.
D. Neither the surgery nor the violin lessons are necessary for the support of the debtor's dependents, under the plain meaning of the statute. All these luxuries can wait until the plan payments are over, at which time the debtors will be free to spend their money as they choose.

ANALYSIS. This one must be a trick question, right? A judge could choose any one of the answers based on his or her own perceptions of necessity, as well as his or her own experiences. Additionally, questions about particular budget items will also be answered in part based on what the rest of the budget looks like. Do the debtors live in a $70,000 home or a $250,000 home? Do they spend other money freely or have they scrimped on other items to make these two expenses a priority?

As a result of all these unknowns, we are guessing here, but you should start the question by trying to eliminate some answers. Based on the cases we have read, it seems unlikely to us that any judge would deny the surgery. After all, nothing short of breathing is at risk here, even if the impairment is slight! When it comes to health, judges are certainly more lenient than with many other categories of items. This would eliminate **D** as an option.

Choice **B** says the violin lessons must cease and some judges would surely agree, but we would eliminate this one next. We think most judges would find that at least the son who might be able to obtain a scholarship for his talents should be allowed to continue, assuming that the lessons are preparing him for his auditions and that those have not yet occurred. Some judges would allow them to continue even for the more distant future, and again, the possible options are endless. This leaves us with two possible correct answers, **A** and **C**. Before moving on to discuss each of those, you should know that many courts (although certainly not all) have found that even if parents pay for private school for minors, children must pay for their own college if their parents are in Chapter 13. Thus, there is a chance that a court could say that these lessons will not save the Kordys money in the long run because the parents cannot pay for the children's college while in Chapter 13 in any event. This does not seem compelling to me, however, because it is just wasteful to throw away a good scholarship. Beware, though! Your own teacher may disagree. The important thing is that you are able to discuss both sides of this issue.

As between choices **A** and **C**, we will not even choose one. It depends so very much on the judge's own view of the importance of these lessons. Certainly some would allow them to continue for both and others would allow them only for Abe perhaps on two grounds. First, Max is already getting an extra benefit through the plan for his surgery. Second, Abe's lessons may result in a scholarship, which would benefit the family in the long run. This problem highlights the judicial discretion issue we discussed. It seems pathetic to deny lessons to the son who is not quite as good or who is perhaps simply younger. On the other hand, you have to draw the line somewhere, and creditors have a right to be paid. This is a basic theme of bankruptcy law, balancing the debtor's right to go on with life against the creditors' right to be paid.

QUESTION 3. (CODE READER) Brian Waters is an above-median debtor who files a Chapter 13 bankruptcy so that he can erase some large credit-card debts but still keep his home and his car. Brian has been a long-time member of his local church and has regularly contributed 10 percent of his annual gross income to the church. If Brian discontinued his 10 percent church contributions, his proposed five-year plan would leave his general unsecured creditors with $1,500 per month in disposable income. If Brian's 10 percent church contributions are allowed to continue, then his monthly disposable income to fund the plan would shrink to $1,000 per month. Brian, however, recently made an additional five-year pledge to his church for the church's capital campaign to build a new building. That pledge amounts to an additional $500 per month commitment on top of the $500 per month that Brian has historically paid his church in donations. Based on this information, what is the amount of monthly disposable income that Brian's general unsecured creditors should be entitled to in his five-year plan?

A. $1,500.
B. $1,000.
C. $500.
D. $750.

ANALYSIS. The correct answer is **D**. That may surprise you, since perhaps it seems that we should either allow none of the contributions, both of the contributions, or just Brian's historic 10 percent rate of contributions. Yet the Bankruptcy Code is fairly clear in §1325(b)(2)(A)(ii) that we should allow eligible charitable contributions of up to 15 percent of the debtor's gross annual income. Under the facts here, that would amount to $750 per month since we are told that 10 percent of Brian's gross annual income yields a payment of $500 per month. (Quick math quiz: What is Brian's gross annual income? It must be $60,000, since $500, his monthly contribution, is said to be 10 percent of $5,000, which is Brian's monthly income. When you multiply that $5,000 monthly income by 12 months, it yields an annual gross income of $60,000.) When we subtract the $750 figure (15 percent of Brian's gross annual income on a monthly basis) from the $1,500 per month disposable income that would otherwise be available to Brian's general unsecured creditors, we end up with $750 per month for creditors in his plan.

What about the fact that the building-fund commitment is brand-new for Brian — should we refuse to allow any of that amount for that reason? Section 1325(b)(2)(A)(ii) seems to make no such distinction, and Congress showed in §548(a)(2) that it clearly knows how to make such a distinction between a debtor's brand-new vs. historical charitable giving when it wants to. *See* §548(a)(2) (requiring prior practice only for contributions that exceed 15 percent of gross annual income); *see also* In re Cavanaugh, 250 B.R. 107 (9th Cir. BAP 2000) (allowing the initiation of a first-time tithing program in bankruptcy). Furthermore, there seems to be no bad faith in any event on Brian's part in increasing his church giving since it was in connection with a church building campaign that just began. Some might argue that debtors should first be fair to their creditors before they are allowed to be generous to their religious and charitable beneficiaries, but Congress has pretty clearly indicated otherwise.

3. *Payments to 401(k) plans for below-median-income debtors*

Recently, courts have been faced with whether to allow a debtor in a Chapter 13 case to make contributions to a retirement plan. The cases seem to fall into two categories, those that say such contributions can wait until after the plan is finished and those that allow some contributions, on a case-by-case basis, as long as they are reasonable. As far as allowing debtors to make these outright contributions, courts are also influenced by whether the employer will match a contribution, thus further improving the debtor's future, and also by the tax implications of the contribution. If there is no or little net benefit to creditors of discontinuing the contributions, then some courts will allow the debtor to continue making the contributions. Sometimes the debtor has borrowed money from his or her 401(k) plan and will suffer a large financial penalty if the money is not paid back. Some courts will allow those payments to continue and some will not, again based on the incentives we hope to create in people and their financial behavior on the one hand, and the desire to pay creditors on the other.

The 401(k) cases pose interesting questions about the future financial well-being of the debtors. Some would argue that encouraging people to save is important to their future rehabilitation and financial health. Others would naturally say that saving for the future is fabulous, once existing creditors are paid. And so the saga continues.

Another issue courts have struggled with is whether the debtor should be allowed some extra money in the budget each month, in case of an emergency, as a contingency fund of sorts. Others have considered whether the debtor can save money for the sake of saving it during the plan. It seems that some plan for emergencies is wise, and might even improve the chance of success under the plan. After all, unexpected expenses frequently come up. Courts are split on this issue, however, with some disallowing contingency funds or savings plans.

4. *Above-median-income debtors and the new disposable income test*

Chapter 13 debtors with a current monthly income above the median income have their expenses deducted "in accordance with" the statutory formula for measuring abuse in Chapter 7 cases in §707(b)(2)(A) and (B).

For above-median-income Chapter 13 debtors, the expense-policing function of an objection to confirmation has been somewhat neutralized by the new law. Congress has substituted a mathematical formula that fixes expense deductions that will routinely be both insufficient to sustain life and (in many cases) in excess of any amount that would survive the reasonable and necessary standard of the prior test. Because current monthly income is not real income and because the expenses that can be deducted for above-median debtors are not real expenses, these numbers will bear no relationship to what a debtor could pay creditors.

For a time, circuit courts disagreed whether a bankruptcy court must only apply the code mechanically, or if courts could exercise discretion by projecting a more realistic disposable income for the debtor than what the mechanical approach would dictate. In 2010, the Supreme Court resolved the issue in a case that clearly illustrated how mechanical application of the code can be problematic. (*See* Hamilton v. Lanning, 560 U.S. 505.) There, a one-time buyout from a former employer inflated the debtor's six-month average of past income. Going forward, the debtor could only count on income from a new job that left her earnings below the state's median income. The debtor proposed a plan paying \$144 per month for 36 months, whereas a mechanical application of the code would require her to pay \$756 per month, an amount that she could not realistically maintain. The Court interpreted the word "projected," as used in §1325(b)(1)(B), in its ordinary meaning, to take into account factors that may affect the final outcome. The Court held that a bankruptcy court "may account for changes in the debtor's income or expenses that are known or virtually certain at the time of confirmation." Thus, bankruptcy courts have discretion to depart from a mechanical application of §1325(b)(1)(B) and apply that section in a forward-thinking way.

A FINAL NOTE ON WHICH EXPENSES CAN BE DEDUCTED: FACT OR FICTION

On a related note, the U.S. Supreme Court also decided whether, in calculating a debtor's "projected disposable income" during the plan period, a bankruptcy court may allow an ownership cost deduction for vehicles only if the debtor is actually making payments on the vehicles. (*See* Ransom v. FIA Card Services, N.A., 562 U.S. 61 (2011).)

In it, Jason Ransom filed for Chapter 13 bankruptcy relief. Among his assets, he listed a car he owned outright, with no loan. On his Statement of Current Monthly Income, Ransom reported a current monthly income of $4,248.56 and an annualized income of $50,982.72, which put him above the median income for his household size in his state of residence, Nevada. However, as the bankruptcy statute and forms seem to allow, Mr. Ransom claimed monthly expense deductions—including the vehicle "ownership cost" deduction at issue in this case—in the amount of $4,038.01 and a resulting monthly disposable income of $210.55.

In his Chapter 13 plan, Ransom proposed paying $500 per month over 60 months, providing approximately a 25 percent distribution on general unsecured claims. MBNA objected to confirmation of the plan, arguing Ransom was not devoting all of his projected disposable income to fund the plan as required under 11 U.S.C. §1325(b)(1)(B).

MBNA argued that Ransom could deduct a vehicle ownership cost only if he actually was making lease or loan payments on the vehicle and because Ransom owned his vehicle free and clear of encumbrances and lease obligations, he was not entitled to the vehicle ownership cost deduction. Thus, MBNA argued, Ransom's projected disposable income should be $681.55 (the $210.55 he reported in disposable income plus $471.00, the amount of the vehicle ownership cost deduction to which MBNA objected).

The Supreme Court held that the car ownership cost deduction "is not 'applicable' to a debtor who will not incur any such costs during his bankruptcy plan." The Court reasoned that §707(b)(2)(A)(ii)(I) authorizes debtors to deduct only those expenses that are "applicable." "Ownership costs," the Court said, "encompass[] the costs of a car loan or lease and nothing more." Therefore, ownership costs are not "applicable" to a debtor who owns a car free and clear. The debtor was not entitled to deduct car ownership costs when calculating disposable income because the debtor was not making loan or lease payments on the car.

Martin's and Keating's Picks

1. Question 1 **D**
2. Question 2 **A or C**
3. Question 3 **D**

24

The Good Faith Test in Chapter 13

OVERVIEW

A. **Overlap with the Disposable Income Test and Other Tests**
B. **Good Faith Factor-Based Tests**
C. **Multiple Filings**
D. **Zero Percent Plans**
Martin's and Keating's Picks

In addition to the disposable income test above, there is another equally powerful and complicated Chapter 13 test. It is called the "good faith" test. Section 1325(a)(3) provides that the plan be proposed "in good faith and not by any means forbidden by law." As simple as this sounds, the test is actually quite elusive.

The "disposable income" test was added to the Code in 1984. Prior to this time, the Code simply required that plans be filed in good faith. Many courts interpreted the good faith requirement to mean that the debtor had contributed all of the disposable income that he or she had. Once the disposable income test was added to the Code in 1984, this left the "good faith" test undefined. The good faith test means different things to different people. Some of those interpretations are discussed here.

A. Overlap with the Disposable Income Test and Other Tests

When the debtor prepares his or her budget, which was the subject of part of the previous chapter (at least as applied to below-median-income debtors), some money falls to the bottom line as disposable income, or funds available to pay creditors. The debtor can then propose the plan. It is implicit in the Code's good faith requirement, as well as the disposable income test, that the debtor will estimate all expenses in good faith and not inflate the expenses. Under some interpretations of the good faith test, the debtor also should engage in some belt-tightening in the budget. If not, the plan may not meet the good faith test. As the good faith test allows one to look at the debtor's overall behavior in a case in terms of expenses, disclosures, and testimony, the test allows for an objection to the plan that is hard to define. In some ways, it is similar to what Justice Potter Stewart said about pornography: "I know it when I see it."[1] Lack of good faith is a smell test, although some of the facts and factors below may tip one off that good faith is at issue.

B. Good Faith Factor-Based Tests

Given the lack of guidance in the Code, some courts have adopted factor-based tests to determine whether a debtor has filed a plan in good faith. Both the Eighth and the Tenth Circuits have adopted the following test, which requires one to balance all the factors:

- The amount of the plan payments and of the debtor's surplus;
- the debtor's employment history, ability to earn, and likelihood of future increases in income;
- the duration of the plan;
- the accuracy of the plan's statement of debts and expenses, the percentage repayment of unsecured debts, and whether any inaccuracies are an attempt to mislead the court;
- the extent of preferential treatment in the plan between classes of creditors;
- the extent to which secured creditor claims are modified;[2]
- the type of debt sought to be discharged and whether any such debt is nondischargeable in a Chapter 7;
- the existence of special circumstances such as inordinate medical expenses;
- the frequency with which the debtor has filed for bankruptcy;
- the motivation and sincerity of the debtor in seeking Chapter 13 relief; and
- the burden which the plan's administration would place on the Chapter 13 trustee.

Now that is a juggling act! After enumerating this eleven-part test, the Eighth Circuit court that drafted the test, stated that "[t]his list is not exclusive

1. Jacobellis v. Ohio, 378 U.S. 184, 197 (1964) (Stewart, J., concurring) (stating with reference to the lack of definition for hard-core pornography the now (in)famous standard, "I know it when I see it").
2. Presumably, this is a legitimate use of Chapter 13 and a sign of good faith.

and weight given to each factor will necessarily vary with the facts and circumstances of each case." (*See* United States v. Estus (In re Estus), 695 F.2d 311, 314-16 (8th Cir. 1982), cited in In re Flygare, 709 F.2d 1344 (10th Cir. 1983).) It is hard to imagine a more fluid test! And be careful: Other circuits have adopted other tests. (*See, e.g.*, Kitchens v. Georgia Railroad Bank & Trust Co. (In re Kitchens), 702 F.2d 885 (11th Cir. 1983); Deans v. O'Donnell (In re Deans), 692 F.2d 968 (4th Cir. 1982); Barnes v. Whelan (In re Barnes), 689 F.2d 193 (D.C. Cir. 1982); Goeb v. Heid (In re Goeb), 675 F.2d 1386 (9th Cir. 1982); and Ravenot v. Rimgale (In re Rimgale), 669 F.2d 426 (7th Cir. 1982)). We repeat just one version of the test here, to give you a flavor for what a lack of good faith might mean. Again, judicial discretion is extensive.

For a sampling of more recent cases on this topic, see In re Welsh, 711 F.3d 1120 (9th Cir. 2013); In re Cranmer, 697 F.3d 1314 (10th Cir. 2012); and In re Puffer, 674 F.3d 78 (11th Cir. 2012).

QUESTION 1. Which of the following would have some bearing on the issue of whether the debtor's plan was filed in good faith?

1. The debtor has been out of work for an entire year.
2. The debtor has tried to discharge a debt for an intentional tort by paying 2 percent distributions to it and the other unsecured creditors.
3. The debtor has proposed to pay the student loan agencies 100 percent under the plan, while paying other unsecured creditors just 25 cents on the dollar.
4. The debtor cannot afford, after paying the mortgage and taxes, to pay anything to the general unsecured creditors.

A. All of the above.
B. None of the above.
C. Just 2 and 3.
D. Just 2, 3, and 4.

ANALYSIS. The answer is **A**. Under the test set out previously, all of these things could bear on whether the debtor has proposed the plan in good faith. Choice **1** is one of the factors in the test and is relevant because if the debtor has truly met hardship in the job market, the court will be more lenient in terms of how much must be paid to creditors, how much to scrutinize the expenses, and whether the plan was filed in good faith. In our experience, this is the least important factor of the four listed, but it is one of the factors in the Eighth Circuit's test. In other words, she has a good reason for filing her case. Choice **2** makes the plan unconfirmable but also demonstrates possible bad faith.

It is very important to understand why choice **3** matters, and this does require some review. As we learned a few chapters back, all priority claims must be paid in full in a Chapter 13 plan, right? Ask yourself whether student loans get priority treatment. We hope you said, "Absolutely not!" They are simply nondischargeable, nothing more. Why is this important? Because the plan discussed in choice **3** proposes to discriminate against creditors with the same legal rights. It proposes to pay the student loans in full, while just paying other general unsecured creditors 25 percent. This is discrimination among similarly situated creditors and is specifically forbidden under §1322(b)(1). (*See* In re Sperna, 173 B.R. 654 (9th Cir. Bankruptcy Appellate Panel 1994).) Apparently, under the aforementioned factor test, this type of discrimination is also a factor in considering whether a plan has been filed in good faith.

Finally, choice **4** matters because the debtor plans to pay the secured and priority debts in full but is unable to pay anything to the unsecured creditors. This is a factor to consider in determining whether the plan has been filed in good faith, as is further discussed in the following paragraphs.

The factors most likely to point to a lack of good faith include: (1) multiple bankruptcy filings; (2) a zero or very small percentage distributions to unsecured creditors; and, most importantly, (3) an attempt to discharge debts in a Chapter 13 that would not be discharged in a Chapter 7 without making much of a distribution on the claims.

C. Multiple Filings

The good faith test is often raised, and used as the basis for objection to a debtor's Chapter 13 plan, when the debtor has filed more than one bankruptcy case. For example, a debtor will sometimes file a Chapter 13 to stop a home foreclosure, and then, before filing a plan, have the case dismissed. As the lender gets close to foreclosing again, the debtor may file yet another case, and may or may not comply with Chapter 13 in the process. Such cases would be filed for delay purposes only and thus would violate the good faith requirements of Chapter 13.[3] This is quintessential lack of good faith. Although one or two previous filings could raise a flag and possibly an objection, it typically takes several to ensure success on a bad faith claim based solely on serial filing.

One controversial topic is the question of whether it is bad faith to file a Chapter 7 case followed by a Chapter 13. We sometimes call this a "Chapter 20," meaning a 7 plus a 13. So why would anyone do something like this? If this is permitted, filing under Chapter 7 would first allow a debtor to discharge all of the nonpriority unsecured debts, so that he or she could concentrate in the Chapter 13 plan on just paying the priority and the secured debts. Assuming that it is acceptable to propose a plan that provides for no distribution to unsecured creditors (something we refer to as a "zero percent plan"), then there

3. Some courts have held that, as abusive as such behavior is, it is not a violation of §1325(a)(3) because this section only applies to a lack of good faith for filing a plan, not a case.

seems to be nothing particularly wrong with a Chapter 20. As it turns out, zero percent plans are just as controversial as Chapter 20s.

D. Zero Percent Plans

The preceding text asks whether it is acceptable to propose a plan that pays no distribution to unsecured creditors at all. Courts disagree about this. Some say a zero percent plan is per se bad faith. Others say this is one factor to consider in analyzing whether a plan has been filed in good faith. Still other courts believe the zero percent plan does not raise good faith issues in and of itself, on the grounds that if the disposable income test is met, there is no issue of good faith.

In the past, plan confirmation was regularly denied by some courts for a lack of good faith when the debtor carried unusually high secured debts (mortgages, car loans) resulting from living the high life. Obviously, uncommonly high secured debts also implicate the disposable income test.

A NOTE ABOUT THE 2005 AMENDMENTS: Now that Congress has eliminated secured debt from the calculation of a person's income and expenses, in both the means test and the disposable income test, it appears Congress is saying that all secured debts (regardless of size) can be paid in full before we worry at all about paying unsecured debts. (*See* 11 U.S.C. §§1325(b)(1)(2), 707(b)(2)(A)(i, ii).) Section 1322(a)(4) also clearly contemplates zero percent plans by permitting the confirmation of a Chapter 13 plan without paying all priority claims in full, as long as all disposable income is used to pay priority claims. This all suggests that a zero percent plan may no longer constitute grounds to challenge a plan's good faith. In some jurisdictions, including those of your two co-authors, zero percent plans have always been common and have rarely implicated the good faith test anyway. In places where a zero percent plan did trigger a good faith challenge, it may no longer do so under the 2005 amendments.

Martin's and Keating's Picks

1. Question 1 **A**

25

The Best Interest of Creditors Test

OVERVIEW

A. The Closer: Chapters 23, 24, and 25

Martin's and Keating's Picks

So far, two Chapter 13 tests we have considered bear on the unsecured creditor distribution, namely the disposable income test and the good faith test. We have focused on how much the debtor must give up to have the plan approved, or, put another way, how much belt-tightening the debtor must engage in, or simply how much the debtor must sacrifice.

The test we are going to learn about now relates to a totally different test, which should at least in theory be more objective. Now we will ask the question, "How much would the creditors get if this person just filed a Chapter 7 instead?" We care about this because if the creditors would get more in a Chapter 7 case, then the debtor should just file a Chapter 7. The money from a Chapter 7 liquidation would be a sure thing and the creditors are entitled to at least that much. We should not allow a debtor to file a Chapter 13 case if the creditors cannot get at least as much in the Chapter 13 plan as they would get from the sale and distribution of the debtor's nonexempt assets, which is what they would receive in a Chapter 7.

Slightly restating the test, in a Chapter 13 case, the creditors must get at least what they would get in a liquidation. If not, the Chapter 13 case is improper. It does not present creditors with the best-case bankruptcy scenario, and the Chapter 13 case would not be in their best interest. Rather, a Chapter 7 case would be in their best interest, thus the name "best interest of creditors test."

Sorry to belabor the obvious, but we find that even our top students will spout off the mechanics of the disposable income test on an exam whenever asked to articulate the best interest test. They seem to think that it is always in the best interest of creditors for them to receive all of the debtor's disposable income. This is true, but the best interest test relates to one thing and one thing only:

What would creditors have received in a Chapter 7?

Disposable income, expenses, and so forth, have no bearing on the best interest test. None. Nada.

Out of the philosophy that creditors should not get less in a Chapter 13 than they would get in a Chapter 7 case, the best interest test was born.[1] But how do we know what creditors would get in a Chapter 7 case? By calculating the value of the debtor's nonexempt assets.

QUESTION 1. Carol Cris, a below-median-income debtor, plans to file a Chapter 13 case to cure the arrears on her home mortgage and get rid of some tax and credit card obligations. The federal exemption scheme is more generous than the state exemptions offered in Carol's state, which offer no homestead exemption at all. Carol owns a home worth $100,000 with a $76,000 mortgage on it as well as approximately $3,000 in household furnishings. She also owns a small home that she rents out. It is worth $100,000 and it has a $50,000 mortgage on it. In addition to curing and paying her home mortgage, her plan provides that she will pay off some tax claims and pay a distribution to her general unsecured creditors. The exact amount they will each get is unknown, but she is contributing a whopping $1,000 per month to the taxes and unsecured claims, over a three-year period. Does her plan meet the best interest test?

A. Yes, she is clearly making a good faith effort to pay down the plan, which should create a very favorable distribution to her unsecured creditors.

B. Yes, assuming that this is a contribution of all of her disposable income, as defined by the Code.

C. No, the unsecured creditors would do better in a Chapter 7 case, in which they would share at least $50,000 rather than $36,000.

D. No, because in the Chapter 7 case, the unsecured creditors would have to share with the secured creditors; thus, they would be better off in a Chapter 13 case.

ANALYSIS. This question is just full of red herrings, which we hope you saw. First, **D** simply makes no sense. Without knowing much about bankruptcy law, one can eliminate it right off the bat because it says that the best interest

1. We generally assume that creditors would get less in most Chapter 7 cases, as compared to most Chapter 13 cases, and in many cases, this is probably true. In any case, the Code requires that creditors not get less in a Chapter 13 case than they would get if this person filed a Chapter 7 case.

test is not met because creditors would be better off in a Chapter 13 case. If creditors are better off in a Chapter 13 case, then the test is met, not vice versa.

Moreover, this thing about sharing with the secured creditors found in **D** is also incorrect. If there is equity in the property, which there is here for both pieces of real estate, then the secured party either continues to be paid by the debtor or sells the collateral and gets paid in full. The secured creditors have no interest in the equity, which goes towards the exemptions (in the case of the home) or to the unsecured creditors (as with the rental property). So **D** is incorrect.

A and **B** are totally irrelevant and relate to the two tests we discussed previously. **A** indicates that the good faith test is met and **B** indicates that the disposable income test is met. Do keep in mind that the debtor has to meet all of the requirements of the statute, and each test is different. Meeting one does not prove that another test has been met.

By process of elimination this leaves **C** as the correct answer, but let's look at why it is correct. How much would the creditors get if Carol were to file under Chapter 7 instead of Chapter 13? This determination requires an exemption analysis. What does she own that is outside her exemptions? This is what creditors would get in a Chapter 7 case, so this is what must be paid out in a Chapter 13 case to meet the best interest test. Creditors would get all of the debtor's nonexempt assets, which are valued here right around $50,000, the value of the equity in the rental property. So this is your base-line, minimum amount that Carol must pay to meet the best interest test. Here, she is paying $36,000 ($1,000 a month for 36 months), which does not do the trick.

One last complication: In a Chapter 7 case, creditors would receive their part of the $50,000 (less the trustee's fees and other costs, of course) right away. In a Chapter 13 case, these amounts would be paid to creditors over time. As a result, creditors are entitled to be compensated for the time value of money, in the same way we discussed for the treatment of secured creditors in Chapter 21. Practically speaking, this means that the debtor must pay the equivalent of interest on these amounts, and assuming the creditors would get $50,000 from a Chapter 7 case, Carol would have to pay more than that. She would have to pay this plus a present value interest rate on this amount under the plan.

Don't let the details confuse you, as the concept contained in the best interest test is not very complex. As set out in the introduction to Chapter 13 found in Chapter 19 of this guide, the debtor is not required to give up his or her nonexempt assets. The model is one of pay out, not sell out. The exemptions are very important in a Chapter 13 case because the debtor must pay the total value of all the nonexempt assets to creditors under the plan. The debtor is, in essence, buying back the nonexempt assets by paying the value of those nonexempt assets to the creditors who would realize that value on sale if the case were a Chapter 7. This means that if the debtor owns $10,000 in unencumbered, nonexempt assets, then the debtor must pay at least $10,000 to unsecured creditors under the plan, plus present value interest as set out above.

QUESTION 2. Carol is now looking for a way to cure the problems caused by her plan. You tell her that her best option is to:

1. sell the rental property and give the proceeds to the trustee for distribution to creditors.
2. extend the plan for two more years and pay it for a total of 60 months.
3. refinance the rental property to raise another $30,000 and then borrow another $20,000 from her mother, so she can pay off the equity to the creditors in cash.
4. proceed with the plan as proposed as the court is a court of equity and can decide to approve the plan anyway, even if it does not meet the best interest test.

A. Either 2 or 3.
B. 1, 3, or 4.
C. 1, 2, or 3.
D. Probably 2.

ANALYSIS. Surely choice **2** would be the easiest thing to do, so perhaps **D** is the best answer. Let's talk about that one first. This plan would tie Carol in for another two years, thereby increasing the already strong chance that she will never finish the plan and won't get her discharge. These little problems aside, this is a really simple way to solve the problem. While neither the court nor the trustee can force Carol to go to a five-year plan, she is free to make this change herself or to propose a five-year plan from the outset.[2] This should work here. She needs to pay $50,000 plus present value interest. Assuming the extra $10,000 would actually cover the present value rate for the five years (which will depend on the rate the court chooses), then choice **2** is best and thus the answer is **D**.

The scenario with the refinancing and the loan from Mom causes some problems. First, it is not clear when creditors would be paid. If it is over time, the $50,000 does not take care of the present value interest. It creates just $50,000. Even if this was not a problem, or this could be solved, Carol would still need to be able to service all this debt to her mother and the new lender. If she could afford to do this, and still put together a feasible plan, then this would allow Carol to stay in a three-year plan, and thus give her a better shot at

2. While the Code states that a plan is normally paid over three years, but can be extended to five years "for cause," this phrase has been interpreted to mean, "if the debtor wants to propose a five-year plan payout." Five years is the maximum. (*See* 11 U.S.C. §1322(d).) Remember that debtors with a current monthly income above the median in his or her state are required to pay a five-year plan. Below-median-income debtors (which will probably be the majority of all Chapter 13 debtors) can choose within a range between a three-year plan and a five-year plan.

completing it and getting a discharge. This makes **A** a viable choice, although probably not the best answer.

What about choice **4**, just going forward with the plan as proposed? This is not a good thing to do here because the court is not free to override the best interest test. Section 1325 states that the court shall confirm (approve) a plan if the best interest, good faith, and disposable income tests are met. Creditors are entitled to the benefit of the best interest test, and not even the court's equity powers can overrule the explicit requirements of §1325. Yes, the court is a court of equity, but Carol would be asking the court to disregard a clear requirement of filing a Chapter 13. This is not a fuzzy requirement, like "good faith"; it involves a simple mathematical computation. Also, where is the equity here? This does not impress us as a situation demanding some extraordinary relief.

What about **1**, selling the property and giving the money to the trustee? The result would be that the claims would be reduced by $50,000 and thus each creditor would get a higher percentage in a Chapter 13 payout. Also, the creditors would get at least as much as they would in the Chapter 7 because her only nonexempt property, at least under the federal exemptions, is the $50,000. This seems to be a decent solution, but somewhat more involved than just extending the plan. Also, she loses the rental property, whereas she could keep it if she extends the plan to five years or borrows the money from her mother. Finally, this alternative will undoubtedly be unsatisfying for the client who will not want to give up the property. This may be why she filed a Chapter 13 case in the first place, so that she could keep her nonexempt property. **D** is still the best answer.

QUESTION 3. (CODE READER) Leila Smith decides that she needs to file Chapter 13 bankruptcy after she is found liable in a negligence tort suit for a judgment of $90,000, which includes $10,000 in actual damages and $80,000 in punitive damages. In addition to the tort judgment, Leila owes $10,000 in credit-card bills. Leila is an above-median debtor who proposes a five-year plan that pays $1,000 per month for a total of $60,000 over the life of the plan with payments on a pro rata basis to each of her $100,000 worth of unsecured creditors. This $1,000 per month represents Leila's projected disposable income based on her current salary and eligible expenses. The value of Leila's nonexempt assets would be $25,000 after subtracting trustee and sale costs. Will Leila's proposed plan satisfy the best interest of creditors test? (Hint: Section 726(a)(4) subordinates punitive damage claims to other general unsecured claims in a Chapter 7 bankruptcy case.)

A. No, because her credit-card creditors would be better off in a Chapter 7 liquidation.

B. No, because her tort creditor would be better off in a Chapter 7 liquidation.

C. No, because both of her unsecured creditors would be better off in a Chapter 7 liquidation.

D. Yes, because $60,000 paid over a five-year plan is clearly worth more, even on a present-value basis, than the $25,000 distribution that unsecured creditors as a group would receive in a Chapter 7 liquidation.

ANALYSIS. The correct answer is **A**. The tricky point here is that even though the statutory subordination of punitive damage claims that is found in §726(a)(4) only applies directly in a Chapter 7 case, the effect of that subordination carries over indirectly to a Chapter 13 case due to the best interest of creditors test. Think of it this way: If Leila filed a Chapter 7 case, the first $20,000 of her $25,000 in nonexempt asset value would go to her credit-card creditors (for $10,000) and for actual damages to her tort victim (for another $10,000), paying those claims at the rate of 100 percent and leaving just $5,000 to pay the $80,000 in punitive damages to the tort victim. In her proposed Chapter 13 plan, the credit-card creditors will get just $6,000 paid over time. That is because the credit-card claims account for 10 percent of the total $100,000 in unsecured claims, and 10 percent of the $60,000 that Leila proposes to pay in her plan is $6,000. That is a violation of the best interest of creditors test and therefore would make the plan nonconfirmable.

Choice **B** is wrong because the tort creditor would be worse off in a Chapter 7 liquidation. In a Chapter 7 liquidation, as described above, the tort creditor would get $10,000 for its actual damages, but only $5,000 for its punitive damages, giving the victim a total recovery of $15,000. In Leila's proposed Chapter 13 plan, the tort creditor would get 90 percent of the $60,000 paid over the five years, which is $54,000. Even when you discount that $54,000 figure to present value, it will be a lot more than $15,000 received today. For that reason, **C** is also incorrect. Answer **D** is incorrect because it ignores the effect of the §726(a)(4) punitive damage subordination on the recovery that the credit-card creditors would receive in a Chapter 7 liquidation of Leila's nonexempt assets.

A. The Closer: Chapters 23, 24, and 25

Mari Max is a single mother who is on Social Security resulting from the death of her husband several years ago. She receives $990 per month in disability payments and has no other income. She recently filed a Chapter 13 case. She owns a regular home on which her monthly payments are current but which has little equity. Her only other significant asset is a mobile home. Some of the payments on the mobile home are past due, and her son has agreed to make these and all future payments, so she can keep the mobile home. If she sold the mobile home, she could get approximately $10,000 for it, after payment of the lien. Ms. Max has a $20,000 judgment against her as a result of an accident she had while driving drunk. She proposes a 5 percent distribution to the person she hit, for a total of $1,000 over the life of her plan. She is paying a 5 percent distribution to all of her unsecured creditors, which total $40,000 (including the drunk-driving judgment). Her plan payments will be approximately $125 per month and her regular monthly expenses are around $775. Rank the possible objections to her plan from the strongest to the weakest.

1. She cannot keep the mobile home because it is not an expense that is necessary for the support of the family, and thus keeping the mobile home violates the disposable income test.
2. The plan is not in good faith because the drunk driving victim is receiving just 5 percent on his claim.
3. The plan fails to meet the feasibility test.
4. The plan fails to meet the best interest test.

A. 1, 3, 2, and 4.
B. 4, 2, 1, and 3.
C. 4, 1, 2, and 3.
D. 4, 3, 1, and 2.

ANALYSIS. In looking at the possible objections to this plan, the easiest way to eliminate a possible objection is probably choice **3**, the feasibility test. It appears that the debtor will have enough income to support herself and her child, while still making the additional $125 payment on the plan. At least it is not obvious that she cannot do so, assuming that her plan payments are only $125. So, choice **3** should appear as the last number in the series, as this seems to be the weakest objection to the plan. Choice **1** also seems somewhat weak. Choice **1** says Ms. Max's son is paying for her mobile home. If he is, this should not bear on what would be reasonable money for her to expend in this particular case. It is not her money that's being used to keep the mobile home; therefore, we would think that choice **1** would be next in line, and not a strong objection to the plan. Do note, however, the tension between the feasibility test and the disposable income test. The debtor's expenses must be high enough to eat up most of the income but not so high as to make the plan infeasible.

What about the good faith test? There's a very strong possibility that the good faith test is not met here because the victim of the drunk driving charges is receiving only 5 percent under the plan. The problem, however, is that some judges will be troubled by this and others will not. We think good faith is a bigger potential problem than feasibility or disposable income, based on the rulings in our own districts, so we think good faith is a stronger objection than either disposable income or feasibility. Choice **4**, on the other hand, that the plan fails to meet the best interest test, is the strongest objection. If the debtor were to sell the mobile home, $10,000 would be raised for the benefit of creditors. The debtor only intends to distribute $2,000 to creditors. As a result, creditors will do better under Chapter 7 than they would under Chapter 13; consequently, the best interest test is clearly violated. As a result, choice **4** should be the first number in the series, choice **2** should be the second answer, choice **1** should be the third, and choice **3** should be the fourth answer. Consequently, **B** is correct.

Martin's and Keating's Picks

1. Question 1	**C**
2. Question 2	**D**
3. Question 3	**A**
The Closer: Chapters 23, 24, and 25	**B**

26

Chapter 13 Plan Feasibility

OVERVIEW

A. Do the Proposed Payments Meet the Plan Obligations?

B. Can the Debtor Make the Payments?

Martin's and Keating's Picks

Section 1325(a)(6) requires the court to find that "the debtor will be able to make all payments under the plan and to comply with the plan." Although it sounds quite daunting (that the debtor be able to make *all* payments), the test is quite lenient. This test, known as the *feasibility* requirement, simply requires that the plan proposed be realistic and that the debtor have a reasonable chance of completing it.

A. Do the Proposed Payments Meet the Plan Obligations?

One aspect of feasibility is quite stringent, namely that the payments proposed under the plan must actually add up to enough money to make the payments proposed in the plan. With the interest requirements and the trustee's fee, this can sometimes be tricky to calculate but the Internet has sites that can help. Or you can just make the payment a little bit bigger and the debtor will get some money back at the end.

QUESTION 1. Tom Tryer plans to pay $500 per month into his Chapter 13 plan, which constitutes all of his disposable income under §1325(b)(2). His plan will go on for five years, or 60 months. His debts include $10,000 in secured debt, plus present value interest for his car, and $10,000 in unpaid taxes that qualify as priority claims. He owes $100,000 to his general unsecured creditors and his plan provides that he will pay that class of creditors a 10 percent distribution. Does his plan look feasible?

A. Yes, because this is all the money that he has and he is paying his plan over the maximum time of five years, so he is in compliance with the Code.
B. Yes, he has just enough money.
C. No, he needs to pay interest on the car and there is not enough money to do so.
D. No, because there would be just enough but he must also pay the trustee's fee of 11 percent.

ANALYSIS. The correct answer is **C**. While **D** is also true in part, in that there are insufficient funds in the plan to pay for the trustee's fee, the answer says there would be just enough, except that he cannot pay the trustee's fee. The truth is that there is not "just enough" because he needs to pay present value interest on the $10,000 car debt, which will not be possible under the current numbers. He also cannot afford the trustee's fee.

How can you tell? He is paying $500 per month for 60 months, which comes to exactly $30,000. Remember, the plan must pay the secured debt, after stripdown, and the priority claim for taxes. This would require a payment of $10,000 for the car, plus $10,000 for the priority claims, plus $10,000 for the general creditors, which is payment of the proposed 10 percent of their claims. However, the secured claim must be paid at its present value, so you have to add interest to the $10,000 to be paid to the secured creditor. That means that the plan is not feasible, because there is no money to pay that interest. Note how this is simply a matter of doing the math. This aspect of feasibility does not ask whether the debtor can afford to pay the plan but only whether the plan payments add up.

Why is **A** wrong? The description in **A** contains facts sufficient to establish that the debtor has met the disposable income test but not the feasibility test. Remember that the debtor must meet all of the requirements of Chapter 13.

Can Tom fix this problem by revising his plan? Sure. All he has to do is decrease the percentage to be paid to the general unsecured creditors to an amount that can be covered by his disposable income.

B. Can the Debtor Make the Payments?

The other aspect of feasibility relates to the debtor's likelihood of being able to pay the payments required under the plan, based primarily on his or her income. This requirement relates to eligibility. You might recall that debtors need regular income to qualify for Chapter 13. The feasibility test is far easier to meet than one might imagine, because courts tend to give debtors a fair chance to rehabilitate their financial lives. There is a similar test in Chapter 11.

QUESTION 2. Ralph Mabee just got his real estate license after working as a manual laborer for 20 years. He then landed an amazing job at Century 21, where he will receive realtor's training. Ralph just got the new job and just filed for Chapter 13. All of his income will come from commissions, and he has yet to sell a house. He has done the math. If he can sell five average-priced homes in his town per year, he can make his plan payments. Is his plan feasible?

A. No, it is too speculative.
B. No, because he has to work at the same job he has been, at least until his plan is paid.
C. Yes, because courts like to give debtors a chance.
D. Probably, if he is able to make the payments while the parties are waiting for the confirmation hearing. If he is making it work somehow, even in lean times, the court is very likely to let him give this a try.

ANALYSIS. The answer here is quite obvious if you keep in mind one of the first test tips: Eliminate those straight yes or no answers. This is going to be a close call, so an answer that starts with "probably" and allows you a way out is more likely to be correct.

Let's start with some of the wrong answers. **A** is incorrect because it is so definitive. The problem does not tell us that Ralph can prove the average commission from a house sale in his area, how many houses new salespeople sell, or the average price of a house in his area, but if he could prove these things, the court might give him a chance, as speculative as all this sounds.

B is worth talking about at some length. It is untrue that the courts make a Chapter 13 debtor do the same job he or she has been doing all along, but courts have struggled with people who would like to drastically reduce their income. What if Ralph made three times as much as this as a manual laborer and could pay a much richer plan if he just continued for another three years? We usually do not force people to work in jobs they hate, but there is always a fear that he is doing this simply because he does not want to work hard just to pay creditors when he could choose an easier life and pay them less. There are cases about musicians who choose lower-paying but more prestigious jobs, mothers who want to go part-time so they can spend more time with the kids, and big-city attorneys who want to move to the woods and become small-town lawyers. The proximity of this decision to the Chapter 13 filing (or in some cases to a Chapter 7 filing, raising the substantial abuse questions discussed in Chapter 17), as well as the huge drop in pay, will raise issues. The drop in pay issue is not suggested by the facts here; thus, **B** is just incorrect.

C is incorrect because the court may allow the debtor to try this, and it may not. There is good chance it will, but it is uncertain, so **C** is wrong. This leaves **D** as the correct answer. The court is likely to let the debtor try, particularly if the debtor makes the first few payments, even while he is not earning commissions. The confirmation hearing will occur about two or three months after the case is filed; thus, a few payments will have come due. This will allow the court to see if the debtor will make the payments, even in lean times.

A question that has come up a lot recently is whether the debtor's plan is feasible when the payments are coming from someone other than the debtor. If the payments are likely to be regular, courts often consider the plan feasible.

QUESTION 3. Jerry Trunk has lost it all: his wife, his job, and his work tools. He is down and out, but has been able to stave off the foreclosure of his home. He has proposed a Chapter 13 plan that covers the regular monthly payments, as well as the arrears to the lender required by Chapter 13. Because he has no income, he proposes that his father make the plan payments, through the sale of his father's restaurant business. His dad does not mind, as he is ready to retire and would have given the restaurant assets to Jerry anyway. The restaurant assets have been listed for sale with a broker. Is this plan feasible?

A. No, because neither the son nor the father will have any regular income from which to pay the plan.
B. This is probably feasible, as long as Jerry's dad signs a promissory note or signs the plan itself.
C. This is probably fine without the signatures, as long as his dad does plan to sell the restaurant, has it listed, and can cover the plan payments from the probable proceeds.
D. This is unlikely to be a feasible plan. While it is acceptable to have someone else pay your plan payments, that person must at least have a regular stream of income. Here the sale of this business is speculative, creating a problem that cannot be solved even under a lenient application of this test.

ANALYSIS. These all look like really good answers, and admittedly, from the very little we have told you about this subject, it is very hard to tell which is correct. You can start by eliminating the two answers that say essentially the same thing and have little to distinguish them, **A** and **D**. Both essentially say that someone here has to have a regular income for the plan to be feasible, and that is not what §1325(a)(6) says. Rather, it requires that the debtor be able to make the plan payments, from whatever source. In one case in the casebook that both of us use, a woman's boyfriend (not even her husband) promised to pay her plan and the court found the plan feasible.

What about the choice between **B** and **C**? We can't expect you to have known this, but the same issue came up in a case before one of our districts in 2003, on the exact facts stated here. The trustee insisted that the father sign the plan and the court found that unnecessary, given that the property was listed for sale, at a price that would more than cover the plan payments. Thus, the correct answer is **C**.

Martin's and Keating's Picks

1. Question 1 **C**
2. Question 2 **D**
3. Question 3 **C**

27

Modification of a Chapter 13 Plan or Dismissal of a Chapter 13 Case

OVERVIEW

Martin's and Keating's Picks

Once the plan is proposed, is the debtor stuck with it? Not exactly. Before actual confirmation, the debtor can modify the plan freely. (*See* 11 U.S.C. §1323.) After confirmation, the court can order a modification at the request of the debtor, the trustee, or any other party-in-interest to increase or decrease the payments or the payment period or to increase or decrease the distributions to be paid under the plan. (*See* 11 U.S.C. §1329.) Obviously, the modified plan must still comply with the Code.

What would justify such a modification? If the debtor is requesting it, perhaps there has been a drop in income or an increase in expenses, either of which could justify modification. Perhaps the trustee or a creditor is requesting modification, because the debtor is making more money now and is no longer in compliance with the disposable income test.

If the debtor has missed a number of payments under the plan, the trustee or a creditor may ask that the case simply be dismissed. The court may dismiss a Chapter 13 case or convert it to a Chapter 7, for cause, including a failure to make payments, unreasonable delay in proposing a plan or otherwise proceeding with the case, or for denial of confirmation, among other reasons. (*See* 11 U.S.C. §1307.)

As you might imagine, after the debtor has failed to pay the plan, the trustee or a creditor may move to convert or dismiss at the same time that a debtor is requesting modification. Believe it or not, if the debtor is really hit with hard times and has met the Code's most minimal requirements, the debtor may be freed from all further payments due to unexpected hardship. Take a look at §1328(b).

Since bankruptcy reform, 60-month plans are mandatory for people with above-median incomes. Because 60 months is the maximum length of a Chapter 13 plan, people can't make up past payments if they fall behind. Thus, some of the flexibility is gone, and more plans may fail. Debtors also must verify under penalty of perjury their income and expenses each year. (*See* 11 U.S.C. §521(f)(4).) This means that if the debtor's income goes up, creditors can demand the overage.

QUESTION 1. Polly Pranz was making $2,500 a month as an accounting clerk when you filed a Chapter 13 case for her over a year ago. Her plan proposed that she pay her car off at a stripped-down value plus interest, cure her home mortgage, pay a few priority tax claims, and pay a distribution of 25 percent to her unsecured creditors, all over 36 months. She recently missed a few payments, was too embarrassed to come in and tell you about it, and is now facing a furious home mortgage lender and a motion by the Chapter 13 trustee. She is now in your office and, as it turns out, she was laid off and forced to take a job that only pays $1,500 a month. Before the layoff, she made every payment like clockwork but is now in quite a bind. She has paid some debts, but has not yet paid off the car, the mortgage cure, or the priority taxes. What are the parties likely to be asking for in this case?

1. The trustee is likely asking for conversion or dismissal.
2. The home lender is probably hoping to either dismiss the case and foreclose or convert the case to a Chapter 7, with relief from the automatic stay.
3. The debtor is likely asking for a hardship discharge under §1328(b).
4. The debtor is probably asking for modification of the plan payments and term.

A. 2 and 4 only.
B. 1 and 4 only.
C. 1, 2, and 4 only.
D. 1, 2, and 3 only.

ANALYSIS. All of these are probably true, except for choice **3**. Thus, **C** is correct. We hope the debtor is not asking for a hardship discharge here, because she would certainly lose. She can only get a hardship discharge after she has met the basic Chapter 13 requirements, which makes sense, right? Otherwise, people could get around the basics by proposing a plan that they could not meet, and then ask for a hardship discharge before the requirements were met. That would be bad policy. Here, Polly has not paid off her secured and priority claims.

Look at the parties' goals. Note that the lender's goal is to foreclose on the house. The lender would like to have the debtor out of bankruptcy completely, or at least in a Chapter 7 case, in which case the lender will be granted relief from the stay. The lender can move for relief from the stay or dismissal in the alternative, and either would allow the foreclosure.

The trustee has probably moved to convert or dismiss but may not actually want that. If there were some way that the debtor could still modify the plan, this would be better for the trustee than just dismissing or converting the case. The Chapter 13 trustee gets no additional fees from converted or dismissed cases. The position the trustee is likely to take will depend on the debtor's payment history and the trustee's faith in the debtor to continue under revised terms.

What about the debtor? The debtor's best option at this point is to modify the plan to eliminate or reduce the unsecured creditor distribution (remember that no specific distribution is required; the debtor must simply comply with the disposable income test and the best interest test, as well as the good faith test) and also to increase the plan term, if necessary. You, as the debtor's attorney, just need to redo the math.

QUESTION 2. Regarding the situation in Question 1, what is the court likely to do?

A. Convert the case and lift the stay for the home lender because secured debts get priority and more say in the case than the other creditors.

B. Allow the debtor to try to comply with the modified plan that you have proposed on her behalf.

C. Dismiss the case, as the debtor already has been given a chance and has failed at bankruptcy.

D. Just do nothing for a few months and see if the debtor can make the plan payments during the delay.

ANALYSIS. This is a discretionary matter over which the judge has almost complete freedom of choice, so it is hard to predict the outcome. This decision will depend on the debtor's track record and the plausibility of her explanation for failure under the prior plan. Having said that, from what we know here, it seems likely that the judge will give the debtor a second chance, because she has a good excuse for failure and a positive prior track record. Thus, **B** is the best answer, with **D** as a close second.

Dismissal (as mentioned in **C**) is an extremely harsh step, not likely to be taken lightly. Moreover, she has not really *failed* at bankruptcy; she just could not quite follow through, essentially through no fault of her own.

The statements in **A** are a little off, and now is a good time to straighten that out. It is true that secured creditors get special rights in bankruptcy as well as out of bankruptcy, and these rights are generally superior to the rights of all other parties-in-interest in a case. These rights are generally protected by ensuring that the creditor's rights are adequately protected, as discussed in Chapter 21. If the court thinks that the new plan provides this protection to the secured party, then the court probably will not convert or dismiss the case but will instead give the debtor a second chance. This can either be through **B**, approving the modified plan, or through **D**, simply putting off the pending motions until we see how the debtor does with the new plan.

QUESTION 3. Mike Staudt filed Chapter 13 bankruptcy after a long illness kept him away from work for several weeks and also caused him to incur a lot of medical-related debt. His main reason for choosing Chapter 13 was to keep his house and his car. As a below-median debtor, he filed a three-year plan with disposable income of $500 per month, which was enough to pay his general unsecured creditors a total of $18,000. That amount was just under one-half of his total unsecured debt of $40,000, and it also met the best interest of creditors test because his nonexempt assets were worth $12,000. One year into his case, Mike won $3 million in the lottery. Mike's attorney then proposed a modification of Mike's case in which Mike would pay all of his creditors early according to the terms of the three-year plan. The attorney for Mike's largest unsecured creditor, the hospital, objected to that modification and proposed instead that Mike pay all of his unsecured creditors 100 percent of their original claims. If you were the judge, which modification would you require?

A. What the hospital is requesting, 100 percent of the original amount owed to unsecured creditors.

B. What Mike's attorney is requesting, which is faster payment of the three-year plan amounts.

C. A compromise between the two: a forced extension of the plan to five years from three years, but still at the rate of $500 per month.

D. No modification at all, because after all, it wasn't Mike's fault that he won the lottery.

ANALYSIS. There is no definite right answer here, because it is not as if the Bankruptcy Code has explicitly covered this situation. However, there is at least one case in which something very similar happened, and the court in that case went with choice **A**. See In re Koonce, 54 B.R. 643 (Bankr. D.S.C. 1985) (allowing creditors in Chapter 13 case to insist on a modification upwards to 100 percent payment when debtor won $1.3 million lottery after the plan had begun). Let's consider the best argument for that outcome. One way to justify that outcome is to imagine that we will do a brand-new best interest of creditors test based on this sudden windfall. In other words, if Mike were to file Chapter 7 today after winning the lottery, of course all of his creditors would get paid in full.

Answer **B** is not nearly as compelling because why should Mike get to walk away with his newfound wealth while his creditors are losing half of their claims through this plan? Choice **C** isn't much better since it still allows Mike to discharge some of his unsecured debt while he sits on a few million dollars. Answer **D** is probably the worst of all, since this is not about "fault" but rather about fairness. Having said that, what if Mike had finished his three-year plan, gotten his discharge, and then a week later won the $3 million? Could his unsecured creditors try to re-open the case and demand full payment after the discharge? That would seem doubtful, even though that also seems unfair. Maybe this is just an example, as the saying goes, that timing is everything!

Martin's and Keating's Picks

1. Question 1 **C**
2. Question 2 **B**
3. Question 3 **A**

28

Overview of Chapter 11 and Its Alternatives

OVERVIEW
A. Comparing the Out-of-Court Workout and Chapter 11
B. Introduction to the Basic Chapter 11 Rules and Major Parties-in-Interest
   1. Major players in a Chapter 11 case
      a. The debtor-in-possession
      b. The United States Trustee's Office
      c. Creditors' committees
      d. Secured creditors
   2. Venue
Martin's and Keating's Picks

Chapter 11 receives lots of press these days. High-profile companies are using it more than ever before. Whatever you may have heard about Chapter 11, it probably does not work the way you think it does. It does not mean creditors have lost their money forever, that employees need to find new jobs, or that the business is closing. It *could* mean these things, but not necessarily.

In beginning our discussion of Chapter 11 and its options, we leave the domain of personal bankruptcy and move into the business side of bankruptcy.[1] Many of the same principles apply (e.g., principles relating to the estate, the automatic stay, the treatment of secured and priority creditors, the feasibility test, and the best interest of creditors test), but there are also many new rules and concepts to master. If learning what makes a business tick interests you, this is the most interesting area of bankruptcy law.

1. As you know, businesses can file a Chapter 7 as well, but many try to keep the business going by reorganizing under Chapter 11 instead. Additionally, individuals can file for Chapter 11 protection, but Chapter 11 is used primarily to restructure businesses.

The debtor-in-possession (the name we give to the debtor who is in Chapter 11) is faced with choices about which parts of the business to continue and which to discontinue, which contracts to honor and which to abandon, as well as many other restructuring options that may not be available outside bankruptcy. Given that these choices must be made relatively quickly, Chapter 11 is an exciting area of the law in which to practice.

Before we even talk about Chapter 11, you should know that businesses have an additional option for trying to sort out financial problems. They can instead try to do an out-of-court workout, which involves restructuring the businesses' debts without a court proceeding. This is done by negotiating with creditors and garnering the consent of the parties. An out-of-court workout can be far superior to filing under Chapter 11 if there are not too many creditors, if no creditor is too aggressive, if the debtor's business and debt structures are not too complicated, and if the debtor has enjoyed good relations with its creditors in the past. Chapter 11 is extremely expensive and an out-of-court workout saves the cost and time of a lengthy Chapter 11 proceeding. Sometimes survival is more likely in an out-of-court workout, given that Chapter 11 will turn off some creditors (and increase antagonism towards the debtor), and also that the costs of a Chapter 11 can put the company further into debt. If the debtor has negotiated with the creditors and they have collectively come up with an out-of-court workout, it may still be necessary for the debtor to file a Chapter 11. The debtor may still need to take advantage of the special provisions only the Bankruptcy Code can give, such as the avoiding powers (*see* Chapter 12), the ability to accept or reject executory contracts and leases (Chapter 33), and the automatic stay (Chapter 7). A plan that is pre-negotiated between the debtor and the creditors is called a prepackaged plan. These are being used more and more frequently.

While some companies may benefit from an out-of-court workout, some are simply too far gone (or in too precarious a position) to have any chance of working out their affairs without a bankruptcy court's help. How can you tell if a client is a candidate for an out-of-court workout? Look back at the prior paragraph and realistically evaluate whether your client fits the bill.

QUESTION 1. Let's check your gut reactions about a company's realistic chance of completing an out-of-court workout. Which of the following factors will most likely dash any hope of a workout?

A. Overall, the debtor has a fair working relationship with its primary secured lender, but is behind on payments.

B. The debtor has a fair number of unsecured creditors who, although naturally hoping to be paid in full, are opposed to disparate treatment among similarly situated creditors.

C. While the debtor has a good working relationship with its employees, the union has indicated that it is opposed to any out-of-court workout or wage concessions even though some wage concessions are needed.

D. The debtor has three different secured creditors that are all antagonistic towards one another.

ANALYSIS. These are all problematic, but the debtor can probably get around the facts in **B** simply by treating all unsecured creditors the same under the workout plan. The facts in **A** could be a problem, but if the debtor's relationship with the primary lender is good, chances are the bank will try to work with the debtor, at least for a while. The facts in **D** don't affect the workout that much. As long as all of the banks like the debtor, that is what counts. The facts in **C**, however, are quite problematic. Absent a change of heart in the union stance, the debtor will not be able to complete a workout that includes wage concessions; therefore, the correct answer is **C**. It is hard to modify union contracts, even in bankruptcy (*see* 11 U.S.C. §1113), so the debtor may find little respite in Chapter 11, as well. This is because unions have strong lobbying power, and also because we traditionally have valued union contracts as a society.

A. Comparing the Out-of-Court Workout and Chapter 11

The terms of an out-of-court workout are left totally up to the parties because there is no need to comply with a federal statute. The debtor simply attempts to determine the type of repayment or forbearance terms with which creditors will agree and negotiates with each creditor individually. Often, a secured loan is in default or is approaching default, so there is a need to work with that creditor first. While many business debtors have more than one secured creditor, most debtors have one primary secured creditor, who provides working capital through a line of credit, in addition to other secured loans. The debtor often has separate equipment loans and perhaps separate real estate loans, but inventory and accounts are often pledged to the primary secured lender to secure a line of credit or revolving loan that is used to generate cash for business operations. If a secured creditor repossesses the debtor's business assets or initiates a court proceeding to replevy these assets, which secured creditors have the right to do on default, the debtor could lose all of the very assets needed to run the business. Thus, the debtor must make peace with the creditor holding these assets as collateral. If an amicable resolution with this cannot be attained, an out-of-court workout is highly unlikely.

Sometimes the threat of a Chapter 11 case in the background can cause creditors to go along with an out-of-court workout. Unsecured creditors in particular may fare poorly in a Chapter 11 case once all the fees and other costs are paid. Also, the debtor could ultimately liquidate, leaving unsecured creditors with little or no assets from which to be paid. Against this backdrop, unsecured creditors might prefer a workout plan. But again, a business typically needs almost 100 percent creditor agreement to make an out-of-court workout viable.

Unsecured creditors are often dealt with as a group in an out-of-court workout. They are typically called to a meeting and asked if they are willing to forgo payments temporarily or even to waive part of their claims, perhaps because doing so will allow the debtor to survive. Because many of these creditors are suppliers who sell to the debtor company, they may want to keep the customer (the debtor) alive, and also get paid part of their unsecured claims. Of course, some of the unsecured creditors could be utility companies and even competitors (who might belong to a trade association to which the debtor owes dues), who may have no interest in keeping this failing company alive.

One of the big disadvantages of an out-of-court workout is that every creditor needs to agree to the workout plan, or the proposed workout plan will probably fall apart. Chapter 11, by contrast, contains rules that allow a court to force the Chapter 11 plan on dissenting creditors. (*See* 11 U.S.C. §1129(b).) Of course, because there are no rules about how much a creditor must be paid in an out-of-court workout, the debtor is free to do different deals with different creditors. Reaching an agreement takes time, however, which is something few companies in poor financial condition have. Moreover, creditors will want to know that they are receiving th4e same treatment as other similarly situated creditors, even though this is not technically required. Additionally, as soon as one creditor steps out of line and starts aggressively pursuing its state court collection rights, the out-of-court workout is less likely to succeed. You'll recall that state collection law places a premium on diligent (and individual) collection efforts, which is why we call the state court collection procedure the *race of the diligent*. Out-of-court workouts are collective in nature and require fairly amicable relations.

If the debtor is able to make the pieces fall into place by negotiating acceptable repayment terms with everyone, the advantages of an out-of-court workout are numerous. Attorneys' fees in Chapter 11 cases can be tens if not hundreds of thousands of dollars, and can sometimes amount to a large percentage of the business's value. Chapter 11 also can take a long time, during which some of the debtor's reputation and goodwill is lost. Finally, the Chapter 11 proceeding itself is a huge burden on management, who must spend endless hours managing the process rather than trying to run the business. Out-of-court workouts, on the other hand, can be quite quick and create much less negative publicity. Overall, out-of-court workouts are much simpler.

One incentive for creditors to go along with an out-of-court workout is that if it doesn't work, the debtor may end up in Chapter 11. Chapter 11 is disadvantageous to creditors because, as you will soon see, creditors can be forced to live with a plan they do not like under Chapter 11. (*See* 11 U.S.C. §1129(b).)

Moreover, secured creditors in Chapter 11 can be forced to accept payments equal to the value of their collateral rather than the full amount of their loan.[2] (*See* 11 U.S.C. §1129(b)(2)(A)(i).) Thus, their liens can be stripped down in Chapter 11, as we discussed earlier in the context of Chapter 13.

It can also take a very long time before unsecured creditors' claims receive any payment under Chapter 11 because a debtor is generally forbidden from paying general unsecured claims except pursuant to a confirmed (court-approved) Chapter 11 plan. While most Chapter 11 plans are confirmed within two years of the filing, it can sometimes take much longer to get a plan confirmed! Thus, unsecured creditors might well prefer an out-of-court plan in which they receive earlier payments, even if they are not paid in full. Finally, in some cases, unsecured creditors will receive very little in a Chapter 11 case, because most of the assets have been pledged as collateral to secured creditors. Thus, an out-of-court workout may pay a better and quicker distribution than a formal case.

Of course, because the debtor and the creditors can figure out the treatment to which they would be entitled in a Chapter 11, many out-of-court workouts look much like a Chapter 11 case, but without the high fees, costs, and expenses of a formal case.

QUESTION 2. Which of the following presents the most formidable challenge to a debtor hoping to do an out-of-court workout?

A. One small supplier refuses to go along with the plan.
B. The debtor has no ultimate plan for improving its business.
C. The primary secured lender plans to repossess the debtor's assets and has rejected the terms of a prior workout plan.
D. The debtors' employees plan to walk out if the debtor files for Chapter 11.

ANALYSIS. The first option that can be eliminated is **D**. Choice **D** does not deal with what would happen if the debtor were to propose an out-of-court workout. It simply says that the debtors' employees will walk out or strike if the debtor files Chapter 11. An out-of-court workout is not a Chapter 11 case; therefore, choice **D** does not present an impediment to a successful out-of-court workout. The other three choices are all problems for the debtor, but some are worse than others. Although the one supplier mentioned in choice **A** does present a problem, it does not present the most formidable problem. There should be some way around this problem, irritating as it is. The debtor may be able to get a replacement supplier or deal with the one supplier

---

2. To be more technical, a plan can be confirmed over objecting classes of creditors under the Code's cramdown provisions.

differently. As long as everyone else is willing to go along with the plan, this should not present an insurmountable problem. Thus, both choices **D** and **A** are incorrect.

Choice **B** definitely presents a challenge to the debtor because the debtor has a much greater likelihood of staying in business (and obtaining consent to a workout plan) if it has a viable exit plan. However, the business plan or exit plan may actually evolve as the creditors are approached in the workout discussions. By far the most formidable challenge to the debtor's workout prospect is choice **C**, repossession by the debtor's primary secured lender. If the secured creditor is determined to repossess the business assets, the debtor is left with little or no choice. The debtor must either fight the creditor in state court or file for Chapter 11 protection. Thus, the correct answer is **C**.

Because of the unique rules and incentives that Chapter 11 creates, there are some situations in which Chapter 11 is so beneficial that it would be much better to go ahead and file bankruptcy rather than attempt an out-of-court workout. For example, as you learned in Chapter 12, certain actions taken by creditors within the 90 days prior to the bankruptcy case can be avoided by a debtor-in-possession. (*See* 11 U.S.C. §547.) Specifically, if a creditor has obtained a lien during the 90 days before the filing, the debtor can avoid that lien if the debtor files a Chapter 11 petition and uses §547 of the Bankruptcy Code to avoid the transfer or lien. In certain cases, the debtor may have provided a security interest to a creditor, thus favoring that creditor over other creditors, and other creditors may choose to file an involuntary bankruptcy petition to reverse the transfer. (*See* 11 U.S.C. §§303, 547.) Another reason the debtor may find it preferable to file a Chapter 11 case rather than attempting an out-of-court workout is that the debtor may need the protection of the automatic stay imposed by §362 of the Bankruptcy Code. As you learned in Chapter 7 of this guide, the automatic stay prohibits the immediate seizure of assets, and prohibits any action to attempt to collect on a debt, or to obtain possession of property of the debtor's estate. (*See* 11 U.S.C. §362.) The debtor may need the protection of the automatic stay during the time it takes to negotiate a plan with creditors. Chapter 11 allows the debtor to operate its business free of collection activity, subject to the need to provide secured creditors with adequate protection of their property interests. This is an issue we will be taking up shortly.

QUESTION 3. Which of the following sounds like the best reason to file a Chapter 11 case?

A. To stop a suit by the city dealing with zoning violations.
B. To stop repossession of all of the debtor's business assets.
C. To stop management from continuing a long-standing dispute among themselves.
D. To stop a suit against one of the debtor's principals or owners.

ANALYSIS. This problem briefly reviews the potential benefits of a Chapter 11 case, through a review of the automatic stay. Choice **A** is not the best answer. A suit by the city may not even be stayed, as it could be a suit to protect the health and public welfare of citizens under §362(b). We can't tell without more facts. While it is seldom wise to incur the costs of Chapter 11 merely to stop one lawsuit, choice **B** describes a very good reason to file and is the correct answer here. If the debtor is about to have its business assets repossessed, filing a Chapter 11 (with the help of the §362 stay) could be the only way to save the business. **C** is incorrect because filing for Chapter 11 will not necessarily resolve a dispute within management. In fact, if the dispute continues, it could impair the debtor's ability to reorganize.

Finally, **D** is also incorrect because the bankruptcy case will only stop suits against the debtor, not the debtor's principals. You might recall from Chapter 5 that a debtor's principal can ask the court for a stay under §105, and the court may grant a stay if it determines that the suit impairs the debtor's reorganization. This would be a long shot, however, and this prospect alone would rarely justify filing a Chapter 11 case.

Another situation in which the debtor may find Chapter 11 beneficial is one where the debtor knows that certain important creditors will not go along with an amicable plan no matter what. In such a case, rather than wasting time and resources trying to negotiate, it will be more efficient to file a Chapter 11 proceeding, and use the bankruptcy system to force a Chapter 11 plan on nonconsenting creditors. Additionally, the debtor may need to borrow funds for its operations going forward. As you will see, Chapter 11 provides particular incentives for lenders and other parties to provide working capital to the debtor during a case. Specifically, under §364, the court can grant security interests that are higher in priority than existing liens, which can be a great benefit to both the cash-starved debtor and the post-petition lenders.

Additionally, the debtor may need to reject (i.e., not perform, or breach) certain leases and contracts, which is something the Bankruptcy Code not only permits but also encourages debtors to do in order to revitalize the business, under §365. The nondebtor party to a rejected contract or lease is left with a general unsecured claim for its damages, a claim that can be dealt with by the debtor in its Chapter 11 plan. (*See* 11 U.S.C. §365.)

Another reason a Chapter 11 proceeding may be preferable is that the ultimate plan may be to sell the debtor's assets as a *going concern* or ongoing operation. The Bankruptcy Code (in §363(f)) allows the bankruptcy court to provide special protections to purchasers of assets sold by the debtor.[3] Specifically, §363(f) of the Bankruptcy Code allows some or all of the assets to be sold free and clear of all liens, claims, and encumbrances, which allows the buyer to purchase the assets without fear that encumbrances, liens, and other

3. This also is true of assets sold by a trustee by the way, whether the assets are sold in a Chapter 7 or a Chapter 11 U.S.C. §363(f).

claims (including future claims) will impede the value of the assets over time. The assets can even be sold free of successor liability claims, meaning claims for which a purchaser of assets could be liable as successor/purchaser of the assets. This is quite hard to accomplish outside of bankruptcy. The policy reason for allowing such a sale is that assets sold free of all claims can be sold at a higher price, thus raising more money for the debtor's creditors.

Finally, a Chapter 11 case may be preferable simply because a debtor may need to restock and rebuild its inventory. This can be accomplished in Chapter 11 because while the debtor is putting together its plan, it will not be expected to pay general unsecured claims. This moratorium on payments can greatly improve the debtor's cash flow, and thus its ability to buy new product.

QUESTION 4. A company that manufactures agricultural pesticides is thinking about filing a Chapter 11 case to address huge liability for tort cases that have been lodged against it, and also to infuse quick cash into the business, which it desperately needs. You are the company's attorney and are working on the cash flow issue, as well as the possible exit plan in the case. You know you'll need allies in the case, and also that some groups will necessarily be opposed to the debtor's efforts. Realizing that one cannot predict an outcome with certainty, and also that positions change throughout a case, who among the following is most likely to oppose the case and the debtor in general?

A. Current suppliers.
B. The debtor's employees.
C. Tort victims.
D. The new lender.

ANALYSIS. Let's go through these one by one. Current suppliers are not likely to be overly hostile. Chapter 11 provides a chance to be paid for current product and also keep the debtor as a future customer. Thus, **A** is not the best answer. Nor is **B**. Just so you know, the employees are not parties-in-interest in the case unless they have unpaid wage claims, so they will not have any standing to be heard. Even if they do have unpaid wage claims, they would likely want the debtor to survive so they can keep their jobs.

The debtor still needs employees' cooperation, of course, and is likely to get it, as well. While it may seem counterintuitive that employees would want to work for a company that is in Chapter 11, it is far superior to losing one's job altogether. The tort victims stand to lose the most here, and thus **C** is the correct answer. The tort victims never did business with the debtor and do not care if the debtor remains in business unless this increases their payout. Moreover, the debtor will likely try to pay a very small distribution to tort claimants, so the bankruptcy could be very harmful to them, especially those that are badly hurt. **D** is incorrect because the new lender will be provided with many incentives to lend to a Chapter 11 debtor and this new lender (who also has no standing in the case unless the lender also is a creditor) will be in favor of the debtor's case. (*See* 11 U.S.C. §364.) Thus, the correct answer is **C**, as the tort victims are likely to be most hostile to the debtor's reorganization efforts.

Believe it or not, some current secured creditors also may prefer Chapter 11. The debtor-in-possession will be required to make many publicly filed disclosures and to inform the court and the parties-in-interest, blow by blow, of its business activities. See Bankruptcy Rule 1007 (requiring the filing of bankruptcy schedules and statements). This allows the secured creditor (as well as other creditors) to monitor the debtor's business activity to a great degree. Secured creditors may also appreciate the fact that in most plans, the debtor does not pay general unsecured claims in full. Thus, unsecured debt is reduced, leaving more money available to operate and pay secured claims. The Chapter 11 case can also reduce delays and state court litigation, which may produce a greater return to all creditors given that the debtor and its assets are often worth more as a *going concern* than in liquidation.

QUESTION 5. What is the greatest benefit that pre-petition secured creditors get out of a debtor's Chapter 11 case?

A. Interest on loan amounts.
B. The possibility of a cramdown or stripdown.
C. Much more disclosure and oversight.
D. An easier path to collecting on the debt.

ANALYSIS. **B** is the easiest answer to eliminate, because cramdown or stripdown is not a benefit to the secured party. By now, you probably know that cramdown is something that the debtor does to the secured party against its will, which results in smaller loan repayments to the secured creditor. This is not a benefit at all, but rather a detriment to the secured party. **A** is also incorrect. Although a secured party may get some interest during a Chapter 11 case, it may *not* get interest if it is undersecured. Moreover, after a plan is confirmed, the debtor may be paying a different rate, which could be lower than the contract rate of interest. Normally, secured parties receive more interest on their loan outside, rather than inside, bankruptcy. Chapter 11 impedes rather than enhances collection efforts, so **D** is also incorrect. This leaves **C** as the correct answer, which can be gleaned from the prior discussion. Debtors-in-possession give creditors a great deal of information in the context of their Chapter 11 cases. This information, which allows parties to evaluate the strength of the debtor's operations and the debtor's likelihood of successfully reorganizing, can be very valuable.

B. Introduction to the Basic Chapter 11 Rules and Major Parties-in-Interest

This section outlines some of the basic principles of Chapter 11, as well as the primary parties-in-interest in a Chapter 11 case. If you represent a Chapter 11 debtor, the first thing you must determine is whether the debtor has a plan for bringing itself out of its financial difficulties. Having an exit plan is the most critical aspect of a Chapter 11 case. This is because Chapter 11 is incredibly expensive. If the case goes on for too long, lawyers' fees can eat up any potential profits and make reorganization impossible. A debtor's attorney must immediately sit down with a potential client and see if there is a feasible plan for getting out of financial distress. Is there a way that divisions can be sold, reduced, or streamlined to make the debtor more profitable? Can unprofitable contracts and leases be rejected? Can the debtor reduce its workforce to become more profitable? Was there a one-time event that caused the debtor to fail?

As with Chapter 7 and Chapter 13, only *pre-petition claims* can be paid at a discount, and even then, only certain kinds of pre-petition claims can be reduced. The debtor will be responsible for paying all of its post-petition obligations on a current basis. Additionally, secured debt may need to be *serviced* (paid) on an ongoing basis, even during the Chapter 11 case. The debtor must calculate these payments into its cash flow. To assess whether a client can come out of Chapter 11 successfully, the debtor must prepare budgets and financial projections, explaining how the case will help its business return to profitability.

The debtor does not need creditor consent to file a Chapter 11 case. Section 109 of the Code discusses the eligibility of a Chapter 11 debtor. While some cases are involuntary, in which creditors force a debtor into Chapter 11, the debtor files most cases. Normally, in those rare involuntary cases, creditors file an involuntary Chapter 7 case, which the debtor later converts to a Chapter 11 case.[4] (*See* 11 U.S.C. §303.) If the debtor is a corporation, its corporate board will do a resolution authorizing the officers to file the Chapter 11 case.

A debtor can file a Chapter 11 reorganization case whether it intends to actually reorganize its business affairs or instead liquidate or sell the company pursuant to Chapter 11. Chapter 11 permits both business reorganizations and the sale of businesses as *going concerns* (meaning ongoing businesses or *turn-key operations*). The debtor can also file a liquidating Chapter 11 plan and sell the assets pursuant to the terms of the plan. Of course, many businesses use a combination of these methods by downsizing business operations, changing the asset base of the business, or simply restructuring business operations to focus on a particular part of the business.

---

4. Regardless of later conversion, very few involuntary bankruptcies are filed under either Chapter 11 or Chapter 7.

1. *Major players in a Chapter 11 case*

a. The debtor-in-possession In most Chapter 11 cases, the debtor's management, not a trustee, runs the case. (*See* 11 U.S.C. §§1104, 1107.) This is obviously different from a Chapter 7 liquidation case, in which a trustee is always appointed. (*See* 11 U.S.C. §701.) Whereas in a Chapter 7 case the debtor and the creditors are mostly concerned with calculating past debts and liquidating nonexempt assets for distribution to creditors, Chapter 11 often focuses on how the debtor's operations can support payments to creditors over time. Absent the appointment of a trustee (a rare and drastic move), the debtor-in-possession retains control of the business and continues to run it. In cases in which there is no trustee, the debtor-in-possession has virtually all of the rights and powers of a trustee under the Bankruptcy Code, which include the right to operate the business, the right to enter into transactions in the ordinary course of business without court approval, and the right to avoid preferential transfers and fraudulent conveyances. (*See* 11 U.S.C. §§1106, 1107.) A Chapter 11 trustee can be appointed in certain unusual circumstances, but most of the time, the debtor-in-possession continues to run the company. Section 1104 provides that a trustee can be appointed for "cause," which can include fraud, dishonesty, incompetence, or gross mismanagement. (*See* 11 U.S.C. §1104(a)(1).)

You learned previously that a trustee in bankruptcy is a fiduciary for all creditors. This means that a trustee in bankruptcy has an obligation to create the largest possible distribution for creditors and to fulfill the duties of loyalty and care to creditors. The debtor-in-possession has these same fiduciary obligations. (*See* 11 U.S.C. §1107.) In fact, the debtor's management (the officers or directors of the company) now has fiduciary duties not only to shareholders but also to creditors. In fact, once the debtor is within the zone of insolvency,[5] the debtor's duty to creditors is paramount and superior in nature to the fiduciary obligations to shareholders.

Over the next several months or years of the case, the debtor-in-possession's obligation is to run the company and comply with the rules of Chapter 11. The debtor's goal is to make a profit and continue its business into the future or, if it so chooses, sell its assets, depending on what approach maximizes the value of its assets for creditors.

b. The United States Trustee's Office You learned a bit about the United States Trustee Program in Chapter 6. The U.S. Trustee is different from a case trustee. The U.S. Trustee is a government officer, essentially a U.S. attorney for bankruptcy cases. (*See* 28 U.S.C. §581.) The U.S. Trustee Program was created to further remove judges from the administration of Chapter 11 cases, and

---

5. *See* Credit Lyonnais Bank Nederland, N.V. v. Pathe Communications Corp., 1991 WL 277613, n.55 (Del. Ch. 1991). Courts have recognized that, at some point before insolvency, justice requires directors to adopt a more moderate sensitivity to risk. *See, e.g.*, In re Ben Franklin Retail Stores, Inc., 225 B.R. 646, 655-56 (Bankr. N.D. Ill. 1998).

thus allow judges to focus on disputes within those cases. The U.S. Trustee Program was created as part of the Bankruptcy Reform Act of 1978, at a time when the jurisdictional powers of bankruptcy judges were greatly expanded, and the Office of the U.S. Trustee was formed to ease the transition to this new system. The U.S. Trustee Program started as a pilot project in 18 districts, and was later expanded nationwide.[6]

The U.S. Trustee's office's duties include: (1) appointing unsecured creditor committees, equity committees, and other committees; (2) appointing a Chapter 11 trustee in the event that the court orders the appointment of a Chapter 11 trustee and creditors do not elect their own choice of trustee; (3) monitoring cases to ensure that debtors file their monthly operating reports and pay their administrative fees; and (4) protecting unsecured creditor interests in cases in which there is no unsecured creditors' committee. Just so you know, the U.S. Trustee has standing to appear and be heard on any issue in a case. (*See* 11 U.S.C. §307.)

The U.S. Trustee Program plays a much larger role in Chapter 11 cases than in Chapter 7 and Chapter 13 cases, particularly in reviewing and approving fees for Chapter 11 debtor's counsel, counsel for the creditors committee, and other professionals who are paid from the debtor's assets. As we have told you, these fees can be quite substantial and in some cases can be in the millions.

c. Creditors' committees You might have wondered how unsecured creditors get any voice in a Chapter 11 case, because their claims are often quite small. The Bankruptcy Code deals with this problem by allowing general unsecured creditors to organize into committees, which are permitted to hire counsel paid from the debtor's assets. (*See* 11 U.S.C. §§1102, 330.) Thus, §1102 of the Bankruptcy Code allows the court to appoint one or more creditors' committees in Chapter 11 cases. By forming an unsecured creditors' committee, the general unsecured creditors gain a powerful and unified voice in the Chapter 11 case, to which a judge is likely to listen. Unsecured creditors' committees are often a counterbalancing force against powerful secured creditors.[7]

The most important activities of the creditors' committee include (1) negotiating the Chapter 11 plan; (2) reviewing the debtor's budgets and other financial information; (3) hiring accountants and other professionals to review the debtor's financial data; (4) reviewing the debtor's cash collateral order and,

6. The goal of removing bankruptcy judges from mundane administrative roles in Chapter 11 cases was only partially achieved. For example, in 1996, bankruptcy judges were given the power to act *sua sponte* pursuant to §105(a) of the Bankruptcy Code. You will recall that §105(a) permits bankruptcy judges to take any action or enter any court order that they believe furthers the purposes of Title 11. Additionally, in 1994, pursuant to §105(d), bankruptcy judges were given the power to hold status conferences, and thus to learn about the case outside the adversarial context. These sections further involve the judges in the administrative process of bankruptcy cases and are used more frequently in Chapter 11 cases than in other types of cases.

7. The unsecured creditors have inferior rights to secured creditors but the committee still has a very strong voice in the case, particularly on procedural and fairness issues.

if applicable, post-petition financing order; and (5) reviewing the debtor's motions to sell assets, assume and assign leases, and engage in other business activities outside the ordinary course of business.[8] (*See* 11 U.S.C. §1103.)

The creditors' committee is often the most important party in the case other than the debtor-in-possession and the primary secured creditor. The committee is appointed by the U.S. Trustee's office. (*See* 11 U.S.C. §1102.) Normally, the 20 largest unsecured creditors receive notice of the meeting to form a creditors' committee, and the U.S. Trustee's office forms a committee from that group with at least three and no more than nine members. Ideally, the committee will have five or seven members. A smaller committee is easier to manage and an odd number of members precludes tie votes on committees.

Like the debtor-in-possession (or the trustee if one is appointed), committee members owe fiduciary duties to the entire general unsecured creditor class, meaning all of the general unsecured creditors in the case. (*See* In re SPM Manufacturing Corp., 984 F.2d 1305 (1st Cir. 1993).) These duties include the duty of loyalty and the duty of care. These duties run not only to creditors that have the same interests as a particular committee member, but to all general unsecured creditors. If an unsecured creditor has a particular interest unique to his or her own position, it may be best for that creditor to refrain from membership in the creditors' committee and to obtain its own counsel. Other creditors that may not be appropriate for the creditors' committee include competitors of the debtor and those involved in litigation with the debtor.

As mentioned previously, the creditors' committee may retain counsel, as well as other professionals (such as accountants), in the case with court approval. These professionals will be paid from the debtor's estate, just as the debtor's own professionals will be paid. As you can see, committee participation levels the playing field and allows the general unsecured creditors (who would not otherwise have a strong voice individually) to be represented and play an active and meaningful role in the case. These professionals are not free for unsecured creditors, however, as they will be paid out of the estate as first-priority administrative expenses, and thus before general unsecured claims.

QUESTION 6. If no committee is appointed in a case, the role of the committee will primarily be filled by:

A. the debtor.
B. the court.
C. the U.S. Trustee's office.
D. the trustee appointed in the case.

8. The creditors' committee is considered a party-in-interest in the case, pursuant to §1103(c)(1). As a result, the committee has a right to be heard on any issue in the case.

ANALYSIS. Absent a showing of *cause* under §1104, there is normally no trustee appointed in the case, so **D** is incorrect. The other answers are all possibilities on some level. As stated in **A**, the debtor does fill some of the same roles played by the committee because the debtor is charged with a fiduciary duty to protect creditors' claims. Its position is sometimes adverse to creditors, however, especially when the parties disagree about the debtor's likelihood of successfully reorganizing. Thus, the debtor often does not fill the shoes of the committee. The court is not supposed to represent any particular creditor or creditor group, and also is not supposed to become deeply involved in the administration of the case, so **B** is also incorrect, leaving **C** as the correct answer. If there is no committee, the U.S. Trustee's office attempts to fill the void. As a practical matter, a very large unsecured creditor often retains its own counsel to ensure that its interests are served by the debtor's plan.

QUESTION 7. The biggest risk in cases where no unsecured creditors' committee is appointed is that:

A. unsecured creditors will not appoint an attorney in the case, but this risk is counterbalanced with the fact that the creditors will not have to pay this expense either.
B. unsecured creditors will have no meaningful way to negotiate the plan.
C. unsecured creditors will not learn of any of the objection deadlines in the case.
D. unsecured creditors will not have a formal and organized voice in the proceeding and thus will be unable to participate in the case in a meaningful way.

ANALYSIS. The biggest risk is **D**. Although it is true that each individual unsecured creditor is a party-in-interest in the case and has a right to be heard in the case, the process is only cost-effective when the committee has organized and appointed counsel. The voice of the committee is the mechanism by which creditors with small claims and little bargaining power are heard. This power, and the lack of it without a committee, cannot be overestimated. Choice **A** contains a true statement, that the unsecured creditors, as a committee, will not get to appoint an attorney if they do not form a committee. But **A** also contains the erroneous statement that this is essentially all right because creditors will not incur the costs of such an attorney. This notion is penny wise but pound foolish. An attorney is critical to being heard in the case and getting the best possible distribution. Moreover, the committee's attorneys' fees will be paid out of the debtor's estate as administrative expenses, just like the debtor's attorneys. Yes, the unsecured creditors will receive more if these fees are minimized, but it's a bit like eating in a restaurant as a group, after which the bill will be evenly split. If everyone else is ordering an appetizer, it won't save much for you to forgo one. Perhaps this is a bit silly, but the main point is that creditors need an attorney to get good results, and if everyone else has one, it is best to have one too, even if it costs money. Thus, the correct answer is **D**. **B** is also a correct answer, but **D** is broader and thus the best answer.

Often, the unsecured creditors' committee also appoints an accountant or other financial advisor in the case. The debtor will undoubtedly have an accountant, and the creditors' committee can best protect its interests by hiring its own accountant to review and verify the debtor's financial information. In larger cases, other committees may be appointed as well. For example, in a publicly traded company, the U.S. Trustee's office often appoints a committee of equity security holders for shareholders. (*See* 11 U.S.C. §1102.) In larger cases, there may also be bondholders' committees or more than one general unsecured creditors' committee, particularly if some creditors have interests that are different from the other unsecured creditors.

d. Secured creditors In some Chapter 11 cases, there is only one secured creditor, which holds a lien on all of the debtor's assets. It is not unusual, however, to have multiple secured creditors with overlapping liens of different priority on the same or different assets. As we discussed previously, if the debtor has just one secured party that holds the first lien on all of its inventory and accounts, we often call that creditor the *primary secured lender*. All secured creditors, regardless of their priority, are entitled to adequate protection of their interests in their collateral. Adequate protection takes many different forms, ranging from monthly payments on the secured debt to simply maintaining the collateral in its present condition.

At the beginning of virtually every Chapter 11 case, the court enters a cash collateral order, which is often negotiated between the debtor and secured parties. This is the subject of a later chapter. However, you should know that every secured creditor has a right to be adequately protected before any of its cash collateral (collateral that turns into cash at some point, including inventory and accounts receivable), is used by the debtor during the Chapter 11 case. Adequate protection is designed to protect the value of the creditor's collateral during the case.[9] (*See* 11 U.S.C. §363(c)(2).) It is very uncommon for a debtor *not* to have pledged these assets (that turn into cash) to a secured party. In other words, most Chapter 11 debtors cannot simply spend the cash they earn in their business, but must ask the court for permission to do so because this cash usually has been pledged as collateral, and is thus the subject of a secured creditor's lien.

As we're sure you have gathered by now, secured creditors in a Chapter 11 proceeding (as in all other types of bankruptcy as well as outside bankruptcy) have very strong bargaining positions. Under a Chapter 11 plan, the debtor

---

9. *See* Chapter 29, Part A.

must either surrender the secured party's collateral, pay the allowed secured claim in full, with a present value interest rate over the life of the plan, or provide the creditor with what is called the "indubitable equivalent" of its secured claim. (*See* 11 U.S.C. §1129(b)(2)(A).) The allowed claim of a secured creditor will be only as large as the value of its collateral, as you've learned in prior parts of this guide, and if the secured creditor is oversecured, it will be entitled to post-petition interest and attorneys' fees to the extent of the value of its collateral pursuant to §506(b). Again, the debtor's primary secured creditor typically plays a very significant role in the Chapter 11 case.

As discussed in the context of Chapter 13 cases, in cases in which the secured party's collateral is worth less than its debt, the secured party's claim will be *bifurcated*. Some of the claim (the deficiency claim, to be more exact) will end up in the general unsecured creditor class under the plan, while the rest (the part supported by the value of the collateral) will be treated and paid as a secured claim. This is at times a great benefit to the debtor, and indeed sometimes allows the debtor to *strip down* the secured party's claim to the value of the collateral, and thus more easily fund a plan. The debtor hopes that each class will vote in favor of its ultimate Chapter 11 plan, or that at the very least, *one class* will vote in favor of its plan.

Without one accepting class, the debtor cannot confirm a plan. If the secured party's deficiency claim is large and dominates the unsecured creditor class, and if the debtor and the secured party are adverse,[10] the large deficiency claim could make it very difficult for the debtor to gain a favorable vote from its unsecured class. Voting is calculated by both number of creditors and by amount, so this formula could cause the whole class to vote no. Consequently, stripping down a secured creditor's claim can make it difficult for the debtor to obtain the unsecured creditor votes that it may need to confirm a Chapter 11 plan. You will learn more about this later.

Remember that an overriding goal of Chapter 11 is to negotiate and confirm a consensual plan, meaning a plan that all classes of claims have accepted. This is done by making peace with the secured creditor classes as well as the unsecured creditor class or classes. Unsecured creditors have a powerful tool in obtaining favorable treatment in the plan, which is known as the *absolute priority rule*. If an unsecured creditor class does not accept the plan and the class is not being paid in full with interest under the plan, then the debtor's equity holders (owners or stockholders) cannot keep their equity interests in the debtor. Instead, the owners must either sell these interests and give creditors the proceeds[11] or distribute the equity interests to the creditors. Naturally,

10. This might result merely *from* the stripdown of the secured claim, which is unlikely to make the secured party very happy. By definition, *stripdown* is accomplished adversely, not consensually.

11. Actually, equity itself may be able to buy back the equity interests in such a situation, a topic discussed in more detail in Chapter 36.

this provides a great incentive for owners to work with the unsecured creditors and to provide a distribution that creditors can live with.

2. *Venue*

In theory, the rules that govern the proper venue where corporate debtors can file a bankruptcy case are pretty straightforward. Those rules are found in 28 U.S.C. rather than 11 U.S.C. because they are jurisdictional rather than substantive in nature. In particular, 28 U.S.C. §1408 provides that a debtor may file bankruptcy in the district where the debtor's domicile, residence, principal place of business, or principal assets reside. Alternatively, a debtor may file bankruptcy in a district where there is a pending case involving an affiliate of the debtor.

In practice, these simple rules have been the subject of some arguable abuse by certain debtors who have strategically used the affiliate alternative to file bankruptcy in venues that have little connection with the nexus of the debtor's main business operations. Indeed, there have been cases in which the debtor has created a strategically located affiliate shortly before filing in order to enable the debtor to file in the debtor's preferred venue by having the newly created affiliate file bankruptcy first.

Why might a debtor prefer one venue over another? There are a number of reasons for this, but here are just a few. First, certain bankruptcy courts are known to have a lot of experience with major Chapter 11 cases, and a large corporate debtor may wish to avail itself of the benefits of having an experienced judge oversee its reorganization. Second, certain bankruptcy courts have a reputation as being "debtor-friendly," and so corporate debtors may gravitate to those venues in the hopes of getting a bankruptcy judge who is prone to favor reorganizations over liquidations. Finally, certain jurisdictions may have favorable precedent on legal issues that are important to a particular debtor, and so the debtor may choose that venue for the predictability of outcome on that issue as compared to a jurisdiction where there is no precedent yet on that matter.

There have been periodic attempts since the enactment of the modern Bankruptcy Code by certain members of Congress to amend the venue provisions to avoid the perceived abuse by some debtors who have used the venue flexibility to their advantage. However, none of these efforts has so far yielded any reform to the venue provisions of bankruptcy law, which remain as flexible (and subject to strategic forum-shopping) as ever.

QUESTION 8. (CODE READER) Debtor Corporation ("Debtor") is a corporation that is headquartered in California, its principal place of business. Debtor's principal assets are located in Indiana. Debtor has offices (but not separate affiliates) in Arkansas. Debtor has one affiliate in Kansas and another affiliate in Missouri. The Missouri affiliate just filed a

Chapter 11 bankruptcy in Missouri last week, but the Kansas affiliate is not in bankruptcy. Which of the following states would NOT currently be a proper venue in which Debtor could file a bankruptcy case?

A. Kansas only.
B. Arkansas only.
C. Arkansas and Missouri.
D. Arkansas and Kansas.

ANALYSIS. As noted above, 28 U.S.C. §1408 says that a debtor may file bankruptcy in the district where the debtor's domicile, residence, principal place of business, or principal assets reside. Alternatively, a debtor may file bankruptcy in a district where there is a pending case involving an affiliate of the debtor. Missouri would therefore be a permissible venue for the debtor to file here because the Missouri affiliate just filed a Chapter 11 there last week. So that eliminates **C** as a possible answer. Debtor has offices in Arkansas, but no affiliates, so that means Arkansas would not be a proper venue to file. Debtor has an affiliate in Kansas, but that affiliate is currently not in bankruptcy, so that eliminates the possibility of Debtor riding the coattails of its Kansas affiliate for venue purposes. That means that **D** must be the right answer since neither Arkansas nor Kansas would be proper venues in which Debtor could file bankruptcy.

Martin's and Keating's Picks

1. Question 1 **C**
2. Question 2 **C**
3. Question 3 **B**
4. Question 4 **C**
5. Question 5 **C**
6. Question 6 **C**
7. Question 7 **D**
8. Question 8 **D**

29

Cash Collateral, Post-Petition Financing, and Other First-Day Orders

OVERVIEW
A. The Cash Collateral Motion and Order
   1. What is cash collateral?
   2. Special rules for the debtor's use of cash collateral
   3. Cash collateral stipulations
B. Post-Petition Financing Orders
C. Critical Vendor Orders and the Doctrine of Necessity
D. Payment of Other Unsecured Claims Before Confirmation
E. Applications to Be Employed as Counsel, Accountant, or Other Professional
F. Cash Management Orders
G. Utilities
H. The Closer: Chapter 29
Martin's and Keating's Picks

Before a Chapter 11 case can be filed, a great deal of preparation is required on the part of the debtor's counsel. The debtor is expected to appear in court just hours after the actual bankruptcy petition is filed, with a handful of motions and other paperwork for the court to approve. These are loosely called *first-day orders* and vary somewhat in form from district to district. First-day orders typically include a motion to approve the appointment of debtor's counsel, and perhaps its accountants, under §330; a motion to use cash collateral under §363(c)(2) (because, as you'll soon see, most debtors have used or pledged[1] their cash to secured lenders); or a motion for post-petition financing

1. When we use the word *pledge* here, we use the word in a very general sense to mean that the debtor has granted a voluntary security interest to a secured party in the asset being described. Some people

(new loans) under §364, a cash management order addressing how pre-petition bank accounts will be handled; a motion to pay trust fund taxes; a motion to pay critical vendors; and perhaps a motion to pay pre-petition payroll.

These motions and proposed orders are presented to the court on very short notice, with a request for almost immediate approval. You'll see why in a minute. Secured creditors receive notice of these motions, as do the largest unsecured creditors. Unsecured creditors are often in no position to actually participate in these matters, however, because they have not yet formed a committee or appointed counsel. Nevertheless, the largest unsecured creditors typically receive notice of the hearings. Before we go into each of these separate motions, let's review the difference between a motion, an order, and a hearing and the purpose of each. When the debtor makes a *motion* before the court, *it is asking the court for permission to do something.* If the court grants the motion, it will enter an *order* approving the motion, often subject to certain conditions. Thus, *the motion requests the entry of an order* approving the motion. The debtor (or whoever is making the motion) drafts the requested order and either attaches it to the motion or brings it to the hearing on the motion.[2] Please try not to forget the difference between the order and the motion, because they serve very different purposes. Students confuse the two, but once you've practiced law you never do. Both the motion and the order will be found on the court docket *if* the motion is actually granted. The motion also must be accompanied by a *notice of motion*, which tells creditors where and when to appear if they would like to participate in the hearing on the motion, and also sets the deadline for filing objections to the motion. If one or more objections to the motion are filed, or if the court itself has questions (which is rare), the court will schedule a *hearing* on the motion, during which the moving party will argue that the motion should be *granted*, and other parties will support or oppose the motion. Sometimes first-day orders are entered without a traditional hearing, given the time constraints.

A. The Cash Collateral Motion and Order

Students often have a hard time wrapping their minds around the following hard and fast rule: debtors-in-possession *must* obtain court approval before

use the word *pledge* in a more technical sense to mean to give property to a pawnbroker to secure a loan by possession, but that is not what we are referring to when we use this word.

2. In most of the jurisdictions in which we have practiced, it is customary to attach a copy of the order that you would like the court to enter when filing the motion. This is true in Pennsylvania, Massachusetts, New Jersey, and New York. In New Mexico and a few other places, however, one does not file the order until it is time to actually enter it — in other words, until the judge has granted the motion.

they can use a creditor's cash collateral. (*See* 11 U.S.C. §363(c)(2).)[3] Why is this rule so hard to understand and remember? Primarily because students do not know what cash collateral is.

1. *What is cash collateral?*

You, however, do know what collateral is. It is a certain kind of property (namely, cash or cash equivalents) that the debtor has pledged to a secured creditor as security for a secured loan or debt. But what company would use its *cash* as collateral? As it turns out, almost every company or business in operation has used its cash as collateral for a loan.[4] That's because the cash comes from (or is generated by) property that is used as collateral. It is the proceeds of other types of collateral. If a secured creditor has a lien on something, its lien automatically continues in whatever the collateral later turns into, including cash. If a debtor has (as most have) used its inventory and accounts receivable as collateral, most of the cash that it uses to run its business comes from these two sources and therefore constitutes cash collateral.

The most common business assets, and the ones that most debtors use in order to acquire a working capital loan (a loan that provides ongoing cash for operations, such as a business line of credit), are the business inventory and the accounts receivable.[5] Other business assets that may or may not be used as collateral for this type of loan include equipment, intangible assets like patents and trademarks, goodwill, customer lists, interests in lawsuits, interests in leases and contracts, and so on. All personal property can be collateral for a loan, but the point of the following discussion is to make sure you understand the two or three main types of collateral.

Equipment is easiest to visualize. Equipment consists of long-term assets used in the business operation. For a retail store, these would include forklifts, cash registers, meat cutters, freezers, computers and so forth. Inventory is also easy to grasp. These are short-term assets, made or held by the business for sale or short-term use in the business. These would include groceries in a grocery store, shoes in a shoe factory, and lumber in a lumber mill. (*See* UCC §9-102(a)(33), (48).)

Accounts receivable are the most important type of assets to learn to identify right now because you may be unfamiliar with them. (*See* UCC §9-102(a)(2).) These are amounts of money (accounts) that other people owe the debtor. In class, one of us will often bring an actual invoice from a business to help students remember what an account is, but examples also help. Picture a corporate

---

3. While the statute actually allows the debtor to use cash collateral *either* with court approval *or* with each creditor's consent, even consensual cash collateral orders are put before the court for approval so that other parties have notice of the use of cash collateral.
4. "Cash collateral" is defined in 11 U.S.C. §363(a).
5. What we are calling *accounts receivable* or *receivables* is referred to in Article 9 of the Uniform Commercial Code (UCC) as simply *accounts*. Businesspeople frequently refer to these as *receivables* or *accounts receivable*, but these words are all used interchangeably here.

cleaning service. The service owns a few big vacuums, a few steamers, and two vans. All of these assets are equipment. It has some inventory in the form of soaps and solutions, which are used by the business on a short-term basis, but are not sold. These assets are inventory, even though the debtor does not sell them directly. They are short-term assets. The vast majority of the valuable assets of the cleaning company are accounts receivable. The cleaning company cleans office buildings every night and then bills customers and requests payment within 30 to 60 days. Each time the debtor cleans an office building, an account receivable (an amount owing to the debtor) is created. When the cleaning company's customers pay these accounts receivable, the customers will send checks or auto debit payments to the company, which will end up in the company's bank account. Voila! The resulting cash is cash collateral if the accounts receivable have been pledged for a loan, which they almost certainly have been!

Let's try another example. Here, the business is a paper factory. What are the paper factory's assets? Assume that all have been pledged to a secured lender on a working capital loan. First, picture the equipment. It would be the industrial equipment, furniture in the employee workrooms, computers, and anything else that is tangible and long term in nature. It need not be used to make paper. Do you see that? How about the inventory? Well, there is the finished paper. There also is the raw material used to make paper. There also is something called work-in-progress, which is paper in the process of being made, but not necessarily in salable form either as raw material or finished product. Can you think of any other inventory? Remember that inventory includes things that are not for sale. It can include the soap in the bathrooms, because this is for short-term use in the business.

Although the soap in the bathroom does not create cash collateral, some of the other assets do. The paper products may be sold directly to the public for cash, in which case the cash that the factory gets in exchange for the paper is cash collateral in a Chapter 11 case. Most of the paper, however, will probably be sold to other businesses, in which case the paper will be sold by the factory on credit. The company will ship to a customer and then bill the customer for the shipment, payment to be made by the paper company's customer within 30 to 60 days. At this point, the obligations of its customers are accounts. As with the cleaning company example above, when the payment is made by the paper factory's customers, the payments are cash collateral of the lender.

QUESTION 1. Which of the following would not constitute inventory for a grocery store?

A. Plastic wrap in the deli.
B. Canned corn.
C. Meat cutters.
D. Cash register tape.

ANALYSIS. **B** can be eliminated first. The canned corn is exactly what you think of when you think of inventory. It is something that the debtor sells as part of its business and is then turned into cash. The cash register tape, as well as the plastic wrap in the deli, are also inventory because the debtor uses them short-term. This is tricky because these things are not sold. Still, they are inventory, eliminating both **A** and **D**, and leaving **C**, the meat cutter, as the correct answer. The meat cutter falls into the other category of tangible assets, equipment. When categorizing tangible collateral, you are often choosing between these two categories, inventory and equipment. The meat cutter is used over a long period of time, and is clearly equipment.

QUESTION 2. On a dairy farm, which of these would be least likely to fall into the category of "equipment"?

A. Staplers in the office.
B. Animal pens.
C. Magazines in the employee break room.
D. A milking machine.

ANALYSIS. The animal pens appear to be equipment, at least based on what you have been told here,[6] and thus, **B** is incorrect. Certainly the milking machines are equipment, so **D** is incorrect. This leaves us with two similar options for what would *not* constitute equipment: the staplers and the magazines in the office. Maybe an easier way to think this through is to consider which of them most likely would be inventory. The magazines are used up quicker than the staplers and we would choose the magazines as the items least likely to be considered equipment. Thus, the correct answer is **C**, with **A** running a close second.

You might wonder why anyone cares which category an asset or piece of collateral falls into. The secured party cares because it must correctly identify its collateral in its filing documents and its contract with the debtor. In this discussion, we are concerned about how assets are characterized for a different reason. We are trying to understand and identify the different types of collateral so that we can learn how cash collateral is created. Although cash collateral can arise from the sale of the debtor's equipment when, for example, the equipment is sold by the business, this is not typically the subject of a cash collateral order. What is most important is the cash collateral that comes from the sale of the debtor's *inventory* and *accounts receivable*. If you can recognize

6. If you took Secured Transactions you might see why these animal pens may be fixtures instead, because they may be attached to the land, but let's not get too carried away here. In this discussion, we have focused most on inventory, accounts, and equipment.

these two types of assets, and distinguish them from other types of assets, you know when to be concerned about the use of cash collateral.

2. *Special rules for the debtor's use of cash collateral*

So now you know what inventory and accounts receivable are, and you also know that if these assets are pledged to a lender to secure a loan or debt, they can become *cash collateral* as that term is used in the Bankruptcy Code. So what? Outside bankruptcy, the debtor is free to use the lender's cash collateral under whatever terms the parties have contractually agreed to. In bankruptcy, the debtor is free to use all of its property in its ordinary course of business, *except* cash collateral, even though it has pledged that property as collateral for a loan, without court approval. For use of cash collateral, the debtor needs court approval or the consent of the secured creditor.

Cash collateral is given special protections under the Bankruptcy Code because it is so volatile and easy for the debtor to dissipate. Thus, the Code requires that the debtor obtain court approval before using any cash in the business in which a creditor has a security interest. Now you may be starting to see why the debtor must move quickly to obtain this approval. Most debtors cannot go one day in business without using the cash generated from the sale of inventory or from the collection of accounts receivable, and most debtors have pledged these assets to at least one creditor.

To gain the right to use a secured creditor's cash collateral in a Chapter 11 business, against the creditor's will, the court must find that the creditor's interest in the collateral will not be harmed or impaired by the debtor's use. In the parlance of §363 of the Bankruptcy Code, this means that the creditor's interest must be *adequately protected*.[7] (*See* 11 U.S.C. §363(c)(2).) We sometimes say that the debtor must provide the creditor with *adequate protection*.[8]

Note that the debtor must provide *adequate protection* to the secured party in other situations as well, which are enumerated in §363. For example, in the context of relief from the automatic stay, if a court finds that all of the requirements of §362(d) are met, and that the secured party is thus entitled to have the automatic stay lifted, the court can still refuse to lift the stay and can order the debtor to make adequate protection payments instead. (*See* 11 U.S.C. §361.) The debtor also must provide adequate protection if it plans to grant new liens on collateral that has already been pledged to an existing creditor. (*See* 11 U.S.C. §364(d).)

Returning to our discussion of the debtor's use of cash collateral, §361 provides at least three nonexclusive ways for the debtor to provide adequate protection to a creditor to gain the right to use cash collateral. First, the debtor can make periodic cash payments to the creditor to protect the secured party from loss. (*See* 11 U.S.C. §361(1).) Second, the debtor can provide the

---

7. Here this phrase is used as a verb form.
8. This phrase, on the other hand, is a noun.

creditor with a lien on new collateral, in addition to the collateral the creditor is already holding, which we call *replacement* or *supplemental liens*. (*See* 11 U.S.C. §361(2).)[9] A third and more controversial way to provide adequate protection is through an *equity cushion*. (*See* 11 U.S.C. §361(3).) Oversecured creditors have an *equity cushion*, which means that the value of the collateral is greater than the face value of the secured party's claim. (*See* 11 U.S.C. §506(b).)

QUESTION 3. Which of the following creditors could be forced to accept an ***equity cushion*** as adequate protection from a debtor that is a bike repair shop and that will continue to use cash generated by accounts receivable in the amount of about $15,000 a month? Assume only the collateral listed in each example.

A. A creditor holding a lien on $310,000 worth of accounts receivable, and with a claim of about $300,000.
B. A creditor holding a lien on $400,000 worth of accounts receivable, and with a claim of about $300,000.
C. A creditor with a claim of about $300,000, with a lien on $500,000 worth of equipment that the debtor is using.
D. A creditor with a claim of $400,000 and with a lien on accounts receivable worth $300,000.

ANALYSIS. The work we did in the earlier chapters of this book will start to come in handy here. First, let's consider a quick question about the basics of cash collateral.

Which of these four creditors would be laughed out of court if it asked for adequate protection? If you need to, reread the options slowly. Careful reading is the key to eliminating one obviously incorrect answer; at least it *will be* obvious once you hear the answer. **C** is the most obviously incorrect answer in the bunch. Why? Because the creditor with a lien on the equipment, assuming no other collateral, is not entitled to adequate protection for the debtor's use of *cash* generated by accounts receivable. Adequate protection is necessary only if the debtor seeks to use cash collateral, and equipment normally does not turn into cash collateral or proceeds. In this choice, the debtor is not proposing to use the debtor's *cash collateral*. Thus, the debtor can use the equipment in the ordinary course of its business without providing adequate protection, at least at this time. If you missed it, go back and read it again.

Now let's examine the other options. We said that an equity cushion can be used to provide adequate protection if the creditor is *oversecured* but not otherwise. Even then, whether an equity cushion will work as adequate protection

9. A supplemental lien is a lien in something new. A replacement lien is where the existing lien is replaced with a lien in something that is more valuable.

depends on how large the equity cushion is. Naturally, if the secured party's claim is $1 million and the collateral is worth $10 million, the equity cushion will suffice. It will provide adequate protection to the secured party. In our problem, one of the creditors is very significantly oversecured and this is the creditor that could probably be forced to accept the equity cushion as adequate protection. Thus, the correct answer is **B**, the creditor holding a lien on $400,000 worth of accounts receivable, and with a claim of only $300,000. This is a significant equity cushion.

Although **A** also has an equity cushion (its collateral is worth $310,000 and its claim is $300,000), this is not the type of equity cushion that will really provide adequate protection to a secured creditor. Without knowing any other facts, this cushion appears too small to protect the creditor from loss. The facts bolster this conclusion. The problem says that the debtor plans to use $15,000 worth of cash collateral per month. While not all of the $15,000 would be lost in any given month (much of it will produce new inventory or accounts receivable), the cushion should at least be equal to the amount of cash that the debtor is using on a month-to-month basis.[10] So, it is doubtful that **A** would be an appropriate way to provide adequate protection to such a creditor.

D is a situation in which the creditor is undersecured. There is no equity cushion at all in this particular case, so there is no equity cushion available to give. Thus, the correct answer, as set out previously, is **B**. The overall lesson is that only creditors who are oversecured and who have large equity cushions in relation to the amount of cash the debtor would like to use on a monthly basis can be forced to accept an equity cushion as adequate protection.

Why are equity cushions a controversial way to provide adequate protection? Well, first of all, as you know from Chapter 11 of this guide, oversecured creditors are allowed to accrue interest and attorneys' fees on their claims. At least in theory, if a creditor starts the case oversecured, it should stay that way because the case is not supposed to impair a secured creditor's position over time. For this reason, equity cushions are not really considered *real* adequate protection in some courts and commentators' minds. Interestingly, the U.S. Supreme Court has explicitly held that it is *not necessary* to preserve an equity cushion, but only the actual property itself. So to the extent that courts find this, it is clearly incorrect. (*See* U.S. Savings Ass'n v. Timbers of Inwood Forest Associates, Ltd., 484 U.S. 365 (1988).) As the Supreme Court reasoned, if there is plenty of collateral to cover the debt, there is no need to make adequate protection payments to protect the creditor against loss, because there is just no way the losses could eat up such a large equity cushion. And as you'll soon see, the debtor may need to use the collateral for other purposes.

We briefly mentioned replacement or supplemental liens as one way of providing adequate protection. These are liens in property in which the

---

10. Courts normally only allow a debtor to use a creditor's cash collateral for a period of 30, or at most 60, days.

creditor currently does not hold an interest. Otherwise the liens would not be in anything the creditor did not already have, and could not be considered *replacements* or *additions*. They would not provide anything new in terms of protection. One concept that is somewhat hard to grasp is that the replacement liens are granted to secure obligations of the debtor to the creditor, but only to the extent of any diminution in the original collateral resulting from the debtor's use.

Here is an example: Assume that the original collateral for a loan is worth $5 million, that the secured party's claim is also $5 million, and that the debtor grants replacement liens in other collateral to adequately protect the secured party in exchange for the use of cash collateral. If the original collateral does not go down in value at all during the case, all of the new collateral is returned to the debtor. If the collateral is reduced in value by just $100,000, then at the end of the case, the other collateral is returned to the debtor, less $100,000 for the creditor, and so on. Collateral is always used in that way. It secures a debt but must be returned once the debt is paid. That is why there is no law against being vastly oversecured. You can never have too much collateral if you are a creditor.

Regardless of how adequate protection is provided, one thing is clear: The debtor cannot operate its business in bankruptcy without cash, and cannot use cash collateral, as all of its cash probably will be, without a court finding that the creditor or creditors with an interest in the cash collateral are adequately protected. If the debtor cannot find some property with which to provide adequate protection to the creditor, then the case is over before it even starts.

QUESTION 4. (CODE READER) Debtor Corporation ("Debtor") has filed Chapter 11 bankruptcy and currently has $500,000 in its account at Local Bank. Debtor does not currently have a loan outstanding with Local Bank, but Debtor does owe $800,000 to Big Bank that is secured by inventory and accounts receivable. All of the funds currently in Debtor's account at Local Bank are proceeds of Big Bank's collateral and therefore qualify as Big Bank's cash collateral. Debtor does not currently have access to other funds with which to operate in Chapter 11 and therefore would like to use the cash collateral that is in its account at Local Bank. Given all of the above, under what circumstances may Debtor use the funds in its bank account at Local Bank in the ordinary course of Debtor's business?

A. If Debtor is unable to provide suitable adequate protection for use of the funds, Debtor may only use the funds if both Local Bank and Big Bank consent.

B. Debtor may only use the funds if Debtor can provide adequate protection to Big Bank that is satisfactory to Big Bank.

C. Even though Debtor's proposed use is clearly in the ordinary course of business, if the court determines that Debtor is unable to provide adequate protection to Big Bank, then Debtor may only use the funds in its bank account at Local Bank if Big Bank allows Debtor to do so.
D. Debtor may only use the funds if the court authorizes such use and Big Bank allows Debtor to use the funds.

ANALYSIS. Before getting to the correct answer here, let's first consider why the other three choices are wrong. Choice **A** is wrong because it incorrectly states that Local Bank, the bank where Debtor has the account in which these funds reside, has any say in the matter. Because Debtor does not currently owe any money to Local Bank, Local Bank has no claim on whether and how Debtor uses those funds. Choice **B** is close to being right but it misstates who has the power to decide whether the Debtor's proposed adequate protection is sufficient. Section 363(e) gives that power to the bankruptcy court, not the secured creditor who has an interest in the cash collateral. Choice **D** is wrong because if Big Bank were willing to allow Debtor to use the funds in the ordinary course of business, then there is no need for the court also to provide permission to Debtor for the same thing. That leaves choice **C**, the correct answer, which accurately states that either the creditor with an interest in the cash collateral must consent or the court must determine that Debtor is providing adequate protection to the affected creditor.

3. *Cash collateral stipulations*

In most Chapter 11 cases, parties do not contest the debtor's motion to use cash collateral. Instead, the debtor and the secured creditor (or creditors) try to work out the terms of cash collateral use consensually, and then present the court with a negotiated order, which is often called a *cash collateral stipulation* or *stipulated cash collateral order*. Thus, the debtor can either move involuntarily for the use of cash collateral or can move to have the cash collateral stipulation approved. Chapter 11, however, is a multiparty proceeding. Even if the debtor and the secured parties agree on the terms of cash collateral use, other creditors may object on the grounds that the order gives the secured party too much, forcing the court to decide whether to grant or deny the motion.

A cash collateral order or stipulation contains many terms that protect the secured party as well as some that protect the debtor. Virtually every stipulation contains a budget prepared by the debtor's management outlining how much cash the debtor can spend during the time covered by the cash collateral stipulation. The budget is the most important thing to negotiate because it determines specifically how the debtor can use the creditor's cash collateral. The debtor can only spend money on the items outlined in the budget, up to the amounts permitted in the budget, perhaps with a 5 percent margin of error overall if that is what the order says. Debtors often propose a larger budget than they actually need during negotiations, knowing that some items will be cut. Items over which there is often a fight include management's fees and salaries, professional fees, and sometimes advertising.

After the ever-important budget, the next most common things to negotiate are the payments to the lender, if there will be any. Many secured parties want to receive ongoing payments during a Chapter 11 case, and if these payments are called *adequate protection payments*, the court will likely approve them.[11] The debtor must think long and hard about whether to offer payments (is this really necessary, or is there other collateral or an equity cushion?), and if so, how much? The creditors' committee (if there is one at this early stage) or individual unsecured creditors can object to the debtor's offered adequate protection payments, but the court may allow the payments anyway. What is the risk to the debtor of promising payments? If the debtor cannot keep them up as the case goes forward, it is unlikely that the court will modify the agreement to reduce the payments against the secured party's will. Missed payments often mark the end of the case, as the creditor's motion to lift the stay will usually be granted.

In addition to the budget and the payments, the stipulation contains many other terms. First, there are the reporting requirements, which require the debtor to tell the secured party on a weekly or even a daily basis what the inventory and accounts receivable are worth. Other reporting requirements might include reports on the level of cash, the daily sales, and the collection of accounts receivable. The debtor is also normally required to prepare financial projections indicating what business it expects to do over the cash collateral period. Usually, the stipulation will require that the debtor meet or exceed its projections, so this is no time for pie in the sky accounting. Remember what the stipulation is for: namely, to allow the debtor to use the creditor's cash collateral, but only if the creditor is not being hurt by the use.

Other things you might find in the stipulation are statements that the debtor is granting the creditor replacement liens as part of the adequate protection (up to the amount of the diminution in the value of the collateral), definitions of what constitutes a default under the stipulation, and what happens upon default, including in some cases relief from the stay for the creditor. Some stipulations also contain an acknowledgment by the debtor that the secured party has a valid and perfected security interest in the collateral and that the debtor has no claims against the lender. As you might be gathering by now, as in most other situations both in and outside bankruptcy, the secured lender holds most of the cards.

Finally, the secured party will look carefully to make sure the debtor is maintaining its collateral and keeping it insured. The secured party will want

11. Keep in mind that in any Chapter 11 case, there are many mouths to feed. If adequate protection payments or regular payments on a secured loan are not necessary to keep the secured party adequately protected, some other creditors might object to the ongoing payments, arguing that the debtor has more pressing needs for the funds elsewhere.

the period for which the debtor is using cash collateral to be as short as possible, so that if the collateral starts to lose value, the debtor's use can be terminated quickly.

QUESTION 5. Which of these is the ***most*** serious infraction by the debtor and thus the most likely to cause the court to immediately terminate a debtor's use of cash collateral?

A. Failure to make a payment.
B. Failure to comply with reporting requirements.
C. Failure to pay insurance on collateral.
D. Failure to meet sales projections.

ANALYSIS. A failure to make a payment is rough, a failure to meet sales projections or to comply with reporting requirements is also quite a bad thing, but a failure to keep the collateral insured will be immediate death to the case. This is nonnegotiable and suggests that the case is going downhill rapidly. Thus, the correct answer is **C**.

QUESTION 6. When negotiating the terms of a cash collateral stipulation, rate the following in importance to the creditor:

1. Amount of cash collateral payments.
2. Reporting requirements.
3. Budget restrictions, meaning cash the debtor is able to use for various categories.
4. Automatic relief from the stay on default.

A. 1, 2, 3, and then 4.
B. They are all equally critical.
C. 3, 1, 2, and then 4.
D. 1, 2, 4, and then 3.

ANALYSIS. This is fairly difficult, because all of these things are important. Lawyers and lenders could disagree about the correct answer, but the question is designed to help you understand why creditors insist on these protections.

Everyone loves money, so payments (choice **1**) would seem to be the first priority. But is this true? Obviously if the choice is between insured collateral and cash payments, it would be shortsighted to favor a small amount of immediate cash over the potential loss of everything. But that's not the choice you are asked to make here.

Cash does seem to be more important than reporting requirements, although reporting requirements are indeed important. Perhaps the reporting requirements are more important than automatic relief from the stay because if the debtor is in default in meeting its projections (which the reporting will show), the court will most likely grant relief from the automatic stay. For me, and the other bankruptcy lawyers on which this question was tested, the tough choice was between the payments and the budget restrictions. In the end, most people felt that negotiating and insisting on compliance with a strict budget that did not allow spending on things outside the approved budget was more important than the amount of the payments. What if the debtor decided to increase manager-insiders' salaries and disregard the approved budget? If this were not an event of default, with severe ramifications, the creditor would lose control of all the cash in the case.

Thus, on balance, the best answer is **C**. The budget restrictions are most important, followed by the amount of the payments, the reporting, and finally, automatic relief from the stay.

B. Post-Petition Financing Orders

Sometimes the mere use of the cash generated by a business is not enough to turn a business around in Chapter 11. Sometimes the debtor needs more cash in the form of new credit. Normally, a debtor needs unencumbered assets (i.e., those not subject to other liens) before it can raise significant cash, but there are some other good options for borrowing money post-petition. We know what some of you are thinking: Why in the world would anyone lend money to a company that is already in bankruptcy? As it turns out, many lenders are happy to do so. The Bankruptcy Code creates an incentive for people to lend money to a troubled company, by providing high priority to money lent post-petition, and by providing special rights to those who procure new collateral post-petition. (*See* 11 U.S.C. §364.)

Before we talk specifically about the special rights that creditors can acquire by lending money to the debtor post-petition, let's look at the different sources a debtor might have for new capital post-petition. Some creditors will have supplied goods or services to the debtor on credit pre-petition, and although most suppliers will have an outstanding unpaid invoice resulting from the bankruptcy case, or may even be owed more money for sales over a long period of time, many suppliers will be willing to continue supplying to the debtor post-petition. A supplier who does so will be entitled to a first-position administrative priority claim for goods and services provided to the debtor on credit post-petition. (*See* 11 U.S.C. §§503(b), 507(a).) The debtor also may be a large customer of such a supplier, making it necessary for the supplier to continue supplying the debtor, or go out of business itself.

Sometimes, owners of the debtor's business also will be willing to put in new cash post-petition to keep the business afloat. Current secured lenders also may be willing to put in additional cash, or perhaps there are new lenders waiting for the opportunity to do so. Finally, people interested in obtaining an equity (ownership) interest in the debtor might provide an influx of new cash.

Some of the Bankruptcy Code's most radical provisions deal with post-petition financing. Section 364 allows the court to grant some unsecured creditors super-priority status for post-petition loans, grant liens on new collateral for new secured loans, and even grant new security interests to new creditors for new lending on collateral that is already pledged to another creditor. Finally, if none of these efforts is enough to generate the cash the debtor needs, the court can *prime* existing secured creditor liens, meaning grant new liens on previously pledged collateral, that are senior in priority to existing liens on the same collateral. Priming is radical and controversial because it basically takes a secured creditor that is in a very protected and secure position and places another lien in front of it, all because the debtor needs new cash to operate and is unable to come up with cash in any other way. (*See* §364(d).) Needless to say, the court would not grant a priming lien unless it believed the new influx of cash definitely would turn the company around. To convince a court of this, the debtor must present the court with a very thorough business plan and financial projections that show how the new cash will allow the company to prosper. The court must also find, in order to prime any lien, that the existing creditor (who is now being primed) is *adequately protected*, despite the priming. This is yet another use of the adequate protection concept. (*See* §361.)

Let's review a quick example. Marty's Produce has borrowed $125,000 from First State Bank. Marty's is now in Chapter 11 and needs another $50,000 to revamp its business. Without the new cash, the business will likely shut down in the next few days. It has pledged all of its inventory and accounts receivable, which are worth approximately $175,000, to First State Bank. There are no other liens on these assets. The debtor's only other assets are unencumbered equipment worth approximately $20,000. Second Bank is very happy to lend Marty's the $50,000 it needs. However, Second Bank insists that it be given a first-priority lien and security interest in the debtor's inventory and accounts. This would leave Second Bank in the very comfortable position of being first for a $50,000 loan with collateral worth $175,000. It would push First State Bank into the second position on the collateral, behind a $50,000 loan on collateral worth $175,000. Can the court tell Second Bank that it must lend and take the second position because First State Bank was there first? No.

No one can force Second Bank to put any money into this case. The court may fail to approve the new loan on these terms because the new loan puts First State Bank in too precarious a position and thus fails to keep First State Bank *adequately protected*, but the court will then have to face the fact that without cash, the debtor may simply close its doors. Tough Hobson's choice here, but of course, without finding that First State Bank is adequately protected, the court has no authority to approve this deal.

Also, debtors-in-possession have to watch out. We know there frequently are few options, but some post-petition financing deals are so bad that it is hard for a debtor to reorganize under their onerous terms.

QUESTION 7. In the previous example, who is most likely to object to the deal as proposed?

A. The U.S. Trustee, as this type of thing is against public policy and should be barred as a matter of public policy in all cases.
B. The unsecured creditors' committee, because unsecured creditors do not want to add new debt to the operations.
C. First State Bank, which currently is fully secured and protected and would be put at risk for nonpayment under this proposal.
D. Another lender, Third Bank, which is willing to put in about $40,000 in the second position, as long as it also obtains a lien on the unencumbered equipment.

ANALYSIS. Starting with **A**, the U.S. Trustee can object to bankruptcy practices that are against public policy. Priming, however, is specifically permitted by the express provisions of the Bankruptcy Code (*see* 11 U.S.C. §364(d)) and thus is not precluded on public policy grounds. Why does the Code provide for this seemingly unfair practice? The reason is that we want to encourage new investments to failing companies to improve the chances of reviving the failing businesses.

B could be correct in certain cases, as any liens the debtor grants post-petition will take unencumbered assets out of the reach of unsecured creditors, who would otherwise receive them in liquidation. This means that if the debtor fails after trying to reorganize, the unsecured creditors will be hurt most directly. In this case, however, it is most likely that the unsecured creditors would be in favor of pumping more money into this debtor. Why? First, many of them may be current suppliers who will rely on the debtor's business in the future. Second, it does not appear that there will be many assets here for unsecured creditors if the debtor liquidates. The $20,000 in unencumbered assets will probably go to administrative claims like the debtor's counsel and accountants, as well as to priority claims. When expensive professionals are involved, $20,000 is a small amount. While there is also some equity in the inventory and the accounts receivable, some of this apparent equity is illusory because it will be lost in the collection and sale efforts if the debtor liquidates.

Thus, it is likely that unsecured creditors would like the debtor to attempt to reorganize, but from what we're told, we can't definitively tell what position they will take.

By comparison, we can be fairly certain that the First State Bank is going to object to the proposal. Oversecured by only $50,000 worth of equity (and by whose estimate we don't know), First State Bank would be put in a precarious position if it were primed. No creditor would take that sitting down, so we know that there would be an objection. Thus, the answer is **C**. The harder question is how the court would rule on this one. It certainly seems that absent ongoing payments to First State Bank, First State Bank is not adequately protected.

Third Bank also may object (choice **D**), but Third Bank does not have standing and will not be formally heard by the court. It is not a party-in-interest in the case, as it does not have a stake in the debtor's financial condition, at least not before it loans money. The existence of Third Bank's offer may cause the court to deny the debtor's motion to prime First State Bank with Second Bank's lien, however. The court may ask the debtor to consider Third Bank's offer instead, because it does not require priming. On the other hand, the court may choose not to second-guess the debtor's judgment. Either way, the correct answer to the question asked is still **C**.

QUESTION 8. (CODE READER) Debtor is a Chapter 11 debtor-in-possession that is desperate for post-petition financing in order to fund its ongoing operations as it prepares to file a Chapter 11 reorganization plan. Secured Creditor is a pre-petition secured creditor of Debtor that is owed $3 million with a perfected security interest in Debtor's equipment, which is currently worth $2.5 million. Secured Creditor is willing to lend $1 million to Debtor post-petition as long as the new loan is secured by a $2 million piece of unencumbered real estate that Debtor owns. However, Secured Creditor says it will only make this new loan if the real estate collateral will also secure any unsecured portion of its pre-petition loan. Debtor is willing to accept Secured Creditor's terms, but the unsecured creditors' committee in the Chapter 11 case objects. What is the best argument against allowing this post-petition loan to be approved under the terms that Secured Creditor proposes?

- **A.** Because §364 of the Bankruptcy Code clearly prohibits it.
- **B.** Because it is an avoidable preference under §547(b).
- **C.** Because in almost every case the DIP will have other attractive post-petition lending options that do not involve favoring certain pre-petition unsecured creditors over others.
- **D.** Because it ends up allowing a de facto preference to one unsecured creditor's pre-petition claim as compared to other pre-petition unsecured claims.

ANALYSIS. What Secured Creditor is proposing here is a controversial form of post-petition lending called cross-collateralization. In a loan involving cross-collateralization, the debtor-in-possession gives the post-petition lender a security interest in property of the estate that secures not only the post-petition loan offered but also any pre-petition debt of the lender that is or may be unsecured. The only federal circuit court to rule directly on cross-collateralization, the Eleventh Circuit, held that it is an impermissible form of post-petition lending.[12] However, there are many bankruptcy courts that have nevertheless approved post-petition loans that involve cross-collateralization.

So what is the best argument against it? Let's run through our four answers now. Choice **A** is not a good answer because §364 neither approves nor prohibits cross-collateralization. **B** is incorrect because in order for a transfer to be avoidable as a preference under §547(b), the transfer must occur within 90 days *before* the debtor files for bankruptcy. The transfer here, which is Debtor's grant of the security interest to Secured Creditor, is occurring after the debtor files for bankruptcy. Nor is **C** a persuasive choice. There certainly may be other, more attractive post-petition lending options available to a debtor-in-possession that don't involve cross-collateralization, but it is probably an overstatement to say that such options would be available "in almost every case."

That leaves **D**, the correct answer in this case. The biggest problem with cross-collateralization is that it violates an overriding principle of bankruptcy that a debtor should not favor one pre-petition unsecured claim over another. Secured Creditor in this case does have collateral for its pre-petition loan, but the collateral is insufficient to fully cover the debt, leaving Secured Creditor with a $500,000 unsecured deficiency claim. To the extent that this post-petition loan is approved with these terms, Secured Creditor's $500,000 unsecured claim would become fully secured, which is a benefit not enjoyed by the other unsecured creditors in the case (which is likely why the unsecured creditors' committee is objecting).

QUESTION 9. Debtor is a Chapter 11 debtor-in-possession that owns a single apartment building worth $20 million. Debtor, with the help of an expert witness, convinces Bankruptcy Judge that a renovation costing $6 million would add $9 million in value to the property. Old Secured Creditor is owed $24 million on a pre-petition loan that is secured by a mortgage lien on Debtor's apartment building. New Lender offers to lend Debtor the $6 million needed to fund the post-petition building renovations, but only if its lien can prime (come ahead of) Old Secured Creditor's lien under Bankruptcy Code §364(d). Should Bankruptcy Judge allow the $6 million loan with the priming lien?

---

12. *See* In re Saybrook, Manufacturing Co., 963 F.2d 1490 (11th Cir. 1992).

A. Yes, whether or not Old Secured Creditor agrees to have its lien primed by New Lender.
B. Yes, but only if Old Secured Creditor agrees to have its lien primed by New Lender.
C. Yes, but if Bankruptcy Judge is wrong in her prediction of the value impact of this proposed renovation, Bankruptcy Judge must take a salary cut to ensure that Old Secured Lender's collateral position will not be diminished.
D. No, because if this renovation costing $6 million would really add $9 million to the value of Debtor's building, then Old Secured Creditor would itself be eager to make such a loan in order to enhance its own collateral position.

ANALYSIS. This question is based on the facts of an actual case, In re 495 Central Park Ave. Corp.[13] Section 364(d)(1) of the Bankruptcy Code allows priming liens, but only if there is adequate protection of the interest of the senior lien that is getting primed. In the case of 495 Central Park Avenue, the bankruptcy judge allowed the projected future increase in value that would be made possible by the priming loan to serve as the adequate protection of the senior lienholder's lien that was getting primed.

Let's look at the possible answers here. If indeed Bankruptcy Judge accepts the expert testimony regarding the impact of the renovations on the value of the collateral, then that increase in value should be sufficient adequate protection for Old Secured Creditor under §364(d)(1). If that's the case, then **B** must be wrong and **A** must be correct. **C** is of course a joke answer, but there is a bit of wisdom in the humor of choice **C** that is captured perhaps more seriously in choice **D**.

After all, can't it be argued that if a $6 million infusion of new capital could truly yield a value increase of $9 million, then someone in the market would have already made the loan? Indeed, if this $9 million projected increase in value was assured, then the first lienholder, Old Secured Creditor, would gladly lend the $6 million for the self-interested purpose of enhancing its own position. That is because such a loan would increase the net value of its security interest and thereby reduce its deficiency claim from $4 million to $1 million — but only if that $9 million prediction of the post-renovation value of the collateral is truly accurate!

Perhaps the lesson here is that if Debtor can't persuade the market that the building ought to be finished, filing Chapter 11 bankruptcy gives Debtor a chance to persuade a bankruptcy judge (instead of the market) that the building renovation should be completed. Since Bankruptcy Judge doesn't stand to lose any of her money if she is wrong, Debtor is likely to find a more

13. 136 B.R. 626 (Bankr. S.D.N.Y. 1992).

sympathetic audience in bankruptcy than it will find in the marketplace where real lenders stand to lose real dollars.

C. Critical Vendor Orders and the Doctrine of Necessity

Recently, Chapter 11 debtors have begun asking for a very controversial type of order known as a *critical vendor order*. Before explaining this type of relief, you should know that one of the big no-no's in Chapter 11 is paying pre-petition creditors before *confirmation* of a Chapter 11 plan. Under the general principle of equality of distribution, it is necessary for a debtor to delay paying its creditors, particularly its general unsecured creditors, until the plan has been confirmed. Generally speaking, then, most unsecured creditors remain unpaid during the time it takes to get the plan confirmed. This rule is not found specifically in the Bankruptcy Code, but the Chapter 11 process is designed to pay pre-petition claims under the confirmed plan. Consequently it is inappropriate to allow a debtor to pick and choose the claims that it would like to pay before confirming its plan of reorganization.

Having said this, the relatively new *doctrine of necessity*, which can result in the entry of a *critical vendor order*, does exactly that. It allows the debtor to choose certain unsecured creditors and to pay their pre-petition claims before confirming a plan. Here is how it works: The debtor brings a request for a critical vendor order to the court along with its other first-day orders, requesting that the court allow the debtor to pay the vendors on a list attached to the motion. The theory of critical vendor orders is that some suppliers will be unwilling to do business with the debtor unless pre-petition debts are paid, and if the vendors stop supplying post-petition, either the business will shut down or the debtor will have to find credit at a more expensive cost.

A few years ago, the Seventh Circuit Court of Appeals decided a large critical vendor case in the Kmart bankruptcy. In that case, Kmart presented the bankruptcy court with a first-day order on limited notice requesting that it be permitted to pay certain critical vendors. No notice was given to the 2,000 vendors who were not favored in the motion and who would not be paid in advance of the other vendors. The motion was open-ended in that it requested permission to pay any creditor that the debtor deemed critical, if the vendor continued to supply on customary trade terms over the next two years. In connection with the motion, the debtor presented no evidence that any particular supplier would otherwise cut the debtor off from supplies or that the post-petition credit from these creditors would be greater than the expense of the pre-petition payments. Pursuant to the motion, which the bankruptcy court ultimately approved, the debtor paid 2,330 suppliers a total of $300 million. These suppliers were chosen from a total of approximately 4,000 suppliers.

Pursuant to the debtor's plan, which was approved several years later, unsecured creditors received 10 cents on the dollar. At the time the critical vendor motion was presented to the court (on the first day of the case), no alternatives were explored, such as purchasing on credit, cash on delivery ("COD"), or through a standby letter of credit. Most shocking, the largest payment made was a \$70 million payment to Fleming, which was obligated to supply the debtor in any event under a long-term contract.[14] Moreover, Kmart accounted for over 50 percent of Fleming's business, suggesting that Fleming would not refuse to continue to supply Kmart once it was in Chapter 11. To the contrary, Fleming was precisely the kind of creditor that we've spoken about: completely beholden to the debtor and almost completely dependent on the debtor to continue its own business. As evidence of this condition, once the Fleming contract expired and was not renewed by Kmart, Fleming itself failed and went into Chapter 11. As a result of all of these factors, it is hard to believe that Fleming would have stopped supplying the debtor. Nevertheless, the bankruptcy court approved Kmart's critical vendor motion under what has become known as the *doctrine of necessity.*

Critical vendor orders are entered under the authority contained in §105(a) of the Bankruptcy Code, which was discussed in Chapter 5. You will remember that §105 allows a court to enter any order that is consistent with the goals and policies of the Bankruptcy Code. (*See* 11 U.S.C. §105(a).) One thing §105 does not do, however, is grant authority to the bankruptcy court to override the rules and provisions specifically enumerated in the Code. Nowhere in the Code does it specifically say that the debtor cannot pay pre-petition claims post-petition, yet every bankruptcy lawyer knows that the rules of equality require that the debtor *not* to pay pre-petition claims once it has filed for bankruptcy.

What the nonfavored vendors requested in the Kmart case was that the payments that were made preferentially to certain vendors during the beginning of the case be brought back into the case as post-petition preferences (*see* 11 U.S.C. §549) and distributed to creditors pursuant to the debtor's plan in a more orderly and equal fashion. The debtor argued that this issue was moot because the payments had already been made and also that the vendors had detrimentally relied on the court's order. The Seventh Circuit disagreed on both grounds, holding that mootness was not an issue here because the debtor could always recover preferential payments, whether the payments were made pre-petition or post-petition. The Seventh Circuit also disagreed on the detrimental reliance argument. Because all suppliers were paid in full, they could not have suffered any detriment. The court further stated that the doctrine of necessity is not supported by §105 of the Code, because §105 does not grant a court the authority to override statutory rules about priorities and

14. We will discuss the treatment of contracts further in Chapter 33. (*See also* 11 U.S.C. §365.)

distribution, or to override provisions dealing with Chapter 11 plans. (*See, e.g.*, §§507, 1122(a), 1123(a)(4).)

As the Seventh Circuit stated, the *doctrine of necessity* is just a fancy "name for a power to depart from the Code." The Circuit Court also looked at several other sections of the Bankruptcy Code, such as §364(b), which authorizes the debtor to obtain credit, but says nothing about how the money will be disbursed or about the priorities, and §503, which enumerates the pre-filing debts that are administrative expenses. As you will learn in Chapters 32 and 34, administrative expenses are entitled to be paid in full during the case, and most of these administrative expenses are post-petition expenses. (*See* 11 U.S.C. §503(b)(1).) Thus, the circuit court distinguished the highly different treatment of those post-petition expenses from the pre-filing debts. The court further noted that the debtor is expected to deal with pre-petition claims during the Chapter 11 plan, and will rarely pay these claims in full.

As a practical matter, critical vendor orders actually interfere with the rehabilitation of businesses because, as creditors get used to such orders, they may refuse to supply a Chapter 11 debtor post-petition, even though the Code already contains many protections for these claims and vendors might have otherwise continued to supply debtors, absent the courts' regular willingness to enter these orders.

QUESTION 10. What is the best legal argument that a debtor should be allowed to pay pre-petition claims of critical vendors during the initial stages of its bankruptcy case?

A. Because the Code explicitly allows the debtor to make such payments.
B. Because §105 cannot be used to override a particular Code provision, but nowhere in the Code does it specifically say that the debtor cannot pay such claims.
C. Because paying such claims does not violate the priority scheme, which can still be followed in the Chapter 11 plan.
D. Because such creditors are likely to be paid in full in a Chapter 11 plan, in any event.

ANALYSIS. **D** is clearly wrong. Most Chapter 11 plans do not pay a 100 percent distribution to unsecured trade creditors. We hope that by now you see that and also can imagine that if some vendors were paid in full in the beginning of the case, these vendors would ultimately be treated quite differently than the general unsecured creditor class under most Chapter 11 plans. The typical Chapter 11 unsecured creditor distribution is often referred to as the "proverbial" 10 cents on the dollar. It is not that all cases pay just 10 cents, as distributions vary greatly. It is just an amount thrown out there to bring home the point that general unsecured creditors rarely get paid in full. Interestingly, in the Kmart case, general unsecured creditors *were* paid 10 cents on the dollar. In any case, choice **D** is incorrect.

Similarly, choice **C** is incorrect because it claims that making these payments does not violate the priority scheme found in §507(a) of the Bankruptcy Code. If you read §507(a), you see that certain creditors are entitled to be paid ahead of other creditors, and that general suppliers and vendors are not listed in §507(a). Assuming that not everyone will be paid in full, priority claims get paid ahead of general claims. As a result, **C** is incorrect. Paying critical vendors 100 cents on the dollar directly violates the priority scheme because it allows other creditors to be paid ahead of priority claims that are supposed to be paid. As you will see very shortly, priority claims get paid in full on confirmation (for the most part) under the Chapter 11 plan. Confirmation is many months down the road from the first day of the case and, as a result, these critical vendor payments *do* violate the priority scheme. (*See* 11 U.S.C. §507(a).)

Choice **A** is also incorrect. Choice **A** states that the Bankruptcy Code specifically allows for critical vendor motions, which it clearly does not. This is why choice **B** is a good choice. Choice **B** says, in essence, that although the Code does not specifically provide for the payment of critical vendor orders, there is nothing in the Code specifically prohibiting such payment.[15] As a result, this is ripe ground for the application of §105(a), which allows the court to enter any order that furthers the provisions of the Bankruptcy Code. This is certainly the most logical reason why it might be acceptable for the debtor to make these payments. On the other hand, the payments violate the spirit of the Code and violate the very important Bankruptcy Code principles of equality of distribution and efficiency in running Chapter 11 cases and should in fact rarely, if ever, be allowed.

QUESTION 11. The strongest and most specific reason why critical vendor orders are inappropriate is that:

A. the orders are unfair.
B. the orders violate specific Bankruptcy Code provisions.
C. the orders, and the vendors that are paid pursuant to them, are within the complete and total discretion of the debtor.
D. the orders violate the spirit of the Bankruptcy Code.

ANALYSIS. The correct answer here is **C**. Critical vendor orders leave it in the complete discretion of the debtor to determine who constitutes a critical

15. Just so you know, the Chapter 11 plan requirements provide that similarly situated creditors must be paid the same. These requirements may well prohibit critical vendor motions. This will be discussed further in Chapter 35.

vendor and who does not. This is a very serious problem. **D** is also true. Critical vendor orders violate the spirit and policies of the Code. However, answer **C** is more specific in that it tells exactly what is so incredibly unfair about this practice to the other parties in the case, and the system as a whole.

A says that critical vendor orders are unfair. Yes, of course this statement is true as well. However, as in most areas of the law, the simple claim that "it's not fair" is not a legal argument. There has to be more than that. "It's not fair" is never the answer to a question asked on a course exam, on the bar exam, or in court, to explain why your client is entitled to the relief that they are requesting. So, although **A** is correct, it does nothing to assist in answering this question.

As a factual matter, **B** is incorrect because, as you saw from the prior discussion, there is nothing in the Bankruptcy Code that specifically precludes the debtor from paying pre-petition general unsecured claims after filing for bankruptcy. The reason that payment of these claims is not permitted is that doing so violates the underlying policies of the Code, primarily because who gets paid in these orders is under the complete and total discretion of the debtor. As we leave critical vendor motions, note that when some general unsecured creditors are paid before confirmation of a plan, and a plan is later confirmed under which general unsecured creditors do not receive a 100 percent distribution, similarly situated creditors are ultimately treated differently in the case. The Bankruptcy Code does not permit this.

D. Payment of Other Unsecured Claims Before Confirmation

Even though a debtor is not supposed to pay pre-petition claims post-petition, except under a confirmed plan of reorganization, some other exceptions to this rule have developed. For example, you learned in Chapter 10 that if a debtor fails to pay taxes that it withheld from its employees' paychecks, the debtor is considered a trustee of these funds, pursuant to §507(a)(8)(C), and thus the debtor is required to pay these claims in full regardless of when the obligations arose. These claims are nondischargeable in any bankruptcy and also carry personal responsibility for some managers. As a result of this rule, courts frequently allow a debtor-in-possession to pay trust fund taxes that just happen to be caught up in bankruptcy.[16] These are pre-petition claims but

16. Regarding pre-petition trust fund taxes withheld but not paid as of the petition date, some attorneys include authority to pay those taxes in the first-day cash collateral order, rather than filing a separate motion and obtaining a separate order. If the funds are statutory trust funds, and therefore not property of the estate, an order probably would not even be required, but some lawyers get one anyway by simply including a provision in the cash collateral motion and order.

would be entitled to priority in a Chapter 11 case in any event, and thus will eventually be paid in full in most plans.[17] Motions to pay pre-petition withholding taxes are much more justifiable than critical vendor motions. First, management will be personally liable for these funds if they are not paid in full and thus paying them will assist management on focusing on the reorganization. Next, because these are priority claims, they are required under §1129(a)(9) to be paid in full under the Chapter 11 plan, so in a sense, it's not really unfair to pay them now.[18]

In addition to the items we've discussed here, the debtor may ask for permission to pay other claims. For example, the debtor may request that it be allowed to honor customer deposits and warranties. In the case of the deposits, these deposits are also entitled to priority pursuant to §507(a)(7). The other reason for doing this, as well as paying the warranty claims, is that part of the debtor's goal is to keep the business running more or less in the same way that it ran before the bankruptcy. As a result, the debtor may not wish to destroy goodwill with its customers. The debtor also may request that it be allowed to pay reclamation claims for the same reason.

Additionally, if the debtor's management is planning the case properly, the debtor will attempt to make sure that it has paid its pre-petition wage claims before the filing of the bankruptcy. This can be done by timing the case so it is filed right after a payroll. If it is not possible to time the filing around payroll (and goodness knows there are many other considerations in play as well), the debtor may make a first-day motion requesting that it be permitted to pay its pre-petition wage claims. It should be obvious why such payments are necessary. The debtor's workforce needs the money badly for one thing, but also may threaten to quit if it is forced to become a pay period behind. These claims are also entitled to priority and making employees miss a paycheck sends them the wrong message about how things are going. The debtor's goal is to not miss a beat, and this would be a serious misstep.

E. Applications to Be Employed as Counsel, Accountant, or Other Professional

As the debtor's lawyer rushes across the street with the packet of first-day orders, she also carries her own application to be appointed as counsel for the debtor. Debtor's counsel also may apply for the appointment of other

17. This concept ignores one reality, namely that many Chapter 11 debtors do not complete a plan or even get a plan confirmed. As a result, despite priority status, the debtor would not pay many trust fund taxes in bankruptcy in any event. Oh well, one can always dream. At least this is better than paying *general* unsecured claims at the time of the filing!

18. This assumes the debtor will be able to pay all administrative claims in full. In some cases, the debtor is unable to even do that. We refer to such a condition as *administrative insolvency*.

professionals, such as an accountant or an investment banker for the debtor. (*See* 11 U.S.C. §327.) It is critical that the debtor's counsel *not be* one of the debtor's creditors at the time that the attorney applies to be general counsel to the Chapter 11 debtor. Section 327(a) of the Bankruptcy Code requires that a debtor's general counsel be *disinterested. Disinterested* means that the attorney is not a creditor of the debtor, and also that the lawyer does not represent any of the creditors or other parties-in-interest in the case. This requires debtor's counsel to do a thorough check for possible conflicts of interest prior to accepting the appointment.

Not becoming one of the debtor's creditors is a bit more complicated. As you may have guessed by now, there is a great deal of work for a debtor's counsel before a case can even be filed. We have been discussing numerous first-day orders that need to be filed with the court immediately on the bankruptcy filing, many of which must be negotiated with other creditors. All of these first-day orders require time and attention on the part of a debtor's counsel, none of which are done for free. The key here appears to be obtaining a pre-petition retainer and applying the retainer on a regular basis. Counsel must be fully paid at the time the bankruptcy petition is filed or counsel will not meet the *disinterestedness* test found in §327(a). Some courts will allow a debtor's counsel to represent the debtor as general Chapter 11 counsel, even though the debtor's law firm has represented one or more of the creditors in the case, or perhaps *still* represents creditors in the case, on different matters. Other courts are stricter on applying the disinterestedness test, however, requiring that the debtor's counsel's firm have no relationship with any of the creditors in the case. As you can well imagine, this frequently eliminates large law firms from Chapter 11 debtor representations. Many courts are more lenient, however, particularly in places like New York City where virtually all of the large law firms have represented most banks and other lenders, at least on a small matter.

Sometimes a law firm or lawyer is hired in a Chapter 11 case for a special purpose; for example, to pursue a large piece of litigation or to handle some other discrete legal matter on behalf of the debtor. If counsel is appointed for these purposes, pursuant to §327(d), then counsel must only be disinterested with respect to the matter for which it has been engaged. Although it is actually the same test as the test for general counsel, general counsel has been engaged in the Chapter 11 to handle all matters. Therefore, any conflict will be a conflict of interest for general counsel in connection with the case.

In the debtor's counsel's application to be retained, counsel will request that it be permitted to submit *interim fee applications* for approval by the court. (*See* 11 U.S.C. §330(a).) These fee applications are required by the Bankruptcy Court, and essentially provide that the court approve all fees for debtor's counsel before the debtor pays the fees. In some jurisdictions, the debtor is permitted to pay these fees on a regular basis and the court approves them retroactively, meaning after the fact. These types of compensation schemes, sometimes called *evergreen orders*, are quite controversial and are frowned upon in other parts of the country. As the name suggests, it is "ever green" for debtor's counsel, as the green keeps flowing and there's no need to obtain court approval before receiving payments in the case.

With respect to the need to ensure that the debtor's counsel does not become a creditor in the case, and has no outstanding fees at the time of the bankruptcy filing, some courts have rejected this strict doctrine under a theory called the *nunc pro tunc* doctrine. The *nunc pro tunc* doctrine provides that if it were an emergency, and debtor's counsel had no way of obtaining either payment or court approval to be retained as counsel before rendering services to the debtor, the court may, at its discretion, approve the fees on a retroactive basis. This means that the debtor's counsel could actually be paid for services rendered before the time that it applied to be debtor's counsel. The *nunc pro tunc* doctrine is an exception to the rule and is not accepted everywhere in the country.

Another thing that the debtor's counsel's application must contain is a statement of the regular hourly rates of the attorneys who will be working on the case, as well as in some districts, a statement of each attorney's educational experience. This same information must be provided in the application to be retained as an accountant for the debtor, as well as in any other application to retain a professional.

QUESTION 12. In terms of meeting the *disinterestedness test*, which of the following situations would be the hardest for debtor's counsel to cure?

A. At one time, debtor's counsel's firm represented a creditor that is now an unsecured creditor in the case.

B. The firm currently represents a creditor that is an unsecured creditor in the case.

C. The firm currently represents a party whom the debtor may later need to sue.

D. The firm has been working for the debtor for a month and is owed $20,000 for those services.

ANALYSIS. All of these situations are problematic, so it is hard to choose the one that is the *most* problematic. Perhaps it is safest to say that **A** raises the fewest problems. Counsel once represented one of the creditors in the case, but no longer represents them; this probably is not a problem. **D** is clearly a problem. The firm cannot be a creditor in the debtor's case. If we think about it, this rule is counterintuitive. Why can't counsel be a creditor in the debtor's case? It would appear that their interests would be the same. Both creditors and the debtor hope the debtor will successfully reorganize. The problem, however, comes when we consider that counsel may need to favor one class of creditors over another and doesn't want to have a conflict in that process. **D** could be cured if counsel waived its prior fees.

B and **C** also present problems. The debtor obviously cannot represent a current creditor in the case, so **B** is problematic. **C** may or may not be problematic, but it is possible that debtor's counsel may decide not to bring the lawsuit against the other party, or the debtor may hire special counsel for this lawsuit. Because both **D** and **C** can be cured and **A** is not a problem, it looks like **B** is the most problematic and cannot be cured. The correct answer is **B**.

F. Cash Management Orders

Some debtors also request the entry of a cash management order in the first-day orders. A *cash management order* is an order permitting a debtor-in-possession to keep certain of its pre-petition bank accounts open. The order also governs the flow of cash between or among debtor-in-possession bank accounts. For example, if a company has retail operations in many cities, it is common for the company to have local depository accounts, with the funds to be swept daily into a central operating account. Because no checks are written from the depository accounts, there is no risk that by keeping the accounts open, outstanding pre-petition checks will be honored post-petition. Why does this matter? Because the debtor is not permitted to *pay* pre-petition claims post-petition, except with court approval, and also is not permitted to *allow* pre-petition claims to be paid post-petition for the same reasons.

On the other hand, it would be burdensome to make the debtor close and reopen a large number of depository accounts and to reset the sweep system for those accounts. Accordingly, in these circumstances, courts routinely allow the pre-petition depository accounts to remain open, in what is called a cash management order. In some jurisdictions where large Chapter 11 cases are rare, cash management orders are uncommon.

G. Utilities

Not surprisingly, most corporate debtors will provide as part of their first-day order some arrangement for the payment of the debtor's utilities. After all, very few debtors could last very long in Chapter 11 without electricity, gas, or water service. Section 366(a) generally prohibits utilities from cutting off service to debtors based on unpaid pre-petition bills. However, there is an important exception to the general rule that utilities cannot stop the debtor's service post-petition even when the debtor is not current with its utility bills. Section 366(c)(2) says that a utility may discontinue a debtor's service in a Chapter 11 case if the utility does not receive adequate assurance of future payment that is satisfactory to the utility within 30 days.

At first, that exception— especially the "satisfactory to the utility" language— sounds like it gives all of the discretion to the utility company regarding the nature and extent of the debtor's assurances regarding payment of future utility bills. After all, what would stop a utility company from insisting on, for example, the next fives years' worth of payments in advance from the debtor as the only arrangement that will give adequate assurance "that is satisfactory to the utility"?

Fortunately for debtors in Chapter 11, even though the statute initially says that the adequate assurances must be "satisfactory" to the utility company, it also makes that requirement subject to §366(c)(3). Section 366(c)(3) provides that on request of a party in interest (presumably the debtor in this case!), and after notice and a hearing, the court may order the amount of an adequate assurance payment under paragraph (2) to be modified. That means that the debtor can always make its own proposal for adequate assurance and hope that the court will deem it adequate. Ultimately, then, §366(c)(3) serves as a check on any overreaching by a utility company regarding how much adequate assurance of future payment by the debtor will be satisfactory to the utility.

QUESTION 13. (CODE READER) Molly's Cookie Factory ("Debtor") files Chapter 11 bankruptcy at a time when it owes $5,000 in pre-petition electric bills to Electric Company. Electric Company has not had a great relationship with Debtor and would prefer not to have to deal with Debtor in the future. Which of the following most accurately describes the rights of Electric Company as against Debtor in the Chapter 11 case?

A. Electric Company has no claim for unpaid pre-petition service but can require a cash deposit or other security as adequate assurance of payment for future service.

B. Electric Company has a pre-petition unsecured claim for unpaid pre-petition service and then can require a cash deposit or other security as adequate assurance of payment for future service.

C. Electric Company can demand that Debtor must pay for any missed pre-petition payments and that Debtor must also must provide adequate assurance of future performance as a condition to Electric Company providing future service to Debtor.

D. Electric Company can demand a cash deposit or other security as adequate assurance that Debtor will pay for any missed pre-petition payments as a condition to Electric Company providing future service to Debtor.

ANALYSIS. Before getting to the correct answer, let's analyze what is wrong with the three incorrect answers. Choice **A** is incorrect because it understates the nature of Electric Company's rights against Debtor regarding the unpaid pre-petition service that was provided. Specifically, it is inaccurate to say that Electric Company has "no claim" for that service when in fact Electric Company will have an unsecured pre-petition claim for the unpaid pre-petition service. Choice **C** is incorrect for the opposite reason, namely, that it overstates Electric Company's rights as to collecting the unpaid pre-petition electric bills from Debtor. It overstates those rights by saying inaccurately that Electric Company can demand that Debtor must pay for any missed pre-petition payments as a condition to Electric Company providing future service to Debtor. Choice **D** similarly overstates Electric Company's rights as to the missed pre-petition payments by saying (again inaccurately) that Electric Company has a right to demand adequate assurance of Debtor's payment for missed pre-petition payments rather than adequate assurance of Debtor's payments for future service. Choice **B**, which is the correct answer, accurately states Electric Company's rights both as to the missed pre-petition payments and as to any payments that Debtor will owe for future electric service.

H. The Closer: Chapter 29

You are feeling euphoric, having just filed your first big Chapter 11 case for Madge's Midnight Rodeo, a fabulous nightclub that has fallen on hard times. It's Friday at approximately 4:00 p.m. When you arrived in court an hour or so ago, the judge invited you into her chambers and entered all of your first-day orders before she left for the day. You just picked up a message on your cell phone from the clerk's office. It seems that only four motions were filed and four orders entered, even though you said you were filing five motions. You have no idea what happened. The judge is gone and the clerk's office is closed. You thought you were getting orders to approve your own fee application, to approve the use of cash collateral, to pay pre-petition wages, to pay critical vendors, and to manage cash through existing bank accounts. You are really hoping that the lost and unfiled motion was not the:

A. application to retain you as counsel.
B. motion to use cash collateral.
C. motion to pay pre-petition wages.
D. motion to use existing bank accounts.

ANALYSIS. The debtor needs all of these orders but the task here is to determine which of these orders the debtor needs the most, on a Friday evening at 4:00 p.m., given that no further orders will be entered until Monday at the earliest. The judge has been very accommodating, perhaps too much so, but that is another issue. You would hate to go to her house on a Friday night.

We can use the process of elimination to figure out the correct answer. Which of these orders do you need the least? Your own application to be retained as counsel is the least important. It even makes you look a bit selfless, forgetting it, and at the most, you will lose a few hours of your pay. No big deal. You can go back and get it entered next week. Thus, **A** is not the answer. The motion to pay wages is very important but unless payroll is tonight or Monday, this one can also wait, making **C** incorrect as well. Of the other two, the bank account order and the cash collateral order, the cash collateral is the more important, right? Tonight will be a big night at the Rodeo, and the debtor simply must use its cash to pay vendors, musicians, and so on. Thus, the correct answer is **B**.

Martin's and Keating's Picks

1. Question 1	**C**
2. Question 2	**C**
3. Question 3	**B**
4. Question 4	**B**
5. Question 5	**C**
6. Question 6	**C**
7. Question 7	**C**
8. Question 8	**D**
9. Question 9	**A**
10. Question 10	**B**
11. Question 11	**C**
12. Question 12	**B**
13. Question 13	**B**
The Closer	**B**

30

The Automatic Stay and Adequate Protection

OVERVIEW
A. The Scope of the Automatic Stay
B. Exceptions to the Automatic Stay
C. Relief from the Automatic Stay
D. Adequate Protection
E. The Closer: Chapter 30
Martin's and Keating's Picks

In Chapter 11, as well as in the other types of bankruptcy, the automatic stay of §362 of the Code reigns supreme as the best benefit of filing a bankruptcy case. This chapter discusses the scope of the stay (*see* 11 U.S.C. §362(a)), its exceptions (*see* 11 U.S.C. §362(b)), and the grounds for relief from the stay (*see* 11 U.S.C. §362(d)), this time in the context of Chapter 11.

A. The Scope of the Automatic Stay

Reviewing what you learned in Chapter 7, the automatic stay stops all collection activity against the debtor and the debtor's property of any kind, as well as all attempts to obtain possession or control of estate property, perfect a security interest, continue suits, and so on. This comes in handy in a number of ways. Attempts by lenders to repossess collateral or to lien property are all stayed. Lawsuits in which the debtor is a defendant[1] are also stayed as to the

1. In one humorous situation, one of us recalls that a debtor called off a deposition in which it was the plaintiff, claiming that the suit was stayed by the automatic stay. After some thought, the defendant claimed this not to be the case (the automatic stay only stays actions *against* the debtor), and the debtor was forced to admit that it was just trying to drum up more money to pursue the suit. Suits in which the debtor is the plaintiff are not stayed by a bankruptcy because the debtor is not being *pursued* in a collection or other matter. (*See* 11 U.S.C. §362(a).)

debtor. If you are A.H. Robins, Firestone Tires, or any other company barraged with lawsuits, this is a tremendous feat in and of itself. The stay is an injunction against all suits and collection efforts, and allows the debtor to breathe a long sigh of relief.

QUESTION 1. (CODE READER) Lee's Lumber supplies building materials to Lowe's and takes back a security interest in everything that it sells to Lowe's. On Monday, Lee's repossessed a warehouse full of lumber, as its loan documents permitted, because Lowe's was way behind on its payments. Two days later, before Lee's had a chance to sell any of the repossessed lumber, Lowe's filed for Chapter 11 protection. The bankruptcy attorney for Lowe's has demanded that Lee's immediately return the lumber, which it refuses to do. Does Lee's have to give back the repossessed lumber?

A. No, because it was repossessed pre-petition.
B. No, because Lee's rights under its loan documents clearly permit it to repossess and sell its collateral as long as the loan is in default.
C. Yes, because Lee's failure to return the lumber once Lowe's asked violates the automatic stay.
D. Yes, but only if Lowe's brings a turnover action under §542(a).

ANALYSIS. What should you eliminate first? Hopefully you chose **B**. Every lender's loan documents allow it to repossess and sell its collateral on default, but this cannot be done *after* the debtor files for bankruptcy. (*See* 11 U.S.C. §362(a)(3) and (4).) That is the whole point of the automatic stay. The stay overrides rights creditors have under a contract or under other provisions of state law, because bankruptcy law preempts state law. Think of rock beating scissors in a game of rock-paper-scissors.

A is so tempting. It is there to teach you an important nuance of the automatic stay. The creditor is free to repossess collateral, or do anything else that its loan documents or state law allows, pre-petition. There was absolutely nothing improper about this repossession. However, the creditor is not permitted to sell the collateral post-petition in order to pay down its debt, or even to retain possession of the lumber after the case is filed given that, until the property is sold by the creditor, the debtor still has an interest in it. It is still property of the estate. (*See* 11 U.S.C. §362(a)(3) and (4).) Thus, **A** is incorrect. **A** would have been correct if the creditor had already sold the collateral prior to the debtor's bankruptcy, because the debtor would no longer have any interest in the collateral after that time.

In the prior editions of this book, **C** was the correct answer to this question. Certainly that is how the majority of courts had approached this issue. However, the United States Supreme Court changed that outcome with its decision in early 2021 in City of Chicago v. Fulton. In *Fulton*, the city of Chicago had impounded the cars of four debtors as leverage to get the debtors to pay parking tickets that they owed to the city. When the debtors filed Chapter 13 bankruptcy, their attorneys demanded that the city immediately return the cars or else be liable for violating §362(a)(3) of the automatic stay. The debtors argued that the city's failure to return the cars upon the debtors' bankruptcy filing was a prohibited act "to exercise control over property of the estate."

The city contended that merely passively holding the cars did not amount to an act to exercise control over the estate property. The city argued that if the debtors wanted their cars back, they needed to file a turnover request under §542(a) of the Bankruptcy Code. There was little doubt that the debtors would be successful in such a turnover action. However, this would require that the debtors file an adversary proceeding against the city. This would entail additional time, cost, and inconvenience for the debtors as compared to the city having an affirmative duty under §362(a)(3) to return the cars as soon as the debtors filed bankruptcy.

The Supreme Court, in a unanimous opinion, held that merely retaining possession of property of the estate does not violate §362(a)(3) because it is not an affirmative "act" to exercise control, but instead just passive possession of the property. The Court concluded that "§362(a)(3) prohibits collection efforts outside the bankruptcy proceeding that would change the status quo, while 542(a) works within the bankruptcy process to draw far-flung estate property back into the hands of the debtor or trustee." Therefore, the correct answer to this question is **D**.

You should note that one automatic stay issue that was *not* before the Court in *Fulton* was whether the city's conditional refusal to return the cars to the debtors was a violation of §362(a)(6). That subsection of the automatic stay prohibits "any act to collect [a pre-petition claim]" against the debtor. In other words, imagine that after the debtors' bankruptcy filings the city of Chicago told these debtors either directly or indirectly, "if you want your car back, you need to pay us your pre-petition parking fines." That would arguably violate §362(a)(6) even though the mere passive holding of the already-repossessed cars would not by itself violate §362(a)(3) under the Court's ruling. However, the attorney for these debtors did not raise the §362(a)(6) argument, so the court did not rule on it.

QUESTION 2. A Las Vegas brothel recently lost its brothel license for failure to pay taxes. The facts in dispute are whether these taxes are actually due. The brothel challenged the revocation of the license and then filed for Chapter 11 while the challenge was still pending. The debtor has demanded return of the license following its Chapter 11 case. What is the debtor's best argument that the state must return and reinstate the brothel license?

A. Refusing to do so is a violation of the automatic stay.
B. Section 105(a) would warrant return of the license, as an exercise of the court's equity powers.
C. The debtor had a contract with the state and the state must continue to perform the contract until the debtor decides whether to assume or reject the contract.
D. Refusing to reinstate the license is a continuing violation of the automatic stay because the debtor still had an interest in the license at the time it filed for bankruptcy and thus the license is still property of the debtor's estate.

ANALYSIS. Building on what you just learned in the prior question, the answer is **D**. Because the dispute about the tax payments is still pending and has not been resolved, the debtor still has an interest in the brothel license. (*See* 11 U.S.C. §541.) **D** is the debtor's best and most complete argument. It explains exactly why the debtor is entitled to have the license reinstated. **A** tells half of that story and is correct, but is not the best argument. **B** is incorrect. It is not necessary to rely on §105(a) in this case because the debtor still has an interest in the license under these facts; thus, §362 would make a refusal to reinstate the license a violation of the stay. Section 105(a) should be used only when there is no particular Code provision that supports your client's argument. Overusing §105(a) suggests some weakness in your argument, as it tips the court to the fact that there is no direct authority for your requested relief. Thus, it is always best to use another (more specific) argument if you have one, rather than relying on §105(a).

C is incorrect and is a precursor to what you will learn in Chapter 33. This statement would be true *if* the state and the debtor were parties to a contract. (*See* 11 U.S.C. §365.) The nondebtor party would need to continue performing the contract until the debtor decided whether to assume or reject the contract. This is not, however, a full-on contractual relationship. It is one of licensee and licensor, and the license can be revoked in certain circumstances. Here the revocation was not effective because the revocation is the subject of a bona fide dispute, leaving the debtor with some remaining interest in the license. Thus, the correct answer is **D**. Note that this situation has nothing to do with protecting the safety of the public, a topic we will now take up.

B. Exceptions to the Automatic Stay

As you learned in Chapter 7, some actions against the debtor are not stayed, meaning that the debtor's sigh of relief is not a sigh of complete relief. (*See* 11 U.S.C. §362(b).) For example, the exercise of police powers taken by a governmental entity to protect the health and public welfare of citizens is not stayed by §362. (*See* 11 U.S.C. §362(b)(4).) We previously noted that if a state or county sues a company to enjoin it from releasing harmful chemicals into a stream, the suit would not be stayed because this action constitutes an exercise of governmental police powers.

QUESTION 3. Which of the following actions would not be stayed by §362?

1. The debtor is a nursing home that has been sued by the state for revocation of its nursing care license, as a result of its failure to comply with state-mandated financial requirements.
2. The debtor is a bar that is subject to license revocation because it served liquor to underage minors.
3. The debtor is a restaurant that has received three warnings that its facilities are out of compliance with city cleanliness standards, and that faces possible loss of its license.
4. The debtor is a movie theater involved in a license revocation proceeding resulting from a fire hazard on the premise.
5. The debtor is a construction company threatened with license revocation because the debtor failed to timely renew all of its truck registrations.

A. Definitely 1, 3, and 4 and possibly 2.
B. Definitely 2, 3, and 4 and possibly 1.
C. Definitely 3 and 4, possibly 1 and 2, but not 5.
D. All of the above.

ANALYSIS. This is a hard question about which no attorney could be certain. When attempting to distinguish between police powers and other things, the *other things* are normally just regular debt collection devices. None of these smack of debt collection, but some also don't quite rise to the level of a public safety issue. Suits must actually protect the public from harm to escape the confines of the automatic stay.

One of us polled several people and we came to some consensus that the restaurant that serves unsafe food and the movie theater that contains a continuing fire hazard are both real threats to the public. Thus, suits to stop these businesses from operating or to correct the problems would not be stayed. We suspect that the bar serving minors might fall into the same category but there was no consensus here. What would the judge need to know? Whether minors who have had a drink or two get in more accidents than adults in the same condition? What is the purpose of the underage drinking law? To protect the minors themselves? Would that be enough to fall within the police powers?

Can the bar owner buy out of this situation by just paying a fine? Does that make it look like a collection effort?

As for the nursing home that failed to meet state financial guidelines, this could be a safety hazard to residents. After all, how can a nursing home hire enough staff to properly care for people if it doesn't have money in the bank? A court recently held otherwise, however, refusing to allow a state to revoke a nursing care license under these facts because the noncompliance issue that the state claimed was violated under state law pertained to financial condition, which the debtor was trying to fix through its Chapter 11 case.[2] Perhaps the court improperly focused on the money issues rather than the staffing issues.

The only one of these examples that clearly falls outside the police powers is the example contained in choice **5**. A failure to register some commercial vehicles on time would not affect the safety of the public, at least as far as we can see. Thus, the correct answer here is **C**.

C. Relief from the Automatic Stay

The sigh of relief the debtor feels on filing is limited not only by the exceptions to the automatic stay but also by creditors waiting in the wings and hoping to have the stay lifted. The stay is a very powerful and general injunction against collection, but individual creditors can move to have the stay lifted as to their own debt, so they can pursue their state law or nonbankruptcy remedies notwithstanding the debtor's bankruptcy. (*See* 11 U.S.C. §362(d).) Stay litigation is so prevalent that some people claim that §362(d) is the most litigated subsection of the Code.

Sometimes the threat of having the stay lifted is no big deal. Let's assume that the debtor is a huge manufacturer of farm equipment, and that it pledged a $20,000 certificate of deposit (CD) to a lender who financed an overseas sales transaction. The debtor owes this lender about $22,000. This lender has moved to lift the stay (or as it is commonly called, has moved for relief from the stay) to liquidate the CD in partial satisfaction of its claim. Does the debtor care about this? Not particularly. The debtor is not using the CD to run the business. It's just money, and not much money at that.

On the other hand, assume the same debtor has financed its operations through a $10 million line of credit[3] that is collateralized by its entire inventory, accounts, and equipment, which have a total value of about $9 million.

2. As you can see through this example, police powers issues often involve issues of federal supremacy as well, pursuant to which a state is told that the Bankruptcy Code, a federal statute, has trumped its laws.

3. This does not mean that the debtor necessarily owes the creditor $10 million at any given time. It just means that the debtor's total loan availability is $10 million.

Assume that the loan balance is about $9 million. If *this* lender moves to lift the stay, does the debtor care? If it wants to stay in business, it does. If the lender in this second scenario gets relief from the stay, it will sell all the assets and the case will be over. The motion for relief from the stay is a threat to the debtor's entire existence, and if granted, will mean saying goodbye to all operations, employees, potential unsecured distributions, and so on.

There are two common ways for a secured creditor to get the stay lifted in order to pursue its rights under state law.[4] The standards for relief from the automatic stay are contained in §362(d)(1) and (2).[5] Under §362(d)(1), or as some of us say, just (d)(1), the stay must be lifted if the court finds that there is "cause, including a lack of adequate protection of an interest in property of the moving party." This test requires that the creditor's interest in its collateral be safe and steady. The creditor is not adequately protected under §362(d)(1) if its position might be worsened through the debtor's use of the collateral. In practical terms, this often means that the debtor has no significant equity cushion in the property, that the property is depreciating in value, or that as a result of this combined condition, the creditor is not protected against loss resulting from the debtor's continued possession and use of the collateral.

Naturally, if the creditor is already undersecured, there is a good chance that there is a lack of adequate protection, but it also may be true if there is a small equity cushion but not one large enough to cover any diminution in the value of the collateral resulting from the debtor's use. Sometimes, even an undersecured creditor *may not* be entitled to relief from the stay if the debtor's use is not further diminishing the value of the collateral, but instead the value of the collateral remains constant. Much of the time, however, an undersecured creditor will not be adequately protected because the collateral will be depreciating and thus, the requirement of (d)(1) will be met. Note that §362(d)(1) is a one-part test.

The second common way to obtain relief from the automatic stay is for the creditor to prove two things: first, that the debtor has no equity in the property (meaning the collateral); and second, that the property is not necessary to an effective reorganization of the debtor. (*See* 11 U.S.C. §362(d)(2).) While (d)(1) often deals with equity in the sense that it requires identifying the size of an individual creditor's equity cushion, (d)(1) focuses on the position of the moving party, and whether there is equity in the property over and above the moving secured party's claim. The equity described in (d)(2) refers to the debtor's *total equity* in the property, which requires calculating all secured claims against the property (not just the moving party's claim) and determining

4. All this really means (to *pursue rights under state law*) is to pursue whatever rights the creditor had before the debtor invoked the federal Bankruptcy Code and interfered with the creditor's foreclosure, collection, repossession, and other rights. The phrase refers to a return to the status quo before the petition was filed.

5. There also is a third way, contained in §362(d)(3), which we will discuss briefly at the end of this section, but §362(d)(1) and (2) are the two traditional and common ways to get the stay lifted.

whether the debtor has any equity over and above all those secured claims. In other words, for (d)(2), we look at the total of all secured claims, not just the amount of the moving party's claim. As you'll see, this distinction makes a big difference.

The second prong of (d)(2) examines whether the property is necessary for an effective reorganization. The court must first determine whether the property is the kind of property the debtor needs for its reorganization, and then determine whether an effective reorganization is likely. This second part of the test is easiest for the creditor to prove after several months have passed without significant rehabilitation of the business. After a certain amount of time has passed, the court may grant relief from the stay where there is no equity, even if this property *would* be necessary for an effective reorganization of this debtor, if an effective reorganization looks unlikely.[6] Note that (d)(2) requires the creditor to prove two elements. Usually, (d)(2) gives the debtor at least a few months (if not a couple of years) to attempt to reorganize, even if the debtor has no equity in the secured party's collateral. On the other hand, (d)(1) requires that the court grant relief from the stay early in the proceeding if it finds that the secured party lacks adequate protection, unless the debtor has another way of providing that adequate protection.

Going back to our first two examples, let's first look at the situation in which the collateral is a $20,000 CD, in which the secured creditor's claim against the collateral is $22,000. This certificate of deposit is not the equity of collateral that the debtor needs to run its business. Moreover, the debtor has no interest in the collateral, as the creditor's claim ($22,000) is larger than the value of the collateral ($20,000). Thus, one of the two tests for granting relief from the stay under §362(d)(2) is met, even though it is the very beginning of the case. Lifting the stay at the very beginning of a case is quite rare because most assets are critical to the debtor's business. The CD is not needed for the reorganization, however, so both elements of (d)(2) are met. This test is consistent with common sense. If the debtor does not need the collateral for its operations (unlike equipment or inventory, for example) and if the debtor has no interest in the collateral anyway, why would we let the debtor keep it? It would make much more sense to just give it to the creditor and let the creditor do what it wants with it, consistent with its state law rights. There are no overriding reorganization goals that would justify keeping the collateral from the creditor under these facts.

On the other hand, in the example in which the debtor financed its operations through a $10 million line of credit collateralized by all of its inventory, accounts, and equipment with a total value of approximately $9 million and a loan amount of approximately $9 million as well, the equities and circumstances

6. Extremely large cases are an exception to the rule that the debtor has just several months before relief from the stay is usually granted. In large cases, debtors are often permitted to remain in operation, despite a lack of equity in a secured party's collateral, for years rather than months. This is true because very large reorganizations are highly complex and often take several years to complete.

are different. The creditor may or may not be adequately protected depending on whether the collateral is depreciating. If the creditor is not adequately protected, the court will need to grant relief or look for other adequate protection. If the collateral is not declining in value, then the creditor would need to use (d)(2) to prove its case, by proving both a lack of equity and that the property is not necessary to an effective reorganization. Because the creditor is required to prove both of these elements and because the collateral is clearly critical to the debtor's reorganization efforts, reorganization policy — as well as §362(d)(2) — mandate that the debtor be given some chance to reorganize its affairs before the creditor is granted relief and effectively shuts the debtor down.

The preceding text focuses on the primary grounds for lifting the automatic stay under 11 U.S.C. §362(d)(1) and (2): (1) there is cause to lift the stay, including a lack of adequate protection; and (2) the debtor has no equity in the property and the property in issue is not necessary for an effective reorganization of the debtor. Section 362(d)(3) contains a unique test for lifting the stay in cases in which the debtor's sole asset is a piece of passive real estate (not a business, but an apartment building). In those cases, the stay also can be lifted by the secured party if the debtor does not, within 90 days (or within 30 days from a determination that the debtor is a single-asset real estate debtor), file a plan of reorganization that has a reasonable chance of being confirmed within a reasonable period of time, unless the debtor has commenced making monthly payments to the creditors in an amount equal to the monthly interest due.

Section 362(d)(3) also allows the stay to be lifted if the court finds that the filing of the case was part of a scheme to delay, defraud, or hinder creditors, after the debtor transferred the property away or filed multiple bankruptcy cases affecting the property.

QUESTION 4. (CODE READER) Bob owns the preeminent horse and buggy service around Central Park. At times, he has been really busy and has done well, but lately there have been few tourists in New York and business has gone way down. His assets consist of approximately $170,000 in equipment (mostly horses, buggies, intercom systems, etc.), as well as accounts receivable from corporate clients worth approximately $30,000. He is behind on his loan payments to his principal lender, who has called a default under his line of credit. The lender's collateral is Bob's equipment and the accounts receivable. The loan balance is now $220,000. Bob recently found a way to reach Japanese tourists and they seem to love his service. Thus, business is picking up. It has not increased enough to pay the whole accelerated loan back to the lender, however, so Bob has put his business into Chapter 11 to buy some time. If the lender immediately moves to lift the stay, what will the court do?

A. On these facts alone, grant the relief under (d)(1).
B. On these facts alone, grant the relief based on (d)(2).
C. Probably not grant the relief at this early time, unless the collateral is losing value in Bob's hands, a fact we are not given.
D. Grant relief, unless Bob can provide the lender with some form of adequate protection, which the facts as stated seem to require.

ANALYSIS. For this one, we recommend calmly going through the statute and looking for facts that support granting the relief. Section 362(d)(1) requires that the secured creditor lack adequate protection. We learned that, whereas most secured parties who are undersecured probably do lack adequate protection, the real question is whether the collateral is losing value. Being undersecured in and of itself is not a *lack of adequate protection* because the only protection to which the creditor is entitled is the maintenance of the status quo— in other words, no loss of collateral value and no diminution of the lender's position.

Because the lender is undersecured, no interest or fees will accrue on the loan, so if the collateral is not losing value and the loan amount is not growing, the lender is adequately protected. Is the collateral losing value? The facts do not tell us this, so **A** is incorrect on these facts alone. The lender will not get relief under §362(d)(1) under the facts given here. This also means that **D** is incorrect. **D** states that the court will grant the relief unless Bob can provide the lender with some form of adequate protection, implying a lack of adequate protection. The facts do not suggest a lack of adequate protection, so **D** is incorrect for the same reasons as **A**: namely, because the lender has not proven its case under (d)(1), a lack of adequate protection. Can you identify facts leading to a conclusion that there is a lack of adequate protection? Look for a worsening of the creditor's position (i.e., failing to maintain and insure the equipment, etc.) when comparing the secured party's claim to its collateral over time.

What about choice **B** and §362(d)(2)? Is this test met? There are two parts to this test: whether there is no equity in the collateral and whether the collateral is not necessary to an effective reorganization. Is there equity? We hope you concluded that there was no equity, because the collateral is worth about $200,000 and the debt is $220,000. So one part of (d)(2) is met. What about the second part? Is this collateral necessary to an effective reorganization? Yes, indeed it is. The debtor needs the horses, buggies, and intercom systems, as well as the cash generated from corporate accounts, to run its business. However, because it is early in the case, the court will probably let the debtor attempt to reorganize for a while, despite a lack of equity. In other words, an effective reorganization is still possible, given that this is early in the case. Thus, **B** is also incorrect and the correct answer is **C**.

QUESTION 5. The debtor is Cherry Hill Estates, which owns a large piece of real estate in Maryland that it has been converting from farmland into deluxe homes. Several of its customers worked for the same dotcom company, which recently went bankrupt, and thus many of these residents defaulted on their obligations to Cherry Hill. Cherry Hill has hit a major cash crunch as a result, and has been anxiously increasing its marketing to get back on track. Things do not look good, however.

Cherry Hill borrowed money from First Bank to buy the land. First Bank's collateral is the land, worth about $2.5 million. First Bank currently is owed $1.8 million. This loan is in serious default. Second Bank lent money to the debtor to do the home construction. Second Bank holds a second mortgage on the land, as well as a security interest in the contract rights that Cherry Hill has with its customers, meaning the profits flowing from the building contracts. Some of these contracts are still in place, and the contracts are worth about $300,000. Second Bank is owed $1.1 million.

What fact would be the strongest in proving a lack of adequate protection on the part of either or both of these lenders?

A. The debtor is not maintaining the buildings it has begun building.
B. The property values in this area are going way up, due to urban sprawl.
C. The debtor is in default on an equipment loan from another bank as well.
D. The debtor is not maintaining its insurance on the property.

ANALYSIS. The answer here is **D**. Failing to maintain insurance is always a lack of adequate protection because if the property is lost or damaged due to fire, theft, vandals, or some other insurable event, the entire property value (and therefore the lenders' collateral) could be lost. Now looking for a lack of adequate protection no longer boils down to looking only at the size of the equity cushion, vis-à-vis the size of the secured party's claims (as is the case with an oversecured creditor) or to determining whether the debtor's use is diminishing the property value (as in the case of an undersecured creditor). Thus, **D** is the correct answer. The debtor is simply not adequately protecting the secured lenders' interests. **A** is probably second best, but you need to think practically about how one maintains ongoing construction. Some knowledge of business is required in these fights over lifting the stay, though much of this knowledge is common sense. Maybe the debtor needs to cover open areas to protect them from rain. Perhaps electrical systems have to be boxed in. In any case, this is important but still less risky to creditors than failing to maintain insurance.

Note how, even if the debtor was not maintaining the ongoing construction, it would have to be quite a serious matter before the rights of First Bank would be impaired enough to make this matter. Quick! Calculate First Bank's equity cushion. First Bank has an equity cushion of $700,000. First Bank will not lack adequate protection until its interest and fees grow to meet the value of the collateral. Even if poor maintenance caused the property to drop in value by $200,000, First Bank still has a large equity cushion and therefore appears adequately protected. Second Bank, on the other hand, could definitely get the stay lifted if the property dropped in value by $200,000 because it doesn't enjoy an equity cushion and the drop in value would drastically reduce its interests in the debtor's property. Its position would be worsened and the status quo (the measure for the undersecured creditor) would not be maintained, and therefore, Second Bank lacks adequate protection. So **A** is the second best answer. It works for Second Bank under (d)(1), but probably not for First Bank.

What about the other two answers, **B** and **C**? **B** actually means that both creditors are probably adequately protected because the land value is going up (appreciating) rather than down (depreciating). This is an argument many debtors try to make in the face of a motion to lift the stay. Debtors typically argue that there is no need to provide adequate protection because market conditions alone are improving the position of the secured creditors who have land as collateral. In any event, the facts in **B** suggest that there *is* adequate protection, not that adequate protection is lacking.

C provides facts that are not relevant to this question. The debtor's default on another loan, whether or not that loan is secured, is not relevant to the adequate protection of these creditors on this other collateral.

As an aside, how much is Second Bank's secured claim? If you came up with about $1 million, leaving an undersecured deficiency claim of approximately $100,000, you're right!

QUESTION 6. In the factual scenario of the previous question, assume that one year has passed and the collateral values are about the same, maybe just a few thousand dollars less than at the beginning of the case. No payments have been made to anyone. First Bank now moves to lift the stay. Can it win?

A. Yes, under (d)(1).
B. Yes, under (d)(2).
C. No, because it still has a huge equity cushion under (d)(1).
D. No, only Second Bank (who has been hurt quite a bit so far) could get relief at this time, because it has no equity cushion and because there is no equity in the collateral.

ANALYSIS. Keep your eye on the question here and go slowly through the statute again. Section 362(d)(1) requires that there be a lack of adequate protection for First Bank to win its motion, and First Bank is still adequately protected. The equity cushion is huge, so First Bank's motion will certainly be denied on the basis of (d)(1), and **A** is incorrect. What about **B**? Is there equity in the collateral? Please try to answer before moving on. The equity we are talking about here has nothing to do with First Bank's equity cushion. Try hard to get this now, as we'll build on it later. To calculate the equity under (d)(2), you need to add up *all* the liens on the collateral, particularly the land, because this is what First Bank holds a lien on. There is *no* equity. The two loans are more than the value of the land, so there is no equity. The second part of the test, dealing with necessity of the collateral for an effective reorganization, is likely to be met as well, as it looks less and less likely that the debtor can successfully reorganize. Thus, the answer here is **B**. First Bank can get relief now under (d)(2), even if it cannot meet (d)(1).

D is incorrect as well. Whether Second Bank can get the stay lifted is immaterial to First Bank's motion. The question is whether First Bank has the right to have the stay lifted. The facts contained in **C** are irrelevant because First Bank has a right to choose which part of §362(d) it relies on to get the stay lifted, and it need meet only (d)(1) *or* (d)(2). The creditor gets to choose between the two tests and can prove either ground for relief. First Bank can get its relief by relying on (d)(2), and thus it need not satisfy the (d)(1) test. Thus, First Bank can get relief from the stay even though its interests are adequately protected.

D. Adequate Protection

A few times in the previous discussion, we referred to times in which a creditor's interest was not adequately protected by virtue of an equity cushion, but we have alluded to the possibility that a debtor may be able to keep the stay in place by offering some other form of adequate protection. This discussion ties into the one we had earlier dealing with the use of cash collateral. Section 361 provides that a debtor may need to provide adequate protection in various instances, including when the debtor is using a creditor's cash collateral, when a debtor is obtaining post-petition financing from a third party and thus priming an existing creditor's lien, and when the secured party has moved to lift the stay under (d)(1). (*See* 11 U.S.C. §§361, 362(d).)

If a court finds that cause exists to grant relief under (d)(1), it can either grant relief from the stay or order the debtor to provide additional protection (adequate protection) to protect the creditor's interest. How? The usual ways include ordering the debtor to make periodic cash payments to the creditor, or ordering that the debtor provide the creditor with additional or replacement liens. (*See* 11 U.S.C. §361.) For example, the debtor may be required to grant the creditor a lien on previously unencumbered assets to the extent of diminution in the creditor's interest in the original collateral, or make some monthly payment to the creditor, and thereby adequately protect the creditor's interests.

E. The Closer: Chapter 30

As you learned in this chapter, a court can refuse to lift the stay even though a lender has met its burden of proof under §362(d). In such a situation, the court can instead order the debtor to make adequate protection payments, while leaving the collateral in the debtor's possession. What is the rationale for allowing these payments, rather than simply letting the creditor take its collateral and sell it?

A. The adequate protection alternative to lifting the stay recognizes that secured creditors often overreact to the debtor's failure and hastily move to lift the stay.
B. The adequate protection alternative to lifting the stay ensures that generally unsecured creditors are not harmed by a premature end to the case.
C. The adequate protection alternative to lifting the stay promotes reorganization.
D. The adequate protection alternative to lifting the stay protects the secured creditor from loss resulting from any diminution in the value of its collateral caused by the debtor's continuing use of the collateral.

ANALYSIS. It is hard for most students to understand why a court can deny a motion to lift the stay and instead just order adequate protection payments under §361. The reason why this can be done is that a decision to lift the stay is based almost entirely on the economic realities. Unlike most litigation, it is not about saving face or proving a point, but about protecting the economic position of the secured creditor. The court would like to give the debtor a chance to reorganize but cannot do this at the expense of the secured creditor or its collateral. If there is a way to let the debtor try to reorganize and also protect the collateral, this is what the judge must do. Thus, the most accurate answer is **D**. The goal of adequate protection payments is to protect the value of the secured party's interest in its collateral. If this is being done, through payments or otherwise, relief from the stay is not justified. Pure and simple, it's all about the dollars and cents.

Martin's and Keating's Picks

1. Question 1	**D**
2. Question 2	**D**
3. Question 3	**C**
4. Question 4	**C**
5. Question 5	**D**
6. Question 6	**B**
The Closer	**D**

31

Operating the Chapter 11 Debtor: The Rights and Goals of the Debtor-in-Possession, and the Grounds for Appointment of a Chapter 11 Trustee or Examiner

OVERVIEW

A. Activities that the Debtor-in-Possession Can Engage in Without Court Approval While in Chapter 11
B. The Appointment of a Trustee
C. The Appointment of an Examiner
D. Maintaining the Debtor's Operations and Structuring a Successful Chapter 11 Case: The Basic Goals and Requirements
E. Overview of Chapter 11 Treatment Rules
F. Overview of Chapter 11 Procedural Rules
G. The Closer: Chapter 31
Martin's and Keating's Picks

In Chapter 28, we introduced Chapter 11 and its alternatives, and the various roles of the parties in the case were discussed. In this chapter, you will pin down what the debtor-in-possession is authorized to do without court approval, and also discuss when a trustee or examiner can be appointed in a Chapter 11 case. This chapter then provides an overview of the operational goals of a debtor-in-possession or a trustee in a Chapter 11 case, as well as an overview of the treatment and procedural rules under Chapter 11. In a way, this chapter previews much of the remainder of the book, especially Chapters 34 through 37. If you don't need the preview, you can skip parts D, E, and F of the chapter.[1]

A. Activities that the Debtor-in-Possession Can Engage in Without Court Approval While in Chapter 11

The debtor-in-possession has almost all the rights and duties that a trustee would have if there were a trustee appointed in the case under §1107(a). The debtor-in-possession is the representative of the estate and a fiduciary to creditors. As a result, the debtor-in-possession has the right to operate the business under §1108, the power to use, sell, or lease property of the estate pursuant to §363, the power to borrow money or obtain credit on behalf of the estate pursuant to §364, and the power to assume or reject, or to assume and assign, executory contracts and unexpired leases on behalf of the estate. The debtor-in-possession also has the power to object to claims on behalf of the estate pursuant to §502, to surcharge the secured party on behalf of the estate under §506(c), to recover property of the estate under §542's turnover powers, as well as all of the avoidance powers already discussed in Chapter 12 of this guide.

Pre-petition management is permitted to stay in place under Chapter 11. This is done to encourage management to file a Chapter 11 case while there is still time to reorganize and also for efficiency reasons. Appointing a trustee immediately would dissuade current management from filing, and make it difficult to continue the operations by creating a large learning curve for the trustee.

In theory, the debtor-in-possession is supervised by the U.S. Trustee's Office, as well as the unsecured creditors' committee appointed in the case, in order to prevent abuses. The bankruptcy court also can hold status conferences to monitor the debtor's activities. Practically speaking, in most other countries, these precautions would not be considered sufficient. Rather, the courts and the system in general would require that an outside party run the company.

During a Chapter 11 case, the debtor is always permitted to engage in business in the *ordinary course of business*. Pursuant to §363(c), a debtor is entitled to operate its business in the ordinary course without notice or a hearing and thus without further court-ordered intervention, just as it normally

1. We are torn here between avoiding repetition and allowing students to be exposed to difficult material several times, to allow it to seep in. You'll miss nothing but a good overview if you skip parts D, E, and F. You might find it helpful to read these parts *after* you have completed Chapters 34 through 37.

would outside bankruptcy. The primary exception is the *use of cash collateral*, which was discussed in Chapter 29 of this guide. When the Code refers to "notice and a hearing," it is referring to §102(1), which requires the debtor to a motion and request a hearing whenever it seeks to do something outside the ordinary course of business.

Naturally, the debtor's counsel must determine which activities are in the ordinary course of business. For most retailers and wholesalers, selling inventory is not considered outside the ordinary course of business. Selling off equipment or entire inventory stocks, however, *would* be outside the ordinary course of business because the debtor doesn't typically sell its equipment (or its entire inventory) in its normal operations. As was briefly discussed in Chapter 29, obtaining unsecured credit for the typical things for which a debtor would have obtained credit pre-petition is probably ordinary-course activity. One question that has arisen is whether, if a debtor is a retailer or a service provider and has numerous locations nationwide, it would be in the ordinary course of business for the debtor to enter into a new lease for premises post-petition. Some jurisdictions allow this practice, while others have held that even though it is ordinary for the debtor to take on new lease space outside bankruptcy, because of the ramifications with respect to these obligations (these will become post-petition obligations that must be paid 100 cents on the dollar), entering into a new lease for premises post-petition is outside the ordinary course of business.

Practically speaking, it seems as if the debtor needs court permission for just about every significant thing that the debtor would like to do. It is always safest to ask the court for permission if the debtor's counsel is unsure whether an activity is in the ordinary course of business.

QUESTION 1. Which of the following can a Chapter 11 debtor safely do without obtaining court approval?

A. Obtain unsecured credit from its regular suppliers.
B. Obtain a short-term bank loan, with its inventory as collateral.
C. Open a new location for its video game chain store.
D. Hire an attorney to handle a piece of litigation against a competitor.

ANALYSIS. The question asks you to determine which of these things would be considered to be activity taken in the ordinary course of business. The answer is **A**. Taking out unsecured credit from regular suppliers is ordinary-course activity. All of the other activities are things that require court approval because they are not ordinary-course transactions. (*See* 11 U.S.C. §363.) The debtor cannot pledge collateral post-petition without court approval, so **B** is incorrect, nor can the debtor open a new store location, or hire special counsel. Thus, **C** and **D** are also incorrect. You might wonder why the debtor would want to hire another lawyer when it presumably already has one. Hiring an attorney for a special purpose is common, particularly if the lawyer has experience with the special situation with which the debtor needs help. A good example would be hiring special counsel to pursue a trademark infringement case. This cannot be done without court approval under §327, however, so the answer is **A**.

B. The Appointment of a Trustee

It has already been said that in the typical Chapter 11 case, no trustee is appointed. Rather, the debtor's management continues to operate the business. There are, however, exceptions to this general rule. Section 1104(a)(1) of the Bankruptcy Code permits the court to appoint a trustee or an examiner[2] in a case in which doing so is "in the best interest of creditors, equity security holders, or other interests of the estate." (*See* 11 U.S.C. §1104 (a)(1).) A trustee may also be appointed in a case for cause, which includes fraud, dishonesty, incompetence, or gross mismanagement of the affairs of the debtor by current management, either before or after the commencement of the case. (*See* §1104(a)(2).) Naturally, when a trustee is appointed in a Chapter 11 case, the trustee exercises all of the rights of a debtor-in-possession, including operating the business. If a trustee is appointed in a Chapter 11 case, the trustee is required to conduct an investigation of the debtor's financial condition and operation. The trustee also holds the attorney-client privilege for the debtor corporation.

The court is required to convert or dismiss any Chapter 11 case for "cause," which now includes for substantial or continuing loss to or diminution of the estate and absence of a reasonable likelihood of rehabilitation, gross mismanagement of the estate, failure to maintain insurance, the unauthorized use of cash collateral, a failure to comply with any of the reporting requirements of the Code, a failure to timely pay post-petition taxes, a failure to file a plan within the time limits set out in the Code, and several other grounds. (*See* §1112(b).)

The 2005 amendments included a drastic departure from the prior §1112, in which only a few things were enumerated as "cause" to convert or dismiss, and in which the court could choose whether to convert or dismiss the case, based on the importance of the infraction in the overall scheme of the case. The section now purports to force the court to convert or dismiss for any of the infractions listed. Read §1112 now.

Also, if the court finds it to be in the best interest of creditors, it can instead appoint a trustee under the same circumstances. (*Id.* §1104(a)(3).)

---

2. Rather than replacing the debtor-in-possession the way a trustee does, an examiner just investigates certain aspects of the case or the debtor's operations. (*See* 11 U.S.C. §1104(c).) Thus, an examiner does not divest the debtor-in-possession of control over the case or the business the way a trustee does. Both a trustee and an examiner must be "disinterested." (*See* 11 U.S.C. §1104(d).)

QUESTION 2. What is the biggest disadvantage to claimholders of appointing a trustee in a Chapter 11 case?

A. The trustee will examine the debtor's financial condition and operations.
B. The trustee's fees will add further administrative costs to the estate.
C. The trustee will have a tremendous learning curve in running the company, and may actually thwart its operations and thus its reorganization.
D. The trustee will normally pursue all avoidance actions on behalf of the debtor-in-possession.

ANALYSIS. Choice **A** is incorrect because it describes a benefit to having a trustee appointed in a Chapter 11 case. A trustee is specifically charged with examining the debtor's financial condition and operations for wrongdoing during the pre- and post-petition periods, and also for information about possible avoidance actions. **D**, which states that the trustee will pursue avoidance actions on behalf of the debtor-in-possession, is also a good reason *to appoint* a trustee, and one of the benefits of doing so. Often, some of the preferential and fraudulent transfers made prior to the case were made to insiders, like management and shareholders, which the debtor-in-possession (and its management) may hesitate to pursue.

Thus, the two answers that are in the running are choices **B** and **C**. The statement made in **B** is true. The trustee will add administrative costs to the estate, and sometimes these expenses will be higher than those that would have been expended by the debtor-in-possession. At other times, however, these professional fees are about the same, whether or not a trustee is appointed. Consequently, **B** describes a possible disadvantage, but is not as significant as the disadvantage described in **C**. Choice **C** is the correct answer here. The trustee often has difficulty determining how to operate the debtor's business post-petition. As a result, appointing a trustee can sometimes be inefficient. In most cases, it is not advisable to appoint a trustee because doing so can make it difficult to keep the debtor operational and thus to reorganize the debtor's business. There are, however, certain cases in which it *is* advisable to appoint a trustee.

QUESTION 3. (CODE READER) In reading §1104, which of the following sounds like a good justification for appointing a Chapter 11 trustee?

1. The debtor's board of directors is constantly fighting, is having trouble making corporate decisions, and cannot be restructured under the current corporate scheme.

2. The debtor's management refuses to pursue preferential transfers to insiders during its case.
3. The debtor's management looted company assets pre-petition, and attempted to place all of the liabilities of a group of corporate entities into the debtor, to the disadvantage of that particular debtor.
4. One of the creditors claims that it would be in its best interest to appoint a trustee.

A. All of the above.
B. 2, 3, and 4.
C. 1 and 3, and possibly 2.
D. 2 and 3 only.

ANALYSIS. Section 1104(a)(2) states that the court can appoint a trustee if it is in the interest of creditors, equity security holders, and other holders. If one creditor claims it would be in its best interest to appoint a trustee, this alone is insufficient to meet the requirements of §1104, as the section requires that the court find under §1104(a)(2) that appointing a trustee be "in the interests of creditors, any equity security holders, and other interests of the estate. . . ." Creditors presumably know what is in each of their best interests, so if more creditors wanted a trustee, they would certainly say so. Thus, answer **4** is incorrect, eliminating both **A** and **B**.

Let's look at some of the other individual options. Option **1** says the debtor's management is in constant dispute over everything. One of us has been involved in a case in which this was the situation, and a trustee was appointed simply because the debtor was unable to continue its operation under current management. In our view, choice **1** should appear in the correct answer. We suppose it is possible that, rather than appointing a trustee, the corporate debtor could simply restructure its board so it could operate, but according to the facts given in choice **1**, this cannot be done.

Choice **3** states that the debtor has looted the company pre-petition by placing the liabilities of other corporate entities onto the debtor and by transferring the debtor's assets to other corporate entities. This certainly justifies the appointment of a trustee and is based on the facts in the case of Sharon Steel Corp., 871 F.2d 1217 (3d Cir. 1989). In *Sharon Steel*, the debtor's management transferred many of the debtor's assets to another corporation controlled by the same management, and also sacrificed the debtor's credit-worthiness to get better loans for other companies. Naturally, the court found this offensive and thus found sufficient grounds to appoint a trustee. *Sharon Steel* also involved preferential transfers that management refused to pursue, thus implicating the facts suggested in choice **2** as well. However, refusing to pursue preferential transfers alone is not sufficient grounds to appoint a trustee. Rather, it is often more appropriate for the debtor-in-possession to simply assign the right to pursue certain preferences to the creditors' committee. Thus, refusing to pursue preferences, in and of itself, is often insufficient to justify appointing a trustee. The efficiencies of having existing management operate the business may override this one particular fact, suggesting that someone else, usually the creditors' committee, could pursue the preferences instead. Thus, the correct answer is **C**.

C. The Appointment of an Examiner

If the court determines that appointing a Chapter 11 trustee would be too disruptive to the debtor's business, §1104 allows the court to appoint an examiner instead. The appointment of an examiner is a less disruptive step by the court and is often preferable because the examiner will investigate the debtor's affairs while the debtor's management continues to operate the company. Interestingly, §1104 makes the appointment of an examiner *mandatory*, on a party's request, if the debtor's fixed, liquidated, unsecured debts, and other debts exceed $5 million. Otherwise, the court has the *discretion* to appoint an examiner for "cause," if any party-in-interest or the U.S. Trustee's office requests the appointment of an examiner to conduct an investigation of any fraud, dishonesty, incompetence, misconduct, mismanagement, or irregularity in the management of the affairs of the debtor.

QUESTION 4. In which of the following cases would the appointment of an examiner be mandatory on the part of the court?

A. All of the creditors have alleged that the debtor mismanaged the debtor's business.
B. All of the creditors claim that the debtor's management has defrauded the debtor.
C. The debtor's fixed, liquidated, unsecured debts are $5.1 million and an examiner has been requested.
D. Many creditors argue that appointing an examiner is in the best interests of creditors.

ANALYSIS. We apologize for the softball, but we want to bring home how very discretionary the appointment of an examiner typically is. The correct answer here is obviously **C**, but if and only if a creditor has *requested* an examiner. If a party-in-interest requests the appointment of an examiner, and the debtor's liquidated, unsecured debts exceed $5 million, the court must appoint an examiner. In terms of the statements made in **A, B**, and **D**, all would justify the appointment of an examiner for cause. However, cause to appoint an examiner is always determined in the discretion of the court. If most of the creditors make these allegations, and they are proven, the court would likely appoint an examiner. However, it would not be mandatory.

In deciding whether the best interests of creditors are served by appointing a trustee or an examiner, the court always uses discretion. If the court believes that cause exists to appoint a trustee or an examiner, the court certainly can appoint one under the standards set out in §1104. Sometimes the cause standard becomes a head count of sorts, with the court trying to determine what percentage of the creditors prefer to have a trustee as opposed to the debtor-in-possession, or in the case of an examiner, what percentage of the debtor's creditors would like to augment the debtor's operation with the services of an examiner, and also would be willing to pay the costs of an examiner. Both trustees and examiners add costs to the estate. Unless there is a reason to suspect wrongdoing, which will result in recovery of assets for creditors, the appointment of a trustee or examiner can decrease creditor distributions by adding additional administrative costs to the estate.

QUESTION 5. The most critical thing that debtor's management brings to the table that neither a trustee nor an examiner will have is:

A. money to contribute to the business.
B. knowledge of the operations of the business.
C. a good relationship with creditors.
D. knowledge of the bankruptcy system.

ANALYSIS. We suppose debtor's management could bring any of these things, but the one that should be true in every case is choice **B**, knowledge of the debtor's business. Management specializes in this one thing. There is no reason to believe that the debtor's management will have any special knowledge of the Chapter 11 process, as this is likely the first time management has been involved in Chapter 11. Thus, **D** is incorrect. Nor is it true that the debtor's management will necessarily have a good relationship with creditors, or money to contribute to the business. Thus, **C** and **A** are also incorrect, and **B** is the right answer.

D. Maintaining the Debtor's Operations and Structuring a Successful Chapter 11 Case: The Basic Goals and Requirements

To make any Chapter 11 case successful, the debtor-in-possession or trustee must accomplish several things. We'll assume for this discussion that there is no trustee and just talk about the goals of the debtor.[3] First, the debtor must be able to keep the business operating by taking advantage of the automatic stay and finding cash with which to operate before confirming its Chapter 11 plan. Second, the debtor must be able to turn the business around by developing a successful business strategy. Third, the debtor must determine which claims are being asserted against it and find a way to pay valid claims. Finally, the debtor must use the Code and any other available law to restructure its debts.

First let's talk about keeping the business afloat. The automatic stay imposed by §362 helps in some respects. Section 362(a) keeps creditors from repossessing or executing on assets in which creditors have a lien. (*See* 11 U.S.C. §362(a)(3) and (4).) It stops ongoing litigation that can funnel assets away from the debtor. (*See* §362(a)(1).) It also allows the debtor some breathing room to concentrate on the actual operation of its business. One thing the automatic stay will *not* do, however, is force a supplier to continue doing business with the debtor. However, if the debtor has a contract with the supplier, the debtor will be able to force the supplier to continue to do business with the debtor. (*See* 11 U.S.C. §365.) Likewise, the automatic stay cannot force anyone to loan new money to the debtor, and will not preclude the exercise of police and regulatory powers of government bodies. (*See* 11 U.S.C. §362(b)(4).) Nevertheless, the automatic stay is a powerful weapon and will help tremendously in keeping the debtor's assets and operations intact, when creditors might otherwise execute on their pre-petition claims.

Another way that the debtor maintains its business early in a case is by finding operating cash. This is done in a number of ways, but first by requesting that the court allow the debtor (through a cash collateral order) to use cash that has been pledged to secured parties as collateral. (*See* 11 U.S.C. §363(c)(2).) Additionally, the cash that the debtor has on hand will go further because the debtor will not be paying its pre-petition claims (except possibly as adequate protection payments to the secured creditors and pre-petition payroll). Another way for the debtor to find money for its current operations is to get court approval for post-petition loans. (*See* 11 U.S.C. §364.)

The second thing a debtor must do to succeed in Chapter 11 is develop a strategy to turn its business around. There are many strategies for changing the debtor's business operations, and this part of Chapter 11 is the most exciting for lawyers. Examples of things that the debtor can do include: building inventory; cutting costs, or just changing the way money is spent; purchasing new and more efficient equipment; rejecting existing equipment leases; selling assets; reducing labor costs; closing locations, and taking advantage of special provisions in the Bankruptcy Code dealing with landlord claims; taking advantage of the automatic stay to prevent termination of contracts and leases that are in default, which the debtor would like to keep in place; and assigning executory contracts and leases, which may be currently leased to the debtor at

3. By that we mean the debtor-in-possession.

below market rates, and which the debtor can sell for a greater price to third parties. (*See* 11 U.S.C. §365.)

The third thing a debtor must do to successfully emerge from Chapter 11 is assess the claims made against it. For the most part, creditors will file proofs of claim with the court[4] and nonbankruptcy substantive law will be applied to determine how much each creditor is owed. In some cases, claims that unsecured creditors assert will be unliquidated (meaning the amount of the claim is not yet ascertained). For example, perhaps the debtor runs a retail store and someone falls down in the place of business and sues the debtor in tort. The litigation to which the debtor is a defendant will be stayed. The creditor or claimant will file a *proof of claim* in the debtor's bankruptcy case and that claim will be adjudicated through the bankruptcy process.[5]

Once the debtor rejects some of its unexpired leases and contracts, the non-debtor parties to the leases and contracts also possess unsecured claims in the bankruptcy for their contract rejection damages. The amount of these claims is adjudicated or determined by the court. (*See* 11 U.S.C. §§501, 502.) In some highly unusual cases, where it will be uncertain far into the future how much a particular claim will be, the court will estimate the claim for the purposes of claim allowance. (*See* 11 U.S.C. §502(c).) Finally, the debtor can seek to equitably subordinate certain claims, meaning taking them out of their normal priority status and turn them into lower status claims. (*See* 11 U.S.C. §510.)

The final thing that a debtor must do in any successful Chapter 11 case, after keeping afloat, restructuring its business, and determining the claims against it, is restructure its debts. (*See* 11 U.S.C. §1129.) In many ways this is the fun part of Chapter 11. Unlike an out-of-court workout, creditors in a Chapter 11 case are entitled to very specific treatment described in the Bankruptcy Code. Fitting within the rules is a bit like playing with a complex Rubik's cube. When you finally get one piece of the puzzle in place, another piece moves.

The rules for treating claims are similar to the ones you learned under Chapter 13, with a few new twists. As you saw under Chapter 13, Chapter 11 contains a *best interest test*. This test requires that creditors in a Chapter 11 case receive no less than they would receive in a Chapter 7 case unless they agree to lesser treatment. (*See* 11 U.S.C. §1129(a)(7)(A).) In some respects, this test makes even more sense in a Chapter 11 context than it does in a Chapter 13

4. Secured creditors are not required to file a proof of claim to protect the secured portion of their claims because the bankruptcy is not permitted to impact lien status except in certain instances. However, if the secured party is undersecured, then a proof of claim is necessary to protect the unsecured portion of the claim. Because no one knows what will actually happen in any given case, most lawyers we know file claims for secured creditors just in case they ultimately become undersecured.

5. In certain cases, where there is insurance to cover such claims, a claim will continue to be litigated outside the bankruptcy case, but the claimant will normally waive all claims against the debtor and agree to only collect against the insurance. (*See* U.S.C. §362(d)(1).) In some cases, the bankruptcy court may lack jurisdiction over such cases and may be required to abstain from hearing them. (*See* 28 U.S.C. §1334(c)(2).)

context. Think about it this way: If the debtor is going to have an opportunity to restructure its debts and pay them over time pursuant to a plan, the creditor should get at least what they would receive in a Chapter 7 liquidation. Otherwise, the debtor is essentially playing with other people's money. Chapter 11 precludes the debtor from taking too many risks with creditors' money because creditor claims are considered higher in priority than equity or shareholder claims. Thus, the debtor must prove that its plan is in the best interest of creditors (because it provides creditors with at least as much as they would receive in a Chapter 7).

QUESTION 6. Which of these statements is ***not*** true?

A. Secured creditors always get paid in full in a Chapter 11 case.
B. Priority claims always get paid in full in a Chapter 11 case.
C. Unsecured claims need not be paid in full in a Chapter 11 case.
D. Unsecured creditors must get at least as much in a Chapter 11 as they would get in a Chapter 7 liquidation, unless an individual creditor agrees to accept less.

ANALYSIS. As the question asks you to identify a statement that is *not* true, start by eliminating anything you know for a fact *is* true. The requirements of the best interest test that were just discussed are exactly what are stated in **D**. Thus, **D** is true and is not the answer. Certainly **C** is true, right? Unsecured creditors need not be paid in full. In fact, this is the point of many Chapter 11 cases, to pay less than the full amount of as many claims as possible. Because allowed secured claims generally must be paid in full, as claims entitled to priority must, the benefit of Chapter 11 (arising from the ability to pay less than the face value of claims) comes from the treatment of general unsecured creditors. Having just said that allowed secured claims as well as allowed priority claims must be paid in full, which of the other two answers is incorrect, **A** or **B**? Go back and read the two choices if you do not know the answer. **A** is not entirely true. Secured creditors will be paid the full value of their collateral, but not necessarily paid the full face value of their claims, because they may be undersecured, right? If choice **A** had said "secured *claims* always get paid in full," as opposed to secured creditors, this might well be true, as §506(a) of the Code defines an *allowed secured claim* as a claim worth the lesser of the face amount of the claim or the value of the collateral supporting the claim. Thus, the correct answer, or rather the answer that is incorrect and thus answers the question posed, is **A**.

The Chapter 11 debtor must pay priority claims in full. This should sound somewhat familiar, as this also is required in a Chapter 13 case. After this, however, the two types of cases (Chapter 13 and Chapter 11) start to diverge. Whatever else a Chapter 11 provides is largely subject to negotiation. This is particularly true of the unsecured creditor distribution.

A typical distribution, for example, might be 10 percent of each claim over five years for a total of 50 percent. However, distributions to unsecured creditors can vary greatly. The distribution can even be based on future events, in what is called a *pot plan*. Under a pot plan, the debtor promises to pay unsecured creditors whatever net profits (or some percentage of these profits) it generates under the life of the plan. Typically, creditors frown on pot plans. They would like to know exactly how much they are getting, rather than taking a chance on the debtor's net profits. Once the distribution has been agreed upon, the creditors' committee will then advocate for the plan among the general unsecured creditor class. As you will later see, sometimes unsecured creditors receive equity in the company as their distribution. In other words, if the debtor cannot pay enough cash to unsecured creditors to cause them to vote in favor of the plan, the debtor may instead pay them in equity, making them the new owners (or more commonly, part owners) of the reorganized company.

Keep in mind that creditors ultimately are placed in creditor classes for the purpose of voting on the Chapter 11 plan. (*See* 11 U.S.C. §1126.) Each secured creditor is placed in a class of its own. (*See* 11 U.S.C. §1122.) Tax creditors are generally treated a bit differently from other priority claimants, and if priority claims are classified, tax claims are classified separately. (*See* 11 U.S.C. §1129(a)(9).) Unsecured creditors are generally placed in one class, unless they are very small, and separately classified for the debtor's administrative convenience. (*See* 11 U.S.C. §1122(b).) There may also be some unsecured debt that is "subordinated." (*See* 11 U.S.C. §510.) This means that some creditors may have agreed in advance that their claims will receive lower treatment than that of other general unsecured creditors, perhaps because they received a very high rate of interest on their claim pre-petition. If there is subordinated debt, this debt will be placed in a separate class as well.

The backdrop for any plan negotiations, be they with an unsecured creditors' committee or a secured creditor, is a party's assessment of what the debtor is likely to achieve before a court over the creditor's objection. In other words, if the debtor would be able to force a certain treatment on a secured creditor, then the secured creditor is likely to agree to that treatment without making the debtor (and the court) go through the expensive and costly litigation involved in pursuing a contested plan. Similarly, if unsecured creditors could be forced to accept a certain distribution, then they're likely to vote in favor of a plan that provides that treatment, without the expense and delay of litigation. The other important backdrop to Chapter 11 plan negotiations is that the creditor must determine what it would get if the plan were to fail and the debtor were to liquidate. General unsecured creditors often receive little in liquidation and are typically motivated to support a plan that proposes more than liquidation payments, but still far less than they are owed.

E. Overview of Chapter 11 Treatment Rules

Naturally, the debtor must restructure its debts according to the rules set out in the Code. As far as the treatment of creditors under a Chapter 11 plan goes, you already know that, unless they agree to other treatment, secured creditors must at least receive the value of their collateral or the amount of their loan (whichever is less) over the life of the plan, with present value interest from the time the plan becomes effective. (*See* 11 U.S.C. §1129(b).) The time period over which each secured claim is paid depends on the useful life of the creditor's collateral, which can extend far beyond the five years mandated by Chapter 13. Priority claims must be paid in full shortly after the plan is confirmed, (1) unless the creditor has agreed to be paid over time; or (2) unless the claim is for priority taxes (*see* 11 U.S.C. §507(a)(8)), which can be paid over five years from the date of the order for relief. (*See* 11 U.S.C. §1129(a)(9).)

Unsecured creditors are not entitled to any particular distribution in Chapter 11. Rather, their distribution is typically negotiated, based on what the debtor can afford to pay creditors while still staying in business. As just discussed, unsecured creditors are sometimes paid from future profits, but at other times are paid with the equity or stock in the new company. Remember how secured creditors are higher in priority than unsecured creditors and also how §507 priority claims are higher in priority than general unsecured creditors' claims? General unsecured claims, which are debt, are higher in priority than equity or ownership claims. This means that the owners (usually shareholders, but sometimes partners) of the company are not allowed to keep their equity interest in the reorganized Chapter 11 debtor unless the unsecured creditor class consents or is paid in full over the life of the plan. (*See* 11 U.S.C. §1129(b)(2)(B).) This is known as the *absolute priority rule*. This rule fosters negotiation and consent. It gives equity owners a huge incentive to negotiate with unsecured creditors to obtain their consent to the plan. We'll discuss the absolute priority rule later, but we wanted you to be aware of it in the background.

F. Overview of Chapter 11 Procedural Rules

Chapter 11 requires that the debtor-in-possession[6] place creditor claims into classes according to their legal rights for the purpose of plan voting. (*See* 11

6. From now on in this guide, we will sometimes call the debtor-in-possession the *debtor-in-possession*, but may also shorten this to simply the *debtor* for simplicity and ease. Please do not forget, however, that when we are talking about a debtor in a Chapter 11, we are always talking about a debtor-in-possession unless a Chapter 11 trustee has been appointed. Courts and practitioners almost always simply

U.S.C. §1122.) Only *impaired* classes, or those that are not paid in full on the effective date of the plan,[7] or whose rights are otherwise affected by the bankruptcy case, are entitled to vote. (*See* 11 U.S.C. §1124.) As you'll see when voting is discussed further, the debtor hopes that every class of impaired creditors will vote in favor of the plan, because it will make the case simpler. However, if each class does not vote yes, the debtor can force the plan (*cram down the plan*) on nonconsenting classes. (*See* 11 U.S.C. §1129(b)(1).)

To cram down, however, the debtor must have at least one accepting impaired class. (*Id.*) Section 1122 requires the debtor to put only claims with similar legal rights in the same class. Although this section does not specifically require that similarly situated creditors be placed in the *same* class, courts expect debtors to do this as well, unless there is a very good reason for doing otherwise. Courts do not allow the debtor to separately classify some claims merely to gerrymander the voting. (*See* 11 U.S.C. §1122.) Sometimes a debtor who believes it will have difficulty coming up with a consenting class will form the classes in a way that ensures at least one impaired class will vote yes. Usually, this involves forming several different classes of unsecured creditors, in hope that one class votes yes. If this is done for the mere purpose of gerrymandering the vote, and ultimately involves discrimination against some creditors, it is not permitted. (*See* 11 U.S.C. §1122.)

Moreover, the debtor is not permitted to send out the plan for voting unless a court-approved disclosure statement accompanies it. (*See* 11 U.S.C. §1125.) Section 1125 provides that the disclosure statement will only be approved if it contains adequate information to allow creditors to determine whether or not to vote in favor of the plan.

G. The Closer: Chapter 31

Comparing the Chapter 11 rules to the out-of-court workout discussed in Chapter 28, which of the following is ***not*** one of the advantages of a Chapter 11 proceeding?

A. In a Chapter 11, the debtor can force dissenting creditors to comply with the plan.

---

refer to the debtor-in-possession as the *debtor* in such cases, even though it is somewhat incomplete, inaccurate, and nondescriptive.

7. This is the date on which the debtor will begin performing its plan obligations, and is usually set at 30 days from the date the court approves the plan. This gives the debtor time to prepare to perform the plan, taking into account any last-minute changes in the plan resulting from the confirmation process.

B. In a Chapter 11, companies have a greater likelihood of success in restructuring the company than they have in an out-of-court workout.
C. In a Chapter 11, the debtor gets the benefit of the automatic stay.
D. In a Chapter 11, the debtor can sell assets free and clear of liens and claims.

ANALYSIS. In this chapter, many of the advantages noted in this question have been discussed. The question is tricky, however, because it is written in the negative and is thus more difficult to read and follow. It asks you to choose the statement that is not correct. **A** *is* correct. One of the biggest advantages of a Chapter 11 case over an informal workout is that the Chapter 11 debtor can cram down or force the plan on dissenting creditors. Conversely, the debtor in a workout cannot force any dissenting creditors to accept the terms of the workout. **C** is also true. The automatic stay is a tremendous benefit to all bankruptcy debtors. **D** is correct as well, as being able to sell assets free and clear of liens and claims increases the value of the assets (and thus the price), a topic covered in more detail in Chapter 33.

The incorrect statement is found in **B**; thus, **B** is the correct answer. While Chapter 11 has many advantages, it is not easy to succeed and confirm a plan. In fact, most Chapter 11 cases do not result in a confirmed plan, as meeting all of the requirements of Chapter 11 is very difficult. Thus, one cannot accurately say that companies have a greater likelihood of succeeding under Chapter 11 than under an out-of-court workout.

Martin's and Keating's Picks

1. Question 1 **A**
2. Question 2 **C**
3. Question 3 **C**
4. Question 4 **C**
5. Question 5 **B**
6. Question 6 **A**

The Closer **B**

32

Claims Against the Estate

OVERVIEW

A. Definition of a Claim

B. Administrative Claims Under Chapter 11

C. The §506(c) Surcharge

D. The Closer: Chapter 32

Martin's and Keating's Picks

Later in this guide, we will look at the ways in which secured claims and priority claims are treated under a Chapter 11 plan. The various protections provided to general unsecured creditors will also be examined. In this section, a few tricky issues dealing with bankruptcy claims as a whole will be briefly addressed. These questions address exactly when a claim arises and can thus be covered in a debtor's Chapter 11 plan. The protection provided to creditors who provide goods and services to the debtor during the post-petition period will also be discussed. As a result, this chapter has two sections: The first addresses what a claim is and when a claim arises, and the second deals with post-petition or administrative claims and how they are handled under the Bankruptcy Code. Another bankruptcy concept, the §506(c) surcharge against a secured party's collateral (which is actually a claim a *debtor* makes against a secured party's collateral), will also be briefly discussed.

A. Definition of a Claim

A *claim* is defined under §101(5) as a "right to payment, whether or not such right is reduced to judgment, liquidated, unliquidated, fixed, contingent, matured, un-matured, disputed, undisputed, legal, equitable, secured, or unsecured." (*See* 11 U.S.C. §101(5)(A).) The definition also includes any "right to an equitable remedy for breach of performance, if such breach gives rise to a right to payment, whether or not such right to an equitable remedy is reduced to judgment, fixed, contingent, matured, unmatured, disputed, undisputed, secured or unsecured." (*See* 11 U.S.C. §101(5)(B).) By now, you might be getting the picture. A claim is defined in the broadest possible way under the Bankruptcy Code.

Debtors want as many obligations to fit within the definition of "claim" as possible. This is because claims can be addressed in a Chapter 11 plan, whereas rights of action that have not yet risen to the level of claims must be dealt with outside the plan, and usually must be paid in full. Most of the time, you can tell whether a claim can be included in a bankruptcy plan (and paid a percentage distribution) by determining whether the events that led to the claim occurred pre- or post-petition.

Using a simple example, assume a man is walking around in Kmart and falls down. No lawsuit has been filed. The next day, Kmart files for bankruptcy. There is no question that even though you don't know the amount, and you don't know whether Kmart is liable, the gentleman who fell down has a claim against Kmart. The action giving rise to the claim clearly occurred prepetition, and although the claim is contingent and unliquidated, it is absolutely and unquestionably a claim in Kmart's bankruptcy. The potential tort victim would typically prefer that this *not* be a bankruptcy claim, because he could be paid in full from the reorganized debtor at a later time, after the claim is adjudicated. Kmart, on the other hand, would prefer that it *be* a claim, so that it can be discharged in connection with its bankruptcy case.

Let's try a trickier example. You own a business and plan to file for Chapter 11 or any other type of bankruptcy. Let's assume your mother guaranteed one of your debts. Pursuant to §502(e)(1)(B), your mother has a contingent claim for reimbursement or contribution based on her guarantee of your debt. There is a chance in this particular scenario that your mother will never have to pay your debt. Regardless of this, however, your mother holds a contingent claim in your bankruptcy assuming you file right now. She has a claim even though you don't know if she'll ever have to pay. Your mother is one of your creditors because she holds a claim in your case.[1]

Some of the toughest cases, in terms of deciding what obligations constitute claims in a bankruptcy and can thus be included in a Chapter 11 plan, involve future tort claims. But before getting to those, make sure you understand why a debtor cares about this. The debtor is hoping to include as many claims or obligations as possible in its bankruptcy, so that when it emerges from bankruptcy, those obligations are included in the Chapter 11 plan and otherwise discharged.

1. There will come a time, however, when a claim like this will need to become matured and entitled to payment, or will be disallowed. Under §502(e)(1)(B), if a contingent claim is still contingent at the time when claims are being allowed and disallowed (the time towards the end of a case at which claims process is being adjudicated), that contingent claim will be disallowed. This will allow the case to be finished and closed out.

Now consider the situations involving asbestos companies and A.H. Robins, the manufacturer of the Dalkon Shield, which caused many women to suffer injuries as a result of the faulty intrauterine birth control device. If A.H. Robins went into Chapter 11 to reorganize its affairs, its Chapter 11 case would be of little use if, after the case was filed, more claimants continued to surface claiming they were damaged by the Dalkon Shield. Given the extremely broad definition of *claim* in the Bankruptcy Code, many courts have found that if a debtor's pre-petition conduct led to the injury, regardless of when the injury is manifest, the resulting injuries, both current and future, constitute claims in the debtor's bankruptcy. Under a test known as the *conduct test*, these claims are pre-petition claims because the injuries resulted from the debtor's pre-petition conduct.

The law in the area of future claims has developed over time, and courts have used several different tests to define the outer limits of a bankruptcy claim. Some courts use a test based on when a claim arises under state law to determine whether a claim has arisen pre-petition. One of these tests requires that the claimant and debtor must have had a pre-petition contract or privity from which the claim arises for a resulting claim to be a pre-petition claim. This is called the *relationship test*. Under this test, a claim by an operator of a forklift manufactured pre-petition but purchased by the claimant's employer post-petition was not considered a pre-petition claim. Using the same test, a claim by the Environmental Protection Agency for environmental cleanup costs that would not be incurred until after confirmation (in other words, would be incurred post-petition, even though the contamination started pre-petition) was held to be a pre-petition claim based on the relationship between the environmental regulating agencies and the parties subject to the regulation.

Another test the courts sometimes use to determine whether a claim is a pre- or post-petition claim is called the *fair contemplation test*. This test does not require that there be a pre-petition relationship between the debtor and the claimant, but instead that the pre-petition interaction between the two be within the *fair contemplation* of the parties at the time of the bankruptcy.

For example, in *Piper Aircraft*, the issue was whether a claim for a defective aircraft sold pre-petition was discharged in Piper's bankruptcy, when the defect causing a resulting plane crash did not even happen until long after the bankruptcy case was over. (*See* In re Piper Aircraft, 244 F.3d 1289 (11th Cir. 2001).) The court held that a claim arises when the conduct giving rise to the alleged liability occurred. The court adopted a hybrid of the *conduct test* and the *relationship test*, finding that in order for a claim to fit within the definition of claim found in §101(5), the events that caused the injury must occur pre-petition and must create some sort of relationship between the claimant and the debtor's product. The court further elaborated that this relationship must be with an identifiable claimant or group of claimants and that the basis for the claim must be the debtor's pre-petition conduct in designing, manufacturing, and selling the allegedly defective or dangerous product. In *Piper Aircraft*, the court therefore found that the claim could not have been discharged in Piper's bankruptcy because there was no identifiable group of claimants, because it was impossible to predict at the time of confirmation of the plan who the future claimants (purchasers of these aircraft and their passengers) would be. In other words, there was no way to know not only who these parties would be, but which planes would crash. The claimants were not ascertainable or identifiable at the time of Piper Aircraft's bankruptcy.

In the *Johns-Manville* case, the landmark asbestos case, the court came to the opposite conclusion, holding that asbestos claims were pre-petition claims because the asbestos causing the injuries was manufactured pre-petition, even though some of the individuals who later suffered from mesothelioma and asbestosis did not have any symptoms at the time of the Manville bankruptcy. (*See* In re Joint Eastern & Southern District Asbestos Litigation, 129 B.R. 710 (Bankr. E.D.N.Y. 1991).) This clearly stretches the notion of what constitutes a claim, but is an excellent example of how far courts are willing to go to fit claims within a Chapter 11 plan.[2] In many other asbestos cases, courts have controversially found that a person who comes down with mesothelioma or with asbestosis years after one of the asbestos companies filed for bankruptcy has lost his or her ability to object to the debtor's bankruptcy. The court found these to be pre-petition claims because the debtor created a channeling trust in its Chapter 11 plan, from which future claimants could recover part of their claims. None of these claims are ever paid in full, and these future claimants are provided with due process in the Chapter 11 case through a future claimant's representative. Whether this constitutes real due process or not is a question with which courts have struggled.

Congress enacted §524(g) to deal explicitly with future asbestos claims. This provision of the Bankruptcy Code provides that a court may enjoin future claimants from pursuing the assets of a debtor who has already been through bankruptcy, as long as the debtor forms a trust pursuant to its plan of reorganization that assumes the liabilities of the debtor for these personal injury, wrongful death, or property damage actions resulting from the manufacture of asbestos. The debtor must also fund this part of the plan with some of the equity in the debtor company and fulfill certain other obligations as well. (*See* 11 U.S.C. §524(g).)

QUESTION 1. Debtor Corporation ("Debtor") is a whiskey manufacturer. One of Debtor's whiskey brands, Killer Buzz, had a defective batch that turned out to be poisonous. That batch of Killer Buzz could cause death or serious injury to any consumer who drank it.

2. In a similar case, called the *Edge* case, a court held that malpractice that occurred by a dentist pre-petition — but did not manifest itself until the post-petition period — was also a pre-petition claim and consequently could be covered under a Chapter 11 plan and otherwise discharged. (*See* In re Edge, 60 B.R. 690 (Bankr. M.D. Tenn. 1986).)

Most of that batch has been successfully recalled from stores. Debtor no longer manufactures Killer Buzz, but some of that brand is still in the hands of consumers who have not yet consumed it. Debtor has faced millions of dollars in lawsuits based on Killer Buzz deaths and injuries, and now Debtor has filed Chapter 11 in order to reorganize and put the Killer Buzz problems behind it. Buyer purchased a bottle of Killer Buzz from a friend after Debtor's bankruptcy filing but before confirmation of Debtor's Chapter 11 plan. Buyer has not yet consumed any of the Killer Buzz in his possession. Under which of the following tests for claims would Buyer have a claim in Debtor's Chapter 11 bankruptcy at this point: the Conduct Test ("Conduct"), the Relationship Test ("Relationship"), or the Fair Contemplation Test ("Fair Contemplation")?

A. Conduct only
B. Relationship only
C. Fair Contemplation only
D. Both Conduct and Fair Contemplation

ANALYSIS. **A** is the correct answer. Buyer has no pre-petition relationship with Debtor because Buyer did not buy the Killer Buzz whiskey until the post-petition, pre-confirmation period. That means that Buyer would not qualify as a claimant in Debtor's bankruptcy under the Relationship Test. So **B** cannot be the right answer. Similarly, there was no reason prior to Debtor's bankruptcy filing for Debtor to think that Buyer would be buying Debtor's whiskey from this third party (or from anyone) in the post-petition world. That would indicate that there is no claim here under the Fair Contemplation Test, which means that we need to eliminate both **C** and **D**. To the extent that Buyer will eventually suffer harm from drinking this whiskey (or even if Buyer learns of the problem before drinking the whiskey and thus suffers only economic harm by paying good money for worthless whiskey), all of that harm or economic damage is due to Debtor's pre-petition conduct in manufacturing the defective whiskey. So that would qualify Buyer as a claimant in Debtor's bankruptcy under the Conduct Test, which is why **A** is correct.

B. Administrative Claims Under Chapter 11

The difference between pre-petition claims and post-petition claims becomes preeminent when determining what claims constitute administrative expenses in a Chapter 11 case. Administrative expenses are the highest priority among the general unsecured creditors. They are paid ahead of all other priority claims, including wage claims, tax claims, claims resulting from a marital settlement agreement, and so on, as well as all general unsecured claims.

Pursuant to §§503(b) and 507(a), administrative claims include many claims that arose during the post-petition period, including fees for the debtor's attorneys, accountants, other professionals, and for the unsecured creditors' committee's professionals. (*See* 11 U.S.C. §§503(b), 507(a).)

Administrative claims entitled to priority pursuant to §§503(b) and 507(a)(2) also include all post-petition claims for goods and services rendered to the debtor or the debtor's estate during the Chapter 11 case. This continues the theme that was previously discussed, that once a bankruptcy is filed, the debtor is fully responsible for all obligations incurred post-petition. This concept is easy to understand when dealing with suppliers who supply goods to the debtor post-petition, as well as utilities, which provide services to the debtor post-petition. All of these claims are *first priority administrative claims* (*see* §§503(b) and 507(a)(2)), and must be paid either in the regular course of the debtor's business or in full on the effective date of the debtor's Chapter 11 plan. In other words, these claims must be paid in 100-cent dollars. The reasons for this are quite clear. People providing post-petition goods and services to a Chapter 11 debtor must be assured of payment to encourage them to participate in the reorganization process. (*See* 11 U.S.C. §503(b).) Moreover, the debtor is responsible for all expenses it incurs after the case is filed, none of which can be paid a discounted distribution.

Soon you will be learning about the debtor's right to assume or reject executory contracts and unexpired leases (*see* Chapter 33). If the debtor rejects an executory contract, or unexpired lease (meaning the debtor decides not to comply with it), then normally the resulting claim becomes a general unsecured claim and is paid along with other general unsecured creditors. (*See* 11 U.S.C. §502(g).) If the debtor instead decides to assume the executory contract or unexpired lease, the assumed contract becomes a post-petition obligation and all of the obligations due under the contract (irrespective of the fact that the contract was originally entered into pre-petition) become first priority administrative expenses in the debtor's bankruptcy. (*See* 11 U.S.C. §503(b).) Because the decision to assume a contract affects the potential distribution not only to all general unsecured creditors but also to priority claimants, the debtor must obtain court approval to assume a contract or lease. (*See* 11 U.S.C. §365(a).) The court pays particular attention to any claim the debtor incurs post-petition to ensure that taking on these obligations does not unfairly interfere with the rights of other creditors.

QUESTION 2. Best Eastern Hotel ("Debtor") is a single-building hotel corporation that files Chapter 11 bankruptcy. In order to save money during its Chapter 11 bankruptcy, Debtor decides to postpone replacing its fire-protection sprinkler system after learning during the Chapter 11 case that the system is no longer working. Unfortunately, there is a fire at the hotel during the post-petition, pre-confirmation period that ends up causing $50,000 in damage to Big Boy's Burgers ("Big Boy's"), an adjacent fast-food restaurant. Assume that Big Boy's will be able to demonstrate that Debtor's negligence in failing to replace the sprinkler system proximately caused the damage to the restaurant property. Will Big Boy's have a claim for the $50,000 in Debtor's bankruptcy case?

A. Yes, it will be a nonpriority unsecured claim.
B. Yes, it will be an administrative expense priority claim.
C. No, because as of Debtor's bankruptcy filing, Big Boy's did not have a claim against Debtor under any of the various tests for claims.
D. No, because these damages caused by Debtor would not qualify as "actual, necessary costs and expenses of preserving the estate" and thus would not be administrative expenses under the Bankruptcy Code's definition.

ANALYSIS. The facts of this question are based loosely on the facts of a famous pre-Code Supreme Court case, Reading Company v. Brown.[3] In that case, just like in this question, the debtor-in-possession negligently caused a fire that damaged a neighbor's property. The issue in the case was whether the damage claim would be an administrative expense priority claim or just a general unsecured claim against the debtor's bankruptcy estate. The Court held that tort obligations of the debtor-in-possession should be treated just like contractual obligations assumed by the debtor-in-possession. Therefore, the Court said, the tort victim's claim should enjoy the same special priority status as any other administrative claim. The correct answer, then, is **B**.

You might be wondering at this point why a Chapter 11 debtor's post-petition, pre-confirmation tort liability should be considered "actual, necessary costs and expenses of preserving the estate" under §503(b)(1)(A). This only starts to make sense if you consider the perverse incentives that the debtor would have if such post-petition, pre-confirmation tort liability were only given the status of a nonpriority unsecured claim. If a Chapter 11 debtor-in-possession knows that its liability for negligence as a debtor-in-possession can be paid in the proverbial 10-cent bankruptcy dollars, then why should the debtor-in-possession spend 100-cent dollars on the necessary precautions to avoid such liability?

To put this in terms of the facts of our question here, why should the debtor spend the money to avoid potential tort liability to third parties when the debtor's estate would not be fully responsible for such liability? In this case, the debtor arguably has self-interested reasons to fix the sprinkler system (namely, to protect its own property), but sometimes the only potential cost that a debtor avoids by spending money on safety precautions is damages

3. 361 U.S. 471 (1968).

that it will owe to third parties that will be harmed if the debtor fails to invest in appropriate safety measures. By assigning administrative expense priority status to negligence claims against the debtor-in-possession, bankruptcy law tries to give debtors-in-possession the proper incentives to spend an appropriate amount of money on safety precautions. If debtors only had to pay "10-cent dollars" for its post-petition, pre-confirmation tort liability, then debtors in Chapter 11 would have perverse incentives to under-invest in safety precautions.

C. The §506(c) Surcharge

In previous parts of this guide, you learned that secured claims are far superior to any other type of claim in bankruptcy, including administrative claims and other claims entitled to priority. As a general rule, secured parties have their collateral to back up their claims and, if there is no equity in that collateral and the collateral is not needed in the debtor's reorganization or if the creditor is not adequately protected, a creditor can obtain relief from the automatic stay to foreclose or repossess its collateral and sell the collateral in satisfaction of its claims. (*See* 11 U.S.C. §362(d)(1) and (2).) You also might recall that over-secured creditors are generally entitled to interest at their contract rate during the post-petition period as well as attorneys' fees under their contract, which is not true of unsecured or undersecured creditors. (*See* 11 U.S.C. §506(b).)

There is a slight exception to both of these rules contained in §506(c) of the Bankruptcy Code. Specifically, §506(c) provides that "the trustee [and thus the debtor-in-possession] may recover from property securing an allowed secured claim, the reasonable, necessary costs and expenses of preserving, or disposing of, such property to the extent of any benefit to the holder of such claims." (*See* 11 U.S.C. §506(c).) This provision is known as the *§506(c) surcharge* provision. It allows the debtor to recover some costs of preserving or selling a secured party's collateral. This is quite radical, given that it has been assumed up to this point that the secured party's collateral is held solely for the secured party, at least until the secured claim is paid in full. When a secured party's collateral is surcharged, however, the secured creditor may not receive payment in full, even though the collateral's proceeds may actually cover the claim. This is because the debtor may be permitted to recover some costs, typically direct costs of sale, before payment to the secured party.

The easiest way to understand what the §506(c) surcharge might cover is to imagine that the trustee or debtor-in-possession sold some of a secured party's collateral and paid for the costs of sale. The trustee or debtor-in-possession is permitted (with court approval) to pay the costs of sale out of the secured party's collateral and then remit the net proceeds to the secured party. This example assumes that the secured party has consented to the sale and is thus the cleanest example of a surcharge that would be allowed by the court. The test for whether a surcharge is permitted is whether the expenses incurred by the debtor-in-possession or the trustee post-petition (1) are necessary; (2) are reasonable; (3) incurred primarily for the benefit of the secured creditor; and (4) resulted in a quantifiable direct benefit to the secured creditor. Thus, a surcharge won't work in every case.

In one case, a debtor-in-possession attempted to surcharge a bank's collateral to pay the debtor's attorneys and marketing commissions. The court found that these services were not necessary or reasonable if they conferred no direct benefit on the secured creditors in the case. (*See* In re Competent Impressions, Common, Ltd., 217 F.3d 1256 (9th Cir. 2000).) In another case, Westwood Plaza, 192 B.R. 693 (E.D. Texas 1996), the court held that the Housing and Urban Development Commission (HUD) could not be surcharged for the cost of operating an apartment complex, even though HUD would receive substantially more under the plan than if the apartment complex were liquidated. The court found that the debtor incurred the expenses directly and primarily to assist the debtor to reorganize and to maintain ownership of the apartment complex. Thus, the court found the benefit to HUD to be only incidental.

Conversely, in another case, Lunan Family Restaurants, L.P., 192 B.R. 173 (Bankr. N.D. Ill. 1996), the debtor operated a number of restaurants and assumed some leases and cured some pre-petition arrearages. At the end of the day, all of the restaurants were sold with the net sales proceeds paid to the lender who held a security interest in most of the debtor's assets. The Chapter 11 case was filed as an alternative to liquidation with the encouragement of the lender. The liquidation value of the leased restaurants outside of Chapter 11 was zero because the debtor could not cure the pre-petition lease defaults in the Chapter 11 case. The lender cooperated in the Chapter 11 and ultimately the court surcharged the creditor with the labor and utility costs of operating the restaurant, to the extent of the direct benefit to the creditor.

If you reread that last phrase, however, you'll see that the rabbit is in the hat. It's unclear what the parties' original intentions were, but it is quite clear that, at the end of the day, the bank received all of the liquidation proceeds. Thus, the court held that the bank received all of the benefits of the sale and the bankruptcy case as a whole. Perhaps the lender could have argued that it would have been faster and just as profitable to simply liquidate the debtor in the beginning. The court ultimately rejected the lender's argument that only costs necessary for the physical maintenance of the collateral could be surcharged to the lender. The court did not permit the lender to be surcharged for the more general costs of the reorganization, however, as these costs did not directly keep the restaurant running. These disallowed costs included the debtor's costs of preparing its tax return, its home office rents, and its general payables.

QUESTION 3. The best way for the secured party to ensure that it will not be surcharged for costs incurred by a bankruptcy estate in which it holds a claim is to:

A. make sure it has plenty of collateral for every loan, as the claims of oversecured creditors cannot be surcharged by the estate.
B. move for relief from the automatic stay early and often and make it crystal clear to the court that the lender does not consent to the reorganization on the first day of the case.
C. refuse to allow the debtor to sell any of the lender's collateral, and ask to lift the stay to sell it itself.
D. tell the court explicitly at the outset that you object to any future surcharges.

ANALYSIS. First, it is unlikely that a secured party's sole goal will be to avoid a §506(c) surcharge, but as these facts are given by the problem, you need to answer the question asked. **B** and **C** are the two best answers, and you will eventually pick between the two. The other two answers are worth discussing, however. **D** is the least helpful suggestion here, as there is no reason to randomly lodge an objection to future surcharges in the beginning of a case. There will be no context for such a protest. The court hears motions, complaints, and applications, but not general thoughts. Moreover, until such a surcharge is actually requested, the court does not know whether the facts supporting a surcharge (benefit to the creditor and so on) are present. If the debtor-in-possession later benefits the creditor, a surcharge will be appropriate, even if the court previously felt that surcharge was inappropriate in the abstract.

Your instinct is correct, however, that it is important for the court to know that you oppose a surcharge. Thus, **B** is a correct answer because part of the reason that the creditor in *Lunan Family Restaurants* was surcharged is that the creditor went along with the reorganization process and did not object to it. So perhaps objecting to the entire reorganization would work for the creditor if the sole goal were to avoid a surcharge.

The answer in **B** is not as good as the one in **C**, however, because objecting to the entire case is simply overkill. It would be almost unheard of for a court to grant a surcharge unless the debtor has sold some of the creditor's collateral. It could be quite beneficial for the creditor to allow the debtor to sell the property, especially if it is sold pursuant to a competitive bidding procedure, but if the sole goal is to avoid a surcharge, **C** is the best answer.

A is partially incorrect, but does contain some good advice in any event. Of course, it is always best for a secured creditor to have lots and lots of collateral, but circumstances change and even if this were true at the beginning of a loan, it is not always true later. The part of **A** that says that oversecured creditors cannot be surcharged is simply incorrect. Any secured party can be surcharged, whether the claim was previously oversecured or undersecured, but if the property is significantly oversecured, there may be sufficient value in the property to pay both the full secured claim and the costs of preservation and sale of the assets. In such a case, these costs would be regular administrative claims in the case, and be paid first after full satisfaction of the secured party's claims. Surcharging is only necessary when the sale proceeds do not cover both the costs of preservation and sale and the full secured claim.

D. The Closer: Chapter 32

The main reason why it matters whether a cause of action or liability constitutes a bankruptcy claim under §101(5) is that:

A. this knowledge allows a claimant to plan for the future.
B. this knowledge allows debtors to plan for the future.
C. this knowledge allows the judge to know what claims must be dealt with in the debtor's plan.
D. this allows the debtor to treat the claim in its Chapter 11 case, and pay a percentage of the claim rather than paying it in full.

ANALYSIS. **A**, **B**, and **C** are all true in one small sense: namely, that knowing whether a liability rises to the level of a bankruptcy claim allows all of the parties in the case to know what the liabilities are and plan for the future. This knowledge is dwarfed by the ramification described in **D**. Why does it matter? Because a claim is treated very differently than a liability that *arises* after a bankruptcy. A bankruptcy claim can be paid a distribution (a percentage of the full claim) rather than being paid in full. A bankruptcy claim can be paid in a Chapter 11 plan (again, in cents on the dollar and over time), after which the debtor can move on with its post-bankruptcy life, free of the liabilities that arose prior to its bankruptcy. For these reasons, a bankruptcy claim is worth less than a claim that arises post-petition. Thus, **D** is the correct answer, and that sums up the relevance of the topics in this chapter.

Martin's and Keating's Picks

1. Question 1	**A**
2. Question 2	**B**
3. Question 3	**C**
The Closer	**D**

33

Reshaping the Estate Through the Assumption or Rejection of Executory Contracts and Unexpired Leases Pursuant to §365, and Through Asset Sales Pursuant to §363

OVERVIEW

A. Assumption or Rejection of Executory Contracts and Unexpired Leases
   1. What are executory contracts and unexpired leases?
   2. Ipso facto clauses
   3. Rejection of executory contracts and unexpired leases
   4. Assumption of executory contracts and unexpired leases
   5. Assuming and assigning executory contracts and unexpired leases
      a. Adequate protection in shopping center leases

B. Sales of Assets Pursuant to §363(b) of the Code

C. The §363 Sales Process: Seeking Out Highest and Best Bids

D. Successor Liability and §363 Sales

E. The Closer: Chapter 33

Martin's and Keating's Picks

A. Assumption or Rejection of Executory Contracts and Unexpired Leases

The Bankruptcy Code contains an amazing benefit to debtors in dealing with contracts and leases (to which the debtor is a party) that have not expired or been legally terminated as of the bankruptcy filing. (*See* 11 U.S.C. §365.) In a nutshell, if a lease is unexpired or a contract is still executory (i.e., performance is still due by each party to the contract), then the debtor can choose whether to perform the contract (to *assume* the contract) or not perform the contract (to *reject* the contract). While the debtor is deciding, the other party (as well as the debtor) must continue to perform. Sometimes, the debtor can continue to stay in leased premises *after rejection*, at a reduced rental rate as well. Moreover, the debtor can sometimes *assign* a profitable lease to another tenant, even if the landlord objects to the type of business the assignee runs. (*See* 11 U.S.C. §365(f).) Very special rules apply to real estate leases, some of which must be assumed more quickly than other contracts and leases and which also are entitled to special protections in some cases. (*See* 11 U.S.C. §365(b)(3) and 365(d).)

Ultimately, if the debtor *assumes* a contract, the debtor agrees to perform into the future, just as if there had been no bankruptcy. If the debtor *rejects* a contract or lease, both sides will be freed from the obligations of the contract or lease, and the other party to the contract, the *nondebtor party*, will receive a general unsecured claim for its rejection damages. (*See* 11 U.S.C. §502(g).) As is the case with all general unsecured claims, the debtor is free to pay only a portion of this claim.

Those are some very basic principles, which we will now explore in greater detail. Executory contracts and unexpired leases are covered in excruciating detail in §365 of the Code. Given that a large portion of many businesses' wealth is now held in the form of contract and lease rights, this Code section has become quite complex. It has become nearly impossible to read in its entirety but, fortunately for us, many of the specific parts still make sense. Try not to get frustrated. This is the meat and potatoes of Chapter 11 practice. Now let's elaborate further on some of the concepts mentioned above.

1. *What are executory contracts and unexpired leases?*

Section 365 gives special rights to the debtor and the nondebtor party, but these rights only apply to leases that have not expired before the filing and to contracts that are still *executory*. Only contracts that are still *executory* can be assumed or rejected. If a contract is no longer executory, then there are two possibilities. First, the nondebtor party may simply be an unsecured creditor for whatever damages he or she may have incurred, meaning that the debtor need not do anything and the creditor must simply file a claim. This would be the case, for example, where the creditor has supplied goods to the debtor pre-petition and the debtor has not paid for them.

The second scenario involving a contract that is no longer executory is the flipside of the first one: namely, where the debtor has fully performed its obligations under the contract and is currently owed the return obligations from the nondebtor party. In this case, the debtor simply has an asset that is part of the estate, the asset being whatever return performance is still owed by the non-debtor party. To use a sales of goods example again, imagine now that the debtor is the seller and has delivered goods to the buyer pre-petition, but the buyer has not yet paid for the goods. The buyer's obligation to pay the debtor the price for these goods is an asset of the debtor's bankruptcy estate. Just like in our first example, there is a contract here, but it is no longer executory.

But what does it mean for a contract to be executory? Many decades ago, Professor Vern Countryman devised a now ubiquitous test for when a contract is executory. Professor Countryman defined a contract as executory and thus subject to possible assumption as follows:

> A contract under which the obligations of both the bankrupt and the counterparty to the contract are so far unperformed that the failure of either to complete performance would constitute a material breach excusing performance of the other.[1]

This test may seem obvious, but is quite complex in its application. The test requires that some performance be due by each party to the contract. While the performance by the debtor can be merely the payment of money, the other party must have something left to do.

QUESTION 1. Classy Cabinets just hammered the last nail in the display cabinets of the Purdy Consulting Firm, and sent Purdy its final bill. But Purdy has now gone bust and filed a Chapter 11 petition. Classy has requested that Purdy assume its contract to build the cabinets. Can the debtor do this?

A. No, because no further performance is due on the part of Classy.
B. No, because no further performance is due on the part of the debtor.
C. No, because the debtor would gain no financial benefit from assuming the contract.
D. Both A and C.

ANALYSIS. All are true except for **B**, making **D** the best answer. **B** is almost true. There is nothing further for the debtor to do here except pay for the work. Classy, however, does not have any future performance due. **A** is correct.

1. Vern Countryman, *Executory Contracts in Bankruptcy: Part I*, 57 Minn. L. Rev. 439, 460 (1973).

Given that all the debtor must do is pay, and that Classy has done all of its work, this contract is no longer executory. **C** also is true. The debtor will not be permitted to assume a contract that is of no financial benefit to it. Put another way, the debtor may not assume a contract if it would be better off financially if it rejected the contract. The debtor would surely be better off rejecting this because it will not have to pay Classy's claim in full, although it need not do so formally because the contract is no longer executory. Thus, the debtor will merely treat Classy's claim as a general unsecured claim, and thus the correct answer is **D**.

2. *Ipso facto clauses*

Once a debtor files for bankruptcy, the nondebtor party must honor an executory contract or unexpired lease to which the debtor is a party.[2] During the initial stages of the case, while the debtor is deciding whether to stay in the contract or be excused from it, the debtor also must honor the contract. The nondebtor party cannot get out of the contract because the debtor has now filed for bankruptcy and may be in financial difficulty. We saw an example of this when Kmart filed for bankruptcy and Martha Stewart attempted to get out of her contractual obligations due to the bankruptcy. As the rule goes, as long as Kmart continues to perform the contract post-petition, Kmart's bankruptcy is no excuse for Martha Stewart not to perform.

It is very common for contracts to provide that if one party files for bankruptcy or becomes insolvent, the other party can cancel the contract. Some clauses even provide that in such an event, the contract terminates automatically. For reasons that may be obvious to you by now (namely, preserving the debtor's assets for the benefit of the estate), the Bankruptcy Code invalidates all provisions that automatically terminate or allow termination upon bankruptcy or insolvency. Section 365(e) reads such provisions right out of the contract. (*See* 11 U.S.C. §365(e).) It is as if these clauses, known as *ipso facto* clauses, are not in the contract at all. Section 365(e) provides that even if there is a provision in an executory contract or unexpired lease providing that the contract or lease may be terminated or modified on insolvency or bankruptcy, these types of provisions are unenforceable. A contract or lease may not be terminated or modified based solely on the insolvency, bankruptcy, or financial condition of the debtor. (*See* 11 U.S.C. §365(e)(1).) The only exceptions to this rule are certain personal service contracts that the debtor wishes to assign to a third party (*see* 11 U.S.C. 365(e)(2)(A)), and contracts to make loans or extend other financial accommodations to the debtor.

2. While the debtor also must continue to perform, the point here is that the debtor's bankruptcy is no excuse for the nondebtor party to stop performing the contract.

QUESTION 2. Comfort Care Nursing Home has a contract with the state of Nebraska to provide services to the elderly, for which the state reimburses Comfort Care. The contract provides that if Comfort Care fails to have at least $500,000 in reserves, the contract may be terminated by the state. The contract also provides that if Comfort Care becomes insolvent or files a bankruptcy proceeding, the contract will automatically terminate. Comfort Care has just filed a Chapter 11 proceeding and the state claims that the contract can be terminated, based on either of these termination clauses. The debtor is behind on its reserves. The court has notified the parties that it intends to decide this issue based solely on the provisions of §365. How will the court rule?

A. The court will hold that the contract is not terminated because both clauses are improper ipso facto termination clauses.
B. The court will hold that the contract is terminated under the reserves clause, but not under the automatic filing clause.
C. The court will rule that either the reserves clause or the ipso facto clause could justify termination of the contract, and thus the court will hold that the contract is or can be terminated.
D. The court will hold that the contract is not terminated because both clauses are improper ipso facto termination clauses, unless the court finds that it is necessary to terminate the contract to protect the health and public safety of the citizens of the state of Nebraska.

ANALYSIS. **C** is easy to eliminate. The text clearly states that a contract provision that allows termination of a contract merely because the debtor is in bankruptcy is not enforceable. **C** states that either ground justifies terminating the contract, which is not true.

B and **D** contain essentially the same concept, namely that the reserves clause may be treated differently than the automatic termination clause because there may be a very good reason for making the debtor meet this financial requirement, one that might overrule the particular provisions of §365(e). Keep in mind that §365(e) provides clearly that any provision purporting to allow termination based solely on the financial condition of the debtor is unenforceable. If this is as far into the Code as the court is willing to look, both **B** and **D** are wrong as well, because the Code invalidates this clause as an ipso facto clause. Thus, **A** is the correct answer.

QUESTION 3. What other Code provision might potentially be useful to the state, assuming the court will look to other Code provisions as well?

A. Section 105(a), allowing the court to make any order that will further the goals of the Bankruptcy Code.

B. Section 365(c)(2), which provides that a party can terminate a contract for future financing. This is such a contract because the state pays Comfort Care for its services.
C. Section 362(b), by analogy or implication, which will allow the state to cancel the contract in order to protect the health and public welfare of the citizens of the state of Nebraska.
D. Section 1104, which allows the court to appoint a Chapter 11 trustee under these facts.

ANALYSIS. This is not an easy question, though some of the answers can be readily eliminated. **D** is the first one that we would eliminate because the mere fact that Comfort Care is behind or below its reserves does not suggest that the grounds for appointing a trustee (essentially fraud, severe wrongdoing, or showing that a trustee would be in the best interests of creditors) have been met. Nothing suggests to us that a trustee should be appointed here. **B** is also incorrect for a couple of reasons. First, the prior question stated that the judge is only willing to look at §365 and this question asks what *other* Code section might help the state. **B** uses §365 and thus is not *another* Code section. Moreover, this is not a financing contract merely because the state pays for the services that Comfort Care provides. To the contrary, the state pays Comfort Care after the services are rendered and thus, the state does not provide any credit to Comfort Care. Comfort Care provides credit to the state by providing the services first and billing for them later. Thus, the correct answer must be **A** or **C**. **A** relies on §105(a), which is usually used by the debtor. It is unlikely that a court would use §105(a) to terminate this contract. This would not further the purposes of the Bankruptcy Code. Thus, the correct answer is **C**. By analogy to §362(b), which allows state action to protect the health and public welfare of the citizens, the court may allow termination of the contract. There is a good chance that none of these will help the state, but if one would be more helpful than the others. We predict that **C** would be the one.

QUESTION 4. Locked and Loaded, an upscale hardware store, has just signed a new lease in a fancy shopping mall. The landlord offered $50,000 in tenant fit-up (remodeling, etc.) and the owners of Locked and Loaded are excited about putting in top-of-the-line fixtures and lighting to enhance their new image. The only trouble is that Locked and Loaded has been sued in a big product-liability suit and needs respite from this and other debts. It has decided to file for Chapter 11 to reorganize some debt, and also delay the litigation. Locked and Loaded figures it will have no difficulty succeeding in its new locale, as long as it can use the landlord's fit-up allowance to enhance its new image. What problem do you foresee for Locked and Loaded?

A. Locked and Loaded is not eligible for Chapter 11 because it is only filing to delay litigation and this would constitute a bad faith filing under §1129(a)(1).
B. Locked and Loaded will not be able to count on the landlord's fit-up allowance because it is a financial accommodation.
C. Locked and Loaded will not be able to confirm a plan.
D. Locked and Loaded will never get an impaired class to vote for the plan.

ANALYSIS. We do not have information sufficient to conclude that either of the conditions described in **C** or **D** are present and thus both are incorrect. We simply cannot tell from these scant facts if either of these is true. **A** is also incorrect. Delaying litigation is a perfectly acceptable reason to file Chapter 11. Many cases have been filed for this very reason and there is absolutely nothing wrong with it. Chapter 11 can be used for financial reasons, for strategic reasons, for policy reasons, or virtually any other reason the debtor chooses.

The correct answer is **B**. Forcing the landlord to honor the promise to give money to Locked and Loaded for new tenant fit-up, after the tenant has filed for bankruptcy, would be forcing the landlord to provide a financial accommodation to a debtor. Courts have refused to uphold similar fit-up promises under §365(e) because these arrangements qualify as financial accommodations. You can think of these fit-up payments as advances on the rent, similar to a loan. Thus, the correct answer is **B**.

QUESTION 5. (CODE READER) You Got Framed ("Debtor") is a painting studio that employs a single artist that specializes in painting portraits for high-net-worth individuals and local politicians. Debtor files Chapter 11 bankruptcy at a time when it has an outstanding contract to paint the portrait of the local town's mayor ("Mayor") for a fee of $20,000 that Debtor has not yet received. The portrait contract says that if either side files for bankruptcy, the contract is null and void. When Debtor files for bankruptcy, Debtor wishes to assume this portrait contract and assign it to another portrait artist across town, who is willing to do the portrait for just $15,000. That way, Debtor figures, it can bring in an additional $5,000 of value for the estate. If Mayor objects, will Debtor be allowed to assume and assign this contract?

A. Yes, because "ipso facto" clauses like the one included in this executory contract are not honored in bankruptcy.
B. Yes, as long as the new portrait artist has a good reputation in the local town.
C. No, unless Debtor can give adequate assurance of future performance by the other artist.
D. No, whether or not Debtor can give adequate assurance of future performance by the other artist.

ANALYSIS. Most "ipso facto" clauses like the one in this portrait contract are unenforceable in bankruptcy. That is why **A** is a tempting answer. However, §365(e)(2)(A) allows the enforcement of an ipso facto clause whenever the contract in question is one in which the promised performance is considered to be too personal to be freely assigned to anyone besides the original party to the contract. When the debtor is the lessee of a commercial lease, this exception would not apply because it normally will not matter to the lessor which party occupies the space and pays the rent. In this question, however, the debtor's promised performance is not to fulfill the obligations of a lessee. Instead, it is to paint a portrait.

Most courts outside of bankruptcy would say that the painting of a portrait is non-assignable because it is too personal to the artist who promised to paint. Therefore, **A** must be wrong. Nor is it enough, as suggested in **B**, that the new artist has a "good reputation" locally. Similarly, **C** is wrong because it would be virtually impossible to give "adequate assurance of future performance" when the future performance is not something fungible like the payment of money but instead painting a picture. That leaves us with **D** as the correct answer.

QUESTION 6. (CODE READER) Bank agrees to loan Debtor a total of $300,000 on an unsecured basis. The loan contract provides that Bank will loan Debtor $50,000 every four months for two consecutive years until all $300,000 has been disbursed. The loan contract also says that Bank's obligation to loan any additional money under the contract will end immediately if Debtor files bankruptcy (a so-called "ipso facto" clause). After the first four disbursements of $50,000, Debtor files bankruptcy. One month following Debtor's filing, the fifth $50,000 disbursement was supposed to be made to Debtor under the original terms of the contract. Will Bank still need to make that fifth disbursement?

A. No, and that would be true even if Bank did not include the "ipso facto" clause in its contract.

B. No, but only because Bank included the "ipso facto" clause in its contract.

C. Yes, because the clause in the contract that cancels Bank's obligation to loan the money is an "ipso facto" clause that is unenforceable in bankruptcy.

D. Yes, as long as the bankruptcy court provides "adequate protection" to Bank for that fifth scheduled disbursement.

ANALYSIS. This question is tricky because it effectively combines an exception with "an exception to the exception." The main exception here is that "ipso facto" clauses (clauses that automatically excuse a nondebtor party's contractual obligation by the mere fact of debtor filing bankruptcy) are not generally enforceable by a nondebtor party when the debtor files bankruptcy even though most other clauses in an executory contract will be enforceable against a debtor that chooses to assume such a contract. However, in this case the ipso facto clause does end up being enforceable (that's the "exception to the exception") because the obligation that the ipso facto clause is nullifying for the nondebtor party here is the obligation to loan more money to the debtor. Section 365(e)(2)(B) is clear that the debtor may not assume a contract in which the nondebtor party is making a loan or other financial accommodation to the debtor. That is why **A** is the correct answer here. Choice **B** is incorrect because even if Bank had not included the "ipso facto" clause in its loan agreement, Debtor would not have been able to assume that agreement for an additional loan disbursement once Debtor filed for bankruptcy. Choice **C** is wrong because it focuses only on the ipso facto clause exception and not the "exception to the exception" that is contained in §365(e)(2)(B). Choice **D** is incorrect because there is no "adequate protection" exception to the rule stated in §365(e)(2)(B).

3. *Rejection of executory contracts and unexpired leases*

Remember that any party to a contract or lease under state law (outside bankruptcy) can breach a contract or lease, as long as they pay the breach damages. Like all parties to contracts and leases, the debtor can choose whether to perform an executory contract or lease, or breach instead. If the debtor does not want to perform an executory contract or unexpired lease, it will simply move to reject the contract or lease. (*See* 11 U.S.C. §365(a).)

A debtor's decision to reject a contract or lease is covered by the business judgment rule. This is essentially the rule that you may have learned in Corporations class. Under the business judgment rule, officers and directors of the company (here the debtor) are free to use their own business judgment in making decisions about how to run the company. While that rule certainly doesn't apply to all activities of a debtor-in-possession, it does apply to a decision to reject a contract or lease. Moreover, there is really no defense to rejection. If the debtor chooses to reject, then the contract or lease is rejected.

In a sense, rejecting a contract or lease is the more conservative or cost-saving way to handle a contract or lease. You will see why in a moment. When a debtor rejects an executory contract or an unexpired lease, the nondebtor party to the lease or contract receives an unsecured claim for its rejection damages. (*See* 11 U.S.C. §502(g).) For most contracts, this claim is equal to the amount of damages that the creditor suffers as the result of the rejection. Damages for rejection of a real estate lease, however, are capped at the greater of one year's worth of rent under the lease *or* 15 percent of the remaining term rent (but never more than three years' worth of rent). (*See* 11 U.S.C. §502(b)(6)(A).)

QUESTION 7. (CODE READER) Yards of Yarn pays $1,000 a month for its Boca Raton lease, of which ten years remain in which to perform. Yards has just rejected its lease, three months into its Chapter 11 case. Under §502(b)(6)(A), what is the maximum amount that the landlord can file a claim for in the Yards Chapter 11 case?

A. $36,000.
B. $12,000.
C. $18,000.
D. None of the above.

ANALYSIS. Answer **A**, $36,000, represents three years' worth of rent. Answer **B** represents one year's worth of rent. Answer **C** represents 15 percent of the lease. So which is correct? Not **B**, because the landlord gets the *greater of* one year's rent or 15 percent of the remaining term (up to three years' rent). The total remaining is $120,000. Fifteen percent of this amount is $18,000, so the landlord gets the greater of $12,000 (one year's rent) or $18,000 (15 percent of the total rent remaining). Note that the $18,000 is still less than three years' rent, which is $36,000. Even if there were 99 years left on the lease, the landlord's claim would still be capped at $36,000. Thus, **C** is the answer.

QUESTION 8. Anheuser-Busch Brewing Company bought a superbox in Sullivan Stadium for $50,000 per year over five years and prepaid all $250,000 of rent under the contract. There are three years left on the contract. The stadium is now in Chapter 11 and has moved to reject the superbox contract with Anheuser-Busch so it can resell the box and thus raise $150,000 it would not otherwise have. Given just these facts, what should the court do?

A. The court should disallow the motion because the debtor is better off financially if it assumes the contract.
B. The court should grant the motion because the debtor believes it is better off if it rejects the contract.
C. The court should disallow the motion because Anheuser-Busch has fully paid for the box and is therefore entitled to use it.
D. The court should disallow the motion because the contract is no longer executory and Anheuser-Busch has no right to use the box anyway, due to Sullivan Stadium's bankruptcy.

ANALYSIS. This is a hard question because it is difficult to remember the reasons for, and the implications of, assumption and rejection. Just remember that a rejection motion is based on a financial decision of the debtor, and very little else. If the debtor feels it would be better off without a contract, then most of the time, the court will permit rejection. This situation is no exception to that general rule and thus the answer is **B**. Compare this answer to **A**, which says that the debtor would be better off assuming the contract. Besides the fact that the debtor generally gets to make its own business decision to reject and has done so here, statement **A** is also factually incorrect. If the debtor rejects this contract, Anheuser-Busch will no longer have use of the superbox for the last three years of its contract. Anheuser-Busch will have a rejection damages claim, which is an unsecured claim, for the $150,000 it paid for the period in which it is no longer able to use the box, on which it will probably be paid a percentage distribution rather than payment in full. The debtor will be able to raise $150,000 in new cash by reselling the box for those three years. Now that's a good deal. If the debtor assumes the contract with Anheuser-Busch, it will not raise the new $150,000. That is obviously not as good, financially.

What about **C**, which states that the court should disallow the motion because Anheuser-Busch has fully paid for the box and is therefore entitled to use it? This statement is not true. Anheuser-Busch does not have a right to continue using the box just because it already paid for it. The debtor can reject the contract and, if it does, Anheuser-Busch will lose its right to use the box. That is the whole point of rejection. If it would be financially favorable for the debtor to unload the contract, the debtor may do so. End of story (except that the nondebtor party will receive a claim in the debtor's bankruptcy). Bottom line: It is always risky to prepay for anything if there is a chance that the party who was paid will go into bankruptcy.

D states that the court should disallow the motion because the contract is no longer executory and Anheuser-Busch has no right to use the box anyway due to Sullivan Stadium's bankruptcy. This is also incorrect, but very tricky. It is not clear whether this contract is still executory or not, but it is very possible that it is not. The debtor has to provide the box, but what does Anheuser-Busch need to do? Use it? Buy concessions? If the debtor is unsure whether the contract is still executory, the debtor can move to reject as a precautionary matter. Whether it is executory and is rejected, or is just a claim, the other party's damages are the same: $150,000. If the contract is still executory, then Anheuser-Busch has the right to continue to use the box that it paid for, unless the debtor rejects the contract. There is nothing about the stadium's bankruptcy that automatically terminates the contract. **B** is still the correct answer. **D** says that the contract is not executory and that Anheuser-Busch still gets to use the box. This last part is clearly untrue, eliminating **D** from the possible choices, and leaving **B** as the correct answer.

4. *Assumption of executory contracts and unexpired leases*

Compared to rejection, a decision to *assume* a contract is a very serious matter in a Chapter 11. When the debtor decides to assume an executory contract or an unexpired lease, the debtor is essentially assuming an obligation to pay or perform the entire contract or lease as it was originally written. Moreover, because assumption of the contract or lease occurs post-petition and the promise to continue performing the contract is made post-petition, if the debtor later liquidates, all of the obligations under the contract become administrative claims with first priority in the case. (*See* 11 U.S.C. §503(b).) These claims must be paid in full in the debtor's plan, which reduces what is available for other creditors.

For these reasons, the business judgment rule does not apply in these assumption cases and the court carefully scrutinizes each and every decision made by the debtor to assume an executory contract or unexpired lease. Because the debtor has until confirmation to assume or reject most leases and contracts,[3] the court normally frowns upon attempts to assume contracts or leases prior to confirmation. The court wants to know exactly what the debtor's reorganization plan is before allowing the debtor to incur extensive post-petition expenses (that could become administrative expenses in the case and, consequently, must be paid in full).

What is the standard for assuming an executory contract or unexpired lease? The debtor is free to assume any contract that is not in default as long as the court will approve the assumption. If the contract or lease is in default, however, the Code contains additional limitations on assumption. The debtor can assume a contract or lease only if the debtor can provide the landlord or other party with adequate assurance of future performance and can show that it can promptly cure any existing defaults under the contract or lease. (*See* 11 U.S.C. §365(b)(1).) Although the nondebtor party has a bit more say in whether the assumption will be permitted, if the debtor meets these tests, the court will allow assumption even over the nondebtor party's objection. Most disputes revolve around whether the debtor can provide adequate assurance of future performance, which is a test designed to protect the nondebtor party and the estate from future defaults under the lease or contract. While the test sounds complex, it basically boils down to determining whether the debtor can make future payments and otherwise perform the contract or lease. (*See* In re Superior Toy & Manufacturing Co., 78 F.3d 1169 (7th Cir. 1996).) This decision is very fact-based.

Under the old law, the deadline for a debtor to decide whether to assume or reject a commercial real estate lease could be extended past the 60 days automatically granted by the court. In fact, many courts allowed debtors to extend this deadline until confirmation of the plan, which essentially is the end of the case.

Under the post-2005 §365(d)(4), the court cannot extend this deadline beyond an initial 120 days from the filing date, and an additional 90 days, for

---

3. The debtor has only 60 days to assume or reject a real estate lease; otherwise, the lease is automatically rejected. This particular provision resulted from a very strong lobby on the part of real estate owners and brokers in drafting the Bankruptcy Code.

a total of approximately 7 months. This could be too short a time for a large retail debtor to decide which premises to give up and which to keep.

QUESTION 9. The debtor, a financial consulting firm, is party to two office leases, one for its main office in King of Prussia, Pennsylvania, and another for a smaller office in Philadelphia. Soon after filing its Chapter 11 case, the debtor moved to assume each of these leases, and the court is considering the motion. Which fact most strongly suggests that at least one of these motions should be denied at this time?

A. The debtor has plenty of time before this decision must be made, as it is still the beginning of the case.
B. The debtor has not yet shown that it can make a profit.
C. The debtor has not yet established that each office is necessary to its ongoing operations.
D. The debtor may need both offices, as it may expand operations.

ANALYSIS. **D** is the easiest to eliminate because it does not answer the call of the question, which is why the motions might be denied. All of the rest of the answers are correct and would all suggest that one or both of the motions should be denied at this time. The question is, which of these reasons is *most* compelling if the motion is to be denied at this time? We find this to be a close call between **A** and **C**. While it would be best if the debtor were already making a profit, that is unlikely at the beginning of the case and not a direct issue in lease assumption, although it is relevant to whether the debtor should take on new administrative claims. No lease should be assumed if the space has not been proven necessary for the debtor's operations. In addition, assumption motions should be prolonged as long as possible so that the debtor can avoid making mistakes and taking on unnecessary obligations in the future. Because this is the beginning of the case, and the debtor still has some time to make this decision, **A** is the best justification for denying the motion at this time. True, the debtor only gets 60 days to decide what to do with a real estate lease, but even given this time frame, these motions are premature. (*See* 11 U.S.C. §365(d).)

5. *Assuming and assigning executory contracts and unexpired leases*

We talked about executory contracts and unexpired leases as if the debtor only had two options, assumption or rejection. In reality, there is also a third option offered in the Bankruptcy Code: The debtor can decide to assume a contract or lease and then assign that contract or lease to a third party. (*See* 11 U.S.C. §365(f).) The reason to do this is that the debtor may not need the lease or contract itself, but may be able to sell its interest in the lease or contract to a third party, thereby turning a potential liability (i.e., a rejection damages claim) into a valuable asset.

For example, assume that the debtor is the lessee in a ten-year lease for retail space for yearly rent of $10 per square foot on a 5,000-square-foot building.

Also, assume there are still six years left on the lease and that the rate for space of this kind has gone from $10 per square foot to $20 per square foot. If you do the math, you will see that the debtor can sell its tenant's interest in this lease for big bucks, essentially for the difference between what it pays for the space and what a third party would have to pay to get space of this kind on the open market. In this example, the debtor could assume the lease and assign its interest for approximately a $300,000 profit, the difference between the total rent due under the lease ($300,000), and the current market price for the space ($600,000). If that asset were being sold along with other assets, such as store fixtures, inventory goodwill, and so on, the proceeds the debtor might receive for the lease could be even higher. In situations in which the debtor intends to assume a lease and assign it, the debtor must prove adequate assurance of future performance. This adequate assurance is required every time the debtor assumes the lease, but for assumption and assignment, this is done by showing that the new tenant will be able to pay the rent into the future. Although the landlord does not have veto power over who the new tenant will be, the landlord can contest the new tenant's ability to provide adequate assurance. Sometimes the landlord will pay the difference in market value to the debtor to avoid losing control over deciding who the next tenant will be.

a. Adequate protection in shopping center leases Special rules apply when the lease in issue is a *shopping center lease*, particularly if the debtor plans to assume the lease and assign it to someone else. (*See* 11 U.S.C. §365(b)(3).) Shopping center lease legislation is more than just special-interest squawking. Tenants in a shopping center often depend on one another to survive, and also depend upon a certain tenant mix within the center. Shopping center leases often contain clauses limiting what each merchant can sell in order to avoid direct market competition. This is why you rarely find a Safeway Supermarket and an Albertson's Supermarket in the same shopping center.

The tricky question in connection with §365(b)(3) is what constitutes a shopping center. The determination is quite factual, and focuses on the interdependency of the tenants and the perceived intent of the landlord in developing a particular tenant mix. In conducting this analysis, courts consider whether these facts are present:

1. There is a combination of leases.
2. All leases are held by a single landlord.
3. All tenants are engaged in the commercial retail distribution of goods.
4. There is a common parking area.

5. The premises were purposefully developed as a shopping center.
6. There is a master lease in existence.
7. There are fixed hours during which all stores are to remain open.
8. The stores share in joint advertising.
9. There is interdependence among the tenants, evidenced by restrictive use provisions in their leases.
10. There are percentage-rent provisions in the leases.
11. Tenants have the right to terminate their leases if the anchor tenant terminates its lease.
12. The tenants participate in joint trash removal or other maintenance arrangements.
13. There is an existing tenant mix.
14. The stores are contiguous.[4]

The most significant of the preceding factors for a court to consider in deciding whether to allow a lease assignment within a shopping center is whether the new tenant will interfere with the tenant mix of the shopping center. In other words, the debtor, a former Home Depot, could not sell and assign its lease to a Wal-Mart, if there already was a Kmart in the shopping center.

QUESTION 10. Chow's Chinese Restaurant is located in one of those village-style retail centers that include restaurants, shops, walking malls, movie theaters, and so on. Chow's has just filed a Chapter 11 petition and plans to move out of the upscale center because the center does not meet its marketing needs. The center already has a Cheesecake Factory, a Spaghetti Factory, and a Baskin-Robbins. Chow's proposes to assume its lease and assign it at a profit to Pete's Pizza and Lemon Ice. Whether the landlord has a viable objection to this assignment because it is a shopping center depends on all of the following factors except:

A. whether there is a master lease.
B. whether stores and restaurants in the center share common advertising, parking, and hours.
C. whether the other tenants are currently paying higher-market rent for their premises.
D. whether there is an existing, planned tenant mix.

ANALYSIS. The question being asked is which of these factors is *not* relevant to whether this lease is in a shopping center. If the lease is in a shopping

4. *See* In re Joshua Slocum Ltd., 922 F.2d 1081, 1088 (3d Cir. 1990). As the court in *Joshua Slocum* stated, Congress' purposes in requiring such additional protections include (i) the avoidance of hardship to the landlord and other tenants caused by the vacancy or partial operation of a debtor's space in a shopping center; (ii) assurance that the landlord will continue to receive payments; and (iii) protection for the landlord and other tenants from substantial disruption of the tenant mix.

center, the debtor may not be permitted to assign its lease to a tenant that would compete with an existing tenant. Pete's could conceivably compete with both Baskin-Robbins and the Spaghetti Factory. If this is not a shopping center lease, the landlord has no right to object to the assignment based on tenant mix. This does not mean that the landlord won't have the right to object on other grounds. The debtor must provide adequate assurance of future performance and the landlord may have an objection on the grounds that the proposed assignee is not financially viable. This question, however, is about shopping center leases.

You need only look through the long list of *Joshua Slocum* factors to decide whether this is a shopping center lease. All of the answer choices are on the list except that found in choice **C**. The amount of rent that other tenants or even that the debtor is paying is not relevant to a determination of whether this is a shopping center lease. It is relevant to whether the debtor will choose to assign the lease, however, because if the debtor's own lease is below market, it can raise money by assigning that interest. This is not the question, however, so the correct answer here is **C**. Incidentally, the fact that the other tenants pay market rent and the debtor (and its assignee) need not would never be a legitimate objection to the debtor's assignment. The landlord made its financial deal and is now stuck with it (perhaps with a new tenant!).

B. Sales of Assets Pursuant to §363(b) of the Code

Generally, a trustee or debtor-in-possession may, with the court's approval,[5] sell property of the estate outside of the ordinary course of business. (*See* 11 U.S.C. §363(b).) This contrasts with the sale of property in the ordinary course of business, allowed under §363(c)(1), for which no court approval is required. Naturally, then, we are not talking about the everyday sale of inventory in this section, but rather about the sale of property that would ordinarily be kept and used by the debtor in its long-term operations. You can think of *§363(b) sales*, as these types of sales are often called, as a natural part of the downsizing process, though this need not be the reason for the debtor's sale. As you will see, sometimes the downsizing efforts are so pronounced that the debtor is attempting to sell its entire operation pursuant to a §363 sale, which is sometimes a problem because it circumvents the Chapter 11 plan process without

5. The exact language of the statute provides that the debtor may sell property outside the ordinary course of business after "notice and a hearing." This indicates that the debtor will file a motion with the court or an application to approve such a sale. An actual hearing is not required, as long as creditors have the right to a hearing if they object to the sale, but if there is no objection, the court can approve the application on the paperwork alone.

giving creditors as much information as they would get if a plan were actually proposed. (*See* 11 U.S.C. §363(b).)

As alluded to previously, the debtor can sell either some or all of its assets pursuant to §363(b). The debtor also can sell all of its assets pursuant to a court-approved Chapter 11 plan under a *liquidating plan*. While selling all the assets is not the model of Chapter 11 that we think of (we think of Chapter 11 as a process by which the company may remain operational, often with the same management), sales of all of a Chapter 11 debtor's assets have become more and more common. Some people even think that this is the most common way in which Chapter 11 is used today (i.e., not to rehabilitate in the traditional pay-over-time sense).[6]

If the property to be sold is encumbered with liens or other interests, a sale "free and clear of any interest in such property" may be permitted by the court after notice and a hearing,[7] provided that one of the five conditions found in §363(f)(1)-(5) is met. Before we get into the particulars, think about what this means in very practical terms. The debtor can sell property out from under the claims and liens of secured creditors and other creditors, with the claims and liens attaching instead to the proceeds of the sale. This avoids valuation and priority disputes that can delay the proceeding and cause the debtor to lose a once-in-a-lifetime chance to sell (at a great price) for the benefit of creditors. The ability to sell free and clear of claims — such as successor liability claims — allows the debtor, and thus the creditors, to get a much higher price for the assets than could be achieved outside of bankruptcy because the assets are cleansed from current and future liabilities that can reduce their value.

The debtor may sell assets free and clear of all liens and claims if applicable nonbankruptcy law would permit a sale of such property free of the interests (*see* 11 U.S.C. §363(f)(1)), and if the creditors holding such liens and claims consent to the sale. (*See* 11 U.S.C. §363(f)(2).) If the claim in question is a secured claim, the debtor may also sell free and clear of the secured creditor's lien, if the property's sale price exceeds "the aggregate value of all liens" on the property. (*See* 11 U.S.C. §363(f)(3).) Thus, the court can approve a sale over a secured party's objection so long as the property's sale price *exceeds* the aggregate value of all liens.

Although this sounds pretty simple, courts are divided about what it means. Does the "aggregate value of all liens" on a debtor's property mean the face value of the secured creditors' claims or does it mean the §506(a) value of those claims? Under the *economic value theory*, courts focus on the fair market value of the property or its stripdown value. Under the *face value theory*,

---

6. Some people have begun asking why debtors don't use Chapter 7 to liquidate, if this is the intention from the start. Is it because they do not feel that a trustee can best achieve good prices for the business? Is it because existing management believes that it can best operate the business while a good price is being sought? These questions do not have obvious answers. What is obvious, however, is that it is important to learn about Chapter 11 sales.

7. Again, for your purposes, this means *with* court approval.

courts instead focus on the amount of the claim secured by the liens. Most recent cases apply the *face value theory*, rather than the more debtor-friendly *economic value* theory.

Courts applying the *economic value theory* reason that the "value" required under §363(f)(3) is the same value that is set by §506(a), which sets an undersecured creditor's secured claim at the value of the collateral. In other words, §506(a) bases the value of a secured party's claim on the economic, or fair market, value of the collateral to determine whether a claim is secured or partially unsecured. Thus, under the *economic value theory*, a sale price that is less than the face amount of the secured creditors' claims could be approved, because §363(b) only requires that the sales price exceed the fair market value of the collateral, not the face value of the claim.

Courts that apply the face value theory, on the other hand, look to the plain language of §363(f)(3), as well as the legislative history, and conclude that Congress really did intend to permit a free and clear sale *only* when there is either consent, state law support, or where the sale price *exceeds* the face amount of a claim secured by a lien.

QUESTION 11. Using logic, which of these statements best supports the argument that the economic value theory is flawed?

A. Whenever the Code discusses value, it means economic value or the fair market value. It never means the face value of a claim, because that would be circular.

B. Focusing on the value of the collateral, under §506(a) parlance, is more consistent with the Code's overall rehabilitative policies.

C. The statute says that the sale price must *exceed* the aggregate value of all liens. Under the economic value theory, any time the sale price is less than the face value of a creditor's claim (which is the only time this theory is used), the value of the property does not *exceed* the aggregate value of the liens, but is instead just equal to the value of such liens.

D. In §506, Congress is talking about entire claims, bifurcation, oversecured, undersecured, and so on. Congress is not using this code section to merely value collateral.

ANALYSIS. Are you sure that you know the difference between the *economic value theory* and the *face value theory*? We are about to find out. Both **A** and **B** are arguments supporting the economic value theory, and the question asks you which of these best refutes the theory. Thus, **A** and **B** are both incorrect. Just so you know, **B** is a true statement, but it does not answer the question. The economic value theory is far more supportive of debtor rehabilitation, as it essentially forces the secured party to accept whatever sale price the debtor receives, assuming the sale is made subject to higher offers and there is adequate advertising and notice. Because the fair market value is determined by what a willing buyer is willing to pay a willing seller in the marketplace, every adequately noticed and advertised sale meets this test under §363(f)(3), making all of the other provisions of §363(f) unnecessary. Somehow this cannot be right. We are taught to construct legislation so that every part has *some* meaning, even if you can't tell exactly what that meaning is.

Both **C** and **D** are arguments *against* the economic value theory, which is what you are looking for, but **D** adds nothing in the logic department because it is circular. We wouldn't blame you too much if you chose this one, however, because many courts have heard this argument. Some have even accepted it! Even if you go back and read §363(f)(3), it is not easy to see that Congress means face value when it refers to aggregate value. While this language is not clear in the affirmative, this language cannot mean that *aggregate value* means *fair market value*. Why? A stripdown value, determined under §506(a), would *equal* the amount of the claim, but not exceed it, as the statute requires. (*See* WDH Howell, 298 B.R. 527, 533-34; *see, e.g.*, In re Canonigo, 276 B.R. 257, 263 (Bankr. N.D. Cal. 2002).) Because fair market value means the actual price realized in the actual sale, that price can never be greater than the value of the liens if it also *sets* the value of the liens. The statute requires that the sale price *exceed* the amount of the liens and this cannot be the case if we define the liens as equal to the size of the sale price. Thus, the answer is **C**. Ah, you have to love this statutory interpretation.

There are two additional statutory grounds that permit a debtor to sell assets free and clear of claims. Under §363(f)(4), property can be sold free and clear of liens and claims that are the subject of a bona fide dispute. To establish a bona fide dispute, the debtor must show that there is "an objective basis for either a factual or legal dispute as to the validity of the asserted interest." Thus, the debtor cannot simply say, "I disagree with the amount of that debt" and expect to then sell out from under the claim and the lien that secures it. Finally, under §363(f)(5), a debtor can sell free and clear of a lien or claim if the interested entity "could be compelled, in a legal or equitable proceeding, to accept a money satisfaction of such interest." Like §363(f)(3), courts have some difficulty construing this provision. If §363(f)(5) is read literally, this exception could swallow the rule. Any property could be sold free and clear of virtually any lien, rendering the other exceptions provided in §363(f) unnecessary. While courts agree that this could *not* have been the intended result of §363(f)(5), they do not agree as to what interpretation the section should be given. Some courts conclude that this section would permit a sale free and clear of a lien only if the lien-holder could be compelled to accept less than full payment for the lien under statutory or equitable law, and a few courts focus more closely on the word "equitable," considering whether equity would compel a sale. Absent one of the conditions described previously, a sale free and clear of liens or other interests may be precluded.[8]

C. The §363 Sales Process: Seeking Out Highest and Best Bids

In a §363 sale, the debtor's goal is to get the best price possible for the assets and maximize the return to a bankruptcy estate. The dollar amount of a bid is not the only factor used to determine what constitutes the highest and best offer, however. The trustee or debtor-in-possession has discretion to determine what constitutes the "highest and best" offer. (*See* In re After Six, Inc., 154 B.R. 876, 881 (Bankr. E.D. Pa. 1993).) Courts have recognized, particularly in connection with negotiated bids, that a lower bid can be accepted when it has other factors in its favor. Courts have upheld decisions to accept lower bids when legitimate business reasons existed to justify the acceptance of the lower bid, such as more favorable payment terms, shorter time frame to complete the sale, fewer contingencies, or doubt as to the ability of the highest bidder to complete the purchase. Thus, the highest bid is not always the "highest and best" bid.

In large sales, there is often a starting bid that is then subjected to the market through advertising and other means. The buyer making this first bid is often called the *stalking horse*. The debtor's hope, as well as the hope of all creditors, is that there will be a bidding war and the price will increase significantly from the stalking horse's original bid. The stalking horse often has incurred substantial costs in reviewing the debtor's business assets and making such a bid. As a result, it is not uncommon for the stalking horse to ask for various forms of bid protection in connection with its bid.

One common form of bid protection is called *overbid protection*, which requires that any higher bid be at least a certain amount higher than the first bid. Another form of bid protection is the *break-up fee*, a fee to be paid to the first bidder in the event that another bidder outbids the stalking horse for the assets. A court being asked to approve a break-up fee must decide whether the break-up fee is worth its cost and also whether the *overbid protection* is so

8. Moreover, when requested by an interested entity and required by a court, a debtor must provide adequate protection of that interest. (*See* 11 U.S.C. §363(e).) Although the term is interpreted flexibly, the Bankruptcy Code provides that "adequate protection" may be provided by: (i) requiring a trustee to make a cash payment or periodic cash payments; (ii) providing the interested party an additional or replacement lien; and (iii) providing the "indubitable equivalent" of the interest in another manner. (*See* 11 U.S.C. §361.) Further, the Bankruptcy Code requires additional and specific adequate protection when a party's interest in estate property is a lease of a shopping center property. Thus, a court's requirement for adequate protection will not always preclude a sale of property. Rather, the debtor-in-possession or trustee might be required to provide the party monetary compensation for its interest, or allow a security interest in the proceeds of the sale.

large that it will actually chill rather than encourage bidding.[9] A reasonable break-up fee would bear some relationship to the amount of time and money the stalking horse put into making its initial bid.

QUESTION 12. The debtor seeks to sell its manufacturing plant, together with its real property, to the person making the highest and best offer. The best offer so far is from Chessy Co. for $3 million. Chessy Co. had all of the assets appraised and hired an accountant to review the records of the debtor for the past seven years. Chessy Co. put down a $30,000 deposit.

The debtor plans to sell to Chessy Co. unless a better offer is made, and has offered the property to the general public on the same terms as to Chessy Co., except that Chessy Co. has requested a $75,000 break-up fee and overbid protection of 10 percent, which would mean that the next highest bid would need to be $3.3 million ($300,000 higher than Chessy Co.'s bid), or Chessy Co. would still be the successful buyer. Should the court approve this deal?

A. It should disapprove the outrageous overbid protection.
B. It should disapprove both the overbid protection and the break-up fee.
C. It should allow the overbid protection but disallow the break-up fee.
D. It should approve both as reasonable expenses needed to get the bidding going.

ANALYSIS. It is very hard to sell assets if there is no stalking horse, so it is difficult to say no to a stalking horse's requested bid protection. The overbid protection here, however, is way too big. It certainly will chill bidding, so the court should probably disallow it, or at least try to get the debtor to negotiate it downward. Understand that if Chessy Co. walks away, there may be no other bidders. Still, typical overbid protection would be 1 to 5 percent, something to compensate the stalking horse for putting its bid, and all its research, up for grabs. Ten percent is too high. The assets may be worth more than $3 million, and considering the economics of bankruptcy sales as they are, it isn't clear

---

9. Courts will look to the following factors to analyze the propriety of break-up fees: whether the fee requested correlates with a maximization of value to the debtor; whether the underlying agreement reflects an arm's-length transaction; whether the debtor's principal secured creditors and the official committee of unsecured creditors support the break-up fee; whether the unsecured creditors oppose the fee; whether the fee affects unsecured creditors in a substantial, adverse manner; whether the fee is a reasonable percentage of the proposed purchase price; whether the dollar amount of the fee is so large that it casts a chilling effect on other potential bidders; and whether safeguards are beneficial to the debtor's estate. (*See* Hupp Indus., 140 B.R. 191, 194 (Bankr. N.D. 1992); Bruce A. Markell, *The Case Against Breakup Fees in Bankruptcy*, 66 Am. Bankr. L.J. 349 (1992).)

that they are worth $300,000 more. It would be unreasonable for the court to approve a scheme under which, if someone bids $3.2 million for the assets, Chessy Co. should still be able to buy them for $3 million. This is the practical effect of the proposed bid protection.

Is the break-up fee also unreasonable? It's hard to say, because we do not know how much Chessy Co. spent on the appraisal and the accountant's due diligence. This $75,000 does not strike us as a huge number in the context of a $3 million sale. Thus, the best answer here is **A**. Although none of the answers is perfect, the court probably should disallow the overbid protection (or try to get the debtor to negotiate it down), but say yes to the break-up fee.

D. Successor Liability and §363 Sales

An obvious advantage of a §363 sale is that the buyer is assured that the assets are free from secured creditor liens and the claims of general unsecured creditors. (*See* 11 U.S.C. §363(f).) Although existing general unsecured creditors *have no* claims in specific property of the debtor, any time a person purchases assets from an ongoing operation, there is a possibility that these assets will cause injury in the future. Under successor liability, a successor-in-interest to a corporation may be liable for the product-liability claims and liabilities of its predecessor where, among other things, the sale is a consolidation, merger, or similar restructuring of the two corporations or the purchasing corporation is a "mere continuation" of the seller, or the new buyer continues the same product line. (*See* Fairchild Aircraft, Inc. v. Campbell (In re Fairchild Aircraft, Inc.), 184 B.R. 910, 920 (Bankr. W.D. Tex. 1995).)

The basic principle behind successor liability is that a claimant in a product-liability suit should not be unfairly deprived of a remedy just because one company has sold its assets to another and then gone out of business. Outside bankruptcy, successor liability claims are frequently and successfully asserted against purchasers who fall into one of the categories described earlier. Chapter 11 debtors, however, have generally been permitted to sell assets free of successor liability claims, through the authority set out in §363(f). Debtors have argued that successor liability claims create an "interest in property" that can be eliminated under §363(f), and that successor liability claimants can be "compelled, in a legal or equitable proceeding, to accept a money satisfaction of such interest." (*See* 11 U.S.C. §363(f)(5).) As tort claims are always paid through a money judgment, many courts have found this argument persuasive.

The big problem, of course, is due process. How can a claim resulting from an accident that has not even happened be a bankruptcy claim in a debtor's Chapter 11 case? Successor liability claims must be treated like any other claims against a debtor. If these really are bankruptcy claims, they must be treated in the bankruptcy case, which may result in the creation of some specific protection for the future claimant. If no such protection is created, the successor may be liable to the successor liability claimant.

QUESTION 13. What would be the best way for a debtor who manufactured airplanes to protect the buyer of its assets against future successor liability claims?

A. Place a sentence in the order approving the sale, stating that the assets are being sold free and clear of all successor liability claims.
B. Create a class of future claimants in the Chapter 11 plan, and set aside assets from which to pay future tort claimants.
C. Make sure all future claimants receive notice of the sale and, thus, an opportunity to object to the sale.
D. All of the above.

ANALYSIS. There is no way to be sure that future claims will not be asserted against the buyer of assets, but there are things that can be done to make it more likely that these future claims will not succeed. Why does the debtor care about this? If the purchaser feels somewhat protected against future claims, the purchaser presumably will be willing to pay more for the assets. Buying free and clear of successor liability claims is one of the big advantages for a purchaser that buys assets from a Chapter 11 debtor. But how is this protection best provided? The most effective step a debtor can take is to provide a remedy to future claimants. The debtor and the purchaser may not eliminate all legal remedies of a person who has not received notice that his or her future rights are being cut off. This would violate due process. Yet the debtor cannot give actual notice to future claimants because they are not yet ascertainable. They have not even been hurt yet! Thus, **C** is impractical. The language in the order mentioned in **A** would be nice, but is not as critical as the step described in **B**. The best thing the debtor can do is to set aside money to pay future claims in its Chapter 11 plan. Thus, the correct answer is **B**. This has been a very cursory treatment of this complex topic, about which many volumes have been written.

E. The Closer: Chapter 33

Mars Stores, a discount department store chain, is in Chapter 11 and considering its restructuring options. It operates 30 stores at the moment, some at a loss and a few at a profit. Its financial projections suggest that if it sold ten of the leases, it could raise $1 million from the assumption and assignment of these leases, and another $500,000 from the liquidation sale of the inventory in the ten closing stores. It believes it can make $2 million in profits from these same stores if it stays in business, a figure arrived at by averaging the net profits of all stores and multiplying by 10. Based on this data, the debtor has moved to assume, but not assign, the ten leases. As the judge in the case, which of these facts do you need to know to rule on this motion?

1. The actual profitability of the ten stores the debtor has chosen to assume here.
2. The overall profitability of all the debtor's stores, in the aggregate.
3. The retail value of the inventory of the ten stores in question and, also, whether the debtor could move the inventory to its other locations.
4. The debtor's realistic prospects for successfully reorganizing.

A. 1 and 4.
B. 1 only.
C. 1, 2, and 4, but not 3.
D. All of the choices.

ANALYSIS. To answer this question, you need to know what it means to assume but not assign the leases. (*See* 11 U.S.C. §365.) It essentially means that the debtor will remain in business at these stores and will not sell them. Given that this is the plan and that, as a result, the leases will become future obligations, the proof offered by the debtor is not what the doctor ordered. Who cares about the average profitability of the chain? What is important is how profitable these stores are, as compared to other stores. And why did the debtor pick these ten stores? Are these the most profitable? The least profitable? What are the plans with respect to the other 20 stores? The debtor must, at the very least, show that *these ten stores* are profitable. Thus, choice **1** must appear in the answer.

You also learned that the debtor cannot take on large post-petition obligations unless it has a good prospect of reorganizing. Thus, choice **4** also will appear in the answer. Choice **3** (that refers to the inventory) seems utterly irrelevant to the motion. The inventory is a small piece of all this, whether it is sold to the public or to another retailer for resale. This would be the subject of a §363 sale, which is not before the court at this time. Thus, **3** is not relevant. The tough call for us is **2**. Does the court need to know the overall profitability of the whole chain to rule on the motion? Technically, no, but we would still like to know why the debtor is choosing to assume these stores over other stores. Choice **2** also may be relevant to whether the debtor has a good prospect of reorganizing. We think this information is relevant enough to make **C**, choices **1, 2**, and **4**, the best answer. Others would disagree and say that the answer is **A**. If ten stores are profitable, then the debtor can assume those ten leases even if it doesn't know how the rest of the chain is doing. We think it is a very close call and a tough question.

Martin's and Keating's Picks

1. Question 1	**D**
2. Question 2	**A**
3. Question 3	**C**
4. Question 4	**B**
5. Question 5	**D**
6. Question 6	**A**
7. Question 7	**C**
8. Question 8	**B**
9. Question 9	**A**
10. Question 10	**C**
11. Question 11	**C**
12. Question 12	**A**
13. Question 13	**B**
The Closer	**C**

34

Introduction to the Plan and the Minimum Chapter 11 Plan Requirements

OVERVIEW

A. Introduction to the Chapter 11 Plan Process
   1. Consensual plans versus cramdown plans
   2. Basic Chapter 11 requirements
B. Priority Treatment Under Chapter 11
C. The Best Interest Test in Chapter 11: Treatment of General Unsecured Claims
D. Feasibility
E. Secured Creditor Treatment Under Chapter 11
   1. The treatment of oversecured and undersecured claims after the filing but before confirmation of a Chapter 11 plan
   2. Secured creditor treatment under the plan
F. The Closer: Chapter 34

Martin's and Keating's Picks

In this chapter, you will learn the basics of Chapter 11 plan confirmation. *Confirmation* is the process by which a debtor-in-possession gets a Chapter 11 plan approved by the court and moves on to its post-bankruptcy life. (*See* 11 U.S.C. §1129.) This chapter outlines the rules with which every Chapter 11 plan must comply, which include basic priority and secured creditor treatment, the good faith test, the best interest test, and the feasibility test. If the plan is consensual, meaning all classes of claims have voted in favor of the plan, this chapter contains all the applicable rules. (*See* 11 U.S.C. §1129(a).) If the plan is not consensual, however, meaning that at least one class has voted against the plan, the debtor must also comply with the rules set out in Chapter 36, for *cramdown* plans. (*See* 11 U.S.C. §1129(b).)

A. Introduction to the Chapter 11 Plan Process

The purpose of Chapter 11 is to allow some companies to stay in business and reorganize their affairs for the benefit of creditors, owners, employees, and other people who do business with the debtor rather than just liquidating the company. Chapter 11 is designed to be a consensual negotiated process. Ideally, creditors will negotiate the treatment they want with the debtor, who will then proceed to propose a plan that pleases as many creditors as possible. The system also recognizes that sometimes not all creditors will agree, and that it may still be best to approve such a plan, if the plan meets certain tests designed to protect the rights of creditors. All of the rules of Chapter 11 are designed to accomplish these competing goals, to allow the reorganization of debtors while at the same time protecting the rights of creditors.

The resulting rules are technical. There are many things to think about as a debtor prepares to draft and circulate a Chapter 11 plan. Long before the debtor drafts the plan, the debtor and its attorneys should attempt to negotiate the treatment that will be provided under the plan to the various creditors. Before starting the negotiations, the debtor will need to place all of the creditors into classes of claims. (*See* 11 U.S.C. §1122.) The classes will later be used to gather and count votes on the plan. Classification and voting are described in Chapter 35. The debtor hopes that all classes of claims will vote yes. The debtor will need at least two-thirds in amount and more than one-half in number in each class in order for the class to be an accepting class. (*See* 11 U.S.C. §1126(d).) If any class votes no, the debtor must comply with the cramdown rules in Chapter 36 as well. In any event, confirmation cannot be achieved at all unless there is at least one impaired accepting class. (*See* 11 U.S.C. §1129(a)(10).)

1. *Consensual plans versus cramdown plans*

If the debtor knows that at least one class will vote no, it is obvious that there will not be a *consensual plan*, and that instead, the debtor will need to *cram down* the plan. (*See* 11 U.S.C. §1129(b).) This is a new way to use the term *cram down* and in this context, the phrase means force the plan on a class of dissenting creditors. Thus, there are two general ways to get a plan through, either with consent (a *consensual plan*), or without consent (a *cramdown plan*). Even if only one class votes no, the debtor will be facing a *cramdown*, not a *consensual*, plan.[1]

1. Here is a brief overview of *cramdown* so you will know what is coming. In a *cramdown plan*, the debtor must meet all of those tests, plus a host of other tests, which explains why it is usually easier, cheaper, and far preferable for the debtor to propose confirmation of a consensual plan. If one of the dissenting classes is a class of secured creditors, the debtor must prove to the court that this class is receiving the present value of its secured claim (based on the value of the collateral under §506(a))

Why does it matter if the plan is consensual if the debtor can get the plan approved without creditors' consent? Is it worth the effort to try to get every class on board? Yes, indeed, for several reasons. First, the court will be much more hesitant to approve a plan that is not consensual for somewhat obvious reasons. In many countries around the world, creditors are the ones to decide if a debtor should be allowed to reorganize or instead be forced to liquidate. This is typically considered a choice for creditors, not the debtor, because the claims of creditors are higher in priority than the claims of equity (owners of the company) or management, which does not even have a recognized interest in the case. If creditors want the debtor liquidated, shouldn't it just be liquidated? If all creditors prefer that the company be liquidated, the answer is most likely yes. But sometimes creditors of different types disagree, and that is where *cramdown* plans come in. These are plans to which some creditors agree and others do not. The court can still approve these nonconsensual plans but only if the debtor meets even more tests, designed to protect all creditors.

2. *Basic Chapter 11 requirements*

In any Chapter 11 plan, the debtor must prove that the debtor proposed the plan in good faith and not by any means forbidden by law, a test similar to the Chapter 13 good faith test. (*See* 11 U.S.C. §1129(a)(1).) The debtor must also prove that the creditors of the debtor are receiving at least as much under the Chapter 11 plan as they would receive if the debtor were liquidated under Chapter 7. (*See* 11 U.S.C. §1129(a)(7).) Can you name that test? This is the same as one of the tests under Chapter 13 and is referred to as the *best interest*

---

over the life of the plan. This test is quite similar to the treatment that secured creditors receive in a Chapter 13 case. The length of the payments is not based upon a three-year or a five-year commitment, however, but on the useful life of the collateral. We'll learn more about this later. (*See* 11 U.S.C. §1129(b)(2)(B).) If the debtor proves that it is providing this treatment to a secured creditor, the plan can be forced on the secured creditor or, as they say, *crammed down* on the secured creditor. If the class being crammed down is a class of general unsecured creditors, the debtor must meet a test called the absolute priority test. This is something with which you have thus far had little experience. Section 1129(b)(2)(B) requires that equity (again, this means the owners of the debtor, the stockholders) cannot keep their ownership interest in the debtor unless every unsecured creditor class votes yes and thus consents to allowing equity to remain in place. What does this mean? It means that (1) the debtor must distribute equity to the creditors, essentially making one or more classes of creditors the new owners of the debtor; (2) the classes must all vote yes; or (3) the owners must pay for this equity by placing liquid funds into the debtor's estate, to be distributed under the plan, equal to the value of such interest. Even this is controversial and, as we will see in Chapter 36, the Supreme Court has held that the debtor's management must not have the exclusive right to buy the equity in the debtor. Instead, other parties also must have a chance to buy the ownership of the company in an auction or other market context, with the equity going to the highest bidder. The Code section itself states that, unless all creditors in a higher class vote yes, the "holder of an interest that is junior to the interest of such class will not receive or retain under the plan on account of such junior interest any property." This means that creditors have claims that are higher in priority than ownership or equity interests. Therefore, unless all creditors (including general unsecured creditors) are paid in full, equity cannot remain in place because this would allow equity (a junior class) to retain an interest in the debtor when a senior class remained unpaid. Confusing? A little, but we'll work on it. As you learn the rules, keep in mind that the system was designed to work best in a consensual situation, but that it also allows the debtor to confirm a plan when there are *holdout*, or nonconsenting, creditors.

test. This test requires the debtor to do what is called a liquidation analysis, pursuant to which the debtor figures out, based on the claims and the sales prices of its assets, exactly how much creditors would receive if it liquidated rather than reorganized. The debtor must show that the plan, as opposed to liquidation, is in the best interest of creditors. In any plan, consensual or not, the debtor must also pay *all priority claims in full*, usually on the effective date of its plan, some future date following court approval of the plan. The debtor must also prove that its plan is *feasible*, which means that the debtor must prove—based on cash flow projections of its future business as well as other financial data—that its plan is not likely to be followed by a liquidation or need for further reorganization of the debtor. (*See* 11 U.S.C. §1129(a)(11).) In plain English, this means that the financial data must show that the debtor can likely afford to pay the plan. These are the basic plan requirements, which will be elaborated upon shortly. Given their preeminence in almost all Chapter 11 cases, this chapter will finish with a general discussion of secured creditor treatment under Chapter 11.

B. Priority Treatment Under Chapter 11

You may recall that under Chapter 13, priority claims must be paid in full pursuant to the debtor's Chapter 13 plan. (*See* 11 U.S.C. §1322(a)(2).) In other words, while these claims can be paid at any time during the Chapter 13 case, they must be paid off in full by the time the debtor completes the plan. (*See id.*) In a Chapter 11 case, the rule with respect to priority claims is similar but also somewhat different. Before going over this treatment in Chapter 11, remember what the possible and likely priority claims are in a Chapter 11. To do this, you will need to get out your Code and turn to §507(a). If you do that, you will see that §507(a)(2) provides that all administrative expenses (including the debtor's and the creditors' committee's professional fees) under §503(b) get second priority.[2] You can skip the third priority provision.[3]

Chapter 11 plans must pay all claims entitled to priority under §507 in full. (*See* 11 U.S.C. §1129(a)(9).) Keep in mind as you go through these that §507 itself requires that all (a)(1) claims must be paid before the next

2. These administrative expenses used to be in the first priority position, and in most Chapter 11 cases, they still are. In the 2005 amendments, domestic support obligations were moved from seventh priority to first, and all other claims (that were previously senior to domestic support obligation) were reduced in priority by one position. This change does not affect corporate or partnership debtors (which would not owe domestic support obligations) but could affect individual debtors who file cases under Chapter 11.

3. This provision pertains to what are known as *gap* expenses, which arise in involuntary bankruptcy cases between the time the creditors file the bankruptcy petition against the debtor and the time the court enters an order placing the debtor into bankruptcy. These claims get priority to encourage creditors to continue to extend credit to the debtor during this time. Because involuntary bankruptcy cases are so rare, we will not spend any further time on this provision.

category, (a)(2) claims, are satisfied and so on. This makes little difference in a Chapter 11, as all must be satisfied by the plan. The fourth priority describes unsecured claims for contributions to wages earned within the 180 days prior to the filing, up to $12,850 per person. (*See* 11 U.S.C. §507(a)(4).) If a debtor was unable to obtain an order of the court allowing it to pay its pre-petition wages pursuant to its first-day motions, or if it was unable to time the filing so that such wages were paid before filing, then the debtor is likely to have claims in this fourth priority category. The fifth is for employee benefit plans earned within 180 days before the filing of the petition, up to $12,850 per person. (*See* 11 U.S.C. §507(a)(5).) A corporate debtor is likely to have claims in these fourth and fifth categories. The sixth category refers to unsecured claims of persons engaged in raising grain, as well as unsecured claims for fish or fish products. (*See* 11 U.S.C. §507(a)(6).) In all of our experience with Chapter 11, we've never had to pay a claim in this category. This is one of those funny categories of claims for which one group had a particularly strong lobby. Category Seven makes claims for customer deposits up to $2,850 entitled to priority. (*See* 11 U.S.C. §507(a)(7).) Claims in the eighth category are for taxes. (*See* 11 U.S.C. §507(a)(8).) We won't go through all of the different types of taxes now, but remember that some taxes get priority for only a short period of time, and others are always entitled to priority. You may notice that a corporate debtor is likely to have claims in any or all of these categories, except (perhaps) marital settlement obligations and that quirky category for fish and grains.

It is not clear why, but a practice has developed in some parts of the country where debtors' attorneys put all administrative priority claims, subject to second (usually actually first) priority under §507(a)(2) pursuant to §503(b), into a separate class of claims pursuant to the plan. In reality, it is not necessary to classify these claims because they remain (for the most part) unimpaired under the Bankruptcy Code.

Technically speaking, under the voting provisions of Chapter 11, which are contained in §1126 of the Code, only claims that are "impaired" are entitled to vote on a plan. Consequently, it is not necessary to classify these administrative claims, because the debtor is not permitted to impair these claims. Essentially, §1129(a)(9) requires that all administrative priority claims be paid in full, unless the holder of such a claim agrees to different treatment. The technical meaning of the word *impaired*, at least as applied to these administrative priority claims, is *not paid in full on the effective date of the plan*. Our own suspicion is that debtors classify these claims separately because they may be asking some creditors to agree to be paid over a longer period of time and, thus, to actually agree to be impaired under the plan.

The precise treatment that the debtor must provide to administrative priority claims pursuant to §§503(b) and 507(a) is different in a Chapter 11 than in a Chapter 13. (Compare 11 U.S.C. §§1129(a)(9) and 1322(a)(2).) Section 1129(a)(9) states that, unless a holder of a particular claim has agreed to different treatment, the plan must pay §§507(a)(1), 507(a)(2), 507(a)(3), 507(a)(4),

507(a)(5), 507(a)(6), and 507(a)(7) claims on the effective date of the plan. The effective date of the plan is a date after the confirmation hearing, on which the plan becomes operable. Debtors often designate the effective date as the date 30 days after confirmation. This 30-day period allows the debtor to prepare for the payment of claims under the plan, and also allows any appeal period to run.

As you can see, compared to Chapter 13, the debtor's attorneys' fees and the other professional fees in the case must be paid earlier in a Chapter 11 case. These claims must be paid on the effective date, unless the holder of these claims agrees to different treatment. In a Chapter 13 case, the debtor has the entire plan period to pay these claims. (*See* 11 U.S.C. §1322(a)(2).) As you might have guessed by now, the first-priority administrative claims under §503(b) consist mostly of these professional fees. Other creditors that are entitled to administrative treatment under the plan will include creditors that have provided goods and services to the debtor post-petition. Most of these creditors will be paid before the plan, in the ordinary course of business during the case, and thus, few of these will remain unpaid at plan time. Those that are still unpaid, however, will hold first-priority claims. (*See* 11 U.S.C. §503(a) and (b).)

Although all other types of administrative and priority claims must be paid in full on the effective date, unless the creditor agrees to other treatment, the debtor is permitted to treat priority tax claims differently. Under §1129(a)(9)(C), with respect to priority tax claims, all the debtor must do is provide the holders of allowed tax claims with "regular installment payments in cash . . . over a period ending not later than 5 years after the date of order for relief." This simply means that the debtor may pay the tax claims over time and with interest, but must have them paid in full within five years of the bankruptcy filing. Most debtors take advantage of this very beneficial provision. Be careful, though! Post-petition taxes, as compared to pre-petition priority taxes, do accrue interest if they are not paid regularly post-filing. We've seen more than a few debtors fail after confirmation because they did not keep post-petition taxes current. Ouch!

Because of these differences in treatment, it is generally advisable for the debtor to separately classify the tax claims because they can be treated differently from other administrative claims. As you might imagine, then, it is typical for the debtor to do so and the tax claims frequently constitute a separate class under a Chapter 11 plan. Even though these tax claims are separately classified under most plans, these claims are not considered impaired, a subject to be covered in Chapter 35. Thus, the holders of these claims do not vote on the plan.

Two new requirements were added by the 2005 amendments for individual debtors filing under Chapter 11. (*See* 11 U.S.C. §1129(a)(14-15).)[4] Finally,

---

4. 11 U.S.C. §1129(a)(15) creates an apparently unintended consequence. It allows the individual debtor to pay the entire Chapter 11 plan with a sum equal to his or her disposable income. This was previously forbidden by the absolute priority rule contained in 11 U.S.C. §1129(b)(2)(B) and discussed in Chapter 35 of this guide.

all transfers of property under the plan must comply with nonbankruptcy law. For example, debtors must comply with state laws that govern the transfer of assets from a nonprofit corporation to a for-profit corporation.

QUESTION 1. After negotiation of a plan of reorganization, Harold's House of Carpets ("Harold's") owes $100,000 in attorneys' fees, $45,000 in employee claims ($15,000 each for three employees, all earned within 90 days of filing), and $100,000 in income taxes ($20,000 a year for the past five years). How much must Harold's come up with in cash on the effective date of the plan to satisfy priority claims?

A. $100,000 in attorneys' fees, $45,000 for employee claims, plus one-fifth of the taxes or $20,000, for a total of $165,000.
B. $100,000 in attorneys' fees, $38,550 for employee claims, plus one-fifth of the taxes or $20,000, for a total of $158,550.
C. One-half of the attorneys' fees, or $50,000, plus $38,550 for the employees for a total of $88,550.
D. $100,000 for attorneys' fees, plus $38,550 for the employees, for a total of $138,550.

ANALYSIS. The attorneys' fees have to be paid in full on the effective date, as do the employee claims (in the amounts allowed by §507(a)(4)), but the taxes can be paid later, in installments, starting after the effective date, as long as they are paid within five years of the filing of the petition for bankruptcy relief. Because the employees can only get $12,850 each for a total of $38,550, the answer is **D**.

QUESTION 2. **(CODE READER)** Under §1129(a)(9), taxes should be paid:

A. over five years after the date of the order for relief and without interest.
B. over five years after the date of the order for relief and with interest.
C. over five years from the date of assessment and with interest.
D. over five years from the date of assessment and without interest.

ANALYSIS. The two variables here are the period over which the taxes must be paid and whether the claims are entitled to interest under the plan. By reading §1129(a)(9)(C), you'll see that taxes must be paid within five years after the date of the order for relief, not assessment, thus eliminating **C** and **D** from the possible answers. What about interest? Section 1129(a)(9) provides that the taxes be paid "over a period ending not later than 5 years after the date of the order for relief, of a total value, as of the effective date of the plan, equal to the allowed amount of such claim." This language referring to "of a total value, as of the effective date of the plan . . ." means that the debtor must pay interest. Reread §1129(b)(2)(A), which applies to secured creditors and states similarly that secured creditors must receive payments totaling at least the value of the allowed amount of such claim, *as of the effective date of the plan*, of such holder's interest in such property. Now compare both these sections to the language of §1322(b), which provides that priority claims in a Chapter 13 are entitled to payment in full without interest. Section 1322(b) requires "*full payment in deferred cash payments, of all claims entitled to priority. . . .*" There is no mention of value as of the effective date of the plan! Therefore, interest must be paid on tax claims in a Chapter 11 but not in a Chapter 13 plan. Thus, the answer is **B**.

C. The Best Interest Test in Chapter 11: Treatment of General Unsecured Claims

You have just covered the minimum treatment for secured and priority claims, and you should now be asking yourself what the minimum treatment is for general unsecured creditors. This question is answered through the *best interest test*. (*See* 11 U.S.C. §1129(a)(7).) You might recall that under Chapter 13, the debtor must prove that he or she is paying as much to creditors under the Chapter 13 plan as creditors would receive in Chapter 7 liquidation. (*See* 11 U.S.C. §1324(a)(4).) The philosophy behind this rule is that a debtor should not be permitted to pay creditors over time if this is going to result in smaller rather than larger payments to creditors. Creditors are thus entitled to at least as much as they would get if the debtor were to simply liquidate its affairs. In a Chapter 13, you arrived at the amount that unsecured creditors get under a Chapter 13 plan by determining the liquidation value of the debtor's non-exempt assets and comparing that number to the amount of money that the debtor would pay to creditors under his or her Chapter 13 plan. This figure was fairly easy to calculate, assuming that the asset values could be ascertained. Chapter 11 contains essentially the same test with exactly the same name. Section 1129(a)(7) provides that, with respect to each impaired class of claims or interests, each holder of a claim has to either accept the plan (this is somewhat unlikely in larger cases because it refers to each and every creditor, not a creditor class), or each holder of the claim must receive an amount as of the effective date of the plan that is not less than what such holder would receive if the debtor were liquidated under Chapter 7. This test requires the Chapter 11 debtor to do a liquidation analysis in order to determine what creditors would indeed receive under a Chapter 7 case. (*See* 11 U.S.C. §1129(a)(7).) In Chapter 11, the debtor (assuming it is a corporation and not an individual) will have no exemptions. Thus, on some levels, the test is simpler to calculate because all one must do is determine the liquidation value of the debtor's property. As the following question suggests, however, this can be a bit more complicated than it looks.

QUESTION 3. Assume the debtor has proposed a plan that will distribute $2 million to its secured and unsecured creditors, over time. Assume that $1 million will be paid to the secured creditors and the other $1 million to unsecured creditors. Now let's assume that liquidation of the debtor's assets will net $2.3 million. For simplicity, also assume there are no administrative or other priority claims. Does the debtor's plan meet the best interest test?

A. Yes, because the plan pays as much as the creditors would receive in a liquidation.
B. Yes, because it would promote the purposes of the Bankruptcy Code to allow for a reorganization in this case, when the numbers are as close as they are, and a great benefit would be achieved by saving jobs.
C. No, because in a liquidation the creditors would get $2.3 million, whereas under the plan they only get $2 million.
D. No, because until creditors vote you cannot tell whether creditors prefer the plan over a liquidation.

ANALYSIS. First of all, right out of the box, **D** is simply not correct. Regardless of how creditors vote, the debtor is required to meet the best interest test contained in §1129(a)(7). This is not an optional test, and cannot be voted around. In other words, even consensual plans must comply with the best interest test. Additionally, both choices **A** and **B** are incorrect. Why? Because the best interest test is a mathematical test. All one must do is compare the distributions that creditors will receive under a Chapter 7 to those they will receive under a Chapter 11. In this particular case, you can see that the creditors would receive $2.3 million in liquidation, but only $2 million in a Chapter 11. Consequently, the correct answer is **C**. **A** is incorrect because it is simply factually incorrect. It states that creditors receive as much under the plan as they would in liquidation, and this is not true. **B** is incorrect because the policies of Chapter 11 cannot override the particular provisions of §1129(a)(7). In other words, regardless of the policies, and regardless of the potential application of §105(a), the debtor is not permitted under any circumstances to override the provisions of §1129(a)(7). Simply stated, the best interest test *must* be met.

QUESTION 4. For this question, assume that the debtor's plan provides for a $2.5 million distribution. It will pay $500,000 to its administrative and priority claims, $1 million to its secured creditors, and $1 million to its unsecured creditor class, which currently holds claims in the amount of $2 million. Pursuant to the debtor's plan the debtor will also assume a large number of executory contracts, meaning that the debtor will perform these contracts post-petition pursuant to their terms. Assume that in liquidation, the debtor would receive $2.7 million for its assets. Also assume, however, that if the debtor were to cease its operations, it would need to reject the executory contracts previously referred to and that this would increase the unsecured class by an extra $1 million, making the general unsecured class total $3 million. Does the debtor's plan meet the best interest test?

A. Yes, because creditors will receive more under the plan than they would receive in a liquidation.
B. Yes, because creditors will vote in favor of the plan.
C. No, because creditors actually receive more in a liquidation ($2.7 million) than they receive under the debtor's plan ($2.5 million).
D. No, because the debtor's plan does not comply with the best interest test.

ANALYSIS. **D** is not the correct answer. The statement in choice **D** simply contradicts the first part of the question. It gives no explanation for the statement but instead restates the statement in the negative. **C** is tempting because it provides that the debtor will pay only $2.5 million in its plan but that liquidation would generate $2.7 million. However, this answer is incorrect because, in calculating the best interest test, what is most important is not the total amount of dollars distributed to creditors under the plan but *the distribution that creditors will receive under the plan.* In this particular case, unsecured creditors will receive a larger distribution under the plan than they will receive in liquidation; thus, **A** is the correct answer. The next question explains this more fully. The plan meets the best interest test. **B** deals with voting, and once again this is not relevant to whether the debtor has met the best interest test.

QUESTION 5. Using the same facts as above, how much is the unsecured creditor distribution in liquidation as compared to an unsecured creditor distribution under the debtor's plan?

A. Under the plan, unsecured creditors receive 30 percent, and in liquidation, they receive 15 percent.

B. Under the plan, general unsecured creditors receive 50 percent, whereas under liquidation, they receive more like 35 percent.
C. Under the plan, general unsecured creditors receive 75 percent, and under liquidation, they receive approximately 50 percent.
D. Under the plan, general unsecured creditors receive a 50 percent distribution, and under liquidation, they receive a 40 percent distribution.

ANALYSIS. The correct answer to this question is choice **B**. Note how this happened. If the debtor were continuing to perform its post-petition contracts, then it would have $1 million less in unsecured claims. As a result of the debtor's rejection of its executory contracts, which is always necessary when the debtor liquidates and goes out of business, the unsecured creditor class group goes from $2 million to $3 million. Also note how creditors are paid. This will require us to review the priority scheme. The first $500,000 of payment goes to the administrative priority class. Additionally, $1 million goes to the secured creditors, leaving us with $1 million under the plan to pay $2 million in claims. This results in a 50 percent distribution.

On the other hand, in liquidation the debtor has $1.2 million left to distribute but must distribute it to $3 million in claims, so the distribution drops to about 35 percent. Thus, creditors do better under the plan and the answer is **B**.

D. Feasibility

Another requirement of Chapter 11 is that the plan be *feasible* or realistic. In other words, the plan must be more than just a pipe dream. The *feasibility* test is contained in §1129(a)(11), which requires that "confirmation of the plan is not likely to be followed by the liquidation, or the need for further financial reorganization, of the debtor or any successor to the debtor under the plan, unless such liquidation or reorganization is proposed in the plan." (*See* 11 U.S.C. §1129(a)(11).) You saw that under the *best interest of creditors* test, the debtor is required to propose a plan that will pay creditors at least as much under the Chapter 11 plan as in Chapter 7 liquidation. The big question that arises, however, is *how certain* it must be that the debtor will be able to actually make the payments proposed in the plan.

The best interest test simply involves comparing the amount of the plan payment to the amounts that would be realized in the liquidation, and calculating the distributions under each. Under the feasibility test contained in §1129(a)(11), the question is whether the debtor will actually be able to make the plan payments. This is what the feasibility test is all about. Because the feasibility test deals largely with the debtor's future business prospects, courts and scholars acknowledge that it is hard to generalize about the feasibility test. Undoubtedly, feasibility deals with the question of the likelihood that the plan will succeed and that the business will survive and prosper at least long enough to make the plan payments. Other than that, the feasibility test is applied by the courts on a case-by-case basis within the very broad discretion of the bankruptcy court.

How does the debtor actually go about proving feasibility? Generally speaking, the debtor presents business projections and projected cash flow statements determining how much money the debtor can generate on a net basis during the plan period. The debtor will also enumerate all other sources of payments for the plan, including asset sales, potential lawsuits, future contracts that will come to fruition, and so on. In addressing feasibility concerns, the debtor may be required to explain to the court (through management or an expert witness) what caused the debtor's financial problems in the first place and what will be or has been done to correct these problems. In other words, the debtor is now required to prove that its cash flow statements and other financial projections are realistic and credible and to show how it will raise the funds necessary to make the plan payments. In some cases, the debtor may even put on financial information regarding the general financial conditions in its industry, if this will help prove the projections.

Reading through the two preceding paragraphs, you can probably imagine ways in which the feasibility test could become controversial. Naturally, if the debtor is relying on future litigation proceeds or contracts to fund its plan, creditors and the court should ask about the likelihood of raising money through the litigation or contracts. Section 1129(a)(11) does not require the bankruptcy court to find that the proposed plan payments will definitely be made.[5] The court need find only a reasonable assurance of commercial viability, not that the plan is guaranteed to succeed. (*See* Kane v. Johns-Manville Corp., 843 F.2d 636, 649 (2d Cir. 1998); In re New Orleans Ltd., 116 F.3d 790 (5th Cir. 1997).) What the court will need to do is determine the adequacy of the capital structure, the earning power of the business, the economics surrounding the business, the ability of management, the probability of the continuation of the same management, and any other related matters that could determine the prospect of a sufficiently successful operation. (*See* In re Georgetown Ltd., 209 B.R. 763 (Bankr. M.D. Ga. 1997).)

Some of the language that courts have used to determine whether a plan is feasible includes: "Is it a visionary scheme that promises more than the debtor can possibly attain? Is it pie in the sky, realistically speaking, regardless of the sincere and honest intention of the plan proponent? Are the debtor's financial statements mere speculation? Most importantly, does it look as though the debtor will continue to operate at a loss throughout the life of the plan?"

---

5. The test simply requires that the case be *unlikely* to be followed by liquidation.

QUESTION 6. Pearl's Dive is a small chain of funky restaurants in the San Francisco Bay area. Two years ago, Pearl's Dive filed a Chapter 11 case because it was in a very large dispute with its primary secured lender about late payments under its working capital loan. The debtor has now proposed to make payments to various creditor groups over a five-year period under its plan. Generally speaking, the plan payments total about $10,000 per month, overall. The debtor has provided financial projections to the court and to the parties-in-interest in connection with its confirmation hearing. To prove that the plan is feasible under §1129(a)(11), the debtor put the president of Pearl's Dive on the stand, who testified as follows: The debtor will generate gross profits of $20,000 per month during the first four years of the plan and thereafter gross profits of $25,000 per month for years five through eight. The debtor's expenses each month will run somewhere between $8,000 and $11,000 depending on the particular month. Included in these projections is a statement by the management of the debtor that, due to new activities, including a sports rink near one of its restaurants, the debtor is anticipating an increase in its net profits of 10 percent over what the debtor has been doing during its Chapter 11 bankruptcy. On cross-examination, the debtor's president also testified that after a lengthy dispute with its primary secured lender, the debtor has agreed that if it misses any payments to the lender, thus defaulting on its mortgage obligations, the lender can immediately foreclose on all of the debtor's assets, without any objection from the debtor. Which of the following facts will the court find *most* relevant to the question of whether the plan is feasible?

A. The debtor's financial projections, showing a gross profit of $20,000 per month during its first four years and $25,000 per month during the second four years.

B. The suggestion that the debtor's profits will increase by 10 percent over the current period.

C. The fact that the debtor has agreed to allow the lender to foreclose on the debtor's assets when it misses a payment.

D. It is impossible to choose from A, B, and C because they are all relevant to the court's determination.

ANALYSIS. The correct answer here is surely **D**, as all of the facts suggested are very relevant to the court's determination. Again, the court has almost unfettered discretion to determine whether the feasibility test has been met and all of these things are particularly relevant. Absent additional facts (including prior decisions by this very court on this very same issue), it would be impossible to choose one, given that the judge's views depend on his or her individual proclivities about such things.

QUESTION 7. Under the same factual scenario, which of the following is likely to be *most* problematic for the debtor in meeting the feasibility test? In other words, which of these things is most difficult for the debtor to overcome in meeting the feasibility test?

A. The fact that, all of a sudden, the debtor is suggesting that its profits will be up 10 percent as soon as the plan becomes effective, although during the entire two-year bankruptcy period these numbers were not achieved.

B. The fact that the debtor has agreed to allow the lender to foreclose, without putting up any defense, when the debtor simply misses one payment.

C. The fact that, on the month-by-month basis, it appears that the debtor will not be making a net payment in certain months. For example, the debtor has acknowledged on cross-examination that in some months its net profits may only be $9,000, while its payment obligations may be $10,000.

D. The fact that the debtor's own management testified in the case, rather than an expert.

ANALYSIS. The answer to this question is choice **B**. Choice **C** suggests that during certain months the debtor will be operating at a net loss. This, in and of itself, should not keep the debtor from meeting the feasibility test. The debtor is not required to prove that it definitively will be able to perform as planned. Moreover, in certain other months, as the debtor's management testified, there should be additional profits over and above what is required under the plan. Thus, the facts in **C** should not keep the debtor from meeting the feasibility test. These numbers do suggest one thing; namely, that the debtor may have proposed too rich a plan given its current earnings. The debtor should be careful not to propose payments that are too high and should also save money for emergencies, just as you saw with individual debtors.

Choice **D** should not keep the debtor from achieving feasibility in its plan. In smaller Chapter 11 cases, it is not always possible for the debtor to afford an expert witness and, moreover, it is not always necessary. In a large number of cases (perhaps the majority) the debtor's own management is the one to testify about whether the plan is feasible. Moving on, choice **A** *does* appear to be problematic. It simply is not realistic for the debtor to be making projections that suggest that it would be making more money during the post-plan period than it was ever able to achieve during the bankruptcy case. Although projections are nice, history is the best measure of whether the debtor can make the plan payment and, consequently, this is a troubling matter. It is very possible, however, that the debtor *could* show that there actually *would* be additional business activity in the area during the post-confirmation period that would allow the plan to go through and to meet the feasibility test. These problems are significant, however, and should not be taken lightly. If at all possible, the debtor should be presenting projections showing net profit amounts that the debtor *has actually achieved*, at least in some points in its history.

The correct answer here, however, is **B.** It is troubling that the debtor agreed to allow the secured party to foreclose if even one payment is missed under the plan. This is an extremely precarious position to put the debtor (and its general creditors) in, and if history is any indication on this issue, the debtor will not be able to make every payment like clockwork. Thus, it is very likely that the case will be followed by liquidation, because the debtor has already agreed to allow the lender to foreclose, without objection, under circumstances that do not appear unlikely. Under similar facts, the Eighth Circuit Court of Appeals has held that such an agreement, along with a few additional facts, could cause a Chapter 11 plan to fail the feasibility test. (*See* Danny Thomas Props. II, Ltd. v. Partnership Beal Bank, SSB, 241 F.3d 959 (8th Cir. 2001).)

E. Secured Creditor Treatment Under Chapter 11

Now that you have covered the basic Chapter 11 rules and some advice about negotiating the plan, it is time to address what is normally the debtor's most complex task in its Chapter 11 case, namely, how it will pay its obligations to secured creditors. As you learned in Chapter 11 of this guide, a creditor's secured claim is generally considered to be only as large as the value of the collateral, unless the collateral is worth more than the loan, in which case the debtor has to pay the amount of the loan, plus interest and fees. This treatment is enumerated in §506(a) of the Bankruptcy Code, which is applicable in all types of bankruptcy proceedings, including Chapter 11 cases. Consequently, as you move through this discussion of the treatment of secured creditors under Chapter 11, keep in mind that if a claim is *oversecured*, it must be paid in full. Conversely, if a claim is *undersecured*, it will be bifurcated for the purposes of the Chapter 11 plan. Essentially, this means that an undersecured creditor will be secured to the extent of the value of its collateral, and any remaining debt over and above the value of this collateral will be placed in the general unsecured creditor class. This undersecured portion of the debt is called a *deficiency claim*. If you are having difficulty remembering what it means to be undersecured or oversecured, or remembering what a deficiency claim is, please go back now and reread Chapter 11 of this guide.

1. *The treatment of oversecured and undersecured claims after the filing but before confirmation of a Chapter 11 plan*

You have just reviewed the most important rule with respect to secured creditor treatment, namely that the secured claim is only as valuable as the value of the collateral. (*See* 11 U.S.C. §506(a).) This is a very important rule because whether a secured creditor is oversecured or undersecured will drastically affect the secured creditor's treatment while the bankruptcy case is pending and before the plan is confirmed. For example, it will take some time for any debtor-in-possession to confirm a Chapter 11 plan. During the time that this confirmation process is at work, the secured party that is *oversecured* will be entitled to accrue interest and attorneys' fees at the contract rates during the case. (*See* 11 U.S.C. §506(b).) Undersecured creditors, as well as all unsecured creditors, are not entitled to accrue interest or fees during the post-petition period. (*See* 11 U.S.C. §506(b).) Additionally, the interest and attorneys' fees provided for in the pre-petition loan document can be paid to the oversecured creditors, but only until the claim becomes as large as the value of the collateral. (*Id.*) At that time, no continuing interest or fees will accrue, and no unsecured claim for interest or fees will be created. Rather, this interest (i.e., unsupported by collateral) will simply fall off the face of the earth. This is how an oversecured creditor (and by negative implication, an undersecured creditor) will be treated during the period in which the debtor is attempting to reorganize its affairs. In other words, these are the rules that are applicable to oversecured claims in Chapter 11, before the confirmation of a Chapter 11 plan.

2. *Secured creditor treatment under the plan*

Once a plan has been confirmed, the treatment for (or payment on) the secured claim is described in the plan itself. At that time, the interest and fees being paid under the pre-petition loan documents will cease, and the prepetition loan terms will no longer apply to the loan, unless the plan provides otherwise. The rules change completely and totally. The secured creditor treatment will be negotiated between the debtor and the creditor. However, the creditor cannot be forced to take less than the terms found in §1129(b)(2)(A). This Code section provides for similar treatment to the secured party to that required in a Chapter 13. In a nutshell, §1129(b)(2)(A) provides that secured creditors are entitled to keep whatever lien or secured interest they have on their collateral and also the *present value* of each of their secured claims (based on the value of the collateral), over the life of the plan. Although this rule (technically speaking) is only required in a *cramdown*, when a secured creditor votes against the plan, secured creditors will normally insist on this treatment. Consequently, this is the default treatment that a debtor will typically provide to a secured creditor. Although a secured party can certainly agree to accept other, less-favorable treatment, few creditors are willing to do so. Thus, secured creditors normally receive the present value of their allowed secured claims in a Chapter 11 plan.

QUESTION 8. New Mexico Educators' Credit Union holds a $1 million loan secured by a lien on the debtor's real property. The loan documents provide for 10 percent interest on the loan with equal monthly payments of principal and interest over the next seven years. The debtor's plan provides for 84 monthly payments in equal installments of principal and interest on the secured portion of the claim, and treats the remaining deficiency claim to be paid as a general unsecured claim. The debtor contends that the real estate is worth $700,000, while the credit union contends that it is worth $1.2 million. Which of the following statements is correct with respect to the permissible treatment of the credit union's claim in the debtor's plan?

A. If the court finds the property to be worth $700,000, the credit union has only a $700,000 secured claim, payable in equal installments over 84 months.
B. If the court finds the property to be worth $700,000, the credit union has a secured claim for $700,000, payable in 84 equal monthly installments of principal, plus interest and fees under the loan documents from the filing date until confirmation, and an unsecured claim of $300,000.
C. If the court finds the property to be worth $1.2 million, the credit union has a secured claim for $1.2 million, plus interest and fees payable in 84 equal installments.
D. If the court finds the property to be worth $1.2 million, the credit union has a secured claim for $1 million, plus interest and fees from the filing date to the plan date payable in 84 equal installments.

ANALYSIS. This problem posts two possible results of the valuation of the debtor's property, one for $700,000 and one for $1.2 million, and asks you to identify the proper treatment for the creditor under both values. If the credit union's claim was undersecured, as is proposed in answers **A** and **B**, the credit union would have a secured claim for $700,000 as well as an unsecured claim for the $300,000. **A** does not mention the unsecured claim and is thus incomplete. **B** recognizes the unsecured claim but then incorrectly states that the credit union will earn interest and fees on its claim from the filing date, which is incorrect under §506(b). Only oversecured claims earn interest and fees at the contract rate from the filing date, so **B** is also inaccurate.

C and **D** ask you to predict the treatment of an oversecured creditor, as these answers set the value at $1.2 million for the $1 million claim. **C** states that, because the real estate was valued at $1.2 million, the credit union's secured claim is worth $1.2 million. That simply isn't true. The credit union is only owed $1 million, so that is the maximum value of the principal on its claim. Remember that you can always have more collateral than you need. This will not increase the amount of principal that you are owed. This means **D** is the correct answer by default. **D** states that the credit union's secured claim is worth $1 million, and also that the credit union is entitled to receive interest and fees from the filing date. This is true under §506(b) because the claim is oversecured. The correct answer is **D**.

QUESTION 9. None of the answers above mentions that the secured party is entitled to receive the present value of its secured claim over the life of the plan, an issue discussed at length in other parts of this book. The secured party, whether it is undersecured or oversecured, is always entitled to the present value of its claim under the plan because:

A. the creditor no longer wants to do business with the debtor.
B. the creditor is secured and secured parties always get interest.
C. the debtor is not paying the secured claim in full right away.
D. lenders choose to loan money only to successful companies and this is not one of those.

ANALYSIS. Present value interest is paid to the creditor to compensate it for not receiving payment in full of its allowed claim right away. It is paid to compensate the secured party for the time value of money, pure and simple. The answer is **C** and the others are simply wrong. To review this in detail, return to Chapter 11.

F. The Closer: Chapter 34

You represent creditors' committees across the country and have done so in the largest Chapter 11 cases ever filed. A newspaper reporter has asked you to choose the most important protection that Chapter 11 provides to unsecured creditors from the following list:

A. The absolute priority rule.
B. The best interest test.
C. The Chapter 11 voting rights.
D. The right to hire and compensate counsel and other professionals.

ANALYSIS. This would be a very close call. One of us asked several people this question and at least one person chose each of the four possible answers as the most important. All are critical to the protection of unsecured creditors, and part of the purpose of this question is to see if you know why this is so. We think the least important of the bunch is the best interest test, choice **B**, because, in many Chapter 11 cases, unsecured creditors would not receive anything in a Chapter 7, so the standard is low. (*See* 11 U.S.C. §1129(a)(7).) Other lawyers disagree that the test is not important, stating that creditors should be allowed to choose to liquidate a company if they think this is in their best interest and can prove that liquidation is better for them. (*Id.*) Creditors gain this right through the best interest test.

The right to an attorney paid from the estate, choice **D**, strikes us as very important, but as a colleague reminds me, this is not unusual. Everyone in the country can hire an attorney if they can afford one. Chapter 11 makes it more affordable, by allowing payment from the estate, but creditors still pay for this right from their distributions. No, **D** does not seem to be the best answer.

Some readers may choose the absolute priority rule, choice **A**. (*See* 11 U.S.C. §1129(b)(2)(B).) Why? Because no one wants the debtor to reorganize more than its owners. This rule, which requires that equity holders buy back their ownership interests unless creditors agree otherwise, motivates owners to put money into the debtor for the benefit of creditors. Without this rule, owners would not contribute to plans, as the argument goes. Thus, this is an important rule, although not the answer we would choose.

To me, voting seems most fundamental to the system, making **C** the answer we would choose. (*See* 11 U.S.C. §1126.) Chapter 11 is designed to be a consensual process and giving creditors the right to vote on a plan fosters agreement. The debtor wants favorable votes, so the debtor aims to please. This is the one place in society where paying for votes is encouraged! Thus, whereas we would choose **C**, any answer is a good one here, as long as you can explain why you chose it.

Martin's and Keating's Picks

1. Question 1	**D**
2. Question 2	**B**
3. Question 3	**C**
4. Question 4	**A**
5. Question 5	**B**
6. Question 6	**D**
7. Question 7	**B**
8. Question 8	**D**
9. Question 9	**C**
The Closer	**C**

35

Voting and Classification: Soliciting Votes for the Plan

OVERVIEW

A. The Disclosure Statement
B. Plan Voting
C. Classification
D. Impairment
E. The Closer: Chapter 35
Martin's and Keating's Picks

It may seem late in the day to discuss plan voting but in reality, if things have been working well in the negotiation stages, a debtor's plan is normally approved consensually. Even before negotiating, the debtor will place all creditors into classes of claims. (*See* 11 U.S.C. §1122.) The classes will later be used to calculate votes on the plan. (*See* 11 U.S.C. §1126.) This chapter describes the classification and voting process. The debtor hopes that all classes of claims vote to accept the plan. The debtor will need at least two-thirds in amount and more than one-half in number of claims voting to gain an accepting class. In any event, as discussed in the prior chapter, confirmation cannot be achieved at all unless there is at least one impaired accepting class. (*See* 11 U.S.C. §1129(a)(10).)

Unless the debtor is a *small business debtor*, as defined in §101(51C), the debtor must obtain court approval of a disclosure statement before circulating the plan for voting. (*See* 11 U.S.C. §1125.) If the votes are not all positive, then the debtor will resort to the *cramdown* tactics referred to in Chapter 36. (*See* 11 U.S.C. §1129(b).) This chapter explains how a debtor-in-possession ensures that its plan voting and solicitation process meets the Bankruptcy Code requirements. As we explained briefly in the introduction to the Chapter 11 materials, the debtor is required to place creditors into classes and, following that classification, to solicit votes from the creditor classes on the plan. Under the 2005 amendments, *small business debtors* follow slightly different and more lenient rules regarding the voting and solicitation process. They also have shorter deadlines for getting a plan approved. The rules for small business debtors are discussed separately in the Chapter 37. Thus, the remainder of this chapter is devoted to the solicitation and voting process for other (non-small business) Chapter 11 debtors.

A. The Disclosure Statement

A plan cannot be circulated for voting unless it is accompanied by a court-approved disclosure statement. Sections 1125(a) and (b) of the Code contain the requirements for obtaining approval of a disclosure statement, as do Bankruptcy Rules 3001(6), 3001(7), and 3001(8). Putting together a disclosure statement can be a difficult task.[1] The debtor must provide creditors with information sufficient to decide whether to vote for the plan. While a large portion of the disclosure simply restates the provisions of the plan, the beginning part of the disclosure statement contains a history of the debtor's operations, as well as an explanation of what went wrong before the bankruptcy filing. The disclosure statement also contains a detailed description of all litigation matters to which the debtor is a party, as well as all of the methods through which the debtor will fund the plan. The description of these funding mechanisms is one of the important parts of the disclosure statement because it explains how creditors will be paid under the plan.

Reviewing some of the other tests that we have discussed in this guide, the disclosure statement explains in detail how the debtor meets the *best interest test*. (*See* 11 U.S.C. §1129(a)(7).) This requires that the disclosure statement contain a detailed liquidation analysis of the debtor, explaining how many claims there would be if the debtor were to liquidate, and the corresponding distribution to creditors. (For an example, see Chapter 34, Section C.) The disclosure statement should also contain a detailed description of how the debtor plans to meet the feasibility test; in other words, a detailed description of its various projections and other financial information.

Once the debtor has drafted its Chapter 11 plan and the accompanying disclosure statement, the debtor circulates the disclosure statement to the major parties-in-interest in the case, notifies everyone in the case that the disclosure statement has been filed, and requests a hearing on the adequacy of the disclosure statement pursuant to §1125(b). The court holds an initial hearing to determine if the disclosure statement contains adequate information, which is aptly called a *disclosure statement hearing*. (*See* 11 U.S.C. §1125.) Once the disclosure statement is approved, it is sent out to all creditors with the plan and

1. Again, this is not as true in a small business case, where the debtor can use a form disclosure statement.

a ballot for voting. Once the votes have been counted, the court holds another more substantive hearing, this time to decide whether to approve (or *confirm*) the plan. (*See* 11 U.S.C. §§1125, 1128, 1129.)

Some creditors, particularly if they are creditors with whom the debtor is in litigation or with whom the debtor otherwise has strained relations, may object to the disclosure statement on the basis that it contains information they find is biased or inaccurate. Some creditors may also object to the disclosure statement because it describes a plan they believe is not confirmable. Consequently, they may wish to tell the court that it would be a waste of estate money to circulate and solicit votes on an unconfirmable plan. As you can see, these are veiled objections to the plan itself, and some courts do not like to hear them. Other courts appreciate the heads-up, as they want to know whether the plan has problems and whether the debtor should consider modifying or changing plan provisions before soliciting votes.

When the court approves a disclosure statement, it essentially holds that §1125(a)(1) has been met, and that the disclosure statement contains adequate information, which is defined as "information of a kind, and in sufficient detail, as far as is reasonably practicable in light of the nature and history of the debtor and the condition of the debtor's books and records, that would enable a hypothetical reasonable investor typical of holders of claims or interests of the relevant class to make an informed judgment about the plan." (*See* 11 U.S.C. §1125.) That's a mouthful, but it essentially means that the disclosure statement must contain adequate information to enable creditors to decide whether to vote in favor of the plan.

QUESTION 1. The debtor, Zarios, owns a huge wholesale distribution center on the coast of Washington State. The debtor was forced to file a Chapter 11 bankruptcy after it was sued by a number of its customers for allegedly supplying spoiled fish in some of its products. The debtor filed for Chapter 11 and plans to restructure its business by closing down some of its smaller operations and by bringing suit against Mike's, who supplied Zarios with the allegedly spoiled fish. In connection with its plan of reorganization, Zarios intends to cram down or strip down the mortgage debt on its primary facility. It claims that the facility is worth $3.5 million, and that the mortgage debt is $4 million. The plan also calls for a significant distribution to unsecured creditors, based on the debtor's future operations as well as its litigation with Mike's. Zarios is also in a fairly large dispute with the IRS, and hopes to reduce some of these claims as well, through litigation.

In its disclosure statement, Zarios explained the cramdown process, included information suggesting that its plan is feasible and meets the best interest test, and also extensively described its litigation with both Mike's and the IRS. In connection with the IRS litigation, the debtor essentially restated in the disclosure statement what was in both the complaint and the IRS answer. In connection with its litigation with Mike's, the debtor included that type of information but also included portions of expert testimony that it intended to present at trial against Mike's, and then predicted that it had an 80 percent likelihood of success in its suit against Mike's.

Based on what you have been told here, who is most likely to object to the debtor's disclosure statement and why?

A. The unsecured creditors' committee, because the disclosure contains inadequate information with respect to the IRS litigation.
B. The IRS, because the disclosure statement incorrectly states the nature of the dispute between Zarios and the IRS.
C. The primary secured lender, who is objecting to the debtor's valuation of the building and thus to the cramdown of its claim under the debtor's plan.
D. Mike's (who is also a creditor of Zarios) because the disclosure statement contains information about the litigation that has not been substantiated.

ANALYSIS. Wow. This is a tough question. Obviously, any party-in-interest can object to the debtor's disclosure statement. But you should ask yourself the following questions. Why does a creditor bother objecting to the disclosure statement? Why does the court require that the disclosure statement be approved before a plan is sent out for voting? What is the purpose of a disclosure statement? How can a debtor-in-possession establish that the disclosure statement contains adequate information to allow creditors to decide whether or not to vote in favor of the plan?

The first thing to do here is eliminate objections that appear to be objections to the plan rather than objections to the disclosure statement. It seems that answer **C**, the lender who is objecting to the cramdown, is probably one of those types of objections. If the disclosure statement contains inadequate information with respect to the valuation of the debtor's facility, only the secured party is really affected by that, at least arguably, and as a result this would not appear to be the creditor with the best argument. If the secured party knows that the value of the building is actually more like $4 million, this does not really affect its knowledge about the plan and how to vote, one way or the other. One could argue that other creditors could be misled and that this misstatement could affect the feasibility of the plan. However, all of these issues can be dealt with in the plan confirmation process that we have previously discussed.

Choice **A** is always a possibility, but if the committee is happy with the proposed distribution to unsecured creditors under the plan, we don't see any reason why the general unsecured creditors' committee would spend the money to object to this disclosure statement. It is in the creditors' best interest to get the disclosure statement approved and sent out, so the case can be completed before more administrative fees mount. Objecting to the disclosure statement is costly and is normally something that only hostile creditors do. It is more efficient to simply ask the debtor for more information. Thus, we don't find the unsecured creditors' committee to be a likely objector to this disclosure statement. Finally, if the committee wanted additional information, it would most likely be about the litigation with Mike's as discussed hereafter, not the litigation with the IRS.

This essentially leaves the IRS and Mike's as the two remaining candidates. Compare what the debtor said about the litigation against each of these creditors in order to come up with the correct answer. Choice **B** states that the description of the IRS litigation simply reiterated what was said in the answer in response to the complaint. All of this information is a matter of public record and, as a factual matter, is obviously correct. It is not biased and tells both sides of the story. This is what the complaint says, this is what the response is, and that's the story. On the other hand, what the debtor said about its litigation with Mike's is very important and directly affects whether creditors should vote in favor of the plan. It is also very subjective. Consequently, it is important to the adequacy of the disclosure statement. The debtor makes an unsubstantiated statement in the disclosure statement that it has an 80 percent chance of success in its litigation against Mike's. Mike's would be the one likely to object because the statement is not substantiated, because it is paying the closest attention to what is said about *it*, and because it may worry that this type of assertion (even unsubstantiated) might somehow prejudice it in the underlying litigation. At the very least, Mike's would object to the bad publicity. Thus, it is very likely that Mike's would object to the disclosure statement. As an aside, Mike's could only object to the disclosure statement here if it were also a creditor of the debtor. As a general matter, only creditors (and the U.S. Trustee) have standing to be heard in Chapter 11 cases. The correct answer is **D**.

QUESTION 2. Using the facts above, how is the court likely to rule on Mike's objection?

A. The objection will be overruled because it is not relevant to the information needed to vote on the plan.
B. The objection will be sustained and the debtor will be required to fix the disclosure statement because it is relevant to creditor votes, particularly on the issue of feasibility.
C. The court is likely to overrule the objection and let the disclosure statement be sent out because this is a question for confirmation, not adequate disclosure in the disclosure statement.
D. The court is likely to overrule the objection because the court will likely see it as a waste of the debtor's time to correct such an insignificant matter.

ANALYSIS. The correct answer here is **B**. This information is highly relevant to creditors in deciding how to vote on the plan and, thus, the court should sustain the objection. The court should either (1) require that the debtor supplement the language in the disclosure statement to say that this is just an estimate and to otherwise let creditors know that this is not sure money under the plan; or (2) require that the debtor substantiate the percentages in the disclosure statement hearing. You can imagine how this might be done if you have experience with litigation. For example, the debtor might simply put on the debtor's special counsel in the litigation to testify about the strengths and weaknesses of the litigation. This approach could always backfire, of course, because Mike's could insist on bringing its own counsel forward to do exactly the same thing, further prolonging the proceedings. Probably the best way to address this situation would be to simply have the debtor change the language in the disclosure statement to indicate that the monies from the litigation are speculative. At a minimum, the court would probably allow Mike's to add its own statement to the disclosure statement, expressing its opinion on the likelihood of success in the case.

Just as a brief aside, by now you should be starting to put the various pieces of Chapter 11 together. Quickly, if you can, think about which test this change might implicate. If you guessed feasibility, you're absolutely right. It sounds as though Zarios is relying on this litigation to make its plan payments. To ward off feasibility issues, the debtor may have decided to take an aggressive stand with respect to what the litigation is worth and to claim that it has a very significant chance of success.

When approving a disclosure statement, the court has to balance several considerations, one of which is that some disclosure statements get so long that creditors are unwilling to read them. If you have ever invested in stock, you may have experienced this when receiving corporate disclosure statements. Very long legal documents do not tend to be read, and consequently there is a point in time when a disclosure statement can defeat its own purpose. Despite this concern, the typical process for dealing with objections to disclosure statements is to simply ask debtor's counsel to add more information with respect to the issues objectors have raised. However, this lengthens the document and increases the chances that it will never be read.

The debtor is not allowed to *solicit votes* on its plan until it has circulated the plan with an approved disclosure statement. (*See* 11 U.S.C. §1125(b).) This does not mean, however, that the debtor cannot negotiate with creditors about plan treatment. The debtor is free to hold meetings to talk about plan treatment, and to discuss various aspects of the plan before its being circulated. Although what is forbidden is soliciting votes on the plan and nothing more, many people consider it inadvisable for the debtor to circulate an actual plan, in plan form, before getting its disclosure statement approved. The entire point of requiring a disclosure statement is to make sure that at the time creditors are considering the plan, they have information sufficient to determine whether the plan is something they should favor. (*See* 11 U.S.C. §1125(a).)

B. Plan Voting

Once the court has approved the disclosure statement and an order approving it has been entered, the debtor is free to distribute the plan and the disclosure statement to creditors for voting. (*See* 11 U.S.C. §1126.) You will recall that when the debtor drafts the plan, the plan will place creditors into different classes. The debtor is hopeful that all classes of creditors will vote in favor of the plan. But what does it mean for a class to accept or reject a plan? How many votes does a debtor actually need? This issue is addressed in §1126(c) of the Code, which provides that a *class* has accepted the plan if the plan has been accepted by creditors that hold at least two-thirds in amount and more than one-half in number of the allowed claims in the class that have voted on the plan. (*See* 11 U.S.C. §1126(c).) This means you need two-thirds in amount and over one-half in number of those who *actually vote* to have a class approve the plan.

QUESTION 3. Barry's Bail Bonds (Bonds) recently filed a Chapter 11 plan. Bonds owes $2 million to its bank, secured by numerous facilities proven to be worth $1.5 million. Thus, Bonds plans to strip down the bank's claim in its Chapter 11 case. There are only two creditor classes voting on the plan. There is the bank's secured creditor class and there is a general unsecured creditor class. Other creditors in the unsecured creditor class include numerous trade creditors who are owed a total of $200,000 and five or six utility claimants who are owed a total of $100,000. Assume that the lender votes against all parts of its claim and that all of the other creditors in the case unanimously vote in favor of the plan. Can Bonds confirm the plan under either the consensual provisions of the Bankruptcy Code or the nonconsensual (cramdown) provisions?

A. Yes, Bonds can confirm a consensual plan because the vast majority of creditors has voted in favor of the plan.
B. Yes, Bonds can confirm a plan but under the nonconsenting cramdown provision, which is possible because the general unsecured creditors voted in favor of the plan.
C. No, Bonds cannot confirm under either the consensual or the nonconsensual provisions because there is no consenting class of impaired creditors under the plan.
D. No, confirmation of the plan is not possible because, even though the unsecured creditor class has voted in favor of the plan, Bonds will be unsuccessful in stripping down the secured party's claim.

ANALYSIS. This question requires you to determine which claims are in each creditor class. Hopefully you saw that the secured creditor class will be only $1.5 million and there will be one voter in that class, the bank, who voted no. Therefore, everyone has voted no in the secured creditor class, and we have one class of creditors not consenting to the plan. Consequently, the plan is a nonconsensual plan, making answer **A** incorrect. The next question is whether Bonds can get even one class to vote yes. Remember that the plan cannot be confirmed unless at least one class of impaired creditors votes in favor of the plan. If you were to articulate which creditors are in the unsecured creditor class and the amount of their claims, what would you actually say? In reality, that class of claims has $800,000 of claims in it. It has $300,000 worth of claims voting yes (trade and utility creditors) and has $500,000 worth of claims voting no. That $500,000 worth of claims comes from the deficiency claim of the secured creditor. Because the voting rules provide that a class has accepted only if two-thirds in amount and more than one-half in number vote yes, the unsecured creditor class also voted no. Consequently, answer **B** is incorrect. How is it that they voted no? Certainly, over half in number of the creditors have voted in favor of the plan; however, two-thirds in amount of claims have note voted in favor of the plan. In fact, $500,000 in claims voted no, namely the secured creditor's deficiency claim. This has dwarfed the other $300,000 of yes votes. Consequently, the correct answer is **C**, and Bonds cannot confirm this Chapter 11 plan because it doesn't have any accepting classes of claims in the case.

As you can see, it is critical to understand how a secured party's claim gets bifurcated when it is undersecured, as well as how plan voting works. Otherwise, you will be unable to tell whether a class has voted in favor or against the plan.

C. Classification

Classification is often a simple matter, as the debtor is required to treat every creditor within a class the same as the other members of that class, and also to only put creditors with the same legal rights into the same class. (*See* 11 U.S.C. §1122.) Section 1122(a) actually requires merely that the debtor classify only *substantially similar* creditors in the same class. It is silent about whether it is acceptable to place similarly situated creditors in separate classes. Courts interpreting the Code, however, have disapproved of classification schemes created for the mere purpose of gerrymandering to ensure an affirmative vote on a reorganization plan. Thus, while the Code does not explicitly state this, the debtor is generally required to put all creditors with the same legal rights in the same class.

What classification issues might come up in a Chapter 11 case? Most arise in situations in which the debtor is trying to isolate hostile creditors into their own class, so that the rest of the similarly situated creditors (presumably friendly creditors) will be in a different class. By so doing, the debtor can get the "friendly," or nonhostile, yet similarly situated creditors to vote in favor of the plan and thereby satisfy the requirement that at least one class vote in favor of the plan. You'll recall that the debtor's goal is to have each class vote in favor of the plan, based on the difficult and time-consuming negotiations that the debtor engages in pre-plan. You also may recall that the debtor can force the plan on dissenting classes, if need be, which we call the *cramdown*, but *only if at least one impaired class votes in favor of the plan.*

The standard that has developed to determine whether a classification scheme meets the requirements of §1122 is whether the classification scheme is in the best interest of creditors, fosters the reorganization effort, and does not violate the absolute priority rule.

As you can see, these are very broad standards. Moreover, whether the scheme fosters reorganization could be in direct conflict with whether it is in the best interest of creditors. What is quite clear is that the debtor cannot separately classify claims to gerrymander votes. Attempts to gerrymander often focus on the proponent's purpose or the state of mind of the plan proponent, rather than on the nature of the claim. Courts sometimes also ask whether separate classification is reasonable based on different legal rights, different legal priorities, or business reasons that are truly relevant to the success of the reorganized debtor. If a separate classification scheme is based on a legitimate reason relevant to the success of the reorganized debtor, such as warranty claims, the court may approve the scheme. If it is done to merely isolate a large deficiency claim of an undersecured party, and thus create an accepting class of creditors in the general unsecured class, separate classification is not permitted.

Why does this matter? The debtor needs to solicit votes from all impaired classes. As we said in the introduction to these Chapter 11 materials, the debtor's goal is to get each and every class to vote yes. If every class votes yes, it will not be necessary to meet the fair and equitable standard of a cramdown confirmation with respect to either the secured or unsecured creditors. This will also make the confirmation process much cheaper as well, because the process will not be a litigious one.

The important thing to keep in mind when classifying claims under §1122 of the Bankruptcy Code is that creditors with similar legal interests should be placed in the same class. (*See* 11 U.S.C. §1122(a).) Additionally, the converse is true. Thus, if a creditor has legal rights that are unique to its own position, it should not be classified with other creditors who are not similarly situated. Because secured creditors normally have different collateral securing their claims (or different lien priority positions), and are subject to different pre-petition rights under their respective loan documents, it is very common for each secured creditor to be classified separately in a Chapter 11 plan.

QUESTION 4. (CODE READER) Which of the following classification schemes most obviously violates the classification rules contained in §1122? Keep in mind that all plans must comply with §1129(a)(9), which also could affect classification.

A. A plan in which these are the classes of creditors: Class 1 administrative claims under §503(b); Class 2 priority claims under §507; Classes 3, 4, 5, and 6, four separate classes of secured creditors; and Class 7, one class of unsecured creditors.

B. A plan in which these are the classes of creditors: Class 1 administrative claims under §503(b); Class 2 priority claims under §507 that do not include taxes; Class 3, a separate class for taxes; Classes 4, 5, and 6, three separate classes of secured creditors; Class 7, one class of unsecured creditors with claims of less than $1,000; and Class 8, which contains all other unsecured claims.

C. A plan in which these are the classes of creditors: Class 1 administrative claims under §503(b); Class 2 priority claims under §507 that do not include taxes; Class 3, a separate class for taxes; Classes 4, 5, 6, and 7, four separate classes of secured creditors; Class 7, a general unsecured creditor class; and Class 8, all deficiency claims held by one of the secured creditors.

D. A plan in which these are the classes of creditors: Class 1 administrative claims; Class 2 priority claims other than taxes; Class 3 priority claims that are taxes; Class 4, all secured creditors classified together; and, finally, Class 5, one class of unsecured creditors.

ANALYSIS. First let's look at answer **A**. There is nothing in answer **A** that violates the classification rules. It is perfectly acceptable to classify Class 1 administrative claims separately from other priority claims, because these claims consist of post-petition suppliers, attorneys' fees, and other creditors, which can't be classified separately in this first position. Moreover, there is nothing wrong with classifying all priority claims under §507, although, as you will see, tax claims can be treated differently, and consequently under §1129(a)(9) are often paid in a different way and thus classified differently. It is necessary to classify secured claims separately, assuming that they all have different collateral and legal rights. This is required by §1122(a). This fact is not given to us, but we can assume that is the case. It would be very uncommon for there to be four secured creditors in this case all holding precisely the same collateral, same legal rights, and also at the same priority. Because creditors holding different forms of collateral are considered to have different legal rights, it is common to classify them separately. Choice **A** provides only one unsecured creditor class. Consequently, there is nothing in **A** that would be inappropriate according to the classification scheme set out in §1122.

Choice **B** contains all of the same options as choice **A**, except that choice **B** also provides that unsecured claims of less than $1,000 will be classified separately. Is this acceptable? Yes. Under §1122(b), a plan may designate a separate class of unsecured claims that is less than or reduced to an amount that the court approves as reasonable for administrative convenience. This is referred to as the *administrative convenience rule*, and allows the debtor to separately classify some small claims and pay them in full, if desired, simply to get them out of the way and to make plan administration less costly and complex. Thus, **B** does not violate the classification rules, even though some unsecured creditors are placed in a separate class for the debtor's administrative convenience.

In choice **C**, the debtor does create a classification problem. What the debtor attempts to do here is take one similarly situated creditor and isolate it by placing it in a separate class. In **C**, the debtor has placed one of the secured creditor's deficiency claims into a separate class. Try to anticipate why this is a problem. The reason is that the deficiency claim is a general unsecured claim, just like all other general unsecured claims. Essentially, that claim is subject to the exact same legal rights as the other general unsecured creditors. Consequently, such a scheme violates §1122 because the debtor's only purpose in isolating this claim is to gerrymander voting on the plan. What the debtor hopes to do in this situation is make sure that it has a class that will accept the plan, even though this deficiency claim could be much, much larger than the other unsecured creditors, and thus could, if the creditor were hostile to the debtor, dominate the unsecured creditor class and cause the unsecured creditor class to vote no. This is exactly the type of classification scheme that §1122 forbids, and many cases have so held. Thus, the correct answer is **C**.

You may have chosen **D** because it seemed inappropriate for the debtor to classify all secured creditors in one class. The debtor can do this, but only if all of the secured creditors have the same priority and the same collateral. Again, we are not told whether this is the case or not. If each creditor has separate collateral (or different priority rights in the same collateral), pursuant to §1122, it would be inappropriate to place creditors in the same class because they have different legal rights. Because we don't know this fact, and we do know that choice **C** is surely inappropriate, the best answer is choice **C**.

IMPORTANT NOTE: All of the answers in the previous problem contained classes of claims that did not need to be classified under the rules of §1123(a)(1); namely, administrative priority claims, other priority claims, and tax claims. While it is the practice to classify such claims in many jurisdictions, none of the creditors in these classes has any right to vote on the plan and thus classification serves no purpose. Moreover, some lawyers would never think of classifying these types of claims, and would even argue that such classification is not permitted because §1123 only specifically mentions claims of other types. We pass no judgment on either practice, but only bring them to your attention.

D. Impairment

We've said that the debtor needs *at least one* accepting class to confirm a plan, but that's really just half the story. The debtor needs at least one impaired class to vote yes. Actually, only *impaired* classes of claims are entitled to vote on the plan. According to §1124, a class of claims is impaired unless the plan "(1) leaves unaltered the legal, equitable, and contractual rights to which such claim or interest entitles the holder of such claim or interest." (*See* 11 U.S.C. §1124(1).) This generally means that a class is impaired if it is not paid in full on the effective date, or its pre-bankruptcy rights are affected by the plan. Because only impaired classes are entitled to vote on the plan, the debtor can only count impaired classes in determining whether one or more classes has voted in favor of the plan.

QUESTION 5. The debtor's plan contains the following classes: Class 1, secured claims of one secured creditor, a creditor who is to be paid pursuant to the terms of its original loan agreement with the debtor; Class 2, another secured creditor claim, who will be paid a crammed-down amount on its claim and the present value of its claim over the useful life of its collateral; and Class 3, the general unsecured creditors, who will receive a 25 percent distribution. In connection with plan voting, Class 1 has voted yes, and Classes 2 and 3 have voted no. Can the debtor confirm the plan?

A. Yes, because a class has voted yes and the debtor can cram down the plan.
B. No, because the debtor has no impaired accepting classes.
C. No, because the general unsecured creditors voted no.
D. Yes, as a consensual plan.

ANALYSIS. Here you should eliminate **D** first. Any time any class votes no, you do not have a consensual plan. Here there are two nonconsenting classes. Of the remaining answers, **B** is clearly the most correct. It is true that Class 1 voted yes, but the class is not impaired. The creditor's rights are exactly the same as they would have been outside of bankruptcy and thus this vote does not count. Thus, **A** is incorrect because Class 1 is not an impaired accepting class. **C** is true, but not the best answer. Although it is true that the debtor cannot confirm a plan because the unsecured creditor class voted no, this is only part of the story. The reason why the debtor cannot confirm the plan is because both impaired classes voted against the plan. If either Class 2 or Class 3 had voted in favor of the plan, cramdown would be possible. Thus, **B** is the correct answer.

E. The Closer: Chapter 35

You recently filed a Chapter 11 case for Franny Fix-it, a hardware chain geared towards women. The principal of Franny, Franny Freid, is anxious to hit the pavement and start drumming up support for her reorganization plan. She knows about the specific voting requirements and wants to get to work right away garnering votes. She has asked you to do a draft plan, as well as a summary of the plan treatment that the two of you have decided to try to negotiate. Franny just picked up a few copies of each, and would like to know how to approach creditors in drumming up votes. Which of the following is she allowed to do?

A. She can pass out draft copies of the plan to the people she is soliciting for votes.
B. She should not circulate the plan itself, but can give out copies of the summary.
C. She should talk about treatment creditors would be willing to accept in the abstract, but should not pass out any paper, or explicitly ask creditors to vote for the plan.
D. She should stay home. Without an approved disclosure statement, Franny should not try to drum up votes on the plan.

ANALYSIS. The issue here is what a debtor can do to negotiate a plan or garner support for a plan, without violating the requirement that a plan be circulated only with a court-approved disclosure statement. (*See* 11 U.S.C. §1125.) The issue is certainly one of degree. One court explained that "there is a spectrum of communication in bankruptcy ranging from a neutral, factual, statement to an actual request to accept or reject a plan. Somewhere on that spectrum a communication crosses the line to become a solicitation." (*See* In re Dow Corning, 227 B.R. 111, 125 (Bankr. E.D. Mich. 1999).) In Dow Corning, after the plan was filed but before a disclosure statement was approved, the debtor issued press releases about the plan, and also sent its executives all over the country to talk up the plan's merits. No plan was distributed, however. In a very close decision, the court said this did not constitute improper solicitation.

So what do you think? It does not seem that Franny must, as **D** suggests, stay home. Surely she can talk to creditors about the plan. On the other hand, the quote above suggests that in her discussions, she should *not* explicitly ask for votes! She seems anxious to do this, so you need to tell her not to. You might even choose to go with her to talk to creditors. The Code itself says not to hand out copies of an actual plan without the disclosure statement, so **A** also is incorrect. The other two answers are in the gray area. Some lawyers would allow Franny to circulate the summary (choice **B**), but we think there is risk in passing out paper. Thus, we would choose the safer path, described in answer **C**.

Martin's and Keating's Picks

1. Question 1	**D**
2. Question 2	**B**
3. Question 3	**C**
4. Question 4	**C**
5. Question 5	**B**
The Closer	**C**

36

Forcing the Plan on Dissenting Creditors: A Different Kind of Cramdown

OVERVIEW
A. Cramdown of a Secured Class
B. The Specific and General Requirements of the Fair and Equitable Test
   1. Duration of payments to the secured party
   2. General fairness and §1129(b)(1)
   3. The present-value interest rate
   4. Obtaining positive votes from at least one accepting class: If you are stripping down, this is harder than it looks
C. The Absolute Priority Rule When Forcing the Plan on Classes of Unsecured Creditors
D. The Closer: Chapter 36
Martin's and Keating's Picks

So far, most of what you have learned about Chapter 11 plan confirmation has pertained to all Chapter 11 plans. The rules and tests discussed in Chapter 34 describe what any debtor must prove to confirm any plan of reorganization, not merely a consensual plan. For example, we learned about *priority claim* treatment, the *best interest test*, the *good faith test*, *feasibility*, and basic *secured creditor treatment*. In this chapter, we will learn what additional steps are required when the debtor wants to *cram down* the plan, meaning *force the plan*, on nonconsenting classes of creditors. (*See* 11 U.S.C. §1129(b).) All of the rules that we previously discussed, namely the *best interest test*, *good faith test*, *feasibility test*, *treatment of priority claims*, and so on, must be met in nonconsensual as well as consensual situations.

This chapter contains practice questions and a discussion of *stripping down* secured creditor claims,[1] about which you have already heard a great deal, as well as a discussion about what the debtor must prove to force the plan treatment on a class of unsecured creditors. Section 1129(b)(1) permits *cramdown* of a rejecting class (be it secured or unsecured), only if at least one impaired class of claims votes in favor of the plan, the plan does not discriminate unfairly between classes, and the plan treatment is "fair and equitable." The *fair and equitable* standard codifies a long line of cases addressing the fair and equitable treatment of creditors under the old Bankruptcy Act. Section 1129(b) of the Code contains the *minimum* requirements for a plan to be found fair and equitable, leaving the court free to impose additional requirements. The rights of secured creditors are contained in §1129(b)(2)(A) and the rights of unsecured creditors are covered by §1129(b)(2)(B).[2]

A. Cramdown of a Secured Class

Section 1129(b) requires that to cram down a secured creditor class, the treatment the secured party receives must be "fair and equitable." Section 1129(b)(1) requires that a nonconsensual plan be "fair and equitable" in general, and §1129(b)(2) states that to be fair and equitable, the debtor must (at a minimum) pay the secured party at least the *present value of its secured claim over the life of the collateral*, and also *allow the secured party to retain its liens during the payment period*. This is a test about which you have now heard a great deal. We will not revisit it all here, but will review a few problems to help you determine if you understand how to meet the fair and equitable test with respect to secured parties. At a minimum, secured claims must receive payment of the full value of the collateral, plus an interest rate designed to compensate the creditor for the present value of its claim.

B. The Specific and General Requirements of the Fair and Equitable Test

You might recall that very similar treatment is required of the debtor in a Chapter 13 case, pursuant to §1325 of the Bankruptcy Code. There are,

1. Remember that many attorneys call this *cramming down* the secured creditor's claim, but many professors feel this unnecessarily confuses students who should use the phrase *cram down* only in reference to forcing a plan under §1129(b), not reducing a claim.
2. This section also describes the minimum treatment required for equity interests, a topic we will not cover here.

however, two significant differences between the treatment provided to secured creditors under §1325 and the treatment provided under §1129. (Compare 11 U.S.C. §1325(a)(5) with 11 U.S.C. §1129(b)(2)(A).) The first difference relates to the length of time over which the debtor may pay a secured party in each type of case. The second difference is that §1129(b)(2)(A) contains an amorphous general fairness standard that is not contained in §1325(a)(5).

1. *Duration of payments to the secured party*

Chapter 13 cases generally last three to five years. (*See* 11 U.S.C. §1322(d).) These time limits are governed by explicit statutory provision. Congress decided that five years is the longest period of time over which an individual Chapter 13 debtor should pay back his or her past debts. In a Chapter 11 case, however, there is no such statutory mandate with respect to the length of time over which a debtor may pay a secured claim. Because a very critical part of secured creditor treatment in Chapter 11 cases is that the secured party retains its security interest while waiting to be paid (*see* 11 U.S.C. §1129(b)(2)(A)(i)), the outer limits of the length of time payments are made to secured creditors is determined by the life span of the collateral. In Chapter 11, plan payments on secured claims cannot continue past the time that the collateral has value, although the payments can be shorter than this useful life of course. A couple of examples might be useful.

Let's assume that for one secured creditor, its collateral is a copy machine. A copy machine's useful life is generally about four years. Assuming that the debtor has already had the copy machine for a year, this particular secured creditor would need to be paid within three years, the period of time in which the copy machine will still have value. Now take an example on the other end of the spectrum, and assume that the secured party has a mortgage on a piece of real estate. Real estate typically doesn't depreciate and thus the debtor could pay the secured party over a much longer period of time. In the case of real estate, the court will apply a reasonableness standard and the cases suggest that such payments should not extend beyond 10 or 15 years. This means, however, that different secured creditors in a case (holding liens on different collateral) will be paid over different periods of time, depending on the useful life of their collateral. Some will be paid over a short period of time; others will be paid over a longer period of time. Imagine that! A bankruptcy plan that spans over 20 years!

QUESTION 1. The debtor owns a bulldozer worth approximately $74,000 and proposes to pay this amount to the secured creditor, with present-value interest, over a five-year period in its Chapter 11 plan. The bulldozer typically would have a lifespan of seven years in the industry from this point forward. The debtor is involved in around-the-clock earth moving, however, and the creditor has objected to the plan, arguing that due to the debtor's heavy use, this bulldozer's useful life is shorter than the plan payment period. If the creditor is able to prove this fact, what should the court do?

A. Confirm the plan anyway because the plan still meets the fair and equitable test, and because what matters is the standard in the industry for equipment of this kind, not the particular useful life of this piece of equipment.
B. Deny confirmation of the plan because what matters here is the useful life of the actual equipment in question, not the theoretical useful life.
C. Postpone confirmation until the debtor can either disprove the creditor's claims, come up with more collateral, or find a way to increase the payments.
D. Deny confirmation because the plan is not feasible.

ANALYSIS. Feasibility is not in issue at this time, so **D** is incorrect. This may become an issue if the debtor is forced to shorten the plan payments and increase the amount of each payment, but at this time, this is not the issue. Here the correct answer is **B**. The fair and equitable test has not been met, an issue explored further in the next question. Bear in mind that the application of the Bankruptcy Code is a very practical process, one that attempts to protect the interests of particular creditors (and their collateral), while at the same time promoting reorganization to the extent possible. Here, *fair and equitable* treatment requires that the secured creditor retain its lien, meaning the property must have value during the entire plan period. The value of the piece of equipment in question is more relevant than any theoretical value. This is true of virtually all valuation issues in bankruptcy. The court will attempt to determine the useful life of this particular piece of equipment and, assuming that industry standards are based on a normal 10- to 12-hour workday, set the useful life of this bulldozer at three and one-half years. For this reason, **B** (rather than **A**) is the correct answer.

Procedurally, once the confirmation hearing has started, the debtor is required to present all of its evidence supporting confirmation. Although **C** sounds like it could be correct, the time for the debtor to contest evidence of the creditor is at the confirmation hearing, not afterward. If the debtor would like more time to either contest the evidence or to try to resolve the dispute, the debtor should ask the creditor to postpone the hearing, rather than requesting that the court do so. It is unlikely that the court would, either at the debtor's request or at its own volition, postpone the hearing midstream to allow one party to get more evidence or settle a dispute. However, the court will sometimes say something along these lines to the debtor:

"I see a problem for you here. Would you like a few minutes to talk this over with your lawyer and the creditor to see if you can resolve it?" This allows the confirmation process to proceed if the issue is a minor one that can be resolved without causing feasibility problems.

QUESTION 2. In the prior problem, what part of the fair and equitable standard has been violated by the debtor?

A. The calculation of the present-value interest rate.
B. The valuation of the creditor's claim.
C. The general spirit of the test, but no particular part of the test.
D. The requirement that the creditor be allowed to retain its liens on its collateral over the life of the plan.

ANALYSIS. **A** and **B** are not in issue as the problem states that the debtor has met these requirements. Thus, the choice is between **C** and **D**. **D** is more specific and is therefore the correct answer. Think about why Congress requires that the creditor be permitted to retain its liens on its collateral in a cramdown. A cramdown is accomplished against the creditor's will. The lien retention provision protects the creditor in the event the debtor defaults on the plan payments during the plan period. If this happens, the creditor should be permitted to repossess its collateral and recover the rest of what it is owed.[3] If the collateral does not retain its value during the entire plan period, the creditor has been denied meaningful lien retention during the plan period. These liens have been eliminated through the debtor's use of the collateral, thus violating §1129(b)(2)(A)(i)(I). Thus, the correct answer is **D**.

2. *General fairness and §1129(b)(1)*

Let's talk a bit further about the answer found in choice **C** in the last question, which refers to the general spirit of the fair and equitable test. Thus far, we have not talked about any general fairness standards embedded in §1129(b), but have focused narrowly on the court-imposed requirements of lien retention, present-value interest, and claim valuation. Section 1129(b) requires that the plan be fair in a general sense, not merely that the specifics of §1129(b) be met. The next problem deals with a very common and practical question of fairness of treatment (frequently found in Chapter 11 cases), namely *negative amortization*. Negative amortization occurs when a secured creditor is being paid the present value of its allowed claim over the life of the plan, but not in equal monthly installments. Instead, the payments are very small in the beginning of the plan, and are later increased. If the payments do not even cover the interest on a monthly or quarterly basis, we call it negative amortization because the

3. What is the creditor owed? This is an issue addressed in the final chapter of this book, dealing with post-confirmation issues.

amount of debt goes up as the plan proceeds, rather than going down. Many plans that propose negative amortization also involve a big payment, called a *balloon payment*, to be paid by the debtor at the end of the plan. This places most of the risk of the reorganization on the secured party, rather than the debtor. In a general sense, does this sound "fair and equitable?"

QUESTION 3. Percy's Used Cars proposes a plan that pays the secured creditor's allowed secured claim, with present-value interest. While the total payments meet the specific §1129(b) cramdown requirements, the plan proposes small payments throughout the four-year plan, followed by a balloon of most of the principal at the end of the plan period. Which potential plan objections can the debtor and its attorneys anticipate?

A. Feasibility.
B. The fair and equitable test contained in §1129(b).
C. The best interest test.
D. The good faith test.

ANALYSIS. From what we have been told here, **C** is not implicated, as the best interest test is typically relevant only to unsecured creditor claims. Although the secured creditor may hold an unsecured (deficiency) claim if it is undersecured, nothing in the problem suggests that the best interest test is at issue. Nor is the good faith test (mentioned in **D**) likely to be implicated. Negative amortization may be unpopular, but it is not forbidden in all cases. Thus, in and of itself, it is not evidence of a lack of good faith in proposing the plan. The correct answer is **B**, as negative amortization often violates the general requirements of the fair and equitable test, even if the specifically enumerated parts of the test (meaning payment of the present value of the allowed secured claim over the life of the plan) are met. (*See* Nauman v. Nauman, 213 B.R. 355 (9th Cir. 1997) (describing a ten-factor test for determining whether a particular negative amortization scheme violates §1129's fair and equitable test).)

Although **A** is not the answer, one can imagine that if the debtor attempts to fix this problem by making larger payments to the secured party earlier in the case, the plan could fail the feasibility test. There is often a reason why the debtor proposes a negative amortization plan, and frequently enough, the debtor is simply short on cash. Fixing one problem often creates another. Therefore, the best answer here is **B**, because negative amortization often violates the general fair and equitable test contained in §1129(b)(1).

3. *The present-value interest rate*

Section 1129(b)(2) also requires that the secured party be paid the present value of its allowed secured claim starting on the effective date of the plan. For many years, courts calculated the present value rate in either a Chapter 11 or

Chapter 13 case by multiplying the allowed secured claim (the lesser of the face amount of the claim or the value of the collateral) by the rate at which a similarly situated borrower, who was not in bankruptcy, could obtain similar credit in the marketplace. In 2004, the United States Supreme Court overruled case law using this standard and held that the rate to be applied in a Chapter 13 case is to be based on the prime rate, plus some added percentage points for a host of risk variables. (*See* Till v. SCS Credit Corp., 541 U.S. 465 (2004).) As the Court explained, [b]ecause bankrupt debtors typically pose a greater risk of nonpayment than solvent commercial borrowers, the approach then requires a bankruptcy court to adjust the prime rate accordingly. The appropriate size of that risk adjustment depends, of course, on such factors as *the circumstances of the estate, the nature of the security, and the duration and feasibility of the reorganization plan* [emphasis added]. The court must therefore hold a hearing at which the debtor and any creditors may present evidence about the appropriate risk adjustment. (*Id.* at 479.)

Most attorneys believe this will simplify things for debtors-in-possession, although the test still seems complex. The court case also seems to say that the application of this test will result in a *risk kicker*, as the interest over prime is sometimes called, in the typical range of 1 to 3 percent, depending on the facts of the case. As the Supreme Court explained, if a court were tempted to assign a larger risk kicker, the plan may be too risky and may not be feasible. The Court also held that the creditor has the burden of proving the amount of the risk, and if nothing but the prime rate is established, the debtor can simply pay the prime rate. *Till* involved a Chapter 13 debtor, but some courts have applied the same interest formula to Chapter 11 cramdown cases as well. Other courts do not believe that *Till* is binding in a Chapter 11 context and have instead used a cramdown interest rate that a hypothetical lender that is forced to make a "coerced loan" to this particular Chapter 11 debtor would use. Whether and how that rate would differ from the *Till* formula's rate is not always clear.

In footnote 14 of the *Till* opinion, the Supreme Court noted that in contrast to Chapter 13 cases, there is sometimes an "efficient" market for exit financing in Chapter 11. In such circumstances, the Court said, it may be more appropriate to use the interest rate existing in such a market, rather than *Till*'s "prime rate plus a risk premium" approach, as the cramdown rate. The Second Circuit heeded this part of the *Till* opinion in a 2017 case, In re MPM Silicones, LLC.[4] In that case, the Second Circuit rejected the bankruptcy court's use of *Till*'s "prime rate plus a risk premium" approach to determine the cramdown rate for a group of secured noteholders in a Chapter 11 case. The Second Circuit decided that there was evidence in that case of an active market for exit financing in which a higher rate of interest was being commanded, and therefore that higher market rate should be used as the cramdown interest rate.

4. 874 F.3d 787 (2d Cir. 2017).

4. *Obtaining positive votes from at least one accepting class: If you are stripping down, this is harder than it looks*

Cramdown plans often involve stripping down a secured party's claim. Reducing or *stripping down* the value of a secured creditor's claim has its costs, however. Remember that any time a creditor is undersecured by a large amount, and the debtor decides to strip down the lien, the undersecured (and thus bifurcated) creditor will have a large deficiency claim, and thus a large voice in the general unsecured creditor class as well. As a result, the creditor may be able to cause the unsecured creditor class to vote no and thus block confirmation of the plan. (*See* 11 U.S.C. §1126(c).)

Remember that *stripdown* of the secured creditor's lien is *optional for the debtor*. In some cases, it may be easier and cheaper (and make little difference in terms of the plan payments) to simply pay a lender the full amount of its claim as a secured claim, rather than attempting to strip down the lien. In many cases, the debtor will have numerous secured creditors and may not want to wage a valuation battle with all of them. Thus, depending on the loan and collateral values, the debtor may choose to dispute collateral values (strip down) with one creditor, two creditors, or perhaps none of its creditors.

The debtor often pays at least some secured creditors pursuant to the original contract terms, if the loan was not in default at the time of the bankruptcy, if the payments have been maintained during the case, and if the collateral has maintained its value. The debtor must evaluate its options on a case-by-case basis. Generally speaking, maintenance of the status quo is easiest to achieve if payments have continued during the case.

QUESTION 4. Assume that the debtor has three secured creditors, Classes 1, 2, and 3, and one general unsecured creditor class, Class 4, which includes trade vendors holding $400,000 in claims, and any deficiency claims arising from the plan. The Class 4 trade creditors (of which there are three) all favor the debtor and the debtor's current proposed distribution. Class 1 and 2 creditors hold claims of $900,000 and $140,000, respectively, secured by first and second priority liens on real property worth $850,000. The Class 3 creditor holds a $75,000 claim secured by a forklift valued at $25,000. The debtor asks you, its attorney, how best to treat the secured creditor claims, given that the debtor wants to achieve confirmation relatively quickly but does not want to throw away money needlessly. You should tell the debtor:

A. that it needs only one impaired accepting class to confirm a cramdown plan, and that if the trade vendors are on board, it should strip down the liens of all three secured creditors and cram down the plan on them, and thereby save a ton of money by paying much lower secured claims and only a percentage of each secured creditor's deficiency claim.

B. to strip down the Class 2 and 3 liens, cram down the plan on them, pay the Class 1 claim in full, and thereby preserve the impaired accepting class.

C. that it can only strip down either the Class 2 or the Class 3 lien because of the voting requirements regarding ballots cast and claims held by each class, and that it makes more economic sense to strip down the Class 2 creditor than the Class 3 creditor.

D. that it should pay all the secured creditors the full face value of their claims and then drastically reduce the unsecured creditor distribution to fund the secured creditor payments.

ANALYSIS. This is a math question, which requires you to determine how the debtor can strip down the claims of some or all of the secured creditors in the case, and cram the plan down on them, without destroying the vote in the unsecured creditor class by creating too many large deficiency claims. Without doing any math at all, you can eliminate **D**, because if you pay the secured claims in full, they may not be impaired. You would then need to rely on the general unsecured creditor class, your only impaired class, to vote yes. Now that the distribution is "drastically reduced" this class will likely vote no, so the plan will not be confirmed. The key is to preserve the yes vote in the general unsecured creditor class, assuming that all of the deficiency claims will vote no (because they will be sore about the stripdown).

The trade class that will vote yes is $400,000, and you need these three trade creditors to continue being the "more than one-half in number." Thus, you need to make sure trade creditors comprise two-thirds of the total unsecured claims and more than one-half in number. As $400,000 is two-thirds of $600,000, the deficiency claims cannot exceed $200,000 if the yes vote in this class is to be preserved. If all of the secured creditors' liens were stripped down, they would have the following deficiency claims: Classes 1, $50,000; Class 2, $140,000; and Class 3, $50,000. You cannot, based on these figures, cram down all three classes. You must pick between Classes 1 and 3, and also strip down (and cram down the plan on) Class 2. Otherwise, the deficiency votes will destroy the yes vote of trade creditors because they total more than one-third of the total amount. Thus, **A** is incorrect. It does not take into account the potential "no" votes of the deficiency claims. **B** is the correct answer because you can strip down both Class 2 and Class 3 liens and still preserve the unsecured "yes" vote.

Now, let's test what you just learned by changing the hypothetical slightly. Assume now that the trade creditors have $300,000 in claims, instead of $400,000. How would this change your answer? Think this through before answering.

We would start by remembering that the unsecured creditor class must have two-thirds in amount voting yes. $300,000 is two-thirds of $450,000, right? It looks like the debtor can strip down enough to create up to, but not more than, $150,000 in deficiency claims. Now the debtor can only afford to strip down one of the liens. It would be most cost effective to strip down the largest one, Class 2, for $140,000. This would make the total unsecured debt $440,000, and $300,000 is more than two-thirds of this amount, so it works! The debtor would be best off in this second hypothetical, stripping down Class 2, but not Classes 1 and 3.

C. The Absolute Priority Rule When Forcing the Plan on Classes of Unsecured Creditors

Unsecured creditors and senior stockholders are protected by a very different cramdown rule. In addition to the best interest test contained in §1129(a)(7), unsecured creditors must either consent to the plan or be paid in full under the plan, or else any party "junior to it" cannot receive or retain anything of value in connection with the plan. A class of unsecured creditors that has rejected the plan cannot have the plan forced on it or *crammed down* unless all of the equity owners are retaining or receiving *nothing* under the plan. (*See* 11 U.S.C. §1129(b)(2)(B).) You might be thinking, well that's OK, because in most Chapter 11 plans, equity holders do not receive any payments under the plan. This, however, misses the whole point of what we call the *absolute priority rule*. What is forbidden is that equity *retain* its equity interests. In other words, if unsecured creditors are either not paid in full under the plan or do not consent to the plan, then equity cannot retain its equity interests under the plan. Rather, these equity interests must be sold or given to creditors. By *equity interests*, we mean ownership interests and all this entails— all profits, all control over the business, all future possibility of getting a return as shareholders or equity holders. This is what current owners are not entitled to retain, unless unsecured creditor classes either consent (meaning vote in favor of the plan) or are paid in full.

This test makes sense because creditors are higher in priority than equity holders and, as a result, creditors must be paid in full (or accept the plan) before equity holders can continue to own the business. If any higher priority class of unsecured creditors has not consented to the plan, then equity holders must give up their ownership interest in the debtor, either to be sold or distributed to creditors, essentially at the option of creditors.[5]

5. This test applies only to dissenting impaired classes of unsecured creditors, however.

Considering that the entire Chapter 11 model assumes that management and equity remain in place during a Chapter 11 case, this should come as some surprise. Whereas the owners and the managers are two different groups of people in very large bankruptcy cases, in the smaller cases, owners typically manage the company. For these cases, the absolute priority rule seems harsh. In reality, this rule essentially means that equity owners must get unsecured creditors to agree to the plan or will lose everything under the plan. Remember that, generally speaking, the debtor's management is controlled by shareholders (also called *equity holders*) and equity holders are attempting to keep their interest in the reorganized debtor. This particular rule, the *absolute priority rule*, creates the greatest incentive of all for owners to get all creditor classes, but particularly all general unsecured creditors, to vote in favor of the plan. As you will see in the next chapter, the new subchapter V small business bankruptcy provisions allow small business debtors to cram down Chapter 11 plans even without complying with the absolute priority rule as long as certain other requirements are met.

Although many courts have interpreted the absolute priority rule strictly, in the manner just described, others have recognized an exception to the rule. This exception is known as the *new value exception* to the absolute priority rule. Under this exception, if the debtor is unable to pay unsecured creditors in full, there may still be another option for allowing management to retain its equity, even if the unsecured creditor class votes against the plan. Do keep in mind, however, that unsecured creditors shouldn't be voting against the plan if they believe that the debtor has given them everything they could realistically get in a plan, and also that they are receiving more under the plan than they would receive in a liquidation. There could still be holdout classes, however, so this exception to the absolute priority rule could be helpful. Make sure you understand the absolute priority rule, and the rationale behind the rule, before you read on and learn about the new value exception.

Under the new value exception, which is not found anywhere in the Code, existing equity holders are sometimes allowed to retain or buy back their equity interests in the debtor by having the equity interests valued and by contributing this amount of cash to the debtor to be used under the debtor's plan. We previously mentioned that the debtor might need new capital to reorganize. As you might imagine, this new capital can actually come from old equity. Old equity holders may invest new money in the debtor and thereby help the debtor reorganize, while at the same time retaining (or buying back) their equity interests through the new value exception.

Although the new value exception sounds straightforward, it has actually been quite controversial. Some courts fear that equity holders may be able to obtain the equity interests in the debtor at a bargain price, because old equity's purchase of these interests has not been subjected to market conditions through an auction or other process. After a long time, during which federal circuit courts were split on whether the new value exception even existed, the U.S. Supreme Court decided the case of Bank of America National Trust and Savings Association v. 203 North LaSalle Street Partnership, 526 U.S. 434 (1999). In that case, the Supreme Court held that while old equity holders *could not* have the exclusive right to buy the equity interests in a debtor, old equity holders may buy back equity interests if these equity interests are first exposed to market conditions, and thus if other parties are also allowed to bid on the equity of the debtor. The Court reasoned that old equity holders could not have an exclusive right to buy the equity in a Chapter 11 business because that exclusive right is itself retention of some interest in the debtor. This is what the statute forbids. (*See* 11 U.S.C. §1129(b)(2)(B).) The Supreme Court noted that the terms *absolute priority rule* and *new value exception* are judicially made law, and are to be reviewed against the backdrop of a larger concern, namely that a Chapter 11 debtor's plan could be too good a deal for the debtor's old owners, who then gain an unfair advantage in the reorganization process.

The Supreme Court in *203 North LaSalle* ultimately held that the debtor's existing ownership would be permitted to bid for equity, but that some form of market valuation must be available to test the adequacy of the old equity holders' proposed contribution. However, the Court did not decide whether a market test would require an opportunity for competing bids or could simply be satisfied by a different valuation procedure. Instead, the Court stated that "it is enough to say, assuming that the new value corollary [exception] exists, that plans providing interest holders with an exclusive opportunity free from competition and without benefit of market valuation fall within the prohibitions of §1129(b)(2)(B)(ii)."

Prior cases interpreting the new value exception (or corollary) to the absolute priority rule had established various requirements for meeting this task. The Supreme Court has articulated an additional test, namely that the equity interest be exposed to market conditions. Before that time, however, courts had articulated the following test, which is still being used as well:

1. The debtor's equity holders' contribution must be in money or money's worth.
2. The contribution must be equal in value to the equity interest being retained under the plan.
3. The contribution must be necessary to the debtor's reorganization.

Courts have found that prong one is not met when old equity holders promise to work for free in the future, essentially contributing sweat equity to the plan, rather than cash. In other words, old equity cannot contribute labor to the debtor to satisfy the new value exception to the absolute priority rule. Nice try, but if you think about it, this is something that many owners plan to do anyway. Thus, courts require that contributions be in money or money's worth.

One of the most interesting things about the new value exception to the absolute priority rule is that, in most cases, the test is not implicated. One of your co-authors, in her own practice, would often suggest that equity holders, if they plan to retain their equity interest in the debtor, go ahead and make a voluntary preemptive contribution of cash into the plan to deter any question about whether the absolute priority test has been met, in advance of plan objections. Some might argue that this is unnecessary, because equity need not meet the absolute priority rule unless unsecured creditors object. However, as we have mentioned elsewhere in the context of this guide, creditors are likely to object to any plan that does not provide them with whatever rights the Bankruptcy Code itself would provide.

Some scholars have suggested that the absolute priority rule comes up most often in the context of a certain type of Chapter 11 case, mainly the single-asset real estate case. In these particular cases, secured creditors are far, far larger than any other creditor in the case. If you think about the business of a single-asset real estate project, you basically have a huge project with a very large mortgage on it, and only a few general unsecured creditors who may have provided telephone services, garbage services, and other services to the debtor. Normally, the debtor is attempting to *cram down* the secured party's claim, and as a result, the project may be way underwater. As we've discussed in prior chapters, the debtor may have difficulty coming up with classes of claims under the plan that will vote yes because a large portion of the secured party's claim will be a deficiency claim in the unsecured creditors' class and will significantly dwarf the claims of the other general unsecured creditors. Consequently, the primary secured lender is often the one that is opposing the debtor's plan and will gain its voting rights through its deficiency claim in the unsecured creditor class. By being in this unsecured creditor class, the undersecured creditor also now has standing to object to the plan on the basis of the absolute priority rule contained in §1129(b)(2)(B).

Interestingly, single-asset real estate cases are not the types of cases that really affect society. In many ways, these cases are unimportant as reorganization cases, as there are no (or few) employees and the businesses generally have little effect on the economy. In fact, in so many ways, these are simply disputes between two parties (the debtor and the mortgage lender), which would probably be better handled in a setting other than Chapter 11. As a result of this, §362(d)(3) contains different standards for granting relief from the stay in the context of a single-asset real estate case.

QUESTION 5. The debtor, Packers Plus, runs a packing and shipping company at the pier in Philadelphia. Pursuant to its plan, the debtor will pay off a small, unsecured loan, pay a large number of workers' compensation claims at 10 cents on the dollar, and pay general unsecured creditor claims at 25 cents on the dollar. The workers' compensation creditors have objected to the plan on various grounds, although the general unsecured creditors are in favor of the plan. The debtor expects to pay off the plan in five years, and possibly make a small net profit during that time. Because very little profit will be thrown off until after the plan is paid off, the debtor's two equity holders propose to put in $5,000 each and to maintain their equity interest in the debtor post-confirmation. Based only on what you know here, what good objections does the workers' compensation class have against confirmation?

1. The plan is not feasible.
2. The plan contains unfair discrimination in its classification.
3. The plan contains unfair discrimination in its treatment.
4. The plan violates the absolute priority rule.

A. Choices 2 and 3 only.
B. Choices 2, 3, and 4.
C. Choices 1 and 4.
D. All of the above.

ANALYSIS. It is fairly clear, as we are on the topic, that this plan violates the absolute priority rule. First, there is no particular justification for the $5,000 per person that the equity holders have proposed as a cash contribution, at least not based on the facts we have. There has been no valuation procedure pursuant to which $10,000 has been chosen as the magic figure that will satisfy the new value exception to the absolute priority rule. Moreover, the debtor's equity interests have not been exposed to any market condition, as no other parties have had an opportunity to purchase this equity for a higher value. Thus, the correct answer should contain choice **4**, which only eliminates answer **A**. What about separately classifying and treating the workers' compensation claims? This is most likely a problem, so choices **2** and **3** are also correct. There is no visible justification for separately classifying and treating these claims differently from other general unsecured claims, except perhaps that there is a large number of them. This does not appear to be a justifiable business purpose, and consequently the classification violates the Bankruptcy Code, as does the disparate treatment. Thus it looks like **2, 3**, and **4** are all correct. The question, then, is whether **B** or **D** is the correct answer because we don't know whether feasibility is also a problem. We actually don't have enough facts to tell us whether feasibility is a problem here, although we would always recommend that a disgruntled creditor object based on anything that seems reasonable. Whether a feasibility objection is reasonable remains to be seen, and thus, choice **1** is not (at this time) a sure thing. The question asks what good objections the workers' compensation class has and not knowing enough about the feasibility issue, the best answer to this question is **B**.

D. The Closer: Chapter 36

Assume that a debtor's plan calls for equal monthly payments to the secured creditor over seven years with interest at 7 percent. The secured creditor has objected to confirmation because the plan does not pay the present value of its claim and calls for payments beyond the useful life of its collateral. At the confirmation hearing, the debtor's chief executive officer and chief financial officer (CFO) testified that the secured creditor's collateral, an enormous turbine generator that the debtor bought three years ago, generally would have a useful life of ten years, but because the debtor recently had the generator professionally overhauled and rebuilt, its useful life is now closer to 15 years. The CFO also testified that, although the debtor missed some payments to the secured creditor in the past, the debtor's projections show that the debtor can make its plan payments. The secured party was unable to get a bank officer to attend this hearing, but on cross-examination, elicited testimony from the CFO that when the loan at issue was first made, the debtor had a clean credit rating and paid interest at the rate of 8 percent. On redirect, the debtor's CFO testified that, as published in the *Wall Street Journal*, the current prime rate of interest is 7 percent. The court should:

A. deny confirmation because the plan doesn't pay the present value of the secured creditor's claim over the life of the plan, as the rate paid in the plan would only apply to a good credit risk.
B. deny confirmation because the debtor is seeking to pay a below market rate (as a bankruptcy debtor, no less) and because the payments extend beyond the useful life of the collateral.
C. confirm the debtor's plan because the plan calls for payments well within the useful life of the collateral and because the evidence suggests that the debtor is paying the present value of the secured creditor's claim, as the creditor failed to prove otherwise.
D. confirm the debtor's plan because the plan appears feasible and because the creditors' committee supports the plan as being in the best interest of creditors.

ANALYSIS. This question combines what you learned about calculating present-value interest and the proper length of plan payments based on the useful life of the collateral. These are the two issues here, so we can first eliminate any choice that talks about something else. **D** discusses feasibility and the best interest of creditors' test, neither of which seem to be at issue here. Thus, we can eliminate **D**. We next try to eliminate other answers that seem wrong. On the issue of the useful life, the useful life of the collateral is either, by anyone's account, 10 or 15 years. The plan payments only extend for seven years so there is no problem with the plan length and we can eliminate **B**.

Given the choice between **A** and **C**, the creditor did not put on a witness and thus failed to meet its burden of proof on the appropriate present value rate. Although it is true that the debtor's own witnesses testified about the rate at the time the loan was taken out, this is not relevant. Interest rates change and this is critical to calculating the present value rate. What is relevant to calculating the present value rate is the prime rate *today*, plus any other risk factors the creditor proves. Here there was no other proof and the answer is **C**. Nice job, if you got that one right.

Martin's and Keating's Picks

1. Question 1 **B**
2. Question 2 **D**
3. Question 3 **B**
4. Question 4 **B**
5. Question 5 **B**

The Closer **C**

37

Small Business Cases Under Chapter 11

OVERVIEW
A. A Brief History of Small Business Bankruptcy
B. Shorter Deadlines for Small Business Debtors
C. Additional Reporting Requirements and Oversight
D. Simplification of the Plan Process
E. Higher Risk of Conversion or Dismissal
F. The Small Business Reorganization Act of 2019 ("SBRA")
Martin's and Keating's Picks

A. A Brief History of Small Business Bankruptcy

When it comes to bankruptcy law's treatment of small business debtors, it is fair to say that the law has come "full circle" on this issue. The Bankruptcy Act of 1898, which was the law in effect prior to the 1978 Bankruptcy Code, had different reorganization procedures for small and large businesses. Large businesses generally used Chapter X, and small businesses tended to choose the more flexible settlement procedures of Chapter XI. However, Congress decided with the 1978 Bankruptcy Code to consolidate both large and small business reorganizations into a one-size-fits-all Chapter 11.

Unfortunately, the complex procedures that the new Chapter 11 created were not well-suited for smaller businesses that depended mainly on the skills and contributions of a single owner-operator. As a result, many such small businesses either tried nonbankruptcy alternatives to reorganize (which were largely unsuccessful) or attempted to reorganize under Chapter 11 but failed. Even those small businesses that successfully reorganized under Chapter 11 did so only after expending a large percentage of the company's assets on the administrative fees that are inherent in the standard Chapter 11 process.

Congress first tried to remedy Chapter 11's poor fit for small businesses through the 1994 amendments to the Bankruptcy Code. These amendments introduced into the Bankruptcy Code the definition of "small business debtor" and allowed a business debtor that was under the $2 million debt limit to opt for that status when filing Chapter 11. The 1994 amendments provided small business debtors a "fast track" that reduced the periods for exclusivity and plan confirmation by 20 days each. The amendments also allowed the debtor to avoid a formal disclosure statement hearing and instead permitted solicitation of plan acceptances with a conditionally approved disclosure statement. A consolidated hearing would then allow the bankruptcy judge to give final approval of the debtor's disclosure statement at the same time the debtor's plan was confirmed.

When very few Chapter 11 debtors chose this new small business option, Congress tried again to separate small business Chapter 11 cases from large ones with the 2005 amendments. These amendments attempted to require small business debtor treatment for those debtors that fit the definition. The 2005 amendments also added some new provisions that tried both to streamline the small business Chapter 11 process and to require additional reporting duties for small business debtors. Despite the mandatory nature of the new small business debtor track in the 2005 amendments, this track remained underutilized by most Chapter 11 debtors who nominally qualified for such treatment. Many small business debtors found the fast-tracked deadlines for small business debtors to be too challenging to meet. Some debtors used clever lawyering to avoid fitting within the small business debtor definition, and others simply avoided Chapter 11 altogether.

Finally, in August of 2019 Congress listened to the recommendations of bankruptcy lawyers and judges and passed the Small Business Reorganization Act of 2019 ("SBRA"). SBRA created an entirely new subchapter of Chapter 11 for small business debtors, subchapter V, that became available in February of 2020. The key difference in subchapter V compared to the 1994 and 2005 attempts by Congress to create a separate small business track for Chapter 11 debtors is that subchapter V creates a number of significant benefits for small business debtors that choose to file under that subchapter. In many ways, Congress borrowed some of the more debtor-friendly features of Chapters 12 and 13 bankruptcy cases and applied them to subchapter V small business debtors.

While the small business provisions added in 1994 and 2005 are still in the Code, the 2019 SBRA has all but replaced these prior small business provisions in practice. The SBRA has been so successful that in many less populous jurisdictions, these SBRA cases now constitute the lion's share of all Chapter 11 cases. Thus, we include a discussion of these prior small business provisions below, but in practice it is most helpful to focus on the 2019 SBRA when considering what type of case to file for small businesses wishing to go into Chapter 11.

Setting the appropriate debt limit for eligibility has been the trickiest challenge for Congress in enacting subchapter V. That issue was highlighted when the pandemic shutdown occurred one month after the new law became effective. Congress originally used the cutoff line that was already in the Bankruptcy Code's definition of "small business debtor," which at the time of SBRA's enactment set the inflation-adjusted debt limit at slightly under $3 million ($2,725,625 to be precise). The prospect of a pandemic-fueled increase in the need for Chapter 11 filings prompted Congress to pass the CARES Act, which temporarily raised the subchapter V debt limit to $7.5 million. One year later, in March of 2021, Congress renewed the heightened debt limit for subchapter V eligibility for an additional year. However, in March of 2022, the one-year renewal expired and as of this writing subchapter V eligibility has returned to its original standard that is tied to the inflation-adjusted figure in the definition of a small business debtor, currently more than $3 million as of the April 1, 2025 inflation adjustments.

To be a small business debtor, a debtor must be engaged in commercial or business activities and have aggregate noncontingent liquidated debt of not more than $3,424,000 (excluding debts owed to affiliates or insiders), and "not less than 50 percent of which arose from the commercial or business activities of the debtor." (*See* §101(51D).) This definition also specifically excludes single-asset real estate debtors.

If a debtor qualifies under the definition of "small business debtor," it can elect to file under the new subchapter V, or instead it can be treated as a debtor under the traditional Chapter 11 track as modified by the small business amendments that were added in 1994 and 2005. Given the special benefits that subchapter V offers to debtors, most debtors that qualify as small business debtors will opt for that subchapter rather than proceeding under the small business provisions that are part of the standard Chapter 11 process. In the sections below, we will first discuss the small business provisions that Congress added to the Bankruptcy Code in 2005. These provisions continue to apply to small business debtors that do not opt for subchapter V treatment. Certain provisions from the 2005 amendments will apply even to those small business debtors that do opt for subchapter V treatment. After discussing the 2005 amendments that affect small business debtors, we will describe the most important provisions that comprise new subchapter V.

B. Shorter Deadlines for Small Business Debtors

Prior to the 2005 amendments, all Chapter 11 debtors were afforded the exclusive right to file a plan for the first 120 days after the entry of the order for relief. If a Chapter 11 debtor filed a plan during this time period, the debtor's exclusive right to file a plan was extended an additional 60 days so that the debtor could seek to obtain acceptance of its plan by all impaired classes of creditors and interest holders without the distraction and competition of non-debtor plans being filed. While creditors could ask the bankruptcy court to shorten these time periods, debtors could likewise seek to have them extended, which bankruptcy courts frequently agreed to do. Before the 2005 amendments were enacted, there were no statutory limitations on the number of times or the duration by which a bankruptcy court could extend a Chapter 11 debtor's exclusive right to file a plan.

In the case of non-small business Chapter 11 debtors, the 2005 amendments largely kept the above-described framework in place with one notable exception: Under the 2005 amendments, bankruptcy courts can no longer extend a non-small business debtor's exclusive right to file a Chapter 11 plan beyond 18 months after the entry of the order for relief or, in the event the debtor files a plan during such period, 20 months after the entry of the order for relief. Following the expiration of these outside dates, the bankruptcy court has no authority to preclude other eligible parties from filing a Chapter 11 plan in the case.[1]

In the case of non-subchapter V small business debtors, the 2005 amendments afford such debtors the exclusive right to file a Chapter 11 plan for the first 180 days after the entry of the order for relief. This time period can be extended for "cause" and/or in accordance with the above-described extension provisions generally applicable in Chapter 11.

Separate and distinct from the issue of exclusivity, a non-subchapter V small business debtor must comply with an independent statutory requirement that a plan be filed within 300 days after entry of the order for relief and that confirmation of such plan must be obtained within 45 days after filing the plan.[2]

QUESTION 1. The plan filing deadline is more critical to a Chapter 11 small business debtor than the exclusivity deadline because:

A. without retaining exclusivity, the debtor's case will be converted or dismissed under §1112(b).

B. without meeting the plan filing deadline, the debtor's case will be converted or dismissed under §1112(b).

1. The Code means this but does not quite say this. (*See* 11 U.S.C. §1121(d)(1) and (2).) Ah, the perils of working with a not very well-drafted statute.

2. *See* 11 U.S.C. §§1121(e)(2) and 1129(e). In reality, the court can extend these deadlines but only if the non-subchapter V small business debtor demonstrates by a preponderance of the evidence that it is more likely than not to be able to confirm a plan within a reasonable period of time. *See* 11 U.S.C. §1121(e)(3). This is arguably tantamount to requiring the debtor to prove feasibility for a plan that has not even been filed. In other words, this is not likely to happen too often.

C. without retaining exclusivity, a creditor could file a Chapter 11 plan that calls for the liquidation of the debtor, or otherwise provides for the creditor to take control of the debtor.
D. if the debtor retains exclusivity, missing the plan deadline is not relevant.

ANALYSIS. Here we are testing whether you understand the difference between a filing deadline and an exclusivity deadline. If you do, this one is easy. The question specifically states that meeting the plan deadline is more important than retaining exclusivity. The main reason this is true is that a debtor that misses the plan deadline can no longer file a plan and reorganize its business. The case is essentially over, and the case can be converted. Thus, **B** is the correct answer. The other three answers all give reasons why exclusivity is more important, which should have made all three easy to eliminate. **A** is actually incorrect in any event. If you pick through §1112(b)(4), the most important part of §1112(b), it never says that losing exclusivity will result in conversion of the case to a Chapter 7. It does however, make missing the plan deadline an infraction resulting in conversion or dismissal. (*See* 11 U.S.C. §1112(b)(4)(J).) **C** says that if a debtor loses exclusivity, a creditor could file a plan in the debtor's case, and that the debtor will lose control of the case. This is true, and this is what it means to lose exclusivity. This is not, however, a reason why the plan deadline is more important than the exclusivity deadline. Thus, **C** is incorrect. Choice **D** demonstrates a lack of understanding of what exclusivity means to a Chapter 11 debtor. Once the plan filing deadline is missed the case is over, as explained previously. Retaining exclusivity in no way cures the problem. Thus, **D** is also incorrect and **B** is the correct answer.

C. Additional Reporting Requirements and Oversight

One of the central assumptions underlying the 2005 small business provisions is that small Chapter 11 cases often do not have active creditors' committees. In fact, only approximately 15 percent of all Chapter 11 cases have creditors' committees. Creditors' committees provide oversight in cases and also put pressure on debtors to finish the case and pay creditors. Given the lack of creditors' committees in so many cases, the 2005 amendments pertaining to small businesses require small business debtors to file a much longer list of documents with the court. This was purportedly designed to further the dual objectives of weeding out cases that had little likelihood of success and also to help smaller debtors reorganize by helping them gather and share basic financial information about their own operations. The idea was that small businesses needed the discipline to do this and such discipline would help the debtor reorganize.

As a result, the 2005 amendments impose far greater financial reporting requirements on small business than on other Chapter 11 debtors. (*See* 11 U.S.C. §1116.) These additional requirements, which also apply to subchapter V small business debtors, include: filing the debtor's most recent balance sheet, statement of operations, cash-flow statements, and federal tax return (if the debtor has these documents); attending extra meetings with the U.S. Trustee's office; filing the bankruptcy schedules within 45 days of the filing (even though bigger companies usually get a longer extension); and preparing and filing reports regarding the debtor's operations that disclose whether the debtor is operating at a profit, describe the debtor's cash flow, and state whether the debtor is current in filing tax returns and paying post-petition taxes and operating expenses. Small business debtors also must deposit all withholding taxes in a separate bank account.

Although it makes some sense to require a little extra information from these smaller companies (which amount to a large percentage of the Chapter 11 cases filed in this country), this is a lot of paperwork to come up with, without many resources with which to provide it. Some feared that the 2005 provisions would quietly overhaul the Chapter 11 systems in a way that would kill rather than save many small companies.

D. Simplification of the Plan Process

The 2005 amendments attempt to simplify the confirmation process for the small business Chapter 11 debtor by allowing the debtor to use form plan and disclosure documents, and also by allowing the debtor to combine the hearings on disclosure and plan confirmation as a way to reduce cost and delay. As we will see shortly, subchapter V simplifies the confirmation process even further by essentially foregoing the need for a separate disclosure statement and instead requiring that the plan submitted by the debtor include a simplified version of information that would normally be a part of a disclosure statement in a non-small business case.

E. Higher Risk of Conversion or Dismissal

Finally, the 2005 amendments require that the court convert or dismiss any Chapter 11 case for "cause," which now includes for "substantial or continuing loss to or diminution of the estate and absence of a reasonable likelihood of rehabilitation," gross mismanagement of the estate, failure to maintain insurance, the unauthorized use of cash collateral, a failure to comply with any of the reporting requirements of the Code, a failure to timely pay post-petition taxes, a failure to file a plan within the time limits set out in the Code, and several other grounds.

This is a drastic departure from the prior §1112, in which only a few things were enumerated as "cause" to convert or dismiss, and under which the court could choose whether to convert or dismiss the case, based on the importance of the infraction in the overall scheme of the case. Even though this expanded list of causes requiring the court to dismiss or convert a case was intended in part to avoid wasting valuable time on hopeless Chapter 11 cases, it may have also had the unintended effect of discouraging potentially salvageable small businesses from filing bankruptcy at all.

Congress's intent in tightening the rules for small business debtors was to provide for quicker action to prevent losses to the estate, and to shift to the debtor the burden of proof regarding the likelihood of reorganization once such losses are shown. Yet the results have been less than positive. The 2005 rules for conversion or dismissal, along with the greater reporting obligations and tighter deadlines, discouraged many small business debtors from using Chapter 11 and helped spur the bankruptcy bar and bench to convince Congress to create a new subchapter V for small business debtors.

QUESTION 2. (CODE READER) The first paragraph of this section contains an oversimplification of §1112(b), which purports to require the court to convert or dismiss a case in certain circumstances set out in §1112(b)(4). A more accurate way to state the rule (although still not perfect) is that:

A. The penalties for conversion or dismissal are now greater under the 2005 law.

B. The court must convert under the facts set out in §1112(b)(4), absent special circumstances.

C. The court must convert under the facts set out in §1112(b)(4), absent unusual circumstances that establish that the conversion is not in the best interest of creditors and the estate.

D. The court must convert under the circumstances set out in §1112(b)(4) unless two other things are both true: first, that there are unusual circumstances that establish that conversion or dismissal is not in the best interest of creditors and the estate; and second, a reasonable likelihood exists that the debtor will confirm a plan within the Code deadlines.

ANALYSIS. If you just worked your way through §1112(b), congratulations. That was not easy. By now you also understand why many bankruptcy professors are asking to teach Contracts instead. What a miserable and incomprehensible section! The answer is **D**, but to get there you must make your way through some complex statutory language. The only way to avoid the so-called "automatic" conversion or dismissal is by proving that conversion or dismissal is not in the best interests of creditors, and also that the debtor is likely to confirm a plan within the Code deadlines. If you look closely, you will find even more exceptions to these exceptions and a drafting mess that is virtually unsurpassed even in the Bankruptcy Code. Both **B** and **C** state part of the rule but not all of it, and even **D** (the correct answer) is incomplete but the closest to the correct rule. **A** doesn't make sense. What does it mean to say that the penalties for conversion or dismissal are now greater under the 2005 law? Conversion and dismissal *are* the penalties. Plus, the section you were asked to read said nothing about this. Thus, **D** is the correct answer.

F. The Small Business Reorganization Act of 2019 ("SBRA")

Probably the most important benefit that Congress included in SBRA for small business debtors under subchapter V is the ability to cram down a Chapter 11 plan under newly enacted §1191 without having to get any impaired class to vote in favor of the plan. Instead, the plan has to provide first, that secured creditors retain their liens and receive the present value of their secured claim over the life of the plan; and second, that all of the debtor's disposable income over the life of the three-to-five-year plan be used to fund payments to unsecured creditors. Even in a cramdown, the subchapter V debtor's Chapter 11 plan still must comply with all of the §1129(a) confirmation requirements other than §1129(a)(8), (a)(10), and (a)(15). This means that the best interest test of §1129(a)(7) still applies, which requires that all creditors in the Chapter 11 plan receive at least as much they would in a Chapter 7 liquidation of the same debtor. Even though the best interest test still applies, a subchapter V debtor is given the opportunity to pay administrative priority claims in full over the life of the Chapter 11 plan rather than at confirmation (as would be the case with a non-subchapter V debtor).

The subchapter V debtor's plan, if it is a cramdown rather than consensual, must not discriminate unfairly among classes of claims and must be "fair and equitable" with regard to all impaired, non-accepting classes of claims. However, the definition of "fair and equitable" is different in one important way under §1191(c) of subchapter V than that term's definition in §1129(b) for cramdowns in non-subchapter V Chapter 11 cases. In a standard Chapter 11 case, the "absolute priority rule" applies in a cramdown as part of the "fair and equitable" treatment of unsecured claims. This means that if a small business filed "regular" Chapter 11 and did a cramdown, the owner of the business would not be able to retain its equity in the company unless the plan paid unsecured claims in full. In a subchapter V cramdown, by contrast, the plan is considered "fair and equitable" even when the owners retain all of their equity, as long as the unsecured creditors are given property that equals the value of the debtor's disposable income for the three-to-five-year length of the Chapter 11 plan.

Disposable income is defined in §1191(d) as all income received by the debtor that is not reasonably necessary for the maintenance or support of the debtor or dependent of the debtor (which is only relevant in individual Chapter 11 cases) or for the payment of necessary business expenses (which is relevant in both individual and corporate small business cases). Both Chapter 11 and Chapter 13 (subject to Chapter 13's debtor limitations) have always been options for individuals who own an unincorporated business. Subchapter V offers a new option for individual small business owners that can often be more attractive than either the non-subchapter V small business path under Chapter 11 or the Chapter 13 option for individuals with regular income. As compared to the traditional Chapter 11 route, subchapter V offers the small business owner who wants to file individually the confirmation benefits that are discussed above, particularly the attractive cramdown option.

As compared to Chapter 13, subchapter V offers an above-median individual debtor a more favorable definition of "disposable income" that avoids the less flexible definition of allowable expenses that above-median debtors must use to calculate disposable income in a Chapter 13 case. Also, an individual subchapter V debtor that can achieve a consensual confirmation under §1191(a) will be granted a discharge at confirmation under §1141(d)(1)(A). If that same individual debtor filed Chapter 13, the individual would not be granted a discharge until the Chapter 13 plan payments were complete.

A subchapter V small business case has its own (even faster!) version of the fast-track timing that Congress created in its earlier attempts to distinguish the Chapter 11 procedures in small business cases from large business cases. The fast track is intended to keep administrative fees lower and therefore make the Chapter 11 process more affordable for small business debtors. The debtor is required to file its plan within 90 days after filing for relief under subchapter V, and there is a required status conference with the judge not later than 60 days after the debtor files its bankruptcy petition. At least two weeks before the status conference, the debtor must file with the court and the trustee and all parties in interest a report "that details the efforts the debtor has undertaken and will undertake to attain a consensual plan of reorganization."

The debtor in a subchapter V case is at least given a number of procedural advantages to make it more likely that the debtor can actually meet the tight subchapter V timeline. There is now a standing trustee in each district to help facilitate the debtor's creation of a consensual Chapter 11 plan in a subchapter V case. The trustee provisions of subchapter V more closely resemble the role of the trustee in Chapters 12 and 13 cases, where the debtor remains in possession but the trustee plays an active role in plan confirmation and plan payments during the course of the Chapter 11 plan (at least in a cramdown confirmation under subchapter V). If the debtor in a subchapter V case can manage to get a consensual confirmation of its plan, then the standing trustee is not involved in distributing payments under the debtor's plan.

Only the debtor in a subchapter V case has the ability to file a plan, unlike in a non-subchapter V Chapter 11 case where the debtor would need to worry about competing plans being filed by creditors after the debtor's exclusivity period has expired. There are no creditors' committees in a subchapter V case, and, as noted earlier, the debtor need not file a disclosure statement. The plan itself needs only to include three elements: a brief history of the debtor's business, a liquidation analysis (which is essential to the best interest test), and projections as to the debtor's ability to make whatever payments are proposed under the plan of reorganization (which is critical to demonstrate the plan's feasibility).

QUESTION 3. Tale of the Lobster ("Debtor") is a restaurant that specializes in high-end seafood dishes. Debtor is a closely held corporation whose stock is all held by Owner. Debtor files a subchapter V small business Chapter 11 case after the pandemic forces Debtor's in-person dining room to shut down for several months. When Debtor files its subchapter V case, there are three classes of claims or interests. Class 1 is Big Bank, a secured creditor that is owed $1 million secured by restaurant collateral that is worth $1.3 million. Class 2 is a collection of unsecured trade creditors that are owed in total $600,000. Class 3 is equity. The plan proposes to cure and reinstate Big Bank's secured claim in Class 1 and to pay Class 2 a total of 80 percent of its $600,000 in claims over a three-year plan period with no interest. Class 3 would retain all of Debtor's equity. In a Chapter 7 liquidation of Debtor, unsecured trade creditors would receive 50 cents on the dollar. If Class 2 opposes this plan, may Debtor nevertheless confirm it?

A. Yes, as long as the plan payments are at least equal to Debtor's disposable income over the three-year plan period.
B. Yes, whether or not the plan payments are at least equal to Debtor's disposable income over the three-year plan period.
C. No, because this plan would violate §1129(a)(10).
D. No, because this plan would violate the absolute priority rule.

ANALYSIS. This question highlights the advantages for a small business debtor that files under SBRA's new subchapter V. We can quickly eliminate **C** and **D** based on the discussions in the text above. In a subchapter V case, a small business debtor can get a Chapter 11 cramdown plan confirmed under §1191(b) without having to get even one impaired class of claims to vote yes, unlike in a regular Chapter 11 cramdown. That makes **C** incorrect. Furthermore, in a subchapter V case the debtor that seeks a cramdown confirmation does not even need to worry about violating the absolute priority rule as do other Chapter 11 debtors. That is why **D** is wrong. However, even subchapter V has its limits for the debtor seeking cramdown. Section 1191(c) requires that in order for a cramdown plan to be "fair and equitable," the plan must provide that all projected income of the debtor is distributed under the debtor's Chapter 11 plan during the three-to-five-year period of the plan. That is why **B** is wrong and **A** is the correct answer.

QUESTION 4. Same facts as the previous question, except now assume that Debtor files its case not under subchapter V but instead as a non-subchapter V Chapter 11 small business case. If Class 2 opposes this plan, may Debtor nevertheless confirm it?

A. Yes, as long as Owner contributed new value using a market test to determine that the amount of the new value contributed was at least equal to the value of the equity being retained by Owner.
B. Yes, as long as the plan payments are at least equal to Debtor's disposable income over the three-year plan period.
C. No, because this plan would violate the best interest test of §1129(a)(7).
D. No, because this plan would violate §1129(a)(10).

ANALYSIS. This question is a reinforcement of the special benefits given to small business debtors that choose to file under the new subchapter V. Since in this question Debtor is filing a traditional Chapter 11 as a small business debtor, then Debtor must meet the requirements of cramdown that are found in §1129(b) rather than §1191. Under §1129(b), a debtor is only eligible for a cramdown confirmation if it meets all of the requirements of §1129(a) except for §1129(a)(8). This plan, however, fails to meet §1129(a)(10), which requires that at least one impaired class of claims must accept the plan that the debtor is proposing. Here the only impaired class of claims is Class 2, and they are opposing this cramdown plan. That is why **D** is correct. That also means that the references in answer **A** to the absolute priority rule and the new value exception to that rule are irrelevant. We never make it to the absolute priority rule and its exceptions in a case like this one where the debtor cannot even meet the fundamental cramdown requirement of §1129(b)(1) that says all §1129(a) requirements except (a)(8) must be satisfied. Similarly, **B**'s reference to the disposable-income test is not relevant to a non-subchapter V Chapter 11 small business debtor cramdown case, but instead only to a subchapter V cramdown. **C** is wrong because even though the best interest test will apply in a cramdown under §1129(b), Debtor did not violate the best interest test here. That is because the unsecured trade creditors would get an 80 percent return in the proposed plan, which is higher than the 50 percent return that they would get in a Chapter 7 liquidation of Debtor.

QUESTION 5. (CODE READER) Same facts as Question 3, except now Debtor is halfway through its three-year subchapter V plan when it realizes that its disposable income projections were too optimistic. Debtor believes that it can still make payments for the remaining 18 months of the plan, except the original payments will need to be cut in half to more accurately reflect Debtor's actual disposable income. At this point in the plan (which you should assume has been "substantially consummated" by now), can Debtor modify its original plan along these lines? (Hint: Read carefully all of §1193.)

A. Yes, as long as the bankruptcy court determines that "circumstances warrant such modification," even if the plan as modified no longer meets the best interest test of §1129(a)(7).
B. Yes, as long as the bankruptcy court determines that "circumstances warrant such modification," and as long as the plan as modified still meets the best interest test of §1129(a)(7).
C. No, because §1193(b) says that any modification of the plan following confirmation must be made before substantial consummation of the plan.
D. No, unless Class 2 agrees to the modification as §1193(d) would require in a case like this.

ANALYSIS. Plan modification is an area where the subchapter V debtor gets a better deal than either a Chapter 13 debtor or a non-subchapter V Chapter 11 small business debtor. Section 1193(a) is better for the subchapter V debtor than a Chapter 13 debtor because only the debtor can propose modifications under subchapter V, whereas under §1329(a) any unsecured claimholder or the trustee may propose post-confirmation modifications to the Chapter 13 plan. That means that a Chapter 13 debtor that sees a sudden increase in income during its Chapter 13 plan could be called back into court to modify its original plan payments upward. On the other hand, a subchapter V debtor that exceeds its initial projections for disposable income during its Chapter 11 plan would not need to adjust its plan payments upwards if the debtor's post-confirmation net profits are higher than expected. The way in which the subchapter V modification provisions are better for the debtor than the comparable provisions for non-subchapter V Chapter 11 cases is that in the standard Chapter 11 case for a small business debtor, the debtor cannot modify its plan once the plan has been substantially consummated. By contrast, §1193(c) allows the debtor to modify its plan even after substantial consummation.

C is wrong because while it accurately summarizes what §1193(b) says, it fails to consider §1193(c)'s generous provision for "certain other modifications." Section 1193(c) allows modifications even beyond the point of substantial consummation as long as the court determines that "circumstances warrant such modifications" and the plan as modified still meets the special cramdown requirements found in §1191(b). **B** accurately captures the requirements of §1193(c) and is thus the correct answer. **A** is wrong because it incorrectly states that the modification can be approved even if the plan as modified no longer meets the best interest test. **D** is wrong because the requirement referred to in §1193(d) that holders of claims get to re-vote on the plan as modified only applies when the plan has been confirmed consensually under §1191(a). This plan, by contrast, was confirmed as a cramdown plan under §1191(b). Thus, the modification rules of §1193(c) apply instead of the modification rules of §1193(d).

Martin's and Keating's Picks

1. Question 1 **B**
2. Question 2 **D**
3. Question 3 **A**
4. Question 4 **D**
5. Question 5 **B**

38

Post-Confirmation Issues: The Effect of Confirmation

OVERVIEW

A. **The Confirmation Order Is Res Judicata as to All Issues Dealt with in the Plan and Also Discharges All Claims Except as Otherwise Provided for in the Plan**
B. **Enforcing the Plan**
C. **The Closer: Chapter 38**

Martin's and Keating's Picks

There is no denying that confirming a Chapter 11 plan is a tremendous accomplishment. It is the day for which most parties in the case have been waiting. Confirmation does not mark the end of the case, but rather the beginning of the post-confirmation period, in which the debtor will attempt to perform the plan, and the debtor's lawyers will be called on to interpret the plan and the order confirming it. (*See* 11 U.S.C. §1142.) These two court documents, along with the Bankruptcy Code, articulate the specific effect that confirmation of the plan has on the debtor, its creditors, and all other parties-in-interest.

This post-confirmation period is mired in complexity. Despite having achieved confirmation, the debtor might do well to don that popular bumper sticker proclaiming, "I've got issues." Surely the debtor will experience post-confirmation issues, and a few of the common ones are discussed here.

A. The Confirmation Order Is Res Judicata as to All Issues Dealt with in the Plan and Also Discharges All Claims Except as Otherwise Provided for in the Plan

Section 1141 of the Bankruptcy Code does a number of radical things. This Code sections binds "the debtor, any entity issuing securities under the plan, any entity acquiring property under the plan, and any creditor, equity security holder, or general partner in the debtor, whether or not the claim or interest . . . is impaired under the plan and whether or not such creditor, equity security holder, or partner, has accepted the plan." (*See* 11 U.S.C. §1141(a).) Thus, the confirmation order entered by the court, approving the plan, is res judicata as to all of the matters addressed in the plan. The only exceptions are orders that violate due process or were accomplished through fraud.

QUESTION 1. The Carsons are creditors of Federated Stores, having sued them years ago in an as yet unresolved warranty action. The Carsons' attorney received notice of the Federated Chapter 11 case but did not file a claim on behalf of the Carsons. The Carsons themselves received absolutely no personal notice of the case, nor did they receive notice of the entry of the confirmation order that purported to discharge their warranty claim. The Carsons have now asked the bankruptcy court for permission to pursue their action post-confirmation. To get past summary judgment under the facts you just heard, the Carsons need to allege:

A. fraud.
B. lack of due process.
C. res judicata.
D. all of the above.

ANALYSIS. The facts you have been given (a lack of personal notice), suggest that the issue here is not fraud but lack of due process. Res judicata is the theory that the debtor will use to try to bar the Carsons' claims, but this theory will *not* help the Carsons. To the contrary, it could bar their claims. The Carsons have no evidence of fraud, nor do they need any. *Either* a lack of due process *or* fraud will justify allowing the Carsons to go forward against Federated, despite the clear mandates of the confirmation order. Therefore, the question will be whether notice to the Carsons' attorney constituted due process, and the correct answer is **B**.

QUESTION 2. Considering the purposes of Chapter 11, the rights of the Carsons, and whatever you know about agency law, do you think the court will permit the Carsons to go forward against Federated despite the confirmation order?

A. Yes, because they had no notice of the case and could not have filed a proof of claim.
B. Yes, because they are creditors and there is no dispute about that critical fact.
C. No, because they received notice of the case through their agent who was under an obligation to pass on that knowledge to his or her client.
D. No, because of the rehabilitative purposes of Chapter 11.

ANALYSIS. We realize you may not feel you know enough about this area to answer the question, which deals with notice, due process, agency, and the effects of a confirmation order. If you think about the lawyer's obligation to his or her clients, however, you should be able to predict **C** as the correct answer. Unfortunately for the Carsons, their lawyer is the one who was supposed to inform them of the Federated case, and the need to file a proof of claim. As fictitious as it may seem, the Carsons have received notice of the case, even if they never heard of it. This is because their agent (attorney) received that notice, and this notice (knowledge) is thus imputed to them as well. The Carsons will not be permitted to go forward against Federated for the reasons stated in **C**.

D is incorrect because if the Carsons had not received this notice through their attorney, there would be nothing about the Code's rehabilitative purposes that could make up for this complete denial of due process. If there were no lawyer in the picture, **A** would have been correct. The Carsons would have received no notice. Because their lawyer did get notice, however, **A** is incorrect. **B** is also incorrect because merely being a creditor is not sufficient in and of itself to avoid the effect of a confirmation order, at least not where their claim is disputed and no proof of claim has been filed. One needs to file a proof of claim in such an instance, something the Carsons did not do. Thus, **B** is incorrect, and the correct answer is **C**.

Section 1141 also states that confirmation discharges all pre-petition and post-petition claims except as dealt with in the plan and also that, except as provided for in the plan, "all property dealt with by the plan is free and clear of all claims and interests of creditors . . . ." (*See* 11 U.S.C. §1141(c).) Courts have struggled with this language in light of the well-accepted rule that a confirmation order is to have no effect on a secured creditor's claim, and that the lien of such a creditor is supposed to survive the reorganization case intact, except as provided for in the plan. Thus, most courts have held that while the plan *can* modify a secured creditor's claim, if a secured party's claim is not treated in the plan, the plan will not discharge the creditor's lien, regardless of what the confirmation order says.

This probably seems obvious as a matter of fairness, but it really isn't all that obvious. Confirmation orders are very powerful, and are often sweeping and broad to protect the debtor's fresh start and future life. Creditors should be extremely careful in reviewing the terms of a proposed confirmation order before the court enters it. In fact, a constant area of confusion is whether a confirmation order, which has res judicata effect, can conflict directly with the Bankruptcy Code and thus grant more rights to the debtor than the Code itself would allow.

For example, some confirmation orders purport to discharge not just the debts owed by the debtor, but also creditor claims against nondebtor third parties, such as the debtor's principals, officers, directors, and guarantors. We briefly discussed third-party stays in another part of this guide and *third-party releases* or *discharges* are a permanent version of the third-party stay. Like third-party stays, they are rarely justified; yet many confirmation orders purport to discharge persons other than the debtor. Some courts have held these third-party discharges valid, even though the Code arguably precludes granting such discharges in §524(e). Specifically, §524(e) says that "discharge of a debt of the debtor does not affect the liability of any other entity on, or the property of any other entity for, such debt."

There are two ways that courts have interpreted the above-quoted language of §524(e). Some courts have read that language to prohibit the inclusion of any third-party releases in a Chapter 11 plan of reorganization. Other courts, however, have read that language simply to mean that the debtor's bankruptcy discharge does not by itself affect the liability of any third parties. This second group of courts therefore does not read that language as precluding the inclusion and effectiveness of third-party releases in a Chapter 11 plan, depending on several other factors. These other factors include things such as how much the nondebtor third party is contributing to the bankruptcy case in order to secure the release, how essential the third-party release is to the debtor's overall reorganization plan, and the level of creditor assent to the plan that includes the third-party releases.

It is worth noting here that §1129(a)(1) specifically precludes court approval of any plan that does not comply with "the applicable provisions of this title." Those "applicable provisions" include, of course, §524(e). Therefore, bankruptcy courts that believe §524(e) prohibits third-party releases could point to §1129(a)(1) as a reason to deny confirmation of a plan that includes such releases. Nevertheless, many courts have approved confirmation orders with third-party releases on res judicata grounds where the affected creditors failed to object to the third-party release provisions in the debtor's proposed plan (even if the court arguably lacked jurisdiction to enter the orders containing such releases). Indeed, courts have consistently upheld such orders in cases where creditors received affirmative notice of the third-party releases and still failed to object to them before entry of the confirmation order. Advice? Read the plan and the confirmation order very carefully before the court enters it!

QUESTION 3. You represent a bank with claims against the debtor in a large Chapter 11 case, as well as against the debtor's parent company, who owns all of the debtor's stock. You just read the confirmation order drafted by the debtor's counsel, which claims to discharge all claims against both the debtor and the parent company, except as provided for in the plan. Your client has approved the plan itself, which contains favorable treatment of the bank claims owed by the debtor. The plan does not cover the parent's debt and does not contain this third-party release provision. In fact, this is the first that you or your client has heard of it. You should:

A. wait until the plan is confirmed, and if the parent won't pay its loans, object to the order then.
B. talk to your client and then file an immediate objection to the form of order with the court and serve the judge's chambers.
C. call the court's chambers and let his or her law clerk or courtroom deputy know that you disapprove of the form of order and why.
D. just let it go. Why be so Type A all the time? And don't bother telling the client about this either. Your banker has been in a bad mood lately and there is no reason to raise nonissues.

ANALYSIS. We hope you found some comic relief here and that you quickly eliminated choice **D**. No, it would not be a good idea to just mull over this one yourself to avoid bothering your client with the "small stuff." This is a very big deal indeed and not telling the client will put you in the same position as the lawyer in Question 1, a great candidate for malpractice. **A** is not much better. You need to talk to your client, but it won't help to take action after the confirmation order becomes final. Choice **A** suggests a course of action that many have taken, only to regret it later. If you want to stop the outrageous order from taking effect, there is no time like the present. You cannot successfully object to the order after it has become final, especially if you were given a copy to review before its entry. The debtor is required to circulate the proposed confirmation order before submitting it to the court for entry, to make sure everyone has notice of its terms and also to ensure that things are not slipped into the order. You may get lucky, as some other creditor might object for you, but you cannot rely on that. Thus, the correct answer is either **B** or **C**.

Do you need to object formally in writing? In most jurisdictions the answer is yes, and given the two choices, **B** is the better answer. In all of the jurisdictions in which we have practiced, the creditor's attorney would first ask the debtor to take out the unapproved language and recirculate the order.

If that failed, the attorney would file an objection with the court, send a copy to the judge's chambers (because time is of the essence), and serve a copy on the main parties in the case. I would never just call and leave a message for the judge, so **C** is incorrect. You need a paper trail, meaning an objection of record. From what you had to choose from, the correct answer is **B**.

QUESTION 4. Big Pharma ("Debtor") is a nationwide pharmaceutical manufacturer that files Chapter 11 bankruptcy when its "Nirvana" painkillers prove to have addictive qualities that cause several thousand addiction-related deaths and subsequent lawsuits against the company. Debtor's individual owners, the Heckler family members, agree to contribute $5 billion of their personal funds to Debtor's bankruptcy case, but only if the Hecklers get third-party releases in Debtor's Chapter 11 plan. Debtor thinks that it will be unable to get a consensual plan with or without the third-party releases and the Heckler family contribution to the case. However, Debtor is convinced that it can at least get a cramdown plan confirmed, but only if it can get the third-party releases included in the plan so that it can also get the Heckler family's $5 billion contribution to help fund the plan. Otherwise, Debtor says it will be forced to liquidate the assets of Big Pharma, and the total value received by creditors will be much less than if this cramdown plan is confirmed. Assuming that Debtor can meet all of the usual requirements for a cramdown plan, should the bankruptcy judge allow confirmation in this case?

A. Yes, because it is clear that creditors as a group will be better off with a cramdown reorganization plan that includes third-party releases than with a liquidation of Debtor that does not involve third-party releases.

B. Yes, because §105(a) clearly gives the bankruptcy court the power to enforce nonconsensual third-party releases in any case where the court believes that such releases are necessary for a debtor's reorganization.

C. No, unless every creditor class affected by the third-party releases votes in favor of the plan so that it is a consensual plan rather than a cramdown plan.

D. No, unless every individual creditor (not just creditor class) that is affected by the third-party releases votes in favor of the plan so that it is a unanimous consensual plan.

ANALYSIS. This question is a simplified version of the Purdue Pharma Chapter 11 case that was decided by the U.S. Supreme Court in 2024. In that case, the bankruptcy court for the Southern District of New York confirmed a Chapter 11 plan that included nonconsensual third-party releases. The District

Court reversed the bankruptcy court, but then a divided panel of the Second Circuit Court of Appeals reversed the District Court and approved the plan. Answer **D** is where the Supreme Court ultimately landed in a 5-4 decision that reversed the Second Circuit and sent the parties back to the Chapter 11 negotiating table.

Answer **A** is probably an overstatement as given. It is not necessarily "clear" under the facts that we have been given that creditors in this case will be better off with this third-party release plan than the alternative. The alternative for creditors would be to take less money now in a liquidation of the company but still preserve their ability to sue the Heckler family members (in real life, the Sackler family members) later on as individuals outside of bankruptcy. The Hecklers, of course, could then file bankruptcy individually. However, their willingness to contribute so much money to the corporate bankruptcy in exchange for third-party releases suggests that their individual bankruptcy cases would have significant nonexempt assets that they would prefer to keep outside of bankruptcy if possible. Furthermore, the Hecklers may also be concerned that the claims against them individually might be deemed nondischargeable under one or more of the exceptions to discharge found in §523 if the Hecklers were to file individual bankruptcy cases.

Answer **B** suffers from the same overconfidence as does **A** with its use of the adverb "clearly" to describe a bankruptcy court's power under §105(a) to enforce nonconsensual third-party releases in any Chapter 11 case where the court believes that doing so will enable the debtor to reorganize. Nevertheless, virtually all of the opinions, both bankruptcy court and appellate, that have upheld nonconsensual third-party releases have relied in some measure on the bankruptcy court's amorphous powers under that catch-all provision in §105(a) that allows the court to issue "any order, process, or judgment that is necessary or appropriate to carry out the provisions of this title." The debtors in the Purdue Pharma case also have argued that the third-party releases in their plan should be upheld under §1123(b)(6), which says that a Chapter 11 plan may "include any appropriate provision that is not inconsistent with the provisions of this title." That argument, however, simply begs the question of whether the third-party releases are "not inconsistent with the provisions of this title" given the language in §524(e) about the effects of a debtor's discharge on nondebtor parties.

You can think of **C** as perhaps a moderate or compromise position in what had been a national bankruptcy debate among the circuits before the Supreme Court settled the matter. This position would allow the third-party releases as long as the affected classes voted in favor of the plan that included the releases, even if not every individual creditor in those classes voted in favor of the plan. Unlike answers **A** and **B**, answer **C** does not assume that the bankruptcy court always knows what is in the creditors' best interest The **C** position would at least require creditor assent to the third-party releases on a group-wide basis using the voting majorities that are required for class acceptance of a plan (two-thirds in amount of claims that vote and more than one-half in number of claims that vote). However, **C** does not go so far as to protect each individual creditor's ability to veto a plan that includes these legally questionable third-party releases.

Answer **D** is clearly the most restrictive position on this issue (from the debtor's perspective) in that it gives each individual creditor the right to veto a plan with third-party releases that would adversely affect the creditor. Yet if we had to choose a "correct" answer on this one (even before the Supreme Court's decision), we would probably choose **D**. Our argument for this position is that third-party releases are really just a form of contract between the non-debtor third party (the Hecklers in this question) and the creditor who is agreeing to release the third party. The creditor is being offered consideration for the third-party release in the form of payments being made in the plan that are funded in part by contributions to the plan made by the third party. Like all contracts, each individual party to the contract must agree to its terms or else there cannot be a contract that is enforceable against that party. Courts that take this approach are treating a creditor's right to veto the plan with third-party releases similarly to a creditor's individual right to veto a plan that does not comply with the best interest test of §1129(a)(7). In both situations, the nonconsenting creditor is given the equivalent of a property right to demand either that it retains its right to recover from the third party outside of bankruptcy (with third-party release plans) or that it retains its right to recover whatever it can get from the debtor though a Chapter 7 liquidation of the debtor (with its entitlement under the best interest test).

In holding that the individual Sackler family members cannot be protected by Purdue Pharma's Chapter 11 bankruptcy discharge, the Supreme Court's majority rejected the argument that §1123(b)(6) (quoted earlier in this Analysis) gives the bankruptcy court the power to discharge the debts of a nondebtor without the consent of the nondebtor whose rights would be affected. The Court also noted the lack of any bankruptcy law history showing support for the idea of third-party releases.

The four-Justice dissent in Purdue Pharma argued that the majority failed to account for the practical implications of its holding, namely that this decision would delay indefinitely any distribution of funds to the great majority of creditor victims who voted in favor of the plan. The dissent also noted bankruptcy law's history of solving collective-action problems in the context of mass tort cases such as this one.

The majority emphasized that its decision was narrow in scope and that its rule banning third-party releases is limited to the case of nonconsensual releases such as those at issue in Purdue Pharma. The big question that remains open and will likely continue to be litigated is what exactly constitutes "consent" by a creditor that is sufficient to make a third-party release effective against that creditor.

QUESTION 5. Same facts as Question 4, except that the plan that includes the third-party releases for the Hecklers provides that any creditor that is eligible to vote on the plan will be deemed to consent to the third-party releases that are included in the plan unless the creditor affirmatively objects to the third-party releases by the same deadline given for the overall vote on the plan. Would such a "no objection" consent to the third-party releases in the plan be enforceable in light of the Supreme Court's Purdue Pharma decision?

A. Yes, because the Court was clear that its decision banning the third-party releases in Purdue Pharma was narrow in scope and is thus limited to nonconsensual releases.
B. Yes, but only as to non-objecting creditors that vote "yes" for the plan.
C. Yes, but only as to non-objecting creditors that vote either for or against the plan.
D. Probably not, because "consent" under the law typically requires more than merely the lack of objection.

ANALYSIS. Let's start by admitting that there is no clear answer to this one. As often happens when the Supreme Court purports to settle a major issue in bankruptcy law, the Court's decision leaves open as many questions as it answers. In Purdue Pharma, the Court was clear that a completely nonconsensual third-party release, such as the one that was at issue in that case, will not be effective as to the creditors involved in the main debtor's bankruptcy case. What the Court failed to do, however, was to articulate what would constitute sufficient "consent" by a creditor so as to make a third-party release enforceable against that creditor. Choices **A**, **B**, and **C** all fail in that each of the choices presumes a level of detail in the Purdue Pharma holding that was lacking. Choice **D** is probably the best choice, not only for admitting the lack of certainty on this question, but also because a number of bankruptcy courts have already ruled after the Purdue Pharma decision that a "no objection" form of consent is not sufficient to make a third-party release enforceable.

B. Enforcing the Plan

The plan forms a new contract between the debtor and the creditors, which replaces all prior contractual obligations between the parties, except as provided for in the plan. Moreover, the bankruptcy court's jurisdiction over the case is quite limited after confirmation, at least as far as the Code is concerned.

The court retains jurisdiction over matters that are pending at the time of confirmation as well as some future matters, and also over matters necessary to administer the estate. This is a far cry from the broad jurisdiction that the court exercised *during* the case, in which it heard business disputes of the debtor, as well as most other matters the debtor needed resolved. Jurisdiction can be expanded through particular provisions of the confirmation order, but this does not mean the court will readily hear a myriad of post-confirmation disputes. Moreover, creditors may choose to sue the debtor in another court, which could mean that nonbankruptcy courts may interpret the confirmation order.

QUESTION 6. You represent Arlington Bank in the case of Virginia Steel. The debtor proposed a plan that met the requirements of §1129, and your client agreed to the proposed terms. The debtor is now circulating a proposed confirmation order, having achieved confirmation in court yesterday. Your client notes that prior to this bankruptcy, it had the right to inspect the debtor's books and records, as well as its physical facility, once a week. Your client wants to schedule an inspection for next week and has asked you to arrange this. This is no problem,

A. as long as everything the client said is actually correct. You are all set and can call for the inspection, because the bank retains all of its inspection rights post-bankruptcy.
B. as long as the debtor agrees that you can do the inspection next week.
C. as long as the plan provides that your client will retain all of its prior inspection rights, or all of its rights under the pre-petition loan documents.
D. because the debtor is required to add these inspection rights into the confirmation order.

ANALYSIS. Choice **A** is flat-out wrong. As stated in the previous paragraph, the rights contained in the bank's prior contract with the debtor have now been replaced with the plan, lock, stock, and barrel. If the plan does not contain inspection rights, then there *are* no inspection rights. **B** is technically correct, but it relies on the debtor's acquiescence. Your client wants the right to continue inspecting in the future, whether he or she has specifically asked for this or not. Sure, the bank can go in next week if the debtor consents, but what about next time? **B** does not answer the underlying question, the practical question. **C** is the correct answer. As long as the plan preserves your client's inspection rights, you're all set. **D** is wrong because the debtor is under no obligation, after yesterday's confirmation hearing, to include extra rights in the confirmation order. As a practical matter, even if you did not negotiate inspection rights into the plan, you may be able to convince the debtor to include them in the confirmation order. Note the word "may"; don't count on it!

QUESTION 7. You represent a steel company that had a $400,000 claim against Diamond, a tool manufacturer, before Diamond's Chapter 11 case. Diamond confirmed a Chapter 11 plan that pays a 25 percent distribution to unsecured creditors like your client. The plan promises 10 percent of the distribution on the effective date of the plan, and another 5 percent a year for the next three years. Diamond has failed to perform as promised. It paid 10 percent on the effective date of the plan but missed its next installment payment. How much can your client sue Diamond for?

A. $390,000, which is the original $400,000 owed, minus what the client has received.
B. $360,000, which is the original $400,000 owed, minus what the client has received.
C. $90,000, the total distribution, less the amount received.
D. $60,000, the total distribution less the amount received.

ANALYSIS. This problem tests two things: first, the notion that the plan, once confirmed, modifies all prior contractual obligations between the parties, and second, calculating the unsecured creditor distribution. The first step is to realize that, even though the debtor did not fully perform, your client no longer has a right to collect the full $400,000. This seems incredibly unfair given that the debtor has failed to perform. It may seem downright criminal, in a way, but this is the way it works. Under the plan, the debtor is obligated to pay your client a total of 25 percent of $400,000, or $100,000. This eliminates both **A** and **B** right off the bat because both of these answers are based on the assumption that the debtor still owes $400,000, perhaps based on the mistaken assumption that your client's rights revert to the original amounts once the plan is breached. Again, this is not the case. Breach or no breach on the part of the debtor, the debtor's full obligation post-confirmation is to pay your client $100,000.

The correct choice between **C** and **D** depends on how much your client has already been paid. Quick! How much, before moving on? That's right, the first payment that was made was for 10 percent of the $400,000 claim (a $40,000 payment), so the debtor still owes your client the difference between that payment and the total 25 percent distribution of $100,000. This balance is $60,000 and the correct answer is **D**. **C** is incorrect because it assumes the first payment by the debtor was 10 percent of the total distribution to be paid, not 10 percent of the total claim. Several students have chosen this answer on past exams, so don't feel badly. Just take your time with the math and check it twice.

C. The Closer: Chapter 38

Black and Drucker, a garden tool manufacturer, just completed a long Chapter 11 case in which all of its assets were sold to Chase Hardware for approximately $4 million. Chase purchased all of the assets free and clear of all liens, claims, and interests of any kind. From the sales proceeds, a group of secured lenders was paid approximately 80 percent of its allowed claims and a very small distribution was paid to unsecured creditors. You represent the debtor and, along with Chase's counsel, are poring over the final version of the confirmation order. Which of these provisions is most important, from the point of view of your client and Chase, to include in the confirmation order?

A. The lenders will retain their inspection rights.
B. The court will retain jurisdiction over all disputes arising under the plan, including successor liability claims.
C. Secured parties will retain their liens.
D. The debtor will retain all post-petition property free and clear of all liens and claims.

ANALYSIS. This question asks you to anticipate what types of issues might come up in a case in which the debtor has sold all of its assets and is free and clear of all liens. To answer the question, you need to be able to picture what a case looks like after the assets are sold and creditors are paid. There is not much left of the case, except some avoidance actions and other actions for the debtor to pursue.

Secured creditors will not need inspection rights (**A**), nor will they need to retain their liens (**C**) because all their collateral has been sold free and is clear of all liens, with the liens attaching to the sale proceeds. They have been paid as much as they are going to get, *taken out* as we say, and no longer have any interest in the debtor or the plan. Thus, **A** and **C** are both incorrect. Between **D** and **B**, the hot issue is going to be successor liability claims in any §363 sale, meaning claims being asserted against Chase flowing from Black and Drucker's products or former business. Thus, the most critical thing (at least from the point of view of Chase and the debtor) to include in the confirmation order is a *retention of jurisdiction clause* so that the bankruptcy court will be the court interpreting the *free and clear language* in the order. As previously discussed, creditors harmed by the assets of Black and Drucker post-confirmation may still sue Chase in another court, but hopefully the retention of jurisdiction language will help Chase get the dispute moved back to the bankruptcy court so that the same court that issued the order can interpret it. The bankruptcy court may refuse to hear these claims, which could arise many years after it has closed the case, but if this language is added to the confirmation order the bankruptcy court may be more willing to reopen the case and resolve the disputes, hopefully in Chase's favor. Thus, the answer is **B**. Note that the retention of jurisdiction clause in **B** is very specific and explicitly mentions successor liability claims. This will help a great deal because it will tell the bankruptcy court what the debtor had in mind when drafting the clause. In other types of cases, it is also quite useful to include a general retention clause because, again, issues will come up.

Martin's and Keating's Picks

1. Question 1	**B**
2. Question 2	**C**
3. Question 3	**B**
4. Question 4	**D**
5. Question 5	**D**
6. Question 6	**C**
7. Question 7	**D**
The Closer	**B**

39

Closing Closers: Some Practice Questions

This chapter contains a practice exam comprising 30 questions. There is no text or black-letter law here, just a chance for you to issue spot and do some problems that contain multiple issues. The questions are designed to give you a chance to practice on questions without reading introductory text first, and to consider questions testing multiple issues. Most professors combine issues when they test, so these questions provide both a review and an opportunity to test your understanding of how different concepts fit together.

We have included a short analysis of the questions at the end of the chapter, but to get full value out of this chapter, analyze these questions fully before looking at our analysis. And again, if any of our questions, in this chapter or others, seem wrong or confusing, send either of us an e-mail and we'll try to fix it for next time.

QUESTION 1. (CODE READER) The trustee in Carson Duly's bankruptcy case has $50,000 to distribute, which he collected from the sale of Carson's nonexempt assets. The total claims are:

- Property taxes in the amount of $40,000 for taxes due two years ago, including late penalties,
- Income taxes in the amount of $10,000 from the past two years,
- Carson's bankruptcy attorney in the amount of $1,000 for preparing his petition,
- Student loans in the amount of $40,000,
- Credit card bills and medical bills in the amount of $20,000,
- The trustee's fees and costs of sale for $3,000,
- Payments to his ex-wife for child support, at $3,000 a month, due for the past three months, and
- Wages for his three security guards for a total of $13,000 (divided equally), for work done in the past month.

What is the distribution in this case for general unsecured creditors?

A. 14.8 percent.
B. 15.8 percent.
C. Nothing, because the priority claims will eat up the entire $50,000.
D. 14 percent.

QUESTION 2. Assume the same facts as in Question 1, but assume that the wife's claims are not child support claims, but property settlement claims. Now what is the general unsecured creditor distribution?

A. 43 percent.
B. The distribution would not change from the prior question, as this does not change the analysis.
C. 21.8 percent.
D. 31.8 percent.

QUESTION 3. Assume the same facts as in Question 1 again. The IRS (which is owed income taxes), as well as a very angry credit card company that is owed $18,000, are each trying to decide whether to challenge Carson's wife's characterization of her claim as support. What difference will this make to them?

A. None to the credit card company because its claim will be paid at the same rate either way, but the taxing authorities should challenge the wife's claim because its distribution will change significantly.
B. Neither should bother challenging this characterization, as it makes no difference in the distribution to either of them.
C. None to the taxing authority because its claim will be paid at the same rate either way, but the credit card company should challenge this characterization because its distribution will increase by approximately $4,500.
D. None to the taxing authority because its claim will be paid at the same rate either way, but the credit card company may want to challenge the wife's claim because its distribution will change by approximately $1,260.

QUESTION 4. Clyde Claussen is having a bad month, after the slow death of his e-business. He has few assets and piles and piles of unsecured debts. In addition, he tells you, he has been accused of criminal battery, the trial for which is scheduled for next week. He is also way behind on his rent and the landlord has threatened eviction. He has a paternity suit pending that is scheduled to go to trial tomorrow. Moreover, the utilities have threatened a shutoff. To top it all off, his doctor has threatened to bring him to court for some past-due medical bills. He wondered what a bankruptcy might do to relieve the pressure. What should you tell him? Will the relief last? Please pick the best answer.

A. All of these troubles will be temporarily stayed until he has time to get his life together, and thereafter, he will have to arrange to pay these debts.
B. All of these troubles will be temporarily stayed until he gets his life together, and he will have to pay some but not all of the debts, if he decides to do a Chapter 7 case.
C. The doctor's suit, the utility shutoff, and the paternity suit will be stayed for a time, but the eviction will not, nor will the criminal battery suit.
D. The doctor's suit, the eviction, and the utility shutoff will be stayed for a time, but the criminal battery suit and the paternity suit will not.

QUESTION 5. If you could make the correct answer in Question 4 just a tiny bit better, how would you do that?

A. The debtor need not pay all of his debts in a Chapter 7.
B. The paternity suit is not stayed but the eviction is.
C. The eviction will be stayed for a time, and will probably resume, but the utility shutoff and the doctor's suit will be stayed permanently.
D. The eviction will be stayed for a time, and will probably resume, the utility shutoff will be stayed permanently, assuming that the debtor makes the required deposit under §366(b), but the doctor's suit will be stayed permanently.

QUESTION 6. **(CODE READER)** Jack and Marie Black own a home in the state of Blackstone worth $200,000, with a $140,000 mortgage on it. Their other assets consist of $20,000 in savings accounts, $30,000 in furniture and household goods, and $200,000 in an ERISA-qualified 401(k) plan. The state of Blackstone offers a homestead exemption of $30,000 per person, exempts unlimited furniture and household goods, and exempts all ERISA-qualified retirement funds. It has not opted out of the federal exemption scheme in bankruptcy. Life looked good until Marie raised millions of dollars for a real estate scheme that unbeknownst to her, turned out to be a Ponzi scheme. This has resulted in huge judgments against the couple. If they have no regular income, but would like to file a Chapter 7, which exemption scheme should they choose?

A. The federal scheme, because they will get to keep their savings account and their house, losing only some of the household goods and furnishings.
B. The state scheme, because they can keep their furniture and household goods, their home, and their retirement funds, and will only lose the savings.
C. The federal scheme, because they can keep half of their savings, their home, and their retirement funds, and will only lose some of their household goods and furniture.
D. It really depends on whether the Blacks prefer to keep most of their cash or their home. The state scheme would save the home, but the federal scheme would allow them to save most of the cash.

QUESTIONS THROUGH 10. Red Lightning Ski Resort is an Olympic-style resort. Its facility was financed through a start-up loan from Farmer's Bank, which is currently owed $2.5 million. The loan accrues interest at 12 percent per annum, and is payable in monthly payments over 30 years. The resort pledged the entire facility as collateral for this loan. The resort recently expanded and took out a second loan on essentially the same terms from Prudential Life Insurance Company, in the amount of $750,000. Unfortunately, the expansion efforts failed because of cost overruns and now Red Lightning is having trouble making a go of it. There has been little snow the past few seasons, exacerbating its financial troubles. Recently, Red Lightning filed for Chapter 11. Both lenders have moved for relief from the automatic stay. The debtor's recent appraisal shows a value for the facility of about $3.5 million. However, this appraisal was taken almost a year ago, before the facility started showing signs of deferred maintenance and tight cash flow. Moreover, the snowmaking system recently broke, leaving gaping holes in the landscaping, where leaking water wiped out huge swaths of trees and grass.

QUESTION 7. Which statement most accurately describes Farmer's Bank's chance of success on its motion for relief?

A. Farmer's has a good chance of obtaining relief from the stay under §362(d)(2) because the debtor has no equity in the collateral and little chance of successfully reorganizing.
B. Farmer's has a good chance of prevailing under §362(d)(1) because the debtor is not taking care of the property.
C. Farmer's has very little chance of success on either ground because of its huge equity cushion.
D. Farmer's has a good chance of success because its position is not adequately protected.

QUESTION 8. Describe Prudential's chance of success on its motion for relief.

A. Prudential has very little chance of success on either ground because of its huge equity cushion.
B. Prudential has an excellent chance of prevailing under §362(d)(1) because the debtor is not taking care of the property, and thus Prudential lacks adequate protection.
C. Prudential has at least some chance of prevailing because it may lack adequate protection based on the debtor's failure to take care of the property.
D. Prudential has no chance of prevailing on its motion because it is in second position and must have lesser rights than Farmer's Bank.

QUESTION 9. For this question only, assume that both lenders did appraisals and that both came in at $3 million on the nose. As a result, the court found this to be the value of Red Lightning's facility. Assume that Farmer's incurred $50,000 in attorneys' fees in the six months following the filing and that at that point, the debtor confirmed a Chapter 11 plan. How much is Farmer's allowed as a secured claim?

A. $3,015,000.
B. $2,700,000, assuming the attorneys' fees are reasonable.
C. $2,700,000 on the nose.
D. $2,551,500, assuming the attorneys' fees are reasonable.

QUESTION 10. Again, assuming a value of $3 million for the building and assuming that Farmer's has the secured claim calculated in the previous question, what is the amount of Prudential's allowed secured claim? Prudential has incurred $40,000 in post-petition attorneys' fees and also gets 12 percent per annum under its contract. A so, assume that unsecured creditors are receiving a distribution of 10 percent. What can Prudential expect under the plan?

A. Prudential's secured claim is $300,000 and it will receive $45,000 on account of its unsecured claim.
B. Prudential's secured claim is $448,500, which includes its post-petition interest and fees, and it will receive $30,150 on account of its unsecured claim.
C. Prudential has no secured claim because the entire value of the collateral went to Farmer's.

D. Prudential has no secured claim because the entire value of the collateral went to Farmer's, and it will receive $75,000 on account of its unsecured claim.

QUESTION 11. The Romeros are in financial trouble, due to Mr. Romero's recent illness and unemployment. Both are working now and bring in a total of approximately $2,000 a month, net, and their "current monthly income" is less than the median income for their state. They have a mortgage payment of $500 a month, which is now ten months in arrears. What payments will the Romeros have to pay for their home during a Chapter 13 plan? Calculate the payments based on both a three-year and a five-year plan, with present value interest of 10 percent, if applicable. (For ease of calculation, assume the false fact that the principal is never paid down when calculating the present-value amounts.)

A. The Romeros need to pay approximately $639 a month for the three-year plan and about $583 for the five-year plan.
B. The Romeros need to pay approximately $583 a month for the three-year plan and about $639 a month for the five-year plan.
C. The Romeros need to pay approximately $625 a month for the five-year plan and $639 a month for the three-year plan.
D. The Romeros need to pay approximately $680 a month for the three-year plan and $625 a month for the five-year plan.

QUESTION 12. The Romeros also have a car on which they are ten months behind. The car was purchased four years ago. The car payments are $350 a month. Currently, they owe $12,000 on the car, which is worth $5,500 according to the NADA website, nada.com. Explain how much the Romeros would have to pay on this car in a Chapter 13 plan. Calculate the payments based on both a three-year and a five-year plan, with present value interest of ten percent if applicable. (Same false fact as in Question 11.)

A. The five-year plan costs approximately $198 per month, and the three-year plan costs approximately $137 per month.
B. The three-year plan costs approximately $100 per month, and the five-year plan costs approximately $110 per month.
C. The three-year plans costs approximately $370 per month, and the five-year plan costs approximately $300 per month.
D. The three-year plan costs approximately $198 per month, and the five-year plan costs approximately $137 per month.

QUESTION 13. The Romeros also owe income taxes for the past two years in the amount of $20,000 ($10,000 per year) and property taxes in the amount of $20,000 (also $10,000 per year) for the past two years. How much are they required to pay for these priority taxes in their Chapter 13 plan? Calculate the payments for the priority taxes, based on both a three-year and a five-year plan, with present value interest if it is necessary, again at 10 percent.

A. The priority plan payments will cost $666 for a five-year plan and $1,111 for a three-year plan.
B. The priority plan payments will cost $500 for a five-year plan and $833 for a three-year plan.
C. The priority plan payments will cost $750 for a five-year plan and $1,166 for a three-year plan.
D. The priority plan payments will cost $833 for a five-year plan and $500 for a three-year plan.

QUESTION 14. Your client, Alex Linden, is a divorced father who supports and has custody of his two young children, whose mother recently died in a car accident. Alex makes $3,000 a month working in the copy center of a large accounting firm. He is nine months behind on his mortgage payments of $800 a month. His monthly expenses are as follows:

Mortgage $800
Car payment/insurance $200
The Academy Private School (after scholarship) $100
Food $500
Medical costs $600
Soccer lessons for one girl $100
Counseling for the girls $100
Utilities $200
Savings $100

He has minimal nonexempt assets. Based on the very little that you know about his situation, what is the biggest impediment to confirmation of a Chapter 13 plan?

A. The food bill looks too high.
B. The soccer lessons and the private school tuition are not reasonably necessary for the maintenance and support of the debtor and his dependents, and thus these expenses violate the disposable income test.
C. The plan does not appear to be feasible.
D. The plan will fail the best interest test.

QUESTION 15. Carole Cole recently purchased a new computer, scanner, and printer on her credit card for $1,300. She has now come to see you and needs to file a liquidation bankruptcy immediately. Is there any risk that she will have to pay for the computer in her bankruptcy?

A. Yes, if Carol knew she was not going to pay for the computer when she bought it.
B. Yes, if the computer is a luxury good.
C. No, because bankruptcy discharges all unsecured debt.
D. No, because a computer is not a luxury good.

QUESTION 16. After Carol saw you and filled out her bankruptcy paperwork, but before you filed her petition with the court, she charged another $200 worth of food and medical supplies to her card. Is there any risk that she will need to pay this amount back?

A. No, because food is never a luxury good.
B. No, because the amount charged is so small.
C. Yes, because she certainly knew she was not going to pay this bill when she charged the food.
D. Yes, assuming she had no intent to repay the bill, but no in the unlikely event that she somehow did plan to pay these sums back.

QUESTION 17. Carlsbad Communications (Carlsbad) is having trouble making a profit. Most of Carlsbad's customers, who are advertisers, have cancelled their contracts because of the way Carlsbad's two local television channels covered a recent international emergency. After the tragic Brussels bombings, which Carlsbad failed to cover at all, viewers ignored these channels and watched CNN. Carlsbad (hereafter the "Debtor") has just filed a Chapter 11 petition. Eastern State Bank is owed $600,000, secured by a first lien and security interest in all of the Debtor's broadcasting equipment, as well as the Debtor's accounts receivable. The Debtor values these assets at $625,000, and Eastern State Bank values these assets at approximately $550,000. The Debtor also has about $50,000 in its bank account, which came from collection of its accounts receivable. The Debtor plans to use the $50,000 to make its payroll tomorrow. Can the Debtor do this? If a court gets involved, is it likely to allow the debtor to use these funds?

A. No, because Eastern State is entitled to relief from the automatic stay.
B. Yes, because Carlsbad can adequately protect Eastern State and thus should be allowed to use the cash collateral.

C. This depends on whether the court finds that the Debtor can adequately protect Eastern State's interests, because the cash is cash collateral.
D. Yes, because the $50,000 in accounts receivable clearly is not Eastern State's cash collateral, and thus the creditor has no right to adequate protection.

QUESTION 18. (CODE READER) Under §362(c)(3), which was added as part of the amendments in 2005, which of the following statements are correct?

1. The restrictions on the stay in a second bankruptcy case do not apply where the debtor's case has been dismissed for abuse under §707(b).
2. The restrictions on the stay in a second bankruptcy case do not apply where the debtor's prior case was a Chapter 12.
3. The restrictions on the stay in a second bankruptcy case do not apply where the debtor filed a Chapter 13 case on December 15, 2020, and then a Chapter 7 case on December 9, 2021.
4. The court can extend the stay past the 30 days provided for but only if it does so for all creditors equally in order to avoid discrimination.

A. 1 and 2.
B. 1 and 4.
C. 1, 2, and 4
D. All the statements are true.

QUESTION 19. Many scholars and others insist that under the 2005 amendments, unsecured creditors could receive smaller distributions than they received under the prior law. Which of these does not contribute to this potential problem?

A. The increased cost of bankruptcy for debtors, due to higher attorneys' fees and added fees for credit counseling and debt management courses.
B. The 2005 anti-stripdown provisions.
C. The fewer reporting requirements for debtors, which allow debtors to hide assets.
D. The 2005 disposable income test, which allows debtors to deduct from their income expenses that they do not actually have.

QUESTION 20. Whether an individual debtor has a "current monthly income" below the median in his or her state will determine:

1. whether he or she will be required to attend credit counseling and a debt management course.
2. whether the debtor can have the bankruptcy filing fee waived.
3. whether the debtor is free to choose between a Chapter 7 or a Chapter 13 case.
4. how the disposable income works in the debtor's case.

A. All of the above.
B. Only statements 2 and 3.
C. Only statement 3.
D. Only statements 3 and 4.

QUESTIONS 21 THROUGH 24. Advanced Porters Limited (APL) provides baggage assistance at airports across the U.S. With rolling luggage all the rage, APL has seen financial problems. Its primary secured lender is Lending for Less (the Bank), who had asked for extra reporting due to APL's tumbling financial condition. Faced with cash flow shortage and a payroll to meet, APL overstated its revenues one month to meet payroll. When the false statement was discovered, the Bank called a default under APL's loan and APL responded by filing a Chapter 11 petition. The first two months of its Chapter 11 case, APL, now a debtor-in-possession (the "debtor"), operated at a continuing loss. By the third month, it had devised a revised business plan, which called for it to reduce its operations to operate only in places that were growing in population, such as the Sunbelt and the West Coast, and more importantly, to restructure its services to provide for wheelchair assistance rather than baggage assistance. Most of the debtor's airport customers are enthusiastic about the change and the debtor has even picked up a few new contracts at airports that it did not do business with before.

Most of these airports are owed money by the debtor and are unsecured creditors in the bankruptcy case. The Bank is owed $10 million, and its collateral (virtually all of the debtor's working assets) is worth $8 million. These numbers have not changed during the case. Now it is five months into the case and the debtor made a profit for the most recent month and broke even the month before. It has had a disclosure statement approved and obtained votes on a plan that pays the Bank $8 million under terms similar to its original loans terms, and 45 percent to unsecured creditors over three years. The unsecured creditor class has voted yes on the plan and the Bank has voted no. The Bank also has filed a motion to convert the case to a Chapter 7, a motion to lift the stay, and an objection to confirmation based on feasibility. The Bank also claims the debtor's disclosure statement is false because it does not fully disclose the false financial statement.

QUESTION 21. As to the motion to convert, it seems most likely that:

A. The motion will be granted because the debtor took a substantial and continuing loss at the beginning of the case.

B. The motion will be granted because the debtor falsified a financial statement.

C. The motion will not succeed because it looks like, despite the continuing losses, converting the case would not be in the best interests of creditors.

D. The motion will not succeed because it looks like, despite the continuing losses, a plan will likely be confirmed.

QUESTION 22. How should the court rule on the Bank's objections to the plan?

A. The feasibility objection should probably be overruled because the numbers look good and the debtor has shown it can operate at a profit, if even just for one month.

B. The court will likely rule in favor of the Bank on the issue of the disclosure statement because the debtor has proved itself to be untruthful.

C. The court should overrule both the objections, the feasibility objection because the debtor is operating at a profit, and the disclosure statement issue because the disclosure statement is not false, and also because this issue already would have been decided in the disclosure statement hearing.

D. The court should allow only the feasibility issue to be raised because the debtor does not have a long enough track record at this point.

QUESTION 23. Assume that the debtor plans to pay the entire $8 million in secured debt during the life of the plan and can meet the §1129(b)(2)(A) requirements for cramdown. Assume also that the collateral values have not changed in the case but that the Bank has not received any payments in the case. How should the court rule on the motion to lift the stay?

A. The motion should be granted because the debtor admits that there is no equity in the collateral under §362(b)(2), but claims that the property is necessary to an effective reorganization.
B. The motion should be granted because there is a lack of adequate protection.
C. The motion should be denied because none of the grounds set out in §362(d)(2) are met.
D. The motion should be denied because the bank is oversecured.

QUESTION 24. In which order should the court hear the pending matters?

A. The conversion motion should be heard first. If it is granted, the court will not need to hear the motion to approve confirmation of the plan or the lift stay motion.
B. The lift stay motion should be heard first. If the collateral goes back to the Bank, the court can simply grant the conversion motion and will not need to hear the motion to approve confirmation.
C. The motion to approve the plan should be heard first. If §1129 is met and confirmation is approved, the conversion motion and the lift stay motion are both moot.
D. The motion to approve the plan should be heard first because if the plan is feasible and meets the requirements of §1129, it is very likely that the conversion motion will be denied because conversion is not in the best interests of creditors, and the lift stay requirements also would not be met.

QUESTION 25. **(CODE READER)** Debtor Corporation ("Debtor") owns equipment that is worth $4.5 million when Debtor files for Chapter 11 bankruptcy. Debtor owes Bank $1.8 million at the time of Debtor's filing, and that loan is secured by a properly perfected security interest in the equipment. At the time of the filing, the equipment is depreciating at the rate of $45,000 per month. Debtor believes that it can show that the equipment is clearly necessary for an effective reorganization of Debtor. Debtor does not have enough cash to pay $45,000 per month in depreciation payments, nor does Debtor have other unencumbered collateral for possible replacement liens. However, Debtor does have effective insurance on the equipment. One month into the case, Bank files a motion for lift of the automatic stay to foreclose on the property. How should the court rule?

A. Grant the motion under §362(d)(1) because of Debtor's current inability to provide Bank with either cash payments or replacement liens to account for the equipment's post-petition depreciation.
B. Grant the motion under §362(d)(2) on the basis that Debtor has no equity in the equipment.
C. Grant the motion under either §362(d)(1) or (d)(2).
D. Deny the motion under either §362(d)(1) or (d)(2).

QUESTION 26. (CODE READER) George Debtor is a heavy drinker, and one night he injures Velda Victim in an accident during which he is driving while intoxicated. Following the accident, Victim sues Debtor and gets a $3 million judgment against Debtor. Before Victim collects the judgment, Debtor files Chapter 7 bankruptcy. During the bankruptcy, Victim successfully petitions the bankruptcy court to declare that the judgment Victim received against Debtor is nondischargeable because it represents a §523(a)(9) injury caused by a debtor's operation of a motor vehicle while intoxicated. After this determination, but before Debtor receives his Chapter 7 discharge, Victim begins garnishing Debtor's post-petition wages. Is this garnishment prohibited by the Bankruptcy Code?

A. Yes, because acts to collect pre-petition claims, even nondischargeable ones, are prohibited by the post-discharge injunction.
B. Yes, because acts to collect pre-petition claims, even non-dischargeable ones, are prohibited by the automatic stay.
C. No, because Debtor's post-petition earnings do not constitute property of the estate.
D. No, because the underlying debt here is not dischargeable anyway.

QUESTION 27. (CODE READER) Secured Creditor is owed $900,000 in principal by Debtor, a corporation, on a loan that is secured by a properly perfected security interest in Debtor's production machine, which is worth $1,080,000 at all relevant points in time. The loan provides for 10 percent annual interest. At the time of Debtor's Chapter 7 bankruptcy filing, Debtor owes a year's worth of unpaid interest in addition to the $900,000 unpaid principal. It takes the Chapter 7 bankruptcy trustee one year following the Debtor's bankruptcy filing and $60,000 in necessary post-petition storage costs in order to sell Debtor's machine for a price of $1,080,000. Assuming that Debtor's Chapter 7 bankruptcy estate ends up paying its unsecured creditors zero cents on the dollar, what is Secured Creditor's total recovery from the bankruptcy estate?

A. $1,080,000.
B. $1,020,000.
C. $900,000.
D. $990,000.

QUESTION 28. (CODE READER) Debby Debtor owns a Volvo hybrid car that she purchased on secured credit a year ago. The car is now worth $47,250. The balance on Debtor's car loan is currently $27,000. The maximum exemption amount that is available by statute for cars in Debtor's state (an opt-out state) is $9,000. If Debtor wishes to redeem her car in her Chapter 7 bankruptcy, what is the combined amount that she will have to pay to the car-loan secured creditor and the trustee in bankruptcy?

A. $36,000.
B. $47,250.
C. $38,250.
D. $29,250.

QUESTION 29. (CODE READER) Carl Debtor (who is a below-median debtor) decides that he would like to file bankruptcy at a time when he has $60,000 worth of nonpriority unsecured debts, $45,000 worth of exempt personal property, and $15,000 worth of nonexempt personal property. He also has a home worth $300,000 on which he owes a mortgage of $300,000, but he is current on his payments there. His disposable income in a Chapter 13 would be approximately $600 per month. He comes to you and asks whether he should file a Chapter 7 or Chapter 13 bankruptcy. Regarding this choice, which of the following statements is accurate?

A. A Chapter 7 would require Debtor to relinquish his nonexempt assets to the estate, but he would not have to forego any post-petition disposable income as he would in a Chapter 13 plan.
B. A Chapter 13 might enable Debtor to give his unsecured creditors less money in total than he would under Chapter 7.
C. In a Chapter 13, Debtor would have to relinquish his nonexempt assets to the estate but at least he would get to keep his house.
D. Both A and B are accurate.

QUESTION 30. (CODE READER) Big Bank makes an unsecured loan to Debtor on Day 93 before bankruptcy. On Day 42 Big Bank asks for a security interest in Debtor's production machine and gets a signed security agreement from Debtor with respect to that machine in order to secure the Day 93 loan. On Day 19 Big Bank files a financing statement against the machine identified in the signed security agreement. When Debtor files bankruptcy on Day 0, has there been a preference?

A. No, because Big Bank made its unsecured loan outside of the 90-day preference period.
B. No, because Big Bank filed its financing statement (and thereby perfected its security interest) within 30 days of when Big Bank attached its security interest and therefore fell within the 30-day grace period of §547(e)(2)(A).
C. No, because Big Bank filed its financing statement within 30 days of Debtor's bankruptcy filing and therefore fell within the 30-day grace period of §547(e)(2)(A).
D. Yes, because even after we adjust the date of transfer of the security interest under the 30-day grace period of §547(e)(2)(A), the adjusted date of transfer still occurred within 90 days of bankruptcy and after the original extension of credit by Big Bank.

Martin's and Keating's Picks

QUESTION 1. The trick to this one is separating out the priority claims from the general unsecured claims by making two columns, one for each type, and then listing them along with their amounts. This question was adapted from a short-answer question that one of us gave that had two additional ambiguities. First, the wife's claim was not identified as a child support claim, so students had to do the calculation assuming both that the claim had priority and then assuming that it did not. Second, the security guards' claims were over the statutory limit so students had to place part of the claim in the priority category and put part in the unsecured category. Watch for questions of this nature.

For this question as written, the following claims go into the priority category: the income taxes for $10,000, the trustee's fees and costs for $3,000, the wife's support claims for $9,000, and the security guards' claims for $13,000. These add up to $35,000, which is then deducted from the total realized from the sale of the debtor's assets, $50,000. This assumes $35,000 is paid to these priority claims and there is $15,000 left to distribute to the unsecured creditors. Unsecured creditors include $40,000 for property taxes that are outside the priority period, $1,000 for the debtor's pre-petition attorneys' fees, which, in most jurisdictions are not entitled to special priority (remember this is why the debtor's lawyer should get paid in advance in a Chapter 7), $40,000 in student loans, and $20,000 in credit card debts. If you add up these unsecured debts, you get $101,000. Divide the $15,000 available to unsecured creditors by the $101,000 in claims and you get a distribution of 14.8 percent. Thus, the correct answer is **A**. The other answers reflect common mistakes that students make.

For example, some students would choose **C**, assuming that some of the unsecured claims get priority, such as the student loans, the old property taxes, or the debtor's pre-petition attorneys' fees. If these other claims were at least $15,000, then there would be no money left for unsecured creditors because all the money would be expended on priority claims. So **C** is wrong. The number you would get if you assumed that the debtor's attorney was entitled to priority for his or her pre-petition claims is 14 percent, making the priority claims $36,000, leaving just $14,000 for the unsecured creditors, and dividing that number by $100,000, for a distribution of 14 percent. Again, this is wrong. Thus, **D** is also incorrect.

QUESTION 2. Now we need to take the wife's $9,000 in claims out of the priority claims and add them to the unsecured creditor class. That makes priority claims total $26,000 and makes unsecured creditors total $110,000. This leaves $50,000 - $26,000 for unsecured creditors, or $24,000. This $24,000 gets divided by the now $110,000 in general unsecured claims, for distribution of 21.8 percent, making **C** the correct answer. Fun, huh? The numbers contained in wrong answers **A** and **D** result from failing to add or subtract the wife's claim to one category or another.

QUESTION 3. This question requires you to first determine who will be paid in full in any case and who will not. Here, the IRS (which holds a priority claim) will be paid in full as the holder of a priority claim, no matter how the wife's claim is characterized, simply because under these numbers, priority claims are being paid in full here. If this were not the case, the wife would come ahead of the priority taxes and it might make sense for the taxing authorities to challenge the wife. Here, the priority tax claim holders gain nothing by challenging her claim, thus eliminating choice **A**. **B** is incorrect because the characterization of the wife's claim as child support or a property settlement will change its priority and will change the unsecured creditor distribution for the credit card creditor, as the answers to Questions 1 and 2 indicate. The difference between a 14.8 percent distribution and a 21.8 percent distribution on an $18,000 claim is $1,260. Hard work, we know! The answer is **D**.

QUESTION 4. This question tests your knowledge of §362(b), the exceptions to the automatic stay. **A** is wrong because criminal suits and paternity suits are not stayed. Also, if Clyde does a Chapter 7, he will not necessarily pay all of his debts, so **A** is wrong for two reasons. **B** corrects one of these defects but is still wrong on the issue of the scope of the stay. **C** contains an incorrect statement of what gets stayed, which is corrected in **D**. Thus, **D** is the correct answer.

QUESTION 5. This question employs a tricky technique that we all use, whether the question is multiple choice, short answer, or essay. It is the compound question in which you are asked to build on the correct answer to the prior question. If you did not have the correct answer to the prior question handy, which you obviously would not in a real exam, you would not know if you got the last one wrong. If you got the previous question wrong, you would likely miss this one as well.

Assuming that you got the correct answer on the last one, even the best answer (**D**) contains a small inaccuracy, dealing with whether stayed collection activity is stayed temporarily or permanently. The correct answer in Question 4, **D**, stated that "the doctor's suit, the eviction, and the utility shutoff will be stayed for a time, but the criminal battery suit and the paternity suit will not." In reality, the eviction will be stayed for a time and will probably resume, the utility shutoff will be stayed permanently assuming that the debtor makes his required deposit under §366(b), but the doctor's suit will be stayed permanently and thereafter discharged. Thus, choice **D** of this answer corrects the misstatement and is the correct answer.

QUESTION 6. This is much easier than the exemption questions in the text, but does pose some tricky issues. First, you need to review §522(d) to remember what exemptions are offered by the Bankruptcy Code, so you can compare them to those of the state of Blackstone. If you do, you'll see that **A** is incorrect in describing the federal scheme in two ways. The federal scheme will not allow the Blacks to save all $60,000 in equity in their home. This is a big disadvantage to the federal scheme as most people want to save their home over all else. The federal scheme also has a limited home furnishing exemption and will not allow the Blacks to save all their furniture. **A** is clearly incorrect. **C** is incorrect because it still says that the Blacks can save their home under §522(d), which is not true.

The tough choice here is between **B** and **D**. Both contain correct statements in isolation. Looking at **B**, the state scheme allows the Blacks to keep the home, the retirement funds, the furniture, and only lose the savings. Looking at **D**, the federal scheme will save most of the cash and the state scheme will save the home. But **B** is the correct answer because the state exemption scheme allows the Blacks to save $60,000 worth of real property, as compared to under $50,000 from the federal scheme. What if liquidity is important to the Blacks? We would still pick **B**. The home is more important than the cash because the Blacks can probably borrow against this equity to raise cash (yes, even after bankruptcy), and could even sell the house after the bankruptcy and keep the equity. They may even be able to borrow from their 401(k) plan. It would not be worth it to save the cash if it meant losing some or all of the equity in the house. So **B** is correct.

QUESTION 7. Farmer's is oversecured by a large amount under these facts: thus, it is going to have some difficulty getting the stay lifted at this time. **A** is incorrect because, under §362(d)(2), any creditor must prove two elements. First, the creditor must prove that the debtor has no equity in the collateral. This will be hard to prove under these facts. There appears to be equity of approximately $25,000, taking the value of $3.5 million, less the total liens of $325,000. It is true that the property appears to be depreciating and in court, a creditor could try to prove this, but none of this proof is described in the answer choices you are given. Second, the creditor has to show (under §362(d)(2)) that the property is "not necessary to an effective reorganization." A court will give a debtor a chance to show it can reorganize before concluding otherwise, if the assets are needed in the business. These certainly are. So **A** is wrong. **B** looks good, but look at the size of Farmer's equity cushion — about a million bucks! Unless the debtor is doing this amount of damage, or close to it, Farmer's is probably adequately protected under §362(d)(1), so this eliminates both **B** and **D** and makes **C** the best answer.

QUESTION 8. Based on years of experience reading the wrong answer on this one, we know **D** is tempting. However, the second lienholder usually has a better chance of prevailing in a motion to lift the stay because its position is more precarious. Remember that Farmer's is in first position with a $2.5 million claim on a building worth something like $3.5 million or a little less. That is a very protected position indeed. Prudential, on the other hand, is owed $750,000 behind that $2.5 million mortgage on the same $3.5 million property, leaving it with a potential $250,000 equity cushion based on an old appraisal taken before the debtor started having severe financial problems. This poor financial condition is an invitation for deferred maintenance and dropping property values. Thus, **D** is the opposite of the truth. Prudential has a decent chance of success not based on (d)(2) (there is still no proof of a lack of equity, let alone proof that the property is not necessary to an effective reorganization), but under (d)(1). Prudential is not adequately protected because its equity cushion (if there is one) is shrinking due to lack of maintenance. This is not a sure winner based on the facts you were given, however, so **C** is a better answer than **B**. Choice **A** is just plain wrong, as Prudential does not have a huge equity cushion. Thus, the correct answer is **C**.

QUESTION 9. Here is how the math works. Start with the $2.5 million claim, add six months of interest at 1 percent ($25,000 per month) for $150,000, then add the $50,000 in attorneys' fees (this assumes they are reasonable), and you get $2,700,000. Choice **B** is correct and better than choice **C**, because §506(a) allows reasonable attorneys' fees to an oversecured creditor and Farmer's is oversecured here. **A** is a wrong answer that one of us took off a student's exam answer (we're not sure where that one came from) and **D** is the answer if you incorrectly figure the interest at $15,000 rather than $150,000 (which many students seem to do). Thus, the correct answer is **B**.

QUESTION 10. Given the answer to Question 9, Prudential has a secured claim for what is left of the value in the collateral after Farmer's is paid, or $3 million less Farmer's claim of $2.7 million, so Prudential's secured claim is $300,000. It will receive another 10 percent as a distribution on its remaining unsecured claim of $450,000, for another $45,000. It will not accrue interest or attorneys' fees on its claims at all during the post-petition period because it is undersecured, as it turns out. Thus, the correct answer is **A**.

QUESTION 11. The key here is remembering that with a home mortgage the debtor cannot strip down the debt, but must make the regular monthly payment and add to that payment an amount that will cure the arrears on the mortgage. Start by taking the regular $500 monthly payment and setting that amount aside. You'll be adding the "cure" amount to that number. The Romeros are ten months (at $500 per month) behind, so that is $5,000. The Romeros need to pay present-value interest on the arrears, which we will (for simplicity's sake) falsely assume accrues at a flat 10 percent per year on the full cure amount (the arrears), even though some will be paid off over time. For the five-year plan, 10 percent of $5,000, or $500, times five years, is an additional $2,500. If we add that number to the $5,000, we get $7,500, and we divide that by 60 months. It costs $125 per month to cure this mortgage. Remember that with a home mortgage, you need to pay this amount plus the regular monthly mortgage, so this costs $625 per month under a five-year plan.

So far it looks like the answer could be either **C** or **D**, so we also need to try the calculation for the three-year plan. For the three-year plan, we need to add present-value interest for three years to the $5,000. To do this, take 10 percent of $5,000 for three years, which is $1,500, and add that to the $5,000 cure amount. You get $6,500, and divide that amount by 36 months, and come up with $180.55. **D** is the correct answer. The numbers in the incorrect answers do not include present-value interest, or they reverse the numbers for the two different plan durations. Remember to use your common sense. Longer plans will have smaller payments, but the debtor will pay more, over a longer period, due to the added interest. The answer is **D**.

QUESTION 12. Ah, stripdown. Ain't it grand? Here, the debtors need only pay the $5,500 value of the car, with present value interest (which we've calculated in that artificial way discussed in the prior question), and can save a big bundle. The numbers in choice **C** assume that the debtor has to pay the whole $12,000 loan with 10 percent interest, and you can see how huge these numbers are. In reality, the debtor will instead pay just the stripdown amount, $5,500 with interest. The correct figures are found in choice **D**, and the calculation goes like this: Take $5,500. Add interest at 10 percent for each year of the plan. That would be $1,650 for three years, or $2,750 for five years. For three years you have $5,500 plus $1,650 (or $7,150 divided) by 36 months, or $198.61. For five years, you have $5,500 plus $2,750 (or $8,250) divided by 60 months, or $137.50. The answer is **D**. This is quite a savings over the numbers found in **C**.

Keep in mind that the 2005 amended version of §1325 imposes new limits on the debtor's ability to strip down a car loan. If the loan is a purchase money security interest on a car purchased within the 910-day period preceding the date of filing of the petition, the debtor cannot strip down the loan. Thus, under that fact scenario, the Romeros would need to pay the full amount owed on the loan plus present-value interest, which is shown in answer **C**. However, under the facts presented to you, the car can be stripped down and **D** is the correct answer.

QUESTION 13. Only $30,000 of these amounts is priority, all of the income taxes under §507(a)(8)(A), and just $10,000 of the property taxes under §507(a)(8)(B). Thus, the number you are working with is $30,000. There is no interest on this claim in a Chapter 13, although there would be in a Chapter 11 case. Thus, the answer is **B**. You take the $30,000 and divide it by 60 months to get $500 per month. Then divide it by 36 months to get $833 per month for the three-year plan. **A** is incorrect because it assumes that all $40,000 is priority. **C** is wrong because it assumes that the debtors will need to pay interest on these amounts in Chapter 13, which is not true. **D** is incorrect because it reverses the correct payment amounts for the three-year and the five-year plan. Again, the monthly payment is always lower if the debtor is paying over a five-year plan than it would be under a three-year plan.

QUESTION 14. Multiple-choice questions test your knowledge of plan issues particularly well, because you need to know all of the tests before you can answer a question as broad as this one. Here, some tests are implicated and some are not, but the question asks you to identify the biggest impediment to confirmation. **D**, the best interest test, is not implicated here because the debtor has minimal nonexempt assets. **A** is also wrong because the amount of money Alex spends on food is not relevant. If Alex has a current monthly income above the median in his state, the 2005 law allocates a specific amount for food and clothing, which is based on the debtor's family size and IRS expense standards, and which is likely below the amount he is spending. If he is below the median, this amount, $500, still seems reasonable for a family of three. **B** could be true. It is possible that because of discretionary expenses, like soccer, he will not pass the disposable income test. However, the statement made in choice **B** is too definitive. It is not clear if the soccer lessons will be an impediment or not, given all the facts we do not know. Just so you know, the school expense described in these facts would be permitted under the disposable income test for above-median debtors, and would be allowed by some courts but not others under the below-median income disposable income test. We find it ironic that some above-median debtors could use private schools (admittedly very inexpensive ones), while below-median income debtors might not be allowed to.

The feasibility test seems to be a more formidable problem. Even before taking into account any incidental expenses, a savings, or contingency funds, or the cost of curing the mortgage under the plan, the debtor's listed expenses are $2,700 and his net income is $3,000. Even if Alex does a five-year cure of his home mortgage, he'll need to pay $180 a month for that. That's $800 a month times nine months for $7,200. He'll also need to pay present value, which we pretend is ten percent. $720 times five years is $3,600. That means Alex needs to pay a total of $10,800 ($7,200 + $3,600) over 60 months to cure the arrears. Curing the arrears costs him an additional $180 per month on top of the regular $800 mortgage payment. In a three-year plan, Alex would need to pay $260 per month to cure the arrears. Either way, he is too close to the bone. So **C** is the correct answer. **B** is a close second.

QUESTION 15. If Carol knew when she bought this stuff that she was not going to pay the debt back, then she is liable for actual fraud and the debt is nondischargeable under §523(a)(2)(A), assuming the creditor can prove this fact. It is true that the §523(a)(2)(C) presumption of fraud for luxury goods would not apply to this situation unless the computer equipment constitutes luxury goods. However, she can still be found liable for actual fraud outside this presumption. Thus, **A** is true and **D** is false. **B** alone is false because it just creates a presumption of fraud that Carol can rebut if she really did intend to pay this back. Hmmm . . . this is hard. **C** is incorrect because unsecured debt is, of course, generally dischargeable, but it will be nondischargeable if it falls into one of the §523(a) exceptions. Thus, the correct answer is **A**.

QUESTION 16. If you got Question 15 wrong, you might have made a similar mistake here. The answer in **A** bears no relation on what the question asks here. This question is about actual fraud under §523(a)(2)(A) and does not deal with the luxury goods exception at all. If Carol had no intention of paying for the food and medical supplies, she is liable for actual fraud, if this intent can be proven. The creditor will be required to prove fraud (unlike luxury goods cases, in which the creditor can rely on the statutory presumption). **A** and **B** both go to the presumption which is not relevant here, and **C** contains a fact not given. Thus, the answer is **D**.

QUESTION 17. **A** is not really what this is all about. Eastern State may or may not be entitled to relief from the automatic stay under §362(d), but the debtor here is trying to determine if it can use Eastern State's cash collateral to meet its payroll tomorrow, by using the $50,000 generated from the sale of its accounts. These items are clearly cash collateral under §363(a), making **D**

incorrect, and making it necessary for the debtor to either have the creditor's approval or get the court to approve the use of cash collateral involuntarily. Whether a court will be willing to do this will depend on whether it finds that the creditor is adequately protected. Here, the facts make this unclear, making **B** incorrect. As we can't tell from these facts if the creditor is adequately protected, the answer is **C**.

QUESTION 18. Statement **1** is correct. The section explicitly provides that if a debtor has a case dismissed for abuse under the means test found in §707(b), then the stay in the new case is not affected by this provision. In other words, the debtor gets the full benefit of the stay, as always. This doesn't help much, however, as all the answers include statement **1**. Statement **2** is true as well. No one knows why but it appears that cases under all the other chapters are implicated in §362(c)(3), but not cases filed under Chapter 12. This looks like an oversight. In any case, statement **2** must appear in the correct answer, eliminating choice **B**. Statements **3** and **4** are both incorrect, leaving **A** as the correct answer. Why? This section limits the stay in cases pending under both Chapter 13 and Chapter 7 within one year, and both the cases described in **3** appear to have been pending within the same one-year period. Statement **4** is incorrect because §362 allows the court the flexibility to extend the stay for one or more creditors but not for others. Although that may seem discriminatory, the section explicitly permits this. We hope you found most of these provisions in the section and thus learned a bit more about both this section and about statutory interpretation.

QUESTION 19. The weird placement of the word ***not*** in this question places a premium on careful reading. You are looking for the 2005 Code provision or policy that is either falsely stated (not actually part of the 2005 Code amendments), or that will not decrease payments to creditors. Alternatively, you could try to locate the things that will lead to smaller distributions for creditors and see what choices are left. Here, we'll look for the ones that most obviously decrease payments to unsecured creditors and eliminate them. Needless to say, you need to have a good understanding of several bankruptcy concepts before you can begin to answer this one.

First, **B** is very likely to lead to smaller distributions for unsecured creditors because debtors, at least in Chapter 13 cases, will need to pay more of their limited resources to their secured creditors now that stripdown has been severely cut back. What is stripdown? See Chapter 21. **D** is also likely to reduce payments to unsecured creditors. The imputation of the means test into the disposable income test means that the debtor can now deduct from his or her income not just actual expenses, but all the deduction categories allowed under the IRS guidelines. Some of these need not be incurred in order to be deducted. (*See* Chapters 17 and 23.) **A** is something we could disagree about. Perhaps most of the money spent on lawyers and credit counselors would have been exempt (*see* Chapter 9), and if so, these added fees would not affect unsecured distributions. They could reduce distributions, however, so **A** is not the best answer. **C**, on the other hand, contains a false statement, namely that the reporting requirements for debtors have decreased under bankruptcy reform. The 2005 Code amendments increase rather than decreases these reporting requirements, making **C** the statement that needs to be eliminated. Thus, **C** is the answer. Whew!

QUESTION 20. Everyone must attend credit briefing (also called credit counseling), so statement **1** is untrue. The bankruptcy filing fee can be waived but only for people living at or below 110 percent of the poverty level, clearly much lower than the median income in any state. On the other hand, the main significance of the means test is that it may limit a debtor's choice to file a Chapter 7, making statement **3** true. Statement **4** is also true, as the disposable income test uses the same median-income guidelines for determining how much a debtor must pay in a Chapter 13 plan. Thus, the correct answer is **D**.

QUESTION 21. Section 1112 does not require conversion of a case for falsifying a financial statement and in any event, the falsification occurred pre-petition, before the bankruptcy. Thus, **B** is incorrect. A substantial loss is grounds for conversion, but this ground can be overcome if converting the case is not in the best interests of creditors. It cannot be overcome merely because confirmation of a plan is likely. (*See* 11 U.S.C. §1112 (b)(1) and (2), as well as Chapter 36 of this guide.) Thus, the correct answer is **C**. Why is converting the case to a Chapter 7 not in the best interests of creditors? Because undersecured creditors will get a 45 percent distribution under the plan and will get nothing if either the conversion motion or the lift stay motion is granted. In either a conversion or a grant of the automatic stay, the Bank will take all of the assets, leaving nothing for the unsecured creditors.

QUESTION 22. **A** looks good but does not answer the whole question. **B** also only answers half the question, and also contains an incorrect statement. The statement is incorrect because the debtor has not proven itself to be untruthful in this case, only pre-petition, and even if the pre-petition infraction mattered, this fact does not necessarily make the disclosure statement incorrect or incomplete. In any event, the court will already have held a hearing on the adequacy of the disclosure statement, and if the Bank objected at that time, and the court approved the statement anyway, the issues will not be revisited here. If the Bank failed to object at that time, it waived its right to do so. **D** does not really answer the question of how the court should rule. It deals only with the procedural question of which evidence the court should hear. **C**, however, contains a correct assessment of how the court should rule on both objections raised. It is somewhat of a close call on the feasibility issue, but as Chapter 34 explains, most courts will let the plan go forward if the plan has a chance of succeeding based on current evidence.

QUESTION 23. **A** should be eliminated right off the bat because it articulates a reason why the motion should be denied. Yes, there is no equity under §362(d)(2)(A), but to grant relief from the stay under this section, a secured party must meet both (d)(2)(A) and (B). There must be no equity, which the plan readily admits by valuing the Bank's collateral at $8 million for the purposes of cramdown, and the property must not be necessary to an effective reorganization. Here the property, the working assets, is necessary to the reorganization, which is effective because it seems imminent after a short period of time in Chapter 11. Thus, **A** is incorrect. **D** also can be eliminated because the Bank is undersecured, not oversecured. It is owed $10 million and has collateral worth $8 million. This leaves **B** and **C**. **B** is tempting because the Bank's undersecured status makes it seem as though the Bank is not adequately protected under §362 (d)(1). However, because the collateral has not lost any value in the case, no payments are needed to keep the Bank adequately protected. Thus, there has been no lack of adequate protection proven under these facts. This leaves **C** as the correct answer.

QUESTION 24. Was this one a softball? Perhaps. It is very likely that all of these matters would be scheduled for the same day, and also that the court will want to hear the confirmation matter first. Keep the goals of Chapter 11 in mind. The purpose is to try to reorganize businesses, not to shut them down. If the rules for reorganizing a business are met, most courts will let the company try to pay the plan and stay in business, even if the feasibility issue is less than clear-cut. The Bank will disagree here but it is possible to create a better result for everyone by allowing the debtor to try to perform its plan obligations rather than allowing the case to be converted to a Chapter 7 liquidation, or allowing the bank to walk away with all of the working assets. Thus, **A** and **B** are both incorrect. Between **C** and **D**, **D** is more accurate. Approval of confirmation does not automatically make the other two motions moot, but it does make it very unlikely that they will be approved. Given that the unsecured creditors have voted in favor of the plan and that the plan complies with the Code regarding the Bank's treatment, the Bank has no grounds to lift the stay. The plan adequately protects its interests. As for the conversion motion, the plan does appear to be in the best interest of creditors. Can you see why? The Bank gets the money it would get in a liquidation, $8 million, albeit over time with interest.[1] The unsecured creditors, which include the Bank for $2 million, get a 45 percent distribution that they would not get at all in a liquidation because the Bank would take all the assets. On the $2 million deficiency claim alone, this is $900,000. Thus, the correct answer is **D**.

---

1. Understand that the Bank does not believe that it will actually get this money. It instead believes that the plan will not succeed. For this reason, it would rather have its $8 million now.

QUESTION 25. This question is a reminder that an equity cushion can often be the source of a secured creditor's adequate protection in a debtor's bankruptcy. In this case, Bank is owed \$1.8 million but has collateral worth \$4.5 million, which gives Bank a \$2.7 million equity cushion in the collateral. Even with a depreciation rate of \$45,000 per month, that amount of equity cushion will last years before Bank would become undersecured. That means that §362(d)(1) would not be available because there is no "cause, including lack of adequate protection" that Bank can point to under these facts. Neither will §362(d)(2) work here for Bank as a basis for getting lift of stay. That's because §362(d)(2) requires both that the debtor has no equity in the property and that the property is not necessary for an effective reorganization, neither of which is true in this case. Therefore, **D** is the correct answer.

QUESTION 26. Before getting to the correct answer here, let's see why the other three answers are wrong. Choice **A** is incorrect because the post-discharge injunction of §524(a)(2) does not begin until the debtor receives a discharge, which has not happened yet here. Therefore, the post-discharge injunction cannot apply to this garnishment action by Victim. Choice **C** is incorrect because the automatic stay's prohibition in §362(a)(6) against "any act" to collect a pre-petition debt is not limited to acts against property of the estate. Therefore, the fact that Debtor's post-petition earnings do not constitute property of the estate does not shield this garnishment from the automatic stay. Choice D is incorrect because the automatic stay, in prohibiting acts to collect pre-petition debts under §362(a)(6), does not make an exception for debts that are non-dischargeable. That prohibition is against any act to collect any pre-petition debt, even if the pre-petition debt is ultimately determinedto be nondischargeable. That leaves **B**, which is the correct answer because under §362(a)(6), acts to collect pre-petition claims against the debtor, even non-dischargeable claims, are prohibited by the automatic stay. Victim will need to wait until Debtor's bankruptcy case is closed or a discharge is granted so that the automatic stay will no longer be in effect. At that point, Victim will be allowed to collect on the pre-petition nondischargeable debt.

QUESTION 27. Choice **B** is the correct answer here, but it takes a combination of simple math and Code knowledge to get you there. Secured Creditor's total claim would equal the \$900,000 in principal, \$90,000 in pre-petition accrued interest, and up to one year's worth of §506(b) post-petition interest (depending on the extent to which Secured Creditor is oversecured). That post-petition interest, to the extent that Secured Creditor is eligible for it under §506(b), would be 10 percent times \$990,000, or \$99,000. If Secured Creditor had the collateral to support it, its total claim could be as high as \$1,089,000. However, the §506(b) post-petition interest here is limited by the collateral value, which is just \$1,020,000 after the trustee subtracts its \$60,000 in storage costs under §506(c). Therefore, the total claim will end up being capped at

$1,020,000 once the post-petition interest stops. Choice **A** is therefore incorrect because under §506(c), the bankruptcy trustee can recover its $60,000 in storage costs from the $1,080,000 purchase price even ahead of the secured creditor's priority in the proceeds of the sale. That leaves just $1,020,000, not $1,080,000, available for Secured Creditor. Choice **C** is incorrect because it fails to fully account for Secured Creditor's $90,000 in pre-petition interest, nor does it account for any of Secured Creditor's §506(b) post-petition interest. Choice **D** is incorrect because even though it gives Secured Creditor all of its pre-petition interest, it fails to account for any of Secured Creditor's §506(b) post-petition interest.

QUESTION 28. Redemption questions can be tricky, and this redemption question is no exception. Choice **A** is incorrect because under §722 Debtor will need to pay her car-loan creditor the value of its secured claim, which is $27,000, and she will also need to pay the trustee to "buy back" Debtor's equity in the car from the estate after subtracting the amount of Debtor's exemption. Debtor's equity in the car is $20,250 ($47,250 in car value minus $27,000 secured loan balance). Debtor can exempt $9,000 of that $20,250 in equity, leaving $11,250 that she must pay the trustee for the rest. The problem with Choice **A** is that it adds the car-loan creditor's claim ($27,000) with the amount of Debtor's exemption ($9,000) instead of the amount of equity ($11,250) that Debtor still needs to buy back from the estate after Debtor uses her exemption. Choice **C** gets this calculation right and therefore is the correct answer: It adds the $27,000 representing the car loan creditor's secured claim with the $11,250 that Debtor needs to pay the trustee to buy back the estate's interest in the car for a total of $38,250. Choice **B** is incorrect because it does not give Debtor any credit for her exemption and assumes that Debtor must pay Secured Creditor $27,000 and then buy all of her equity back from the trustee for another $20,250 with no $9,000 subtraction for the value of Debtor's exemption in the car. Choice **D** is incorrect because even though it correctly assumes that Debtor owes the trustee $11,250 to buy back Debtor's equity in the car from the estate, it wrongly assumes that Debtor's $9,000 exemption comes ahead of secured creditor's $27,000 secured claim.

QUESTION 29. The Chapter 7/Chapter 13 choice is a key issue for consumer debtors contemplating a bankruptcy filing. Under these facts, choice **A** is an accurate statement and thus the correct answer. That's because §541(a) essentially defines property of the estate as all of a debtor's nonexempt assets, but then §541(a)(6) says that the debtor's bankruptcy estate does not include any of the debtor's post-petition income. Section 1306(b) specifically allows the debtor to stay in possession of property of the estate in a Chapter 13 bankruptcy, but the debtor's Chapter 13 plan will typically need to be funded with the debtor's post-petition income. Choice **B** is incorrect because §1325(a)(4)'s "best interest of creditors test" requires that unsecured creditors must receive at least as much in a Chapter 13 bankruptcy as they would in a Chapter 7 liquidation bankruptcy for the same debtor. Choice **C** is incorrect because, as noted above, §1306(b) specifically allows a Chapter 13 debtor to stay in possession of property of the estate. Choice **D** is incorrect because **B** is incorrect.

QUESTION 30. This question tests how well you know the operation of the 30-day grace period that is found in §547(e)(2)(A). Let's first consider why the three incorrect answers are wrong. Choice **A** is incorrect because a preference does not require that the extension of credit must occur within the 90 days before bankruptcy. The key event that must occur within the 90-day preference period is the repayment of the loan, not the making of the loan. Choice **B** is incorrect because merely qualifying for the 30-day grace period of §547(e)(2)(A) does not necessarily mean that a creditor will escape preference liability. Choice **C** is incorrect because it misstates the starting and ending points for §547(e)(2)(A)'s 30-day grace period. To qualify for that grace period, the creditor must perfect its security interest within 30 days after attachment. So the starting point for the 30-day grace period is attachment and the thing that must happen within the 30 days is perfection, not the debtor filing for bankruptcy. That leaves **D**, the correct answer. Choice **D** is correct because merely qualifying for the 30-day grace period of §547(e)(2)(A) (as was true here) does not necessarily mean that a creditor will escape preference liability. In this case, even after qualifying for the 30-day grace period, Debtor's transfer to Big Bank is deemed to occur on Day 42 rather than Day 19 before Debtor's bankruptcy filing. However, even a transfer by Debtor to Big Bank on Day 42 will qualify as a preference because it is still a transfer on account of an antecedent debt that occurs within 90 days of Debtor's bankruptcy filing.

Congratulations on reaching the end of this book, and good luck in your course.

Index

Absolute priority rule
- debtors-in-possession, 367
- dissenting creditors, 452–456
- secured creditors, 306
- unsecured creditors, 452–456

Abuse test, 201–215
Accountants
- applications to be employed as, 332–335
- creditors' committees
  - appointing, 303

Accounts receivable, 311–312
Actual fraud, nondischargeability, 151–152, 176
Adequate protection
- automatic stay, 344–351
- cash collateral, 314–320
- lack of, 73–74
- post-petition financing orders, 322
- shopping center leases, 396–397

Administrative claims, 375, 414, 438–440
Administrative convenience rule, 439
Adversary proceedings, 51n1
Agency law, post-confirmation issues, 475–476
Allowable expenses and means test, 203–204, 212–214
Allowed secured claims, 28, 365
Annuities, 80
Antecedent debt, 129, 133
Anti-modification clauses, 241–242
Appeals, 43–44
Article III judges, 40, 42
Articles of Confederation, 48
Asbestos claims, 372–373
Asset sales, 398–405
- bidding, 402–404
- break-up fees, 402–404
- economic value theory, 398–402
- face value theory, 398–402
- free and clear of liens, 398–399
- overbid protection, 402–404
- overview, 398–402
- stalking horse, 402–404
- successor liability, 404–405

Assignment
- of executory contracts, 395–398
- of unexpired leases, 395–398

Assumption
- and assignment, 395–398
- of executory contracts, 393–395
- of unexpired leases, 393–395

Attorneys
- applications to be employed as, 332–335
- investigations, 52
- obligations, 54–55
- sanctions for false certification of petition, 94

Attorneys' fees, 55, 334, 415
Automatic stay, 61–75
- adequate protection, 344–351
- cause, relief for, 345
- child support, 63–64
- collateral, 63
- debtors-in-possession, 362–364
- divorce, 64

Automatic stay (*cont'd*)
  domestic support obligations, 163–164
  duration, 73
  equity, relief for lack of, 73–74, 345–347
  exceptions, 62–68, 342–344
  extending, 69–70
  insurance, relief for lack of, 349–350
  marital obligations, 64
  obtaining, 71
  one prior dismissed case, 69
  passive real estate, 347
  paternity, 62
  police powers, 342–344
  pre-petition debt, 61
  property not necessary for effective reorganization, relief for, 345–347
  purposes, 61–62
  relief from, 73–74, 344–351
  repeat filers, not available to, 71
  repossession, 61
  scope of, 339–342
  security interests, 62
  taxes, 63, 341–342
  two or more prior dismissed cases, 69
Automobiles. *See* Motor vehicles
Avoiding powers, 123–142
  defined, 123
  fraudulent transfers, 124, 138–140
  preferential transfers. *See* Preferential transfers
  strong-arm powers, 140–141
  unperfected security interests, 124, 140–141

Badges of fraud, 18
Balloon payments, 448
Bankruptcy Act. *See* Bankruptcy Code
Bankruptcy appellate panels (BAPs), 43–44
Bankruptcy Clause, 39, 46–47
Bankruptcy Code. *See also specific Chapter*
  automatic stay, 61
  creditors' committees, 302–305
  enactment, 39
  exemptions, 15–16
  fraudulent transfers, 35, 138–140
  overview, 3
  post-petition financing orders, 322
  reading, 31
  small business debtors, 34
  state opt-out provisions, 15–16
  structure of, 57
  trustees, 358
  undue hardship, 165–166
  valuation, 238–239
Bankruptcy Court
  appeals, 43–44
  equity powers, 45–46
  jurisdiction, 39–43
  terms of judges, 42–43
Bankruptcy Reform Act of 1978, 17, 302
Bankruptcy Rules
  attorneys' fees, 55
  schedules and statements, 299
BAPs (Bankruptcy appellate panels), 43–44
Best efforts test. *See* Disposable income test
Best interest test (Chapter 11), 416–419
  debtors-in-possession, 364
  disclosure statement, 430
  dissenting creditors, 443
  overview, 416
Best interest test (Chapter 13), 271–278
  Chapter 7 compared, 272–278
  disposable income test compared, 271
Bidding, asset sales, 402–404
Bifurcation, 234–236, 306
Break-up fees, 402–404
Business inventory, 311

Capitalism, 25
Cars. *See* Motor vehicles
Case administration, 51–59
  Bankruptcy Code, 57
  Chapter 7, 55–56
  Chapter 11, 56–57
  Chapter 13, 56
  creditors' meeting, 55
  new requirements of 2005 Bankruptcy Code amendments, 52–55
Cash advances, nondischargeability, 153–155
Cash collateral, 310–321
  accounts receivable, 311–312
  adequate protection, 314–320
  business inventory, 311
  debtors-in-possession, 356
  defined, 311–312
  overview, 311–312
  special rules for debtor's use of, 314–318
  stipulations, 318–321
Cash management orders, 335
Chapter 7 (liquidation)
  administration, 55–56
  Chapter 13 compared, 225–227
  discharge, 143–147
  dismissal. *See* Dismissal
  home mortgage payments, 74–75
  involuntary bankruptcy, 217–222
  "keep and pay" option, 183–184, 190–193
  motor vehicles, 94
  overview, 27–28
  post-petition assets, 80–81
  prior discharge, 178–179
  reaffirmation. *See* Reaffirmation
  redemption, 184–186
  "ride through" option, 183–184, 190–193
  secured property, 183–184
Chapter 9, 30–31
Chapter 11 (reorganization)
  adequate protection, lack of, 73–74
  administration, 56–57
  administrative claims, 375, 414, 438–440
  advantages of, 296
  alternatives, 291–308
  asset sales. *See* Asset sales
  automatic stay. *See* Automatic stay
  best interest test. *See* Best interest test (Chapter 11)
  bifurcation, 306
  cash collateral, 310–321
  cash management orders, 335
  claims. *See* Claims
  classification, 436–440
  confirmation, 409
  consensual plans, 410–411
  counsel's application for retention, 332–335
  cramdown, 424
  cramdown vs. consensual plans, 410–411
  creditors' committees, 302–305
  critical vendor orders, 327–331
  debtors-in-possession. *See* Debtors-in-possession
  discharge, 144–146
  disclosure statement, 430–435
  examiners, 361–362
  executory contracts. *See* Executory contracts
  feasibility, 419–423
  first-day orders, 309–338
  first priority administrative claims, 375
  goals, 362–366
  good faith test, 411–412
  impaired claims, 413–414
  liquidating plans, 399
  major parties-in-interest, 300–308
  multiple filing cases, 68–72
  ordinary course of business, 356–357

Chapter 11 (reorganization) (*cont'd*)
out-of-court workouts compared, 293–299
oversecured claims, 423–424
overview, 29–30
plan, 409–427
police powers, 62–64
post-confirmation issues. *See* Post-confirmation issues
post-petition assets, 80
post-petition financing orders, 321–327
pre-petition claims, 300
primary secured lenders, 305
prior discharge, 178
priorities, 412–416
procedural rules, 367–368
purposes of, 294–295
race of the diligent, 294
relief from stay, 73–74
rules, 300–308
secured creditors, 305–307, 423–426
small business debtors, 459–466
stripdown, 306
taxes, 412–416
treatment rules, 367
trustees, 358–361
undersecured claims, 423–424
unexpired leases. *See* Unexpired leases
United States Trustee's Office, 301–302
voting. *See* Voting
Chapter 12
discharge, 146
eligibility, 32–33
overview, 29
prior discharge, 178
Chapter 13
administration, 56
advantages, 233
best interest test. *See* Best interest test (Chapter 13)
changes made in 2005 amendments, 226–227
Chapter 7 compared, 225–227
confirmation, 227
debt limits, 229–231
discharge, 143–147
disposable income test. *See* Disposable income test
domestic support obligations, 252
duration of payment, 225
eligibility, 229–231
exempt assets, 226
feasibility, 226, 279–289
good faith test. *See* Good faith test (Chapter 13)
home mortgages, 241–242
means test, 227
modification or dismissal, 285–288
motor vehicles, 94
non-exempt assets, 225
overview, 28–29, 225–227
pay-out cases, 225
personal property loans, 234–240
post-petition assets, 80
post-petition wages, 226
prior discharge, 178
priorities, 249–254
regular income, 229–231
secured creditors, 233–246
secured debt, 226
sell-out cases, 225
taxes, 249–251
Charles factors, 70–71
Child support and automatic stay, 63–64. *See also* Domestic support obligations
Claims, 371–381
administrative claims, 375, 414, 438–440
allowed secured claims, 28, 365
asbestos claims, 372–373
assessment of, 363
conduct test, 373
contingent, 32

defined, 371–374
discharge, 145–146
fair contemplation test, 373
first priority administrative claims, 375
general claims, 106
general unsecured claims, 106
impaired claims, 413–414
matured, 31–32
oversecured claims, 423–424
pre-petition claims, 300
proof of, 364
relationship test, 373
Section 506(c) surcharge, 378–380
secured claims, 115–122
undersecured claims, 423–424
unliquidated claims, 31–32
unsecured claims, 106, 416–419
Classification, 436–440
Code. *See* Bankruptcy Code
Co-debtor stay, 46
Collateral
automatic stay, 63
cash collateral. *See* Cash collateral
defined, 5
Collection, 9–20
execution process, 9–12
fraudulent transfers, 16–19
state law exemptions, 12–16
Common law liens, 6–7
Concealment of records, nondischargeability, 173–174
Conduct test, 373
Confirmation
Chapter 11, 409
Chapter 13, 227
payment of unsecured claims before, 331–332
post-confirmation issues. *See* Post-confirmation issues
Consensual plans, 410–411
Constitution
Bankruptcy Clause, 39, 46–47
Eleventh Amendment, 46–47
Indian Commerce Clause, 46–47
Constitutional Convention, 48
Consumer bankruptcy cases, preferential transfers in, 131–132
Contingent claims, 32
Contracts. *See* Executory contracts
Conversion
Chapter 13 plans, 285–288
small business Chapter 11 cases, 464–466
Core jurisdiction, 40–41
Corporations
Chapter 7 (liquidation), 27
Chapter 11 (reorganization), 29–30
discharge, 146
exemptions, 85
Court. *See* Bankruptcy Court
Cramdown
Chapter 11, 410–411, 424
debtors-in-possession, 367–368
dissenting creditors, 443–444, 448–452
secured creditors. *See* Stripdown
Credit briefing, 52
Credit card charges, nondischargeability, 153–155
Credit counseling, 52
Creditors
best interest test. *See* Best interest test (Chapter 13)
committees, 302–305, 463
dissenting creditors. *See* Dissenting creditors
failure to list on paperwork, nondischargeability, 158–159
meetings, 55–57
oversecured creditors, 118–120, 315–320
secured creditors. *See* Secured creditors
undersecured creditors, 118–120, 315–320

Creditors (*cont'd*)
unsecured creditors. *See* Unsecured creditors
Criminal proceedings, automatic stay, 62–64
Critical vendor orders, 327–331
Current monthly income, 203–203, 206–214

Debt management course, nondischargeability for failure to complete, 179
Debtors-in-possession (DIPs), 355–369
absolute priority rule, 367
activities without court approval, 356–358
assessment of claims, 363–364
asset sales. *See* Asset sales
automatic stay, 362–363
best interest test, 364
cash collateral, 356–357
Chapter 11 procedural rules, 367–368
Chapter 11 treatment rules, 367
cram down, 368
defined, 300
examiners compared, 361–362
goals, 362–366
impaired classes, 367–368
maintaining operations, 362–366
ordinary course of business, 356–357
overview, 291–292
pre-petition management, 356–357
restructuring of debt, 364
supervision, 356
trustees compared, 362
Debt restructuring, 364. *See also* Chapter 11; Chapter 13
Defenses to preferential transfers, 132–133
Destruction of records, nondischargeability, 173–174
DIPs. *See* Debtors-in-possession
Discharge, 143–147
actual fraud, 151–152, 176
cash advances, presumptive fraud, 153–155
claims, 145–146
corporations, 146
credit card charges, presumptive fraud, 153–155
debt management course, failure to complete, 179
domestic support obligations, 146, 159–164
drunk driving, 164–165
embezzlement, 156–157
exceptions, 150–167
false financial statement, fraud based on, 152–153
false oath, 170–172
falsification of records, 173–174
fiduciary capacity, fraud in, 156–157
fraud, 147, 151–152
intentional torts, 164–165
larceny, 157–158
limitations, 146–147
LLCs, 146
luxury goods, 147, 153–155
objections to, 169–181
paperwork, failure to list creditor on, 158–159
partnerships, 146
policy, 143–144
post-confirmation issues, 474–478
pre-bankruptcy planning, 174–178
pre-petition debt, 145
presumptive fraud, 153–155
prior discharge within past six or eight years, 178–179
records, loss, destruction or failure to keep, 173–174
scope of, 145–147
student loans, 146, 165–166
taxes, 146, 150
timing, 144
transfers with intent to hinder, delay or defraud creditors, 174–178

unexplained loss of money, 172–173
Disclosures, 51–52
Disclosure statements
approval, 430–435
best interest test, 430
hearings, 430–431
objections, 430–435
Disinterestedness test, 332–335
Dismissal, 197–215
Chapter 13 cases, 285–288
for failure to cooperate in case, 197–200
for insufficient paperwork, 53–54
means test. *See* Means test
small business debtors, 464–466
Disposable income test, 255–264
401(k) plans, 262–263
above-median income debtors, 262–263
below-median income debtors, 257–258, 262
best interest of creditors test compared, 271
class issues, 259–262
current version, 256–264
deductible expenses, 263–264
good faith test compared, 265–266
overview, 226
prior version, 255–256
retirement funds, 262
status quo, maintaining, 256–262
Dissenting creditors, 443–458
absolute priority rule, 452–456
best interest test, 443
cramdown, 443–444, 448–452
fair and equitable test. *See* Fair and equitable test
feasibility, 443, 446–447, 456
good faith test, 443
new value exception, 453–456
priorities, 443
Divorce and automatic stay, 64. *See also* Domestic support obligations
Doctrine of necessity, 327–331
Domestic support obligations (DSOs)
and automatic stay, 163–164
Chapter 13, 252
defined, 35–36
discharge, 146, 159–164
nondischargeability, 159–164
priorities, 108–110, 252
property settlement obligations, 159–163
support obligations, 159–164
Driving under the influence, nondischargeability, 164–165
Drunk driving, nondischargeability, 164–165
DSOs. *See* Domestic support obligations
Due process, notice to creditor, 158–159, 474

Economic value theory, 398–402
Eleventh Amendment, 46–47
Embezzlement, nondischargeability, 156–157
Employee Retirement Income Security Act of 1974 (ERISA), 81, 94
Encumbrances. *See* Liens
Enforcement of plan, post-confirmation issues, 481–483
Equity
absolute priority rule, 452
automatic stay, relief from for lack of, 73–74, 345–347
in property, 13, 78–79
Equity cushion, 315–318, 349–350
Equity powers, 45–46
ERISA (Employee Retirement Income Security Act of 1974), 81, 94
Evergreen orders, 333
Examiners, 361–362
Exceptions to discharge. *See* Nondischargeability
Execution process, 9–12

Executory contracts, 384–407
assignment, 395–398
assumption, 393–395
defined, 385–386
ipso facto clauses, 386–389
overview, 385
rejection, 391–393
Exemptions, 85–103
Chapter 7, 85
Chapter 11, 85–86
Chapter 13, 85–86
corporations, 85
federal law, 86–91
homestead. *See* Homestead exemption
household goods, 86–91, 96–100
individual retirement accounts, 93–94
jewelry, 86–91, 96–100
liens, voiding, 99–100
LLCs, 85
married persons, 86
motor vehicles, 14–15, 86–91, 93–96, 96–100
in New Mexico, 88
pour-over exemption, 86–91
security interests, voiding, 99–100
state law, 12–16, 86–91
valuation of estate, 93–98
wildcard exemption, 86–91

Face value theory, 398–402
Failure to keep records, nondischargeability, 173–174
Fair and equitable test, 444–452
balloon payments, 448
duration of payments, 445–447
feasibility, 446–447
general fairness, 447–448
liens, 444
negative amortization, 448
present-value interest rate, 448–449, 457–458
voting, 448–452
Fair contemplation test, 373
False financial statements, nondischargeability, 152–153
False oath, nondischargeability, 170–172
Falsification of records, nondischargeability, 173–174
Family farmers and fishermen, 29, 32–33
Farmers, 29, 32–33
Feasibility
ability of debtor to make payments, 280–283
Chapter 11, 419–423
Chapter 13, 226, 279–283
dissenting creditors, 443, 446–447, 456
fair and equitable test, 446–447
proposed payments meeting plan obligations, 279–280
Fiduciary duties of creditors' committees, 303
Filing fee, waiver, 52–53
Final judgments, 41
First-day orders, 309–338
cash collateral. *See* Cash collateral
cash management orders, 335
critical vendor orders, 327–331
defined, 309
doctrine of necessity, 327–331
overview, 309–310
payment of unsecured claims before confirmation, 331–332
post-petition financing orders, 321–327
Fishermen, 29
506(c) surcharge, 378–380
401(k) plans, disposable income test, 262–263
Fraud
actual fraud, nondischargeability, 151–152, 176
cash advances within 60 days of filing, nondischargeability, 153–155

credit card charges within 60 days of filing, nondischargeability, 153–155
false financial statement, nondischargeability, 152–153
false oath, nondischargeability, 170–172
in fiduciary capacity, nondischargeability, 156–157
nondischargeability, 147, 151–152
presumptive fraud, nondischargeability, 153–155
Fraudulent transfers
avoiding, 124, 138–140
badges of fraud, 18–19
Bankruptcy Code, 34, 138–140
elements, 17–20
insiders, 18
nondischargeability, 174–178
pre-bankruptcy planning, 174–178
purpose of law, 16
Uniform Fraudulent Transfer Act, 16–20
Fresh start property, 82

General abuse test, 202, 212–213
General claims, 106
General unsecured claims, 106
Gerrymandering, 436
Going concerns, 297, 300
Good faith test (Chapter 11), 411–412
Good faith test (Chapter 13), 265–269
disposable income test compared, 265–266
dissenting creditors, 443
factor-based tests, 266–268
multiple filing cases, 268–269
overview, 226
zero percent plans, 269

Hearings
disclosure statements, 430–431
motions and orders distinguished, 310
Home mortgages, 74–75, 241–242
Homestead exemption
limitations, 90–93
overview, 13–15
state vs. federal law, 86–91
valuation, 96–99
Household goods
exemption, 86–91, 96–100
means test, 204
valuation, 96–99
voiding liens and security interests, 99–100

Impairment, 413–414, 440–441
Income, means test, 202–203, 206–214
Income taxes
automatic stay, 63
priorities, 108–112
Indian Commerce Clause, 46–47
Indians, sovereign immunity, 46–48
Individual retirement accounts (IRAs)
property of estate, 81–82, 92–93
state law exemptions, 14
In rem jurisdiction, 47–48
Insiders
defined, 131
fraudulent transfers, 18–19
landlords, 34
Insolvency defined, 17
Inspection rights, post-confirmation issues, 482–483
Insurance, automatic stay and lack of, 349–350
Intentional torts, nondischargeability, 164–165
Interest rate, present-value, 239–240, 448–449, 457–458
Interim fee applications, 333
Involuntary bankruptcy, 217–222
Involuntary liens, 6–7, 99–100
Ipso facto clauses, 386–390
IRAs (Individual retirement accounts). *See* Individual retirement accounts

Jewelry
exemption, 86–91, 96–100
valuation, 96–99
voiding liens and security interests, 99–100
Judges
Article III, 40, 42
term for bankruptcy judges, 42–43
Judgments, 9–10
Jurisdiction, 39–49
Bankruptcy Court, 39–43
core jurisdiction, 40–41
"related to," 40
in rem jurisdiction, 47–48

"Keep and pay" option, 183–184, 190–193

Landlords, 34
Larceny, nondischargeability, 157–158
Learning theory, 1–2
Leases. *See* Unexpired leases
Legal and equitable interests in property, 78–79
Levy, 10–11
Liens
asset sales free and clear of, 398–399
common law liens, 6–7
execution process, 10
fair and equitable test, 444
involuntary liens, 6–7
mechanics' liens, 7
replacement liens, 314, 316–318
state law exemptions, 15
statutory liens, 6–7
supplemental liens, 314, 316
voiding, 99–100
voluntary liens, 6–7
Limited liability companies (LLCs)
Chapter 7, 27
discharge, 146
exemptions, 85
Liquidating plans, 399
Liquidation-style bankruptcy, 27. *See also* Chapter 7
LLCs. *See* Limited liability companies
Loss of records, nondischargeability, 173–174
Luxury goods, nondischargeability, 147, 153–155

Married persons, exemptions, 86
Matured claims, 31–32
Means test, 200–215
abuse test, 201–215
allowable expenses, 203–204, 212–214
Chapter 13, 227
consumer bankruptcy, 200
current monthly income, 202–203, 206–214
current test, 201–215
general abuse test, 202, 212–213
household goods, 204
money left over after allowable expenses, 20
motor vehicles, 210–212
prior test, 201
rebuttable presumptions, 205–206
totality of circumstances test, 202, 212–213
Mechanics' liens, 7
Modification
Chapter 13 plans, 285–288
small business Chapter 11 cases, 464–466
Motions, 310
Motor vehicles
exemption, 14–15, 86–91, 93–95, 96–100
means test, 210–212
valuation, 94–95, 96–99
voiding liens and security interests, 99–100
Multiple filing cases
Chapter 11, 69–72
good faith test, 268

Municipalities, 30–31
Mutilation of records, nondischargeability, 173–174

National Conference of Commissioners on Uniform State Laws, 16
Native Americans, sovereign immunity, 46–49
Necessity doctrine, 327–331
Negative amortization, 448
New Mexico
  exemptions in, 88
  larceny in, 157–158
New value exception, 132–133, 453–456
No-asset cases, 27
Noncore proceedings, 41–42
Nondischargeability
  actual fraud, 151–152, 176
  cash advances, 153–155
  credit card charges, 153–155
  debt management course, failure to complete, 179
  domestic support obligations, 159–164
  drunk driving, 164–165
  embezzlement, 156–157
  false financial statement, fraud based on, 152–153
  false oath, 170–172
  falsification of records, 173–174
  fiduciary capacity, fraud in, 156–158
  fraud, 147, 151–152
  fraudulent transfers, 174–178
  intentional torts, 164–165
  larceny, 157–158
  luxury goods, 147, 153–155
  paperwork, failure to list creditor on, 158–159
  pre-bankruptcy planning, 174–178
  presumptive fraud, 152–155
  prior discharge within past six or eight years, 178–179
  records, loss, destruction or failure to keep, 173–174
  student loans, 165–166
  taxes, 146, 150
  transfers with intent to hinder, delay or defraud creditors, 174–178
  unexplained loss of money, 172–173
Non-exempt property, 10
Nonpossessory security interests, voiding, 99–100
Non-purchase-money security interests, voiding, 99–100
Nunc pro tunc doctrine, 334

Orders, 310
Ordinary course of business
  debtors-in-possession, 356–357
  defense, 132–133
Out-of-court workouts, 293–299
Overbid protection, 402–404
Oversecured claims, 423–424
Oversecured creditors, 118–120, 315–320
Oversecured loans, 243

Paperwork, 52–55
Partnerships, discharge, 146
Passive real estate and automatic stay, 347
Paternity and automatic stay, 62
Pay-out cases, 27–30, 225
Personal property loans, 234–240
Personal property purchase money security interest (PMSI) loans, 235, 236–237
Plan feasibility. *See* Feasibility
Plan voting, 435–436
Police powers
  automatic stay, 342–344
  Chapter 11, 62–64
Possession, debtors in. *See* Debtors-in-possession
Post-confirmation issues, 473–485
  agency law, 474–476
  confirmation order, 484–486
  discharge, 474–478

Post-confirmation issues (*cont'd*)
due process, 474
enforcement of plan, 481–483
inspection rights, 482–483
res judicata, 474–478
Post-petition assets, 82–83
Post-petition financing orders, 321–327
Post-petition wages, 226
Pot plans, 365
Pour-over exemption, 86–91
Practice questions, 487–513
Pre-bankruptcy planning, nondischargeability, 174–178
Preemption, 45
Preferential transfers, 124–138
consumer bankruptcy cases, 131–132
defenses, 132–133
defined, 124
new value exception, 132–133
ordinary course of business defense, 132–133
setoff preferences, 135–138
substantially contemporaneous exchange for new value exception, 132–135
Pre-petition debt
automatic stay, 61
claims, 300
discharge, 145
Present-value interest rate, 239–240, 448–449, 457–458
Presumptive fraud, nondischargeability, 153–155
Primary secured lenders, 305
Priming, 321–327
Prior discharge, 178–179
Priorities, 105–112
absolute priority rule, 306, 367, 452–456
administrative claims, 438–440
Chapter 11, 412–416
Chapter 13, 249–254
dissenting creditors, 443
domestic support obligations, 108–110, 252
income taxes, 108–112
overview, 25
post-petition financing orders, 321
property taxes, 110–111
social engineering, 105–108
student loans, 109–111
taxes, 108–112, 249–251, 415–416
trust fund tax, 111–112
UCC, 141
Proof of claims, 363–364
Property of estate, 77–84
annuities, 81
breadth of, 77–78
fresh start property, 82
individual retirement accounts, 81–82, 93
legal and equitable interests in property, 78–79
post-petition assets, 82–83
retirement funds, 80–82, 93
valuation, 94–99
Property taxes, priorities, 110–111
Purchase money security interest (PMSI) loans, 235, 237–238

Questions, 487–513

Race of the diligent, 294
Reaffirmation
formal requirements, 189–190
"keep and pay" option, 190–193
overview, 189–193
principles, 189
"ride through" option, 190–193
Records, loss, destruction or failure to keep, nondischargeability, 173–174
Redemption, 184–186
Referees, 40
Rejection
of executory contracts, 391–393
of unexpired leases, 391–393

Relationship test, 373
Relief from automatic stay, 73–74
Reorganization-style bankruptcy, 29–31. *See also* Chapter 11
Repayment plans, 28
Replacement liens, 314, 316
Replacement value, 238
Reporting requirements, small business debtors, 463–464
Repossession and automatic stay, 61
Res judicata, post-confirmation issues, 474–478
Restructuring of debt, 364
Retail value, 238
Retirement funds
  disposable income test, 262
  property of estate, 80–82, 93
  state law exemptions, 14
"Ride through" option, 183–184, 190–193

Sales of assets. *See* Asset sales
Savings Incentive Match Plans for Employees (SIMPLEs), 93
Schedules of assets and liabilities, 53
Section 341 meetings, 55–57
Section 363(b) sales. *See* Asset sales
Section 506(c) surcharge, 378–380
Secured claims, 115–122
Secured creditors, 115–122
  generally, 115–117
  absolute priority rule, 306
  advantages of, 116–117
  in bankruptcy, 116–117
  bifurcation, 234–236
  calculations, 120–122
  Chapter 11, 305–307, 423–426
  Chapter 13, 233–246
  classification, 436–440
  comfort of being secured, 117–118
  home mortgages, 241–242
  outside bankruptcy, 116
  personal property loans, 234–240
  stripdown. *See* Stripdown
  UCC, 116
  unsecured creditors compared, 5–7
  valuation, 238–239
Secured debt and means test, 204
Security interests
  automatic stay, 62
  avoiding unperfected security interests, 124, 140–141
  UCC, 124
  voiding, 99–100
Sell-out cases, 27–28, 225
SEPs (Simplified Employee Pensions), 93
Setoff preferences, 135–138
Sheriff's sales, 11
Shopping center leases, 396–397
SIMPLEs (Savings Incentive Match Plans for Employees), 93
Simplified Employee Pensions (SEPs), 93
Small business debtors
  avoiding status, 460
  Chapter 11, 461–463
  conversion, 464–466
  creditors' committees, 463
  deadlines, 461–463
  defined, 34, 459
  dismissal, 464–466
  election of status, 459–460
  oversight, 463–464
  plans, 460–461, 464
  reporting requirements, 463–464
  simplification, 454
  voting, 429–430
Social engineering, 105–108
Solicitation of votes, 431, 434, 437, 441
Sovereign immunity, 46–49
Stalking horse, 402–404
Statements of affairs, 53
Statute of Elizabeth 1570, 16
Statutory liens, 6–7
Stipulations, cash collateral, 318–321
Straight bankruptcy, 27

Stripdown. *See also* Cramdown
absolute priority rule, 452–456
applicability, 242
bifurcation, 234–236
Chapter 11, 306
dissenting creditors, 444, 448–452
limitations, 236–237
new approach, 242–247
oversecured loans, 243
terminology, 235
undersecured loans, 243, 246
Strong-arm powers, 140–141
Student loans
discharge, 146, 165–166
nondischargeability, 165–166
priorities, 109–111
undue hardship, 165–166
Substantially contemporaneous exchange for new value exception, 132–135
Successor liability, asset sales, 404–405
Supplemental liens, 314, 316
Support. *See* Domestic support obligations

Taxes
automatic stay, 63, 341–342
Chapter 11, 412–416
Chapter 13, 249–251
classification, 438–440
discharge, 146, 150
income taxes, priorities, 108–112
nondischargeability, 146, 150
priorities, 108–112, 249–251, 415–416
property taxes, priorities, 110–111
trust fund tax, priorities, 111–112
Torts, nondischargeability, 164–165
Totality of circumstances test, 202, 212–213
Trustees
asset sales. *See* Asset sales
Chapter 11, 358–361
United States Trustee's Office. *See* United States Trustee's Office
Trust fund tax, priorities, 111–112
Turnkey operations, 300

UCC. *See* Uniform Commercial Code
Undersecured claims, 423–424
Undersecured creditors, 118–120, 315–320
Undersecured loans, 243, 246
Undue hardship, 165–166
Unexpired leases, 384–407
assignment, 395–398
assumption, 393–395
defined, 385–386
ipso facto clauses, 386–389
overview, 385
rejection, 391–393
shopping center leases, 396–397
Unexplained loss of money, nondischargeability, 172–173
Uniform Commercial Code (UCC)
accounts receivable, 311–312
priorities, 141
secured creditors, 116
security interests, 124
Uniform Fraudulent Conveyances Act, 16–17
Uniform Fraudulent Transfer Act, 16–20
United States Trustee's Office
Chapter 7 duties, 28
Chapter 11 duties, 56–57, 301–302
creditors' meetings, 56–57
debtors-in-possession, supervision of, 356
examiners, request for appointment of, 361–362
small business debtors, oversight of, 464
Unliquidated claims, 32
Unsecured claims, 106, 331–332, 416–419

Unsecured creditors
  absolute priority rule, 452–456
  classification, 438–440
  execution process, 9–12
  secured creditors compared, 5–7

Valuation
  Bankruptcy Code, 238–239
  of estate, 94–99
  homestead exemption, 96–99
  household goods, 96–99
  jewelry, 96–99
  motor vehicles, 94–95, 96–99
  personal property loans, 238–239
  replacement value, 238
  retail value, 238
  secured loans, 238–239
  wholesale value, 238
Value defined, 17
Voiding liens and security interests, 99–100
Voluntary liens, 6–7
Voting, 429–442
  classification, 436–440
  disclosure statement approval, 430–435
  fair and equitable test, 448–452
  gerrymandering, 436
  impairment, 440–441
  plan voting, 435–436
  small business debtors, 429–430
  solicitation of, 431, 434, 437, 441

Wholesale value, 238
Wildcard exemption, 86–91
Workouts, 293–299
Writ packages, 12–13

Zero percent plans, 269

www.ingramcontent.com/pod-product-compliance
Lightning Source LLC
LaVergne TN
LVHW082018200926
848481LV00010B/2882